William Palmer

# Egyptian chronicles

With a harmony of sacred and Egyptian chronology and an appendix on

Babylonian and Assyrian antiquities, Vol. I

William Palmer

**Egyptian chronicles**
*With a harmony of sacred and Egyptian chronology and an appendix on Babylonian and Assyrian antiquities, Vol. I*

ISBN/EAN: 9783742864901

Manufactured in Europe, USA, Canada, Australia, Japa

Cover: Foto ©ninafisch / pixelio.de

Manufactured and distributed by brebook publishing software (www.brebook.com)

William Palmer

# Egyptian chronicles

# EGYPTIAN CHRONICLES

WITH A HARMONY OF SACRED
AND EGYPTIAN CHRONOLOGY, AND AN APPENDIX ON BABYLONIAN
AND ASSYRIAN ANTIQUITIES

BY

WILLIAM PALMER, M.A.,

AND LATE FELLOW, OF MAGDALEN COLLEGE, OXFORD

In Two Volumes

VOL. I.

LONDON
LONGMAN, GREEN, LONGMAN, AND ROBERTS
1861

# CONTENTS

OF

# THE FIRST VOLUME.

## CHAPTER I.



## CHAP. II.

## CHAP. III.

### ERATOSTHENES (B.C. 240—194).

# INTRODUCTION.

Most persons who have at all attended to Egyptian antiquities will remember with interest how slight an accident it was which led Belzoni to his grand discovery of the tomb of Seti I., the father of Rameses the Great. In the wild desert-valley of Biban el Malouk, the bareness of which contrasts so strangely with the green plain on the other side of the Assassif when in crossing by the mountain path one sees from the top both sides at once, at the foot of one of those lateral ridges in which are many of the kings' tombs, he noticed a slight depression of the sand, as if the rains, which even in the Thebaid fall in some years, had there soaked through to some cavity. So he dug, and came first upon a descending gallery; and then, after trying the rock at which it seemed to end and which sounded hollow, he broke his way through it, and found himself in the most perfect and the most magnificent of all the royal tombs — one unentered by Greek visitors under the Ptolemies, and connected with reigns of the highest historical interest (for Seti I. and his son Rameses II. are the chief elements of the Sesostris of Herodotus and Diodorus)—the gorgeous paintings of which, partly historical and partly relating to the dead, preserved intact in all the freshness of their colours, have been the source of the most striking of those facsimiles of Egyptian sepulchral paintings which are now to be seen in the museums of Europe.

The present writer cannot promise to conduct his readers to discoveries so interesting at once to the eye and to the imagination as that of the tomb of a Sesostris; but his work originated in an accidental observation of something as simple in its way as that depression in the sand which was remarked by Belzoni. It was—only in an intellectual instead of a material sense — as if one had been standing on the beaten track of Egyptian history, and had spied on the path itself, where every passer-by should have seen it or trodden upon it, a key to the entrance of some conspicuous but unexplored monument, thrown, as if on purpose, above 2000 years ago at the very threshold of the door it was to open. And this key having been picked up and used, the first chamber into which it gave admittance led to a second, and the second to a third, and this again to others, till at length there were six in all. And as the reader will have himself to enter each of these in turn he will be better able to understand and to judge of what he finds in them when he has previously been made acquainted with that hint from which each of the six reconstructions or explanations of as many Egyptian Chronicles has been successively obtained.

But first it may be proper to enter into some preliminary details, explaining how a remark which might have been made equally at Oxford, or at Rome, or wherever else one chanced to light upon the text which suggested it, and which might have been equally followed out to its consequences by any classical scholar, however ignorant of Egyptian antiquities, came to be made in a boat on the Nile, so that the author while pursuing afterwards his discovery to its consequences was not under the disadvantage of being totally unacquainted with Egypt and its monuments, but had laid in the country itself a foundation to which it was easy to add from published works and from an inspection of the chief museums of Europe. At the same time the narrative now to be given will sufficiently account for all those shortcomings which will no doubt be detected by competent judges in what may be said on points of detail respecting the monuments and the results hitherto obtained from their study.

Having been advised to winter in some southern climate, the author went in the autumn of 1853 to Egypt, rather than to any other country, and to Cairo, not with any idea of studying antiquities or of making the usual voyage up the Nile, but in quest of a Greek MS. of the 17th century containing an account of the deposition of the Russian Patriarch Nicon, in which the writer of the MS., Paisius Ligarides, an ex-archbishop of Gaza, and originally an ex-pupil of the Propaganda, had acted a chief part. For some years previously the author had been collecting materials for a life of that great man, to whose memory justice has never yet been done. From his fall an *uncanonical* Supremacy, as it may well be called, though it has never yet touched the details of doctrine or ritual, has attached to the Autocrats of Russia; and as the Patriarchs and Bishops of the East either assisted personally in the mixed council which degraded Nicon, or assented by their silence, it may seem that from that time the claim of spiritual independence, long before damaged at Constantinople by the Greek Emperors and the Sultans, was surrendered for the whole Greek and Slavonian Church. Whatever may be the lesson which a well-instructed piety ought to draw from this fact, the history of that crisis within the Russian empire is one in itself of the highest and most dramatic interest. And the personal character of Nicon loses nothing by comparison with those of the great champions of the Western Church, such as St. Thomas of Canterbury and Pope Gregory VII. To call him a saint indeed would in Russia be offensive to the sectaries (the *Staro-obratzi*), who hated him for his enlightenment; and to formalists, who might object that he was condemned by a mixed Synod, and with the assent of the whole "Eastern-Catholic" Church, so that his enemies could not even imagine for him any other resource than that of appealing to the elder Rome; and most of all it would be offensive to the flatterers of the civil power, and to the power itself, which has never yet acknowledged its sin; while in the West, though the existence of sanctity in spite of outward separation is admitted to be possible, it would be scandalous and improper for private persons to call any man a saint who lived and died in separation from Rome. But, though Nicon be thus cast out both by the Greeks and by the Latins (and necessarily by private persons of the latter), it is permissible to observe that according to records of him preserved among his enemies, but neither noticed nor understood, he was called by an angel a "holy man of God," and was named in a dream by Christ himself to a widow woman sent to succour him as "my servant Nicon." But if the testimony of two such witnesses be true, the first question, whether for the Greek or for the Catholic, will be not as to the need of any form of canonisation, but as to the credibility of the Russian narrative in which these things are stated.

We are now far enough from Egyptian antiquities; but this was the subject on which the author was employed, and on account of which he went to Egypt. And if health and time allowed, his intention was, after translating the MS. of Paisius, to go on to Jerusalem to re-examine there with more attention than before certain details, with a view to an "Historical account of the Question of the Holy Places," which he had in great part written since the French in 1850 opened and reopened that difference with a hope in which they succeeded only too well. As it was, though he completed in the spring of 1854 his local researches at Jerusalem, the war having already broken out put an end to that public interest which had been attracted to the question out of which it originated. But to return to Egypt:—

On arriving at Cairo it was discovered that the MS. in quest of which the author came had not long before been sent to Russia to M. Mouravieff, whose History of the Russian Church, translated into English by Mr. Blackmore, had been edited by the author. M. Mouravieff had desired to obtain a transcript of the MS. for his own use; but the Greek Patriarch, after one out of its three divisions had been transcribed, finding the transcript to be disfigured by frequent errors, and the original to be difficult to read, and having a Bishop then going to Russia for alms, sent the original itself, to be kept as long as needed for use, and then returned. Thus the author found only the transcript of the First Book, which the Patriarch readily gave him to translate, regretting that he could only promise the rest whenever it was returned, if he thought it worth coming for again, and if he had not seen it in the mean time in passing through Russia. For if the war had not broken out it had been part of a former plan to go from Syria to Mosul, and through Georgia and the Caucasus to the Volga, and so up to Moscow and to St. Petersburg; and the late Prince Woronzoff two years before in the Crimea had promised to facilitate that journey. But as things turned out, after two or three months spent at Cairo partly in translating, and partly in a tedious confinement from the gout, early in 1854 an American stranger introducing himself to the author invited him to join in a short voyage up the Nile, all the preparations for which were already made, but there was still room for a fourth person. This proposal having been accepted, and only just before embarking, one of the party, as he was seeking very different commodities, found by chance in the same shop and purchased a thin quarto on Egypt by an American named Gliddon, a publication of little value, but containing two things which Murray's handbook does not. The first of these was a translation of that short document (preserved by Syncellus) which is called the Old Egyptian Chronicle, and which is the subject of Chapter I. of this work. The other was a page exhibiting the hieroglyphical signs used like letters or syllables in such words and names as are written phonetically. Sir Gardner Wilkinson in Murray's handbook had given a useful series of the hieroglyphical names of the Egyptian kings, so far as their order seemed to him to have been made out. On comparing these with the hieroglyphical alphabet in Gliddon's publication, it appeared that nothing could be easier than to recognise and to spell by their help the personal names of kings. And this was quite enough to give great interest even to a cursory inspection of the ruins on the banks of the river, as it would enable one to see in each case what were the latest names on the outermost portions added to any temple, or on other parts rebuilt, and what the earlier as one advanced inwards towards the original nucleus or sanctuary, and so to form some idea as to the monumental traces left both by dynasties and by individual kings.

One other piece of good fortune there was of the most trivial kind, without which the writer might have gone up to the first Cataract and down again to Cairo almost without setting foot out of the boat. This was his having taken with him by chance, and without any thought of wanting them again so soon, a pair of list shoes. But only two or three days after embarking the gout returned, and it was not till reaching Assouan that he was able to go on shore, nor till some time after returning to Cairo that he could wear a common shoe. But beginning from Assouan, by the help of a list shoe tied from the heel over the instep, and of such donkeys as the villages afforded, he was enabled to visit most of those ruins and tombs which were seen by his companions. So the Russian Patriarch Nicon, an American stranger, Mr. Gliddon's reproduction of the Old Chronicle and his hieroglyphical alphabet, and a list shoe, were together the fingers as it were of a hand which took the author from his previous occupation, and put him upon a work totally different, for which he had not before felt the slightest inclination, and which was about the last that he would have thought himself either fit or likely to undertake.

Any general description or narrative such as belongs to a volume of travels would here be out of place; and most readers are already familiar with those peculiarities of climate and scenery which make the charm of a winter in Egypt. But some features more or less connected with the subject of this volume may be rapidly glanced at. It is interesting then to be met at once at Alexandria by the conspicuous column of Diocletian (misnamed Pompey's pillar), reminding one that to the era of his accession, which may be taken also to mark the last persecution and the triumph of Christianity, all the later chronology and history of Egypt and of the Coptic and Abyssinian Churches is attached. The sites of Naucratis and Sais, which are passed in going from Alexandria to the Nile by the Mahmoudieh Canal, carry one back in thought to the seventh century before Christ, when the Greeks first penetrated into Egypt and obtained an emporium on the Canopic or Western branch of the Nile, and to the travels of Herodotus two centuries later, when he saw the palace of the kings of the Saite dynasty and their tombs and other monuments still entire. So we enter Egypt at the present day nearly by the same route with the Greeks.

Higher up, after getting upon the Nile, when one first comes in view of the desert of the Libyan hills, the colour of the sand is so yellow that a shortsighted person might imagine it to be a tract of ripe wheat. Hereabouts, in the lower part of the steep bank, on the Libyan side, one sees in places thin strata, as streaks, of yellow sand alternating with black earth, a peculiarity which takes the mind back to those very early ages when the river and the desert were still contending for the surface even at the water's edge, and it was only in some seasons, perhaps, that an inundation overspread the banks with mud, which was again in turn covered by sand swept over it by the wind. Then, without dwelling on the first distant view of the pyramids of Gizeh, sometimes called the Granaries of Joseph, as the canal along the foot of the Libyan hills is called his River (and these works really date from his time), or the noble obelisk of Sesortasen I. (invisible from the river but within a short ride to the N.E. from Cairo,) which marks the site of the Temple at Heliopolis, and which was first set up at least 40 or 50 years before Joseph was sold into Egypt, — without dwelling, again, on later reminiscences of the Assyrians and the Romans connected with the Egyptian Babylon, or on traditions of the Holy Family and of St. Peter and St. Mark connected with the same Babylon and with the Fountain of Matarieh on the Roman road near Heliopolis,—or lastly on the numerous and beautiful mediæval mosques of Fostat and Cairo, and the tombs of the Mamelukes, so rich and picturesque, with all the transitions from the Roman and Byzantine to the Saracenic and Pointed architecture,— without dwelling on any of these things, but confining ourselves to the voyage on the Nile, let us recall if we have seen, or paint to ourselves from description, some of the most striking features of the scenery; the broad surface of the river — the black steep bank — the creaking wheels for raising water to irrigate the lands — the narrow flat strip covered with growing crops above the bank sometimes of a dark blue-green sometimes of a yellow-green — the bare stems of palms rising from this strip, some upright like slender shafts, others slanting in different ways, and all with the green tufts at their heads showing as against a background against the sky or the yellow sand of the desert or the rock rising behind: then the frequent mounds, like small hills, marking the sites of ancient towns, and often still occupied by modern villages — each village on its mound (which during the inundation becomes an island) amid a clump of palm-trees full of pigeons — the houses and walls all of sunburnt-bricks of black earth such as were used by the ancient Egyptians — the doorways, too, slightly converging towards the top as in all the old Egyptian buildings — their roofs not flat as in Syria, but rising into a multitude of picturesque turrets which are dovecotes and which give to the villages a castellated appearance — the contrast in places, where both are seen together, of the broad expanse of the river and treeless flats of the most vivid green in islands or on the shores with some portion of the yellow sand of the desert. From the hill and the old rock tombs above Osiout, formerly Lycopolis (and wolf-mummies are still visible in the tombs), this contrast is heightened by a double city, that of Osiout itself at one's feet—one of the chief places of modern Egypt, with its port full of life, connected with cultivated tracts on the shore and in an island beyond, and with the river with the picturesque sails of the vessels (pointed like hares' ears crossing one another) upon it—and a little to the left the mediæval and modern necropolis, a perfect town of Saracenic tombs and small mosques and cupolas, standing apart without any sign of life or vegetation near it in the midst of the desert. Then in places the Libyan and Arabian mountains (sometimes both, but oftener only the Arabian) approach close to the bank, and narrow the course of the river; at others the river widens and bends so as to resemble a huge lake: in some places again it is divided into several channels and half lost between extensive islands. When the Arabian hill comes near, the entrances to ancient tombs are often visible to the passing boats in the rock above. For those who have the use of their feet a walk along the steep bank — by no means to be mounted or descended at every point — is an agreeable preparation for breakfast in the early morning while the Arab crew tow the boat up the stream, crying out to keep time and singing as they haul. On the deck too, and in rowing, they are not sparing of their songs. Sometimes perhaps a funeral from some village may be crossing the river, with the wailing of hired mourners, and a car drawn by oxen to convey the dead from the landing-place to the cemetery on the opposite bank; so that the modern funeral bears a close resemblance to the ancient, the greater conveniences offered for burials by the more desert side and the hill-bank having perpetuated the custom of ferrying the dead across the water. The form and colours also of the cattle in the pastures, the innumerable flocks of wild geese on the river, and the barley, wheat, and dhourra of different heights in the cultivated tracts, remind one constantly of the cattle and crops sculptured and painted in the tombs, and of the geese living and dead which make so great a show in the same sculptures and paintings, that they quite take precedence of the kine and the beef. Buffaloes in the fields and negro slaves occur on the monuments, mixed as now with handsome cattle of the Apis form and breed, and with the native Egyptians; but now one sees also lines of camels with their packs on the banks of the river and in the city, and in the cultivated lands crops of maize, which are absent from the monuments.

Any one of the larger Egyptian temples which is tolerably preserved, as those of Denderah and Edfou, with the remains of its *δρόμοι*, or avenues of approach, its pylons and propylæa, its hypæthral courts, its inner halls of columns, and its innermost sanctuary, the original nucleus of all, is sufficiently imposing. But those of Thebes, on both banks of the river—viz. the great ruins of Gourneh, of the Ramesseum, and of Medinet Habou, besides the vocal colossus of Memnon and its fellow, and the royal and private tombs on the west side, and the ruins of Luxor, and above all those of the great temple of Ammon at Karnak, on the east side—are absolutely overwhelming to the eye, and even to the imagination. No other ruins in the world can be compared with these; and it is utterly inconceivable that such buildings and such a capital should have been seen by Herodotus still complete, and passed over undescribed. This silence alone

— even if there were no other concurrent indications—would be sufficient proof that the parenthetical notices of his having ascended the Nile to Thebes, and even to Syene, were inserted late in life, and after a second visit to Egypt. But the mention of the temple of Karnak affords a good opportunity for breaking off from these desultory allusions and reminiscences, and turning to that which properly belongs to the present Introduction, namely, the *historical* instruction to be obtained from a rapid and superficial glance at such monuments as meet the eye of the ordinary tourist, or such as any one who has been in Egypt may afterwards notice with more attention in one or other of the chief museums of Europe.

To generalise, then, from the author's own experience, it is easy to observe that the traces left by different Roman emperors become gradually more numerous and more important as one goes back from the Antonines (their's are the latest hieroglyphical names) towards the time of Cleopatra, a temple in honour of whose delivery of a son born to Julius Cæsar (a son named on this monument Ptolemy Cæsar) is seen near Hermonthis. The latest works of those executed under the Roman emperors show plain signs of inferiority and decay in point of number, magnitude, and style, and especially in the hieroglyphical characters themselves; while the earliest, consisting of magnificent reconstructions of temples, or additions, bearing the names of Augustus and Tiberius as deities, with dates equally belonging to the life of Christ on earth, and even it may be to his actual presence as an infant in Egypt, are quite in keeping with the constructions of the Ptolemies. And the temples built, rebuilt, or added to by the Ptolemies show that under them Egypt enjoyed material prosperity, and that it was their policy heartily to support the priesthood and the national superstitions, accepting in return the same divine honours which had been given to the earlier Pharaohs, and which passed from themselves, in like manner, to their Roman successors. Of the Persian fire-worshippers scarcely a single name is likely to meet the eye of the traveller (unless he visits the ruins of Jupiter Ammon in the Great Oasis, where he will see the cartouches of Darius), though the reconstructed sanctuary of the great temple of Karnak, bearing the names of Philip Aridæus and Alexander II., speaks distinctly both of the destruction caused by the last Persian conqueror, Ochus (in B.C. 345), and of the inauguration of a new policy under the first Macedonians, who were received as deliverers. The intervention of a time of native independence between the first Persian dynasty of Cambyses and his successors and the last Persian conquest of Ochus is clearly marked by the names of *Nepharoot*, *Hakori*, and the two *Nectanebos*, some or all of which, in one place or another, will be likely to present themselves. Of the Saites of Dyn. XXVI the monumental remains, both in museums and in Egypt, especially in the neighbourhood of Memphis, are so abundant, and of such admirable workmanship, as to prove that their age contrasted favourably with the times preceding it. Of the Ethiopians comparatively little is seen, but enough to catch the eye at Thebes, and to show that whatever violence and cruelties may have accompanied their conquest, they identified themselves in religion, at least, with the native kings whom they supplanted. And for such travellers as go up to the Second Cataract there are plain signs at Gebel Barkal (the site of the ancient Napata) that the native monumental history of Ethiopia begins only from Tirhakah, the contemporary of Hezekiah, and that the religion and civilisation of the Ethiopians were of Egyptian origin, not that of the Egyptians of Ethiopian. The same results, too, from Lepsius's examination of the Nubian pyramids, both those near Gebel Barkal, and of other groups still higher up the river. But for the time between the Ethiopian conquest (B.C. 746) and the first two kings of the Bubastites, Shishonk I. and Osorchon I., (that is, during 44 + 19 + 48 =) 111 years of Dynasties XXIV, XXIII, and XXII, and the last 80 or 90 years of Dyn. XXI of the Old Chronicle, in all for about 200 years of the Bubastites or Tanites, and the first Saites, scarcely anything is seen. It is only to the recent discoveries of M. Mariette in the Apis-cemetery near Memphis, which was visited by the author on his return to Cairo, and the numerous stelæ of which are now in the Louvre, that we are indebted for the knowledge of a number of monumental names filling up the break in this part of Egyptian history. The monumental records of the conquests of Shishonk I. on the outer walls of the great temple at Karnak have become familiar to the public through engravings since the time when Champollion first pointed out in the long series of tributary or vanquished kings, countries, and cities, the scutcheon of the "king of the country of Judah (*Judah-melek-ka*)." But it is for the three great Theban Dynasties, XVIII, XIX, and XX, anterior to the time of Shishonk I. and Rehoboam, and covering (348 + 194 + 228 =) 770 years, from B.C. 1748 to B.C. 978, that the architectural remains, especially at Thebes, are so abundant, and the links of mutual connection so numerous, as to afford something like a continuous monumental history, while the temples, palaces, and tombs of many of the kings of these dynasties are on so vast a scale, and their wars and conquests and tributes recorded are so considerable, as to strike every beholder with amazement. Especially the great temple of Ammon at Karnak, consisting of an endless accretion of successively-added chambers, columnar buildings, and halls, intermediate and outer pylons, propylæa, obelisks, hypæthral courts, dromoi of ram-headed sphinxes, and even lesser outlying temples, each with its own similar additions, attached like faubourgs to the outskirts of the greater, affords of itself quite an epitome of Egyptian history both of a positive and of a comparative or negative character. The kings whose works both in this gigantic and complex ruin and in those on the opposite side of the river stand out in boldest relief are, as might be expected, Rameses II. and Seti I. of the fifteenth century before Christ, and Rameses III. of the fourteenth, the chief elements of the compound Sesostris. But those of an earlier king, viz. Amenoph III., the Memnon of the Greeks, who was contemporary with Joshua, if they had remained entire, would have been scarcely less stupendous. As it is, both his palace-temple and his tomb on the west side of the river have been utterly destroyed by some successor hostile to his memory, and his temple at Luxor on the east bank has been appropriated and added to by later kings, and much damaged besides by modern barbarism. A still earlier king, Thothmes III. (the fourth or fifth of Dyn. XVIII, according as his elder sister and her consort Thothmes II. are reckoned or omitted), is set by the monuments in a light in the highest degree remarkable. It is from his death that the narrative of the Exodus in the Scriptures commences: he was himself the chief oppressor of the Hebrews: and it is in a tomb of his reign that the Hebrews with their semi-Nubian taskmasters are still to be seen painted in the act of making bricks for the temple of Ammon. This king is shown by the monuments to have been one of the greatest *builders* that ever reigned in Egypt. And further they show that he was also one of the greatest conquerors. The list of his tributes from vanquished peoples, which was sculptured with much detail on the walls of the great temple at Karnak, with an enumeration of his campaigns, is still in part preserved, and has been illustrated by Mr. Birch of the British Museum. A portion of these inscriptions is now in the Louvre. Thus it appears that the development of Egypt as the great military power of the world commenced under the first kings of Dyn. XVIII, almost immediately upon the overthrow of the Shepherds, and that it seemed to be just reaching its climax when the Hebrew bondsmen had attained their greatest numbers, and their bondage had become most severe. And those modern writers who, to suit their own theories, have made Rameses II. to have been the great oppressor of the Hebrews, and his son and successor Menephthah, or Amenoph, to be the Pharaoh of the Exodus, have in some features of the history come nearer than they deserved to the truth. For the real oppressor of the Hebrews was a king who for his conquests, his long reign, and his innumerable monuments, is scarcely, if at all, inferior when compared with Rameses II., and not at all inferior to Rameses III. (though it is true that the architectural *proportions* of the works of Thothmes III., as being earlier, have been surpassed by his later rivals); and it was in the first year of the son and successor of this king, really named Amenoph, when the pride of Egypt was already at its zenith, that the power, as it were, of Sesostris was broken or bruised by the overthrow in the

Red Sea, so that it was not till two centuries later that it again threatened to overrun Asia.

Of monumental lists, such as those of the Chamber of Kings, the most ancient of all, which belonged to the buildings of Thothmes III. in the temple at Karnak (what remains of it is in the Imperial Library at Paris), and those of the Abydos Tablet in the British Museum, which also went back beyond the head of Dyn. XVIII, it is unnecessary to speak, as no portion of these lists is now to be seen by travellers either at Karnak or at Abydos; and, even if it were otherwise, they would not enable one to form any clear notions as to the earlier history of Egypt. Those monumental lists, however, of Dyn. XVIII and part of Dyn. XIX which are still in their places in the Ramesseum and at Medinet Habou are intelligible at once, and highly interesting, as occurring on the very spot where one is surrounded by separate inscriptions and monuments of the same kings whom they enumerate in order. For the times above Dyn. XVIII the ordinary traveller can no longer work his way upwards as before. The monuments seem to fail: and he is besides perplexed by having for his guide the lists of Africanus, which contain before Dyn. XVIII seven interpolated dynasties of kings besides the eight really belonging to the original Manetho. And even if any one were to make a bold guess that the *anonymous* dynasties are perhaps fabulous, and thereupon were to attempt to refer all royal names anterior to Dyn. XVIII to those dynasties which give the names and reigns in detail, he would be little better off than before. For he would see in one place or another, or find mentioned by persons more learned than himself, many names of kings which cannot be identified in Manetho's lists. He would be obliged therefore to content himself with observing that of the Shepherds who were overthrown by the founder of Dyn. XVIII he had seen no traces whatever (though traces of one of them, the second Apophis, have in truth been found at Tanis), unless indeed he were deceived for a time, like the author, by the plausible assertion that the names *Papa*, *Aan*, and *Assa* occurring the first of them in many parts and the other two in tombs near

Memphis, were those of the Shepherds Apophis, Janias, and Aseth. He would find however in different places, especially in the remarkable tombs of Beni-Hassan, a number of names easily identifiable with those of Dyn. XII of Africanus (XV of the original Manetho), among which the obelisk of Heliopolis would secure his due pre-eminence to that of Sesortasen I. At Chenoboskion and elsewhere he would find names which through Papa-Maire he might connect with Dyn. VI of Africanus (XIII of Manetho). In tombs near the pyramids of Memphis he would find frequent traces of their builders of Dyn. IV of Africanus (XI of Manetho), as well as other names identifiable in Dyn. V of Africanus (XII of Manetho). But with these Memphites and "Elephantinites" (a mixture of designations in itself sufficiently perplexing) he would find others of whom he could make nothing. And of the names of Africanus' first three dynasties, two of "Thinites", and one of the earliest Memphites, he would find no certain traces at all.

On the whole, the traveller who has been on the look-out for historical indications will feel it to be pretty certain that up to the head of Dyn. XVIII he has been tracing backwards a single succession of sovereigns who ruled both Upper and Lower Egypt, and during a number of centuries Nubia also, though with clear traces in certain titles of the kings and in the double crown (one white and the other red) of there having been in earlier times at least two kingdoms in the Upper and Lower Countries. But above Dyn. XVIII he will feel quite unable to form any clear opinion not only as to the extent of territory ruled by particular kings, but even as to the relative order of priority and posteriority to be attached to whole groups or dynasties. At the same time he may reasonably think that thus much at least is shown by the monuments, that before the commencement of Dyn. XVIII, and consequently also before the commencement of the Shepherd supremacy which it overthrew, there had reigned at least two kings as suzerains over all Egypt, viz. Sesortasen I, the 2nd king of Africanus's Dyn. XII, and Papa-Maire, the 4th of Dyn. VI (dynasties XV and XIII of Manetho). And, if he has visited Wadi Mogara in the Sinaitic peninsula, the representations and titles of *Sahoura* and of *Snefrou* seen there (and apparently more ancient than those of *Khoufou*, the builder of the great pyramid, and of *Ra-en-tseser*) will seem to possess some importance, so that he will not wonder to find afterwards that Lepsius, in his arrangement of the Berlin Museum, has referred them to Dyn. III of Africanus (X of Manetho), and placed them as the earliest monumental kings, the earliest, that is, who are known not only by their mere names in lists of later date, but by their own contemporary monuments.

The outline thus sketched may be taken to represent the utmost extent of information likely to be collected from any cursory inspection of the monuments themselves, that is, of such of them as may fall under the notice of the ordinary traveller, even if he adds to his voyage up the Nile a supplementary acquaintance with some or all of the principal Egyptian collections at Paris, London, Leyden, and Turin, to which must now be added also that of Berlin. And whatever further conclusions and inferences may have been arrived at by those who have been able to make a more complete survey of all known monuments, and to read whatever is historical in their inscriptions, it is clear enough, and generally confessed, that some clue is still wanting, beyond what the monuments alone have hitherto furnished, before we can make out even in a general and broad way the true mutual relations of the earlier Egyptian dynasties, whether contemporaneous or successive.

While reading one day on board the boat in Mr. Gliddon's book the text of the Old Chronicle, in which it is pretended that a series of XXV Sothic cycles had been completed at the end of the last native dynasty, when the Persian Ochus reconquered Egypt, and considering the different items by which the sum of (1461 × 25 =) 36,525 years was made out, the author's attention was drawn to one clause in which it is said that "here 443 years of the Sothic cycle in XV generations are entered or registered," the place being just above fifteen historical dynasties of kings and just below fifteen other earlier mythological dynasties of Gods and Demigods. The "XV generations" thus placed in the middle space were reckoned to no one of the thirty dynasties among which all the rest of the 36,525 years were distributed. The question suggested itself — To *what* Sothic cycle are these 443 years or XV generations said to belong? and the first step thought of towards finding an answer (since the whole series was pretended to consist of Sothic cycles) was to distribute the sums named into successive spaces of 1461 years each, in order to see whether the 443 years would prove to be connected either with the beginning or the end of any one of the XXV spaces. But then the objection occurred that in truth the whole fancy on which the document was based was mere nonsense; and that there was no *real* "Sothic cycle" in the series from beginning to end. So long indeed as a true Sothic epoch were kept to, it was open to multiply Sothic cycles to any imaginable extent by calculating back into past time or forwards into futurity. But as soon as any one pretended to make a Sothic cycle or series of cycles begin from or end at any other than the right day and in the right year for a Sothic epoch, there was no longer any Sothic cycle in the case, but merely a space or period of 1461 Egyptian years, equal indeed in its length to a Sothic cycle, but yet a totally different thing. For a Sothic cycle is not merely a space of 1461 Egyptian years, but it is that particular space of 1461 such years, and that only, which begins from the conjunction of the movable new-year or Thoth 1 with the heliacal rising of Sirius, fixed to July 20 of our Gregorian Calendar for that part of Egypt which is just above Memphis. But this conjunction occurs only once (and then for 4 years successively) in 1461 movable or 1460 fixed Julian or Canicular years: and July 20 in the first of those 4 years, and in that year alone, is the Sothic epoch. Consequently, though it might suit the humour of the Egyptians to put off an impossible conceit upon the Greeks who knew little or nothing about the Cycle, for the Egyptian priests themselves the expression "the Sothic Cycle" was no more ambiguous than that of "the month," or "the year," or "such a year of the king," which meant of course the current month, the current year, and such a year of the reigning king. For the author of a chronicle ending with Nectanebo, or at any date between the Sothic epochs of July 20 in B. C. 1322 and July 20 in A. D.

139, "the Sothic Cycle," if put simply without reference to any other past or future cycle, and connected with certain particular years, could mean only the cycle actually current, which began from the former and which would run out at the latter of the epochs above-mentioned.

After this discovery — if the perception of a truism can be called a discovery — it followed naturally to observe further that in constructing a fanciful scheme which should pretend to exhibit a cycle or a series of cycles ending at any other date than a true cyclical epoch the first operation (implied by the very terms of the scheme) must be to cut off all those years of the true current Cycle which were yet to run out below the date fixed upon, and to throw them back, so that they might be reckoned as past instead of being looked forward to as future. This then was what the author of the Old Chronicle had done; and, with an ironical humour common among the Egyptians, he had told his readers to their faces the nature of his trick, ticketing and labelling the key to it, and tying it to the lock, or rather leaving it in the lock itself. The event at which the series of the Chronicle ostensibly ends, viz. the conquest of Ochus, to whatever year before Christ it were referred, would necessarily leave *more* than "443 years of the Cycle" below it still to run. But when 443 years were counted upwards from July 20 in A.D. 139, the end of the Cycle which began with July 20 in B.C. 1322, the date which came out, viz. B.C. 305, being that at which Ptolemy Lagi first assumed a crown, both proved sufficiently that the key was now fitted to the lock, and brought out the full idea of the Chronicle, of which only one half, and that of itself pointless, had been seen before. For before all that appeared to be signified was this, that the world had run itself out with the last native dynasty, an idea which might be appropriate as a fanciful lamentation for Egyptian patriotism, but which had no propriety as addressed to Greeks. But now one saw that by throwing up distinctly the last 443 years of the Cycle which were still to run, without noticing those other years of the interval between Nectanebo and the Lagidæ which in some form or other were necessarily thrown up too, the effect was to draw down as it were the conquest of Ochus and make of it one point (the interval being in appearance sunk) with the commencement of the Macedonian dynasty. And the whole sense was this, not only that the old world came to an end with Nectanebo, but also, as a corollary, that a new world with all its hopes and promises was commencing at the date of the Chronicle with the Lagidæ.

The reader cannot fix his attention too closely upon this first step, since when it is fully understood it will make it easy to follow out in Chapter I. the analysis and reconstruction of the Old Chronicle. And when once the Old Chronicle is understood it will in turn serve as a key to all the other Egyptian schemes whether earlier or later.

The six Egyptian schemes examined and explained in this work are in order of time as follows:—First, there is the Hieratic, attached by implication to the cyclical epoch of B.C. 1322. Then the Old Chronicle, similarly attached for its own date to B.C. 305. Another scheme preserved by Diogenes Laertius is of uncertain date, later than Alexander, since it ends at his Egyptian accession, and probably also somewhat later than the Old Chronicle. The "Ægyptiaca" of the original Manetho, the Theban list of Eratosthenes, and the scheme of Ptolemy of Mendes (or whoever else was the Manetho of Africanus,) may be referred to dates not far distant from B.C. 268, B.C. 216, and B.C. 100 respectively. With respect to the last (supposing Ptolemy of Mendes to have been really the author) it was an error to leave it doubtful whether Ptolemy did not write as late as the time of Augustus, since his work seems to be alluded to, and that not as belonging to any contemporary or quite recent author, by Diodorus and Suidas; and Suidas himself is placed by Clinton before the contemporaries of Augustus. His "Manetho of Mendes" therefore must have been earlier still.

All the six schemes are expressed in terms of the movable year of 365 days: and this *of itself* involves a difference of some 7 or 8 months from the reckoning of the sacred Scriptures and Josephus which began from the autumn, since at the date at which the Egyptian reckoning of true human time began, viz. in B.C. 5361, the movable Thoth was at

April 26. Further, three of the six schemes, viz. the Hieratic, the Old Chronicle, and that of Ptolemy, are *cyclical*, pretending to exhibit a series of complete Sothic cycles. And of the three, one, the earliest of all, the Hieratic, ends at a true cyclical epoch; the other two do not. The two latter consequently throw up those years of the Cycle current when they were made which were yet future. But all the three alike insert a sum of 341 fictitious years in order to make time seem to have begun from a cyclical epoch, which in truth it had not done. Two other schemes, those of Manetho and Eratosthenes, are *uncyclical:* and lastly one, that preserved by Diogenes Laertius, is a *compound* sum of years, partly cyclical and partly uncyclical. And, as none of these three last-mentioned schemes pretend to exhibit a single series of complete cycles, they all three omit those 341 fictitious years which are indispensable to such schemes as are cyclical.

Those elements of Egyptian reckoning in terms of the movable year which are common to all the six schemes, cyclical and uncyclical alike, are 3139 years (divisible into 2922 and 217) from the beginning of human time to Menes, and 903 years of kings from Menes to the Sothic epoch of July 20 in B.C. 1322. To these common elements the three cyclical schemes (the Hieratic of B.C. 1322 a copy of which was contained in the Turin Papyrus, that of the Old Chronicle, and that of Ptolemy of Mendes or the Manetho of Africanus) add the 341 fictitious years mentioned above, not prefixing them, however, at the head of all, but interposing them between the first 2922 years and the 217 really following. Five out of the six schemes add a continuation of 978 years of kings from the Sothic epoch of B.C. 1322 to the conquest of Ochus in B.C. 345; and two of the five go on 13 years further to B.C. 332. The two later of the three cyclical schemes throw up besides all those years of the Cycle current in B.C. 345 or 332 which were still future at the one or other of these dates. The two schemes which are not cyclical (those of Manetho and Eratosthenes) contain nevertheless the one a sum of 1435 the other a sum of 443 years really unchronological, but presented as chronological to the

Greeks, and borrowed or imitated from the years thrown up in the cyclical schemes, though without seeking or admitting any cyclical result. Lastly, the mixed scheme preserved by Diogenes Laertius, while it prefixes a round *month* of XXX fictitious cycles or spaces equal in length to cycles, subjoins to these without any mixture of fictitious or concurrent years the true chronological and uncyclical reckoning of the Egyptians from the beginning to Alexander, viz. (3139 + 903 + 978 + 13 =) 5033 movable years.

Besides those peculiarities which have already been specified, the Hieratic scheme, really consisting of three cycles or (2922 + [341 + ]217 + 903 =) 4383 movable years ending July 20 in B.C. 1322, was made to exhibit the much greater sum of 36,525 nominal years, or XXV nominal cycles, by multiplying the first 2922 years or two nominal cycles by 12 into months. From the XXIV pseudo-cycles or (2922 × 12 =) 35,064 months so obtained, and called years, the author of the Old Chronicle suppressed one pseudo-cycle. This he did in order to make room for a fourth true cycle of the world which had been growing since the composition of the Hieratic scheme and was current in his own time, while he retained from the Hieratic scheme its sum of XXV nominal cycles or 36,525 years. So then, as he suppressed 1461 months, and retained the remaining 33,603, these last were in value no longer months but became equal to 1 month and $\frac{1}{23}$rd of a month each. In the scheme of Manetho too, in its mythological part, there is a great sum of 24,000 nominal years derived like those of the Chronicle from the Hieratic scheme, but without any suppression and consequent change of their value, these 24,000 being simply months, and equal to 2000 movable years. Only, as Manetho did not choose to retain the whole cyclical sum of 35,064 months from the Hieratic scheme, he restored the first 900 and the last 22 of the 2922 years multiplied in it by 12 to their original and true character of full years.

Without the key to the composition of the Old Chronicle, and its date, the attempt to make out or to reconstruct any of the other five schemes from such notices of them as we possess would have been much more hopeless than that of a comparative anatomist who from some fragments of bones of three or four different creatures mixed together should undertake to delineate the whole skeletons and bodies of each. Cuvier, it is said, from small portions of bones did actually make drawings of whole skeletons which were afterwards fully verified. And in the case of living creatures a man of science and a good draughtsman, used to deal with proportions and analogies, has something to go upon. But in the case of schemes of chronology partly true and partly fabulous the attempt to reconstruct any one of them and to exhibit it entire from mixed notices and fragments relating to several would be mere guesswork, unless the parts of each were of themselves distinct, and nearly complete, and unless there was a very close symmetry or analogy between the different schemes. But that which makes the reconstruction of the Egyptian Chronicles not only less difficult than the task of the comparative anatomist but even easy, and certain of success, is this, that the measure and reckoning of time in all of them is the same, and the elementary sums of years on which they are all based are the same, so that with only slight data as to the peculiarities of any one scheme one can either fill up what is wanting in particular parts, or cut off what is redundant, with something like mathematical certainty. Every year day and hour being fixed as in a framework within the measure of the four Sothic cycles commencing from July 20 in B.C. 5702, (that is 341 movable years according to Egyptian reckoning before man was upon the earth,) and ending at July 20 in A.D. 139, and the schemes themselves being historically successive, and each of them in turn based upon those which had preceded, every point in any one of them can be compared with every point in any other: and to whatever extent particular years may in any scheme be misplaced or misrepresented, they are always there, and can be found out and compared with the same years in each of the other analogous schemes, and brought back to their true and original places, and to their true and original form and designation. Nor does this hold only of those schemes which are cyclical; but even those (for instance, that of the original Manetho) which are not cyclical, being still constructed with materials common to the cyclical schemes, and in terms of the same movable year, are hence equally explainable and recoverable by a knowledge of the original elements common to both, and by comparison with the schemes that are cyclical.

After what may be called the abstract or cyclical chronology, supposing the construction of each scheme to have been made out, as in the first four chapters of this work, and to be understood, if any one inquires after those results which are properly historical, and which will be to the general reader more intelligible, and more interesting, they are these: —

I. First, the Old Chronicle (p. 7, &c.) gives *without names* a series (not to be supposed to correspond uniformly to actual reigns) of lxxvi royal *generations*, averaging 24¾ years each, divided into xv *dynasties*, the whole in a space of 1881 movable years from the commencement of the native monarchy, Feb. 22, B.C. 2224, to its extinction, Nov. 16, B.C. 345.

II. The original Manetho (pp. 123, 91, and 441) enables us to cover with names and *actual reigns*, in a rough and general way, the greater part of the blank dynasties of the Chronicle. Only for the iv generations of its Dyn. XVII, called Memphite, and for the viii Theban generations of its Dyn. XX, Manetho leaves us quite at fault. For *parts* of Dynasties XVIII, XIX, XXI, and XXVI too there is need of some further resources than are supplied by his lists. On the other hand Manetho gives names and reigns for a number of early dynasties, viz. one of Tanites (called in the lists of Ptolemy Thinites), three called Memphite, and one called by Ptolemy "Elephantinite" (perhaps Heliopolite), in all for five dynasties in *Lower* Egypt, which are not recognisable in the series of the Chronicle. And again for *Upper* Egypt Manetho gives three dynasties, one of viii Diospolites with names and reigns, and two others without names or reigns but with xvi "Diospolite" kings to the one and lxxvi [xxxvi] called by Ptolemy Xoites (really Nubians) to the other, which are equally unplaced in the series of the Chronicle. Manetho then out of his XXIII dynasties of kings has eight in all which though absent from the Chronicle must be supposed to have been contemporaneous with the first three dynasties and the first 477 years of its kings. And in fact, though he seems to make for the kings in all a sum of 3555 years, he himself marks for his Egyptian reader the same sum with the Chronicle, viz. 1881 years, (of which 477 are anterior to Dyn. XVIII) as alone successive or chronological. What is more, he alludes to and marks the duration of each of the first three sovereign dynasties (XVI, XVII, and XXVII) of the Chronicle, viz. 190, 103, and 184 years, the first sum of the three being marked indeed only indirectly, but the other two distinctly (pp. 264 and 285).

The reigns in Manetho's first six dynasties of kings (the early dynasties of *Lower* Egypt), being made to average over 30 years each, suggest the suspicion — a suspicion justified also by finding monumental names not in his lists intermixed near Memphis with those of his Memphites and " Elephantinites " — that either there were many more kings than he has named, or that they reigned fewer years. Both these suspicions will turn out to be true at once. On the other hand, whether the actual reigns of the early dynasties, and even the dynasties themselves, of *Upper* Egypt were more numerous than is acknowledged by Manetho or not, the names and reigns of their kings being omitted by him — at least for two out of three dynasties — are plainly to seek from other sources.

Below Dyn. XVIII, while there is a general agreement or parallelism, a comparison of Manetho's *reigns* with the *generations* of the Chronicle reveals some discrepancies in the designations of dynasties, and some considerable differences in their subdivision and duration. And these are connected with remarkable dislocations; Manetho having allowed himself (and the Chronicle itself in its Dyn. XXVII had set him the example) to suppress years and kings in certain places, while he balanced his suppressions by unhistorical insertions elsewhere; and this to such an extent that, but for the Chronicle, any attempt at an exact rectification would have been hopeless.

Manetho has also before Menes four dynasties of Manes

or ghost-kings, an enigma upon the meaning of which the Chronicle throws no light.

III. Eratosthenes, under whose name are to be understood the priests, the composers of his list, throws great light on the relations of Manetho's first ten dynasties of kings both to one another and to the first three dynasties of the kings of the Chronicle. As his plan was to take for his basis and to fill up with names the *generations* of the Chronicle he does not help us to place any *additional* monumental names of those omitted by Manetho in the early dynasties of *Lower* Egypt, but he takes Manetho's names as they stand, only reducing the fictitious and extravagant reigns to the average length of the generations of the Chronicle. But for the early dynasties of *Upper* Egypt he does give as many as eleven names or generations of kings omitted by Manetho (pp. 374, &c. and 401). The chief value, however, of his list lies in this, that whereas, if he had simply filled up with names from Manetho the first three dynasties and the first 477 years of the kings of the Chronicle, he would have given us no fresh light except on the one most important point of the composition of its Dyn. XVII, (for its Dynasties XVI and XXVII are identifiable of themselves in Manetho's Dynasties VIII and XVII, I and XV of Ptolemy) his informants by taking in xv generations and 443 unchronological years of the Chronicle (being those 443 of the Cycle which it names as such and throws up), by omitting the Shepherds of its Dyn. XXVII, and lastly by encroaching upon Dyn. XVIII to the extent of 156 years, have managed to place as many as xxii generations and reigns with (443 + 184 + 156 =) 783 years besides those which represent, or which should have represented, the first three sovereign dynasties of the Chronicle. And their whole work is arranged so symmetrically that, after commencing with the 190 years of the Tanites of Dyn. XVI of the Chronicle (VIII of Manetho, but I of Ptolemy) as a common root or source, an equal space of 443 years is twice measured off, first to a selection from the early kings of *Lower*, and then to a selection from the early kings of *Upper* Egypt (p. 298). On examining more closely these selections it appears that Dyn. XVII of the Old Chronicle unites the two (p. 314), its four sovereign generations being taken two of them (which are represented by *Sahoura* and *Snefrou*) with 39 years from the latter part of Dyn. X of Manetho (III of Ptolemy), the third (that of Phiops) with 21 or 22 years from the end of his Dyn. XIII (VI of Ptolemy), and the fourth [Sesortasen I.] with 42 years from the head of his Dyn. XV (XII of Ptolemy). Thus through their later reigns the relative places of Dynasties X and XIII, and through its first reign the relative place of Dyn. XV of Manetho is fixed; and it appears that the early local Memphites of Lower Egypt, if they had the full sum of 214 years, began (214 – 103 =) 111 years before Dyn. XVII of the Chronicle, that is 79 years after the epoch of Menes; and again that the "Memphites" of Central Egypt, supposing them to have ended about 22 years after the death of Phiops and to have had the sum of 197 years, which however is shown by the Papyrus to be too great by 16, began (197 – 22 = 175 – 22 = 153 – 39 =) 114, or (114 – 16 =) 98 years, before Dyn. XVII of the Chronicle, that is 92 years after the epoch of Menes; while the Diospolites of Dynasty XV (XII of Ptolemy), after the death of their first or second king Sesortasen I., were for their remaining 133 years contemporary with the Shepherds of Dynasty XXVII of the Chronicle, the death of Sesortasen I. being about (260 – 184 =) 76 years after the commencement of Dyn. XVII of *Manetho* (XV of Ptolemy) corresponding in its last 184 years to Dyn. XXVII of the Chronicle. And parallel in a manner with these Diospolite contemporaries of the Shepherds, in that one of the two spaces of 443 years which stands first and is given to Lower Egypt, Eratosthenes exhibits the Memphite pyramid-builders of Manetho's Dyn. XI (IV of Ptolemy), who besides are expressly said to have followed through a change of the reigning family the earlier Memphite line of Dyn. X (III of Ptolemy), two reigns of which have already been identified with the first two generations of Dyn. XVII of the Chronicle. Respecting the later Tanites and the "Elephantinites" or Heliopolites who make Manetho's Dynasties IX and XII (II and V of Ptolemy) Eratosthenes shows that they might be omitted as of secondary importance; while their relative position in Manetho's lists, and the mixture of names of the "Elephantinites" with those of the Memphite pyramid-builders in the tombs near Memphis, shows thus much at least, that the earliest of the second group of Tanites were less than 190 years before the commencement of Dyn. XVII of the Chronicle, while the Elephantinites or Heliopolites probably began together with the second line of local Memphites (though they may possibly have begun earlier), and were together with them and with the successors of Sesortasen I. in the Thebaid contemporary with Dyn. XXVII of the Chronicle. In Upper Egypt again eight kings or generations, hinted to be Diospolites, are enumerated by Eratosthenes before he gives the first reign of Manetho's Dyn. XV (XII of Ptolemy); and Manetho also has in his lists before that dynasty an anonymous line of "xvi Diospolites," who must be supposed to have *begun at least* before it. If then it were inferred from the list of Eratosthenes that eight of these sixteen Diospolites (though not likely to be the same eight which he names to represent the whole line) were in fact earlier than the reign of Sesortasen I., the fourth generation of Dyn. XVII of the Chronicle, these first eight might seem to have begun ($8 \times 24\frac{3}{4} =$) 198 years (according to the average length of the generations of the Chronicle) before the reign in question, and ($198 - 22 = 176 - 39 =$) 137 before the first generation of Dyn. XVII of the Chronicle, and so only 53 years after the epoch of Menes. But as the last name of the eight in the list of Eratosthenes is identified by the monuments with the immediate predecessor of Amosis and Dyn. XVIII, the whole xvi reigns of Manetho, taken together, cannot be calculated to have begun more than ($16 \times 24\frac{3}{4} =$) 396 years before the end of Dyn. XXVII of the Chronicle, that is ($396 - 184 = 212 - 103 =$) 109 before the beginning of its Dyn. XVII, or ($190 - 109 =$) 81 below the epoch of Menes. And if this estimate be assumed to be correct — it is more likely to be somewhat too high than too low — it results that the establishment of petty kings at Memphis, in Central Egypt, and in the Thebaid, took place nearly at one and the same time, the estimated dates being 70 [corrected to 79], 76 [corr. 92], and 81 [corr. 97?] years after the epoch of Menes. And, reasoning from the short intervals in this progression southwards, one may infer with some probability that kings had begun to reign in Heliopolis (Castor, or whoever is the original "*Barbarus*," names a line of "Heliopolites") a little earlier than at Memphis, and perhaps some secondary line nearer to Tanis, and thence called Tanite (if these were not themselves the earliest Heliopolites), may have commenced a little earlier still. But there may well have been more lines of early kings who are now represented only by Manetho's two Dynasties IX and X (III and IV of Ptolemy) under the designations of Tanites and Memphites. On this subject the Manes of Manetho, Dyn. VII of Ptolemy, and the fragments of the Turin Papyrus, have already thrown some light; but much remains still obscure, which can be cleared up only by fresh discoveries.

Lastly, after the generations taken from Manetho's Dynasties XIV and XV (XI and XII of Ptolemy), Eratosthenes has within the 443 years of Upper Egypt three more generations and names, one of which may be called double, as if to represent Manetho's Dyn. XVI (XIV of Ptolemy). And he has so connected indirectly these three or four generations with the sum of 184 years, while Dyn. XVI of Manetho (XIV of Ptolemy) is directly connected with the same sum, as to hint pretty clearly that these kings also, who in actual number were a prodigious multitude, were contemporary with the three or four generations and the 184 years of Dyn. XXVII of the Chronicle.

The list of Eratosthenes in several of its parts shows traces of conformity with the selection of kings exhibited in the Thothmes Chamber of Karnak (pp. 293 and 501), a conformity the more interesting as this list is known to have been made out at Thebes. Its most remarkable feature of making two equal compartments, one for early kings of *Lower*, and one for those of *Upper* Egypt, is seemingly imitated, on a reduced scale, from the same Thothmes Chamber. Thence too a like arrangement may have been borrowed in much earlier times by the hieratic papyri, in which instead of about xxx there were as many as cxliii kings in each of the two corresponding divisions.

IV. The latest Egyptian scheme is that of the Manetho of Africanus (pp. 91 and 437), identifiable perhaps with Ptolemy of Mendes. This, being taken alone, and ascribed to the original Manetho, has hitherto been a most fertile source of error and confusion. But when studied in its true character and analysed by the help of the Chronicle, of the genuine Manetho, and of Eratosthenes, it makes us ample amends. For after its peculiar and purely fictitious additions (required by its cyclical scheme of reduced years) have been detected and set aside, its remaining additions throw a new and unexpected light on those four dynasties of Manes or ghost-kings in the scheme of the original Manetho which otherwise, though they might suggest various surmises, must have remained inexplicable. And, again, the original Manetho and the Manetho of Ptolemy together contain such an exhibition of the lists of kings belonging to the oldest of all Egyptian schemes, the Hieratic, that by their help we are enabled to reconstruct with tolerable certainty — at least without room for any great error — the fragments of the Turin Papyrus (pp. 465—512).

V. This is perhaps the most interesting result and reward of all the preceding investigations. For it is one thing to infer (as in Chapter I. p. 32) that there probably existed an earlier scheme, from which the Old Chronicle was derived and altered, and that its construction was probably of such and such a kind, and another to have before us the scheme itself, with its general features still plainly discernible though much mutilated in detail. And now we *have* before us the scheme itself (pp. 508—512), fixed by its idea and nature to the date of July 20, B.C. 1322, and in a copy the actual writing of which cannot be supposed to be later than the end of the 13th century before Christ, that is, 800 years before a similar papyrus was shown by the priests of Phthah at Memphis to Herodotus. This, being by far the most ancient and authentic of all writings concerning Egyptian history, sheds, even in its present mutilated state, a flood of light not only upon the mythological dynasties of the original Manetho, and upon those of his Manes and other kings, as well as upon the additions of Ptolemy, but also on some of the phenomena presented by the monuments, especially on the Thothmes Chamber of kings. Some of its historical revelations are very curious. We learn from it, first, that 330 or 331 kings were *rightly* named to Herodotus as having reigned from Menes to Sesostris (Sesostris here being Rameses III.), but that their years when added up together instead of being above 11,000, as Herodotus supposed, reckoning each king as a full life-generation, were in all only 3750. Again, it shows that, instead of exaggerating, the original Manetho had greatly curtailed both for Lower and for Upper Egypt the number of the kings before Rameses III.; and that for *Upper* Egypt he had also vastly curtailed the sum of their years; while for all the early kings of *Lower* Egypt, on the contrary, whether named or omitted, the sum of their years was not only given in full, but with some exaggeration. The Papyrus reveals further — since the early kings of Lower Egypt, of whom Manetho makes xlix in six dynasties, were really no fewer than (xlix + xl =) lxxxix — that either the local dynasties were more numerous than Manetho has represented, or the reigns were shorter by one half or nearly one half, or associations in the throne were continual; or, lastly, two or three such causes, but not all to an equal extent, may have concurred together. At the lowest the kings of Lower Egypt would have reigned on an average about 15 years each. But respecting the kings of Upper Egypt the Papyrus shows that, while in those groups which may more properly be called dynasties they seem to have reigned on an average above 20 years each (though this average may be only apparent if there were many associations), there was also a multitudinous group of no fewer than (cxliii + xix =) clxii kings who, though possessing the royal title, reigned only from 1 to 4 years each. And, the whole of this multitude being derived from the first two kings of Dyn. XV of the original Manetho (XII of Ptolemy), they are consequently confined for their extreme chronological limits between the commencement of the last generation of Dyn. XVII of the Chronicle and the end of its Dyn. XXVII, that is, within a space of less than (42 + 184 =) 226 years; though Manetho connects with them the sum of only 184 years, which was the time of the domination of the Shepherds in Lower Egypt. Besides these general results, the Papyrus enables us to make out, or very nearly, the full series of (ix + ix) xviii reigns out of which Manetho has made his Dyn. XII (V of Ptolemy) of only ix Elephantinites, with 248 years, which appears to have been the true sum. It gives us again the full list of the reigns answering to Manetho's Dyn. XIII (VI of Ptolemy), showing that in this he gave all the first vi reigns, but suppressed iv short reigns after the name of Nitocris, while he added to the sum total of the dynasty 16 years, its true sum being only 181. It adds historical certainty to the long reign of Phiops (Papa Maire) of 94 years, while the monuments, marking only his 16th or 18th year, hint a distinction between those many years which he must have reigned previously as a local king in central Egypt and the last 21 or 22 of his life during which he was suzerain, making the 3rd of the 4 generations of Dyn. XVII of the Chronicle between Snefrou and Sesortasen I. In him we recognise the Mœris of Herodotus, the first Egyptian king "who did anything very remarkable," and the immediate predecessor *as suzerain* of the earliest Sesostris the conqueror of Nubia. He was born in B.C. 2074, that is, 85 years after the birth of the patriarch Abraham, shortly after his sojourn in Egypt, and before the destruction of Sodom and Gomorrhah; he succeeded to the title of local king in central Egypt (his territory including the Fayoum) at the age of only 6 years, and he was already 40 years of age when the supremacy passed from Tanis to Memphis. This was in B.C. 2034; when Abraham was 125 years old, and Isaac 25; so that, if the sculptures of the first two Memphite suzerains *Sahoura* and *Snefrou* which are still seen at the copper-works of Wadi Mogara in the Sinaitic peninsula and elsewhere are really the most ancient contemporary inscriptions known, these earliest of Egyptian monuments are to be referred to dates for Sahoura between the 125th and 144th (B.C. 2034 and B.C. 2015), and for Snefrou between the 144th and the 164th year of Abraham, (B.C. 2015 and B.C. 1996). The numerous monuments of Papa Maire himself will belong to the 21 years between the 164th of Abraham (the 64th of Isaac and the 4th of Jacob) and the 85th of Isaac or 25th of Jacob (B C. 1997 and B.C. 1975); while the monuments of Sesortasen I. and of his father-in-law and colleague Amenemhe I. will belong to the (16 + 42 =) 58 years ending in B.C. 1932 in the 128th of Isaac, which was the 68th of Jacob. The Turin Papyrus has preserved also the sum of the years for the viii kings of Dyn. XV of Manetho (XII of Ptolemy), so that we can make out with general certainty the reigns, and assure ourselves that the 43 and the 16 years nominally given to his Dyn. XIV (XI of Ptolemy) are really to be restored and added to the 160 of his Dyn. XV, which has been improperly curtailed, though after this restoration there is an overplus of 6 years, its true hieratic sum being 213 not 219 years. In the case of this dynasty the lists of Eratosthenes and the monuments, which are numerous, combine their evidence, so as to enable us to distinguish the successive or chronological years underneath the gross sum made by adding up the reigns, most of which were in part associate (see p. 391). The Papyrus, too, in conjunction with the monuments and with the lists of Ptolemy, throws light on the peculiar character of Dyn. XVI of Manetho (XIV of Ptolemy) and on that half of the Thothmes Chamber which answers to it, by showing both that it was derived from the first kings of Dyn. XV (XII of Ptolemy), that it was locally connected with Nubia, and also that, unlike other dynasties, instead of a single succession it consisted of a selection from a number of groups, and of individual kings, to be found in full only in the hieratic lists.

VI. Lastly, it is only through a previous knowledge of the elements entering into the composition of the Chronicle and other schemes that one is able (p. 21) to decompose with certainty the sum of 48,863 years mentioned by Diogenes Laertius into a prefixed month of XXX fictitious Sothic cycles and an uncyclical sum of 5033 vague years attached to it, which last is the Egyptian reckoning of true human time from the beginning to Alexander, that is from April 22 in B.C.

5361 to Nov. 16 in B.C. 332. This brief but invaluable summary is at once the complement of all preceding reconstructions and explanations and the proof of their accuracy.

Besides the six Egyptian schemes themselves, which thus illustrate mutually one another, the knowledge of them enables one to explain—upon the whole satisfactorily—and to account for the relations of Herodotus (p. 557–600) and Diodorus Siculus (p. 619–679) and nearly all other statements which occur in different authors.

The last three chapters of this work, in which some account is given of the sacred and mixed chronology of Africanus, of Eusebius, and of Anianus, with the last of whom are associated Panodorus and Syncellus, may be regarded as appendices intended to enable the reader to judge with more accuracy of the text of the Egyptian lists exhibited by each of these writers. The knowledge of their peculiar reckonings, joined to that of the six schemes properly Egyptian, enables one to refer nearly all the different texts and variations to their true sources and connections, and to distinguish all such readings as are due only to the pen of Eusebius or of Anianus from the genuine text or variants of one or other of the Egyptian Chronicles. Moreover, the scheme of Anianus (though historically worthless) supplies a true connection and common measure of heathen-Egyptian and Christian chronology. Even with his arbitrary and illegitimate reduction of the old Egyptian to his own sacred reckoning, his recognition of the true character and amount of the "years of the Cycle" thrown up by the Chronicle, and his ejection of 483 years, in consequence, from his Egyptian series above the last Persian conquest (p. 8), is extremely valuable, as adding at the end of all the testimony of a native Egyptian and Christian writer to the correctness of that observation out of which this whole work originated, and which, however like a truism, had not merely been unnoticed by other Jewish and Christian writers (so far as the author is aware) from Josephus downwards, but had been contradicted in effect by them all; since all have treated those 483 years as really belonging to some very early period of Egyptian history, whether before or after

Menes, to say nothing of other years equally unchronological to which the same error has been extended.

It is to be regretted that Anianus, instead of first making out his own sacred scheme, like Eusebius, and then forging such an Egyptian scheme and such a reduction of the nominal years of the Chronicle as should agree with it, did not do with the whole scheme of the Chronicle as Africanus seems at one time to have done with one length of the lists of Ptolemy, namely, take it as his guide, so as not to depart from it unnecessarily, or upon the whole, in dealing with those parts of sacred chronology where there seemed to be breaks in the Scriptures, or where there was a variety of conflicting readings or reckonings in Jewish and Christian authors. Perhaps, if he had understood the true value of the nominal years of the Chronicle, and how many of them in all were really reducible, and that 341 other years were not to be reduced as months, still less to be reckoned as full years, but to be ejected as fictitious, he might have noticed how closely the true chronological sum of the Chronicle approached to that made by Clemens of Alexandria (he differs in one of his reckonings by only 12 years), and might have been moved by so close an agreement to make the Egyptian reckoning his standard for ruling such doubts as might account for the difference.

As it is, that scheme of sacred chronology which has been drawn out in Chapter I from the Greek Scriptures and Josephus harmonised (p. 22—28) must be viewed (as it is in truth) as a totally separate work, unsupported by the express concurrence of any former writer. And it must be examined and tested without any regard to its close agreement with the Egyptian reckoning, which was not yet fully understood by the author when it was first made out. If, however, it should stand the test of criticism, or if, which is also possible, any inaccuracies discoverable in it should be found to balance one another, the discovery of an independent heathen reckoning much more ancient seemingly than the fourteenth century before Christ, and so probably preserved from the very beginning, will add such weight to that sacred reckoning with which it coincides that it will have a natural claim to prevail over all others; and there will no longer be the same objection as heretofore against reckoning in years of the world; but, on the contrary, it may be convenient to reckon profane chronology downwards, in terms of the movable Egyptian year reduced to those of the anticipated and uncorrected Julian or Canicular, with which the sacred reckoning of Hebrew years will then be parallel, provided only some eight months be restored at the head of the Egyptian reckoning, to carry it back from the movable Thoth 1, which in B.C. (5702 – 341 = ) 5361 was at April 22, to the fixed Hebrew commencement of Tisri 1, in the autumn preceding.

A few words must still be added respecting the monuments. What may be learned from them at once, and on a superficial inspection, has been stated at the outset. But the reader may wish to know also how they bear upon the written lists and chronicles, after these latter have been studied and compared together.

First, then, besides various names—especially those of the builders of the three great pyramids—identifiable in Manetho's Dynasties X, XI, XII, and XIII (III, IV, V, and VI of Ptolemy), the monuments have made known some at least of those early kings of Lower Egypt whom Manetho has banished to his Manes, and as many as 19 or 20 kings of Upper Egypt and Nubia belonging to his anonymous Dyn. XVI (XIV of Ptolemy), though in both cases a clue is wanting to the order of succession.*

* Since this has been in type, M. Mariette (in the *Revue Archéologique* of July, 1860) has announced the discovery near Memphis of a priest's tomb, containing in two rows as many as forty royal cartouches. Among these he thinks he finds from Dyn. I (that is, of Africanus) one name, *Miebaes*; from Dyn. II *Kaiechos*, *Binothris*, *Sethenes*, *Nephercheres*, and *Sesochris*; from Dyn. III *Necherophes*, *Soyphis*, and *Siphuris*; from Dyn. IV *Shouphou*, *Ratoiches*, and *Chaphra*; from Dyn. V *Usercheres*, *Nephercheres*, *Mencheres*, *Tatcheres*, and *Ounos*; and from Dyn. VI *Othoes* and *Phiops*. Then follow, he says, at once the kings of Dyn. XII, preceded by two names (*Mentuhotep* and *Ameni*) of Dyn XI, and followed by one other name (*Ra-Sevek-kar*) either of the same dynasty or of Dyn XIV. And, lastly, there are six names (of which the latest is *Rameses II.*) from Dyn. XVIII. He observes that the names of Dyn. XII with the other three inclosing them are distinguished by an inversion of order, the name of *Mentuhotep* being placed in immediate juxtaposition with that of *Amosis* the head of Dyn. XVIII. He adds (though

There is also a whole line of names in the Tablet of Abydos (now in the British Museum), which is omitted by Manetho, and which may perhaps be the same with that group of xviii kings which followed next after Dyn. XIII of Manetho (VI of Ptolemy), in the hieratic papyri. The fourteen names still preserved, and nearly all entire, not having been given elsewhere in the body of this work, are here subjoined. They read as follows (the first seemingly was preceded by 12 other cartouches, now broken away):— 13. . . . *ef*; 14. . . . *neterkar*; 15. *Menkar-ra*; 16 *Nepherkar-ra*; 17. *Nepherkar-ra Nebbi*; 18. *Tatkar-ra Mamou*; 19. *Nepherkar-ra Chentou*; 20. *Meren-hor*; 21. *Snepherkar*; 22. *Karen-ra*; 23. *Nepherkar-ra Rerlou*; 24. . . *nepherkar*; 25. *Nepherkar-ra Sab-en-Pepi* (or *Pepisneb*); 26. *Snepherkar Annou.* After these, at the commencement of the lower line, there were eight cartouches, now lost, and then five names of Manetho's Dyn. XV, and those of Dyn. XVIII (XII and XVIII of Ptolemy).

For Manetho's earliest "Diospolite" dynasty, Dyn. XIV (XI of Ptolemy), which equally with his Dyn. XVI is anonymous, the full number of sixteen names—perhaps, indeed, one or two more than sixteen—seems to have been found (p. 369); and of these thirteen, at least, are exhibited in the Thothmes Chamber of Karnak, in their true relative order of succession. They are also fixed by their tombs to have been strictly and locally Diospolites, in like manner as the kings of Manetho's Dynasties X and XI (III and IV of Ptolemy) were strictly and locally Memphites.

Respecting the war with the Shepherds, about the time of

the known names indicated scarcely leave room for so many new *names*) that 12 out of the 40 *cartouches* are *new*. The names being merely a selection, and the tomb itself being of the time of Rameses II, this discovery may perhaps add little or nothing to our actual knowledge. Still it is valuable as giving names from the early dynasties in their proper order, the dynasties named or indicated by M. Mariette according to the numeration of Ptolemy and Africanus, being really Dynasties VIII, IX, X, XI, XII, XIII, XIV, XV, XVI, and XVIII of the original Manetho. The Shepherds only of his Dyn. XVII (XV of Afric.) are altogether omitted (as was sure to be the case), the kings of Dyn. XV, with others of the Upper Country who outlasted them, being no doubt intended to stand out prominently as the only *legitimate* claimants of all Egypt during the time of the strangers.

the commencement of Dyn. XVIII, some valuable information has been preserved by contemporary inscriptions, and by an hieratic papyrus. In particular, the name of the local predecessor of Amosis in the Thebaid, *Ra-Sekenn*, is ascertained; and it is one which appears in a corresponding position both in the Thothmes Chamber and in the written list of Eratosthenes. The capture of Avaris, which Manetho puts before the first year of Amosis, seems, on the contrary, to be fixed to his *fifth* year (p. 197); and the name of one, at least, of the Shepherd kings has been found on sculptured fragments in the ruins of Tanis, and found, too, in connection with the name of Sutech (a form of Typhon) whom the Shepherds are said in an hieratic papyrus to have worshipped to the exclusion of all other deities. This throws light both on the impiety imputed afterwards to them and to their Memphite tributaries, and on the assertion of Manetho that Avaris was " from the first *Typhonian*," and upon the statement made in other words to Herodotus, that Egypt for 150 years was subjected by destiny to a Typhonian influence.

The true place of the fifteen years suppressed by Manetho on Dyn. XVIII is fixed by the monuments of the Sun-worshippers; and the name of Chousan-Atin with one or two others equally omitted by the lists are now restored with certainty between Amenoph III. and Horus (p. 177, &c.). But for the interval between Horus and Rameses I. monumental names to justify or to replace those of Manetho's lists are still to seek (p. 218).

In Dyn. XIX Manetho has twice consolidated a number of *actual reigns* of which the author of the Chronicle had made together only one *generation;* and he has besides transposed one king, Rameses III., and blended him into one fabulous person with Seti II. the first legitimate, but not the first actual, king of the dynasty. But this dynasty, by the help of the monuments, is now made out satisfactorily, so that both the small number of five *generations* given by the Chronicle to its 194 years is explained and justified, and the incredible *reigns* assigned for it by Manetho are corrected and filled up to their true number (pp. 222—234).

The Diospolites, too, of Dynasty XX of the Chronicle

(pp. 235–241), from whom Manetho has cut off 93 of their 228 years, transferring them to a new Tanite dynasty of his own, are exhibited by the monuments with their full number of viii *generations*, or xii *actual reigns*, though the order of some of the later reigns is still open to doubt. Whether the 93 years cut off by Manetho really belonged concurrently to a distinct family of Tanites (the remaining 42 years of his Dyn. XXI are certainly transposed), future discoveries may show.

But as regards the nine kings of Manetho's Bubastite Dyn. XXII, for whom he gives only three names and 120 years, the monuments have both supplied the six names wanting, and have shown that the nine taken together had many more years than 120, so as to correspond rather to the two Tanite or Bubastite Dynasties XXI and XXII of the Chronicle, with vi and iii generations respectively, and with 121 and 48 years (p. 244).

Next, the monuments enable us to restore Petubast, put up by Manetho over the heads of Osorchon and Psammis (these two reigns are Dyn. XXIII of the Chronicle), to his true place as head of the Saite Dynasty XXIV, which no doubt had three kings answering to its three generations in the Chronicle, and not one only (p. 246).

The monuments show too that the last king of the three Ethiopians, Tirhakah, reigned on, and was the only sovereign known at Memphis many years after the date assigned for the end of his dynasty, which seems to have been that of his withdrawal to Napata. So that there would be no room left for the Sethon of Herodotus, even if the date of the overthrow of Sennacherib had not been, as it was, much earlier, and soon after the accession of Tirhakah (pp. 248 and 578).

In Dyn. XXVI again (p. 250), though it needed no help from the monuments to set aside Manetho's first three names, help was absolutely needed to fill up the first two generations of the seven of the Chronicle, and to show the historical character and the value of the name Ammeris prefixed to this dynasty by Ptolemy, and preserved only in the lists of Eusebius.

The pedigree of the Chief Architects of all Egypt (p. 593)

extending over a space of above 800 years and affording at once a correction and supplement to the generations reckoned by Herodotus from Sesostris (Rameses III.), and a proof of the true length of the interval between Shishonk I. and Amasis, confused by the transpositions of Manetho, is not the least valuable nor the least curious of those comments on the written lists which have been supplied by the monuments.

And lastly, it is remarkable to find the Apis-bulls, the deification of which when living was the very climax of religious darkness and degradation, serving after many ages by their tombs and epitaphs towards the illustration of certain points in sacred history, and so towards the glory of God and of His truth. Their tombs, the earliest of which as yet found (p. 217) belong to the middle of the 16th century before Christ, present a series of stelæ (often dated) with royal names almost continuous down to the times of the Ptolemies and Cæsars.

The author is well aware that so far as his work treats of the monuments there may be cause for regret that it did not originate with some one better qualified. Still it seemed impossible to leave that branch of the subject untouched without disappointing the reader in his natural expectations. And after all it is a question only of a little more or a little less of imperfection. For our knowledge of the monuments (even the knowledge of those who are esteemed authorities) being as yet in itself imperfect and progressive, the utmost that can be hoped for even from the most competent writer is that he should state fairly the results already obtained at the date of his publication, that he should map out the ground as yet unexplored, and that he should give a point to further researches by throwing out such guesses and theories as it may be worth while for others to take pains either to establish or to refute. As regards then this part or element in his work the author only hopes that its imperfections may not so preponderate as to prevent its being found on the whole a useful accompaniment to that more essential portion which treats of the written Chronicles. He desires at the same time to return thanks to all those from whose kindness or courtesy he has received any assistance or information. Among these are Mr. and Mrs. Lieder at Cairo, M. Mariette, Dr. Lepsius, M. De Rougé, and Sir Gardner Wilkinson. But his more particular thanks are due to Signor Orcurti at Turin for facilitating his study of the Royal Papyrus, to Professor Brugsch at Berlin for looking over with him his verified facsimile, and communicating some valuable remarks of his own, and to Mr. Birch of the British Museum for revising that English reconstruction of the same papyrus which is now printed as well as for many other kindnesses. Of the use that has been made of published works it is unnecessary to speak, as it will appear of itself whenever they are named or referred to, and the author has already disclaimed all pretence of treating of the monuments as an original authority. But it is only fair towards one eminent and talented writer, Baron Bunsen, whose theories are not much favoured by the Egyptian Chronicles, to acknowledge (and the more fully on that account) how greatly the author has been indebted to his work. Embodying as it does quite an apparatus of necessary documents, instrumental treatises, and materials, it has been invaluable to one who, from living an unsettled life, has often had access to no other Egyptian library than a bundle of his own MS. notes and such few books as he could carry about with him in his portmanteau.

And now it may be asked What then after all is the true place of Egypt in universal history? In order to receive a reply to this question the reader shall be invited to go up in thought to the area of the Capitol at Rome — the spot where Romulus is said to have opened his Asylum — within a stone's throw of which the greater part of this work was written. And first, casting a glance up the steps on our left as if to the six-columned façade of Jupiter Capitolinus, let us reflect on the prodigious change which has been made by Christianity. Here was once the temple to which Roman conquerors ascended in their triumphs; to which not the spoils only of the earth with its chieftains, but the very gods of the nations were, in a manner, led as captives. And what was it — besides or under the name of Jupiter — that was here worshipped by the conquerors themselves? Their own ancestor Romulus — the offspring of violence and lust, itself deified as Mars — suckled by a wolf — called to reign by eagles or vultures — a leader of robbers and outcasts — who cemented the foundations of his new city with the blood of his brother. They worshipped too the city itself — that is their own spirit of pride, cruelty, ambition, and force, personified in the goddess Roma.

From this same spot, however, a religion has gone forth teaching gentleness, humility, charity, purity, and hope after death. It has gone forth, and has subdued and remoulded not only the heathen empire of the Romans, but also those barbarous nations of the West and North by which that empire was finally overrun. We see now on the site of the temple of Jupiter a church built in His name to whom as a man the sceptre of the world belonged not by robbery but of right, but whose birth, and infancy, and youth, and whose whole life of beneficence, and lowliness, and patience, and suffering are unspeakable contrasts to the filthy and cruel and proud fables attaching to the cradle of worldly power. This church is tenanted by the votaries of chastity and obedience, and more especially of poverty (connected with it is the chief convent of the Franciscans), and the object of popular devotion which in it has supplanted Mars and Romulus and the she-wolf and the eagle and Jupiter, and Rome herself, is the image—in itself a coarse image in olive wood from Gethsemane—of a new-born child. Let any one who pleases meditate on the contrast embodied in this nativity as the germ of universal empire.

Here then we are at the very centre of history, the source from which the religion, the laws, the civilisation, the literature, and in great part the languages of the West, have been evolved. And the nations of the West have now attained such a superiority of energy and influence, that through them all the future history of the habitable globe is linked to Rome. Looking down towards the Forum and the sites of the Julian and Æmilian Basilicas, we see the source of our civil law. To our right is the Palatine hill with those ruins from which all "*palaces*" are named. Just behind us to the left was the temple of Juno Moneta, whence are derived the words *money* and *mint*. The area of the Senate-house below our feet with its outer porch for the tribunes of the people, and the remains of the Rostra and the Comitium, in close connection beyond, are the germs of all our mixed forms of government. The columns of the temple of Vespasian and the arch of Titus, with the spoils of the temple of Jerusalem still borne upon it, and the huge Coliseum in the distance, built, in part by the labour of captive Jews, for the triumphs of Christ, remind us of that mysterious dispensation by which the kingdom of God was taken away from the first husbandmen and given to the Gentiles, while Jerusalem, from the entry of the Caliph Omar (in A.D. 636-7), is trodden under foot, till the times of both divisions of the Gentiles now (in 1860) fulfilling be quite fulfilled.

Let us sit down either here in the Tabularium fronting the Forum, or in the corner of a garden attached to those Prussian houses on the citadel which front the Palatine, and let us ascend in thought the stream of time, beginning from this spot itself. All the modern world runs back into the Roman Empire. But the Roman empire — what account did it give of itself? How far could it trace its own existence? and what knowledge would mankind have had of its own origin, and of the growth of its civilisation and its religions, if it had had to ask only of Rome, or of such sources as the Romans condescended to adopt and to connect with themselves?

The appearance of Rome *as a power* cannot be put higher than the war with Pyrrhus in Italy (B.C. 280); and the fabulous or semi-fabulous period of its annals hardly ends before the burning of the city by the Gauls (in B.C. 390). But even if we go up to Romulus, we are no higher than the middle of the 8th century before Christ. Above this the Romans had only a genealogy of some thirteen petty kings at Alba, descended from Æneas and a band of fugitives from Troy. This Greek fable takes us back 430 years more, to B.C. 1183, before which time the gods only, as Saturn, Picus, Faunus, and Hercules, were thought to have reigned in Italy. So, if the world had been limited to merely Roman sources, its authentic history would scarcely have gone back four centuries before Christ. But by passing off from the Romans to the Greeks, a kindred people, whose civilisation and greatness was earlier than that of their conquerors, the commencements both of history and of fable are carried back somewhat higher. The Greeks had authentic records to about the date of the foundation of Rome — let it be said to the first Olympiad, — with a mixture of historical traditions and fables for a further space of four centuries, up to Eratosthenes's date for Troy. Above that point there is nothing but mere fable, and some lists of reigns or genealogies certainly not historical but embodying perhaps traces of history. So they counted seventeen generations and 698 years from Troy up to the foundation of Argos; and another Pelasgic genealogy carried up the kings of Sicyon somewhat higher; while some hints were given which might serve Italian antiquaries; as when it was said that Thesprotus and Pelasgus were sons of Lycaon. This, if understood of the earliest Pelasgus, might imply that the *Pelasgian* migration into Greece and Italy took place about eighteen generations, making as was pretended 698 years, before Troy. So we are at the year B.C. (1183+698=) 1881, or even at B.C. (1250+698=) 1948. But at the same time we are more than 1100 years above all authentic Greek history; and the origin of the Greek gods and heroes, of their very names and worship, is put in their fables not only in the space between Inachus and Troy, but in part even below Troy, in the space before the first Olympiad.

We must therefore make another recommencement, and pass off from the Greeks, as we before passed off from the Romans, into that Asiatic empire which was overthrown by Alexander the Great, and with which the Greeks had previously been in contact during 230 years. Herodotus then, "the father of history," who flourished about B.C. 450, a little after the great invasions of Greece by Darius and Xerxes, gives such notices as he had been able to collect respecting the Lydian, the Median, and the Babylonian monarchies, all of which were subdued by *Cyrus*, the founder of the Persian empire, as also respecting the kingdoms of the Assyrians and the Egyptians which had already fallen under the attacks of the Medes and the Babylonians before they became dependencies of Persia. The Lydian kings, by whom the Greek cities on the coast of Asia Minor had been subjugated in the 6th and 7th centuries before Christ, he traces back from the capture of Sardis by Cyrus, in B.C. 547, to the accession of *Gyges*, 171 years earlier, in B.C. 718. And of the five reigns of the Lydian "Mermnadæ" he gives a detailed account. Before them he places a series of xxii other kings who reigned 502 years, the first of them, *Agron*, being the fourth descendant of Hercules. So the commencement of these Heraclidæ would be in B.C. 1220; and the birth of Hercules himself, four generations earlier, might be set about B.C. 1350, since elsewhere Herodotus says that Hercules was 900 years before his own time. And he mentions still earlier Lydian kings of the time of Hercules as descended from Lydus, the son of Atys, "before whom the country was called Mæonia." The names of the father and grandfather of Agron, being *Ninus* and *Belus*, may hint that the Lydian Heraclidæ were really a branch from the first kings of the Assyrian empire. The kings of the Medes, who were subjected to the Persians in B.C. 559 by Cyrus, Herodotus traces back for 150 years (28 being included during which a horde of Scythians were masters of Upper Asia); and of each of the four Median reigns he gives some details. So the epoch at which the Medes and the Babylonians became independent of Nineveh seems fixed by him to B.C. 709, before which time the Assyrians of Nineveh, he says, had ruled all Upper Asia during a space of 520 years. Some later writers have 526 years. So that the Assyrian empire should have begun about B.C. (709 + 520 =) 1229, or a little earlier, which agrees well with the date assigned for the commencement of the Lydian line of Agron, derived from Ninus and Belus. But the local kingdom of Nineveh or Assyria, and that of Babylon too, may be allowed to have been much more ancient than the Assyrian *empire* properly so called, though Herodotus says nothing of their earlier kings, just as we know from Herodotus that, after the Assyrian *empire* had ended, the kings of Assyria still reigned on in Nineveh, their own capital, which, after having been once before all but taken and unexpectedly delivered by the irruption of the Scythians, was at length, on their expulsion, reduced by Cyaxares and Nebuchadnezzar. And in fact later writers, as Ctesias, who was physician to Artaxerxes Mnemon, and who ended his Assyrian history in B.C. 398, went back with lists of Assyrian and Babylonian kings and dynasties to the year B.C. 2009, or even higher. And the mythological reckonings of Berosus and Alexander Polyhistor (who was the freedman of Sylla) ended, as it seems, and their historical lists began, as far back as 1903 years before Alexander, that is, in B.C. (330 + 209 + 68 + 141 + 526 + 215 + 458 + 62? + 224 = ) 2233. But these lists, those of Ctesias at least, were *mere* lists of names; and if we are to judge of them from the excessive average length of the reigns, and from the acknowledgment that nothing was known of the kings, they can scarcely be regarded as historical. For Egypt Herodotus distinguishes a space of "less than 900 years" between his own time and the death of Mœris, "the earliest king who did anything to be recorded." But he fails to make out any connected account of the eight or nine centuries so specified. His consecutive notices of Egyptian history begin only with the Saite kings who, in the 7th century before Christ, first engaged a corps of Greek mercenaries, and opened the Canopic mouth of the Nile to Greek traders; while before Sesostris, and his predecessor Mœris, he has a fable of 330 generations of kings in lineal succession, who were all *faineants*, but who reigned, as he supposed, or as he was given to understand, during a space of above 11,000 years.

Such being the account which heathen antiquity, as known to us through the Greeks and Romans, had to give of itself, going back with a detailed narrative in no case much above seven centuries before Christ, nor even with lists of kings really consecutive and historical, it is certainly no slight accession to our knowledge, when we find the Egyptian chronicles taking us back with specific details, and even with contemporary monuments and inscriptions, above 2000 years before Christ; and with lists of names manifestly historical and some well marked facts 200 years higher; and even above the epoch of Menes (B.C. 2224), up to within a few months of the creation itself, exhibiting an exact measure of time; agreeing with the Alexandrian LXX and Josephus harmonised; showing the epoch of the Flood marked accurately, though unnamed (2263 movable years and 6 months, or 2262 Canicular years, below the beginning); and with a number of generations of deified antediluvian and postdiluvian ancestors before Menes agreeing very closely with that in the Sacred Scriptures.

Nor is this a slight addition to our interest, that in remounting the course of time it is not till we have reached the age of Homer, and have nothing more remaining in Greek antiquity but mere fables, that we find ourselves just entering upon the *latest* part of a long period of seven or eight centuries during which Egypt was the chief power of the world. Owing to the peculiar character of its people, to the abundance of materials fit for sculpture and building, to the climate, in which nothing seems to decay, and, above all, to the care bestowed on the preservation of the dead and on the decoration of their tombs, the Egyptians, for nine or ten centuries before the death of Solomon, are actually in some respects better known—at any rate, they are more vividly and more minutely brought before the eye—than the Greeks and Romans of classical times, or even than our own Saxon and Norman ancestors. Their manufactures, their clothes, their works of art, their tools and instruments, their household implements and furniture, are in many cases preserved. Their occupations and amusements, indoors and out, their processes of agriculture and of art, their crops and their cattle, their hunting, fowling, and fishing, their battles and sieges, their chariots and horses on land, their vessels on the water, their buildings and gardens, their entertainments, their religious and other public ceremonies, and especially all that relates to embalming and sepulture, and to the soul after death, are represented either by painting alone, or by painted sculptures, with every variety of detail. Jewellery of the 16th, and even of the 19th century before Christ, ivory and alabaster boxes and vases, and even a royal diadem in gold, of the time of the patriarch Jacob, a literary work on morals written during the life of Abraham, the actual copy and papyrus being not much later, and other like curiosities, seem so astonishing, that one is at a loss to think what is to be found next. And in point of history, there are contemporary inscriptions and sculptures recording the establishment of copper works in the Sinaitic peninsula, with victories over some local tribes, during the life of Abraham, above 2000 years before Christ; there are records again, half a century later, of the earliest Egyptian conquests in Nubia; and from the 18th century before Christ, while the Hebrews were multiplying under bondage, inscriptions already alluded to above are preserved, recording extensive conquests both in Asia northwards as far as Nineveh, and southwards among the black tribes of inner Africa, with representations of the different races, Asiatic and African, showing their dresses, their complexions, and the tributes imposed, among which one sees gold-dust, ivory, leopards in cages, monkeys, ostriches, and camelopards.

But, after all, it is not merely the comparatively remote antiquity to which Egyptian history ascends, nor the abundance of minute details vividly brought before us by the monuments and tombs, that constitutes its main interest. It is conceivable, though it is not true in fact, that authentic and minutely detailed histories should have been preserved by other nations, as, for instance, by the Etrurians, the Aztecs, or the Chinese, and that some of these should have gone back even to the first settlement of their respective countries. Yet the importance of such histories would have been as nothing compared with that of the peoples and empires out of which modern Christendom has been formed. It is not in the mere knowledge that such a race has possessed this or that country so long, with such a form of religion and government, and with such manners and customs, and that it has passed through such or such varieties of fortune, that the essence of history consists; nor even in the knowledge of such literature, philosophy, religion, art, commerce, and civilisation as may be conceived by possibility to have existed among outlying peoples. What makes the true interest and importance of history is its more or less near connection with the final ends and relations of ourselves and of that humanity of which each one of us is a part. This religious interest it is which alone, in the highest and truest sense, is political and philosophical, though it be little thought of by the politicians and philosophers of the world. It is because the people of God was from the time of Nebuchadnezzar downwards contained within the great empire of the world, mixed up with it, and subjected to its rulers, that so high and direct an interest attaches to the four successive empires of the Babylonians, the Persians, the Macedonians, and the Romans. And for later times the interest of secular history, as distinct from ecclesiastical, is in principle the same.

It is only from such a point of view that the importance of Egyptian history can be rightly appreciated. The first step towards appreciating it is to consider that inward antagonism and outward combination of natural and supernatural good and evil which has been working from the beginning, and that Divine appointment by which both inanimate creation, in all its parts and in innumerable ways, and living creatures too, and men, cities, and nations, are at once what they are in themselves, and also often types and emblems of other and greater things beyond themselves. For as a man paints different objects, and instructs children with words and colours, so the Almighty Creator makes creation itself, and, what is more wonderful, even free human agents and nations, to be types and anticipations pregnant with divine instruction.

From the confusion of tongues downwards, but more especially from the reign of Nebuchadnezzar, Babylon, the city of confusion, was the appointed and lively symbol of all other capitals and empires and of that city or society of the evil world which were to be developed out of the Babylonian empire, or were to succeed it in course of time, and to stand in the same relation to the Church, whether Hebrew or Christian, as it had stood, containing, and in some respects oppressing it, as by a captivity. But for the significancy of Egypt and Egyptian history we go back to a still higher and earlier antagonism than that between Babylon and Jerusalem, between the world and the Church. Egypt takes us back to the very beginning of the world and of mankind, and exhibits the whole anticipatory outline of that awful drama which began with the Fall, and with the death of our first parents, and will end only with the Resurrection, and the final triumph of the Second Adam.

First, in the country itself there is something typical, by which it is the Paradise of this world, and the contrast to that "Desert" into which the Church flees from persecution, and in which she is nourished and preserved from her pursuer. Like the garden of Paradise, the rich black soil of Egypt produces almost spontaneously double crops and the most abundant harvests. But its fertility is caused not by the fourfold river of life, but by a river which with its seven streams and mouths symbolises the great dragon of the waters, with seven heads antagonistic to the seven horns and seven eyes of the Lamb. Its abundance of bread, then, is like that of the cities of the plain which were overthrown with fire and brimstone from heaven. And it is expressly joined with them when the world subject to Satan is spoken of as "Sodom and Egypt, in which also the Lord was crucified."

Such being the typical character of the country itself, its history is in accordance with the same. Not only was the devil suffered to develop in Egypt from the earliest times, and on the greatest scale, that false religion and idolatry by which the nations have been deceived, and that proud and cruel and blasphemous tyranny by which they have been enslaved, but these developments of evil were brought into close contact and combination with the divine economy of mercy and long-suffering which was working for good. No sooner was Abraham, the father of the faithful, called out of the apostasy of the postdiluvian world, than he was sent down into Egypt; and the Egyptians, whose idolatry was not yet perhaps fully developed, were warned, as it were, and plagued with moderate plagues, for the sake of the Church, which at length they are to let go free and untouched, bearing with her the spoils of the world, to her heavenly Bridegroom. And two centuries later, before the nation and its rulers were exhibited as the obdurate and permanent enemies of God, and their land as the kingdom of darkness, the Patriarch Joseph, himself a type of Christ, was sold into Egypt, not only to make known in the most striking way the Divine power and mercy, but also to reform and reclaim them (if that had been possible) with all the influence of worldly authority. So he ruled them for eighty years, "informing the counsellors of Pharaoh after the will of God, and teaching his satraps wisdom." And his memory was held in honour, by the Shepherd suzerains at least, for fifty years after his death. During all this time the Spirit of God strove with men, who were not finally moulded into special vessels of wrath and types of evil till they had also been visited with repeated warnings of judgment and mercy, and had had a long time given them for repentance, and had rejected the most extraordinary invitations. But after their hearts had turned so that they hated the Lord's people, when a new dynasty arose which had not known Joseph, the Hebrews (and in them the future Church) were oppressed in Egypt for ninety-four years with a most bitter and cruel bondage, till at length, after plagues foreshadowing what are yet to come in the last days, the power and pride and malice of the chief empire of the world and its king were overwhelmed in the passage of the Red Sea, when Israel saw their enemies dead on the sea-shore, to afflict them no more for ever.

Yet all these events, so great, so sublime, so awful in themselves, and the actors in them too, as Joseph, and Moses, and Pharaoh, and the two peoples of Israel and Egypt, were but pictures and types of other events and persons and peoples far greater, which lay beyond in futurity. One might have thought, certainly, that after the Exodus, whatever symbolism was to attach to Egypt, it was now perfect, and that Egypt henceforth would be named only in reference to the past, as *having been* not as *still being* a mysterious embodiment of the kingdom of darkness. But the contrary was the case. And this was shown to be so when Christ, the true Joseph, was taken down in his infancy into the literal Egypt, as if otherwise the Scripture would not have been adequately fulfilled, which said, "Out of Egypt have I called my Son."

Bearing now in mind the typical character of the land itself and its people, let us take a brief survey of its religion in its relation to the Creator of the world, and to Satan, and to the destinies of mankind.

To the eye of the mere carnal man there is at first sight a parallelism between the religion of the old Egyptians and that of the Hebrews and of the Christians, which is imposing, and which may even be turned against Catholic Christianity. What is still more striking is this, that in a number of points their religious developments seem to go beyond those of the Hebrews, and to be anticipations of what was only after many ages to be manifested in the Christian Church.

The Egyptians claimed for themselves to have been the first of all men to *name* the gods, to set up altars, temples, and images, and to offer sacrifices: and though this claim, if taken to the letter, and understood of all the points mentioned, is certainly false, still it may be true that they were really the first to *invent* names of *false gods*, other than deceased ancestors, that they were the first to build temples, to raise altars of hewn stone, and to institute *stated* national worship and sacrifices with a ritual, a kalendar, and sacred books, under a sacerdotal caste, and that other nations learned and imitated these institutions from them. Nay, it may be admitted further that many details of the ceremonial law of Moses were borrowed from Egypt.

In their theology they named first three deities which answer, in some sense, to the three Divine Persons in the doctrine of the Trinity, an unoriginated father (*Phthah*), a son of that father (*Ra*) of whom the visible sun was the symbol, and a divine spirit (*Cneph*). Then, with a certain correspondence to the doctrine of the Incarnation, there was a deified humanity from which all mankind was derived, which was slain by its enemy, and in which all the scattered members were to be collected together and renewed through a son—a son of the woman—who was no other than the original humanity itself, and in whom it was to triumph eventually over its adversary. The mysteries of the death and *passion* (*τὰ πάθη*) of Osiris, and the lamentation of Isis, were celebrated annually in Egypt, with images, ritual ceremonies, readings and singings, lights, processions, and a representative embalming and burial, much as the ceremonies of Holy Week are now celebrated by Christians. Isis, the deified woman, the "great mother," and the "queen of heaven," answered to her who obtains similar titles and worship in the Christian Church. Then there were a multitude of lesser deities—deified ancestors—to whom worship was paid, anticipating the Saints, and other spirits and powers which may be compared to the Angels. All these had their peculiar names and associations, and their supposed spheres of influence and patronage. They had their images, too, like the images and sacred pictures of the Christians. Nor did the parallel stop here; but a special influence or inhabitation of the image, and special preferences of particular images were recognised, like what is heard of miraculous images and pictures now. Nor did they shrink from avowing, that the will and device or feeling of men had the power to attract, as it were, into images of their own fabrication divine spirits and influences, as is expressed in a remarkable passage of St. Augustine (*De Civitate Dei*, lib. viii. c. 23) of which the following is a translation:—

"The Egyptian Hermes, whom they call Trismegistus, thought and wrote [of images] differently from Apuleius. Apuleius denies them to be gods. But that Egyptian makes a distinction, and says that some deities are originated by the chief god, others by men. He asserts that visible and palpable images are, as it were, embodiments of deities; and that they are inhabited by spirits which enter into them on human invitation, and have a certain power. To establish, then, by certain methods an association between these invisible spirits and visible objects made of bodily matter he says is to make gods; and he asserts that this great and wonderful power of making gods has been actually received by men. So that, as the father and lord, or by whatever name they call the supreme god, has made other eternal and celestial gods like himself, so human nature also should make its own gods after the likeness of its own countenance. Knowest thou not, O Imhotep (so he continues), that Egypt is an image of heaven, or rather, I should say, that in it is brought down and repeated all that is done in heaven; and that, in a word, our country is the temple or sanctuary of the whole world?"

With such an outward parallelism, it is no wonder if some, as the Mahometans and the Jews, and others besides them, blinded by hereditary aversion and voluntary ignorance, identify either absolutely, or, with a doubtful qualification, Catholic Christianity with Pagan idolatry. And it is clear that, so long as a man goes no further in the matter than to assert the existence of a positive prohibition, equally binding on Jews and Christians, and notoriously acknowledged and obeyed since the Babylonish Captivity by the Jews, but as plainly set aside by the Christians, it is impossible to defend Catholic Christianity against the Mahometan or the Jewish objector. If there be nothing else that makes the essential difference between piety and idolatry but the letter of an outward law, then indeed there is, *so far*, no difference between Christian and Pagan idolatry. But this goes too far; since in that case the heathens, who *without any positive prohibition* made and honoured symbolical images, were *so far* guiltless, and only the Jews and the Christians are guilty, if they do that which *to them* is forbidden. But if, apart from any positive prohibition, there be a radical antagonism and contrariety between the Pagan system and the Christian, not in respect of images only, but in all those points in which the two systems seem at a distance to be like and parallel, then it is to be considered on what authority it is so positively asserted that not the spirit only but the letter of the outward prohibition of images is binding on the Christian Church, though she herself teaches a contrary interpretation.

What, then, is the essential difference between the true religion and the false (the false meaning here heathenism), both in the whole, and, by consequence, in all details? What is that point which, after making the most of their likeness and parallelism, is observable at once as a plain contrast, intelligible to all? It is this, that in heathenism the idea of *sin*, in its strict sense, as an offence against a personal Creator and Lord, is absent, and with it the ideas of *punishment* threatened by his justice, and of *reconciliation* offered by his mercy. The Almighty is thus left out, and indirectly denied, and the author of sin and evil is indirectly, and so far as is possible, worshipped in his stead. *Indirectly*, and *so far as is possible.* It is important to attend to these words, that the nature of the false religion may become intelligible. To deny God absolutely was impossible, when all nature, and the constitution of man himself, and of human society, proclaimed Him, and represented under an infinite variety of symbols His acts and attributes. On the other hand no finite being, though he were the first-created of all angels, and though in glory and power he transcended, to any conceivable degree, all other created beings, could measure himself directly with his Maker. Satan himself could not either dissemble the existence of the Divine attributes, or claim them all as his own, and say of himself, "I am the eternal, the infinite, the almighty, the creator and preserver of all things both material and spiritual, who will punish sin and its author, and who have provided a reconciliation for sinners." Between two men, or between any other two creatures or objects which are at all like and equal, there may be a question of identity, which is which, or of competition and of rival claims. But between God and a creature this is impossible even to imagine. In what way, then, could the serpent take to himself the honour of God, and cause God to be virtually denied by men? In this indirect way only, if admitting the existence of the Divine operations and attributes he could lead men to forget or deny that they belong to a separate pre-existing personality, and to associate them with the universe, so that the general idea of the works of God, through which His attributes are known, should be taken to be itself God. One general *idea* being thus made of God and creation together, there was no longer for the heathen any manifest contradiction or absurdity in ascribing to the Divine Universe, within which God Himself was mentally included, and as it were imprisoned and enslaved, those infinite powers and attributes which *could not* be claimed to himself by any single separate being. This is what is rightly named Pantheism: and in spite of the seeming variety and inconsistency of false religions (in which Judaism and Mahometanism are not now included, being rather like heresies) Pantheism is the original source out of which they have all arisen, and the common principle and spirit into which they may all be resolved. Nay even Judaism and Mahometanism too, and all Christian sects and heresies, whether the outward form of *a* Church be preserved or not, after the first mad and fierce fanaticism of their rebellion or separation, subside for their permanent basis either into Pantheism itself, or into a "Catholicism," or Universalism, which repeats against the Church the same process of *denial by inclusion* which heathenism first devised against God, and from a similar necessity. But in the first ages of the world, the universe itself having been substituted for a supreme and distinct Creator, it followed, as a consequence, that all its parts and powers, from the most ancient and powerful of spirits down to men and beasts, and to the lowest of creeping things on the earth, and even to plants and inorganic bodies, were inherently divine, and were all capable of being made the objects even of an outward worship. And, this being so, all the worship which was so paid, under whatever names of deities, and with whatever forms, redounded, indirectly at least, to the true author and suggester of the delusion, and to his subordinate ministers.

Such being the false religion, even if one deity were named first as the eternal self-originating father, the source of all other *forms* of being, with other attributes of the true God, and with no other name than simply "God" (ὁ θεὸς), which seems to be the case with the Egyptian *Phthah*, still this deity, not being the *creator* of matter by his own free will, but confusedly co-ordinate with it, and the author only of its *forms* and changes, and that under necessity, is not really like (which could only be if he were identical with) the First Person in the Blessed Trinity, but the highest and nearest and so also the most blasphemous approach towards a direct *particular* antagonism (that is, if there were any real being underneath). And this is well shown when it results as by necessary consequence that if on the one hand the "lord and father and supreme god" of the Egyptian theology, that is *Phthah*, is called the source of all other deities and of the forms of all things, on the other hand and from another point of view he may be said himself to be the offspring of *mud* (see p. 51). In the same way if *Ra*, the sun-god, is called the Firstborn, the son of Phthah, who does the same things with his father, and equally with him forms and rolls the egg of the universe, still that original blasphemy by which the father himself was only conjointly with matter eternal, and subject to necessity, is reproduced in the son who is of the same nature; and, what is more, the visible material sun being regarded not only as the symbol but as the coeval tabernacle or body of Ra, the son of the Egyptians is not strictly co-eternal with his father, but is so begotten that *time* measured by the visible sun begins with his existence. Of the divine spirit, *Cneph*, which proceeds from the father and the son, and does the same things with them both, forming like them the mundane egg, and moulding as a potter out of clay the first man, the like holds good. And in this also there is a distinctive peculiarity in the pantheistic trinity, that not only is it possible (in virtue of the co-eternity of matter) to refer each of the three deities to a mother without a father, but also to invert their order, so that when Cneph, the spirit, forms the egg of the universe Phthah himself is said to issue from the mouth of Cneph. And whatever is said of any one deity, it is said only from one point of view; and from another point of view the same may be said of almost every other; and almost all divine titles and attributes, not only of these three but also of the inferior human deities, are variable and interchangeable with an endless and inextricable confusion.

If we descend to Osiris and Isis, Typhon, and Horus, who seem to present a parallel to Adam and Eve, to the enemy who slew Adam, and to the seed of the woman who overcomes the enemy and reunites into one body the members of the slain Adam, the likeness vanishes, and only a frightful transposition of parts and characters remains when it is noticed that according to the Egyptian myth there is neither *sin* in the man who is slain, nor in the woman, nor any suggester of disobedience, nor any judgment upon all three, nor promise of mercy to the woman and her husband as to sinners. But human nature is slain, as if under some blind destiny, by an enemy whose malice is spontaneous, the enemy insinuated being the true God. It is from destiny too, not from the promise of a just but merciful judge, that the woman expects a seed, not to atone for the *sin* but to avenge the *wrongs* of the first father, and to overcome in some sense that enemy who inflicted death. This seed then, in the fullest and ultimate sense, is equivalent to antichrist, since the enemy to be overcome is no other than He who first inflicted the penalty of death, who drowned mankind with a flood, and who scattered over the earth the members of that humanity which he had slain. All this the Egyptians ascribed to the malignant deity Typhon. And the deified humanity which they worshipped was not the true seed of the woman who is at once the propitiation for sin, and the second Adam, the Lord from heaven, giving resurrection to them whom he has redeemed and incorporated into his own body; but it is the first Adam himself, whose hope of self-vindication and victory lies not in a Divine Incarnation, but in the power of natural generation, by which the race condemned to die escapes as it were for ever out of the hands of its enemy, till all forms and beings under the wheel of destiny having run their round of generations and changes are reabsorbed into the primæval elements of Phthah and mud, thence to repeat the same changes over again. The Egyptians then worshipped the dead Adam instead of Christ the Living Spirit; and they worshipped the powers of natural generation, especially the male principle in men and beasts, with its obscene emblems and accompaniments, parading as a sacred mystery the irreverence of their ancestor Ham. And Isis their "universal mother" and "queen of heaven," instead of resembling the Church or the immaculate Mother of God, was in one aspect (when identified with matter with the attribute of maternity) a deification of mud; and in another aspect, as the first woman the sister and wife of Osiris, she was the deification of the dead Eve, without any confession of sin, or any other hope than that of multiplying through her daughters a succession of sons all living but to die.

But it was after death that the most terrible and significant of contrasts was exhibited. It must certainly be confessed that some truths which were rather veiled to the mere intellect and imagination among the Hebrews — though they lay at the root of all their religion, and were implied whenever they named the "God of their fathers," or "the God of Abraham"—were brought out prominently and painted in lively representations in the Egyptian tombs. The continuance of the soul after death, its judgment according to its observance or breach of the moral law written on the conscience of mankind, the comparative happiness of the good who are acquitted or "justified," and the torments of the bad, are all portrayed. There is the balance exactly trimmed, with the feather of Ma in one scale and the heart of the deceased containing his works in the other: there is the recording deity Thoth with his pen and his scroll on which is written every word and deed of every year and day and hour of the life now passed. The accuser also is present. The Judge is seated at the further end of the hall; and on one side are the 42 assessors, representatives from all parts of the Egyptian world, looking on and taking part in the judgment. The deceased, conducted by the conductors of souls, is seen entering at the doorway. The view of the preparations for the trial, the balance, the accuser, the written record, the assessors and the judge, with the thoughts of his own conscience, are overwhelming; he cannot face the sight, but covers his eyes with his hand. Here then at any rate there is a striking parallel to the truth, or rather the truth itself. And scenes not unlike mediæval representations of hell and purgatory are painted perhaps in the same chamber. But what underneath all this is the true sense and purpose? Why should the father of lies and blasphemies and of all impurity set before the eyes and imaginations of his votaries so *true* and wholesome a warning? Why should he cause them to proclaim, and in so impressive a way, that moral law which he is constantly tempting men to break, and join with it the ideas of trial and most rigid justice, even though the true Lawgiver and Judge be absent, and the tremendous contrasts of happiness and tortures, which even though prepared by destiny are still to be suffered or enjoyed? The answer is not far to seek. We need only notice the form in which the soul replies to its accuser. It mentions no propitiation; it knows no hope of mercy; it makes no excuses. When that ordeal which was so terrible even at a distance, but which was inevitable, has commenced, when the records of Thoth are referred to and the accusations heard, it replies to each only by a categorical and reiterated denial. "I have not done this; no, nor this, nor this;" and so on. And having denied a long list of crimes objected with great accuracy and minuteness the soul is justified (except in some rare cases) by the flattery of the living, and is represented in another scene as conducted to behold the face of the gods of the lower world. But at the same time there is an insinuation underneath that if any one, even the least, of those accusations were perchance true — if any one of those reiterated and absolute denials were false — if but so much of guilt existed as could turn the scale against a feather—there was no resource, and no hope for the soul, which must then become the prey of its accuser. Thus did he who is the true enemy of mankind mock his victims, and only for the sake of this fiendish irony exhibit among the dead truths which among the living it was his constant study to obscure.

The Judge too — since some appearance of a judge was necessary to the idea — and the felicity of being presented as justified to the gods are in keeping with the same mockery. For he who is set as judge is no other than Osiris the first and dead Adam, whose sentence cannot absolve those who are already condemned in himself, whose hope, whether for himself or for his descendants, consists only in this, that they may live on in a manner through generations successively begotten and successively dying. So the dead were gathered to their fathers and to their gods, and "Osirified" or incorporated into the dead Adam. After this it may be felt what resemblance there was in truth between the mysteries of the passion of Osiris and the ceremonies of Holy Week, between the lamentation of Isis and the sorrows of the Virgin Mother and of the Church whose soul was pierced with a sword beside the Cross.

The parallelism of the worship and deification ascribed by the Egyptians to their dead ancestors with the worship and invocation of Christian Saints shows on a nearer view the same contrariety. The ancestors of the Egyptians, as for instance the XII antediluvian patriarchs called in the Old Chronicle Gods, and the VIII postdiluvian called Demigods, share the deification of the first Osiris (Seb in the Chronicle) in virtue of their unity with him, and he shares deification with the created universe in which empty names and a dung-beetle (the symbol of Phthah) and the serpent and mud are worshipped, but the Creator of men and angels is omitted or made to share, to share too after changing places with the enemy and murderer of mankind. But the Christian Saints and Martyrs are not thus honoured in connection with a denial of God and with blasphemy, nor as dead ancestors, for having been the propagators of a natural life which they themselves have lost, but as living members of Christ the Second Adam into whom they have been incorporated, and by union with whom they are quickened and glorified and in a certain sense deified. And these not apart from God but in God and Christ and only by their prayers to the true God (which one idea is a subversion of all heathenism) help forward the Church on earth towards the same glory. Those other spirits and powers too which the Egyptians worshipped and with which they dealt by their magicians and oracles, if they were anything at all, were devils, rebels against God, and intent only on seducing men into and fixing them in their own rebellion, and on counteracting the designs of Divine mercy. But the Angels of God who are honoured and invoked by Christians are His faithful servants and His ministers towards them that shall be heirs of salvation.

Lastly, the temples and altars and sacrifices, the institution of the priesthood, the worship and ceremonial, the sacred books and pictures used and honoured by the Egyptians, were all in and for the sake of their blasphemous Pantheism; but the churches, the altars, the priesthood, the sacrifice, the worship, the ceremonial, the sacred books, the sacraments, and the images and pictures of the Christians, being instituted by God or by his Church, are used and honoured in and for the sake of the true faith.

After all, there is such a complexity in human nature that even they whose minds and consciences seem most darkened, who by their birth and nationality are most fixed in ignorance, and prejudice, and hatred against the truth, have within them all the while an undercurrent of ineffectual knowledge and conscience which makes them at times bear witness against themselves. In the case of the ancient Egyptians this is shown by the extreme sensitiveness with which they distorted, or related by contraries, and shifted to unhistorical dates, all that bore upon their relations to the Hebrews, to the Shepherd kings, and even to their Memphite tributaries. The land of Goshen or Avaris was, as we have seen, "*Typhonian* from the beginning." Egypt during the time of the Shepherds and the Hebrews was subjected by destiny to a Typhonian influence, and oppressed by impiety and tyranny. The king, Amenophis, returned from the Red Sea "without a battle," as not daring to conflict with some evil but superior deity, and fled *with the gods of Egypt* and the sacred animals to Ethiopia, when destiny had decreed a certain time of power to the *Hierosolymites.* And before that, out of fear of evil consequences to Egypt, to the king, and to himself, from oppressing "*the lepers,*" the prophet Amenoph, the son of Pepi, had been driven even to suicide. And again, among their fables there was one that once *all the gods* (the gods, that is, of Egypt and of heathenism) in terror of Typhon hid themselves from him under the forms of different animals. Such was the way in which they themselves would sometimes account for the origin of their worship of brute beasts, and birds, and fishes, and creeping things of the earth; by a fable which in one instance at least was literally verified, when the legion of devils — not, however, without first obtaining permission — entered into the herd of swine. But the most remarkable hint of latent knowledge and conscience is found in a story told somewhere of the ancient Egyptians to this effect; that when things went very much amiss, when they found no benefit from their sacrifices, nor from their magical arts and divinations, nor could obtain help or relief from the demons whom they served, they would sometimes turn, as it were, upon their deceivers. And, first taking the sacred animals of the temples out of sight (that the people might not be scandalised), they would secretly whip, and torment, and even kill them, as if thereby they might afflict and compel the spirits with which they were associated. And if this failed they would as a last resource threaten the gods themselves, crying to them that they would "shake the heavens;" that they would "reveal the secret;" and this threat was their last and most potent adjuration. That is, in plain words, they threatened that they would be no longer accomplices; that they would upset the whole establishment of imposture and falsehood; and would publicly confess that the gods of Egypt were only miserable devils and dead men, powerless before another whom they had called the enemy and Typhon, but who nevertheless was the Almighty and the only true God.

Viewed in its most important aspect, as representing the kingdom of darkness upon earth, Egypt besides a general unity with other heathen empires, and a special pre-eminence among them all, has also an historical connection with those four great empires which it anticipated as having once like them included and oppressed the Lord's people, which it far surpassed in its religious antagonism, in which it was finally merged and incorporated, and together with which as part of the Roman world it was subdued by the Fifth Empire of the Church. But it has also two more particular points of junction and relationship to the earliest and the latest forms of that Greek and Roman heathenism which Christianity supplanted. And these deserve to be noticed.

First, the polytheism (perhaps of other nations also but certainly) of the Greeks and Romans was borrowed originally from Egypt. Herodotus tells us distinctly of a time when the Pelasgian ancestors of the Greeks knew only in a general way "the Divine Nature (τὸ θεῖον), the Gods (τοὺς θεοὺς), or God (τὸν θεὸν)," the plural form not implying originally or of necessity any false religion, any more than the Hebrew *Elohim*), but had no idea of particular deities, nor names for them. He says also that all or almost all the names of the Greek gods were Egyptian; that their use came in only gradually, and was at first a matter of doubt, till the oracle of Dodona, founded and served by two black or dark Egyptian priestesses, having been consulted, it answered that the new names were to be received. And even after that, he continues, they knew little more of the gods than the mere names, till the poets Homer and Hesiod and others added a multitude of fables, and gave some distinctness to their persons and characters. The institution of sacrificing and making libations with prayers was no doubt older among the Pelasgians, and derived to them in common with the Egyptians themselves from the patriarchal religion. But the earliest style of Greek architecture accords with the assertion of the Egyptians that altars in hewn stone and temples were from them; since the Doric column shows plain traces of an Egyptian origin. The heathenism of the Greeks and Romans, however, viewed as a positive religion, was always of a very loose and superficial kind, consisting partly of the remains of a vague superstition, but chiefly of poetical fables animating and embellishing the life of a world which knew neither God nor hope, but only nature and their own passions. Among the Romans it was also a political imposture. And it is only by reverting to its source in Egypt that the original and proper depth and system and the intense impiety of the false religion can be understood.

The end of the false religion—in opposition to that of the true—being to glorify the enemy by leading men and nations more and more astray from God, and enslaving them to evil lusts, this end was not only aimed after in Egypt through an outward ceremonial and a powerful priesthood, with the worship of everything in the world except the true object of worship, but it was especially sought and attained by the deification and worship of the living ruler. The monarch was the keystone of the whole fabric. To him the deceiving serpent — the dragon, to whom the religion as such belonged — delegated his own seat, his power, and great authority. That evil character of pride, ambition, selfishness, and cruelty, which the false religion naturally formed was enthroned and deified in him. As the centre of human society, the source of that law and order without which society itself could not exist—nor consequently its highest forms of perversion be developed — the monarch was not inappropriately compared to the sun. And he was not merely so compared metaphorically, but he was actually worshipped as the earthly Sun-god. The kings of Egypt from very early times took the title of *Ph-Ra* or Pharaoh, which is the name of the Sun-god with the article prefixed. And as the throne-name nearly always commenced with the symbol of the sun, *Ra*, so the personal name was preceded by the title *Si-Ra*, "Son of Ra," so that if one puts the two together they may be rendered equally and indifferently "Sun-god, son of the Sun-god," or "Pharaoh the King, Son of Pharaoh the King" who preceded him. They took also separately the title "God" (*Neter*); and the name of a deceased king is constantly followed by the title *Neter Nepher* "the Good God." And as they took both the abstract title "God," and also the particular title of the Sun-god, which corresponded in their theology to the Second Person of the Blessed Trinity in the true, so also in relation to the human economy the king took during life the title of "*Horus;*" that is, he claimed to be, or to represent in his generation, the expected seed of the woman, the god-man who should avenge the wrongs of humanity and overcome the enemy, the great hope of the world, and the Giver of Life to the world, that is Antichrist.

So complete was the absorption of all into the person of the monarch, that no word answering to *people*, such as was familiar to the Greeks and Latins as well as to the Hebrews, is known to have existed in the Egyptian language. That vein of thought and feeling which runs through the Psalms of David, not only noticing the existence and the rights of the poor and the oppressed, but making it the special attribute of the righteous and merciful Lord and of the religious king to watch over them and do them right, and which dwells on anticipations of food to be measured to the hungry, rest to the weary, comfort to the afflicted, exaltation to the depressed and lowly, and discomfiture and abasement to the cruel and the proud, is the most remote than can be conceived from the tone and attitude of an Egyptian king. This latter meets and embraces the gods themselves in his sculptures more as a brother and an equal than with any humility as a worshipper. He receives from them all that can gratify his own pride and ambition. They give to him never-ending life, and the empire over all the world: they give him victory over all his enemies, and put their necks under his feet: and he on the other hand massacres in their presence "his vile enemies." And as with the people below, so with the gods themselves who might seem to be above; the delegation of their honour to the king as their living representative or embodiment is so complete, that at the very first sight of the walls and sculptures of any Egyptian temple the beholder is struck by the impression that the king its builder is not only *one* of the gods of Egypt, and of that temple, but that he has a far greater share in it than all the gods to whom it is ostensibly dedicated, and than all the gods of Egypt put together.

The same blasphemous titles, and the same deification and worship, with temples, altars, sacrifices, libations, and incense to their honour, passed from the Egyptian Pharaohs to the Ptolemies, and at length to the Roman emperors in the time of Herod, under whom Christ was born. At that same time the development of sin in the world, Jewish and Gentile, had reached its height. Among the Greeks and Romans even superstition was almost extinct: all after death was a blank: the mythology of the poets was disbelieved, and openly ridiculed: nothing remained but materialism, scepticism, pride, cruelty, avarice, ambition, and unblushing sensuality. So while the more ancient and more substantial form of the false religion was still fully preserved in Egypt, the practical service of its author was established equally under a variety of less philosophical, less superstitious, and less positive, but equally atheistic and immoral, traditions over the rest of the Roman world, which was, as it were, the outer court of the nations to that central sanctuary or common temple, that reproduction of heaven upon earth, which the Egyptians recognised in their own country. Just, too, at the same time, the popular constitution of Rome, after lasting for five centuries, was transformed into a monarchy. And not merely were the characteristics of the old Egyptian kings, their tyranny, cruelty, and pride, too faithfully repeated, and on a vaster scale, by the Roman people, whether under popular or imperial government, but in the emperors the concentrated profligacy of the heathen world, boasting itself in enormities unheard of before, and almost inconceivable, publicly enacted, and even surrounded with the forms of legality, was enthroned, and deified, and worshipped.

This empire, then, of the Cæsars one may either call the beast to which the old serpent had delegated his seat and power, or under it we may see the dragon himself, the true Typhon, now come to his full growth. We may see him standing before the mystical woman, the contrast to Isis, seeking to devour her seed, the counterpart to Horus, as soon as he should be born. Tiberius might be called the upper, and his vassal Herod the under jaw of the monster. And afterwards, while the new people of God multiplied as of old in Egypt under persecution, the whole power of this world, with that of the flesh and the devil which it wielded, was bent throughout the empire, and in Rome itself the capital, to put down the rising religion. For three centuries, or nearly, the struggle was continued. One after another the bishops of Rome, the chief pastors of the Church, stood up, face to face, against the deified emperor, armed with all the power of the world and of hell. They were men of no public rank; they possessed no political power; they were not like their successors of the fourth and fifth centuries, who dealt as equals with the great men of the earth, and surpassed the heathen philosophers and rhetoricians of their time by their learning and eloquence. The early Popes did nothing of this kind. They merely taught and confessed their faith with simplicity, disobeyed the laws, refused to worship the gods or the emperor, and were condemned and decapitated. One persecutor after another succeeded in the throne, and for the most part — which is remarkable —

fared no better in his death than those whom he had persecuted. At length the Cross of Christ triumphed. In one of the temples of Egypt, part of which had been converted into a church, the author remembers finding this inscription scratched at the entry, "'Ο σταυρὸς ἐνίκησε, καὶ ἀεὶ νικᾷ·" "The Cross has conquered, and is to conquer for ever;" with other words recording that "this good work [of converting the temple into a church] was done when Theophilus was Pope [of Alexandria]." The Church throughout the empire and at length at Rome itself, raising her head above the waves of persecution, and emerging as it were from the Catacombs, overthrew and reconstituted the whole fabric of society and religion. Then the emperors themselves became Christians: and at length by the spontaneous force of events, after the dissolution of the Western empire, the city of Rome with a certain territory became the absolute possession of the Church, so that from thenceforth she reigned in a manner among the believing Gentiles, till their times should be accomplished, and her chief pastors were able to instruct and reprove with a suitable independence the kings and nations whom they had converted to Christ.

Rome having thus from the capital of the heathen become the centre of the Christian world, it is not difficult to see a certain overruling providence in the fact that the emperors, thinking only to embellish their capital and to borrow from antiquity monuments for their own glory, should have transported thither as many as eleven obelisks erected originally in Egypt to the Sun-god or to other deities, and not least to the kings themselves. These obelisks, covered most of them with hieroglyphics, represent various points of time from the first persecution of the Hebrews in Egypt itself down to the final persecution of the Christians at Rome. They are collectively from seven Egyptian sovereigns, beginning with Thothmes III. (B.C. 1655), and ending with Domitian whose obelisk originally set up in Egypt now stands in the Piazza Navona, bearing upon it in hieroglyphics all the same titles of blasphemy which were taken by the early Pharaohs. Thus there is one king and horn as it were for each of the seven heads of the beast which is the Roman empire. Of the intermediate obelisks four are of Rameses II. the great Egyptian conqueror (B.C. 1460) as if answering to the four heads and lesser horns of the third or Macedonian empire incorporated like the rest into the Roman. Then there is one plain obelisk which stood on the spina of the Circus of Nero, and was there a silent witness of the martyrdom of St. Peter. It stands now in front of his church, and witnesses annually the conflux of the Christian world to his tomb. A pair of smaller obelisks, also plain, which once stood before the Mausoleum of Augustus, but now the one of them near Santa Maria Maggiore and the other on the Quirinal, remind us of the two horns of the Medo-Persian beast or empire. Then on the Monte Citorio there is an obelisk of Psammetichus I. (B.C. 663), under whom Egypt first became known to the Greeks. It was brought to Rome as a trophy after the deaths of Antony and Cleopatra, and marks the epoch of the undisputed empire of Augustus, when deification and worship were first offered from Egypt to a ruler beyond the sea. Lastly, in the Piazza della Minerva, near where stood the temple of Isis, there is an obelisk of Apries, to whom the Jews fled (in B.C. 586) after the burning of the Temple, an obelisk which about 19 years hence may witness the expiration of the seven mystical times if reckoned from the 1st (associated) year of Nebuchadnezzar. All these obelisks having been found lying overthrown and broken among the ruins of pagan Rome, and having been repaired and re-erected on appropriate sites by different Popes, now stand surmounted by the Cross as trophies of the triumph of the Church, after her long warfare of above 2000 years, from the accession of Amosis the king who knew not Joseph (in B.C. 1748) to the edict of Constantine in A.D. 311. And they may be regarded as huge monumental nails or pins visibly clasping and riveting together into one whole, at Rome its centre, the past history of the Pagan and the Jewish with the history both past and future of the Christian world.

# EGYPTIAN CHRONICLES.

## CHAPTER I.

### THE OLD CHRONICLE.

THE idea of a succession of worlds, and of a certain period of time ending the existing world and introducing a new one, is common to the mythologies of India and Egypt. Whether derived from early prophecy, or, by generalisation, from the fact that the world had already once ended and recommenced at the Flood, this idea had a foundation in truth. The very expression of the Egyptians, in Greek ἀποκατάστασις, i. e. restoration and renewal, is connected by St. Paul with the Second Advent of Christ, "whom the heavens," he says, "must receive till the restoration of all things, ἕως τῆς ἀποκαταστάσεως τῶν πάντων." As the old world was drowned with water, and a new one recommenced from Noah and his family, so, we are taught, this present world after a fixed but secret period is to be dissolved by fire. "The earth with the works that are in it shall be burned up." God will "make all things new;" "new heavens and a new earth;" a new Paradise with its Tree and River of Life; a new City, called the New Jerusalem, whose citizens are the spirits of just men made perfect, reunited to their glorified bodies, whose life is that of the Second Adam, and whose light is the intellectual Sun Himself, the uncreated effulgence of the eternal Father.

But among the ancient Egyptians this idea was corrupted and expressed in terms suited to their own pantheism. They held that the Divine Universe of spirit and matter runs a round of developments and transformations, till at length all forms are reabsorbed into the primary element, whether watery or fiery, and the Deity, having thus re-entered into himself, after a pause, goes forth again into energy, and repeats the same successive developments and transformations as before. The same theogony, and formation of plants, animals, and men, the same persons even, and historical events, are to recur. The sun-god Ra first emerges from the abyss of primæval waters, (Νοῦν, Νεῖλος, Μὼτ,) and reigns for a period alone. He is the *son* of the Divine heat (Φθᾶ,"Ηφαθτος, "Ηφαιστος), which conjointly or confusedly with *gas* or water is unoriginated paternal deity (ὁ Θεός); and together with them both a third is named, also eternal, Κνῆφ or Ἀγαθοδαίμων, "the conserving soul of the universe." To Phtha, Ra, and Cneph indifferently they might ascribe the formation of the first man. Sitting, as a potter at his wheel, Cneph (at Philæ) moulds clay, and gives the spirit of life to the nostrils of Osiris. From Osiris is formed Isis, his sister and wife, the mother of all living. In this pair first we have the dualism of sex; and the idea of sex, abstracted from the first parents of mankind, and thrown back upon universal nature, gives two other deities, Cœlus and Terra, Chronos or Kronos and Rhea, in Egyptian Seb and Nutpe, who are fabled to be the father and mother of gods and men, of animals, and of all things, though really derived themselves from their so-called offspring Osiris = Adam, and Isis = Eve. Thus Seb "owes it to Osiris that he is his father." And besides these, there is yet another deity, not really different, being equally constituted by abstraction from the first man, who is called by Herodotus Pan. This is the male principle in universal nature. His consort, equally called his mother, is Mout or Demeter, being the female personification of primordial matter, whether moist (for Μὼτ or Μοὺτ is associated with moisture, like Chaos,) or dry, as suits better the derivation of the Greek name Δημήτηρ. The idea of sex abstracted from the first human pair may even be thrown back upon the three primary deities Phtha, Ra, and Cneph, which then become hermaphrodite, and are divided each into a pair; though originally neither these, though masculine, nor elementary matter, though feminine, had consorts associated with them. The first human pair having being thrown back into pairs of anthropomorphous deities, the original Osiris and Isis, formed by the divine potter as parents of all, disappear in name, and are represented by Seb and Nutpe; while Osiris, Typhon, and Horus, the progeny of Seb and Nutpe, answer rather to Cain, Abel, and Seth in the old world, and to the three sons of Noah in the new. At any rate Osiris blends together the characters of Adam as the protoplast, of Abel as literally slain by his brother, (for the slayer of Adam could only by metaphor be called a brother,) and of Noah as the father of husbandmen and vinedressers, and of the existing world. From Osiris-Seb (whether he be viewed as Adam or Noah) are derived downwards all the successive generations of Egyptian gods and demigods, patriarchs, kings, and other men; each dynast in turn in the early generations being identifiable at once with Seb and Osiris as father of those following, with Osiris again by sharing the same mortality, and with Horus as renewing his father's life, and being the hope of the coming world. So each ancestor in turn went, it was said, to the original Osiris as patriarch of the dead, and to his intermediate "Osirified" fathers, and was himself Osirified like them; all making one collective Osiris, waiting for that reunion and restoration which was to come through successive generations by the great expected Horus, who was to take up into himself the old and to be himself the new Osiris.

And when at length the whole predestined series of generations of gods, demigods, and men, and of years or cycles of years should be completed, and the heavens themselves, and the heavenly bodies which influence earthly *γενέσεις*, i. e. especially the sun, moon, and five planets, should return to the same relative places from which they had started, then they expected the aqueous or igneous resolution and re-absorption and reproduction of all things.

The period assigned to the *ἀποκατάστασις* was originally and properly, as we may collect, a space equal to two Sothic cycles, viz. 2922 vague Egyptian years, this being the duration of the old world, or rather the sum of the lives and reigns of the antediluvian patriarchs, survivors of the Flood, with something still added in order to cast the whole into the cyclical form, which it approached near enough to suggest. So Herodotus (Lib. ii. c. 123) and Plato (Phædr. p. 248, 8) tell us that the circle for the transmigrations of the soul, or at least for the highest souls, was 3000 years, the round number being probably put for the exact number of two Sothic cycles, 2922, which approaches to it. Or it may be that the number 3000 means not two Sothic but two Phœnix cycles, amounting to 3012 years; the difference being this, that the Sothic cycle of 1461 vague years, though it brought back the first day of Thoth of the movable year to the same point in the canicular or Julian year from which it had started, did not bring back the new year to the same point of the zodiac and of the seasons. To accomplish this a space of about 1506 vague years was needed, which being divided into three parts of about 500 years each, answering to the three Egyptian seasons, was called the Phœnix Cycle. This cycle itself being manifestly later than the Sothic Cycle, to which it was a sort of supplement, our inference from the mention of 3000 years that the original and proper ἀποκατάστασις was made to consist of two Sothic cycles, might have been legitimate, even though the same idea were found more clearly connected with Phœnix than with Sothic cycles, and were in that form alluded to by Plato or Herodotus. But the schemes of chronology which we are about to analyse show beyond a doubt that originally the reigns of XIII Gods, answering to the XIII antediluvian patriarchs, were made to occupy two full *Sothic* cycles, or 2922 years; a fact which of itself suggests the thought that the earliest of these schemes may have originated at a date not far removed from the epoch of the Sothic Cycle in B.C. 1322.

But, besides their expectation of a literal end and reproduction of the universe, the Egyptians had a secondary and improper form of the same idea; according to which, *something like* a recommencement of the world, and a reappearance of the human gods and demi-gods in the persons of kings and heroes of like characters and actions, was fancied to take place after periods of time short of 2922 fresh years to be added to the ἀποκατάστασις of the old world. They admitted partial or lesser *ἀποκαταστάσεις*, and returns of like characters and events, resembling the avatars of the Hindoos; resembling, also, those true recurrences of similar persons and events, which appear in sacred history as types of greater persons and events still to come. Thus, after 500 years, one great season, or the third part of a Phœnix cycle, a king and conqueror like Rameses II. might be regarded as an avatar of his predecessor Sesortasen I., the first Egyptian conqueror; and, though only 120 years, or one great month later, Rameses III., going over nearly the same ground, might be identified with Rameses II.: and 500 years after Rameses II., Shishonk I. might seem to reproduce both: and thus three or four or more kings might all blend into one mixed and fabulous character of Sesostris; just as in the earlier mythology one deity, as Cronus or Osiris, may be connected with several antediluvian and postdiluvian ancestors, and even with other collateral personages, and with heavenly luminaries, and elements and powers of nature besides. Thus at B.C. 1322, when the Sothic Cycle may probably have been in use some 480 years, i. e. one great season, from about B.C. 1800, or 500 years at most, from B.C. 1820, though the existing world had by no means completed two spaces of 1461 years each, like the two given to the antediluvians, but only one, and not even that without 341 fictitious years to make time begin from a cyclical epoch; still, at the end of a cycle, the first ever really ended, and at the beginning of another, the first ever really begun, Egyptian priests might compliment, and probably did compliment, the reigning Pharaoh, their earthly sungod and Horus, with the fancy that he was the auspicious beginner of a new line of kings, to be the gods and heroes of a new world. And in later times, the precedent having once been set, even without a conjuncture so suitable as that of the renewal of the real Cycle, still, if any great occasion prompted the thought, imaginary cycles, or sums of years equal to cycles, could always be multiplied so as to exhibit an imaginary *ἀποκατάστασις* to be completed in any year selected by the constructor.

It was by the adoption of an Egyptian idea in the

consulship of Pollio, B.C. 40, the year that the sceptre passed out of the hands of Judah, that Virgil expressed unconsciously, in language like that of sacred prophecy, the groaning of all creation for the promised Son, the expected peacemaker and king: —

"*Ultima* Cumæi [or Thebaici] venit jam carminis *ætas*,
Magnus ab integro sæclorum nascitur ordo.
Jam *redit* et Virgo, *redeunt* Saturnia regna,
Jam nova progenies cœlo demittitur alto.
Tu modo nascenti puero, quo ferrea primum
Desinet, ac toto surget gens aurea mundo,
Casta fave Lucina, tuus jam regnat *Apollo*.
Teque adeo decus hoc ævi, te consule, inibit,
Pollio, et incipient *magni* procedere *menses*."

. . . . . . . . . .

"Ille Deûm vitam accipiet, *Divis*que videbit
*Permixtos Heroas*, et ipse videbitur illis,
Pacatumque reget patriis virtutibus orbem.
Pauca tamen suberunt priscæ vestigia fraudis,
Quæ tentare Thetim ratibus, quæ cingere muris
Oppida, quæ jubeant telluri infindere sulcos;
Alter erit tum Tiphys, et altera quæ vehat Argo
Delectos heroas; erunt etiam altera bella,
Atque iterum ad Trojam magnus mittetur Achilles."
[or, Atque iterum in terris geret ingens bella Sesostris.]

. . . . . . . . . .

"Aggredere, O magnos, aderit jam tempus, honores,
Cara Deum soboles, magnum Jovis incrementum!
Aspice convexo nutantem pondere mundum,
Terrasque, tractusque maris, cœlumque profundum;
Aspice, venturo lætantur ut omnia sæclo!"

The same Egyptian compliment that Virgil in his fourth Eclogue addressed to the opening dynasty of Augustus and the Cæsars, and indirectly and unconsciously to a greater birth than any thought of by Pollio or Octavius, the Egyptians themselves, 265 years before, had addressed to the successors of Alexander the Great, when Ptolemy Lagi, in B.C. 305, first took the crown and title of king. And their complimentary anticipations were not altogether out of season. For in like manner as Augustus, after the civil wars, after a stormy deluge and reign of Typhon, gave peace to the Roman world with a prospect of stability and prosperity, so in Egypt, too, at an earlier period, after the extinction of her last native dynasty, and the odious domination of the Persian fire-worshippers, the Macedonian Ptolemies introduced a new era of material prosperity, conforming readily to the national religion, rebuilding and founding temples, confirming the priesthood in their possessions and privileges, and accepting for themselves, in return, the same deification which had been given to the ancient Pharaohs.

The conceit that an old world had ended with the last native Egyptian dynasty, and a new world with all its promise was beginning with the kingdom of the Lagidæ, was embodied in a Greek document very different indeed in form from the spirited Eclogue of Virgil, yet wrapping up, under a dry and enigmatical husk, a kernel of information both interesting and valuable. The substance of this document has been preserved by George Syncellus, a writer of the ninth century, who gives it, probably from the Manetho of Africanus, thus:

"There is extant among the Egyptians a certain old Chronicle, the source, as I suppose, which led Manetho astray, exhibiting XXX Dynasties, and again CXIII generations, with an infinite space of time (not the same either as that of Manetho), viz., three myriads, six thousand, five hundred and twenty-five years, first, of the Aeritæ, secondly, of the Mestræans, and thirdly, of Egyptians, being word for word as follows:—

(*Dynasty I. to XV. inclusive of the Chronicle, of Gods:*)

"*Time* of Phtha there is *none*, as he shines equally by night and by day, [but, all generations being from him,]

[First, Dyn. I.] Ἥλιος [i. e. Ra, the sungod], son of Phtha, reigned three myriads of years . 30,000

Then [Dyn. II. to XIV. inclusive, and generations II to XIV inclusive;] Κρόνος [or Χρόνος, i. e. Seb], and all the other XII Gods [who are the Aeritæ perhaps of Eusebius and Africanus], reigned years . . . . 3984

| | |
|---|---|
| Then [Dyn. XV.] VIII Demigod Kings, [the Mestræans of Eusebius and Africanus], reigned [as VIII generations but one dynasty] years | 217 |
| And after them XV generations *of the Cynic Cycle* were registered in years . . . . | 443 |
| Then Dyn. XVI. of Tanites, generations VIII, years. | 190 |
| Then Dyn. XVII. of Memphites, generations IV, years of the same generations . . . | 103 |
| After whom there followed— | |
| Dyn. XVIII. of Memphites, generations XIV, years of the same generations . . . | 348 |
| Then Dyn. XIX. of Diospolites, generations V, years | 194 |
| Then Dyn. XX. of Diospolites, generations VIII, years of the same generations . . . | 228 |
| Then Dyn. XXI. of Tanites, generations VI, years. | 121 |
| Then Dyn. XXII. of Tanites, generations III, years | 48 |
| Then Dyn. XXIII. of Diospolites, generations II, years of the same generations . . . | 19 |
| Then Dyn. XXIV. of Saites, generations III, years | 44 |
| Besides whom is to be reckoned— | |
| Dyn. XXV. of Ethiopians, generations III, years of the same generations . . . | 44 |
| After whom again there followed— | |
| Dyn. XXVI. of Memphites, generations VII, years of the same generations . . . | 177 |
| And then after— | |
| Dyn. XXVII. | |
| [Here the designation, generations, and years are purposely omitted; but the years are implied by the sum total which follows below to be certainly . . | 184] |
| Dyn. XXVIII. of Persians, generations V, years of the same generations . . . | 124 |
| Then Dyn. XXIX. of Tanites, generations... years | 39 |
| And lastly, after all the above— | |
| Dyn. XXX. of one Tanite King, years . . | 1 |
| [Generations CXIII, years | 36,525] |

Sum of all the years of the XXX Dynasties, three myriads, six thousand, five hundred and twenty-five." [Kings, 1881 yrs.]

"These 36,525," says Syncellus, "being divided by 1461, give the quotient XXV, and exhibit the *ἀποκατάστασις* of the zodiac fabled by the Egyptians and the Greeks, that is, its circuit from starting round to the same point, which point is the first minute (*λεπτὸν*) of the first degree (*μοίρας*) of the zodiacal sign containing the vernal equinox, called by them Aries; as is said in the *Γενικὰ* of Hermes, and in the *Κυραννίδες*," (spurious and late writings mentioned here only by Syncellus). "And hence," continues Syncellus, "one may see how irreconcilable such accounts are both with our Divine Scriptures, and with one another, when this, *which is accounted the oldest Egyptian document*" (of all that have been written in Greek), "introduces first a *time* absolutely infinite, which it gives to Ἥφαιστος, and then for the other XXIX" [rather he should have written, "and then for the XXX"] "dynasties 36,525 years; although Ἥφαιστος, or Phtha, reigned in Egypt many years after the Flood and the building of the Tower of Babel, as we shall show hereafter in the proper place."

"*Φέρεται παρ' Αἰγυπτίοις παλαιόν τι χρονογραφεῖον, ἐξ οὗ καὶ τὸν Μανεθῶ πεπλανῆσθαι νομίζω, περιέχον λ' δυναστειῶν ἐν γενεαῖς πάλιν ρῦγ' χρόνον ἄπειρον, καὶ οὐ τὸν αὐτὸν ὃν Μανεθῶ, ἐν [ἐτῶν] μυριάσι τρισὶ καὶ ͵ϛφκε', πρῶτον μὲν τῶν Λὐριτῶν [Αἐριτῶν], δεύτερον δὲ τῶν Μεστραίων, τρίτον δὲ Αἰγυπτίων, οὕτω πως ἐπὶ λέξεως ἔχον·*

(*Θεῶν βασιλεία κατὰ τὸ παλαιὸν χρονικόν·*)

*Ἡφαίστου χρόνος οὐκ ἔστι, διὰ τὸ νυκτὸς καὶ ἡμέρας αὐτὸν φαίνειν·*

*Ἥλιος Ἡφαίστου ἐβασίλευσεν ἐτῶν μυριάδας τρεῖς·*

*Ἔπειτα Κρόνος, φησί, καὶ οἱ λοιποὶ πάντες Θεοὶ δώδεκα ἐβασίλευσαν ἔτη ͵γ<sup>ϡ</sup>πδ'·*

*Ἔπειτα Ἡμίθεοι βασιλεῖς ὀκτώ, ἔτη σιζ'· καὶ μετ' αὐτοὺς Γενεαὶ ιε' Κυνικοῦ Κύκλου ἀνεγράφησαν ἐν ἔτεσι υμγ'·*

*Εἶτα Τανιτῶν ιϛ' δυναστεία, γενεῶν η', ἐτῶν ρϛ'·*

*Πρὸς οἷς ιζ' δυναστεία Μεμφιτῶν, γενεῶν δ', ἐτῶν ργ'·*

*Μεθ' οὓς ιη' δυναστεία Μεμφιτῶν, γενεῶν ιδ', ἐτῶν τμη'·*

*Ἔπειτα ιθ' δυναστεία Διοσπολιτῶν, γενεῶν ε', ἐτῶν ριδ'·*

*Εἶτα κ' δυναστεία Διοσπολιτῶν, γενεῶν η', ἐτῶν σκη'·*

Ἔπειτα κα' δυναστεία Τανιτῶν, γενεῶν ϛ', ἐτῶν ρκα·
Εἶτα κβ' δυναστεία Τανιτῶν, γενεῶν γ', ἐτῶν μη'·
Ἔπειτα κγ' δυναστεία Διοσπολιτῶν, γενεῶν β', ἐτῶν ιθ'·
Εἶτα κδ' δυναστεία Σαϊτῶν, γενεῶν γ', ἐτῶν μδ'·
Πρὸς οἷς κε' δυναστεία Αἰθιόπων, γενεῶν γ', ἐτῶν μδ'·
Μεθ' οὓς κϛ' δυναστεία Μεμφιτῶν, γενεῶν ζ, ἐτῶν ροζ'·
Καὶ μετὰ κζ' .... [Cod. B. has Μετὰ τὰς κζ' δυναστείας]

Here the designation, generations, and years are purposely omitted; but the years may be filled up with certainty from the sum given below, thus:

Καὶ μετὰ κζ' [δυναστειαν ...., γενεῶν δ' ?, ἐτῶν ρπδ']
. . . . κη' δυναστεία Περσῶν, γενεῶν ε', ἐτῶν ρκδ'·
Ἔπειτα κθ' δυναστεία Τανιτῶν, γενεῶν [γ' ?] ἐτῶν λθ'·
Καὶ ἐπὶ πάσαις λ' δυναστεία Τανίτου ἑνὸς, ἔτη ιη'·

"Τὰ πάντα ὁμοῦ τῶν λ' δυναστειῶν ἔτη Μ. [μυριάδες] γ' καὶ ͵ϛφκε' [δηλαδὴ τρισμύρια, καὶ ἑξακισχίλια, καὶ πεντακόσια, καὶ εἴκοσι πέντε ἔτη· τῶν δὲ ιε' δυναστειῶν τῶν βασιλέων τὰ πάντα ὁμοῦ ἔτη χίλια ὀκτακόσια ὀγδοήκοντα καὶ ἕν.]

"Ταῦτα ἀναλυόμενα, εἴτουν μεριζόμενα παρὰ τὰ ͵αυξα' ἔτη εἴκοσι πεντάκις, τὴν παρ' Αἰγυπτίοις καὶ Ἕλλησιν ἀποκατάστασιν τοῦ ζωδιακοῦ μυθολογουμένην δηλοῖ, τοῦτ' ἔστι τὴν ἀπὸ τοῦ αὐτοῦ σημείου ἐπὶ τὸ αὐτὸ σημεῖον, ὅ ἐστι πρῶτον λεπτὸν τῆς πρώτης μοίρας τοῦ ἰσημερινοῦ ζωδίου, Κριοῦ λεγομένου παρ' αὐτοῖς, ὥσπερ καὶ ἐν τοῖς Γενικοῖς τοῦ Ἑρμοῦ καὶ ἐν ταῖς Κυραννίσι βίβλοις εἴρηται· ἐντεῦθεν δὲ οἶμαι καὶ Πτολεμαῖον τὸν Κλαύδιον τοὺς προχείρους κανόνας τῆς ἀστρονομίας διὰ κε' ἐτηρίδων ψηφίζεσθαι θεσπίσαι, ὡς τοῦ Αἰγυπτιακοῦ ἐνιαυτοῦ καὶ τοῦ Ἑλληνικοῦ διὰ ͵αυξα' ἔτους ἀποκαθισταμένων, εἰ καὶ διὰ ͵αυοϛ' ἐτῶν τὸ κανόνιον τῶν κε' ἐτηρίδων ἐξέθετο, διὰ τὸ μὴ ἀπαρτίζειν τὸν ͵αυξα' ἀριθμὸν εἰς κε' ἀλλὰ λείπεσθαι ιδ'. Τὴν μέντοι μονάδα περιττὴν ἔθετο, διὰ τὸ πλήρη τὰ τοῦ α' ἔτους ἐγκεῖσθαι κινήματα καὶ μὴ ἀπ' ἀρχῆς αὐτοῦ, ὥσπερ καὶ ἐπὶ τῶν μηνιαίων κινημάτων. Ἐντεῦθεν δέ ἐστι καὶ τὸ ἀσύμφωνον τῶν τοιούτων ἐκδόσεων πρός τε τὰς θείας ἡμῶν γραφὰς καὶ πρὸς ἀλλήλας ἐπιγνῶναι, ὅτι αὕτη μὲν ἡ παλαιοτέρα νομιζομένη Αἰγυπτίων συγγραφὴ Ἡφαίστου μὲν ἄπειρον εἰσάγει χρόνον, τῶν δὲ λοιπῶν κθ' [he should have written τῶν δὲ λ'] δυναστειῶν ἔτη τρισμύρια ͵ϛφκε', καίτοι τοῦ Ἡφαίστου πολλοῖς ἔτεσι μετὰ τὸν κατακλυσμὸν καὶ τὴν πυργοποιίαν τῆς Αἰγύπτου βασιλεύσαντος, ὡς δειχθήσεται ἐν τῷ δέοντι τόπῳ."—*Syncell. Chronogr.*, p. 51.

The Chronicle thus described contains within itself, in its structure, and especially in its date, after a fashion not uncommon in Egyptian enigmas, both an account of its own origin, and a key to its purpose and meaning; so that on these points we need only to analyse and question the document itself. But in order to give the reader an idea of the way in which, probably, it has been preserved and transmitted to us, we must draw somewhat on conjecture:—

It seems, then, that as the earliest systematic account of Egyptian antiquity written in Greek, it was followed more or less by later writers, and first by Manetho, who yet differed from it considerably in details, making most of the thirty dynasties, instead of the last fifteen only, to consist of mortal kings, all seemingly successive, and carrying up Menes and the commencement of the monarchy 1674 years above the date at which it was set by the Chronicle. The vast sums of years given by Manetho not only to the sun, or to gods and demigods, but to Manes also, and to ordinary kings, having excited the ridicule of the Greeks, Eratosthenes, the second Librarian at Alexandria, attempted at the king's desire to reduce them to the limits of the Chronicle, except that he yielded so far to the priests, whom he consulted, as to include within the times of the monarchy those XV generations and 443 years "of the Cynic Cycle" which in the Chronicle were entered between the Demigods and Menes. But all above or beyond these, whether in the Chronicle or in Manetho, he disallowed as ante-historical and fabulous. Somewhat later, Ptolemy of Mendes, or whoever was the editor of the Manetho of Africanus, undertook to explain the origin of those myriads of years which seemed so incredible, reducing them, as *months*, to one-twelfth of their apparent bulk: but at the same time, as if to compensate for this concession, he not only retained and reasserted, but he even extended, the vast antiquity claimed by Manetho for Egyptian history and civilisation. And as the Chronicle, which Manetho had plainly used as one of his sources, exhibited both an older and a fuller form of those myriads of years which it was now proposed to explain and reduce, and for reduction its larger sum (Manetho having 6000 or 7000 years less) was the more convenient, it was natural for Ptolemy of Mendes to give some account of a document which he meant to follow. In this way probably it was, that Africanus found an account of the Chronicle in the preface to that edition of Manetho from which his Lists are taken; and Eusebius and Syncellus derived their knowledge of it from him, each, perhaps, in copying adding a word or two of his own.

The expressions *φέρεται παρ' Αἰγυπτίοις*, "is extant among the Egyptians," and *ἐξ οὗ καὶ τὸν Μανεθῶ πεπλανῆσθαι νομίζω*, are clearly from Africanus, and not from Syncellus; nor even from Eusebius; for Eusebius shows himself to have no other knowledge of Manetho than what he gained at second-hand from Josephus or from Africanus. And long before the time of Eusebius, before that of Africanus, or even of Josephus, not only the Old Chronicle, but the genuine work of Manetho also had ceased *φέρεσθαι*, that is, to be popularly known in their own original forms. So far as they were known, it seems to have been only through that abridgment and re-edition of Manetho, the compiler of which had used both the true Manetho and the Chronicle as his materials.

The words "an infinite space of *time*," and others like them at the end of the extract from Syncellus, where the infinite reign of Phtha is hastily and inaccurately sneered at, as if it were an infinite number of years *in time*, and where the writer promises to show that *Ἥφαιστος*, as king of Egypt, reigned long after the Flood and the building of the Tower of Babel, are plainly from the Christian extractor, not from the text of Ptolemy. But when it is added, that the vast space of time reckoned in the Chronicle is "not the same either as that of Manetho," this remark, though in its wording from Africanus, is probably in substance from Ptolemy himself. For Ptolemy, in bringing forward the Chronicle, and preferring its sum for reduction to that of Manetho, though he followed Manetho for his lists of names and for historical details so closely, that his work was still Manetho's in name, could not but notice the difference existing between the sums of his two sources, and signify his reasons for reducing the sum of the one rather than that of the other.

The astronomical explanation of the ἀποκατάστασις given by Syncellus, who connects it with the Greek and Babylonian zodiac, and with a return to the sign of the Ram, the sign of the vernal equinox, *need* not be viewed as a mere comment of his own, or as derived from the Γενικὰ of Hermes, or the Κυραννίδες, which he cites in illustration; but the same *may* have been found by Africanus, or even by Ptolemy himself, conjoined with the Chronicle; the Babylonian and Greek zodiac being certainly known in Egypt when the Chronicle was composed; and it being perhaps natural that its author, writing in Greek and for Greeks, should give to the Egyptian idea of the ἀποκατάστασις a Greek form. Supposing that he did so, it by no means follows that the commencement of the world according to the Egyptian reckoning, or the first epoch of the Sothic Cycle, had any connection with the sign of Aries, or with the vernal equinox; or that the idea of the ἀποκατάστασις was originally expressed among the Egyptians themselves in terms borrowed from the Babylonian zodiac. Thus much only may fairly be argued, that whether the Chronicle itself, or only its transcriber, first connected the commencement of its period with the sign of Aries, the writing in which this connection occurs cannot well be older than the time of Alexander the Great, or his first successors. The idea itself of the ἀποκατάστασις, and its connection with the number of xxv Sothic cycles, is quite another thing. But it is possible also that the mention of the sign of Aries may be only a gloss added afterwards, as an explanation to Greek readers.

In the same way, the three designations Ἀερίται, Μεστραῖοι, and Αἰγύπτιοι, as if from three successive names of the country of Egypt, have excited suspicion, because Mizraim is named by Moses as the ancestor of the Egyptians, and Africanus, and others after him, see this name in the adjective form Μεστραῖοι. It certainly is possible that these designations were added only by Syncellus, who may have borrowed them from that latest Manetho or Sothis of Anianus and Panodorus which he uses so largely, and that the text of Africanus and of Ptolemy had them not; though Africanus, by the way in which he introduces the name Mizraim seems to allude to the Μεστραῖοι. But, on the other hand, even if these designations were found by Africanus in the text of Ptolemy, and it be granted that the source of the Μεστραῖοι is to be looked for in the writings of Moses, there would be nothing so very wonderful in this, considering the time at which Ptolemy seems to have lived, when the LXX. version was well known. But there is really no valid reason for denying that all the three designations may have belonged to the Chronicle from the beginning, and that without the word Μεστραῖοι being borrowed from the Mosaic writings at all; for we shall see below that the Phœnician Sanconiathon, writing from Egyptian sources about 1000 years before the epoch of the Chronicle, gives the name Μισὼρ as that of the father of Thoth, and ancestor of the Egyptians.

We may now proceed to consider the Chronicle itself; and first the sum of its years, consisting of 30,000 given to the sun, + 3984 of XIII gods, + 217 of VIII demigods, + 443 of the Sothic Cycle, + 1881 of kings from Menes to Nectanebo, making in all 36,525; which sum divided by 1461, gives XXV cycles as the period of the ἀποκατάστασις.

Why, it will be asked at the outset, is the ἀποκατάστασις defined as taking place after XXV rather than after any other number of cycles; especially when we have already collected from passages of Herodotus and Plato that the original and proper period of the ἀποκατάστασις, at least for the human soul deified, was only two cycles of years? This question has been answered by various hypotheses. Some say, because the canicular, like the uncorrected Julian year, being somewhat too long, would really cause a precession of the equinoxes and solstices to the amount of one day in about 130 years, and so to the amount of one whole year in about (365 × 130 =) 47,450 years; and that this is what the Egyptians meant when they spoke of the ἀποκατάστασις, though they erroneously supposed one day to be gained in 100 instead of 130 years, and so made the whole period to be only 36,525 ($365\frac{1}{4} \times 100$) instead of 47,450 years. But this theory rests on no grounds to begin, and fails besides to connect itself distinctly with that period of XXV cycles which it is put forward to explain. Others have supposed that the number of XXV cycles, i. e. 36,525 years, may have originated in the idea of multiplying the Sothic into the Apis Cycle, the latter being a luni-solar cycle in use among the Egyptians from at least as early a time as the first known epoch of the Sothic Cycle (B. C. 1322). And certainly the fact that the sum of XXV Sothic cycles does seem to represent such a multiplication, supplies a very intelligible reason for *adhering* to this same definition of an ἀποκατάστασις, so long as both cycles continued to be in use, even though the idea of multiplying them into one another were not originally or alone the *source* of the definition. But in truth, at the point at which we now are, this discussion of the origin of the number of XXV cycles is premature: we have not yet those aids for forming a judgment which we shall shortly obtain: so we must be content merely to notice the existence of different opinions, and to remark that the connection of the ἀποκατάστασις with this or that period of time, whether variable or uniform, longer or shorter, is noways essential to the idea of the ἀποκατάστασις in itself, or to its application, as in the Chronicle, to any particular epoch. *Some* definition of course it needs, in order to exhibit a period of time; and the sum which the Chronicle actually presents, from whatever source derived, being that of XXV Sothic cycles, or 36,525 years, our only business with this sum at present is to analyse it, and resolve it into its elements.

We cannot perhaps set about this better than by putting ourselves in thought in the place of the Egyptian constructor of the Chronicle at that point of time at which it seems to end, viz., at the end of the last native dynasty, or the conquest by Ochus, and ask ourselves what we have to do in order to exhibit an imaginary ἀποκατάστασις in XXV Sothic cycles ending at this point? Now, as the Sothic Cycle, which is by no means any or every period of 1461 vague years, did not really end at or near this date (B. C. 345,) but was still current, and had many years, let us say 483 years, still to run, to July, A. D. 139, its true epoch; the first thing to be done, plainly, is to cut off and throw back to some point above well-known history these 483 years of the real Cycle. Next, it will be natural to survey the chronological materials at our disposal, running back from Nectanebo to the head of the Monarchy, before we think of placing the 483 years cast up from below; and going down, in like manner, from the beginning of all known time as many perfect cycles, or rather, as many times 1461 years, as our reckoning may allow, till we come to a fractional number, which will be sure *not* to coalesce with the years reckoned upwards from Nectanebo, and the years "of the Cycle" thrown up, into a sum divisible by 1461. For it would be absurd to suppose that either the sum of our own chronological reckoning should of itself fall exactly into a number of spaces of 1461 years each, or, that the world in point of fact should have begun from an epoch of the Sothic Cycle. So, when we come to this fraction, we shall have to cut off or to add, according as it presents too many years or too few. And lastly, if after this operation our whole number of cycles, or spaces like cycles, falls short of XXV, we must add as many more whole cycles, purely fictitious, as are wanted.

This is, in fact, what the author of the Chronicle seems (at least at first sight) to have done. First, he ran up from Nectanebo to Menes 1881 years, and placed before these, let us say, the 483 years of the true Cycle which in B. C. 345 were still to run. Then, looking back to the beginning, he found two complete cycles, or spaces of 1461 years each, which he gave to Chronos, the first deified ancestor and first measurer of human time, and to XII other Gods, in XIII generations, seemingly answering to the XIII patriarchs of the antediluvians, or of the old world. After these 2922 years there came a fraction of 217 before the foundation of the monarchy by Menes; and this he gave to VIII Demigods, representing no doubt VIII generations of postdiluvian patriarchs of the line of Mizraim. But this fraction of 217, with the 1881 years of the monarchy from Menes to Nectanebo, and the 483 of the Cycle thrown up as aforesaid, making altogether a sum of 2581, short of two more complete cycles by 341, he threw in 341 fictitious years, adding them to the 2922 of the XIII Gods, where they could cause no confusion; whereas, if they had been added to the 217 of the Demigods, no one could have any longer distinguished the original fraction, nor so much as guessed what addition or curtailment had been needed in order to make time from the beginning seem to run in the form of Sothic cycles. Having thus obtained four complete cycles of human time, but wanting XXI more, the author prefixed and added XXI more whole cycles of time purely fictitious, or, as it might seem, cosmical, not reckoned by men, nor by deified ancestors of men, but by the Sun-God alone; though in order to give him the round sum of 30,000 rather than 30,681 years, the fraction 681 was detached, and added to the two cycles of the XIII (human) Gods, again without danger of any confusion. So their years were swelled by the double addition both of 681 from above and of 341 from below; and yet further by 40 detached from the 483 of the Cycle; so as to amount in all to the sum of (681 + 2922 + 341 + 40 =) 3984 instead of 2922 years. The purpose of the last-mentioned addition was this, that the interval of 40 years between the conquest by Ochus and the assumption of the crown by Ptolemy Lagi might be sunk, as it were, and suppressed; and that the latter epoch of the two, viz. B.C. 305, might be marked in the structure of the Chronicle by the specification of "443 years of the Cycle" as thrown up; whereas, if the 40 between B. C. 345 and 305, equally thrown up, had been included in one and the same sum, the specification of "483 years of the Cycle" would have pointed only to the end of the last native dynasty B.C. 345; and the commencement of a new world would have been given to the Persians, instead of those conquerors and successors of the Persians for whom the compliment enigmatically contained in the Chronicle was intended.

The specification, indeed, of 40 years as the precise interval between Nectanebo and Ptolemy Lagi, or the first of the 443 years of the Cycle thrown up above Menes, is not contained in the structure of the Chronicle, but rests on other grounds. The Chronicle, we are informed (for though Manetho is named, the Chronicle must have been originally meant), ended its thirty Dynasties 15 years before the *cosmocracy* of Alexander; that is, as it seems, 15 years before B.C. 330. Again, if we allow the 124 years of the Persian Dynasty XXVIII of the Chronicle to commence with the 5th of Cambyses, Jan. 1, B.C. 525, a date for which nearly all are agreed, it follows that its Dynasty XXX (124 + 39 + 18), 181 years later, ends Nov. 18, B.C. 345; still, if any one thinks he sees reason for it, it is certainly open, so far as the structure of the Chronicle goes, to substitute any other number that he prefers for the 40 in question, subtracting from the 341 also contained in the years of the XIII gods, as many years as he adds to the 40, or adding to the 341 as many as he subtracts from the 40, the purpose of the Chronicle being, as has been explained, to present the ἀποκατάστασις as if there were *no* interval between Nectanebo and the Lagidæ. But this one point being assumed (and at present only on the grounds stated), that the interval between Nectanebo and the Lagidæ was 40 years, and that the author of the Chronicle so reckoned it; we have now the whole scheme of the Chronicle, as it is given from Africanus by Syncellus, explained by our own analysis of its internal structure, having ourselves gone through the process of constructing it. The 36,525 years then stand thus:—

30,681 + 2922 + [341] + 217 + 1881 + 483 to A.D. 139, or<br>
{ 30,681 + 2922 + [381] + 217 + [443] + 1881,<br>
{ 30,000 + 3984 + 217 + [443] + 1881 to B.C. 345.

Cutting off the XXI cycles of 30,681 years entirely fictitious prefixed, ejecting the 341 inserted for cyclical purposes between the XIII gods and the VIII demigods, and restoring the 40 and 443 years of the Cycle current under the Ptolemies to their proper place, between B.C. 345 and A.D. 139, we obtain the Egyptian chronology of the world at a date at least as early as that of the Chronicle, i.e., before the settlement of multitudes of Jews at Alexandria, or the translation of the Hebrew Scriptures into Greek, as follows:—

2922 years of the XIII antediluvian Patriarchs + 217 of

VIII post-diluvian Patriarchs of the line of Ham and Mizraim, + 903 years from Menes to the epoch of the Sothic Cycle, B.C. 1322, + 978, or thence to the last Persian conquest by Ochus, B.C. 345, + 40 to the assumption of a crown by Ptolemy Lagi, B.C. 305, + 443 to the cyclical epoch A.D. 139, making in all from Chronus, who should be Adam, to the expiration of the Sothic Cycle in A.D. 139, 5493; or to our era (i.e. to B.C. 1, Aug. 24, within 4 months and 7 days of it) 5364 vague or civil years of 365 days each.

If this analysis and its consequences stand the test of criticism, and it appear that later writers, as Manetho, Eratosthenes, Ptolemy of Mendes, Diodorus, Josephus, Africanus, Eusebius, Anianus and Panodorus, and Syncellus, have, either of themselves or by following others, transferred dynasties, generations, and years of the gods and demigods of the Chronicle to kings after Menes, the imposture or the error will be sufficiently refuted by the mere statement that such is the case. And if, further, any writers, ancient or modern, should have swelled the antiquity of Egyptian history, not only by transferring years of gods and demigods, but also by similarly transferring years of the Sothic Cycle lying between B.C. 345 and A.D. 139, and belonging to the Ptolemies and Cæsars, and other years purely fictitious, to a succession of antediluvian or even of pre-Adamite Pharaohs, such an error may be coupled for the future with that of the French Academicians of the last century, who in the Zodiac of Dendera, of the times of the Ptolemies, found proof that Egyptian civilisation went back thousands of years, to an antiquity incompatible with the truth of the sacred Scriptures.

Having obtained then an Egyptian reckoning of time from the beginning, not derived from any translation of the Hebrew Scriptures, the thought naturally occurs to compare this with the chief systems of sacred chronology, and to see how far it agrees with any of them.

But first it will be well to notice the testimony given by another Egyptian computation to the accuracy of the foregoing analysis of the Chronicle, and to the actual existence among the Egyptians of that scheme of chronology which has now been extracted from it. Testimony indeed there will be enough hereafter; for the Chronicle is the first of a family of documents, all derived from the same sources, and all repeating the same elements with variations. But without anticipating the examination of these, we have in Diogenes Laertius, a writer of the time of Augustus, a computation constructed on a different idea, and exhibiting a sum of years very different from the 36,525 of the Chronicle, (a sum by the way much more like than 36,525 to what would result from a calculation of the precession of the equinoxes), viz. 48,863 years, which are reckoned from Phtha to Alexander the Great, without any pretence of an ἀποκατάστασις. "Αἰγύπτιοι μὲν γὰρ Νείλου γενέσθαι παῖδα Ἥφαιστον, ὃν ἄρξαι φιλοσοφίας, ἧς τοὺς προεστῶτας ἱερέας εἶναι καὶ προφήτας· ἀπὸ δὲ τούτου εἰς Ἀλέξανδρον τὸν Μακεδόνα ἐτῶν εἶναι μυριάδας τέσσαρας καὶ ὀκτακισχίλια ὀκτακόσια ἔτη ἑξήκοντα τρία." (*Diog. Laert. in Præf.*)

What may be the precise age of this computation, or from what source Diogenes obtained it, we cannot determine. It occurs between references made respecting the Egyptians and Babylonians to Aristotle and Sotion; and the passage in which it occurs is very similar to another concerning certain astronomical observations, going back 2903 years before Alexander, which were sent from Babylon by Callisthenes to Aristotle; during which 2903 years, it is added, there had been so many eclipses of the sun, and so many of the moon. Of the Egyptians, in like manner, Diogenes Laertius asserts, that they made 48,863 years from Phtha, son of Nilus, to Alexander: and that during this time there had been observed so many eclipses of the sun, and so many of the moon. So there is some appearance that the Egyptian computation also of 48,863 years may have been communicated by Callisthenes or some one else to Aristotle, and may have passed from him to Diogenes Laertius: and in that case, the chronology contained in it will of course be older among the Egyptians than the time of Alexander, or than that of the author of the Chronicle. On the otherhand, there is also some appearance that the sum of years named by Diogenes Laertius was, in the fictitious or cosmical part of it, a variation suggested by the sum of the Chronicle itself. For the sum of 48,863 contains, first, for its fictitious part, thirty times 1461; i.e. a full Egyptian month of thirty "Great Days," or cycles, instead of the twenty-one fictitious cycles of the Chronicle, or its thirty thousands of years assigned to the Sun-God: the number *thirty* having a plain relation both to the sun and to the moon; while neither the number *twenty-one*, in connection with *cycles*, or great days; nor that of a *thousand*, in connection with *thirty* as its multiple, had any peculiar sense or propriety. And after the aforesaid month of cosmical cycles, being 43,830 years, the remainder of the 48,863, being 5033 years, resolves itself into a simple and honest addition of the periods of true or human time reckoned by the Egyptians from the beginning of the world to Alexander, without any insertion of 341 fictitious years to make the world seem to have begun from a cyclical epoch, without any allusion to the idea of the *ἀποκατάστασις*, still less with any throwing up of years still future, in order to exhibit a feigned *ἀποκατάστασις*, ending at a point not really the epoch of a Sothic cycle. For 5033 years are equal to those 2922 + 217 + 1881 years which alone in the Chronicle belong (properly and originally) to the XIII gods, the VIII demi-gods, and the last XV dynasties, of the kings from Menes to Nectanebo, with 13 more years only, from the conquest of Darius Ochus to Alexander, i. e., seemingly, to the autumn of B.C. 332, when he first entered Egypt. And those years of the Chronicle which we distinguished in its internal structure as true human time, chronologically reckoned, if added to thirty cycles of cosmical time, together with 13, instead of 15, years on from Nectanebo to the *cosmocracy* of Alexander, make exactly the sum total of Diogenes Laertius (43,830 + 5033 =) 48,863 years; and the comparison of the two schemes will be as follows:—

XXI Cycles or 30,681 + 2922 [+ 381] + 217 [+ 443] + 1881 + 15 = 36,525
XXX Cycles or 43,830 + 2922 ——— + 217 ——— + 1881 + 13 = 48,863

In both cases alike, the sum of real Egyptian years, reckoned chronologically, will be 5364 to Aug. 24, B.C. 1, four months and seven days before the vulgar era.

Having thus strengthened our foundation, we may go on

confidently to compare, as was proposed, Egyptian with sacred chronology, observing, however, first, that in reckoning to the XV dynasties of kings from Menes 1881 years, we have supplied, from the sum total of the Chronicle, the particular sum of 184 for the years of one dynasty, which stands as XXVII, next before that of the Persians, without having the sum of its years named.

But for a scheme of sacred chronology with which to compare the Egyptian, what method is to be followed? The simplest rule will be this:—Let it be supposed open to us, and to every man, to take for a basis whatever text, or system we prefer; only, when this is done, let us consent to sacrifice in this our basis every *peculiarity*, by making first its excesses and deficiencies compensate one another, so far as possible, and only afterwards, in case of need, cutting off or filling up any residual excess or deficiency; preferring also, *cæteris paribus*, the elder to the later writer or text, and the original text to the translation. With these principles, we shall select the historian Josephus, as being at once the most ancient and the best qualified writer of all who have left anything like a continuous reckoning connecting sacred with profane history. And, as he is often inconsistent with himself, citing sometimes the shorter numbers of the Hebrew text, which already differed from the Greek, but generally following a longer chronology, which gave to many of the patriarchs 100 years more before the birth of their son, we shall take for our basis the longer or Greek, not the shorter or Hebrew, reckoning of Josephus.

Josephus, then, for the time before the Flood, making XXVI *centuries*, agrees so far with the LXX., but differs from both the Hebrew and the Samaritan texts. Still, as these two texts are not identical, and as besides the question of the longer or shorter chronology before the Flood has no historical importance, and between the Flood and Abram relates to a period which is mostly ante-historical, we need not in these periods dwell minutely on any questions of detail, nor scruple to admit anything which is not strictly peculiar to our author. We observe, however, that in his *decads* and *units* for the time before the Flood Josephus has the '56 of the

Hebrew, not the '62 of the LXX., his whole number being 2256 not 2262.

After the Flood it is, by a peculiarity of his own, that he interposes 12 instead of 2 current years between the Flood (let us understand with Africanus the commencement of the year of the Flood, not the end) and the birth of Arphaxad; but this excess is compensated below, all but one year, when, by another peculiarity of his own, he cuts off 9 years from the decads and units of Nahor.

In giving six centuries more than the Hebrew gives to the first six postdiluvian patriarchs, and 50 years more than the Hebrew to Nahor, he has with him both the Samaritan text and the Greek LXX. against only the Hebrew. But in adding yet another 50 years to the decads of Nahor, while cutting off his 9 units, he is peculiar; and after allowing the suppression of the 9 units to tell in compensation for part of his excess of 10 years above, he has still an excess of 51 years, peculiar to himself, before Abram. This excess being cut off, he will exhibit 940 full years (or 941 current) from the *end* of the 600th of Noah, the year of the Flood, to the birth of Abram; a result agreeing exactly with the Samaritan text, and differing from the LXX. only by the absence of 130 years which it gives to the second Cainan. But on this point Josephus has not only the Samaritan and the Hebrew texts, but also the earliest Christian fathers, as Africanus and Eusebius, in his favour, and only the LXX. against him. For the *name* of Cainan, in the genealogy given by St. Luke, does not necessarily imply that 130 *years* are to be reckoned twice over, once to Arphaxad and again to Cainan; Cainan being named in the Scriptures both as the youngest son of Shem, and at the same time elsewhere as the son of the first-born of Shem Arphaxad. It is possible, therefore, that Shem himself may have "raised up seed" to his first-born; and that 130 years may be reckoned rightly to Arphaxad as including Cainan, or to Arphaxad and Cainan conjointly, but not separately to both. So to Abram from Adam the Greek sum to be collected from Josephus is 2256 + 940.6$^{m}$. = 3196, less by 6 years than the sum of the Septuagint, which is 2262 + 940.6$^{m}$. = 3202 full or 3203 current years.

Beginning afresh from Abram, and now reckoning from Nisan, commonly paralleled with our March, not as before from September, he has, with general consent, 505 years to the Exodus + 40 of Moses + 5 of the wars of Joshua, to the division of the Promised Land; in all 550. For the survival of Joshua he gives 20, and for the Elders of that generation who outlived Joshua 10 more, making 30 years; with which, from whatever source, he very reasonably and probably fills the gap left in the text of the book of Joshua. Nor is there anything peculiar in his mention of "18 years of anarchy" before the first judgeship of Othniel, though hereby he may have led later writers astray; for 18 years of anarchy there were, before the constitution of a judge, between Joshua and Othniel, viz., 10 during the survival of the Elders, and 8 more during the first servitude under Cushan Risathaim, which last are not to be reduplicated, if they are reckoned, as they usually are, with the other servitudes in the time of the Judges. After the 30 of Joshua and the Elders, he has for the 450 years of Judges, reckoned by St. Paul "to Samuel the Prophet," only 426, omitting uniformly, by a peculiarity of his own, 4 years from the servitude under the Midianites, and all the 20 years of Samuel's minority after the death of Eli, while the ark abode at Kirjath Jearim. Then he allows only 12 years, manifestly too few, for the time during which Samuel judged Israel alone from the assembly at Mizpeh to the demand for a king: then 40 years, however divided, of Saul, part conjointly with Samuel and part alone: then 40 of David (of which he commonly drops the fractions composing one year whenever he divides the reign, and reckons to or from the conquest of Jerusalem): then 80 years of Solomon, doubling by a peculiarity of his own, and in plain contradiction to the Scripture, the reign of that king; then 260 to the capture of Samaria in the sixth year of Hezekiah + 134 more to the burning of the Temple by Nebuchadnezzar, reckoning all the years named in the reigns of the kings of Judah from Hezekiah downwards as perfect years, though the 70 years of penal sabbaths of the captivity following show clearly that 490 were the true interval, to be reckoned from the separation of Samuel from

Saul, and the commencement of that neglect which lasted "all the days of Saul," i. e. all the time that he reigned alone, the last 20 years of his reign. The excesses and deficiencies hitherto noticed compensate one another, and may be corrected by simple transposition, the four years too many reckoned to the kingdom of Judah being thrown back to fill up the servitude under Midian from 3 to 7 years; and one half of the reign of Solomon being thrown back to the times of Samuel, viz., 20 years to cover the time of his minority, while the ark abode at Kirjath Jearim, and 20 to increase the years of his judgeship from 12 to 32, which will give time for him to have become old and greyheaded between the assembly at Mizpeh and the demand for a king. Thus to the burning of the Temple, or rather, to the end of the 11th year of Zedekiah a little earlier, from the birth of Abram, reckoning from Nisan to Nisan, we have 1572 years. Then follow 70 years of the captivity, which may be reckoned from a double or even treble commencement to a double or treble end; for they may be reckoned either from the deportation of Daniel in the fourth year of Jehoiakim, and the first of Nebuchadnezzar in Syria, to the edict of Cyrus in his first year, after the death of his uncle; or from the deportation of Jeconias and Ezekiel to the edict of Cambyses; or, lastly, from the end of the 11th of Zedekiah, before the burning of the Temple, to the end of the 4th year (not the second) of Darius Hystaspes. Josephus himself reckons accurately enough, making only 52 between Nisan 1 preceding the burning of the Temple and the edict of Cyrus, thus: 25 years for the remainder of the reign of Nebuchadnezzar, + 2 of Evil-Merodach, + 4 of Neriglissar, + 9 months of Laborosoarchod, + 17 years of Nabonadius; in all $48.9^{m}$. from the burning of the Temple to the capture of Babylon, + 3 years to the edict of Cyrus. But Josephus, in one place, speaking at once of Nebuchadnezzar's first Syrian campaign (with which he not untruly connects the commencement of the 70 years' captivity), and of the burning of the Temple by the same Nebuchadnezzar in his 19th year afterwards, some ambiguity in his language (and in that of 2 Paralip. xxxvi.), has given occasion to later writers to make 70 years between the burning of the Temple and the edict of Cyrus; and they complicate the error by putting this edict in the first year of his first Babylonian or even of his Persian accession, which was really 21 years before the capture of Babylon, and 24 before the death of his uncle Darius and his third and last accession as sole monarch at Babylon and Ecbatana.

From the accession of Cyrus as sole ruler, and the end of the 70 years as reckoned from the fourth of Jehoiakim, or 52 from the eleventh of Zedekiah, Josephus uses all those reckonings of the heathen, as the years of Nabonassar, of the Seleucidæ, of the Greek Olympiads, and of the Roman Consuls and Emperors, which the Scripture also uses, or refers to as known, and of which the most exact and scientific form is that preserved or digested by Hipparchus and Claudius Ptolemy in the Astronomical Canon. The years of this, too, are in form Egyptian. According to this reckoning, there are of Persians, from the capture of Babylon and the joint Babylonian accession of Cyrus with his uncle Darius (antedated from January 5, B.C. 538), 209 years, or from the accession of Cyrus sole after his uncle's death, 206, or from the end of the fourth of Darius Hystaspes, December 31, B.C. 518, 188 years to the death of Darius Codomannus in B.C. 330. Then 300 years of Macedonians, to the deaths of Antony and Cleopatra, and the reduction of Egypt, in the year after the battle of Actium, B.C. 30; and lastly, from thence 99 (30 + 69) to the burning of the Temple by Titus, in A.D. 70.

Josephus has also other parallel and Jewish reckonings, which come to the same thing. So he makes 414 Hebrew years from the death of Seraiah the high-priest slain by order of Nebuchadnezzar at Riblah, in the autumn of B.C. 587, to that of Onias, the high-priest, slain at Antioch in the winter three years after the accession of Antiochus Epiphanes. And again, he subdivides the same space by the death of Jaddua the high-priest, who died, he says, a little after Alexander the Great, 263 years after the death of Seraiah. But 263 Hebrew years, reckoned from the autumn of B.C. 587, or 263 Nabonassarian or Egyptian years, reckoned from the spring of B.C. 586, end in the autumn of B.C. 324, where the death of Alexander is technically put: and thence 151 more take us on to the winter of B.C. 173, which certainly seems too early; and it may be that Josephus reckoned as if Seraiah were put to death after the 19th of Nebuchadnezzar, in B.C. 586, and Onias in the winter of B.C. 172, which seems the more probable date. Again, "from the deliverance from Babylon," for which we must correct from Eusebius, "the carrying away into captivity to Babylon," to the assumption of royalty by the high-priest Alexander Josephus reckons 481, or rather (as we again correct from the Armenian version of Eusebius' Chronicon) 484 years. But from B.C. 587 484 take us to B.C. 103; whence he reckons to Pompey 1 + 27 + 9 + 3 and 3 months, in all 40 years and 3 months; which being counted from B.C. 103, give us rightly the year B.C. 63, and the beginning of the fourth month. Thence he makes 27 current years to the capture of Jerusalem by Herod and Sosius, which so was in the winter of B.C. 37, three years after Herod had been made king by the Romans, and in the 27th current year after Pompey. And again, he makes 24 current years of Hyrcanus + 3 years and 3 months of Antigonus, to the death of this latter, who was slain by Antony sometime after the capture of Jerusalem, i.e. in the summer of B.C. 36, before his Parthian expedition. Again, Josephus gives 126 years to the dynasty of the Asmoneans, which being reckoned back from the death of Antigonus in B.C. 36, take us for the commencement of the dynasty to B.C. 162, when the convention made with Judas Maccabeus by Antiochus Eupator and Lysias was ratified by the concurrence of the Roman commissioners then in Syria.

The result of the whole, to recapitulate, is a sum of 2256 years *full* to the end of the year including the Flood, reckoned from September to September, or 2257 years *current* to the birth of Arphaxad: and from a little before the birth of Arphaxad, reckoning now from the spring instead of the autumn, from Nisan to Nisan, 940 years to the birth of Abram, + 550 to the division of lands, + 30 of the survival of Joshua and the Elders, + 450 of Judges and servitudes, or other intervals, to Samuel the prophet, + 32 of Samuel alone, + 20 of Saul with Samuel, + 490 to the end of the 11th of Zedekiah, in the spring of B.C. 587, a little before the burning of the Temple, + 52 to Nisan 1 in B.C. 535, or 70 to Nisan 1 in B.C. 517, between 2 and 3 months after the end of the 4th of Darius Hystaspes: for his 4th (Nabonassarian) year ended Dec. 31, B.C. 518. Thence in Nabonassarian or Egyptian years, from Dec. 31, B.C. 518, the remainder of the Persians, being 188 years, + 300 of Macedonians, + 29 of Augustus, in all 517, to Aug. 24, B.C. 1; but from Nisan 1 in B.C. 517, where our Hebrew reckoning ended, only 516 years, 5 months, and some days to the same date, Aug. 24, B.C. 1, or 517 years to Nisan 1, A.D. 1, of the vulgar era.

The sum total is 5355 Hebrew or solar years, beginning from September B.C. 5356, and ending in Sept. B.C. 1; or 5356 years from Sept. B.C. 5356 to Sept. A.D. 1 of the vulgar era. But these 5355 Hebrew or Julian years being equal in terms of the vague Egyptian year to 5358 years and 243¾ days, i.e. about 8 Egyptian months, ending perhaps 10 or 11 days later than Aug 24 (the end of the vague Egyptian year in B.C. 1), we have this sum of our sacred chronology, collected from the Scriptures and Josephus, to compare with that native Egyptian reckoning of 5364 vague years ending Aug. 24, B.C. 1, which we obtained both from the Chronicle, and also from the sum 48,863 given by Diogenes Laertius.

But if we deduct 5358 Egyptian years and 243 days, or nearly 8 months, from 5364, we have for the remainder five years, four months, and some days; which is, in fact, the same thing as to find that the two reckonings absolutely coincide, except that the Egyptian agrees with the Alexandrine LXX. in having six years (before the Flood) more than the Hebrew text and Josephus (2262 instead of 2256), though this excess of six years is reduced to five years and about four months by the Egyptians putting down their *natale mundi* from the Hebrew epoch in September B.C. 5362, to the next following commencement of their own movable year. For Thoth, the first day of the vague year, being in B.C. 5362 and 5361 not in autumn, but at April 26, it was clearly necessary for the Egyptians either to cut off eight months (supposing them to have had originally the same reckoning with the Hebrews), or to add and antedate by four months, if they chose to make the world to begin from the first day of their own year: and this we may be sure they would choose to do, even apart from any scheme which should superadd the idea that all time, both cosmical and human, had run from the beginning in the mould of the Sothic Cycle; in which case, of course, a commencement from any other point than that of the new year could have no place.

Some approximation we might have expected, knowing, as we do, that the traditionary dates of the Babylonians also, and of the Chinese, for the Flood, agree very nearly with that of the Greek Scriptures; but this appearance of exact agreement with one of the most important varieties of the sacred text, connected, too, with Egypt as having been preserved or originated there by the LXX. and followed by the earliest Christian chronologers, as Africanus, and Hippolytus, is so very singular a result, that at first it excites wonder and suspicion rather than satisfaction; and when these subside, they are followed by curiosity as to the way in which such an agreement may have come to exist. Had then the Egyptians preserved, independently, a reckoning of time, both before and after the Flood, identical with that of the Hebrews? or had they learned anything from the patriarchs Abraham or Joseph? Were the early genealogies given by Moses equally known to the Egyptians when he wrote? or did the priests of Egypt at some later time borrow from the Hebrews, or from the sacred books of the Hebrews? And again, as respects the difference between the decads and units of the Hebrew text and the Greek, the '56 or the '62 in the sum of the years before the Flood:—Did a traditional reckoning preserved in Egypt influence the Hebrew translators? or did they find in books brought from Jerusalem, and follow in their translation, some older reading than that of the present Hebrew and Samaritan texts, agreeing exactly with Egyptian tradition? and, if so, whence is the present reading of the Hebrew and

Samaritan texts? May it be from a Babylonian source, seeing that the reckoning of Berosus to the Flood very nearly agrees with the Hebrew, much as the Egyptian reckoning agrees with the Greek text? These are questions naturally suggested by the result arrived at, but beyond our power to answer. Only, it may be remarked, that the 130 years of the second Cainan, which are found in the LXX. and not in the Hebrew or Samaritan texts, and which any one might suspect to have been added in Egypt, are now seen to have had no native Egyptian source. Also, we may add, that while the Chronicle itself, and still more, any statements traceable to the time of Aristotle and Alexander, are older than the Jewish settlements in Egypt, and the translation of their Scriptures into Greek, the existence of other schemes similar to that of the Chronicle, and containing the same chronological elements, can be traced, as we shall see, to a point of time 1000 years earlier than its epoch. And this being so, it seems probable that the same were already familiar to the priests in the time of Moses, whether derived in part from Hebrew, or only from native sources.

We may now return to that question of the nature and origin of the period of XXV cycles, as exhibiting the *ἀποκατάστασις*, which we passed over above as unnecessary and premature. With the help of the ascertained elements of this period in the Chronicle, and of certain hints from other sources, we may have a better chance of success.

We know that under the Ptolemies and the Romans, the idea existed that the vast periods of the Egyptians, of the Chronicle and of Manetho in particular, had been swelled to their apparent bulk by counting, for the earlier spaces of time, *months*, under the name of years. We are told by Diodorus Siculus (B.C. 60) of some of his own contemporaries, men of learning and sagacity, and by Eusebius, in the fourth century after Christ, of certain Christian writers, who had attempted to reduce those vast periods as if from months to years. Later still, in the fifth century, the Egyptian monks Anianus and Panodorus, according to Syncellus, blamed Eusebius for having slighted such attempts, and put forth a scheme of their own based on the same principle of reduction. But from Herodotus, and Plato, and Aristotle, and also from the remains of the Turin Papyrus, of the 13th or 14th century before Christ, we know that vast periods, very similar to those of Manetho and the Chronicle, had, for ages before Herodotus, been reckoned by the Egyptians to their earlier dynasties of gods and demigods, before coming to ordinary kings. And as Africanus ascribes to the Phœnicians also a period of above 30,000 years, probably the same with that of the Chronicle, and so, by its nature, connected with the Sothic cycle, and with Egypt, we may infer that they borrowed this, together with most of their cosmogony and theogony from the Hermetic books, which their oldest writers on the subject followed. So, then, this definition of the period of the ἀποκατάστασις is nothing devised by the author of the Chronicle for his own purpose; but it had preexisted long before, either as a derivative form, or perhaps as itself the original form of the vast periods of the Egyptians; and it became in time the basis of the Chronicle, and through it of other later varieties. Herodotus and Plato, or Eudoxus, no less than other later writers, had heard that the earliest Egyptian "years" were *months* of 30 days: "Εἰ δὲ καὶ ὅ φησιν Εὔδοξος ἀληθὲς, ὅτι Αἰγύπτιοι τὸν μῆνα ἐνιαυτὸν ἐκάλουν, οὐκ ἂν ἡ τῶν πολλῶν τούτων ἐνιαυτῶν ἀπαρίθμησις ἔχοι τι θαυμαστόν." (*Proclus in Timæum, p.* 31. l. 50.) Diodorus Siculus adds more particularly that, according to some, the long reigns of the earlier *Gods*, who had above 1200 years each, were composed of *months* of 30 days, not real years; and those of the later Gods, who had over 300 years each, were composed of *seasons* of four months each (and 300 seasons alone would give them equally with the earlier 100 real years each), the native Egyptian year being divided into three seasons (τριμερέσιν ὥραις) of spring, summer, and winter (ἐαρινῇ, καὶ θερινῇ, καὶ χειμερινῇ), not four, like the Greek. Later writers, after the introduction of the Julian year, as Eusebius, and Anianus, and Panodorus, not attending to this peculiarity, tell us that the *oldest* times, of the gods, were reckoned by the Egyptians in months of 30 days, and those of the demigods, who came after them, in seasons of "*three* months" each.

But for us it is enough to be informed that the years given to the gods, whether earlier or later, were confessed by some of the Egyptians, in the time of Plato and Diodorus, to be properly Egyptian months of 30 days (carrying with them, if obtained by division of Egyptian years, their fraction of the five ἐπαγόμεναι). But as for the demigods, it is evident that, *in the Chronicle at least*, their years are neither months nor seasons capable of reduction, so that what was told to Diodorus about season-years does not apply to them: for 217 years divided between VIII demigods gives to each an average reign of only 27 years and a little over, which are manifestly true years. And for reduction we can have to do, in the Chronicle, only with those 30,000 + 681 + 2922 years, making XXIII cycles, which, in it, belong properly to Ra and to the XIII gods.

Now if we suppose an Egyptian priest, at some date near the cyclical epoch of July 20, B. C. 1322, to have occupied himself with reducing his tradition of all past time to terms of the Sothic Cycle, he would first go back as many vague years of 365 days each as had been reckoned since the addition of the *epagomenæ* (contemporary perhaps with the calculation of the Sothic Cycle itself). Then he would have to reduce to similar years as many earlier years as had had only 360 days each. Then again, if there had ever been a still earlier reckoning of months only, of alternately 30 and 29 days, he would have to distribute these into years of 365 days each. And lastly, no doubt, he would have to cut off or add, at top, some fractional number of months or days, to make the whole series begin from the first day of Thoth, the first month of the movable year. And supposing him thus to have obtained those 3042 (2922 + 217 + 903) vague years which we have found in the Chronicle, ending July 20, B.C. 1322; and further to have added the fractional number of 341 years, to make all time begin from a Sothic epoch, so as with this addition to have three complete cycles, ending July 20, in the Julian year B.C. 1322, and beginning July 20, B.C. 5702 (for 903 + 217 [+ 341,] + 2581 + 341, making 4383 vague, are less by 3, that is, are only 4380, in Julian years); and yet again, supposing him to have assigned to the old world two out of his three cycles, reckoning to the antediluvians, under whatever designations, 158 years more than their actual survival of the Flood, he would have in these two cycles by themselves a distinct and perfect ἀποκατάστασις, much more real than any which the arrival of the cyclical epoch might prompt him to feign 1120 or (by the help of his addition of 341) 1461 years later. The fact that the first elementary reckoning of time, after that by *days*, is by *months*, or lunations, joined with a tradition of the longevity of the Patriarchs, and an idea of what was becoming for a succession of deities as compared with ordinary men, and for a real and physical as compared with a merely imaginary ἀποκατάστασις, might suggest the idea of multiplying the years of the Gods by twelve. And this being done for their two *whole* cycles only, no inconvenience nor confusion would follow, such as would have followed if any *part* of a cycle had been reckoned in months and the rest of it in real years; but it would be for those that understood merely a varied form for expressing the true reckoning; it being all one, both for the whole number and for every subdivision of it, to give uniformly the true figures, or to multiply them uniformly by twelve; to name two cycles, or spaces equal to cycles, of Egyptian solar years, or twenty-four cycles of Egyptian month-years. And the number 35,064 (XXIV cycles) of such years, together with 341 fictitious, and the fractional number of 217 real years, being given to the gods and demigods, these all, with 903 of the monarchy since Menes, would make for the uninitiated a sum total of XXV cycles, or 36,525 years, ending July 20, B.C. 1322; but for the initiated, who knew that they were to divide the XXIV cycles by 12, and eject the 341 years interpolated, the true chronological sum understood would be (2922 + 1120 =) 4042 years.

It is probable, then, that the definition of the ἀποκατάστασις by the number of XXV nominal cycles originated merely in the fact that, when the cyclical epoch of B.C. 1322 first suggested the fancy, actual reckoning went back only two real cycles and 1120 years (besides a fraction of months to be cut off), and when this space was filled up to three cycles, the first two cycles admitted well, the third, on the contrary, did not admit, the process of equable multiplication. So XXV cycles of nominal, or III of full years, was then the natural definition of an ἀποκατάστασις; and very probably the great sums still discernible in the Turin MS. (two of which make together about 36,620 years, or about 100 more than the sum of the ἀποκατάστασις, and reach, perhaps, if they admit of being so added together, to the epoch of the MS.), may be connected with this earliest form of the scheme, which above 1000 years later was taken as his basis by the author of the Chronicle.

Twenty-five cycles, or 36,525 years, being the period of the compound and partial ἀποκατάστασις feigned at the true cyclical epoch of B.C. 1322, this same definition would be likely to remain in possession, both by prescription, and also perhaps because it seemed equivalent to a multiplication of the lunisolar Apis Cycle of 21 years into the Sothic Cycle of 1461. Else, if it had been the second instead of the first Sothic epoch since the old world, when the idea first occurred, the period of the feigned ἀποκατάστασις would have been fixed at XXVI, or, without any multiplication into months, at IV Sothic cycles, and 37,986 instead of 36,525 nominal years. But XXV cycles being the number in B.C. 1322, if it were desired at the next cyclical epoch, i. e., in A.D. 139, when time had moved on one complete cycle, to renew the same fiction of an ἀποκατάστασις without changing its definition from XXV to XXVI cycles, it would be necessary to strike out one whole cycle of the month-years of the gods above, to make room for the new cycle of real years to be taken in below. And this change would destroy the nature and symmetry of the scheme. For the years of the gods or antediluvians appearing then as XXIII nominal cycles instead of XXIV, neither the whole sum of their true years, 2922, nor any of its chronological subdivisions, would be any longer obtainable from it by dividing by 12, but only by dividing by 11½ths, a fraction which has no relation to months or to any other component parts of the year. And the same would be the case if, instead of the next true cyclical epoch, some other date short of it, as B.C. 345 or 305, were taken for the end of an ἀποκατάστασις in the same number of XXV cycles.

The symmetry of the original scheme would equally be destroyed, and the month-years would equally lose their character, by the suppression of 978 or 1018 of their number, to make room for the years which had grown between B.C. 1322 and Nectanebo or the Lagidæ. And this being so, it would be all one whether the complement of 483 or 443 years more were left to stand as before as years of the gods, or were separated as years of the last cycle of the whole series, really future, but thrown up, as in the Chronicle, to make the ἀποκατάστασις end 483 or 443 years short of the true expiration of the Cycle.

We can understand now why the author of the Chronicle not only suppressed one cycle out of the original XXIV of month-years, but separated also from the remaining XXIII cycles 2922 years as the sum out of which they had sprung, and gave this sum only to his XIII gods representing the antediluvians (for we need not notice fractional numbers seemingly added to them, but really separate), while the XXI cycles still remaining out of the XXIV originated by multiplication, having lost not only the character of month-years, but all relation to the 2922 now become again full years, are given in truth, all of them (though ostensibly only the round number of 30,000 is given) to the sun as years merely nominal, fictitious, or, if any one please, cosmical, answering no other purpose than that of telling towards the traditional sum of ἀποκατάστασις which it is desired to exhibit.

Besides the succession of real years in three distinct sums, of 2922 for the old world, 217 for the interval between it and Menes, and 1881 years of the monarchy from Menes to Nectanebo, we have also to consider in the Chronicle its assignment of these three spaces of time to three distinct classes (ἔθνη) of rulers (besides the Sun-God), viz. Gods, Demigods, and ordinary mortal Kings, perhaps connected with three peoples of Ἀερῖται (antediluvian Egyptians), Μεστραῖοι (i. e. descendants of Misor, who is named by Sanchoniathon), and Αἰγύπτιοι (i. e. the Egyptians of the times of the monarchy). These three classes are subdivided further into XXX Dynasties and CXIII generations.

Before considering this triple arrangement of designations,

dynasties, and generations in detail, it is to be remarked of the god Phtha, Ἥφαιστος, to whom later schemes give a reign with a certain number of years, making him either the first dynasty, or the head of the first dynasty, and the first generation, that in the Chronicle, on the contrary, his name is set at the head of all only to be connected with the notice that, as he *has no relation to time*, he has *no reign* measurable by days and years, nor constitutes any one of the XXX Dynasties, or of the CXIII generations. From him are all generations, and in his timeless reign all temporal dynasties and reigns are comprehended. But the first principle with the Egyptians being not a pure spirit, creating matter from nothing, but, to speak plainly, a confused compound of rarefied matter and spirit, or intellectual fire, it was open to them to make their theogony and cosmogony begin from either the one side or the other of this compound. The author of the Chronicle inclines to the less materialistic method, but according to other later writers, as we learn from Diodorus Siculus, Phtha himself sprang from the material watery principle Νοῦν, Νεῖλος, or Μῶτ, i.e. mud: and the followers of this school would naturally give a reign in time to their Phtha son of Nilos, no less than to other originated deities his successors.

Besides Phtha there is another deity not of human origin, Cneph or Agathodæmon, who in the lists of Manetho and his re-editors stands third among the gods, with a reign assigned him in years; but in the Chronicle he is unnamed, not because his existence was unrecognised, but because he also, like Phtha from whom he is derived, had no distinct relation to *time* as measurable in days and nights. Time, according to the Chronicle, is measured by the sun; and originally by the sun alone, but secondarily also by man, both such as he is now upon the earth, and earlier by demigods and gods, of whom the first is therefore perhaps named in Greek Κρόνος, or Χρόνος. So the earliest of the CXIII generations, which all have relation to time, and the first reign and dynasty of the XXX Dynasties in time, is given by the Chronicle to Ra the Sun-God: and after him we proceed at once to Cronus and XII of his descendants and successors, who are XIII more generations; and each one of them is in himself a dynasty; so that thus far generation, reign, and dynasty are all one: and it is to these XIII Gods of the family of Cronus that the first 2922 years of real human time, according to Egyptian reckoning, have been ascertained above to belong.

Now apart from any hint contained in the name Mestræans, if that be admitted to be from the author of the Chronicle himself, as it may well be, and not merely a gloss of Africanus or Eusebius, the historical position of the three spaces of time, the 2922, the 217, and the 1881 years contained in the Chronicle, having been ascertained, it follows that the dynasties and rulers named by it *must* virtually correspond to the rulers of mankind and of Egypt during the times to which they severally belong. This would be so, even if all the three spaces were covered alike by generations or reigns of ordinary length (as the first 903 years after the Flood in Berosus seem to have 84 apocryphal kings with average reigns of only 10 years). But when we find the rulers of the first two periods in the Chronicle, its XIII Gods and VIII Demigods, answering closely to the true generations of the antediluvian and postdiluvian patriarchs in number, and therefore also in the average length of the reigns and generations; and when we know besides, as we do, that the Pantheon of the Egyptians and of other nations, which they said had all borrowed from them, was peopled, in part at least, with deified ancestors;—for even the heavenly luminaries, and the elements and powers of nature, and notions of the true God still remaining, or of angels and demons, so far as they were invested with humanity and sex, were identified with human ancestors; — we cannot doubt that Κρόνος or Χρόνος is the first man who reckoned time upon the earth, when the sun ceased to reign alone, and that the XII Gods his descendants are meant to answer to the XII patriarchs of the antediluvians, the three sons of Noah being included as three successive generations, so as to suit the consecutive nature of the Chronicle, and so as to give a true average length to these generations of 174 years, instead of 205, which would be their average length if only eleven generations were to be reckoned in all, and one of the eleven, like that of Noah in the Mosaic history, had the anomalous length of 500 years.

When we say an average length of 174 years, this is only for such as knew the true date of the Flood, the end of the old world, an epoch by no means to be named nor even directly alluded to by any Egyptian. Else, the old world being carried down to within 217 years of Menes, and not only 500 years of the survival of the patriarchs, but even 158 years beyond, being added to their reigns, so as to give it a cyclical termination, the XIII generations and dynasties would seem to have an average of nearly 225 years each; and the single Dynasty XV of the VIII generations of Demigods following with its 217 years would be in keeping with the lengths of the XIII dynasties preceding, though they each contain only a single dynast with an average length of between 224 and 225 years for his joint generation, reign, and dynasty. And thus the VIII Demigods, if divided into consecutive generations and reigns within their apparent limits of 217 years, would have an average of only $27\frac{1}{8}$ years for each reign and generation, being less than that of the XV merely human generations or lives "of the Cycle," which follow with an average of $29\frac{2}{15}$ years to each. But for the initiated, who knew the true epoch of the Flood, and that the generations of the VIII postdiluvian "Mestræans" really commenced from thence, or within a little after, and continued concurrently with those of the antediluvians during 658 years reckoned for cyclical purposes to the old world, the true length of these generations would be given not by 217, but by (658 + 217 =) 875, divided by VIII; and thus it would be not $27\frac{1}{8}$ but $109\frac{3}{8}$ years, analogous to the average length of $117\frac{1}{2}$ years shown by the first VIII generations of the line of Arphaxad, which have 940 years to the birth of Abram, 65 years below Menes. But that there were some among the Egyptians who understood this, without borrowing from the Hebrew Scriptures, appears from the fact that the epoch of the Flood is alluded to as known, or indirectly indicated, in some of their schemes, as we shall show: and the exact chronological reckoning underlying those schemes in which it is not alluded to, as this scheme of the Chronicle, is a sufficient sign that it *must* have been known, so that the suppression itself is significant.

That the epoch of the Flood was alluded to as known in that earliest scheme of the *ἀποκατάστασις* which made XXIV cycles of 35,064 month-years, and one more of full years ending at B.C. 1322, may be inferred from a fragment of the Turin Papyrus, in which the sum of 23,220 month-years is named, extending, as it seems, from the first dynasty of Ra to the elder Horus. But, according to our synchronistic scale, the end of the year of the Flood, whether alluded to or not, if reckoned as if nothing had been cut off at top, should be after 2262 Julian years, or 2263 vague years and 200½ days (supposing the *natale mundi* to have coincided with Thoth 1 of the movable year), while the end of the two cycles of the Gods, or antediluvians, is 658 vague years and 164½ days later. So it seems the epoch of the Flood divides the XXIV cycles of 35,054 month-years into two sums, one of 2263 × 12 = 27,156 + 200½ days, for which fraction of 6 months and 20½ days the Egyptians might substitute two whole seasons or 8 month-years more (making the whole sum 27,164), and the other of 658 × 12 = 7896 month-years + 4 (making the whole sum 7900). And if we now mark off 23,220 from the first of the two sums, we have the whole scheme of the *ἀποκατάστασις* to B.C. 1322 standing thus:—

23,220 + 3944 + 7900 [+ 341] + 217 + 903 = 36,525.

But the new sum of 3944, inclosed and marked by the last year of the 23,220 above, and the epoch of the Flood below, is resolvable into 681 + 2922 + 341, and is identical with the gross sum of years reckoned in the Chronicle to the XIII Gods, except that the Chronicle has 3984 instead of 3944, the difference consisting in the 40 years interval between Ochus and the Lagidæ, thrown up without being named to the times of the Gods. (And here, as we may notice in passing, we have an important confirmation of the assertion made on other grounds that the true length of this interval according to the Chronicle is 40 years, lying between B.C. 345 and 305.) And if we deduct from the 7900 month-years following 1120, i. e. enough with the 341 fictitious years following to make one whole cycle (suppressed by the author of the Chronicle to make room for the new cycle grown or growing since B.C. 1322), we have in the remainder, 6780, exactly the sum which will unite with the 23,220 above into the round number of 30,000 nominal years given in the Chronicle to the Sun. So we see the author of the Chronicle found his work already in a manner done to his hand in the older scheme, which, though it probably distributed its vast spaces of month-years in a way different from his, and one of which we find traces in Manetho, in Herodotus, and in the Turin Papyrus, still marked, for the initiated, both the number 2922, the source of all its month-years; the number 341, being that of the fictitious years needed to make all time begin from a cyclical epoch; and lastly the number 156, which probably is meant for the number of years reckoned for cyclical purposes to the old world, beyond the true survival (500, according to the Hebrews, for Shem, but 502, it should seem, according to the Egyptians, for Ham) of the antediluvians. For 525 still remaining out of the 3944 are not added for any special purpose, but merely because they are the complement needed for a fractional number 936 below the Flood. And this sum of 525 in the older scheme is analogous to the whole sum of 681 in the scheme of the Chronicle. In the Chronicle the round sum 30,000 containing, besides XXI cycles, the broken number of 780, this broken number requires for its complement another of 681, which, therefore, may be reckoned to the Gods without ceasing to be distinguishable as really part of the cycles of the Sun. And in like manner in the older scheme the 7900 month-years below the Flood, after giving first 1120 to coalesce with the 341 prefixed to the new world, but meant to be also referable at will to the beginning of the old and of all time, and then four complete cycles in 5844 month-years, have a fractional number of 936 requiring to be met by a corresponding fraction of 525 in the time before the Flood.

What the author of the Chronicle had to do, then, after suppressing one whole cycle, was little more than to eject those month-years which still stood after the epoch of the

Flood, throwing them all back to the beginning and to the reign of the Sun, and to let those month-years of the older scheme, which indicated the numbers of full years underlying its larger sums, *become* themselves the full years which before they had only indicated; as will appear from the following parallel: —

Original Scheme of B.C. 1322:—

$$\frac{21{,}915+1305}{23{,}220}+\frac{156+2922+341+525}{3944}+\frac{936+5844}{6780}+\frac{1120+[341]}{1461}+\frac{217\quad+\quad903}{1120}\text{ to B.C. 1322.}$$

The Chronicle of B.C. 305:—

$$\frac{23{,}220+[6780]}{30{,}000}+\frac{156+2922+[341]+525}{3944}+\text{[transposed]}+\text{[suppressed]}+\frac{217\quad+\quad903}{1120}+\frac{978+40+443}{1461}\text{ to A.D. 130.}$$

or

$$30{,}000\quad+681+2922+[341]+[40]+\text{[transposed]}+\text{[suppressed]}+217+[443]+420+483+978\text{ to B.C. 341.}$$

The 7900 month-years of the older scheme below the epoch of the Flood would give to VIII postdiluvian Demigods average reigns of $987\frac{1}{2}$ month-years each, besides one eighth part of 217 full years, viz., 27, making in all $1014\frac{1}{2}$ nominal years, or $(82\frac{1}{3} + 27 =)$ 109 full years. Or, if it was in the older scheme that the years of the Demigods were reckoned (partly at least) in seasons, then the VIII would have each about 247 such season-years + 27 full years from the 217, and perhaps also about 42 more from the 341, in all about 314 nominal years, agreeing with the words of Diodorus, "not less than 300": while the 27,164 month-years of the old world, reckoned only to the epoch of the Flood, might give a reign of about 11,900 at the head of all to the Sun, if there were after him only XIII Gods, like the series of the Chronicle, with average reigns of 1200 nominal years to each, like those alluded to by Diodorus. Whether he had over 11,000, or 9,000, or any other number, there is no doubt that Ra, the Sun-God, stood at the head of the series, as his name is still preserved in the fragments of the Turin Papyrus: and in the Chaldean scheme of Berosus, also, as quoted by Eusebius from Alexander Polyhistor, there is a parallel arrangement, 1058 full years being put first, before monarchy is said to have arisen; and then ten generations of rulers, with an average of about 100 full years to each reign. In Manetho the Sun seems to have had 900 real, or 10,800 month-years; and in the pseudo-Manetho of Anianus and Syncellus Phtha, or Ἥφαιστος, reigns 11,000, and Ra, Ἥλιος, 968 years. But we have no certainty as to the number of the Gods and Demigods of the older scheme.

For such as knew that the time of the old world was purposely prolonged in the Chronicle to the length of two cycles, the 217 years interval between these two cycles and Menes, though not containing really eight divine or heroic births and reigns, nor eight reigns and seven successive births, would still contain in some sense the reigns of the Patriarchs of the line of Mizraim, i. e. parts of the lives of six, or five at least, out of the eight born since the Flood. For, according to the parallel Hebrew reckoning of the line of Arphaxad, the birth of Terah, the eighth, falls just within the 217 years preceding Menes; and six out of the eight are found surviving or living during some part or other of the same period; while the first two or three (for two at least of the line of Mizraim must have died before the 217 years began) were necessarily to be numbered with the six who actually touched or occupied the period, unless they were to be omitted. And this undue compression of the postdiluvian Demigods was involved, as a consequence, in the undue expansion given to the antediluvian Gods by adding to their reigns, for a cyclical purpose, the whole 500 years of their survival, and 158 years beyond. And these 158 years, as the length of life was shortening after the Flood, make just the difference that the son and grandson of Shem or Ham die before instead of dying after their progenitor. And the reigns of the postdiluvians collectively being made to begin later by 158 years than the true date of the death of Shem or Ham, Mizraim and his son, though reckoned of course at the head of the Demigods, must be in truth already dead; dead too before their father and grandfather Ham. Such were the gods of the Egyptians; such the honours which, even in deifying them, they offered to their ancestors! whereas, according to the truth of history, the most merciful Creator, even while shortening life for sin, and hastening the penalty of death, provided that the eyes of the father should be closed by his son, and that the son should succeed, for a time at least, to the seat and honour of the father.

In the succession of Gods, Demigods, and mortals (Ἀερῖται,

Μεστραῖοι, Αἰγύπτιοι) of the Chronicle, we have the same descending scale in point of dignity and longevity (the undue compression of the demigods being understood and allowed for) as in later times, in Virgil's Eclogue, and in the Sibylline verses, is connected with the idea of the ἀποκατάστασις. The times of Κρόνος and the other XII Gods of the old world are the "Saturnia regna;" the time of the VIII Demigods suits for the silver age of heroes, such as Hercules, who were afterwards to be added to the Gods; and the kings, the successors of Menes, degenerate into ordinary men. But the distinction of four successive degrees, as of gold, silver, brass, and iron, each decreasing in worth, which from the time of Hesiod was familiar to the Greeks, and which in the book of Daniel is applied to the four great pagan empires, does not appear in the Chronicle; nor does this idea seem to have been of Egyptian origin; though it would have been easy to exhibit a fourfold division, by classing first those IX deified ancestors who belong exclusively to the old world, then the IV who are at once antediluvian and postdiluvian, and thirdly, the VIII postdiluvian ancestors born since the Flood, the fourth place belonging, as now, to all the ordinary generations after Menes. In the scheme of Manetho, indeed, a little later, we do find a fourfold division of Gods, Heroes, Manes, and mortal Kings, though there is nothing to connect them with the four metals; and in Eusebius' or Africanus' account of the re-edition of Manetho by Ptolemy of Mendes "*five peoples*" are named, seemingly of Gods, Demigods, Ἀερῖται, Μεστραῖοι, and Αἰγύπτιοι, the Gods and Demigods being no longer themselves the Ἀερῖται and Μεστραῖοι, but the Ἀερῖται being the Manes, and the Μεστραῖοι the older Egyptians, before the country was renamed, as is pretended, from the king called Rameses Ægyptus.

The number of XII Gods, deified ancestors of the old world, and descendants of Κρόνος, reminds one of the XII Gods of the Greeks and Romans, and of the earlier XII Gods of the Egyptians mentioned by Herodotus. Herodotus says that these XII were older than the Demigods, but less ancient than the VIII Gods, from whom they were derived, Pan and his consort Mout being of the VIII, and older than

Hercules, who was of the XII, by some 2000 years. Whether he means that there were two distinct classes, one older of VIII, and another less ancient of XII Gods the progeny of the VIII, or rather that an older group of VIII had been increased to the later group of XII by the addition of four names, that of Hercules being one, is not agreed. The number VIII suggests the thought of the succession of VIII generations after Κρόνος or Adam to the Flood, or of Adam and the VII descendants of Cain, who were founders of cities, giants, inventors of music, metallurgy, and other arts. The addition of four, increasing the original number of the Gods from VIII to XII, suggests the thought of Noah and his three sons, who certainly form a later group by themselves, intermediate between the old and the new worlds. Then, as has before been observed, the VIII Demigods, to say nothing of their name Mestræans, answer well to the probable number of postdiluvian ancestors of the line of Ham before Menes. So we are tempted to look for some VIII and IV, making XII greater Gods; and again for VIII Demigods, all derived from one ancestor, like a series of Gnostic Æons, in the popular and monumental pantheon of Egypt, to correspond with the generations of the Chronicle and of the Hebrew Scriptures. But nothing of this kind is to be found. An ogdoad indeed of gods *and goddesses* there is in Seb, Osiris, Typhon, and Horus, with their consorts, answering in certain respects to the ogdoad of the first family both of the old and of the renewed world. We may fancy ourselves, too, to discover the VIII greater Gods of Herodotus in Phtha, Ra, Cneph, Seb, Khem, Osiris, Typhon, and Horus; and if Hercules, Chons, was one of the XII, his father Ammon would not fail to be also of the number; so that only two may seem to be wanting; and we may form conjectures more or less probable as to these. But whatever be our luck in such conjectures, we shall be as far as ever from any such strict genealogical succession as marks the Gods and Demigods of the Chronicle. Nor, if we reflect, could it be otherwise; seeing that the Egyptian pantheon was not peopled merely by the successive deification of ancestors, but it blended other personages of kings and heroes with ancestors, condensed many distinct persons into one, again divided one person into many, and above all mixed largely with its human element another totally distinct, viz. the deification of the elements and powers of nature, which would not fall into any long series of generations.

But while the gods and demigods of the Egyptian monuments and popular mythology were of mixed, and in their human element mostly of postdiluvian and late origin, and therefore exhibited no genealogical series, it might still be possible for the author of the Chronicle to make out such a genealogical succession of gods and demigods, as he needed to cover his 2922 and 217 years, from native Egyptian sources; and it will be worth while to show this clearly; as some, not perceiving what proofs the Chronicle contains within itself of its own genuineness and antiquity, reject it at once as a forgery for no other reason than this, that they see in its XIII Gods and VIII Demigods a manifest parallel to the Patriarchs of the Hebrew Scriptures, while yet nothing of the sort appears on the surface of Egyptian mythology.

Now it may be assumed that whatever knowledge was possessed by the Babylonians respecting the early history of mankind, the same was not altogether hidden from the Egyptians. And Berosus, a contemporary both of Alexander the Great and of the author of the Chronicle, whose Χαλδαϊκὰ seem to have served as a model for the Αἰγυπτιακὰ of Manetho, enumerates ten generations of kings of antediluvian Chaldæa in 1200 vague years, which, with 1058 before monarchy is fabled to begin, make 2258 vague, or about 5 months over 2256 Julian years, agreeing almost exactly with the Greek Scriptures; except that, like Josephus and the Hebrew text, Berosus has '56, not '62, for the decads and units of the sum of years to the Flood; and that he *adds* the fraction of 4 or 5 months (instead of cutting off like the Egyptians 7 or 8 months) to make time begin with the beginning of the vague Nabonassarian year. And though the fancy of making the ten kings to begin only after 1058 years, and to be not all named from the same city, seems to distinguish them from Adam and the IX Patriarchs his descendants, still, Xisuthrus, the tenth, being clearly identified with Noah by the Flood and the ark, the very number ten, and the relation of succession in which they stand one to the other, show that Alorus, the first of them, is no other than Adam; while the deity who warns Xisuthrus, and bids him prepare the ark, being named *Κρόνος*, whom the Egyptians and Phœnicians name as the first deified ancestor, and Xisuthrus himself, on quitting the ark, being immediately deified, with his wife and daughter and pilot, a similar deification seems implied for all the intermediate kings or patriarchs. The list of Berosus, as given in passages quoted from Apollodorus and Alexander Polyhistor, is as follows:—

| | | |
|---|---|---|
| "Ἔτη ἀβασίλευτα, σάροι ρε', νῆροι δ', καὶ σῶσσοι η' . . . . | (vague years) = | 1058 |
| (a Sarus being 3600 day-years, a Neros 600, and a Sossus 60.) | | |
| α'. Μετὰ ταῦτα πρῶτος ἐγένετο βασιλεὺς Ἄλωρος ἐκ Βαβυλῶνος Χαλδαῖος, καὶ ἐβασίλευσε . . . . | . σάρους ι' = | 100 |
| β'. Ἀλάπαρος . | σάρους γ' [the sum requires ιγ'] = | 30 |
| γ'. Ἀλμηλὼν ὁ ἐκ Παντιβίβλων . | . σάρους ιγ' = | 130 |
| δ'. Ἀμμενὼν ὁ Χαλδαῖος . . | . σάρους ιβ' = | 120 |
| ε'. Μεγάλορος ἐκ Παντιβίβλων [al. Ἰδοτιών.] . | . σάρους ιη' = | 180 |
| ς'. Δαὼν ποιμὴν ἐκ Παντιβίβλων . | . σάρους ι' = | 100 |
| ζ'. Εὐηδορὰχ ἐκ Παντιβίβλων . | . σάρους ιη' = | 180 |
| η'. Ἀμέμψινος, Χαλδαῖος . . | . σάρους ι' = | 100 |
| θ'. Ὠτιάρτης, Χαλδαῖος . . | . σάρους π' = | 80 |
| ι'. Ξίσουθρος . . . . | . σάρους ιη' = | 180 |
| | | 2258 |

"[Τῷ δὲ Ξισούθρῳ] Κρόνος προσημαίνει μὲν ἔσεσθαι πλῆθος ὄμβρων Δαισίου πέμπτῃ ἐπὶ δέκα· κελεύει δὲ πᾶν ὅ τι γραμμάτων ἦν ἐχόμενον ἐν Ἡλίου πόλει τῇ ἐν Σιππάροισιν ἀποκρύψαι," κ.τ.λ. (So it is in Abydenus; but in Alex. Polyhistor thus:) "Ἐπὶ τούτου Ξισούθρου μέγαν κατακλυσμὸν γενέσθαι· ἀναγράφεσθαι δὲ τὸν λόγον οὕτως· τὸν Κρόνον αὐτῷ κατὰ τὸν ὕπνον ἐπιστάντα φάναι μηνὸς Δαισίου τῇ ιε' τοὺς ἀνθρώπους ὑπὸ κατακλυσμοῦ φθαρήσεσθαι· κελεύ-

*σαι οὖν διὰ γραμμάτων πάντων ἀρχὰς καὶ μέσα καὶ τελετὰς ὀρύξαντα θεῖναι ἐν πόλει Ἡλίου Σιππάροις, καὶ ναυπηγησάμενον σκάφος ἐμβῆναι μετὰ τῶν συγγενῶν καὶ ἀναγκαίων φίλων, ἐνθέσθαι δὲ βρώματα καὶ πόματα· ἐμβαλεῖν δὲ καὶ ζῶα πτηνὰ καὶ τετράποδα"* . . . (And then, after a story of his twice sending out "some birds," and a third time, when they returned no more, he continues:) *τὸν δὲ Ξίσουθρον ἐννοηθῆναι γῆν ἀναπεφηνέναι· διελόντα δὲ τῶν τοῦ πλοίου ῥαφῶν μέρος τι, καὶ ἰδόντα προσοκείλαν τὸ πλοῖον ὄρει τινὶ, ἐκβῆναι μετὰ τῆς γυναικὸς καὶ τῆς θυγατρὸς καὶ τοῦ κυβερνήτου· προσκυνήσαντα δὲ τὴν γῆν, καὶ βωμὸν ἱδρυσάμενον, καὶ θυσιάσαντα τοῖς θεοῖς, γενέσθαι μετὰ τῶν ἐκβάντων τοῦ πλοίου ἀφανῆ· τοὺς δὲ ὑπομείναντας ἐν τῷ πλοίῳ, μὴ εἰσπορευομένων τῶν περὶ τὸν Ξίσουθρον, ἐκβάντας ζητεῖν αὐτὸν ἐπὶ ὀνόματος βοῶντας· τὸν δὲ Ξίσουθρον αὐτὸν μὲν οὐκέτι ὀφθῆναι· φωνὴν δὲ ἐκ τοῦ ἀέρος γενέσθαι κελεύουσαν ὡς δέον αὐτοὺς εἶναι θεοσεβεῖς, καὶ παρ' αὐτῶν [αὐτὸν] διὰ τὴν εὐσέβειαν πορεύεσθαι μετὰ τῶν θεῶν οἰκήσοντα· τῆς δὲ αὐτῆς τιμῆς καὶ τὴν γυναῖκα αὐτοῦ, καὶ τὴν θυγατέρα, καὶ τὸν κυβερνήτην μετεσχηκέναι· εἰπεῖν τε αὐτοῖς· ὅτι ἐλεύσονται πάλιν εἰς Βαβυλῶνα, καὶ ὡς εἵμαρται αὐτοῖς ἐκ Σιππάρων ἀνελομένοις τὰ γράμματα διαδοῦναι τοῖς ἀνθρώποις· κ. τ. λ. Ἐλθόντας οὖν τούτους εἰς Βαβυλῶνα τά τε ἐκ Σιππάρων γράμματα ἀνορύξαι, καὶ πόλεις πολλὰς κτίζοντας, καὶ ἱερὰ ἀνιδρυσαμένους, πάλιν ἐπικτίσαι τὴν Βαβυλῶνα."*—*Euseb. Pamph. Chron.* 5. 8.

If it be said that, as regards Berosus and the Babylonians, the dispersion of the Hebrews since Shalmaneser or Esarhaddon, and Nebuchadnezzar, the long government of Daniel the "Master of the Magi," and the proclamations of Nebuchadnezzar, Darius, Cyrus, and Artaxerxes, acknowledging the true God of the Hebrews, might well have left traces, so that Hebrew truths should have mixed with Chaldean tradition, we need not deny that this is so; especially when we find in Berosus not only the distinct mention of the Flood, but even minute details, little varied from the sacred narrative. Still, even thus, whatever was well known to Berosus, might, in the age of the Lagidæ, be known also in Egypt to the author of the Chronicle.

But though Berosus gives us a fair parallel with which to

illustrate the Divine Generations of the Chronicle, at least for the time before the Flood, we have a far older and more important illustration in passages of Sanchoniathon, preserved by Porphyry and Eusebius. The works of this Phœnician writer were translated in the time of Nero by Philo Byblius, himself a Phœnician Greek, for the express purpose of showing that, according to the oldest Phœnician and Egyptian testimony, the gods were almost all dead men, Philo being one of the followers of Diagoras Melius, who for this opinion were called Atheists. Sanchoniathon is named by Athenæus with Mochus, as one of the very oldest writers of Phœnician history; and Porphyry (ap. Euseb. Præp. Ev. i. 9, 10,) gives an account of him as follows:—

"'Ιστορεῖ δὲ τὰ περὶ 'Ιουδαίων ἀληθέστατα ὅτι, καὶ τοῖς τόποις καὶ τοῖς ὀνόμασιν αὐτῶν συμφωνότατα, Σαγχωνιάθων ὁ Βηρύτιος, παρὰ 'Ιερομβάλου τοῦ ἱερέως θεοῦ 'Ιευὼ, ὅς" (that is, Hierubbaal, not Sanchoniathon, who was later), "'Αβελβαλῷ τῷ βασιλεῖ Βηρυτίων τὴν ἱστορίαν ἀναθεὶς, ὑπ' ἐκείνου καὶ τῶν κατ' αὐτὸν ἐξεταστῶν τῆς ἀληθείας παρεδέχθη· οἱ δὲ τούτων" (that is, of Jerubbaal, Abelbaal, and their contemporaries) "χρόνοι καὶ πρὸ τῶν Τρωϊκῶν πίπτουσι χρόνων, καὶ σχεδὸν τοῖς Μωσέως πλησιάζουσιν, ὡς αἱ τῶν Φοινίκης βασιλέων διαδοχαὶ μηνύουσι. Σαγχωνιάθων δὲ (ὁ κατὰ τὴν τῶν Φοινίκων διάλεκτον Φιλαλήθης), πᾶσαν τὴν παλαιὰν ἱστορίαν ἐκ τῶν κατὰ πόλιν ὑπομνημάτων καὶ τῶν ἐν τοῖς ἱεροῖς ἀναγραφῶν συναγαγὼν, καὶ συγγράψας, ἐπὶ Σεμιράμεως γέγονε τῆς 'Ασσυρίων βασιλίδος, ἣ πρὸ τῶν 'Ιλιακῶν ἢ κατ' αὐτούς γε τοὺς χρόνους γενέσθαι ἀναγέγραπται. Τὰ δὲ τοῦ Σαγχωνιάθωνος εἰς 'Ελλάδα γλῶσσαν ἑρμήνευσε Φίλων ὁ Βύβλιος. Μέχρι τοῦδε Πορφύριος." (Euseb. Præp. Evang. i. and x.) And then Eusebius continues of Philo the translator: "'Ο δὲ Φίλων εἰς θ' βίβλους τὴν πᾶσαν τοῦ Σαγχωνιάθωνος πραγματείαν διελὼν, κατὰ τὸ προοίμιον τοῦ α' συγγράμματος αὐτοῖς ῥήμασι προλέγει περὶ τοῦ Σαγχωνιάθωνος ταῦτα· Τούτων οὕτως ἐχόντων, ὁ Σαγχωνιάθων ἀνὴρ πολυμαθὴς καὶ πολυπράγμων γενόμενος, καὶ τὰ ἐξ ἀρχῆς, ἀφ' οὗ τὰ πάντα συνέστη, παρὰ πάντων εἰδέναι ποθῶν, πολὺ φροντιστικῶς ἐξεμάστευσε τὰ Τααύτου, εἰδὼς ὅτι τῶν ὑφ' ἥλιον γεγονότων πρῶτός ἐστι Τάαυτος ὁ τῶν γραμμάτων τὴν εὕρεσιν ἐπινοήσας, καὶ τῆς τῶν ὑπομνημάτων γραφῆς *κατάρξας, καὶ ἀπὸ τοῦδε ὥσπερ κρηπῖδα βαλόμενος τοῦ λόγου, ὃν Αἰγύπτιοι μὲν ἐκάλεσαν Θωὺθ, Ἀλεξανδρεῖς δὲ Θὼθ, Ἑρμῆν δὲ Ἕλληνες μετέφρασαν."* Then Philo says that later writers and hierophants after Thoth had darkened everything with multiplied allegories and fables: "*Ἀλλ' οἱ μὲν νεώτατοι τῶν ἱερολόγων τὰ μὲν γεγονότα πράγματα ἐξ ἀρχῆς ἀπεπέμψαντο, ἀλληγορίας δὲ καὶ μύθους ἐπινοήσαντες, καὶ τοῖς κοσμικοῖς παθήμασι συγγένειαν πλασάμενοι, μυστήρια κατέστησαν, καὶ πολὺν αὐτοῖς ἐπῆγον τῦφον, ὡς μὴ ῥᾳδίως τινὰ συνορᾷν τὰ κατ' ἀλήθειαν γενόμενα. Ὁ δὲ, συμβαλὼν τοῖς ἀπὸ τῶν ἀδύτων εὑρεθεῖσιν ἀποκρύφοις Ἀμμουνέων*" (seemingly the Phœnician word of which *ἀδύτων* is the rendering), "*γράμμασι συγκειμένοις, ἃ δὴ οὐκ ἦν πᾶσι γνώριμα, τὴν μάθησιν ἁπάντων αὐτὸς ἤσκησε, καὶ τέλος ἐπιθεὶς τῇ πραγματείᾳ, τὸν κατ' ἀρχὰς μῦθον καὶ τὰς ἀλληγορίας ἐκποδὼν ποιησάμενος, ἐξηνύσατο τὴν πρόθεσιν, ἕως πάλιν οἱ ἐπιγενόμενοι ἱερεῖς χρόνοις ὕστερον ἠθέλησαν αὐτὴν ἀποκρύψαι, καὶ εἰς τὸ μυθῶδες ἀποκαταστῆσαι· ἐξ οὗ τὸ μυστικὸν ἀνέκυπτεν οὐδέπω φθάσαν εἰς Ἕλληνας.*" . . .

"*Προδιαρθρῶσαι δὲ ἀναγκαῖον, πρὸς τὴν αὖθις σαφήνειαν καὶ τὴν τῶν κατὰ μέρος διάγνωσιν, ὅτι οἱ παλαιότατοι τῶν βαρβάρων, ἐξαιρέτως δὲ Φοίνικές τε καὶ Αἰγύπτιοι παρ' ὧν καὶ οἱ λοιποὶ παρέλαβον ἄνθρωποι, θεοὺς ἐνόμιζον μεγίστους τοὺς τὰ πρὸς τὴν βιωτικὴν χρείαν εὑρόντας, ἢ καὶ κατά τι εὐποιήσαντας τὰ ἔθνη· .... Ἐξαιρέτως δὲ καὶ ἀπὸ τῶν σφετέρων βασιλέων τοῖς κοσμικοῖς στοιχείοις καί τισι τῶν νομιζομένων θεῶν τὰς ὀνομασίας ἐπέθεσαν. Φυσικοὺς δὲ ἥλιον καὶ σελήνην καὶ τοὺς λοιποὺς πλανήτας ἀστέρας, καὶ τὰ στοιχεῖα, καὶ τὰ τούτοις συναφῆ, θεοὺς μόνους ἐγίνωσκον, ὡς αὐτοὺς τοὺς μὲν θνητοὺς τοὺς δὲ ἀθανάτους θεοὺς εἶναι.*"

Suidas, following Philo and Porphyry, says of Sanchoniathon, that he wrote "*κατὰ τὰ Τρωϊκά,*" about the time of the war of Troy; and gives as his writings an Account of the Physics of Thoth translated into his own Phœnician tongue, an Egyptian Theogony, and some other pieces: "*Περὶ τῆς Ἑρμοῦ Φυσιολογίας, ἥτις μετεφράσθη πατρίᾳ Τυρίων τῇ Φοινίκων διαλέκτῳ, Αἰγυπτιακὴν Θεογονίαν, καὶ ἄλλα τινά.*"—*Suidas in voc. Sanchoniathon.*

Sanchoniathon, then, writing, at latest, in the twelfth or thirteenth century before Christ, gives us, so far as the fragments preserved from him go, a mixed Phœnician and Egyptian mythology derived from much older sources, the Hermetic books of the Egyptians being shown by internal evidence, no less than by the testimonies above recited, to be its basis; though the contents of these books were by no means simply translated and borrowed; but they were altered and paralleled in many points, so as to suit the Phœnician nationality, Thoth himself, and Isiris or Osiris, being spoken of as if they were Phœnicians first, before they became Egyptians. Ham, indeed, under whatever name, was a common ancestor to the two peoples; but for Mizraim, the son of Ham, ancestor of the Egyptians, we should expect the Phœnicians to substitute their own ancestor Canaan; and in the next generation we should expect to find the sons of Canaan, who may be the Phœnician Κάβειροι. If the Nile was deified by the Egyptians, who worshipped only a freshwater Ὠκεανὸς, this would not be suitable for the maritime Phœnicians, who owed everything to the sea, but nothing to any great river; so that it would be only *mutatis mutandis* if they worshipped, together with Typhon and Nereus, an elder and a younger Pontus or Neptune, and made Sidon and Poseidon their offspring. We might also expect to find here and there some Greek gloss or interpretation of the translator, or of transcribers in Greek times, especially after we have had a hint from Philo himself that the works of Sanchoniathon had been corrupted and obscured. And some manifestly Greek additions we do find in the fragments preserved; as when, after the mention of Cronus, i.e. Noah or Ham, giving Egypt to Thoth, son of Misor, to be his kingdom, it is added, that "Cronus also gave Attica to his daughter Ἀθηνᾶ," i.e. Neith, a donation which certainly formed no part of the original text.

Bearing these qualifications in mind, we may examine how far there may be in the fragments of Sanchoniathon any series answering to that of the Gods and Demigods of the Old Egyptian Chronicle.

First, the unoriginated god Phtha, who is named in the Chronicle at the head of all, is recognisable also in the fragments of Sanchoniathon, which have been preserved to us, thus:

"Τὴν τῶν ὅλων ἀρχὴν ὑποτίθεται Ἀέρα ζοφώδη καὶ πνευματώδη, ἢ Πνοὴν ἀέρος ζοφώδους, καὶ Χάος θολερὸν ἐρεβῶδες· ταῦτα δὲ εἶναι ἄπειρα, καὶ διὰ πολὺν αἰῶνα μὴ ἔχειν πέρας."

It is easy to see that, under this language, which seeks to make one "principle" of matter in a rarefied form (ἀέρα) and spirit (πνοὴν, πνεῦμα), there are really *two* principles, so that one man, putting the spiritual element first, might make it form and all but originate matter, while another might make Phtha himself to be the offspring of Nilus, or mud. The language of Sanchoniathon, like that of the Chronicle, inclines towards the less materialistic side; for after introducing as his first principle spiritual gas, or gaseous spirit, of which Chaos is only a varied form, he continues with spirit (πνεῦμα) alone in the following words: —

"Ὅτε δέ, φησιν, ἠράσθη τὸ Πνεῦμα τῶν ἰδίων ἀρχῶν, καὶ ἐγένετο σύγκρασις, ἡ πλοκὴ ἐκείνη ἐκλήθη Πόθος· αὕτη δὲ ἀρχὴ κτίσεως ἁπάντων."

That the self-reflection of the unoriginated Being is the beginning of generation, and indirectly of creation, is here confusedly implied. The Chronicle is clearer; for it names Ra, the Sun-God, distinctly "*son* of Phtha," son without a mother; while the same formation of the Mundane Egg is ascribed to him (and to Cneph also) as to Phtha himself. The text proceeds: "Αὐτὸ δὲ (i. e. τὸ Πνεῦμα) οὐκ ἐγίνωσκε τὴν αὐτοῦ κτίσιν," which plainly agrees with the Chronicle, making Phtha unoriginated as well as infinite, without relation to time or space: "Καὶ ἐκ τῆς αὐτοῦ συμπλοκῆς τοῦ Πνεύματος ἐγένετο Μώτ· τοῦτό τινές φασιν ἰλύν· οἱ δὲ ὑδατώδους μίξεως σῆψιν· καὶ ἐκ ταύτης ἐγένετο πᾶσα σπορὰ κτίσεως, καὶ γένεσις τῶν ὅλων."

Mout is well known in the Egyptian Pantheon as material nature, the great universal mother, mother of gods and men: and it is to be noted, that though Μὼτ is material nature in its primary element *mud*, it is no longer the inert passive mud, or air, or gas, or chaos, first spoken of, and confusedly compounded with Πνεῦμα; for that pre-existed from the beginning; but mud now instinct with life and form; as if the Divine Universe of spirit and matter, originally an inert compound, by self-reflection on its own compound principles (ἠράσθη τῶν ἰδίων ἀρχῶν), and by Πόθος, produced Μὼτ as a daughter, instead of the abstract Ra as a son. The ἐμπεριχώρησις is such, that when Phtha is said to mould the egg, the Sun-God may be said to spring from it; and on the other hand, when Cneph is said to form it, Phtha himself is in some sense contained in it, and issues from the mouth of Cneph.

"Ἦν δέ τινα ζῶα οὐκ ἔχοντα αἴσθησιν, ἐξ ὧν ἐγένετο ζῶα νοερὰ, καὶ ἐκλήθη Ζωφασημὶν, τουτέστιν οὐρανοῦ κατόπται· καὶ ἀνεπλάσθη ὁμοίως ὠοῦ σχήματι, καὶ ἐξέλαμψε Μὼτ, ἥλιός τε καὶ σελήνη, ἀστέρες τε, καὶ ἄστρα μεγάλα." But the formation of the mundane egg out of matter now instinct with form and life, is specially ascribed to Phtha in the Egyptian mythology, the egg itself being identical with Μώτ: and for this cause the scarabæus, or dung-beetle, which was supposed to be only male, or without sex, and to be self-engendered, and which is constantly seen rolling the ball or egg which it has formed, was taken to be the special emblem of the self-originating and world-forming God Phtha.

Ra, the Sun-God, who in the Chronicle is named as son of Phtha, and so also is the first of its CXIII generations, and to whom, as the measurer of time, the first reign in time, and the first dynasty of the XXX is given, appears also in the passages quoted from Sanchoniathon; and there, too, as in the Chronicle, he appears as already inherent in the visible sun; though he may be inferred to have pre-existed as the abstract intellectual sun, or effulgence of Phtha, when he also is said to mould that mundane egg whence spring the sun, moon, and stars, and to have Atmu, Mentu, and Su for his offspring, and the sun and moon for his two eyes. For Sanchoniathon, speaking of the second generation of mortal ancestors afterwards deified, i. e. of the generation of Cain and Abel and Seth, whose sacrifices are mentioned also by Moses, says that "they worshipped the Sun, thinking that god the only lord of heaven, and therefore calling him Beelsamin." The passage itself, in Greek, will be given below.

A third deity, not named in the Chronicle, because without relation either to cosmical or to human time, but understood, no doubt, together with Phtha and Ra by its author, and named by Manetho and his re-editors in their Lists, is distinguishable also in Sanchoniathon, who ascribes the first deification of his emblem, the basilisk or uræus, to Thoth. The passage, slightly abridged, is as follows:—

"Τὴν μὲν οὖν τοῦ δράκοντος φύσιν καὶ τῶν ὄφεων αὐτὸς ἐξεθείασεν ὁ Τάαυτος, καὶ μετ' αὐτὸν αὖθις Φοίνικές τε καὶ Αἰγύπτιοι· πνευματικώτατον γὰρ τὸ ζῶον πάντων τῶν ἑρπετῶν, καὶ πυρῶδες, ὑπ' αὐτοῦ παρεδόθη. .... Καὶ πολυχρονιώτατον δέ ἐστι, οὐ μόνον τῷ ἐκδυόμενον τὸ γῆρας νεάζειν, ἀλλὰ καὶ αὔξησιν ἐπιδέχεσθαι μείζονα πέφυκε. Καὶ ἐπειδὰν τὸ ὡρισμένον μέτρον πληρώσῃ, εἰς ἑαυτὸν ἀναλίσκεται, ὡς ἐν ταῖς ἱεραῖς ὁμοίως αὐτὸς ὁ Τάαυτος κατέταξε γραφαῖς· διὸ καὶ ἐν ἱεροῖς τοῦτο τὸ ζῶον καὶ ἐν μυστηρίοις συμπαρείληπται.... Φοίνικες δὲ αὐτὸ Ἀγαθὸν Δαίμονα καλοῦσιν· ὁμοίως καὶ Αἰγύπτιοι Κνὴφ ἐπονομάζουσι· προστιθέασι δὲ αὐτῷ ἱέρακος κεφαλὴν, καὶ διὰ τὸ πρακτικὸν τοῦ ἱέρακος. Καί φησιν ὁ Ἐπήεις ἀλληγορῶν (ὁ ὀνομασθεὶς παρ' αὐτοῖς μέγιστος ἱεροφάντης, καὶ ἱερογραμματεὺς, ὃν μετέφρασεν εἰς Ἑλλάδα φωνὴν Ἄρειος Ἡρακλεοπολίτης) κατὰ λέξιν οὕτως· Τὸ πρῶτον ὂν θειότατον ὄφις ἐστὶν ἱέρακος ἔχων μορφὴν, ἄγαν ἐπιχαρές· ὃς εἰ ἀναβλέψειε, φωτὸς τὸ πᾶν ἐπλήρου ἐν τῇ πρωτογόνῳ χώρᾳ αὐτοῦ· εἰ δὲ καμμύσειε, σκότος ἐγίνετο· ἔμφασιν διδοὺς ὁ Ἐπήεις ὅτι καὶ διάπυρόν ἐστιν, διὰ τὸ φάναι διηύγασε· φωτὸς γὰρ ἴδιόν ἐστι τὸ διαυγάσαι. .... Ἔτι μὴν οἱ Αἰγύπτιοι ἀπὸ τῆς αὐτῆς ἐννοίας τὸν κόσμον γράφοντες περιφερῆ κύκλον ἀεροειδῆ καὶ πυρωπὸν χαράσσουσι, καὶ μέσον τεταμένον ὄφιν ἱερακόμορφον· καί ἐστι τὸ πᾶν σχῆμα ὡς τὸ παρ' ἡμῖν Θῆτα· τὸν μὲν κύκλον κόσμον μηνύοντες, τὸν δὲ μέσον ὄφιν συνεκτικὸν τούτου Ἀγαθὸν Δαίμονα σημαίνοντες."—*Euseb. Præp. Ev.* i. 10.

Then, to parallel those XIII Generations and Dynasties of the Chronicle which we have shown to be reckoned to as many deified ancestors of the old world (three generations instead of one being made for the three sons of Noah), we find in Sanchoniathon a human genealogy, which slightly abridged will stand as follows:—

I. (Parallel to the first generation and Dynasty after Ra, viz. that of Cronus, in the Chronicle):—"Εἶτά φησι γεγενῆσθαι ἐκ τοῦ Κολπία" (i. e. perhaps קול־פי־יה) "ἀνέμου *καὶ γυναικὸς αὐτοῦ Βάαυ*" (perhaps really an Egyptian word signifying spirit, breath), "*τοῦτο δὲ Νύκτα ἑρμηνεύειν*" (בית pernoctare, and בותא, noctua, have a final letter more) "*Αἰῶνα καὶ Πρωτόγονον, θνητοὺς ἄνδρας· εὑρεῖν δὲ τὸν Αἰῶνα τὴν ἀπὸ τῶν δένδρων τροφήν.*" (As if it were said that the original Deity, *πνεῦμα*, at once father and mother, begat the first men: "*Τοῦ γὰρ καὶ γένος ἐσμέν.*")

The name Protogonus necessarily indicates the protoplast, i. e. Adam, who becomes Seb, or Cronus, for the Egyptians: and Αἰών, if masculine, being merely another name for the same person, might have the sense of *Χρόνος*; or if feminine, as what follows lower down seems to imply, it will agree in sense with *Ζωή*, Eve; and it seems connected with her, in spite of the masculine form, by the circumstance that she devises food from trees; though certainly there is herein no *necessity* for any special allusion, as vegetables and fruits alone were the food given to man at the beginning.

II. (Generation and Dynasty III., that is, the second generation and dynasty after Ra, in the Chronicle):—"*Ἐκ τούτων τοὺς γενομένους κληθῆναι Γένος καὶ Γενεάν, καὶ οἰκῆσαι τὴν Φοινίκην·*" (just as later Osiris, son of Seb, in the second generation of men, was fabled to have been the colonist and cultivator of antediluvian Egypt: and Cain in the second generation, in the Book of Genesis, is said to have founded the first city:) "*Αὐχμῶν δὲ γενομένων, τὰς χεῖρας ὀρέγειν εἰς οὐρανοὺς πρὸς τὸν ἥλιον· τοῦτον γάρ, φησι, θεὸν νομίζειν μόνον οὐρανοῦ κύριον, Βεελσαμὶν καλοῦντας, ὅ ἐστι παρὰ Φοίνιξι Κύριος Οὐρανοῦ, Ζεὺς δὲ παρ' Ἕλλησι.*"

III. (Generation and Dynasty IV., that is, the third generation and dynasty after Ra, in the Chronicle):—"*Ἑξῆς ἀπὸ Γένους Αἰῶνος καὶ Πρωτογόνου*" (here we see that Αἰών is in sense feminine, since Γένος is the son of the two) "*γεννηθῆναι αὖθις παῖδας θνητούς, οἷς ὀνόματα Φῶς, καὶ Πῦρ, καὶ Φλόξ· οὗτοι ἐκ τῆς παρατριβῆς ξύλων εὗρον πῦρ, καὶ τὴν χρῆσιν ἐδίδαξαν.*"

IV. (Generation and Dynasty V., that is, the fourth generation and dynasty after Ra, in the Chronicle):—"*Υἱοὺς δὲ ἐγέννησαν οὗτοι μεγέθει τε καὶ ὑπεροχῇ κρείσσονας*" (plainly answering to the giants of the old world in the Book of

Genesis), "ὧν τὰ ὀνόματα τοῖς ὄρεσιν ἐπετέθη ὧν ἐκράτησαν· ὡς ἐξ αὐτῶν κληθῆναι τὸ Κάσιον, καὶ τὸν Λίβανον, καὶ τὸν Ἀντιλίβανον, καὶ τὸ Βραθύ."

V. (Generation and Dynasty VI., that is, the fifth generation and dynasty after Ra, in the Chronicle):—"Ἐκ τούτων ἐγεννήθησαν Μημροῦμος καὶ Ὑψουράνιος. . . . . Εἶτα τὸν Ὑψουράνιον οἰκῆσαι Τύρον·" (So Babylon also, in Berosus, is built before the Flood, and rebuilt after it:) "καλύβας τε ἐπινοῆσαι ἐκ καλάμων καὶ θρύων καὶ παπύρων·" (this last word may indicate an Egyptian source:) "στασιάσαι δὲ πρὸς τὸν ἀδελφὸν Οὔσωον·" (Esau and Cain, perhaps, in one. As Cain was a keeper of sheep, the Egyptian designation Sôs, shepherd, elsewhere written Οὔσσως by Eusebius, might be suitable:) "ὃς σκέπην τῷ σώματι πρῶτος ἐκ δερμάτων ὧν ἴσχυσε συλλαβεῖν θηρίων εὗρε. . . . Δένδρου δὲ λαβόμενον τὸν Οὔσωον, καὶ ἀποκλαδεύσαντα, πρῶτον τολμῆσαι εἰς θάλασσαν ἐμβῆναι·" (this is clearly Phœnician, and if the name, or the life, is at all connected with Esau, may hint that the first navigators were Ἐρυθραῖοι:) "ἀνιερῶσαι δὲ δύο στήλας Πυρί τε καὶ Πνεύματι" (i.e. to Phtha under these twin forms of Heat and Spirit, or to Phtha and Cneph, who, with Ra Baal-shamaim, make the three mentioned above:) "καὶ προσκυνῆσαι· ἅμα τε (αἷμά τε?) σπένδειν αὐταῖς ἐξ ὧν ἤγρευε θηρίων. Τούτων δὲ" (i.e. Mimroum and Hypsouranios) "τελευτησάντων, τοὺς ἀπολειφθέντας ῥάβδους αὐτοῖς ἀφιερῶσαι, καὶ τὰς στήλας προσκυνεῖν, καὶ τούτοις ἑορτὰς ἄγειν κατ' ἔτος." (As if the fifth generation of mankind were already deified after death by the survivors.)

VI. (Generation and Dynasty VII., that is, the sixth generation and dynasty after Ra, in the Chronicle):—"Χρόνοις δ' ὕστερον πολλοῖς ἀπὸ τῆς Ὑψουρανίου (i.e. of Cain?) γενεὰς γενέσθαι Ἀγρέα καὶ Ἁλιέα (Hunter and Fisher, this and the next three generations being named from modes of life), τοὺς ἁλιείας καὶ ἄγρας εὑρετὰς, ἐξ ὧν κληθῆναι ἀγρευτὰς καὶ ἁλιεῖς."

VII. (Generation and Dynasty VIII., that is, the seventh generation and dynasty after Ra, in the Chronicle):—"Ἐξ ὧν γενέσθαι δύο ἀδελφοὺς σιδήρου εὑρετὰς καὶ τῆς τούτου ἐργασίας· ὧν θάτερον τὸν Χρυσὼρ" (perhaps the elder Thoth of Egypt, Thoth Pnubi, or the Golden, Χρυσὼρ being the translation of Πνοὺψ?) "λόγους ἀσκῆσαι καὶ ἐπῳδὰς, καὶ μαντείας· εἶναι δὲ τοῦτον τὸν Ἥφαιστον·" (i. e. not Phtha, but the smith-god of the Greeks. The inventions ascribed to this Generation and the next, the eighth, are identical with those of two of the sons of Lamech, the fifth descendant of Cain, Jubal being the father of musicians, and Tubal-Cain, whence, perhaps, the Latin Vulcanus, the father of smiths; while the name Διαμίχιος, though derived by some from מְחִי, machina, as if it were Ζεὺς Μηχανικὸς, sounds like a corruption of Lamech:) "εὑρεῖν δὲ ἄγκιστρον καὶ δέλεαρ, καὶ ὁρμιὰν, καὶ σχεδίαν· πρῶτον δὲ πάντων ἀνθρώπων πλεῦσαι·" (perhaps because his art was the assistant of Κρόνος, i. e. Noah, in the war with Uranus in fabricating the ark:) "διὸ καὶ ὡς θεὸν αὐτὸν μετὰ θάνατον ἐσεβάσθησαν· καλεῖσθαι δὲ αὐτὸν καὶ Διαμίχιον·" (so here we have another confessed deification:) "οἱ δὲ τοὺς ἀδελφοὺς αὐτοῦ τοίχους φασὶν ἐπινοῆσαι ἐκ πλίνθων." (The sailing, except for the word σχεδίαν, seems of Phœnician, the bricks are certainly of Egyptian origin.)

VIII. (Generation and Dynasty IX., that is, the eighth generation and dynasty after Ra, in the Chronicle):—"Ἐκ τοῦ γένους τούτου γενέσθαι νεανίας δύο, Τεχνίτην καὶ Γήϊνον Αὐτόχθονα·" (Artisan, and Earthly Aboriginal:) "οὗτοι ἐπενόησαν τῷ πηλῷ τῆς πλίνθου συμμιγνύειν φορυτὸν, καὶ τῷ ἡλίῳ αὐτὰς τερσαίνειν· ἀλλὰ καὶ στέγας ἐξεῦρον." (These are manifestly the sun-baked bricks of Egypt, made with earth and chopped straw, not the burnt bricks of Babylonia, still less any of Phœnicia. So the older bricks also were Egyptian; and the substance of the whole genealogy hereby shows itself to be, not from Sanchoniathon, nor any other Phœnician or Greek writer, but from those Hermetic books which Sanchoniathon followed.)

IX. (Generation and Dynasty X., that is, the ninth generation and dynasty after Ra, in the Chronicle):—"Ἀπὸ τούτων ἐγένοντο ἕτεροι, ὧν ὁ μὲν Ἀγρὸς ὁ δὲ Ἀγρόηρος ἢ Ἀγρότης (Field and Fieldman) ἐκαλεῖτο· οὗ καὶ ξόανον εἶναι μάλα σεβάσμιον, καὶ ναὸν ζυγοφορούμενον ἐν Φοινίκῃ· παρὰ δὲ Βυβλίοις ἐξαιρέτως Θεῶν ὁ Μέγιστος ὀνομάζεται·" (so this ancestor is not only deified, this being a thing of course, but he is even styled the Greatest of the Gods:) "ἐπενόησαν δὲ οὗτοι αὐλὰς προστιθέναι τοῖς οἴκοις, καὶ περιβόλαια, καὶ σπήλαια. Ἐκ τούτων ἀγρόται καὶ κυνηγοί·" (this generation has the occupation of Noah, as the two preceding have the occupations of the sons of Lamech, who are in the eighth generation from the beginning, in the line of Cain:) "οὗτοι δὲ καὶ Ἀλῆται καὶ Τιτᾶνες καλοῦνται."

X. (Generation and Dynasty XI., that is, the tenth generation and dynasty after Ra, in the Chronicle):—"Ἀπὸ τούτων γενέσθαι Ἄμυνον καὶ Μάγον·" (of whom Amun, as the father of Misor and Sydyk, called also below Isiris and Chnaa, the ancestors of the Egyptians and the Phœnicians, should be Ham: and the name Ἄμυνος may be taken from the Egyptian Amoun, Amoun-Khem:) "οἳ κατέδειξαν κώμας καὶ ποίμνας·" (Ham, perhaps, the ancestor of the Egyptians and Phœnicians, being the father of such as live in villages and towns, κώμας, and Magus, who may stand for Shem the father of the Magi, being the father of such as keep flocks.)

At this point we have one generation less than the eleven which should be reckoned from Adam through Seth to any one of the three sons of Noah inclusively; a difference which disappears, if we suppose the line of Cain, in which chiefly were the founders of cities, the giants, men of renown, and inventors of arts, to have been followed by allusion in the generations given above, rather than the line of Seth. It is even conceivable that Noah himself should have been descended, though in the female line, from Cain as well as from Seth; and on that supposition he might be made to stand ninth from the beginning by one reckoning, as he stands tenth by the other.

In these X Generations (which would be XII if the 600 years of Noah and his sons were divided into four average generations instead of two actual) we have a close parallel to the XIII Generations and Dynasties of the XIII Gods (Seb or Cronus and his descendants) in the Chronicle, and a perfect parallel to the X which are given in the book of Genesis, if one passes from the last descendant of Cain, the eighth from the beginning, to Noah and Ham and to the new world.

And as the VIII Demigods of the Chronicle, though thrust down, and apparently confined to 217 years, between the two complete cycles of the antediluvians and Menes, yet really begin from the Flood, and are concurrent for 658 years with the survival, real or fictitious, of the antediluvians, it follows that the sons and grandsons of Amunus and Magus in Sanchoniathon are to be paralleled with the first and second of the eight generations of Demigods in the Chronicle; although the name of Mizraim or Osiris (Μισὼρ,῎Ισιρις) having been blended later with the characters of antediluvian deities, he is lost from this place in the popular mythology (in the older he is not yet named), and it is only his son Thoth that heads the series of Demigods in the lists of Manetho or his re-editors. The two generations after῎Αμυνος and Μάγος appear thus:—

XI. (Generation XIV., fourteenth after Ra, and first of the VIII Demigods, in the Chronicle):—"Ἀπὸ τούτων" (i. e. ἀπὸ Ἀμύνου καὶ Μάγου) "γενέσθαι Μισὼρ καὶ Συδὺκ, τουτέστιν, Εὔλυτον καὶ Δίκαιον." (Sydyk being identified with Canaan, son of Ham and father of Sidon, both as the ancestor of the Phœnicians, father of their Κάβειροι, and also as brother of Μισὼρ, father of Thoth and ancestor of the Egyptians, it is interesting to notice how the name is varied, so as to have a sense contrary to that of the name Canaan. For "Canaan," i.e. "*Humiliatus*," implies rather degradation and servitude, in agreement with the curse of Noah, "a servant of servants shall he be to his brethren:" but his own Phœnician posterity name him mystically "Sydyk," i.e. "The Righteous," or the "Justified." Elsewhere, though with a confusion of chronology as if both were descendants or successors of Thoth, "Chnaa," i.e. Canaan, is named distinctly by his proper name as brother of Isiris, and as being "the first Phœnician.")

XII. (Generation XVI., i.e. fifteenth after Ra, and second of the VIII Demigods, in the Chronicle):—"Ἀπὸ Μισὼρ Τάαυτος· ὃς εὗρε τὴν τῶν πρώτων στοιχείων γραφήν· ὃν Αἰγύπτιοι μὲν Θὼθ, Ἀλεξανδρεῖς δὲ Θωὺθ, ῞Ελληνες δὲ Ἑρμῆν ἐκάλεσαν. Ἐκ δὲ τοῦ Συδὺκ Διόσκουροι, ἢ Κάβειροι, ἢ Κορύβαντες, ἢ Σαμοθρᾷκες. Οὗτοί, φησι, πρῶτοι πλοῖον εὗρον."

Here, with the generation of Thoth himself, ends the consecutive genealogy deduced from Protogonus and Æon, i. e. from Adam and Eve: and the fact that it ends here is some sign that thus far Sanchoniathon may have been following not only the Hermetic books, but that most ancient part of them which was really derived in substance from Thoth himself, who like other authors would naturally go down to his own time. And in this succession of deified ancestors, through all the period of the old world, until after the generation answering to Noah, no single name of any deity of the popular Egyptian Pantheon has occurred. Only at the outset we have learned that Thoth symbolised by the scarabæus with the egg that it forms and rolls, by the visible sun, and by the serpent or uræus, four deities not of human origin, identifiable with Phtha, Ra, Cneph, and the goddess Mout. But when Sanchoniathon, or rather, as we may suppose, Thoth himself, begins afresh, and goes back, as he does, from his own generation, to give a separate account of the *existing* world, deducing it not from Protogonus and Æon and the material cosmogony, but from Uranus, and Cronus the elder, i. e. from Noah and the Flood, we do find in this separate *postdiluvian* mythology either plainly, with Egyptian names, or under their known Greek equivalents, or by necessary inference, or under Phœnician parallels, those same deities of the popular Pantheon which the Egyptians claimed for themselves and for Thoth the credit of having first invented. And as the former consecutive genealogy extends through those 500 or 600 years after the Flood, within which the sources of the separate mythology following are chronologically contained, and the two accounts are distinctly connected together by the name Sydyk, i. e. Canaan, father of the Phœnician Cabeiri and brother of Misor, and so uncle of Thoth, it is possible to ascertain with some exactness the relation of the popular Pantheon, in its earlier form, to the succession of real postdiluvian ancestors.

Sydyk, who is son of Amunus and father of the Cabiri, according to the Genealogy, is, according to the Mythology, father of the same Cabiri (especially of Asmounius or Asclepius, the youngest of them), by a Titanid, daughter of Κρόνος. Cronus therefore, the chief deity of the Phœnicians (and the chief of deified ancestors in the Chronicle), is necessarily one with Amunus of the tenth Generation in the Genealogy, that is, he is one with Ham. And this is confirmed, when we find that Κρόνος the younger (for there are two) is, as Ham ought to be, one of three brethren named Κρόνος β', Βῆλος, and 'Απόλλων, who have also three Phœnician contemporaries, Pontus, Typhon, and Nereus. But 'Απόλλων being Horus, and there being no room for literal contemporaries of Ham and his two brothers, Amoun or Amoun-Khem, Typhon or Baal, and Horus will be the Egyptian triad of Thoth and Sanchoniathon, answering to the three sons of Noah. But Amoun (the hidden deity) and Khem (the generator) are already in Sanchoniathon, as commented by Eusebius, divided into two, Πὰν, i. e. Khem, being named as the son of Uranus and brother of Cronus, while yet there is no room for more than two literal brothers of the younger Cronus, Ham, nor for any literal brother at all of the elder, who must necessarily be Noah, and so one with 'Αγρότης, the Husbandman of Generation IX. in the Genealogy. But Κρόνος the elder is certainly the Egyptian Seb. Being the sole father of the existing, no less than Protogonus or Adam of the old world, he might have been presented without human ancestors (humanity having been reabsorbed into nature) as sprung from some θεὸς καὶ θεά, like ἄνεμος Κολπίας and Βάαυ; or from the grosser pantheistic duad Heaven and Earth; after which Heaven, as an unnatural father, might war on his consort and her offspring. This would have been intelligible: and in purely Egyptian mythology, as known from other sources, 'Ελιοῦν Ὕψιστος, i. e. antediluvian humanity, Οὐρανὸς, i. e. heaven personified, and the elder Κρόνος, i. e. the ancestor of existing humanity, are all one deity under one name, Seb, who is indifferently either Uranus or Cronus; and his consort has one name, Nutpe or Rhea, the goddess Mout (Γῆ or Δημήτηρ) having a different connection. But in Sanchoniathon, whether he were following Thoth or varying from him, the allegory is complex and confused. Κρόνος, the Humanity of the existting world is deduced from two earlier generations of antors; his grandparents being not simply spirit, like Ἄνεμος and Βάαυ, and his parents the pantheistic duad, Heaven and Earth, which again would have been intelligible; but his grandfather, blasphemously named Ἐλιοῦν Ὕψιστος, God the Most High, is antediluvian Humanity slain by a beast (neither the deceiving serpent nor the true dragon, Apepi, of the deluge, but some *other* enemy), and afterwards deified. His immediate father is again a man, who by the name Ἐπίγειος Αὐτόχθων, Aboriginal Man on the Earth, while yet derived from an older humanity, is fixed to be no other than Cronus himself reduplicated. And this reduplication with its consort being thrown back upon nature, and identified with the pantheistic duad, and renamed (after death and deification) Heaven and Earth, Noah or Cronus, now become his own father, becomes also, through the material heaven and the power moving it, his own enemy; and in his father is even one with the enemy, the monster, which slew his grandfather Elioun Hypsistos: an inextricable confusion of contrary relations.

The whole series of this mythology is expressly connected by Sanchoniathon not only with the existing postdiluvian world, but with the times of Thoth himself and the Cabiri, and even of the generation next following; for he introduces it with these words:

"Contemporary with *these*," i. e. strictly speaking, with the progeny of the Cabiri, who are the last mentioned, but no doubt the sense is, "contemporary with these later generations, there existed one *Elioun Hypsistos* and a female named *Beryta*, who settled at Byblos (so that this form of the myth is evidently from some native of Byblos): "Κατὰ τούτους γίνεταί τις Ἐλιοῦν, καλούμενος Ὕψιστος, καὶ θήλεια λεγομένη Βηρούθ· οἳ καὶ κατῴκουν περὶ Βύβλον.

"Ἐξ ὧν γεννᾶται Ἐπίγειος ἢ Αὐτόχθων, ὃν ὕστερον ἐκάλεσαν Οὐρανόν· . . . γεννᾶται δὲ τούτῳ ἀδελφὴ ἐκ τῶν προειρημένων, ἣ καὶ ἐκλήθη Γῆ." (Eusebius, from Diodorus and Euemerus, adds that this Aboriginal Man of the Earth was afterwards, when deified, called Uranus or Heaven either for having been knowing in the stars, or for having been the first to sacrifice to the Celestials, that is, to his own earthly antediluvian ancestors.—*Euseb. Præpar. Evang.* II. ii. p. 60.)

"Ὁ δὲ τούτων πατὴρ, ὁ Ὕψιστος, ἐκ συμβολῆς θηρίων τελευτήσας ἀφιερώθη· ᾧ καὶ χοὰς καὶ θυσίας οἱ παῖδες ἐτέλεσαν.

"Παραλαβὼν δὲ ὁ Οὐρανὸς τὴν τοῦ πατρὸς ἀρχὴν, ἄγεται πρὸς γάμον τὴν ἀδελφὴν Γῆν, καὶ ποιεῖται ἐξ αὐτῆς παῖδας δ', Ἶλον, τὸν καὶ Κρόνον, καὶ Βέτυλον, καὶ Δαγὼν, ὅς ἐστι Σίτων, καὶ Ἄτλαντα." (Under these Phœnician names Κρόνος only is at once identifiable with the Egyptian Seb; but Eusebius helps us to name another, viz., Πάν, i.e. Khem, whom Herodotus also names among the VIII most ancient Gods; for he says, from Diodorus and Euemerus, that "Uranus by Ἑστία, i.e. Onka or Vesta, had sons Pan and Cronus, and daughters Rhea and Demeter."—*Præpar. Evang.* II. ii. p. 60) "Καὶ ἐξ ἄλλων δὲ γαμετῶν ὁ Οὐρανὸς πολλὴν ἔσχε γενεάν·" (and so he continues to give the fable at length; according to which Uranus, by the deluge, seeking to destroy the mother Earth his consort, with her children, his son Cronus, i.e. man, sprung from the slain antediluvians, and now disentangled from his confusion with heaven personified, takes part with his mother; and aided by male and female prudence, the elder Thoth and Athene or Neith, his daughter, at length defeats Uranus, mutilates and slays him, and reigns in his stead; after which, as a thing of course, he also deifies and worships him. That is, without allegory, man, by foresight and skill in making the ark, surmounts the deluge; sees the power of the heaven for mischief cut off; the waters being confined to some central abyss, and issuing only in beneficent sources of rivers; and so he rules the earth freed and recovered from the Flood. The elder Thoth and Neith, and the elder Athor (Astarte), Ἑστία or Onka, Pan himself, and others, as Ζεὺς Δημαροῦς posthumous son of Uranus, and his son Melcarth the Tyrian Hercules, (who must be Amoun and Khons,) and others named in connection with Uranus and the elder Cronus, must all (except one consort, Rhea Nutpe) be either merely allegorical personages, or reduplications, for whom there is no room literally in the ark, any more than for "the daughter and pilot and select friends" of Xisuthrus, who are named by the Chaldean Berosus.

Putting together the Egyptian deities which we have hitherto found in Sanchoniathon, and which may possibly be from the earliest Hermetic books, we have now before us the following series: —

I. Φθᾶ, under Πνεῦμα or Πνοή in the Cosmogony, with the symbol of the scarabæus implied in what is said of the Mundane Egg: also under Πνεῦμα and Πῦρ, worshipped by Ousous in Generation V. of the Genealogy.

II. Ῥᾶ, under Ἥλιος Βεελσαμὴν, worshipped as the only Lord of Heaven in Generation II. of the Genealogy.

III. Κνήφ, "the Conserving Soul of the Universe," in Greek Ἀγαθοδαίμων, under the symbol of the serpent, or uræus, deified by Thoth.

Also a goddess, Μὼτ, the universal mother, mother and consort at once of Khem or Pan, the Generator. She is expressly named in the Cosmogony, and is not different from the Mundane Egg moulded by Πνεῦμα. Then in the Mythology, which must be compared with the last four Generations of the Genealogy, there are mentioned or indicated

IV. Σήβ, under Ἐλιοῦν Ὕψιστος, Οὐρανὸς, and Κρόνος α′ in the Mythology, and under Ἀγρότης, Gen. IX. of the Genealogy. Also, connected with these; we have

V. Χὲμ, whom Eusebius calls Πὰν, under one of the Phœnician names of the four sons of Uranus in the Mythology: as such he seems to be the brother of Κρόνος α′, but really he is is a form of Κρόνος β′. Further, there occur

IX. Θὼθ, i.e. Thoth or Hermes the elder, counsellor of Κρόνος, perhaps one with Χρυσὼρ or Πνοὺψ of Generation VIII. in the Genealogy.

X. A form of Ἀμοῦν, under Ζεὺς Δημαροῦς a late son of Οὐρανὸς after his defeat, born in the house of Dagon (Χὲμ?), brother of Κρόνος α′, and so parallel with his three sons; and one therefore with that one of them who is named Ἄμουνος.

XI. Χὼνς, Ἡρακλῆς son of Ἀμοῦν, under Melcarth the Tyrian Hercules, son of Ζεὺς Δημαροῦς, parallel seemingly with Μισὼρ and Συδὺκ sons of Ἄμυνος, but really perhaps parallel with Thoth and the Cabiri, a generation lower.

XII. Perhaps Ἰοὺρ, Ὠκεανὸς, or Νεῖλος, under the Phœnician Πόντος, contemporary of the sons of Κρόνος β′. Also there are the goddesses

a. [Γῆ or Δημήτηρ, who is the same as the goddess Μὼτ,

already mentioned above, and mother and consort at once not of Seb but of Khem or Min, who is Pan.]

b. Nutpe, consort of Seb (who is at once Uranus and Cronus), under 'Ρέα consort of Κρόνος α'.

c. Onka, a Phœnician goddess, known also in Egypt, under 'Εστία, named by Eusebius as consort of Οὐρανός.

d. "Αθωρ the elder, 'Αφροδίτη Οὐρανία, under Astarte daughter of Uranus.

e. Νεἶθ under 'Αθηνᾶ the daughter of Κρόνος α'.

All these, and others not clearly identifiable with Egyptian names or deities, are either merely allegorical personages, or else they are reduplications.

VI. 'Αμοὺν, under "Αμυνος of Generation X. in the Genealogy, son of 'Αγρότης of Generation IX.; and under Κρόνος β' chief of the three sons of Κρόνος α', deities derived from the three sons of Noah, this the chief of them being Ham or Chem.

VII. Τυφὼν, under Βῆλος second son of Κρόνος α'; for "Baal" is also in Egyptian a form of Typhon; but by name also, as the second of the three aqueous deities contemporaries of the three sons of Κρόνος β', viz. Πόντος, Τυφὼν, Νηρεύς.

VIII. "Ωρος, i.e. Horus the elder, son, not grandson, of Seb, or Κρόνος α'; under 'Απόλλων, third of the three sons of Κρόνος α'.

Supposing this list, obtained from Sanchoniathon, the earliest as is thought of heathen writers (apart from any hieroglyphical papyri or inscriptions which may be older), to contain the chief personages of the mythology as it was left by Thoth himself, we may discern in it perhaps those VIII greater and more ancient Gods, to whom, according to Herodotus, Hercules was added later, with three others, so as to make XII: and the name of Hercules (Chons) we have before us already. Another name, Osiris, not deified it seems as yet by Thoth, appears nevertheless uniformly from an early period (seemingly from 200 years before the head of Dyn. XVIII., i. e. from about B. C. 2000, if on the altar of Pepi), as the first of the three sons of Seb, in the place where we find in Sanchoniathon Cronus II. or Amoun. Osiris is not indeed entirely absent from Sanchoniathon. He is mentioned as one of the successors of Thoth, who taught and added to his mythology several generations after him: but as it is added at the same time that he was "brother of Canaan the first Phœnician," we see that Osiris (whether the name be etymologically the same or not) is really one and the same person with Misor, the immediate father of Thoth, who was living perhaps still when Thoth compounded his mythology: but after some few generations later, at the time when he is inconsistently said to have lived, he was himself added to the group of mythological deities, probably at the same time with Hercules, and put up into the place of Κρόνος β' or 'Αμοῦν; and Amoun, even if he had not ranked with the greater Gods already, would by inference be understood to belong to them, since Chons or Hercules was his son. Having still a third Egyptian name, Thoth, given in Sanchoniathon to a contemporary and counsellor of the elder Cronus, we may suppose that this elder Thoth was also advanced at the same time with Misor and Chons, the name perhaps of Thoth having been given to him by Thoth the son of Misor on account of the propriety of its signification; for *tat* or *thoth* signifies *hand*, and he was the hand and skill which devised and made (as the pilot in Berosus was the skill and power which animated and preserved) the ark. Or he may have been originally unnamed, being derived from the Χρυσὼρ or Πνοὺψ of Gen. VIII. in the Genealogy; and the name of Thoth the son of Misor may have been thrown back upon him from the similarity of his character, so that Thoth himself, the son of Misor, besides becoming a Demigod afterwards, was first deified in him. After these three there remains only one name more to look for, and we shall have found in Sanchoniathon not only the VIII but all the XII Gods of Herodotus. And as we find in Sanchoniathon not only Typhon but other aqueous deities, Pontus the elder or Poseidon, and Nereus, it is probable that these saltwater deities may have been for the maritime Phœnicians the representatives, *mutatis mutandis*, of an Egyptian freshwater 'Ωκεανὸς, 'Ιοὺρ, or Hapi, the Egyptians owing everything to their river, but regarding the salt sea as an emblem of desolation, and salt as the "foam of Typhon."

As for the six consecutive generations of Demigods in the

Chronicle between that of Thoth, the son of Misor, and Menes, we have certainly no regular series to parallel with them from Sanchoniathon; still we have a slight compendious indication of nearly as many generations down to the mention (the addition, as we understand it) of Isiris brother of Canaan in the Mythology; and this we may suppose was at any rate not later than the time of Menes; seeing how the name of his son Thoth is connected with the first dynasty of Tanite kings, pervading it in a manner according to the list of Eratosthenes.

II. "Ἐλθὼν δὲ ὁ Κρόνος (that is, Ham, it is said) *εἰς Νότου χώραν, ἅπασαν τὴν Αἴγυπτον ἔδωκε θεῷ Τααύτῳ, ὅπως βασίλειον αὐτῷ γένηται.*" In this passage Ham, the great patriarch of the Egyptians, is represented as giving Egypt to Thoth; as if, at the point of time alluded to, Misor was already dead, and Ham surviving; while, when the passage itself was written, Thoth himself is already deified.

"*Ταῦτα δέ, φησι, πρῶτοι πάντων ὑπεμνηματίσαντο οἱ ζ´ Συδὺκ παῖδες Κάβειροι, καὶ ὄγδοος αὐτῶν ἀδελφὸς Ἀσκληπιὸς, ὡς αὐτοῖς ἐνετείλατο θεὸς Τάαυτος.*"

III. ["*Ἐκ τούτων γεγόνασιν ἕτεροι οἳ καὶ βοτάνας εὗρον, καὶ τὴν τῶν δακετῶν ἴασιν, καὶ ἐπῳδάς.*"] "*Οἱ ἀπὸ τῶν Διοσκούρων*" are mentioned also as building ships before the death of Cronus, after the foundation of Byblos.

IV. ["*Θαβίων τις.*"]

V. "*Ταῦτα πάντα Θαβίωνος παῖς πρῶτος τῶν ἀπ' αἰῶνος γεγονότων Φοινίκων Ἱεροφάντης ἀλληγορήσας, τοῖς τε φυσικοῖς καὶ κοσμικοῖς πάθεσιν ἀναμίξας, παρέδωκε*

VI. *τοῖς ὀργιῶσι καὶ τελετῶν κατάρχουσι Προφήταις· οἱ δέ, τὸν τῦφον αὔξειν ἐκ παντὸς ἐπινοοῦντες,*

VII. *τοῖς αὐτῶν διαδόχοις παρέδοσαν,*

VIII. *καὶ τοῖς παρεισάκτοις· ὧν εἷς ἦν Ἴσιρις τῶν γ´ γραμμάτων εὑρετής, ἀδελφὸς Χνᾶ, τοῦ πρώτου μετονομασθέντος Φοίνικος.*"

So that this mention of Osiris is put in at least the sixth, but very probably in the seventh or eighth, generation from Ham. As for the demigods of the popular mythology which grew up after Thoth during these six generations, we can name some of them with certainty, as Manetho or his re-editors in their lists give names which we have not yet found, and which in some of those lists are expressly named Ἡμίθεοι, though there is no reason to suppose that their number was ever exactly *eight*. Thoth himself appears at their head, then Anubis, Anhour, who is Mars, and an Apollo, who may be Horus son of Isis. They name also Ἀμμὼν and Ζεὺς and Ἡρακλῆς, which seem more doubtful, Σῶσος, who may be Su, son of the Sun, and Τιθόης. One might conjecture that Σοῦχος, or Sebek, in later time at least, would be added; and the name Ἀσκληπιὸς occurring for the youngest of the Phœnician Κάβειροι, we should expect to find Imhotep in a corresponding place among the popular demigods or Κάβειροι of Egypt. Four Bulls appear with reigns among the fragments of the Turin Papyrus; but the deification of the sacred animals, according to Manetho, took place only under the kings, after Menes. **Also in the same MS. it seems that a *Horus* was named as the last of the divine rulers, immediately before Menes.**

The myth of Uranus and Cronus, which had spread to the Greeks before the time of Hesiod, is parallel in some respects to that of Typhon and Osiris, which seems to have supplanted it at a later date than that of the first composition of the Hermetic books. The difference between the two is this, that while the myth of Uranus and Cronus refers only to the enemy, the evil, and the strife connected with the Flood and the origin of the existing world (and to this, as we have seen, the earliest mythology of Thoth was confined), the later myth of Osiris, Isis, Typhon, and Horus (connected with whom we first find Anubis the successor of Thoth), is the embodiment of a much more ancient story connected similarly with the beginning of the antediluvian world. It may sound paradoxical at first to hear it said that the later event was supplanted by the earlier, the Flood by the Fall; but with a little reflection we shall see that this may well have been. Sin and its punishment, with whatever age connected, were disagreeable subjects, which sinners would at all times ignore and forget if they could. But in the first generations after the Flood, to ignore or forget that tremendous catastrophe was plainly impossible. The recommencement of mankind from a single father, and a single family, while that father and his sons were still living, must have been the great fact ever present to the imaginations of all; while the true cause of the destruction of the old world must have been known with a painful distinctness to the first authors of apostasy in the new. The story of the Fall, the original source of all death and misery, even if misrepresented, as it was in later fables, with a blasphemous transposition of parts and characters, could offer but poor comfort in reproduction by natural generation, and in the hope of some future antichrist, to a race which had almost witnessed the Flood; while the source and sting of death, and of the Flood itself, lying in the original transgression, the sensitiveness of sinners may have concentrated itself upon the Fall, which last its actual remoteness, and the nearer, engrossing, and overwhelming fact of the destruction and recommencement of the world, helped to hide from view. The Flood too, much more than the Fall, was capable of being represented in a light favourable to self-complacency. For carnal and irreligious men it might be said that man by his foresight and skill had surmounted the utmost malice of his enemy, surviving even the confusion of the elements, the war of heaven against earth, and the reabsorption of the world into primæval Chaos. But as time went on, and the newness of the existing world was less felt, as successive generations left further and further behind them that mountainous fact which at first had hidden all the past, older facts of human history even more momentous than the Flood itself would begin, like higher but more distant mountains, to re-appear; till at length the relative proportion of the Flood was so lessened by distance, that it became possible even to ignore and to forget it as a particular fact, a disagreeable fact, in history, just as the overthrow in the Red Sea was forgotten and ignored; while the existence of disorder in nature animate and inanimate, and of enmity, suffering, and death, in one word, of evil, in the moral world, was a permanent fact which met the eye and mind everywhere, and required to be accounted for: and whatever account were given of it, the story must from its very nature go back virtually to the commencement of the old world and the first origin of mankind.

Death, being universal, must have begun in the first *father;* and there must have been some other *enemy*, not a man, to slay him: and as he still lives in posterity, he had a *son* by the first mother to survive, and in some sense to avenge him. Men also, in the plural, being at variance, naturally hostile, brother striving against brother, and brother slaying brother, the parts divided between the first man and some other enemy will, in the first generation springing from him, be divided between the first *brothers*. These essential elements of the story being reproduced perpetually, *mutatis mutandis*, in successive generations, a myth embodying them might approach very closely to historical truth without deriving either its names or incidents from historical tradition oral or written. The Egyptian mythology seems in its historical basis to have been in the first instance (as has been said above) wholly postdiluvian; and its human ancestor, *Κρόνος α'*, in the first instance could be no other than Noah, there being no other ancestor probably in the existing world who had died when it was composed. Some time later Ham or Cronus II., the ancestor of the Egyptians and Canaanites, supplanted his father as absolute and universal ancestor, leaving to Noah, between the race of Cain above and the race of Ham below the Flood, only that character of the unnatural father, which had formerly belonged to Uranus. The germ of this is perhaps traceable in Sanchoniathon, who makes *Κρόνος α'* suspect his brother and his children, and slay some of them "so as to astound the Gods." But in the form in which the Greeks received and preserved it this idea is expanded, and becomes the most important part of the myth, Cronus II., or Zeus, i. e. Ham, Ἀμοῦν of the Egyptians, dethroning his real father Cronus I. or Noah, just as Cronus I. before him had dethroned his mythical father Uranus. And so elastic is the character of the mythical ancestor, that he is equally capable of taking up into himself what is historically later, or running back himself into what is historically older. Thus in Sanchoniathon even Cronus I. (before Ham has distinctly supplanted him), the first ancestor and great god of the Egyptians and Phœnicians, is made to be one with Abraham, and, by a confusion of Abraham with Israel, even with

Jacob, sacrificing his only son Ἰεοὺδ (i. e. Ἀγαπητὸν), after the fashion of later Phœnician kings, to his father Uranus, and circumcising himself and his family. And yet again the son of this Cronus, Cronus II. or Ham, a little later is carried back and identified with Uranus and Elioun, i.e. with antediluvian Man, and with Adam himself: and Osiris his son, the father of Thoth, having been put up into the place vacated by his father, becomes by his father's elevation to the head of the antediluvian world, the first brother (i. e. Abel) who was slain, of the three brothers the sons of Adam. And the idea of Humanity slain by its enemy having once been attached to the name of Osiris as son of Cronus and brother of Typhon, it followed lastly, since Humanity had already been slain in the father before it was slain in a son, and by an enemy not human before it was slain by a literal brother, to exalt Osiris, in virtue of his connection with Humanity as slain, to be himself the protoplast, and so identical with Cronus himself, and the source with his consort Isis of that personification of Heaven and Earth, Seb and Nutpe, of which Osiris with his two brothers Typhon and Horus, or with his brother Typhon, is ordinarily in the later mythology named the son.

When the VIII Demigods of the Chronicle, instead of being each one of them by himself a dynasty, like the XIII Gods preceding, are put all of them into one dynasty, XV, this, as has been noticed above, is so arranged, in order to suit the short space of 217 years, into which they are all compressed by reckoning all the time of their survival, and 158 years more, to the XIII antediluvian Gods. Else, if the VIII had had the whole space they really cover allowed them, viz. (658 + 217 = ) 875 years, with an average of 109½ years each, they might have claimed to be each one of them a dynasty by himself, with almost as much reason as the XIII Gods preceding.

The 443 years "of the Cycle" having no place chronologically where they stand, it would be needless to mention them again here, were it not that they are also described as *fifteen generations*, and so seem to add fifteen to the series of human generations from Cronus to Nectanebo. But in truth they are not to be reckoned any more than that "generation" of the Sun-God which stands first of all. These fifteen generations share the nature of the 443 years to which they belong. It is only to give this space of time thrown up a certain similarity to the rest above and below it, that it is thus distributed into fifteen generations at 29½ years each, the generations being, like the years themselves, merely nominal, and at the epoch of the Chronicle as yet future. And if those who have been misled by these generations had been more attentive, they might have seen in the very fact that these alone out of all the CXIII are neither indicated to be *reigns*, nor referred to any one of the XXX Dynasties, a hint of their real nature, over and above that direct information which is given respecting them, when they are described as years or generations "of the Sothic Cycle."

So then in all, before the commencement of the monarchy, we have XV dynasties, one of the Sun-god, XIII of as many antediluvian patriarchs called Gods, and the fifteenth of VIII postdiluvian Demigods; and 37 generations, from which one of the Sun-god and 15 merely nominal being subtracted, the remaining 21 are human, covering (2922 + 217 =) 3139 vague years of Egyptian reckoning, from the beginning to Menes.

To come at last to that part of the Chronicle which gives, in XV more dynasties and 76 generations or reigns, the 1881 (vague) years of the monarchy from Menes to Nectanebo:— Its essential idea requiring the exhibition of a certain continuous space of time, and nothing more, it would necessarily in its dynasties and generations or reigns, whether of Gods, Demigods, or Kings, be strictly successive: and having once exhibited that succession of time which it needed, it would be little likely to touch parenthetically on any of those historical details which were foreign to its purpose. Thus, if it were the case in early times in Egypt, as in other neighbouring countries, that there were a number of kings at once reigning in different parts, in Lower, Middle, and Upper Egypt (and we have the express testimony of Manetho and of others that this was so), the author of the Chronicle would have for those early times to make out his consecutive series either from the kings of some one Egyptian kingdom, or from those of a number of dynasties which successively obtained pre-eminence. And in doing this, if he did not find ready to his hand at every time a distinct and recognised supremacy of one kingdom over the rest, he would have to elect; and if it should have happened that the chief sovereignty during any space of time attached rather to personal character than to any one family or local capital, he would for this space of time be obliged, perhaps, to put together into one dynasty of his own a succession of kings not belonging to the same family or capital, nor occurring together as one series elsewhere. On the other hand, as it was clearly irrelevant to his purpose either to exaggerate or curtail the times of the monarchy or its subdivisions; and the details of history, even so far as they were unavoidably alluded to, were only incidentally connected with his purpose; we have no reason to suspect his estimate of the antiquity of the monarchy, whether always united from the first, or in early times subdivided; unless, indeed, there be any thing to throw a doubt either on his personal ability or means of information. On the contrary, when any native author, such as Manetho or Berosus, makes the national history his professed subject, and offers it to the notice of foreigners, it is to be expected that he will exaggerate rather than curtail the pretensions of his nation both to antiquity and to every other pre-eminence worthy of admiration.

In the list of xv dynasties of kings made out by the author of the Chronicle, on the principle above stated, each dynasty is designated from the capital or nationality of its kings, and has added to this designation the number of its *generations* (not necessarily identical with that of its actual reigns as known from other sources), and lastly the sum of its duration stated in complete years. Such, at least, is the form in which it has reached us. Only it is remarkable that one dynasty of the xv, numbered as XXVII, is altogether anonymous, and is named merely to be coupled with that of the Persians, and to be passed over without specifying either the capital or nationality of its kings, the number of its generations, or the sum of its years. The sum of its years, indeed, 184, it is easy to supply from the total sums of 36,525 for the *ἀποκατάστασις*, and 1881 for the monarchy; and the number of its generations would have been recoverable with equal ease and certainty from the sum total of CXIII, but for the accident that the number of generations is wanting not only to this one dynasty, but also to another, XXIX, from which it has dropped out probably by mere accident. So that all we can collect for certain in the first instance is, that the generations of the two dynasties XXVII and XXIX are together *seven*. Further, it is noticeable that the average length of the generations in the XV dynasties is by no means uniform, but of mixed and artificial adjustment, so as neither to represent the number of actual kings when there chanced to be any very short reigns, nor, on the other hand, to *add* kings when the reigns were really long, merely to prevent long reigns, or years of anarchy or usurpation thrown in, affecting the average. Thus, in Dynasty XXVIII of Persians, where Manetho names VIII kings, the Chronicle, like the Canon of Ptolemy, has only V generations: and though none are named, it manifestly alludes to the five kings Cambyses, Darius, Xerxes, Artaxerxes, and Nothus, consolidating with theirs the short reigns of the false Smerdis, Artabanus, Xerxes II., and Sogdianus. So too usurpers, queens, regents, and even collaterals, who reigned without being distinct generations, may sometimes be omitted. Another cause affecting the average length of the reigns in different dynasties is this, that years of confusion, or of a doubtful character, are added sometimes to that dynasty to which they chronologically adhere. So the time of anarchy or dodecarchy, or continuance of Ethiopian influence, (for Herodotus gives his Ethiopian "above 50 years,") is manifestly prefixed to the Memphitico-Saite Dynasty XXVI, founded by Psammitichus I.

Without closer inquiry into the causes affecting its variations, the average length of reigns or generations, as it stands in each dynasty, is as follows: In Dyn. XVI, 8 generations in 190 years have 33¾ years each; in XVII, 4 in 103 have 25¾; in XVIII 14 in 348, have 25; in XIX, 5 in 194 have 39 years each; in XX, 8 in 228 have 28½ each; in XXI, 6 in 121 have 20 each; in XXII, 3 in 48 have 16 each; in XXIII,

2 in 19 have $9\frac{1}{2}$ each; in XXIV, 3 in 44 have $14\frac{2}{3}$ each; in XXV, 3 in 44 have $14\frac{2}{3}$ each; in XXVI, 7 in 177 have $25\frac{2}{7}$ each; in XXVII, 4 (as we conjecturally supply) in 184 have 46 each; in XXVIII, 5 in 124 have 25 each; in XXIX, 3 (as we conjecturally restore) in 39 have 13; and lastly, in XXX, one generation has 18 years. Or, if any one rather suppose that the anonymous Dynasty XXVII has 5 or 6 generations, with an average of 37 or $30\frac{2}{3}$ years, he must give Dyn. XXIX 2 generations with $19\frac{1}{2}$ years each, or only one with 39 years. Putting all the xv dynasties together, the 76 generations of kings from Menes to Nectanebo have one with another in 1881 years an average of $24\frac{2}{3}$ each.

But we have still to inquire what may be the proper local or national designation of the anonymous Dynasty XXVII? and further, what may be its true place? for the Memphitico-Saite dynasty preceding, and the Persian following it, belong both of them to times during which Egypt was known to the Greeks; and manifestly there is no room for any dynasty at all, still less for one with 184 years, either between Dyn. XXVI and the Persians, or between the Persians and Dyn. XXIX. So Dyn. XXVII has either been stripped of all particulars *and* misplaced by a complication of accidents, or it has been made anonymous and all but suppressed, and coupled with the dynasty of the Persian fire-worshippers, under whom Egypt had suffered so much, and whom the Macedonians had overthrown, *purposely*. That this last is really the case we cannot doubt, when we reflect that Dyn. XVIII is known to have been preceded by a dynasty of "strangers," Shepherds, who according to Manetho "took Memphis, made both Upper and Lower Egypt tributary, and held the native kings in their hands;" while, according to Herodotus, the memory of those Memphite kings who were contemporaries and vassals of the Shepherds was so odious to the later Egyptians, that they did not willingly so much as name them. And Josephus, quoting not from Manetho as re-edited by others, but from the original Manetho himself, gives us six Shepherd kings, with their names and years, as immediately preceding in Manetho another series identifiable with Dynasties XVIII and XIX of the Chronicle. Dyn. XXVII then of the Chronicle is to be put up to its true place between XVII and XVIII, and filled up thus: "Ἔπειτα κζ′ [which properly, however, should have been ιη′] δυναστεία Ποιμένων [Παλαιστίνων, Ἀράβων, or Φοινίκων] ξένων βασιλέων, γενεῶν δ′, ἐτῶν ρπδ′." It is true that Josephus, as has just been said, gives from Manetho not 4 but 6 kings, who are not at all too many for 184 years (they have according to Manetho 259.10ᵐ.); and we *know* that in other dynasties, as in XVI, Manetho has preserved the true number of kings, while adding to their years, so as to justify a suspicion that here also his 6 kings may be the true number, and his sum of 259.10ᵐ. for their years an exaggeration. But on the other hand Manetho has 4 kings for only a part (20 or 21 years) of the 39 years of Dyn. XXIX; and only one of these 4 has so short a reign as would *certainly* be suppressed in the Chronicle; while it is highly probable that the Shepherds, if really strangers, may have settled in the Delta some time before they "took Memphis" and became lords paramount of all Egypt: and their kings seem, from other indications, to have been longlived. So it may be safest to leave both the names and the figures of Manetho as they stand in Josephus, only borrowing from them the last 184 years of the last four of the six reigns, to form Dynasty XXVII of the Chronicle.

Having thus restored and filled up the dynasties, we may consider their general order and designations, noticing first, that the Chronicle seems to describe all the native dynasties from their capitals, naming not always the city with which any family of kings was directly connected by origin, or which they preferred to be their personal residence, but rather that one of the most ancient and permanent capitals of Lower, Middle, or Upper Egypt, with which their own city, if different, was more naturally connected. In this way the author, speaking generally, recognises only *three* great capitals, viz. those of Tanis, Memphis, and Thebes: and in introducing these three, he seems to follow a certain order of historical succession. The monarchy, according to the Chronicle, begins not from any inconsiderable place in

Upper Egypt, exhibiting no traces of having ever been a capital, nor from the unexplained migration of some citizen of such a place to found the first dynasty in Lower Egypt, and reign with his successors in a capital from which they are not named; but it begins from Tanis, the Zoan of Sacred Scripture, in the Delta, a city which still in the time of the Romans showed traces of its ancient greatness. And with this the notices of Sacred Scripture agree, recording in the history of Abram how Hebron, where he found the children of Heth, had been built somewhat earlier, "nine years before Zoan in Egypt," as if Zoan were then the Egyptian city of most note for power and antiquity. And even so late as the time of Moses, under the first kings of Dyn. XVIII, the miracles preceding the Exodus are connected, not with Memphis, still less with Thebes; but with "the land of Zoan," and "the field of Zoan." And even Manetho himself, whose designation of Menes as Θενίτης, Θεινίτης, or Θεεινίτης (possibly a purposed variation from Τανίτης), has led all later writers into error on this important point, goes much further by the details which he relates to show that the Egyptian monarchy began from Tanis, if we are to choose between Tanis and This (Teni,) than any mere name, even if This were ever so clearly and uniformly written from the first, could go towards proving the contrary. For after Menes, who, according to Herodotus, founded Memphis, Manetho relates of the second king of his first dynasty of Thinites, Athothis, that he built the palace there, and of the fourth king, that he began the earliest of the pyramids at Κωχώμη (Ka-khem?) which is intelligible enough if the development of Egypt was from the north southwards; the first offshoot from Tanis being Heliopolis, on the same eastern side of the Nile, then Memphis growing up as its cemetery on the opposite western side, and precisely for that reason because it was to the west, under the Libyan hill. There being neither rocks nor quarries about Tanis, to move up to the vicinity of Heliopolis and Memphis, where they had both the mountain on the eastern side for quarrying, and the desert sand and hill on the west side for burial, was natural: and so the earliest kings having built only with bricks of earth, a later king may have "introduced the use of squared stones." But, if they had been reigning at This or Abydos from the first, it is inconceivable that they should have moved down to the vicinity of Memphis to seek a place either for their quarries or their tombs. Again, under a very early king, Boethos or Bochos, second of his second dynasty of Thinites, Manetho records the deification of the bulls Apis and Mnevis of Memphis and Heliopolis, and of the goat of Mendes; and the opening of a chasm by an earthquake near Bubastis, these four places being all within the same part of Egypt with the capital, if Tanis were then the capital, but quite remote from This or Abydos. And the Phœnician Sanchoniathon, as we have seen, relates that Cronus, i. e. Ham, "going southwards" (from Phœnicia), "gave Egypt to Thoth, the son of Misor, to be his kingdom," hinting plainly that its settlement and the origin of its monarchy was from the north. So strong, indeed, are the indications from on all sides, that even they who persist in making Dyn. XVI of the Chronicle, and I and II of the Manetho of Africanus and Eusebius, to be Thinite, explain away their own supposition by allowing that the capital of all these early kings was in lower Egypt: only, they say, it is possible that Menes, and in him his successors, were by family origin from This. But the Chronicle certainly does not name its dynasties from the origin of individuals, nor even from the favourite residences or birth-places of their kings; but beginning from Tanis in the north it moves southwards in its second dynasty of kings (Dyn. XVII) to Memphis: and even its fourth, Dynasty XVIII (the shepherds of XXVII being the third), is still called "Memphite," no doubt for some reason allowable in the eyes of a native of Lower Egypt, though it is more commonly and more properly called Diospolite; while the Memphite priests who conversed with Herodotus thought they had some pretext for ignoring it altogether as Ethiopian; an astonishing hint of the depth and tenacity of the jealousies subsisting between the ancient capitals ages after they had both been to a great extent supplanted by other cities. Dynasties XIX and XX are in the Chronicle Diospolitan. In XXI the kings are again from

Lower Egypt; and though we know from other sources that they really made Bubastis their chief residence and capital, and left there their chief monuments, the dynasty is named in the Chronicle Tanite, from Tanis, the elder capital of that part of Egypt to which Bubastis belonged. In like manner Dynasties XXII, XXIX, and XXX, are all named Tanite, though there may have been some family connection of the kings of XXIX with Mendes, and of XXX with Sebennys, so as to afford later writers, such as Manetho the Sebennyte, and Ptolemy the Mendesian, some colour for complimenting their native cities by giving titles from them to the last two dynasties. Sais being on the western arm of the Nile, the kings of Dynasty XXVI of the Chronicle, nidisputably Saites by origin, residence, and burial, are named by it Memphites; and undoubtedly Memphis under them, as Tanis under the Bubastites, retained its ancient honour and titular primacy; and they left monuments, as is related by Herodotus, no less at Memphis than at Sais. The only exception to his general method of designating the dynasties admitted by the author of the Chronicle is in the case of Dyn. XXIV, which he names from the personal connection of its kings, Saite; but his special motive for doing this is discernible. It is a feeling like that which made him all but suppress the dynasty of the Shepherds: for Bocchoris, who lost miserably his kingdom and his life, being burned alive by the Ethiopian Sabaco, could do no credit to any of the ancient capitals: it was better, therefore, to confine such a reign and family to its own local origin and connection.

Of the 40 years between Nectanebo and the Lagidæ and the 443 between B.C. 305 and A.D. 139 thrown up; of the reasons for throwing them up not in one sum but separately, indicating the 443 years, and describing them as belonging to "the Cycle," and as being (i.e. being equal to) XV generations, but neither making any generation of the 40 nor distinguishing them at all; as also of the proof that the interval between Nectanebo and B.C. 305 is really intended by the author of the Chronicle to be 40 years, and the epoch of the conquest by Ochus to be B.C. 345, enough has been said above. It has also been noticed how the presence of an addition of precisely 40 years in the years reckoned to the XIII Gods by the Chronicle, is incidentally revealed by the structure of that earlier scheme of the ἀποκατάστασις, which made 24 cycles of month-years out of two of full, and ended its 25th cycle at B.C. 1322. To these topics then we need not return in detail. But, as the result and conclusion of this whole examination of the Chronicle, we shall apply the Egyptian scale of the Chronicle to that sacred scale which we have obtained from the Scriptures and Josephus, so that the true expiration of the 443 years of the twenty-fifth cycle, and the end of the last day of the epagomenæ of the Egyptian vague year, may coincide with some point in the morning of July 20 of the Julian year after Christ 139, according to the vulgar era. Then, reducing the Egyptian vague years to Julian by marking the first of Thoth one day later in the Julian calendar every fourth year as we go backward, and having thus gone up with a joint synchronistic reckoning in terms of the Julian calendar from A.D. 139, B.C. 305, and B.C. 345, to Thoth 1, coinciding with April 24, in the Julian year B.C. 5355, we shall then add, for convenience, to our sacred scale those 6 years by which the Egyptian scale seems to exceed the sum of Josephus, and to agree with that of the LXX. for the time before the Flood. Thus our sacred reckoning, instead of falling short of the head of the Egyptian by 5 years and some 4 months, will accompany the Egyptian up to its head at Thoth 1, coinciding with April 26, in the Julian year B.C. 5361, and rise some 8 months higher to the autumn preceding, in B.C. 5362, these 8 months being a fraction cut off by the Egyptians in order to begin with the first day of their vague year. This being done, we may re-descend the combined scale from April 26, B.C. 5361, noticing as we go the more important dates and synchronisms, which will come out as follows:—

First, instead of the true date of the end of the year of the Flood, in Sept. B.C. 3100, or of the last survivor of the patriarchs born before the Flood (in B.C. 2600), or that of the Dispersion, or of the Settlement of Egypt, being marked, 2920 Julian years, a space equal to two Sothic cycles, are given by the Egyptians to the XIII Gods, in faint allusion to the old world, which so is prolonged to April 26, B.C. 2441, 658 years and nearly 8 months after the completion of the year of the Flood; 158 years and 8 months after the death of Shem; and 80 years before the death of Peleg.

Next, 217 years only from the above date (but 875 from the end of the Flood), being given to VIII postdiluvian generations of Demigods, the head of the Egyptian monarchy appears with Menes, at March 3, B.C. 2224, in the 876th year after the year of the Flood, 65 years nearly before the birth of Abraham, whose 75th year will end two months after the 140th of the Tanite Dynasty XVI of the Chronicle, (which ends Jan. 27, B.C. 2084,) and the birth of Isaac will be in the beginning of its 165th year, B.C. 2059.

The birth of Jacob, in B.C. 1999, will be in the beginning of the 36th year of the Memphite Dynasty XVII of the Chronicle; the sale of Joseph, then aged 17, to Petephra (i.e. beloved by Ra, the god of Heliopolis), in B.C. 1891, will be early in the 41st year of Dynasty XXVII of the Shepherds; his exaltation when aged 30, in B.C. 1878, will be early in its 54th; his reception of his father and brethren, B.C. 1869 (Jacob being then 130 years old), will be in its 63rd; and the death of Joseph, B.C. 1798, in its 134th. The commencement of Dynasty XVIII of the Chronicle, which it designates as Memphite, but which others call Theban, and even Ethiopian, when "another king arose who had not known Joseph," appears at Nov. 4, B.C. 1748, 50 years and about 7 months after Joseph's death. The birth of Moses, 3 years after that of Aaron, is in the 14th year of this dynasty, B.C. 1734; his flight from Egypt in its 54th, B.C. 1694; his mission from the burning bush on mount Sinai at the end of its 93rd, i.e. on or after Nov. 12, B.C. 1655; and the Exodus in its 94th, at the passover of B.C. 1654; the death of Moses in its 134th, B.C. 1614; that of Joshua in its 159th, B.C. 1589; the death of the last of the Elders who outlived Joshua in its 169th, B.C. 1579. So the 8 years of the first servitude under Cushan-Rishathaim, king of the "Shasoo" of Arabia, and of Mesopotamia, lie between the 169th and 177th years of Dynasty XVIII, B.C. 1579, and B.C. 1571;

the 40 of Othniel reach to its 217th in B.C. 1531; the 18 years of servitude under Eglon, king of Moab, are from its 217th to its 235th, B.C. 1531 to 1513; the 80 of Ehud and Shamgar are from its 235th to its 315th, B.C. 1513 to B.C. 1433; the 20 of servitude to Jabin, king of Canaan, are from its 315th to its 335th, B.C. 1433 to 1413. In the 14th of Deborah, Aug. 19, B.C. 1400, we find the commencement of a new dynasty of the Chronicle, viz. XIX, the first which it names Diospolite. The 7 years of servitude to Midian begin in the 27th, and end in the 34th of this dynasty, B.C. 1373 to 1366. The 40 of Gideon end in its 74th, B.C. 1326; the 3 of Abimelech in its 77th, B.C. 1323. The epoch of the Sothic Cycle, July 20, B.C. 1322, in the 2nd year of Tola, is at the end of the 78th year and the beginning of the 79th of Dynasty XIX; 903 vague years, or 902 years and between 4 and 5 months of Julian reckoning, from Menes; 978 vague years, or 977 years and nearly 4 months Julian, before the conquest by Darius Ochus. The 23rd year of Tola ends in the 100th of Dynasty XIX, B.C. 1300. The 22 years of Jair end in its 122nd, B.C. 1278; the 18 of servitude to the Ammonites end in its 140th, B.C. 1260; the 6 of Jephthah in its 146th, B.C. 1254; the 7 of Ibzan in its 153rd, B.C. 1247; the 10 of Elon in its 163rd, B.C. 1237; and the 8 of Abdon in its 171st, B.C. 1229. The 40 years of the Philistines, which include the 20 of Samson, end in the 17th year of Dynasty XX of the Chronicle, also Diospolite, B.C. 1189; the 40 of Eli end in the 57th of the same, B.C. 1149; the 20 of Samuel's minority in the 77th of the same, B.C. 1129; the 32 during which Samuel governed alone in the 109th of the same, B.C. 1097. The first 20 of Saul, reigning conjointly with Samuel, end in the 129th year of the same, B.C. 1077; and from this point commence the 490 years of neglect, to be followed by 70 of penal desolation. The remaining 20 years of Saul, reigning alone, end in the 149th of Dynasty XX, B.C. 1057; the 7th of David in Hebron ends in its 156th, B.C. 1051 (so that Jerusalem was reduced in the autumn following); the 40th of David ends in its 189th, B.C. 1017; and the 4th of Solomon (in which the Temple was founded) is completed in the

193rd of this dynasty, in the spring of B.C. 1013. Solomon's 40th year ends nearly together with the first year of the Tanite Dynasty XXI of the Chronicle; for the 1st day of the movable Thoth was in B.C. 977 at April 25. The 5th of Rehoboam nearly coincides with the 6th of Dynasty XXI, ending in the spring of B.C. 972. So then the first king of Dynasty XXI is apparently the Shishak or Σουσακεὶμ, to whom Jeroboam fled *before the death of Solomon* (the expression in the LXX. *may* imply that this was only just before the death of Solomon), and who took Jerusalem in the 5th year of Rehoboam. But if any one think that the words of Scripture imply that Jeroboam fled into Egypt *before* the last year of Solomon's reign, he may consider that, even if this were so, it is not necessary to suppose that the epoch at which the Chronicle puts the commencement of its Dynasty XXI is also that of the first accession of its first king, supposing him to be the Shishak of the Scriptures. It is possible that there may have been about this time two royal houses, one of Diospolites in Upper Egypt, and one of Tanites in the Delta; and that the author of the Chronicle puts the commencement of a new Tanite dynasty only at B.C. 978, and no higher, because it was then only that the Tanite family, which may have been independent, or only nominally dependent on the Theban kings, for some time before, became the undisputed sovereigns of Upper Egypt also, and of Thebes, where the reduction of Judæa by Shishonk I. is still seen recorded on the walls of the great temple of Karnak. In this case this same Shishonk of the Theban temple, nay, and even his father or fathers before him, may have been reigning at Tanis or Bubastis many years before the death of Solomon, whose Egyptian queen may have been of the Diospolite family, then declining, and seeking to strengthen itself; while Hadad and Jeroboam may have fled to the Tanite princes of the Delta: and not only the name Shishonk, but that of Tahpenes, the queen, whose sister was given in marriage to Hadad some 20 years perhaps before the death of Solomon, may be thought to look the same way. But to return: Dynasty XXII of the Chronicle, also of Tanites, begins March 26, B.C. 857, and ends March 15, B.C. 809; Dynasty

XXIII of Diospolites ends March 9, B.C. 790; Dynasty XXIV of Saites ends Feb. 26, B.C. 746. The capture of Samaria, 256 years after the accession of Rehoboam, early in the 6th of Hezekiah, will be in B.C. 721, after the end of the 25th year of the Ethiopian Dynasty XXV of the Chronicle; and the 14th of Hezekiah will be still current at the end of its 34th year, in the spring of B.C. 712. So then the "king of Egypt" called Σωὰ, Sua, or Σηγὼρ, in the Book of Kings, who was reigning somewhat earlier than the spring of B.C. 724, and another called Tirhakah, *Τάρακος*, "king of Ethiopia," who was reigning in the 14th of Hezekiah, are put by the Scriptures within the space of this Ethiopian dynasty, which however may have ruled Egypt indirectly as suzerains, if not directly and personally, for a longer period than 44 years. Herodotus says expressly that Sabaco (under which one name he means all the three Ethiopian kings) ruled over Egypt for "50 years." Nor would this be in contradiction with the Chronicle, the author of which no doubt reduced the foreign dynasty within the narrowest limits justifiable, making it begin from the actual conquest, but making it end, perhaps, as soon as Tirhakah ceased to reside personally in Egypt; and his monuments in Nubia show that in his later years he fixed his capital at Napata (now Mount Barkal), of which he was in a manner the founder, and which is far above the second cataract.

The 177 years of the "Memphite" Dynasty XXVI of the Chronicle, which follows next after the Ethiopians, (Dyn. XXVII of the Shepherds being to be restored to its true place above, between XVII and XVIII), will lie between Feb. 15, B.C. 702, and Jan. 2, B.C. 525, containing at its head some continuance of Ethiopian supremacy, and a subdivision of Egypt between rival princes, called by Herodotus a dodecarchy, by Diodorus Siculus anarchy. Herodotus gives 54 + 16 + 6 + 25 + 44, in all 145 years, to the 5 reigns of this dynasty (whose kings made their personal residence chiefly at Sais), from Psammitichus I., who was really its founder, to Amasis inclusively. So, if Herodotus were rightly informed, the actual commencement of the dynasty would be Feb. 8, B.C. 670, towards the end of the 27th year of

Manasseh, 32 years later than its commencement in the Chronicle; and these 32 years reckoned to it by the author of the Chronicle would cover whatever continuance there was of Ethiopian sovereignty, and the time of subdivision, anarchy, or dodecarchy. But according to the monuments there seem to have been only 138 years to the five reigns, which so began in B.C. 663.

In the 95th year of this dynasty, beginning Jan. 23, B.C. 609, 112, years from the capture of Samaria, we find the defeat and death of Josiah; and consequently we must suppose a king named Necho, the Nekos of Herodotus, to have been then on the throne, either alone, or perhaps associated with his father; for Psammitichus, according to Herodotus, had a long reign of 54 years. But if we reckon up from Jan. 5, B.C. 525 with Herodotus (who was in Egypt about B.C. 450, that is 145 years before the epoch of the Chronicle), 44 years of Amasis, + 25 of Apries, + 6 of Psammis, + 16 of Nekos, in all 91 years, it appears that the 16 years of this king should lie between Jan. 26, B.C. 616, and Jan. 22, B.C. 600. By the monuments, however, which correct Herodotus, there are 7 years less, and the reign of Necho lies between B.C. 609 and 594, so that the date of the death of Josiah appears early in the second year of his reign: and the Prophet Jeremiah names this same Necho as the King of Egypt defeated by Nebuchadnezzar, at Carchemish, 3 years and some months later, in the 4th of Jehoiakim, B.C. 605.

Again, after the destruction of the Temple, on the 7th day of the 5th month, in the 19th of Nebuchadnezzar, i. e. in B.C. 587, and after the death of Gedaliah, two months later, the remnant of the Jews are said to have fled to Hophra, or Apries, king of Egypt. Now according to Herodotus, the reign of Apries, of 25 years, lies between Jan. 19, B.C. 594, and Jan. 13, B.C. 569; but according to the monuments it seems to lie between Jan. 18, B.C. 588 and Jan. 13, 569. So the monuments too (as well as Herodotus) exhibit this synchronism. Of the lists of Manetho, and other writers later than the author of the Chronicle, we need say nothing for the present.

The Persian Dynasty XXVIII of the Chronicle beginning from Jan. 2, B.C. 525, with the 5th year of Cambyses (this year containing both the 6 months of Psammenitus and the conquest of Egypt), the 4th of Darius Hystaspes. with which ended the 70 years' captivity, Dec. 31, B.C. 518, will be its 8th; and its 124th and last will end Dec, 2, B.C. 402, with the 3rd year of Artaxerxes Longimanus. The 39 years of the Tanite Dynasty XXIX beginning thence, will end Dec. 23, B.C. 363, after Ochus had already reigned 2 years in Persia as associated with his father.

And, lastly, the 18th of the Tanite Dynasty XXX of the Chronicle will end Nov. 18, B.C. 345, 6 years before the murder of Ochus by Bagoas; 9 before the Macedonian accession of Alexander, and the accession of Darius Codomannus in Persia; 11 before the crossing of Alexander into Asia in B.C. 334; 13 before his first entry into Egypt in B.C. 332; 14 before the Egyptian Era of Alexandria and the battle of Arbela; and, lastly, 15 before "the *cosmocracy* of Alexander," the cosmocracy being reckoned from after the death of Darius, Nov. 14, B.C. 330. Also, as we have seen, a point of time 443 vague years above July 20, A.D. 139 of the vulgar era, i.e. Nov. 8, B.C. 305, is marked in the Chronicle, by the specification and entry above of "443 years of the Cycle," as being the epoch of some event connected with its scheme; and this event, we understand at once from the date, must be the assumption of a crown by the Lagidæ.

## CHAP. II.

### MANETHO.

On the overthrow of the Persian Empire, and the foundation of the Græco-Syrian and Egyptian kingdoms, it was natural that the conquerors should show some curiosity about the antiquities of those nations with which their own race was to blend: and under kings who founded the library of Alexandria, and drew to it the most learned men of Greece, such as Demetrius Phalereus, Eratosthenes, and Apollodorus, and caused the sacred books of the Jews, settled in multitudes in their capital, to be translated, it was not likely that any long time would pass before some member of the Egyptian priesthood, master of both languages, would offer to his sovereign, in Greek, a detailed account of the national religion, philosophy, and history. This was done by Manetho, a native of Sebennys, one of the chief priests at Heliopolis, who is said to have dedicated his Αἰγυπτιακὰ (probably about B.C. 276) to Ptolemy Philadelphus, a little after Berosus, under similar circumstances and influences, had dedicated his Χαλδαϊκὰ, in three books, to Antiochus Θεός. Berosus was advanced in age when he wrote, as he had lived, according to his own account, under Alexander the Great; and after the death of Alexander he had travelled and resided in Greece: and Manetho, though younger, seems to have been already at the head of the Egyptian priesthood under Ptolemy Lagi, if, as is probable, the Manetho of Sebennys consulted about the image of Pluto brought from Pontus and identified with Serapis be the same as the historian. (*Plutarch De Is.*, c. 28.) It is supposed that Manetho had the work of Berosus before him when he wrote, (Syncellus says he wrote *κατὰ μίμησιν Βηρώσσου*,) so that he may have borrowed from it, and may have made his own work purposely parallel with it, or counter to it, in some details.

Besides being acquainted with the Chaldaica of Berosus, Manetho, according to the opinion of Africanus, adopted by Eusebius, followed to a certain extent "the Chronicle," (the oldest thing of the kind extant in the Greek language,) though he varied much from it, both in his sums of years and in other details.

The work of Manetho established its author as the chief and most copious authority on the subjects of which he treated, just as Berosus had become the great authority on Chaldæan antiquities. But though this was so, and though his name is extolled by later writers when Egyptian history is mentioned, it seems that, from some cause or other, his genuine work was superseded about the time of the Christian era by an abridged and altered edition, which still went under his name. From an Egyptian list compiled by Eratosthenes, but copied by Syncellus from Apollodorus, and from a notice taken by Syncellus no doubt from the same source, that "the chronographer had collected from Manetho" a certain sum of the years of the Kings to Nectanebo or Alexander, we see that the genuine work of Manetho was still extant, and no other mentioned, as late as the year B.C. 141, when Apollodorus ended his chronography. But Diodorus, who was in Egypt in the time of Ptolemy surnamed *Νέος Διόνυσος*, Ol. 180, B.C. 58, makes no mention of Manetho: and Josephus, writing against Apion at Rome under Domitian, quotes with such emphasis from "Manetho *himself*," as perhaps to imply that the Manetho then most known, and quoted by his adversary Apion and by others, was not the original, and that it was only recently, and owing to a special cause, that he had himself become acquainted with the genuine text. For a fire having consumed the Portico of Octavia with its library, the Emperor Domitian, no great patron of learning at other times, showed, as Suetonius relates, an extraordinary zeal for the reparation of this damage, causing duplicates of some books, and fresh copies of others made on purpose, to be brought from different libraries, especially from the great library of Alexandria, where the genuine work of Manetho himself had been originally deposited, and was certainly preserved, and whence a copy of it, or even the original itself, was then in consequence brought to Rome. Plutarch and Ælian, who also quote the genuine Manetho, became acquainted with him no doubt through the same accident as Josephus, as they too are known to have been at Rome. But in the East itself we have no clear mention of the genuine Manetho later than the time of Apollodorus. And already in the first century of the Christian era Tatian, a Christian writer born in Babylonia, when touching on Egyptian history in such a way as to make one expect that he is about to name Manetho, names *not* Manetho but another writer, Ptolemy of Mendes, as the great authority on this subject:—"*Αἰγυπτίων δέ εἰσιν ἀκριβεῖς χρόνων ἀναγραφαὶ, καὶ τῶν κατ' αὐτοὺς γραμμάτων ἑρμηνεὺς Πτολεμαῖος, οὐχ ὁ βασιλεὺς, ἱερεὺς δὲ Μένδητος.*" (*Euseb. Præp. Ev.*, x.12.) And then, after quoting him for the synchronism of Amosis, Moses, and Inachus, he adds that *Apion* also, the same writer against whom Josephus was writing at Rome when he quoted with such emphasis Manetho himself, follows Ptolemy of Mendes, being, as it would seem, not long after his time:—"*Μετὰ δὲ τοῦτον Ἀπίων ὁ γραμματικὸς, ἀνὴρ δοκιμώτατος, ἐν τῇ δ' τῶν Αἰγυπτιακῶν...φησὶ δ' ὅτι κατέσκαψε τὴν Αὔαριν ὁ Ἄμωσις, κατὰ τὸν Ἀργεῖον γενόμενος Ἴναχον, ὡς ἐν τοῖς Χρόνοις [Χρονικοῖς?] ἀνέγραψεν ὁ Μενδήσιος Πτολεμαῖος.*" But if Apion, who was himself by birth an Egyptian, and the author of a work entitled like that of Manetho *Αἰγυπτιακὰ*, quoted not Manetho, but Ptolemy, this agrees well with the language of Tatian, who says that in his time Ptolemy was the great authority. What is still wanting is, first, something to show more distinctly that the work of Ptolemy was in fact an abridgment and re-edition of Manetho; and then further, something to explain how it came to pass that the genuine work of Manetho himself should have been so little circulated and so completely supplanted even in Egypt by a later re-edition.

As to the first point this may help us, that Ptolemy of Mendes is said to have written *Αἰγυπτιακὰ in three books*, which so far agrees with the title and division of Manetho; while Suidas, besides the original "Μανεθῶ Σεβεννύτης" of Sebennys, has also another "Μαναίθως Μένδης" of *Mendes;* the Mendesian Manetho being no doubt Ptolemy. And whereas from the time of Africanus downwards those lists and conjoined notices which he has preserved have been in possession of the name of Manetho, though they show by internal disagreements, and by mentioning both Manetho and other sources, as the Chronicle, that they cannot possibly be the original work of Manetho himself, the same lists of Africanus, by their brief chronicle-like form, answer well to the title Χρόνοι, Χρονικὰ, given by Tatian and others to the work of Ptolemy; the extracts given by Josephus from the original Manetho being in a very different diffuse style. In this too the Manetho of Africanus agrees with the character given to Ptolemy of Mendes, that he marks a number of Greek synchronisms, especially that of Amosis and Inachus, for which Ptolemy is expressly quoted by Apion and Tatian, and by other Christian writers following Tatian: and it is related of Ptolemy that he was exact in his Greek chronology, having profited no doubt by those writings of Eratosthenes, Apollodorus, and others, which were all posterior to the time of the original Manetho. Lastly, it is significant, though not perhaps of itself conclusive, that whereas the two last native dynasties, XXIX and XXX, are in the Chronicle both called *Tanite*, in the Manetho of Africanus the first of them is named, from the native city of Ptolemy, "*Mendesian*," the second, from that of Manetho, "*Sebennyte;*" though neither the one city nor the other is ever mentioned elsewhere as having been the actual capital or royal residence even for a single reign.

As regards the other question, how the original work of a writer of such note as Manetho came to be superseded by an abridgment and re-edition, we have some grounds at least for a probable conjecture. It seems certain that Manetho, by his myriads of years divided among Gods, Demigods, Heroes, and Kings before and after Menes, had obtained more ridicule than admiration from Greek readers; and his account not seeming satisfactory, Eratosthenes, the second librarian at Alexandria, himself the father of Greek chronology, attempted at the king's desire to reduce the dynasties of Manetho to one consecutive series of kings within the limits allowed by the Chronicle. And this he did, *except that* he yielded so far to the priests whom he consulted, as to include within the times of the monarchy those "XV generations and 443 years of the Cynic Cycle" which in the Chronicle were entered between the Demigods and Menes. But all reigns above or beyond these, whether in the Chronicle or in Manetho, he disallowed as antehistorical and fabulous, or as at best only contemporary and subordinate. It may be imagined that this method was not to the taste of the native priesthood, and that they would not accept such an exposition of their history made, with whatever extorted assistance, by a Greek; an exposition, too, which gave no account of many kings who had certainly existed. So, somewhat later, Ptolemy of Mendes (or whoever was the author of the Manetho of Africanus), thinking that the chief stumbling-block for the Greeks lay in the "myriads of years," undertook to explain the origin of these myriads which seemed so incredible, confessing them to be merely months, reducible to one-twelfth of their apparent bulk: but at the same time, as if to compensate for this concession, he not only retained and reasserted, but he even amplified the vast antiquity claimed by Manetho for Egyptian history and civilisation after Menes. And as the Chronicle, which Manetho had plainly used as one of his sources, exhibited both an older and a fuller form of those "myriads of years" which it was now proposed to explain and reduce, and for reduction the larger sum was the most convenient (Manetho having some 6000 or 7000 years less than the Chronicle), it was natural for Ptolemy of Mendes to give an account in his preface of a document which he meant to use. In this way probably it was that Africanus came to find in that re-edition of Manetho which he followed not only lists really extracted from Manetho, with additions and alterations, but also an Introduction giving some account of the principle of reduction on which this re-edition of Manetho was based, and of the Chronicle, the sum of which, though departed from by Manetho, was now returned to, and preferred by the writer to that of Manetho himself.

Thus much premised, we shall exhibit from Eusebius and Syncellus all that is certainly from the Manetho of Africanus, omitting what relates to the Chronicle, and to the reduction of those myriads of years which seemed incredible; notices which, though taken no doubt by Africanus from the same *book* with his Manethonian lists, i. e. from its *introduction*, actually name Manetho as not the same but another writer. Neither shall we notice those alterations which Eusebius, for purposes of his own, has made in copying out the lists of Africanus; nor anything which Syncellus may have found only in that latest pseudo-Manetho, the Sothis of Anianus and Panodorus, which he himself chiefly follows. But after placing before the reader in outline the Manetho of Africanus, we shall compare therewith those earlier notices which we have of the original work of Manetho the Sebennyte, and see how far they help us to decompose the later work of Ptolemy, and to reconstruct out of materials afforded by it the outline of the original.

We extract then from Eusebius, as making towards our purpose, the following words and enumerations (*Chron.* l. i. c. 19, 20, *Lat. Vers. ex Armen. Ed. A. Mai.*):

" Here it will be convenient to insert also the Egyptian accounts *from Manetho*, who seems to be the chief authority for that branch of history: [From the

INTRODUCTION

prefixed to the Manetho of Ptolemy of Mendes used by Africanus:]

[I.] "The first *God* of the Egyptians is Vulcan [Phtha];
From him was the Sun [i. e. Ra];
After the Sun, Agathodæmon [i. e. Cneph];
Then Saturn [i. e. Seb],
Then Osiris,
Then Typhon, brother of Osiris,
*Lastly* Horus, son of Osiris and Isis.

" These *first* reigned over the Egyptians.

[II.] " *Then* there reigned in succession others [i. e. other

*Gods*] down to Bytis, in a space of years amounting [for all the Gods together] to . . 13,900.

[Of which 900 are originally full years, equal to 10,800 month-years; and the rest are month-years, equivalent to 1083 full years and 4 months; making together 1983 full years and 4 months.]

| | | |
|---|---|---|
| [III.] | " *After the Gods* reigned Heroes years . . | 1255 |
| [IV.] | " And again other Kings [also Heroes? or, xxx Kings, Diospolites?] ruled years . | 1817 |
| [V.] | " Then other xxx Kings, Memphites, years | 1790 |
| [VI.] | " Then other x Kings, Thinites, years . . | 350 |
| [VII.] | " After these there followed a rule (*Dominatio*, dynasty) of Manes and Heroes [or, cvi Kings, Nubians?] during years . . | 5813 |

"The sum [after the Gods] amounts to 11,000 [month] years;" [equal to 916 full years and 8 months:]

"And the whole space of time during which, as the Egyptians say, the Gods, Heroes [i. e. Demigods], and Manes reigned, is reckoned to be 24,900 years." [Of these 900 only being originally full years, and the rest months, the true sum of full years is 2900.]

"Then follows [i. e. in Africanus] an enumeration of *thirty* Dynasties from Menes to Nectanebo II., which we" (continues Eusebius) "shall give immediately."

But instead of taking these from Eusebius, who has so altered them, especially the last fifteen or sixteen, that Syncellus imagined he must have used a different "edition" of Manetho from Africanus, we here have recourse to Syncellus.

"Of the dynasties of Egypt *after the Flood*, according to Africanus:" [Africanus understanding those of the Gods and Demigods to belong to the antediluvian world:]

[BOOK I. OF MANETHO,

according to the re-edition of Ptolemy of Mendes, who had thrown back all that related to the vii mythical groups of Gods, Demigods, and Manes, as well as other matter relating to the Old Chronicle, into an Introduction prefixed to the Three Books.]

"After the Manes and Demigods" [whose dynasties are understood by Africanus to be *after* the Flood, but before Menes], "is reckoned,

" *Dyn. I.* [*VIII.*] *of* VIII *Kings: of whom*—

1. Menes, a Thinite, first reigned years . . . . . 62
2. Athothis, his son, who built the palace at Memphis . 57
3. Kenkenes, his son . . . 31
4. Ouenephes, his son (under whom was a great famine. He first began to build the pyramids at Kochome) . 23
5. Ousaphaidos, his son [Ousaphaes, *Euseb.*] . . . . 20
6. Miebidos, his son (Niebaes, *Euseb.*) ' . . . . . 26
7. Semempses, his son, in whose time there was a great plague [" many prodigies, and a very great plague," *Euseb.*] . . . . . 18
8. Bieneches, his son (Oubienthes, *Euseb.*) . . . . 26

"Sum 253 263

[Eusebius introduces this dynasty with some additional words of Africanus, alluding to a plurality of writers instead of one Manetho, thus: "Of whom the first was Menes, a ruler who merited renown; from whom *they* that have registered the kings of each race deduce the succession as follows:—' 1. Menes of This, and his descendants, seven in number,' &c."]

" *Dyn. II.* [*IX.*] *of* IX *Thinites:*

1. Boethus (Bochus, *Euseb.*) *in whose time* the earth opened near Bubastis, and many perished . . . years 38
2. Kaiechos (Chous, *Euseb.*), in whose time the Bulls Apis at *Memphis*, and Mnevis at *Heliopolis*, and the Goat of *Mendes*, were [first] accounted to be Gods . . 39

Carried forward 77

Brought forward 77

3. Binothris (Biophis, *Euseb.*), in whose time it was decided that women might reign . . . . . . 47
4. Tlas . . . . . . . 17
5. Sethenes . . . . . 41
6. Chaires . . . . . . 17
7. Nephercheres, in whose time it is related mythically that the Nile ran for eleven days mixed with honey . . 25
8. Sesochris, whose height was five cubits and three palms 48
9. Chéneres . . . . . 30

" Sum 302 302

[Syncellus adds] " Sum of Dyn. I. and II. after the Flood, 555 years, κατὰ τὴν β' ἔκδοσιν Ἀφρικανοῦ, according to the second edition of Africanus " [alluding by the word "*edition*" to his previous designation of the lists of Africanus and Eusebius as " the two principal editions of Manetho." The β' is probably the addition of some copyist, derived from the same source, viz. the previous mention of the two editions τὰς β' ἐκδόσεις, of which that of Africanus was *one*, but *not* the *second*.]

" *Dyn. III.* [*IX.*] *of* IX *Memphites:*

1. Necherophes (Necherochis, *Euseb.*), in whose time the Libyans revolted, but, panic-struck at a portentous increase of the moon, returned to obedience . . 28
2. Tosorthrus (Sesorthus, *Euseb.*) This king is regarded as an Esculapius by the Egyptians for his knowledge of medicine; and he *introduced* the method of building *with hewn stone:* he also paid attention to writing . . 29

Carried forward 57

Brought forward 57

3. Tyreis . . . . . 7
4. Mesochris . . . . . 17
5. Soyphis . . . . . 16
6. Tosertasis . . . . . 19
7. Aches . . . . . . 42
8. Siphouris . . . . . 30
9. Kerpheres . . . . . 26

"Sum 214 214

[Syncellus adds] "Sum of the three dynastics according to Africanus, 769 years."

"*Dyn. IV.* [*XI.*] *of* VIII *Memphites of another lineage:*

1. Soris . . . . . . 29
2. Souphis, who built the greatest pyramid, ascribed by Herodotus to Cheops. He was also contemptuous towards the Gods: and he wrote the sacred [i.e. hieratic] book which I bought, as something of great value, *when I was in Egypt* . . . . . 63
3. Souphis . . . . . 66
4. Mencheres . . . . . 63
5. Ratoises . . . . . 25
6. Bicheres . . . . . 22
7. Sebercheres . . . . 7
8. Thamphthis . . . . 9

"Sum 277 284

[Syncellus made the sum 277, for he adds] "Sum of the four dynasties 1046, according to Africanus."

"*Dyn. V.* [*XII.*] *of* IX *kings from Elephantine:*

[Perhaps a purposed mistranslation of the Egyptian word *Abt*, the East, meaning the eastern side of the Nile, or Heliopolis, opposite to Memphis:]

1. Ouserchercs . . . . 28
2. Sephres . . . . . 13

Carried forward 41

Brought forward 41

3. Nephercheres . . . . 20
4. Sisires . . . . . 7
5. Cheres . . . . . 20
6. Rathoures . . . . . 44
7. Mencheres . . . . . 9
8. Tancheres . . . . . 44
9. Ounos [or Obnos] . . 33

"Sum 248 218

[And Syncellus found 248, for he adds] "Sum, with the 1046 of the four preceding dynasties, 1294 years." [So probably either Sisires had 37, or Mencheres 39.]

"*Dyn. VI.* [*XIII.*] *of* VI *Memphites:*

1. Othoes, who was slain by his guards . . . . . 30
2. Phios . . . . . . 53
3. Methou-Souphis . . . 7
4. Phiops, who began to reign at the age of six and reigned to 100 . . . . .100
5. Menthe-Souphis . . . 1
6. Nitocris, the most courageous and most beautiful woman of her time, of fair complexion (ξανθὴ), who built the third Pyramid . . 12

"Sum 203 203

[Syncellus adds] "Sum, with the 1294 of the five dynasties preceding, 1497 years;" [which shows that he cast up 100, and not only 94, for Phiops.]

"*Dyn. VII. of* LXX *Memphites, 70 days.*

"*Dyn. VIII. of* XXVII *Memphites, who reigned 146 years.*

[The "146" is the genuine reading, though Syncellus must have found 142, for he subjoins]. "The sum of the eight dynasties is 1639 years;" [i.e. the 1497 last made + 142.]

"*Dyn. IX. of* XIX *Heracleopolites, who reigned 409 years; of whom the first, Acthoes, a king more tyrannical than any of his predecessors, did much evil to the people throughout all Egypt, till at last he went mad, and was killed by a crocodile.*

"*Dyn. X. of* XIX *Heracleopolites, who reigned 185 years.*

"*Dyn. XI.* [*XIV.*] *of* XVI *Diospolites, who reigned 43 years; after whom—*

Ammenemes reigned . . 16

"Here Manetho ends his *First Book*, containing in all of kings CXCII, and of years 2300, and 70 days;" [this notice being not, like the sums of the dynasties, from Syncellus, but from Africanus, or even from Ptolemy of Mendes himself.]

## "BOOK II. OF MANETHO.

"*Dyn. XII.* [*XV.*] *of* VII *Diospolites:*

1. Sesonchosis, son of Ammenemes . . . . . . 46
2. Ammanemes, who was slain by his own eunuchs . . 38
3. Sesostris, who in nine years subdued all Asia, and Thrace in Europe, and set up everywhere stelæ as memorials of his reduction of each people, with emblematical signs of manhood or effeminacy, according as they had shown the one or the other; so that this king is accounted by the Egyptians the first [i.e. the greatest] after Osiris . 48
   [Eusebius adds, "He is said to have been four cubits three palms and two fingers high;" which seems to be the same notice as Diodorus Siculus attaches to his Rameses-Sesoosis-Sesostris, whose stature was four cubits and four palms.]
4. Lachares [in Eusebius Lamaris or Lampares], who built the Labyrinth in the *Arsinoite* Nome for his tomb 8
5. Ameres . . . . . 8
6. Amenemes . . . . . 8

Carried forward 156

Brought forward 156

7. Scemiophris, sister [of the preceding] . . . 4

"Sum 160 160

"*Dyn. XIII. of* LX *Diospolites, who reigned 453 years.*

"*Dyn. XIV.* [*XVI.*] *of* LXXVI [XXVI, XXX, *or* XXXVI?] *Xoites* [*or Diospolites? Kusites, or Ksoites,* i. e. *Nybians*], *who reigned* 184 *years.*

"*Dyn. XV.* [*XVII.*] *of Shepherds. These were* VI *Phœnician kings*" ["*Arabs,*" i. e. *Shasoo, in the Scholiast on Plato,* "*Peleth-im,*" i. e. *probably Philistine or Pelethite, in Herodotus*], *who took Memphis: of whom—*

1. Saites first reigned . . 19
   And from him was named the Saitic Nome [i. e. the Set-ic or Sethroitic, not the Saitic of which Sais was the capital on the western arm of the Nile]. And these kings built a city in the Sethroite Nome, whence they subdued Egypt.
2. Bnon . . . . . 44
3. Pachnan . . . . . 61
4. Staan . . . . . . 50

Carried forward 174

Brought forward 174

5. Archles . . . . . 49
6. Aphobis [Aphophis in Eusebius] . . . . 61

"Sum 284 284

[So this is no doubt the true sum of the dynasty in the Manetho of Africanus.]

"*Dyn. XVI. of Shepherds, Greeks* [Ἕλληνες, *perhaps a purposed mistranslation of the Egyptian designation Hanebou, which in later times is given to the Greeks*]; XXXII *kings, who reigned years* 518.

"*Dyn. XVII. of* XLIII *other Shepherd kings and* XLIII *Theban Diospolites. The Shepherds and the Thebans reigned together years* 151.

"*Dyn. XVIII. of* XVI *Diospolite kings; of whom:—*

1. Amos "in whose time Moses went out from Egypt," says Africanus, "as we demonstrate;" [to which Syncellus subjoins,] "But, as the reckoning and sum here made force me to say, Moses, in his time, was still quite young." [The 25 years given to this king in the list of Eusebius, are omitted by Syncellus, either through some inadvertence of his own, or owing to some defect in that copy of Africanus from which he transcribes.] [Years omitted . ]
2. Chebros . . . . . 13
3. Amenophthis [Ammenophis, *Euseb.*, and with only 21 years] . . . . . 24
4. Amensis or Amessis . . 22
5. Misphris [Miphres, *Euseb.*] . 13
6. Misphragmouthosis (in whose

Carried forward 72

Brought forward 72

time was the flood of Deucalion) . . . . 26

7. Touthmosis . . . 9
8. Amenophis [this is the reputed Memnon and the vocal stone] . . . 31
9. Horus . . . . 37
10. Acherres . . . . 32
11. Rathos . . . . 6
12. Chevres . . . . 12
13. Acherres . . . . 12
14. Armesses . . . . 5
15. Ramesses [Σίθως-Ῥαμεσσῆς?] 1
    [Then Ramesses II, or "Armesses Miammous," follows in the list copied by Josephus from the original Manetho with 66 years and 2 months; and in the list of Eusebius, copied or altered from Africanus, with 68 years. This long reign, either through his own inadvertence, or rather by some defect in his copy of Africanus, is wanting in the list transcribed by Syncellus . . ]
16. Amenophath . . . 19

"Sum 263 262

[It seems, then, that Syncellus made the sum of the dynasty 263 years, though the figures of our present text make by addition only 262.]

"*Dyn. XIX. of* VII *Diospolite kings:*

1. Sethos, [ὁ καὶ Ῥαμεσσῆς] reigned years . . 51
2. Rapsakes ["his eldest son," *Joseph.*] (Rampses, *Euseb.*) . . 61
3. Ammenephthes, or Amenephthes . . . 20
4. Ramesses, or Rameses . 60
5. Ammenemes . . . 5
6. Thouoris, called by Homer Polybus, hus-

Carried forward 197

Brought forward 197
band of Alcandra, in whose time Troy was taken . . . 7

"Sum 209 204

"In this second book of Manetho are kings xcvi, and years 2121." [This notice is from Africanus, or from the compiler of his edition of Manetho.]

## BOOK III. OF MANETHO.

"*Dyn. XX. of* xii *Diospolite kings who reigned years* 135.

"*Dyn. XXI. of* vii *Tanite kings:*

1. Smendes, reigned years 26
2. Psousennes, or Psousenes 46
3. Nephelcheres [Nepherecheres, *Euseb.*] . . 4
4. Amenophthis . . 9
5. Osochor . . . 6
6. Psinaches . . . 9
7. Psousennes or Sousennes 14

"Sum 130 114

"*Dyn. XXII. of* ix *Bubastite kings:*

1. Sesonchis [Sesonchosis, *Euseb.*] . . . 21
2. Osorthon . . . 15
3. }
4. } Other three . . 25 [29]
5. }
6. Takelothis . . . 13
7. }
8. } Other three . . 42
9. }

"Sum 120 116

"*Dyn. XXIII. of* iv *Tanite kings:*

1. Petubates [Petubastes, *Euseb.*] . . . 40
2. Osorcho [Osorthon, *Euseb.*], whom the Egyptians call Hercules . 8
3. Psammous . . . 10
4. Zet . . . . 31

"Sum 89 89

"*Dyn. XXIV.*

Boechoris, a Saite (in whose time a lamb spoke), reigned years . . 6

". . 990 years." [This is no doubt a note of Africanus, reckoning probably up from his own time, A.D. 220, to the first Olympiad, and finding that it fell *not* under Bocchoris, but, as he thought, in the last year of Petubastes above.]

"*Dyn. XXV. of* iii *Ethiopian kings:*

1. Sabacon, who took Bocchoris prisoner and burned him alive, and reigned years . . 8
2. Sebichus, his son . . 14
3. Tarkos [Tarakos, *Euseb.*] 18

"Sum 40 40

"*Dyn. XXVI. of* ix *Saite kings:*

1. Stephinates [Stephinathis, *Euseb.*, who also puts first of all "Ammeris, an Ethiopian," with 12 years] . . 7
2. Nechepsos . . . 6
3. Nechao . . . 8
4. Psammitichus . . . 54
5. Nechao II. (He took Jerusalem and carried the king Jehoahaz captive into Egypt). . 6
6. Psammouthis or Psammitichus II. . . 6
7. Ouaphris (to whom, after Jerusalem had been taken by the Assyrians, the remnant of the Jews fled) . 19
8. Amosis . . . 44
9. Psammecherites, or Psammach . . . — 6m.

"Sum 150.6m. 150 6m.

"*Dyn. XXVII. of* VIII *Persian kings:*

| | | |
|---|---|---|
| 1. Cambyses in the fifth year of his reign over the Persians conquered Egypt and reigned over it | 6 | |
| 2. Darius, son of Hystaspes | 36 | |
| 3. Xerxes the Great | 21 | |
| 4. Artabanus | — | 7m. |
| 5. Artaxerxes | 41 | |
| 6. Xerxes | — | 2m. |
| 7. Sogdianus | — | 7m. |
| 8. Darius, son of Xerxes | 19 | |
| "Sum 124.4m. | 124 | 4m. |

"*Dyn. XXVIII., Amyrtæus a Saite, reigned years* 6.

"*Dyn. XXIX. of* IV *Mendesian kings:*

| | | |
|---|---|---|
| 1. Nepherites | 6 | |
| 2. Achoris | 13 | |
| 3. Psammouthis | 1 | |
| 4. Nepherites, or Neforotis | — | 4m |
| "Sum 20.4m. | 20 | 4m. |

"*Dyn. XXX. of* III *Sebennyte kings:*

| | |
|---|---|
| 1. Nectanebes, who reigned years | 18 |
| 2. Teos | 2 |
| 3. Nectanebos | 18 |
| "Sum 38 | 38 |

"*Dyn. XXXI of* III *Persian kings:*

| | |
|---|---|
| 1. Ochus in the 20th year of his reign over the Persians conquered Egypt and reigned over it years | 6 |
| 2. Arses | 3 |
| 3. Darius | 4 |
| | 13 |

"Sum of the years of Book III., 1050." "Here Manetho ends." [These two notices are both at least as early as the time of Africanus, whose Manetho, as completed and re-edited by Ptolemy of Mendes, had not only XXX but XXXI dynasties.]

With this scheme of the Manetho of Africanus, as collected from Eusebius and Syncellus, we have now to confront such earlier notices as refer certainly to the work of the original Manetho.

Now that the original Αἰγυπτιακὰ of Manetho the Sebennyte were divided into *three books* is a point on which all are agreed; and if he wrote, as Syncellus says he did, "κατὰ μίμησιν Βηρώσσου," in imitation of Berosus, whose Χαλδαϊκὰ were in three books, it was probably this fact that suggested to him a similar distribution of his own work. However this was, Josephus gives us "from Book II." of Manetho a passage containing an account of the Shepherd Kings, and the same list of six names which forms Dyn. XV of Africanus. And this dynasty appears also in Book II. of the Manetho of Africanus, so that even if Josephus did not mention afterwards, as he does, "another book of the same Egyptiaca," which from the narrative being connected with

Dyn. XIX seems to be the third, we might infer that the division of the three books marked in the Manetho of Africanus is derived from the original work of the Sebennyte. Only as regards Book III. the sum given for its years, viz. 1050, is inconsistent with the division implied above when the sum of Book II. is put at the end of Dyn. XIX. For if Book III. of the Manetho of Ptolemy and Africanus began with Dyn. XX, it would have only 853, or at most 859 years, to the end of Dyn. XXX, that is, fewer than 1050 by 197 or 191. Besides which we shall see hereafter that if Book II. of the Manetho of Africanus be supposed to include the whole of Dyn. XIX, it will have too many years for the sum of 2121 assigned to it. We may suppose, therefore, that Book III. really began some few years after the commencement of Dyn. XIX; as for instance, if it began from the flight of the brother of Sethos, identified with Danaus, so as to include the times of the "Egyptians," as named from Sethos Egyptus. This peculiarity would then account for the sum of Book II. being put down seemingly too low at the end of the dynasty. In this case Book III. of the original Manetho (who certainly identified Sethos with Egyptus), probably commenced at the same point of Dyn. XIX as Book III. of the Manetho of Africanus, and made about the same sum of 1050 years, there being no reason to suspect any *great* difference for the last twelve dynasties (from XIX to XXX inclusive) properly composing Book III. between the Manetho of Africanus and the original.

Syncellus says of Manetho that "he writes of five Egyptian *peoples* distributed into XXX *Dynasties* of *Gods*, *Demigods*, and *Manes*, and of *mortal men*, mentioned also by Eusebius in his Chronicon: "Μετὰ δὲ ταῦτα καὶ περὶ ἐθνῶν Αἰγυπτιακῶν πέντε ἐν λ' δυναστείαις ἱστορεῖ τῶν λεγομένων παρ' αὐτοῖς θεῶν καὶ ἡμιθέων, καὶ νεκύων, καὶ θνητῶν, ὧν καὶ Εὐσέβιος ὁ Παμφίλου μνησθεὶς ἐν τοῖς χρονικοῖς αὐτοῦ φησὶν οὕτως·" κ.τ.λ.

It is true that in this passage he means by Manetho the pseudo-Manetho or Sothis of Anianus and Panodorus; but what he says refers equally and rather to the original Manetho, and to the Manetho of Africanus, which exhibited

*Manes* and other mythical kings before Menes, whereas the Manetho of the book of Sothis seems to have passed at once from the Demigods to Menes. But however this was, if only the number of dynasties in the three books of the original Manetho be allowed to have been *thirty*, like the number in the Chronicle, (and the latest pseudo-Manetho of Anianus *returns* to this number, not having the thirty-first dynasty of Africanus,) it seems certain that *some* of these XXX dynasties must have contained the Gods, Demigods, Manes, and mythical Kings. Not only in the Chronicle, which Manetho is said to have followed, but in the Turin Papyrus a thousand years older than the Chronicle, in Herodotus, in Diodorus, and everywhere in short, down to the latest pseudo-Manetho of Anianus and Panodorus, we find the Egyptians pretending a *continuous succession* of dynasts and dynasties from Ra, the Sun-god, down to Menes and the living sovereign of the day. Even in the Manetho of Africanus, though the whole number of *thirty* dynasties, derived by the original Manetho from the Chronicle, is given to kings after Menes, and though the earlier groups of Gods, Demigods, Manes, and mythical Kings, are not distinctly numbered as dynasties, words are retained in connection with them which amount to the same thing. And it is easy to see that the author of this scheme, writing between two and three centuries after the Mosaic books had been translated into Greek, meant tacitly to let the earlier dynasties of the original Manetho, the Gods, Demigods, and Manes, stand as a separate series for the times of the old world, as was rightly understood by Africanus; while in compensation for his reduction of their vast periods as from months to real years, he numbered a complete series of thirty postdiluvian dynasties from Menes to Nectanebo II. with a thirty-first added, to cover the years (already mentioned by the original Manetho) between Nectanebo and Alexander. And possibly the spurious letter of Manetho to Ptolemy Philadelphus "*Augustus*" (Σεβαστῷ), and the explanatory hint of antediluvian history having been derived from *stelæ* buried in the land of Assyria, ἐν γῇ Σιριάδι, which Syncellus gives from the later pseudo-Manetho or Sothis, may have belonged originally to the compilation of Ptolemy of Mendes, since the story has its roots in Berosus, and seems to be alluded to by Josephus in connection with Manetho. But in the time of the original Manetho there was nothing as yet to require any such covert modification of the long-established fable that there had been one unbroken succession of dynasties in Egypt from Ra downwards to Menes and his successors.

Assuming then that the seven groups given by Eusebius from the Manetho of Africanus, and belonging by the very fact that their years are month-years *unreduced* to the original Manetho, are in fact his first VII dynasties, forming part of his first book, but prefixed to the three books as part of a separate Introduction by the compiler to the Manetho of Africanus, it follows that these have been displaced by seven out of those XXXI dynasties of kings after Menes which now fill the three books of the Manetho of Africanus and Ptolemy. And our business, if we would recover the original Manetho, is to distinguish in the lists of Africanus *which* are the twenty-three genuine, and which are the seven interpolated dynasties, and to eject these latter, bringing down the seven mythological dynasties into their room. As a step towards this we shall first look for such internal indications as the lists of Africanus may afford of themselves; and then test them by the help of five sources older than the time of Ptolemy of Mendes, viz., the Chronicle, Eratosthenes, the Monuments, the Turin MS., and the citations in Josephus.

Now, at the first glance one gives to the thirty-one dynasties of Africanus, they divide themselves into two distinct and opposite classes, one class having every mark of historical reality, the other none whatever, or next to none; the one forbidding, the other provoking suspicion. In the first class the names of the kings are given with the years of each reign: in the second class the dynasties are either wholly anonymous, or all but anonymous, with the mention perhaps of a single name. Of the first class are Dynasties I, II, III, IV, V, VI, XII, XV, XVIII, XIX, XXI, and the rest to XXX inclusive, in all twenty, being three fewer than we are prepared to allow as genuine. Of the second or anonymous class are VII, VIII, IX, X, XI, XIII, XIV, XVI, and XVII, in all ten, being three more than we are seeking to eject as fictitious. But without looking far, there are some slight signs which may already hint which three of the ten are *less* open to suspicion than the rest. For Thebes being one of the great capitals, giving its name to a number of dynasties, it is perhaps unlikely that the *first* Theban dynasty named should be spurious; and Dyn. XI has one name distinctly connected with the kings of Dyn. XII; and if he were the first king who ever reigned at Thebes, he certainly would have been set at the head of a dynasty, even though a fictitious dynasty had been prefixed. Then again in Dyn. XIV (though it is slightly uncertain owing to a defect in the MSS whether it may not belong to XIII), the sum of years given, 184, is the sum of one of the dynasties of the Chronicle, of one too which it purposely avoids describing in detail; so that this, though equally anonymous, may be either the same, or some other contemporary with it, under which the same space of time is alluded to. And, thirdly, although Dyn. XX is altogether anonymous, still, as it is within the period of the ascertained consecutive dynasties governing or claiming to govern all Egypt (from Dyn. XVIII downwards), it is less *probable* that any dynasty merely fictitious should be inserted here than at a more remote antiquity; and there are other grounds, as we shall see, which quite preclude the supposition.

I. Of the dynasties of the Chronicle, Dyn. XVI with its VIII kings headed (since it is the *first* of mortal kings) by Menes, clearly proves the historical character, if proof were needed, of Dyn. I. of Africanus, which has the same number of kings, and the same place at the head of the monarchy, though it adds 63 years to the 190 of the Chronicle, and varies the designation from "*Tanite*" to "*Thinite*" (the Egyptian name of This, *Teni*, facilitating the change). Dyn. II of the Chronicle, being "Memphite," justifies one at least, we may suppose the earliest, of the Memphite dynasties of Africanus. Dyn. XXVII of the Chronicle identifies itself with the last 184 years of the last four out of the six kings of Dyn. XV of Africanus. Dyn. XVIII and XIX of the Chronicle identify themselves with XVIII and XIX, and XX of the Chronicle with XX and part of XXI of Africanus; and the remaining dynasties of the Chronicle XXI, XXII, XXIII, XXIV, XXV, XXVI, XXVIII, XXIX, and XXX are identifiable upon the whole with Dynasties XXII, XXIII, XXIV, XXV, XXVI, XXVII, XXIX, and XXX of Africanus, though the subdivision of the chronological space covered by these dynastics, and their designations and lengths, vary considerably in Africanus from those of the Chronicle. Dyn. XXVII of the Chronicle having been put back to its true place, and Dyn. XXVIII of Africanus, intended, no doubt, as a substitute for it, being neglected, as having nothing really answering to it in the Chronicle, the whole series of dynastics from XVIII to XXX inclusive is parallel, and the chronological space covered by them identical, as we shall find, in the two schemes, except that three years of the 1404 (for so many there are in the Chronicle) have in the list of Africanus been thrown back to the very commencement of the monarchy, and six other years of the same 1404 are in the list of Africanus represented by the six of its Dyn. XXVIII, which chronologically have no separate place of their own, but are contained in the years of the Persians. So then Dyn. XX of Africanus, although anonymous, is by comparison of the scheme of the Chronicle placed beyond all reach of suspicion.

II. In that portion of the list of Eratosthenes which has been copied by Syncellus from Apollodorus (a detailed analysis of it shall be given hereafter), there are joint allusions to the Chronicle, Manetho, and the monuments. Dyn. I of Africanus is identified with XVI of the Chronicle, and its due number of 190 years is *restored*, though the eight kings are for certain intelligible reasons compressed to five. Dyn. II of Africanus is also alluded to, its sum being indicated, and its last two reigns making together the first Memphite generation of Eratosthenes, the particulars of the gigantic stature of Sesochris fixing his identity. Dyn. III appears more fully; also IV and VI. To V there is no allusion, though its historical character is unquestionable; but Eratosthenes had only a certain limited number of generations and of years to fill, and could not even allude to all. Nothing whatever appears to indicate that the anonymous dynasties VIII, IX, and X (to say nothing of VII) had ever existed; but before coming to names plainly belonging to Dyn. XII, he has no less than eight kings connected with Thebes by the surname "*Ammon*odotus" given to the first of them. So he justifies our anticipation that the *first* Theban Dynasty in Africanus, viz. Dyn. XI, although nearly anonymous, would scarcely turn out to be fictitious. After the names connected with Dyn. XII, there follow yet three names belonging neither to Dyn. XII, nor to XV, nor to XVIII of Africanus, before Syncellus breaks off, so that these three names should represent that third dynasty of Africanus (guessed from the sum 184 to be Dyn. XIV) which with XI and XX, though anonymous, is to be allowed as genuine. As regards the rest of the list of Eratosthenes, though the names are not given, we know the number of years and of generations still to follow, and comparing these with the names of Manetho, and the space of Manetho and the Chronicle still remaining unfilled, we may collect that he must certainly have filled up both Dyn. XX and all the other remaining dynasties of Africanus after XVII, omitting, beyond a doubt, the Shepherds of Dyn. XV, and *possibly* also Amyrtæus, if he perceived that his Dynasty XXVIII of six years was a mere representation, in a place where it could not stand, of years omitted at the head of Dynasty XXVI.

III. On the existing monuments and papyri there are (in the names of Menes and Athothis), traces though not contemporary, of Dyn. I of Africanus; probably also on some fragments of the Turin papyrus, if not elsewhere, there are names of Dyn. II. The names of the uppermost line to the left in the Karnak Chamber of Kings, seem to have been identified by Eratosthenes or his informants with Severcheres of Dyn. II and other kings of Dyn. III of Africanus. The names of Choufou or Shouphou (Χέοψ or Σοῦφις) and Mencheres, of Dyn. IV, have been identified beyond a doubt in the pyramids of Gizeh. Names of Dyn. V, called Elephantinite (or ἐξ Ἐλεφαντίνης), are found mixed with those of Dyn. IV in the tombs of the pyramid-field near Memphis, showing pretty clearly that they were more closely connected with

Memphis or Heliopolis than with Elephantine, and at the same time attesting the historical character of the dynasty, though unnoticed by Eratosthenes. The names of the kings of Dyn. VI also occur, especially in central Egypt. Of the anonymous dynasties VII, VIII, IX, and X, there is no trace. But at Thebes, or in its neighbourhood, there are names and tombs of early kings exceeding in number those eight for which alone Eratosthenes could find room before the representatives of Dyn. XII, and justifying the *sixteen* Thebans of Dyn. XI in the lists of Africanus; so that Manetho must be supposed in this dynasty *of Upper Egypt* rather to have curtailed its years, than to have multiplied its kings; whereas in Dyn. I. of Africanus (XVI of the Chronicle,) we have found him doing the reverse. And Eratosthenes, who there reduces, here expands his years. Dyn. XII. appears fully on the monuments; and so does another dynasty or group of kings (among whom the names Sevekhotep and Neferhotep are frequent) plainly connected by lineage with the founders of Dyn. XII, and by locality with Nubia and Upper Egypt. This monumental group answers well enough to that anonymous but genuine dynasty of Africanus which we have guessed, from the sum 184, to be Dyn. XIV. On separate monuments eight or ten names only of these kings have as yet been found; but on the right side of the Thothmes Chamber of Karnak there are no less than XXX of them; and it is conceivable that XXVI was the number in the original Manetho, (the Karnak Chamber sometimes gives also princes,) and that the LX of his Dyn. XIII was meant by Ptolemy to include all the kings, in number about 60, who are represented on both sides of the same Karnak Chamber. Of the Shepherds of Dyn. XV, there is only one name, Apophis, certainly identified, on some fragments of the temple at Tanis; and the emblem of the god Sutech or Typhon accompanies this name. And this may probably be the second Apophis, who was last of the Shepherds, and whose short reign, omitted by Manetho, gave occasion to a transposition of an earlier Apophis, with 61 years, from the fourth to the sixth place: for we shall see hereafter that such a transposition has been made in the lists of Africanus. The kings of XVIII, XIX, and XX, (not of XXI, though the *years* covered by it are placed beyond all doubt by the Chronicle,) and again of XXII, XXIII, XXIV, XXV, XXVI, and of XXVIII, (for Amyrtæus reigned over part of the Delta, though within the 124 years of the Persians,) and lastly of XXIX and XXX, are to be read on the monuments.

IV. The Turin Papyrus after Gods, as Ra and Horus, and Demigods, as Thoth and Ma, in vast periods, myriads of years, like those of the Chronicle and Manetho, offers names and sums of years connecting themselves with the general order of Manetho's dynasties as recoverable from the lists of Africanus. Menes, for instance, and Athothis stand first after the Gods and Demigods (the last of whom is a Horus), for the commencement of Dyn. I. Baichos, Kaiechos, Bi-netrou, Sethenes, Choires, and Nephercheres, are perhaps identifiable for Dyn. II, Aches for Dyn. III, Soris and Mencheres for IV, Mencheres, Tatcheres, and Onnos for V. A reign of above 90 years, probably 94 (but certainly not 100 as Eratosthenes has made it, and as Syncellus casts it up in Dyn. VI of Africanus), followed by a reign of only one year and the name Nitocris, sufficiently identify Dyn. VI. A Mentuhotep may represent XI. The whole eight kings of Dyn. XII with the sum of the dynasty are distinguishable; and, lastly, there are found a prodigious number of kings with extremely short reigns, among whom the throne-name of Amenemhe I, and the names Sevekhotep and Neferhotep are frequently repeated; and who are clearly connected by lineage with the first kings of Dyn. XII, and by locality, as has been said already, with Nubia and Upper Egypt, the names being the same, only with the addition of many more of kindred elements, as the thirty names of the right-hand side in the Thothmes Chamber of Karnak. So these names may be supposed to represent Dyn. XIV of Ksoites or Diospolites, according as the one name or the other was connected with the sum of 184 years by the original Manetho.

Besides names and figures and affinities, and a certain general order in the Turin papyrus, showing that hieratic papyri of the same kind were among the sources used by Manetho, there is in it a further peculiarity which may possibly throw light on one of the most obscure points in the earlier part of Manetho's scheme, viz. the nature and origin of his "Manes and other mythical Kings," registered by him before Menes. Of these there seem to be four dynasties in an order the inverse to that of the Chronicle, one with an indefinite number of kings (perhaps *Theban*) in 1817 years, another with XXX *Memphite* kings in 1790 years, the third with ten *Thinite* kings in 350 years (being 35 years to each king of these ten), and after all these a fourth with a vast sum of 5813 years. But in the Turin MS., besides a number of ancient names of kings answering in their general character to those of Dyn. I and II, in which the syllable Ra does not as yet enter into composition, and names identifiable or spaces connected with names sufficient to correspond to those dynasties I, II, III, IV, V, VI, XI, XII of Africanus which are more or less identifiable, there are also intermixed and following a number of other names not to be found in the list of Africanus. And whatever be the principle on which the hieratic MS. was written, it is clear that its multitude of names even in the earlier dynasties, and still more after Dyn. XII, in what one may call the Nubian branch, was not fabricated to cover a fabulous number of generations of ordinary length; as Herodotus understood the 330 names of kings, read to him doubtless from a very similar papyrus, to be intended to cover a space of 11,000 years. On the contrary, a great number of the reigns, where the figures have been preserved, are extremely short, so that a number of them being put together give in one case an average of only seven years, in another of only two years and a half. It is open then to imagine that the principle on which the MS. was constructed was that rather of a genealogy of each family that had reigned, not only grown men who had actually reigned being given, but also those whose descendants more or less remote had reigned or might reign, and even infants, who while they lived had stood for a time in the line of succession. All such names crowned only after death in Amente, or on paper, might, when ejected from his own list by Manetho, be thrown up above Menes, and described as Manes, i. e. kings whose reigns were only

after death, nominal, in Amente, not in the upper world.]
And the large sum of 5813 years (to say nothing of the three sums preceding), need make no objection to this hypothesis, as the great sums in Manetho, and in the Chronicle, and in other sources, are, as now understood, divisible by twelve. So 5813 will be reducible to 484.5$^{m}$.; 1817 to 151.5$^{m}$.; 1790 to 149.2$^{m}$.; 350 to 29.2$^{m}$. And in full years the ten kings supposed to be ejected from the Thinite [or Tanite] lists would have not quite *three* years each: the thirty kings ejected from the *Memphite* lists would have not quite five years each; and thirty ejected from the Theban lists probably about the same. So there would be an excess of about 70 kings in the hieratic MS. as compared with the dynasties of Manetho hitherto accounted for: and the average quite agrees with what we see in the Turin MS. So to the end of Dyn. XII the MS. might have 143 names in something under six columns answering to the 73 names of Manetho. After that 484 years and 4 months at not quite the same average of five years would give 106 more kings, seemingly ejected from that part of the hieratic MS. which follows after Dyn. XII, and in which the Nubian lineage connected with Dyn. XII, (and so also with Dyn. XVIII and XIX below, and approaching nearest to the time when the papyrus was written,) is treated with such prodigious development. If we suppose 36 kings of this same lineage, who actually reigned, to be these on the right hand side in the Karnak Chamber, and 36 or 26 to be the true number of the Ksoite or Diospolite kings (perhaps a double or treble line) with 184 years in Manetho, we shall have 36 + 106, i.e. 142 at most, (for there may have been fewer,) to add to the 143 obtained before, making 285 for the whole number of kings contained in the Turin papyrus in its XII or XIII columns, supposing, as seems probable, that it contained no names of Dyn. XVIII. The addition of 46 more would still be wanting to complete the 331 kings of Herodotus from Menes to Rameses II. or III. inclusive.

V. It is now time to transcribe and compare with that part of the lists of Africanus with which they correspond some long passages of narrative containing the lists of two dynasties, and the first two names of a third, happily preserved to us by Josephus from Book II. of "Manetho himself."

"We once had a king named Timæus. In his time, I know not why, God was unpropitious, and some men of ignoble race from the parts to the East in a strange way had the confidence to invade our country, and *easily, without a battle*, subdued it. And having *subjected* to themselves them that had been its princes, they *afterwards* cruelly burned the cities and demolished the temples of the gods. And all the inhabitants of the country they used most barbarously, killing some and *reducing* others with their whole families *to slavery*. At length they made one of themselves king, whose name was Salatis. And he resided in Memphis, exacting tribute both from the *Upper* and the Lower country, and having garrisons in the fittest places. Especially he attended to the strengthening of the eastern frontier; foreseeing that the Assyrians, whose power was then getting very great, would desire to invade the same kingdom. And having observed in the Saitic (i. e. Setic or Sethroitic) Nome, a city very conveniently situated to the east of the Bubastic arm, which from some ancient theological reference was named Avaris [i. e. Ἀβαρόπολις, or Hebræopolis], he built it and made its walls exceedingly strong, and garrisoned it with a force of 240,000 men. Thither he was used to go in the summer season, both to collect his tributes in corn and to pay his troops, and also by constant exercises and reviews to strike terror into the peoples beyond the frontier.

| | |
|---|---|
| "Salatis died after a reign of years . . . | 19. |
| Another, Bnon [Βαιὼν, *Sync.*] succeeded him, and reigned . . . . . . . . . | 44. |
| Then another, Apachnas . . . . . . . | 36.7m. |
| Then again Apophis . . . . . . . . . | 61. |
| And Janias . . . . . . . . . . . | 50.1m. |
| And *lastly* Assis . . . . . . . . . . | 49.2m. |
| | [Sum 259.10m.] |

"And these six were the first among them who became rulers, ever warring upon [πολεμοῦντες, persecuting] Egypt, and seeking more and more to pluck out its root. The whole people of them collectively were called Hyk-shôs, i. e. Shepherd-kings; for *Hyk* in the hieratic dialect means a king, and *Shôs* both in the hieratic and in the vulgar idiom is a shepherd or shepherds, and so put together they form *Hyk-shôs*. Some say that they were Arabs" [Shôs or Shasou being the common designation of the Asiatic nomads, and first and chiefly of the Arabs, as Bedouin is often used now]. "These above-named kings of the people called Shepherds, *and their posterity*, held Egypt (Manetho says) 511 years.

"After these things *the kings*, he says, who were in *the Thebaid and* in the *rest of Egypt* rebelled against the Shepherds, and they had a great and long war, till in the time of a king named Alisphragmuthosis" [seemingly corrupted in the MSS. from Misphragmuthosis, as is written elsewhere by metathesis for Miphra-Thuthmosis, the fifth name in the list of Dyn. XVIII], "the Shepherds, he says, having been by him defeated, lost all the rest of Egypt, and were hemmed in within a place which was 10,000 *arouræ* in circumference, named Avaris. All this space, Manetho says, the Shepherds surrounded with a vast and strong wall, that they might hold there in security all their possessions the spoils of Egypt.

"And Thummosis (Θμουθῶσις, Θμῶσις), the son of Alisphragmuthosis, endeavoured to reduce them by siege, blockading the place with 480,000 men; but at length, despairing of success by that way, he made a convention with them that they should depart unmolested whither they would; whereupon they, with all their families and possessions, being in number not fewer than 240,000, went out from Egypt into the desert towards Syria; but, fearing the power of the Assyrians, (for the Assyrians were then masters of Asia,) they built, in the country which is now called Judæa, a city large enough to contain all that multitude of their people, and named it Jerusalem."

"(In *another book* of the Αἰγυπτιακὰ Manetho says that 'This nation' of the people called Shepherds, 'are in our hieratic books called *bondsmen*.')"

"After the people of the Shepherds had gone out from

Egypt *to Jerusalem, Tethmosis,* the king who had driven them out of Egypt, reigned after their expulsion

| | | |
|---|---|---|
| "[Tethmosis i. e. Amosis] . . | years | 25. $4^m$. |
| And his son Chebron succeeding reigned . | | 13. |
| After whom Amenophis . . . . . | | 20. $7^m$. |
| After him Amesses, [his] sister, . . . | | 21. $9^m$. |
| After her Miphres [i. e. Thothmes III. Miphra-Thuthmosis] . . . . . . | | 12. $9^m$. |
| After him Miphramuthosis [i. e. the same as above, reduplicated, but really Amenoph II.] | | 25.$10^m$. |
| After him Thmosis . . . . . . | | 9. $8^m$. |
| After him Amenophis . . . . . | | 30.$10^m$. |
| After him Horus . . . . . . | | 36. $5^m$. |
| After him Acenchres [his] daughter . . | | 12. $1^m$. |
| After her Rathotis [her] brother. . . . | | 9. |
| After him Acencheres . . . . . | | 12. $5^m$. |
| After him another Acencheres . . . | | 12. $3^m$. |
| After him Armais . . . . . . | | 4. $1^m$. |
| After him Ramesses . . . . . . | | 1. $4^m$. |
| After him Armesses Miammous . . . | | 66. $2^m$. |
| After him Amenophis . . . . . | | 19. $6^m$. |
| | | [Sum 333.] |

" After him [reigned] Sethosis, who is also Ramesses, who was strong in cavalry, and had a fleet on the sea.

" This king made his brother Armais his deputy to govern Egypt, giving him all the prerogatives of royalty with only these restrictions, that he was not to wear the crown, nor ill-treat the queen, the mother of the young princes, nor touch any of the other royal concubines. And having thus provided, he himself invaded first Cyprus and Phœnicia, and afterwards Assyria and Media, and subdued them all, some by force of arms, and others without a blow, by the mere terror of his power. And being elated by his successes, he advanced still more confidently, subduing the cities and countries towards the East.

" And when now a long time had passed, Armais, who had been left in Egypt, began to do without scruple just the contrary to all his brother's injunctions; for he took the queen by force to himself, and lived freely with the other concubines as his own, and wore at the suggestion of his friends the crown, and openly set up for himself against his brother.

"But the chief of the priests of Egypt wrote and sent a letter to Sethosis, informing him of all, and that his brother Armais had set up for himself; wherefore he immediately returned to Pelusium, and recovered his own kingdom. And the country was called from *his* name "Egypt;" for Manetho says that Sethosis was called Egyptus, and his brother Armais Danaus."—*Jos. Contr. Ap. lib.* i. c. 14, 15.

In this passage the Shepherd kings, conquered by Amosis the founder of Dyn. XVIII, are purposely made to cover and include the Hebrew bondsmen oppressed by Mephres-Tethmosis III. or Misphragmuthosis, and suffered to leave Egypt in the first year of his son and successor Amenoph II., 94 years after the overthrow and expulsion of the Shepherds. And the Shepherds thus confounded with the Hebrews are made to settle in Judæa and build Jerusalem, which was really taken and "built" by the Hebrews only in the time of king David.

In another passage extracted by Josephus, Manetho, *ἐκ τῶν ἀδεσπότως μυθευομένων*, gives avowedly an account of the Hebrews, whom he represents as a mixed people of lepers and other unclean outcasts, partly descended from the Shepherds, expelled long before, and partly of Egyptian origin. He confounds both them and the Shepherds with certain sun-worshipping Shasou, who ruled Egypt between the reigns of Amenoph III. and Horus; and represents their Exodus, under a leader who is Joseph and Moses blended into one person, as a victorious expulsion by Sethosis-Rameses the head of Dyn. XIX, son of Amenoph the last king of Dyn. XVIII, above 333 years of his own reckoning (really above 348) from the expulsion of the Shepherds, 254 from the true Exodus of the Hebrews, and 173.3$^{m}$. after the 13 years of the admitted subjection of Egypt to impious Asiatics, which intervene really between Amenoph III. and Horus. He even preserves Amenoph II. and III. as if surviving under the same name in the later Amenoph, father of Sethosis, to enjoy the poetical retribution. Josephus, however, though he perceives that anyhow there will be inconsistency and absurdity, and complains that the Amenophis introduced is a fictitious king, whose epoch and reign Manetho dares not fix, thinks it least absurd to understand the Amenophis son of Rampses, and Rameses or Rampses (who however should be also Sethosis) son of Amenophis, who figure in the passage about to be given, to be the third and fourth kings of Dynasty XIX, for he introduces the extract as follows:

"Manetho, relating that our ancestors [he means the Shepherds] came with many myriads into Egypt, and subdued it, and acknowledging that after that they" [but Manetho merges the Hebrews in the Shepherds, and the true Exodus in the expulsion of the Shepherds 94 years earlier, and by no means acknowledges the Hebrews at all in that former narrative] "went out and occupied the present Judæa, and built Jerusalem and its Temple, thus far follows ancient histories;" [so Josephus was willing to have it believed;] "but *afterwards* giving himself license by saying that he will write the stories *commonly credited* about the Jews, he inserts worthless tales, seeking to confound with us a multitude of Egyptian lepers and other unclean outcasts. For adding also a king Amenophis, a false name, and on this account not daring to fix the time of his reign, (though he gives the years of the rest with precision enough,) he hangs upon him certain fables, forgetting how he had written that the *Shepherds* went out to Jerusalem about 518 years before. For Tethmosis [i. e. Amosis] was king when they went out. But from him the interval to the two brothers Sethos and Hermæus, surnamed Egyptus and Danaus, is 393 years" [i. e. reckoning at top the year of the expulsion of the Shepherds, and at bottom the 59 of Sethos, which are so inadvertently reduplicated]. "And after expelling the latter,

"Sethos reigned years . . . . . 59
"And the eldest of his sons, Rapsakes . 66

[And 393 + 125 make 518.] "Having then already confessed that our fathers went out so many years earlier, and then having invented and put in an interpolated king whom he names Amenophis, he goes on and says:

"This king desired to behold the Gods, like Horus, one of the kings who had reigned before him;" [alluding probably to the same story as is given by Herodotus, only with the name of Hercules instead of Horus, Horus the God being the predecessor intended, rather than the king of Dyn. XVIII;] "and he communicated his desire to a priest named like himself Amenophis, son of Papis, who seemed to partake of the divine nature by his wisdom and prescience. And this his namesake told him that he might have his wish and see the Gods, if he would first cleanse the whole country from lepers and all other unclean persons then in it.

"The king, well pleased, collected together from all Egypt all such as had any defect in their bodies, to the number of 80,000; and these he put into the quarries on the east side of the Nile, to work there and to be kept separate from the rest of the Egyptians. Now there were among them, he says, some learned men of the priests who were affected with leprosy. And that Amenophis, the sage and prophet, who has been mentioned already, began to fear lest the wrath of the gods should be provoked both against himself and the king, if it should appear that violence were done them; and he added this prediction, that certain people should come *to the aid* of the unclean, and should be masters of Egypt for 13 years. Not daring, however, to say this to the king, he wrote all in a paper to leave behind him, and put an end to himself, at which the king was greatly distressed and dispirited.

"And then he writes word for word thus: 'After a considerable time, those people becoming impatient of the hardships they endured in the quarries, the king was petitioned to set apart for their relief and shelter the city of Avaris which was *then* empty, *as* it had been evacuated by the Shepherds, and he granted it. Now that city, according to the theology, is from of old Typhonian' [i. e. under the influence of a malignant deity].

"They having come thither, and having this place convenient for a revolt, set up as their leader a certain man formerly of the priests of Heliopolis, named Osarsiph," [a name altered from Joseph,] "and bound themselves by oath to obey him in all things. He first made them a law that they should neither worship the gods, nor abstain from any of the sacred animals, not even from those most venerated in Egypt, but should sacrifice and eat all alike; and that they should intermarry with none but such as had sworn to their covenant. Having made such laws as these, and many others directly opposed to the customs of the Egyptians, he gave command that all their multitude should work at strengthening the walls of the city, and hold themselves in readiness for the war which he designed against Amenophis the king; while he, taking to him some more priests and others of those similarly unclean, sent an embassy, which he headed himself, to the Shepherds who had been driven out by Tethmosis, to the city called Jerusalem, and informing them of all that had befallen himself and the rest who had been ignominiously treated with him, he asked them to join him, and with one consent to attack Egypt. He promised first of all that he would reinstate them in Avaris, their ancestral country, and supply their host with all things needful in abundance, and fight for them," [ὑπερμαχήσεσθαι, take their part and protect,] "as occasion might require, and assured them that he would without difficulty make the country subject to them. They joyfully agreed, and marching all of them at once, to the number of 200,000 men, within a short time arrived at Avaris.

"Amenophis, the king of Egypt, when he heard of their invasion, was in great consternation, remembering the prophecy of Amenophis, the son of Papis. And having first assembled the multitude of the Egyptians, and having consulted with their chiefs, he sent for the sacred animals, for those, that is, which have the highest honours in the temples, and gave orders to the priests in each locality to hide the images of the gods as carefully as possible. And *his son Sethos*, also called Ramesses, from Rampses, his [own] father, being then a boy of five years old, he put out to be taken care of *by his friend.* Then *crossing* and marching with the rest of the Egyptians, being 300,000 most valiant men, he came up with the enemy, who advanced to meet him, but he did not join battle; for he scrupled lest he should be fighting against the Gods. *So* he turned, and came back to Memphis; and taking with him Apis and the other sacred animals which he had sent for, and which had been brought thither, he went straight up the country into Ethiopia with all his army and the multitude [i. e. all the principal people] of the Egyptians; for the king of the Ethiopians was under obligations to him, and was ready to serve him. [But in truth Ethiopia during all the time of this dynasty had no separate king.] Wherefore, receiving him and all the accompanying multitudes, he supplied their wants with all such provisions as the country afforded, and allotted them a sufficient number of cities and villages in which to pass the 13 years for which he was destined to be deprived of his throne; and further, he encamped an Ethiopian army of observation on the frontier, to assure the safety of King Amenophis.

"While these things were passing in Ethiopia, the Jerusalemites (Σολυμῖται) having come down, and having joined the leprous Egyptians, they both together treated the inhabitants with such barbarity, that the [earlier] domination of the first-mentioned [the Shepherds] seemed to have been a golden time to such as saw the impieties and atrocities now committed. For they not only set fire to the cities and villages, nor were content with insulting or mutilating the images of the gods, but they even roasted and ate the sacred animals which were worshipped, and forced priests and prophets to sacrifice and slay these, or cast them out naked [from their offices and possessions]. And it is said that the priest who instituted their polity and laws, being by origin an Heliopolite, named Osarsiph" [i. e. Joseph, son-in-law of the chief priest of Heliopolis, made to derive his name from Osiris], "from Osiris the god worshipped in Heliopolis, when he went over to these people, changed his name, and was called Moses."—*Jos. Contr. Ap.*, lib. i. c. 26.

"Manetho says again that 'After this, Amenophis returned from Ethiopia with a great force, and his son Rampses too, heading another army of his own; and both together encountering the Shepherds (Shasoo) and the unclean, they routed them, slew multitudes, and pursued the rest to the borders of Syria.'"—*Jos. Contr. Ap.*, lib. i. c. 27.

These extracts preserved by Josephus suffice to show how Manetho interposed in his narrative lists of kings supplied by the hieratic MSS.; and how their methodical exactness in enumerating for each reign its years, months, and even days (in which last point they were not followed by Manetho), contrasted with the mythical character of his own text. So that both opinions held concerning him are justified; on the one hand, that his work was of great historical value; on the other, that he was an impudent fabler, in whose stories different persons, names, times, and events are blended and confused together, so that they need to be analysed and separated into their original elements. And when this is done, even these stories are valuable, as being of pure Egyptian origin, quite unlike the later fables of writers who had become acquainted through the LXX. version with more or less of the contents of the books of Moses. And, though fables, they are each in their details a tissue of allusions to real history. Into a closer examination this is not the place to enter: but we see now what is meant when it is said that the Chronographer *collected* out of Manetho a certain sum of years; since he had need to pick out the historical lists derived from the hieratic papyri from the fabling narrative in which they were interposed.

In the passages given by Josephus there are the full lists of two dynasties, viz. XV and XVIII, of Africanus, and the first two names of XIX. But if these are taken together with the narrative, and if all the statements of the narrative are supposed to be consistent, and of equal authority, there ought to be a succession of other Shepherd kings during exactly 251 years and two months ($511-259.10^{m}.= 251.2^{m}.$) between the death of Assis the last of the six Shepherds of Dyn. XV of Africanus, and the accession of Alisphragmuthosis, Misphragmuthosis, Tethmosis, or whatever name be given him, who founded Dyn. XVIII, and reigned 25 years and 4 months "after expelling the Shepherds." But from the sum which, as we shall see below, he "collected," it is clear that the Chronographer, that is

Eratosthenes, gave no place to any such anonymous "descendants" of the six Shepherds above-named, nor to any interval of 251 years between them and Dyn. XVIII. And, what is more, even the re-editor and amplifier of Manetho, Ptolemy of Mendes, or whoever else he was, though he had here an opportunity of building one, or if he pleased two fresh dynasties, with 251 years, out of a distinct assertion of Manetho, gives instead two dynasties of "*other* Shepherds," (we need not dwell upon the designation Ἕλληνες,) not even adding from Manetho "descendants of the preceding," the one dynasty with 518, the other with 151 years. So he agrees with Eratosthenes in entirely neglecting the express assertion of Manetho's text, that the whole domination of the six Shepherds *and their descendants* from first to last covered a space of 511 years. In the same way there are 13 years mentioned, during which Amenoph, the father of Sethos, was driven from his throne; and some years of Armaus-Danaus, during the absence of his brother Sethos, whose 59 years are said to be all "after the recovery of his kingdom, and the expulsion of his brother Danaus." The Chonographer then had to divine what was the truth; and he decided that, whatever facts might be alluded to under the stories connected with these years, the 19 years of Amenoph (at the end of Dyn. XVIII of Africanus) and the 59 of Sethos (at the commencement of XIX) were alone to be admitted and reckoned. So neglecting with him, and even with the author of the lists of Africanus, the incidental statements of the text of the original Manetho, and extracting only those lists of kings which are given with the years and months of each reign, we obtain through Josephus a distinct confirmation of our inference already made on other grounds, that the Diospolitan Dynasty XVIII, which expelled the Shepherds, followed immediately after that which stands as XV in the lists of Africanus. This latter then was really Dyn. XVII in the series of the original Manetho (for there is no doubt that he numbered and distinguished the XXX Dynasties, though he by no means exhibited them in a tabular form, which would have been only parading the inconsistency of his general narrative). And that such was also the true historical succession is confirmed from other sources, of which one, and a remarkable one, is this:— Syncellus mentions that it is a point "agreed upon by all, that Joseph came into Egypt under Apophis," the fourth, according to the original Manetho of Josephus, of the six Shepherd kings. But this fact, agreed upon by all, and yet reconcileable with the chronology of none (for it agrees neither with that of Africanus, nor with that of Eusebius, nor, taking the list as it stands in Josephus, even with that of Syncellus himself), must be supposed to rest upon some other anterior foundation. And if we reckon back from the commencement of Dyn. XVIII in B.C. 1748, 94 years before the Exodus, according to our joint scale of sacred and profane chronology collected from the Egyptian Chronicle and Josephus, we find the 130th year before the accession of Amosis, that is, the year of Joseph's advancement coinciding nearly with B.C. 1878, to be according to Manetho's list of the six Shepherds in Josephus the 31st year of Apophis; and so, Joseph having been born, as it appears, in the first year of the reign of Apophis, his coming into Egypt in his own 17th year falls also naturally in the 17th year of the reign of the same king, B.C. 1892.

Hitherto we have been going on the assumption that the original Manetho made in his three books XXX dynasties in all, and that within these, and naturally in Book I., the seven mythological groups given by Eusebius from Africanus were included. And to make room for the restoration of these seven groups as dynasties to their proper places, we have been bringing together indications from six distinct sources, which have concurred to justify the ejection of the anonymous Dynasties VII, VIII, IX, X, XIII, XVI, and XVII of the lists of Africanus.

We shall now begin afresh; and forgetting for the moment what first suggested or has since justified the ejection of these seven anonymous dynasties, we shall *assume*, as if *arbitrarily*, that those twenty-three dynasties of Africanus which are numbered I, II, III, IV, V, VI, XI, XII, XIV, XV, XVIII, and so on to XXX inclusive, were alone originally the dynasties of ordinary kings from Menes, and that they were numbered by Manetho himself as Dynasties VIII, IX, X, XI, XII, XIII, XIV, XV, XVI, XVII, XVIII, respectively, and so on, the dynasties from XVIII to XXX inclusive being identical as regards their numbering in the two schemes. To this assumption, presented as a mere arbitrary hypothesis, we shall apply a test which is furnished by Syncellus, but which he derived probably through Apollodorus from Eratosthenes.

"Manetho," says Syncellus, "the most celebrated historian of the Egyptians, writing of the same XXX Dynasties," (the same, that is, with those of the Chronicle described and copied out from Africanus just before,) "or at least taking them for his base, differs much from them in his spaces of time, as may be seen both from what has been said above, and from what shall be said further. For from the contents of his three books, that is to say, from the CXIII generations in XXX dynasties, *the Chronographer*," [ὁ χρόνος being a corruption from ὁ χρονογράφος written contractedly], "*collected* a sum total of 3555 years, ending about 15 years before the *cosmocracy* of Alexander." "Ὁ δὲ Μανεθῶ περὶ τῶν αὐτῶν λ' δυναστειῶν γράψας, ἐκ τούτων δηλαδὴ λαβὼν τὰς ἀφορμὰς, κατὰ πολὺ διαφωνεῖ περὶ τοὺς χρόνους πρὸς ταῦτα [ταύτας?] . . . . Τῶν γὰρ ἐν τοῖς γ' τόμοις ριγ' γενεῶν ἐν δυναστείαις λ' ἀναγεγραμμένων αὐτῶν [αὐτῷ, corrigit Buns.], ὁ χρονογράφος τὰ πάντα συνῆξεν ἔτη ͵γφνε' . . . λήξαντα πρὸ τῆς Ἀλεξάνδρου τοῦ Μακεδόνος κοσμοκρατορίας ἔτη που ιε'."—(*Sync. Chronograph.*, p. 52.)

It is clear that, in this passage, the sum of years spoken of by Syncellus is that of the kings, and that consequently they were collected *not* from *all* "the XXX dynasties" of the original Manetho, but from those only of the XXX which contained the years of kings from Menes, Syncellus here identifying the original with the Manetho of Africanus, in which the years of the kings form the whole contents both of the three books and of the thirty dynasties. The CXIII generations of the Chronicle being certainly not reproduced in any sense in the Manetho of Africanus, while they are distinctly exhibited, though in a varied form, by the latest pseudo-Manetho of Anianus and Panodorus, often followed by Syncellus, it would be natural to suppose that the ascription of the CXIII generations to the original Manetho was also a confused addition of Syncellus's own. But there is reason to think that Manetho really reckoned CXIII average generations of time (not CXIII names or reigns of kings). For 3555 divided by 113 gives an average of 31 years and about 5 months, which *of itself* agreeing neither with the general average of the Chronicle for its reigns or royal generations, which is $24\frac{1}{4}$, nor with the average of Herodotus for lives, which is $33\frac{1}{3}$, would rather discourage the thought that Manetho reckoned in any such peculiar generations of his own. But when we look into the sums of his dynasties of kings, we find that, in the first six, that is, in *all* the ancient dynasties of *Lower* Egypt, their forty-eight kings in 1491 years have, one with another, *reigns* not merely of $24\frac{1}{4}$ years each, the full average of the Chronicle, but of something over $30\frac{1}{4}$ years, being very nearly that peculiar average of $31\frac{52}{113}$ which is obtained on division of 3555 by 113; (and Dyn. I. of Africanus actually has for its reigns the full average of $31\frac{1}{8}$;) while the 113 kings of all the other following dynasties, exclusively of Dyn. XIV of Afric., have, if taken together, in 1880 years, an average of only $16\frac{72}{113}$ years to each. So we may suppose that his idea was to give CXIII average *generations*, in the sense of *lives*, not *reigns*, to the monarchy; but that, for some reason connected with the symmetry of his scheme, he made his generations somewhat shorter than they would have been, had he followed the usual calculation of three to a century, and somewhat longer than the analogous "XV generations of the Cycle" occurring in the Old Chronicle.

"The Chronographer" is no doubt Eratosthenes, though it was through Apollodorus, probably, as has been said above, that Syncellus derived his information. It is plain that Eratosthenes, in setting about the task imposed on him by the king, would have, as a first step, to consider and compare the sums and averages given to the kings after Menes by the Chronicle and by Manetho respectively. The sum of the former being 1881 years, ending 15 years before the cosmocracy of Alexander, the sum of the latter, as he collected it, turned out to be 3555, ending, as Syncellus understood, at the same point. Eratosthenes found in the Chronicle in all XXX dynasties and CXIII generations; but the 1881 years of kings occupied only XV of these XXX dynasties, and only LXXVI of the CXIII generations; and these LXXVI generations alone were average *reigns* of 24½ years, the XV dynasties of kings having each separately its own peculiar average artificially determined, but from the facts of its actual history. In Manetho's three books he found again the XXX dynasties, containing, like those of the Chronicle, not only kings after Menes, but Gods and Demigods besides. But here the kings after Menes occupied not XV only, but XXIII of the dynasties; and not LXXVI only out of CXIII, but a complete series of CXIII average life-generations of their own, besides others uncounted, which might belong to the Gods, the Demigods, and the Manes. And the dynasties of Manetho being filled with actual reigns, it was only in the first six that these actual reigns seemed to be identified, *on the whole*, with as many of his CXIII abstract *life generations*, though each dynasty by itself, like those of the Chronicle, has its own peculiarities.

Now, let us take the sum of 3555 collected by Eratosthenes from the original Manetho, and apply it as a separate test to the XXX dynasties of the kings in the lists of Africanus, as they stand, only cutting off Dyn. XXXI, as being manifestly of subsequent addition. According to the sums given by Africanus for the contents of the three books of his Manetho, viz. 2300 (or 2303) + 2121 + 1050, making in all 5471 or 5474 years of kings after Menes, there are 1916 over the sum of 3555. And even after deducting from this excess 1862 years, the sum of the seven dynasties we have ejected, there still remains an excess of 54 years, interpolated, as it would seem, in the re-edition of Ptolemy and Africanus, into the genuine dynasties of the original Manetho, supposing the sums given by Africanus for the three books to be correct, or all but correct.

But if we take the actual sums of the XXIII genuine dynasties as cast up by Syncellus (and these as varieties, even if inconsistent with the sums given for the Books, must be from some source), substituting only for his sums in Dyn. XV and XVIII of Africanus the sums of "Manetho himself" preserved by Josephus, and making one other correction from the text of Africanus, and from the Turin Papyrus, in the sum of Dyn. VI, we obtain the following as an approximative and conjectural restoration of the scheme of the original Manetho:—

## BOOK I.

| | | |
|---|---|---|
| Dyn. I. Of VII Gods from Phtha to Horus, Horus being last: Dyn. II. Of other Gods to Bitys, making [with the preceding] years . . . | | 13,900 |
| Dyn. III. Of Demigods, years 1255 [for which, to suit the sums given below, we may substitute . . . . . . | 1230] | |
| Dyn. IV. Of other Kings [Manes, viz. XXX Thebans ejected from the hieratic lists?] years . . . . . . . . . | 1817 | |
| Dyn. V. Of [Manes] XXX Memphites [ejected like the preceding,] years . . . . | 1790 | |
| Dyn. VI. Of [Manes] X Tanites [ejected like the preceding] years . . . . . | 350 | |
| Dyn. VII. Of Manes [CVI Nubians or Ethiopians similarly ejected?] years . . . . | 5813 | |
| Sum of years of the Demigods and Manes | | 11,000 |
| The sum total [of the VII mythological Dynasties, amounts to years] . . . . . . | | 24,900 |
| Dyn. VIII. [XVI of the Chron. with 190 years, I of Afric.] of VIII Thinite *kings*, years . . | | 253 |
| Dyn. IX. [II of Afric.] of IX Thinites . . | | 302 |
| Dyn. X. [XVII of the Chron. during 39 of its 103 years, III of Afric.] IX Memphites . . . | | 214 |
| Dyn. XI. [IV of Afric.] of VIII Memphites . . | | 277 |
| Dyn. XII. [V of Afric.] of IX Elephantinites . | | 248 |
| Dyn. XIII. [XVII of the Chron. during 22 years, VI of Afric.] of VI Memphites . . . | | 197 |

Dyn. XIV. [XI of Afric.] of XVI Diospolites, with 43, and after them Amenemhe I. with 16 years . 59

Sum of the kings in Book I., LXVI, and of years 1550

Which sum of 1550 years divided among LXVI kings will give to each reign an *apparent* average length of something under 20 years and 6 months.

## BOOK II.

Dyn. XV. [XVII of the Chron. during 42 years, XII of Afric.] of VII Diospolite Kings, years . 160
Dyn. XVI. [XIV of Afric.] of XXXVI [?] *Ksoites* 184
Dyn. XVII. [XXVII of the Chron. with 184 years, XV of Afric. with 284 years] of VI Shepherds . 259.10$^{m}$.
Dyn. XVIII. [XVIII of the Chron. with 348 years, XVIII of Afric.] of XVI Diospolites . 333

Sum of the years in Book II. . . . 936.10$^{m}$.
and of the kings (XXIX + XXXVI =) LXV, or LXVI.

(Or if the first fifteen years of Dynasty XIX are to be included, the sum in that case instead of 936 years and 10 months will be 951 years and 10 months.) The *apparent* average length of the reigns with XXXVI kings to Dynasty XVI is something under 9 years; but the average for the XXIX kings of the other three dynasties, without Dynasty XVI, is 25 years and a half.

## BOOK III.

Dyn. XIX. [XIX of the Chron. with 194 years] of VII Diospolites, years 15 + 194 = . . . 209
Dyn. XX. [XX of the Chron. during 135 years of its 228 years] of XII Diospolites . . . 135
Dyn. XXI. [XX of the Chron. during the last 93 of its 228 years] of VII Tanites, years [93 + 37 thrown up from below =] . . . . 130
Dyn. XXII. [XXI of the Chron. with 121 years] of IX Bubastites . . . . . . . 120
Dyn. XXIII. [XXII and XXIII of the Chron. and XXIV during 21 of its 44 years] of IV Tanites 89

Dyn. XXIV. [XXIV of the Chron. during 6 of its 44 years] of one Saite . . . . . . 6

Dyn. XXV. [XXV of the Chron. during 40 of its 44 years] of III Ethiopians . . . . . 40

Dyn. XXVI. [XXVI of the Chron. from the middle of its 27th year to its end] of IX Saites . . 150.6m.

Dyn. XXVII. [XXVIII of the Chron.] of VIII Persians, years 124, with 4 months cast down from above= . . . . . . . . . . 124.4m.

Dyn. XXVIII. [not in the Chron.] of one Saite, years [all unchronological, or cast down from above] . . . . . . . . . . 6

Dyn. XXIX. [its last 19 years = the first 19 of XXIX of the Chron.] of III Mendesians [Tanites?] years [1 + 4 months, unchronological, cast down from above + 19 historical =] . . . . . 20.4m.

Dyn. XXX. [XXIX of the Chron. during its last 20 years, and XXX] of III Sebennytes? . . 38

Sum of kings in Book III. LXVII, and of years 1068.2m. (Or, if the first fifteen years of Dynasty XIX are to be included in Book II., the sum of the years of Book III. will be 1053 years and 2 months). The *apparent* average length of the reigns is not quite 16 years.

The apparent sum of all the actual kings from Menes in the three books is (LXVI + LXV + LXVII =) CXCVIII, and that of the years is (1550 + 936.10m. + 1068.2m. =) 3555; giving CXIII life-generations at something less than 31 years and a half to a generation, but to CXCVIII reigns, if all be thrown together, giving an *apparent* average of scarcely 18 years. But we may subtract Dyn. XVI [XIV of Afric.] with its LXXVI kings and 184 years, (which will be safer than counting it with a conjectural reading of only XXIX, XXXVI or XXXVI kings to answer to the right hand side of the Karnak Chamber, these being supposed to represent two or three concurrent lines thrown together;) and again we may substract three kings at least either from Dyn. XXI or from Dyn. XXVI, as reduplications; and after these reductions the remaining CLVIII kings will have in the remaining 3371 years an apparent average of something over 20 years each. [Probably then the kings for the 184 years of the excluded Dyn. XVI were not really more than IX in any one single line; and, even if three lines were compressed into one, they would not be much above XXVI, which may be reconcileable with the appearance of XXX cartouches on the right hand side of the Karnak Chamber.]

The 3555 years of the kings, reckoned from Menes in XXIII dynasties by Manetho, end at the same point of time with the 1881 years of the kings reckoned from Menes in XV dynasties by the Chronicle, viz. at Nov. 18, B.C. 345, 14 years before Manetho's date for Alexander, that is, before the foundation of Alexandria, in B.C. 331, (for he throws up and so marks 14 years,) or 15 years before the *cosmocracy* of Alexander in B.C. 330, which is the reckoning of the Chronicle. But if we include also his seven mythological dynasties, the sum total of Manetho's scheme will amount to 28,455 years.

The scheme thus obtained is certainly in its details only conjectural and approximative; for it is not probable that the sum of years left by Ptolemy of Mendes, or cast up by Syncellus, was exactly that of the original Manetho (fractions only being equalised) in every dynasty except those two in which Josephus has helped us both to eject years added by Ptolemy, and to restore years and kings dropped out in the list of Africanus. And in Dyn. VI of Africanus (XIII of the original Manetho), though the text of Africanus expressly excludes the first 6 years of the 100 of Phiops from his reign, and the Turin Papyrus gives him not 100 but 90 and some units, which are lost, it is open to any one to argue that Eratosthenes, who gives him 100 *to his "generation,"* was herein following Manetho, and not considering only the exigencies of his own scheme of generations. No alteration, some may say, should have been introduced, except perhaps from Josephus, into the sums of Syncellus, which are either all to be followed consistently, or all debated, each on its own grounds, separately. But even though we leave to Dyn. VI of Africanus the 203 years given it by Syncellus, the sum of 3555 years found by Eratosthenes may still be said to be exactly exhibited, if only we suppose Eratosthenes to have understood that the 6 years of Dyn. XXVIII, that is, of Amyrtæus, are really only concurrent years included under the 124 of the Persians, and consequently to have omitted them from his reckoning. But there is another quarter in which errors of detail, however compensated, may be presumed to exist; when we consider that while the sums of the other dynasties have been taken from the lists of Africanus, with the fractions of the original Manetho rounded off to full years, the sums of four dynasties XV, XXVI, XXVII, and XXIX of Africanus are exhibited with fractions of 10, 6, 4, and 4 months respectively. Of these fractions the last three only are given anomalously, from whatever motive or accident, in the lists of Africanus; the first has been introduced incidentally by ourselves from the text of the original Manetho supplied by Josephus. And it can only be by accident that this fraction of ten months brought in by ourselves unites exactly into a whole year with the other fraction of two months which would otherwise have remained on adding up the sums of the three later dynasties. But in truth, in such an attempt at reconstruction as the present, and with such imperfect means at our disposal, *perfect* success, and the exact exhibition of arithmetical coincidences in detail, are grounds rather for suspicion against the process than for confidence in the result.

The general outline of Manetho's scheme having now been ascertained, it may be compared with those earlier cyclical schemes of B.C. 1322 and B.C. 305, the later of which, that of the Chronicle, he is said, with some variations, to have followed.

If one thought only of the times of the monarchy, which come last in the whole series, and compared the scheme of Manetho with that of the Chronicle, going back from the last year of Nectanebo II, it might seem at first sight as if Manetho's process had been to cover with additional kings, thrusting back Menes, first the "443 years of the Cycle" thrown back by the Chronicle, then its 217 of Demigods, then a round thousand of its 3984 years of the XIII Gods, and lastly 14 years besides, so as to have in all (1660 + 14 =)

1674 additional years of kings. And of these the last-mentioned number 14 might perhaps suggest a suspicion that either Apollodorus or Syncellus had misunderstood the reckoning and allusion of Eratosthenes; and that the 3555 years collected by the latter really covered the interval of 14 years between Nectanebo and the foundation of Alexandria in B.C. 331, which Manetho may have preferred to make his closing point rather than the "*cosmocracy*" of Alexander a year later. But this on examination will not turn out to be the case.

The mythological dynasties at the head of Manetho's scheme show that his first and greatest variation from the Chronicle was this; that whereas the Chronicle had picked out from the month-years of the older scheme of B. C. 1322 the precise number 2922, out of which they had all sprung, and had given these only (with certain heterogeneous fractional numbers of 681, 341, and 40 added) to its XIII Gods, suppressing one pseudo-cycle of 1461 month-years, and giving the remaining 21 pseudo-cycles of month-years (all except the 681 nominally detached) to the Sun; Manetho, on the contrary, wished to return towards the older method, and to re-distribute among Gods, Demigods, and Manes (the last, perhaps, an addition of his own) the myriads of month-years alienated from them by the Chronicle, so as to impose upon the imagination of his Greek readers. But the ejection in the Chronicle of one twenty-fourth part, one cycle we may call it, out of the original XXIV pseudo-cycles of month-years, in order to make room for the new cycle of real years growing since B. C. 1322, having destroyed the symmetry of the remaining sum of month-years, and their aptitude for division by 12, Manetho could not conveniently take them from the Chronicle as they stood, and redistribute its 33,603 month-years (30,000 + 681 + 2922) among his Gods, Demigods, and Manes. Had he done this, the true space of 2922 real years, underlying all the month-years, would neither have been recoverable on division by 12, as from the 34,064 month-years of the older scheme of B. C. 1322, nor would it have been indicated separately, as in the Chronicle. It was necessary, therefore, to make some change; and the change that he made was this:—Distinguishing in that original sum of 2922 real years, out of which all month-years, of whatever scheme, had grown, three sums of 2000, 900, and 22 respectively, he discarded not only the fancy of exhibiting an ἀποκατάστασις, but all idea of cyclical symmetry, and multiplied by 12 the two thousands only, so obtaining a sum of 24,000 month-years, resolvable at will, with all their subdivisions, into true years, and giving these with the 900 *unmultiplied* prefixed, in all 24,900 mixed or nominal years, to his Gods, Demigods, and Manes. Probably the 900 full years, equivalent to 10,800 of the month-years of the older schemes, made the reign of Phtha, if Phtha had a reign *in time*, and Manetho, like the informants of Diodorus, made him the offspring of Μὼτ or Νεῖλος. But the 22 real years still remaining, as *he* had no intention of giving precisely two cyclical spaces (i.e. 2922 real years) to the Gods, or to the old world, he made to be the first 22 years of Menes, at the head of the ordinary monarchy.

At the point, then, at which he ends his mythological dynasties, Manetho is short by 22 of the end of the first 2922 real years of human time, whether multiplied by 12, as in the older scheme of B.C. 1322, or by $11\frac{1}{2}$, as they are in the Chronicle; and he had before him, in the Chronicle, to convert into years of kings, if he pleased, after these 22 years, its 341 fictitious solar years added for a cyclical purpose, its 40 thrown up from between B.C. 345 and 305, its 217 of Demigods, and lastly its 443 thrown up from between B.C. 305 and A.D. 139, the true end of the Cycle which commenced in B.C. 1322. So he might have made out of these in all 1041, or, with the 22, 1063 fresh years of kings, in themselves partly real and partly fictitious (but as years of kings all chronologically fictitious, since Menes was thrust up to their head), before coming to the 1881 true and chronological years of the monarchy, as given by the Chronicle.

This, it seems, was not room enough for the materials he meant to use. So discarding those 341 fictitious years which in the earlier schemes had been inserted for a cyclical reason, but in his own uncyclical scheme had no propriety, he borrowed from the Chronicle its device of throwing up years "of the Cycle," that is, of the real current cycle, and used it not now for any cyclical purpose, but in order to obtain a sufficient framework of fictitious time, labelled as such for those that could understand, in which to place as consecutive dynasties of kings really contemporaneous and included historically within the 1881 years following. For this purpose, besides 22 years of the Gods, and the 217 of the Demigods, and the 443 of the last part "of the Cycle" *named* and thrown up by the Chronicle, he covered with kings a reduplication of those 978 years of the same Cycle which had passed between its commencement in B.C. 1322 and Nectanebo II.; so that, had he only retained those other 40 years of the Cycle from between B.C. 345 and B.C. 305 which the Chronicle had cast up *unnamed*, and had added to its Gods, he would have had exactly one cycle of fictitious years thrown up or reduplicated from between B.C. 1322 and A.D. 139, besides those 22 and 217 real years which he also added to the times of the monarchy. And then, reckoning downwards from the beginning, he would have had three cyclical spaces, two of real and the third of fictitious time, before coming to the true uncyclical continuation of 1120 years ending at the epoch of the real Cycle in B.C. 1322, with 978 thence to Nectanebo II., and 14 more on to Alexander and the foundation of Alexandria. But this he avoided, no doubt purposely; and, instead of retaining the whole 40 years of the interval between Nectanebo and the Lagidæ as thrown up by the Chronicle, he retained and added to the times of the early kings only 14 of these 40 years. Thus he at once avoided falling partially into a cyclical form, and marked the foundation of Alexandria, in the autumn of B.C. 331, as his own epoch for the close of native Egyptian history and the commencement of the times of the Macedonians.

The three schemes, of B.C. 1322, of the Chronicle of B.C. 305, and of the original Manetho, may now be compared with one another as follows:—

In the scheme of B.C. 1322, A, the first 2922 years of real time, as reckoned by the Egyptians, × 12, become 35,064 nominal years, really months, divisible into 23,220

+ (681 + 2922 + 341) + (1120 + 6780); or into 32,142 + 2922; or into 10,800 + 24,000 + 264.

In the scheme of the Chronicle, B, the same first 2922 real, or 35,064 month-years, by the suppression of one pseudo-cycle of 1461 of their number, become 33,603, this being the same thing as if 2922 had been multiplied by $11\frac{1}{2}$ instead of 12. And 33,603 nominal years of the Chronicle are divisible into 30,681 + 2922; or into 9900 + 23,000 + 253.

In the scheme of Manetho, C, the same first 2922 real years are exhibited by 900 full years (which would equal, if multiplied by 12, 10,800 of the month-years of A) + 24,000 month-years + 22 full years (which, if multiplied by 12, would equal 264 of the month-years of A).

Then, as regards the 1120 more years of real time following upon the first 2922, and reaching to the cyclical epoch, July 20, B. C. 1322, the scheme connected with that epoch, A, prefixes to these 1120 real years 341 other fictitious years, in order to fill them up to 1461, and make time seem to have run from the first in Sothic cycles. The complete cycle of 1461 years thus obtained (being the third, or the twenty-fifth, according as the first 2922 real years are reckoned simply, or are multiplied by 12), is divisible into [341] + 217 + 903.

The scheme of the Chronicle, B, has the same addition of the 341 fictitious years; and its third space of 1461 full years thus obtained, is consequently in truth, and for the initiated, composed of the same elements as in the older scheme A, and is divided or divisible (for the 341 do not stand out of themselves) into [341] + 217 + 903. But *in appearance* its third cycle of full (or twenty-*fourth* of mixed) years is constituted very differently, viz. of [341] + [40] + 217 + [443] + 420, this last number being the first 420 only of the 903 years. The true cyclical epoch of B. C. 1322 is put back by 483 years to an imaginary point answering to B. C. 1805, in order that a *fourth* cycle of *full*, or twenty-fifth of mixed years, may seem to end in B.C. 345, 483 years before the true cyclical epoch of A. D. 139.

The scheme of Manetho, C, not being cyclical, omits the 341 fictitious years inserted as a cyclical complement in the two older schemes; or rather it substitutes for them a greater number of fictitious years of its own, viz. 978, these being the first 978 years "of the Cycle," the years, that is, which had passed from B. C. 1322 to Nectanebo II., reduplicated and thrown back, in like manner as the remaining 40 past and 443 future years of "the Cycle," i. e. of the cycle current in Manetho's time, had been thrown back by the Chronicle. And of these latter Manetho retained the 443 as thrown up; but of the 40 years' interval between Nectanebo II. and the Lagidæ, as thrown up in the Chronicle, he retained only 14 years, partly, as has been explained above, in order to mark his own closing point to be the foundation of Alexandria, and partly to avoid making one precise cycle of anticipated years.

Setting aside all amplification by the help of month-years, the four schemes of A, B, C, and that preserved by Diogenes Laertius, which may be called D, will stand parallel to one another thus:

| | | | |
|---|---|---|---|
| A. | (1935 + 328.9m + 658.4m) | +[341] — — + 217 + 903 | to B. C. 1322. |
| B. | 2922 | +[341]+[40]+217 +[443]+420+483+978 | to B.C. 345. |
| C. | 900 + 2000 + 22 | +[978 + 14 +443]+ 217 + 903 +978 | to B.C. 345. |
| D. | 2922 | — — — + 217 + 903 +978+13 | to B.C. 332. |

To kings from Menes the older scheme, A, probably gave only 903 years, from B.C. 2224 to B.C. 1322; the Chronicle, B, and the authors of the computation in Diogenes Laertius, D, continued with 978 years more to B.C. 345, so making in all 1881, with 15 or 13 on to Alexander the Great in B.C. 330 or B.C. 332. Manetho alone made to Nectanebo II. 3555 years of kings from Menes, who so seemed to be put back by him (443 + 217 + 14 + 978 + 22 =) 1674 years from the anticipated Julian year B.C. 2224 to B C. 3897. But of these 3555 years all but the last 1881 are either years anterior to Menes, belonging originally to Gods and Demigods; or else they are years unhistorical and fictitious, years posterior to Nectanebo, or even years of Ptolemies and Cæsars yet future, anticipated and thrown back by the Chronicle to times before Menes, but made by Manetho to follow him; or lastly, they are years absent from all the earlier schemes, reduplicated and thrown back, i. e. fabricated, after the example of the Chronicle, by Manetho himself.

Placed after an imposing series of mythological dynasties, the *kings* of Manetho were plainly meant to be all taken for consecutive; and it might have been enough for his purpose merely to enumerate the groups of their dynasties in the order in which the cities of Tanis, Memphis, and Thebes rose successively to importance, without alluding to the fact that some dynasties were contemporary. Not content with this, he has added here and there short notices implying that each king and dynasty reigned successively over all Egypt. But for us who have found in the origin of his other spaces of time a confession that all the dynasties of kings are contained chronologically within the space of 1881 years, the only problem is to discover the true historical place and duration of each.

That there were in early times a number of kings reigning at once in different parts of Egypt is not only most probable from the analogy of neighbouring nations, but it is alluded to by Herodotus as a fact; perhaps also in the book of Psalms; (cv. "ἄρχοντας αὐτοῦ," his princes, and "πρεσβυτέρους" or σατράπας·) and it is distinctly asserted from Egyptian sources by others, as by Artapanus, who with reference to the end of Dyn. XV of Africanus (XVII of Manetho) and the commencement of XVIII says that in those times there were many kings reigning in Egypt, "πολλοὺς γὰρ τότε τῆς Αἰγύπτου βασιλεύειν." And hence Africanus makes no difficulty even to admit that all the XXXI Dynasties of Ptolemy of Mendes might have reigned since the Flood and the Dispersion: "Quod si temporum copia adhuc exuberet, reputandum sedulo est plures fortasse Ægyptiorum reges unâ eâdemque ætate extitisse: namque et Thinitas regnavisse aiunt et Memphitas, et Saitas et Æthiopas, eodemque tempore alios. Videntur præterea alii quoque alibi imperium tenuisse, atque hæ dynastiæ suo quoque in Nomo semet continuisse; ita ut haud singuli reges successivam potestatem acceperint, sed alius alio loco eâdem ætate regnaverit. Atque hinc contigit ut tantus cumulus annorum conficeret." (*Euseb. Chron.* i. c. 19, *e Versione Lat. ex Arm. Ed. Mai.*)

But what is most of all to the purpose is this, that Manetho himself in his narrative not only, at the commencement of the dynasty of the Shepherds, speaks of them as subjecting the native princes of Egypt, in the plural, (τοὺς ἡγεμονεύσαντας ἐν αὐτῇ χειρωσάμενοι,) but also at its end shows that the same native rulers had continued all along, though as vassals or tributaries: "At last," he says, "the kings of the Thebaid and of the other parts of Egypt rose up against the Shepherds, and there followed a great and long war, which ended in their expulsion." "Μετὰ ταῦτα τῶν ἐκ τῆς Θηβαΐδος καὶ τῆς ἄλλης Αἰγύπτου βασιλέων γενέσθαι φησὶν ἐπὶ τοὺς Ποιμένας ἐπανάστασιν," κ.τ.λ. And still more precisely in an hieratic MS., approaching in antiquity to the time itself, it is said that at the moment, seemingly, when independence was first asserted there was *only one* native king surviving in all Egypt, besides the Shepherd Apophis at Avaris; and that one was a king named Raskennen, who reigned in Upper Egypt; the same, no doubt, whose name (found also in the list of Eratosthenes) stands last in the lowest line on the left hand side of the Karnak Chamber.

Subdivision of Egypt during 477 years, B.C. 2224-1748

This then being clear both from the fictitious spaces in which many of Manetho's dynasties are arranged, and from direct testimony of others, and even of Manetho himself, it is next to be noticed that the *limits* within which all the concurrent dynasties of early times were confined are open to no doubt; for all agree that a single monarchy for all Egypt was founded by Menes. So no secondary dynasty can be made to begin before his; nor is it probable perhaps that any one began until after his death. On the other hand it is a point equally agreed upon that the kings of Dyn. XVIII united all Egypt, and Nubia too, under a single sceptre; and we see them on the monuments all wearing indifferently the two crowns of the Upper and Lower country, and the imperial crown or *pshent* compounded out of them both. But the space between the accession of Menes and that of Amosis, head of Dyn. XVIII, consists according to the Chronicle of 190 + 103 + 184, in all 477 years, of its Dynasties XVI, XVII, and XXVII, of Tanites, Memphites, and Shepherds.

In this space of 477 years the first point is to identify, if possible, in Manetho's lists the three leading dynasties of the Chronicle; which done, we may try to place the other secondary dynasties. About the first there is no difficulty, Dyn. I of Africanus (VIII of Manetho) being clearly identical with the Tanite Dyn. XVI of the Chronicle. And, further, as these two dynasties, beginning from the same point, and having the same number of VIII kings, are absolutely coincident the one with the other, it appears from their collation that Manetho (the later author of the two) has added 63 years to the true length of the reigns, giving the eight kings an average of 31½ years each, instead of one of 23¾ (somewhat below the ordinary average of 24⅓) which they have in the Chronicle. And on examination it appears that Manetho has done nearly the same by all those first six dynasties of his kings (I to VI inclusively of Africanus) which really belong to Lower Egypt; these dynasties having in all 49 kings and 1491 years, which give over 30 years to each king.

Dyn. VIII. viii Tanites, 190 years, March 3, B.C. 2224, to Jan. 14, B.C. 2034.

The Memphite Dyn. XVII of the Chronicle cannot be identified with any *one* of the dynasties of Manetho; but from an examination and comparison of the list of Eratosthenes it appears that his informants understood it to consist of two kings and 39 years taken from Dyn. X of Manetho (III of Africanus), or from the uppermost line on the left side of the Karnak Chamber, of one king, Papa Maire, from Dyn. XIII of Manetho (VI of Africanus), or from the second line on the left side of the Karnak Chamber, with the last 22 years of his long reign, and of one king, Sesortasen I, with 42 years, from Dyn. XV of Manetho (XII of Africanus). And the monuments justify this succession, showing clearly that Papa Maire and Sesortasen at least (to say nothing of Sahoura and Snefru) were sovereigns of all Egypt before the domination of the Shepherds; and Herodotus names Mœris as the immediate predecessor of the conqueror of Ethiopia.

Passing over Dyn. XVII, and coming to XXVII of the Chronicle, this again is easily identified with Dyn. XV of Africanus (XVII of Manetho). And after having detected Manetho adding to the years of Dyn. XVI of the Chronicle, one might suppose that here also the 259 years and 10 months of the six kings should be reduced to 184, the sum of the Chronicle. But there are signs against this; for it is most *probable* that the Chronicle had only *four* generations to the 184 years of its Dyn. XXVII, and *three* to its Dyn. XXIX; and the additions made by Manetho to the first six of his dynasties, all that belong to Lower Egypt, are followed by curtailments in the next three (XI, XII, XIV of Africanus) belonging to Upper Egypt: and after this he would scarcely begin again to exaggerate merely to do honour to the Shepherds, nor favour them above native Thebans, even though these latter were from Upper and the Shepherds from Lower Egypt. It is also more probable that the Shepherds had been for some time settled in the Delta when they became dominant, than that they came in as invaders and took Memphis at once. It is safer, therefore, to let the figures of Dyn. XVII of Manetho (XV of Africanus) stand as they are, and to suppose that only the last 184 years of its last four reigns correspond to Dyn. XXVII of the Chronicle.

Eratosthenes, a great authority, having been persuaded to add to the times of the monarchy the XV generations or 443 years "of the Cycle" thrown up by the Chronicle, in spite of the difficulty of transposing them so as to stand below Menes, and of blending them with the coherent series of dynasties into which they were to be interpolated, it is natural to inquire whether then there was really any great difficulty in placing all Manetho's ten dynasties anterior to Dyn. XVIII in the space of 477 years? In order to examine this question fairly the first six dynasties of Manetho must, as a general rule, be reduced from his exaggerated average of life-generations of above 30 years each to reigns of 24½ years each, the average of the Chronicle and of Eratosthenes; and the three dynasties of Upper Egypt which follow will have to receive a proportionate expansion.

Dyn. IX. ix Tanites, 174 years. Jan. 14, B.C. 2034, to Dec. 27, B.C. 1861; or, Jan. 30, B.C. 2095, to Dec. 17, B.C. 1922?

The first dynasty of Tanite Kings, after its 190 years, might well enough be succeeded in the same city by a second of the same lineage, or a younger branch beginning from the time when the Memphites became predominant. But in this case, after 103 years, or little more, we should expect it to cease, the Shepherds who then became masters residing in that part of the Delta, and the name of the last

Shepherd king being still visible in the ruins of Tanis. But the IX Kings of Manetho with the full average of 24½ would have in all 220 years, continuing during 117 years under the Shepherds, which, though unlikely, is certainly *possible*, as the Shepherds made their own special residence not at Tanis, nor at Memphis, but at Avaris. In the list of Eratosthenes, however, the *last* two kings of Dyn. IX of Manetho (II of Africanus) are detached, and, being consolidated into one generation of 79 years, stand at the head of the earliest Memphite dynasty; while the remaining sum of the second dynasty of Tanites, 224, unreduced by Eratosthenes, is *indicated* as complete long after, viz. ten years after the commencement of the 184 years of the dominion of the Shepherds. Seemingly, too, Eratosthenes begins his Memphites with the first cartouche of the uppermost line on the left hand side of the Karnak chamber. His variation seems to correct a curious and gross blunder in the original compilation of Manetho's lists, as if Manetho, without attending to the truth of history or to the monuments, had either copied or miscopied from some hieratic MS., so as to put the rubric dividing his Dyn. VIII of Tanites from X of Memphites two names too low, making the head of the Memphites, who reigned perhaps no long time after the death of Menes, to become the last king but one of a dynasty which began long after his time. But even after accepting from Eratosthenes this correction, the VII kings who remain will claim 173¼ years, and will last 70½ into the time of the Shepherds, or, it might be, somewhat less, if the actual reigns fell short of the usual average. Another idea is suggested by the fact that the end of this dynasty is indicated by Eratosthenes only 10 years after the end of Dyn. III of Africanus, viz., that though it be called Tanite, this designation may be used in a wide sense, like those of Memphite and Diospolite afterwards, and may mean only that its kings were by origin and locality connected with Tanis, and with that part of the Delta of which Tanis was the capital; not that they actually reigned in the same city with the kings of Dyn. I of Africanus. But perhaps, for example, there were two cities of Tanis, divided by the water, as Memphis and Heliopolis were separated, with a greater interval, by the Nile; and these may have had at once two lines of kings. In this case the VII kings of the second dynasty of Thinites (Tanites), if their actual average equalled 24½ years, may have commenced 60½ years before the end of the first dynasty, and may have ended, as Eratosthenes hints they did, 10 years after the end of Dyn. III of Africanus, and 10 therefore also after that of Dyn. XVII of the Chronicle.

Dyn. X. IX Memphites. 214. Feb. 11, B.C. 2145, to Dec. 20, B.C. 1932.

Dyn. III of Africanus (X of Manetho) the first of Memphites, is clearly paralleled by Eratosthenes, and its IX kings seem to be identified by him with the earliest names on the left hand side of the Karnak chamber. According to the general average they might claim 222⅔ years, but Manetho gives them only 214, which is probably then their actual number.

Dyn. XI. VIII Memphites. 177. Dec. 20, B.C. 1932, to Nov. 6, 1755.

And Dyn. IV of Africanus (XI of Manetho) not only seems to follow III, but can be shown to have done so: and being thus connected with it, Dyn. IV helps much to fix the place of III, and the epoch of its commencement. In the lists of Eratosthenes the kings of Dyn. IV follow, as here, next after those of III, and occupy in Lower Egypt the chronological place of the Shepherds of Dyn. XXVII of the Chronicle. Herodotus says that they were impious and tyrannical, and that their memory was so odious, that the Egyptians would scarce name them if they could avoid it. Exactly the same is said by Manetho of the Shepherds, who are altogether omitted both on the monuments and in the lists of Eratosthenes, and are all but omitted by the Chronicle, while the kings of Dyn. IV also are omitted from the monumental succession in Upper Egypt. During their time Egypt, according to Herodotus, was subjected by destiny to a Typhonian influence; and the dominion of the Shepherds is connected by Manetho also with destiny and with a malignant deity; and the city of Avaris, where they lived, and the whole region of the Sethroitic arm of the Nile, is according to him Typhonian, the special province of Typhon. The Memphite kings of Dyn. IV, according to Herodotus and Manetho, built the pyramids; and according to Herodotus the same pyramids were *also* ascribed to the Shepherd Philition, who contemporaneously fed his flocks "in those parts," i.e. in Lower Egypt.

Lastly, in Manetho's heading of Dyn. IV, naming it Memphite, it is added "of another lineage," i. e. *not* a continuation of Dyn. III, which they are implied to have succeeded. And in Dyn. XV it is noticed of the Shepherds that they "took Memphis;" and elsewhere it is implied that native rulers, not only in the Thebaid but in the rest of Egypt, were continued under the Shepherds; so that if, as was natural, they put nominees and creatures of their own into the place of that Memphite family which they had violently dispossessed, one understands how the kings of Dyn. IV came to be "of another lineage," and so to constitute a new dynasty, and how their memory in later times shared the odium attaching to that of the Shepherds. And though such great works as the pyramids at Memphis or the labyrinth in the Fayoum may suggest an idea that the kings who built them must have been sovereigns of all Egypt, this idea has no real cogency. On the contrary, the peculiar circumstances of the famine, and the permanent changes occasioned by it, may well account for the fact that under the kings of Dynasties IV and XII of Africanus public works in Egypt suddenly assume gigantic proportions, and that, from that time forth, the kings become more absolute, and have greater multitudes of men at their disposal both for civil and for military service. On the other hand the "Ethiopian stone," i. e. the granite, used for casing the third pyramid hints that the Suphises and Mencheres lived after the conquest of Nubia, and not before those kings Mœris and Sesostris (i. e. Papa Maire and Sesortasen I.), whose predecessors "had done nothing remarkable." But if the eight kings of Dyn. IV of Africanus, who might claim 198 years, are to be reduced so as to cover only the 184 of the Shepherds, or somewhat less, and Dyn. III of Africanus cannot be supposed to continue after the capture of Memphis and the commencement thereupon of the Shepherd domination, it follows, that the commencement of the 214 years of Dyn. III must be put up 111 years before the end of Dyn. I of Africanus; that is, it will have commenced about 79 years after the accession of Menes, a date not at all improbable.

Dynasty V of Africanus (XII of Manetho), which, with Dyn. XII. in East Bank

Memphites? 228 years. Feb. 12, B.C. 2149, to Dec. 17, B.C. 1921; or, Jan. 1, B.C. 1982, to Nov. 5, B.C. 1751.

its IX kings, must be reduced from 248 to 222¾ [228 or 218] years, having a separate designation (ἐξ Ἐλεφαντίνης), causes no difficulty. Its kings were certainly connected with Memphis (for their names occur mixed with those of Dynasty IV of Africanus in the tombs about the pyramids), and if they reigned at Heliopolis they might be regarded as Memphites of the *East* bank; for "*Abt*," the Egyptian word for the east, is also the name of Elephantine. Since they are a separate line, there is no difficulty in supposing them to have commenced at any date not earlier than the commencement of Dynasty III; and this is a point on which light can be thrown only by the monuments, or by hieratic papyri. But if they began later, and lasted together with the Memphites of Dynasty IV through, or almost through, the 184 years of the Shepherds, they would have begun 86 or 94 years before the termination of Dynasty III of Africanus (X of Manetho), and also 90 or 84 before the termination of Dynasty XVII of the Chronicle.

Dyn. XIII. vi Memphites. 181 years. Feb. 8, B.C. 2133, to Dec. 25, B.C. 1952.

Dynasty VI, again, of Africanus, though called Memphite, must be a separate line by itself, both because we have already had one succession of Memphites reaching down to Dynasty XVIII; and also because it is separated from that succession in Manetho's lists by a dynasty with another designation. So the name "Memphite" is used in a wide sense. And, in fact, the monuments connect the kings of this dynasty chiefly with central Egypt, while from the lists of Eratosthenes it is found to contribute one name, that of Phiops with his last 22 years, to make the third of the four Memphite generations of Dynasty XVII of the Chronicle. And the monuments mark the 18th year of the sovereignty of this king *over all Egypt;* which sufficiently shows that he reigned before the Shepherds and their Memphite contemporaries, of Dynasties XV and IV of Africanus. If we let the last three reigns of this dynasty stand as actual reigns, only with 94 not 100 years to Phiops, and reduce the first three, in conformity with the average of 24¾, to 74¼ years, the whole dynasty having then 181¼ years ending 29 years before the end of Dynasty XVII of the Chronicle, it must be supposed to have begun 108¼ years before the end of Dyn. I of Africanus, i. e. only 82, or 81 after Menes, in the very same years, perhaps, according to our scale of averages, with the earliest Memphite dynasty, the two being a double offshoot, at one and the same point, from the trunk line of Tanis. As for the notice of Manetho that Nitocris, the last name in Dynasty VI of Africanus, "built the third pyramid," this is of no weight, since we know both that it was the purpose of Manetho to present all the dynasties as successive, and that, whenever it suited his purpose to make them so, his assertions are fabulous. Still, since even falsehood must have had some source, one may reasonably inquire after the source of this notice; and we may perhaps find it, if we put together the following facts:—Herodotus was told that the third pyramid was built by Mycerinus; and rightly, for his name and sarcophagus have been found in it. He says, also, that some pretended it was built by a certain beauty named Rhodopis (compare the words *ὡραιοτάτη, ξανθὴ τὴν χροίαν*, in the lists), of the times of the Saites of Dyn. XXVI. He saw himself "*at Sais*" the wooden coffin, in the form of a cow, of the daughter of King *Mycerinus*, whom he naturally identified with the builder of the third pyramid, whereas, in truth, it was a Saite king of Dyn. XXVI, who had taken to himself exceptionally the name of Mencheres; and two *Nitocrises*, mother and daughter, appear in the same family as Pallades, and as connected with the kings Necho II. and Psammitichus II.; and with the latter of these two kings, the Greek name of Doricha or Rhodopis also seems to be connected. The pyramid of Mycerinus is said to be of double construction, as if a smaller pyramid, built for one sepulchre, had afterwards been made the nucleus of a larger. The reign of Mycerinus having been cut short according to Herodotus, this agrees with the idea that his pyramid might be enlarged and finished afterwards, perhaps by his daughter, perhaps by a queen such as Amessis, certainly not by Nitocris of Dyn. VI. But it is to be remarked that Manetho, having given Mycerinus a reign of 66 years, long enough to complete any one of the pyramids, says not of Nitocris that she *finished*, but simply that she built, "*ἤγειρε*," the third pyramid, which is a plain falsehood, blending well with the Greek story of Rhodopis, but contradicted both by Herodotus and by the pyramid itself. However, if any one wish to make the best of the case for Manetho, and if the construction of the pyramid admit of the hypothesis, it is open for him to imagine that Nitocris of Dyn. VI of Africanus may have "built" a small pyramid (since pyramids were built from the time of the third successor of Menes), which afterwards became the nucleus of "the third pyramid" built and completed, under Dyn. IV of Africanus, by Mencheres. And though it is true that the use of granite can be traced as high as the time of Papa Maire (the Mœris of Herodotus),—for he is said by Pliny ("Phios and Smarres," he writes the names) to have set up two plain obelisks, of no great size, still perhaps to be seen at Rome, and an altar of black basalt, bearing his name, is preserved in the museum at Turin,—still it is not likely that the use of "Ethiopic stone," such as partly faced the third pyramid, was introduced on any great scale before the time of Sesortasen I., the successor of Papa-Maire as sovereign of all Egypt, and the first conqueror of Nubia.

Dyn. XIV. xvi Diospolites, [illegible]. Feb. 11, B.C. [illegible], to Nov. [illegible], B.C. 1748. [illegible]

To come now to the three dynasties of Upper Egypt, XI, XII, and XIV (as it seems) of Africanus, numbered XIV, XV, and XVI by the original Manetho:—For the earliest Diospolite dynasty, Dyn. XIV of Manetho (XI of Africanus,) the number of kings given is XVI; and a series of XIII names, probably representing these, and nearly justifying the number, appears on the left-hand side of the Karnak Chamber, with a shorter line, viz., the kings of Dyn. XII of Africanus, following one another in a contrary order, interposed in the midst of them. The XIII names are—1. A prince named *Enantef* or *Nantef* (which in Greek might be Enantæus or Myrtæus): his name alone, of them all, is not inclosed in a cartouche. 2. *Mentuhotep I.* (perhaps the same whose throne-name is *Ra-neb-teti*). 3. *Enantef II.* 4. *Enantef III.* (whose other name perhaps is known). 5. Perhaps (for the name is not preserved) *Enantef IV.*, with the addition *Aa*, and the throne-name *Ra-tap-ma-kherp*; for the sarcophagi of two of these kings, brothers, the one of whom buried the other, have been found at Thebes, and with other objects from the same tomb, bearing their names, are now in the museums of London, Paris, and Leyden. 6. *Enantef V., Ra-her-per-ma-kherp*, whose sarcophagus is preserved. 7. Perhaps *Mentuhotep II.* (for this name is again effaced). 8. *Ra-s-neferkar.* 9. *Ra-neb-cheru* (whose family name, elsewhere found conjoined with this, is *Mentuhotep III.*; his 46th year is marked on a stele from Abydos in the Turin museum, and in one of the monumental lists at Thebes, at the Ramesseum, his name appears as the sole intermediate link between Menes and Amosis head of Dyn. XVIII). 10. *Ra-nub-cheper* (whose family name, elsewhere conjoined with this, is *Enantef*). 11. *Tseser-en-ra* (the same name with that of a Memphite king of Dyn. III of Africanus, who built one of the pyramids). 12. *Sescht-en-ra* (to whom Bunsen gives the family name *Aah-hotep*). 13. *Ra-s-kennen*, whose family name is *Taanaken*, and who is known to have been the immediate predecessor of Amosis, the founder of Dyn. XVIII. There are also on the monuments two or three other names seemingly connected with these, such as *Ra-spen-neb*, *Ka-mes*, and an earlier *Ra-s-kennen*, which will bring up the list to the full number of sixteen kings.

But these XVI kings have in fact *no years* assigned to them by Manetho; for the 43 years nominally given to them are probably intended only to mark off so many years really belonging to Dyn. XII of Africanus but detached because after those 43 years the remaining kings of the dynasty were no longer lords of Memphis and of all Egypt. Else, to divide 43 years between XVI kings, giving less than 2 years and 8 months to each, and that too after all their predecessors have averaged something over 31 years each, is plainly absurd. But if we give them 24½ each, the full average of the Chronicle and Eratosthenes, they will cover 396 years. And supposing them to end, as the monuments seem to show that they did end, immediately before the commencement of Dyn. XVIII, they will even so have begun as early as the 81st year after Menes, that is, very little later than the other two branch-lines from the original trunk of Tanis, viz., that of the Memphites of Memphis itself, and that of the Memphites of Central Egypt, Dyn. III and Dyn. VI of Africanus; for we need not now speculate about the date of the origin of his Dyn. V.

Dyn. XV. viii Diospolites, 191. Jan. 3, B.C. 1989, to Nov. 17, B.C. 1799.

The VII kings of Dyn. XV of Manetho (XII of Africanus) are also named Diospolite; and we have seen that the first of them, Sesortasen I., is shown by the list of Eratosthenes to make the last of the four "Memphite" generations of Dyn. XVII of the Chronicle. The monuments justify both designations, connecting, on the one hand, Sesortasen I. with the earlier Memphite kings Siscrirenra and Aan; and on the other showing that Thebes itself was not the ordinary residence either of himself, or of his co-regents Amenemhe I. and II., or of their successors of Dyn. XII of Africanus, but was ruled by a line of local kings (Dyn. XI of Africanus) of secondary importance, while the monuments and tombs of the later kings of Dyn. XII appear rather in the Fayoum. Still, after they had lost the sovereignty over Memphis and Lower Egypt, they might rightly be called Diospolites, as sovereigns of all *Upper* Egypt; as before, for some similar reason, they were styled Memphites.

According to Manetho the VII kings of his Dyn. XV (Dyn. XII of Africanus) have 160 years, with average reigns of nearly 23 years each, Amenemhe I. (counting whom there would be VIII kings with 176 years, and an average of 22 years to each) being named only as an appendage to the preceding dynasty. But in the Turin papyrus the VIII kings of this dynasty, Amenemhe I. being the first, have a sum of 213 years, 1 month, and 17 days. The separate reigns, as partly still legible in the papyrus, partly restored conjecturally by comparison of such traces as remain in the papyrus with the Greek lists, should succeed one another in some such way as follows:—

16. Jan. 3, B.C. 1989, to Dec. 30, B.C. 1974; or 9, to Jan. 1, B.C. 1980.

I. *Amenemhe I., Ra-s-hotep-het.*—The papyrus, after the sign for years, and seemingly in direct connection with it, in fragment No. 64, retains distinct traces of the number ix. (Bunsen quotes Seyffarth for [x]ix, but there is neither any trace of a x, nor appearance of room for it.) Manetho gives only xvi years. In an inscription on a stele now at Paris, "the 8th year" is named in connection with two kings at once, Amenemhe I. and Sesortasen I.; and again in another inscription, also at Paris, the "9th year of Sesortasen I." is marked, the name of Amenemhe I. also, but without any other titles, being prefixed. Hence it seems that whether Amenemhe I. reigned in all only 16, or more from some earlier accession, he had for his last 7 years *at least*, perhaps even for the full 16 years, Sesortasen I. for his colleague on the throne of Upper Egypt, [~~where he appears originally as contemporary with, and as some think subordinate to a king named Mentuhotep (whom we have placed in Dyn. XI of Africanus)~~.] Eratosthenes seemingly gave these two kings Amenemhe I. and Sesortasen I. under two names (Peteathyres and another which has fallen out) as *two* of his *generations* numbered XXXI and XXXII, but with only *one* joint *reign* of 42 years, a sum, as we may infer, representing the whole time during which Sesortasen I., whether jointly with Amenemhe I. and II. or alone, was sovereign of all Egypt, after the death of Papa Maire. Of any earlier years which either Amenemhe I. may have reigned in Upper Egypt before Sesortasen became his colleague, or Sesortasen in Lower Egypt either before or after his alliance with Amenemhe I., whose daughter probably he married (since he is called 'Αμμενεμίδης), Eratosthenes takes no notice; but it is certainly quite possible that from their earliest accessions Amenemhe I. may have reigned 19 years or more, and Sesortasen I., not 42 only, or 45, or 46, but even 48 or 49 years. The 42 years of Eratosthenes are probably identical chronologically with the 43 given to the contemporary Dyn. XI of Africanus by Manetho, some fractional months and days, amounting nearly to half a year, having been cut off in compiling the one list, but filled up in the other.

II. *Sesortasen I., Ra-cheper-ka.*—In a fragment of the Turin papyrus, numbered 67, and supposed to have contained the figures for this and the four following reigns, there are traces, after the uppermost sign for "years," of the number xl, and most probably also of viii; certainly either of viii or v. (Bunsen gives the number xlv as "still legible.") Africanus gives this king only xlvi years, which

48. Jan. 1, B.C. 1979, to Dec. 20, B.C. 1932. Or 42, Dec. 31, B.C. 1974, to Dec. 20, B.C. 1932. Erat.

would agree well with Bunsen's reading of the papyrus, if we suppose that the papyrus made xlv years, and a fraction exceeding vi months. It appears that in his 41st or 42nd year he associated his successor, as there is an inscription which names conjointly the 44th year of Sesortasen I. and the 3rd year of Amenemhe II. The xlii years then given by Eratosthenes to Amenemhe I. and Sesortasen I. jointly, if they end at the death of the latter, include the first five at least of Amenemhe II., who in that case might be reckoned chronologically to reign only 33 instead of 38 years. The xlii years begin probably, as has been said above, from the date when Sesortasen I. became sovereign of all Egypt, which we collect from Eratosthenes, and indirectly also from Herodotus, was upon the death of Papa Maire. And it may be that his alliance and union with Amenemhe I. was either made in the same year with this event, or a few years before.

38. Dec. 22, B.C. 1940, to Dec. 13, B.C. 1902. Or 23, Dec. 20, B.C. 1932, to Dec. 14, B.C. 1909. Erat.

III. *Amenemhe II., Ra-nub-karu.*—In the papyrus, after the sign for years, there is the greater part of a sign which, when perfect, must have been either x, xx, or xxx, followed, it may be, by units, and by fractional months and days. We may conjecture that the sum of the years marked was [xx]x[viii], so as to agree with the number in the lists of Africanus. Colonel Felix concluded from a stele which he saw at Alexandria, but which unhappily has been lost since, that Amenemhe II. was son of Amenemhe I., whence Bunsen argues that Sesortasen I. and Amenemhe II. were brothers: but this would not follow merely because Sesortasen I. is called "son" of Amenemhe (he might be son-in-law); and it is sufficiently disproved by the fact that Amenemhe II. was associated by Sesortasen I. only in his 41st or 42nd year, and reigned himself 38 years afterwards. It is true that Eratosthenes gives him only xxiii years, but this is perhaps an error, since the monuments mark his 35th year: and further, by marking the concurrence of his 3rd year with the 44th of Sesortasen, and that of his 35th with the 3rd of Sesortasen II., they seem to forbid any deduction from the 38 years of his whole reign beyond 5 or 6 imperfect years of concurrence with Sesortasen I. (if Sesortasen reigned xlv and some months), and 6 years, possibly with some months over, which might be reckoned as 7 imperfect years, at most, of concurrence with Sesortasen II. But after deducting 5 or 6, and 6 or 7, there still remain 26 years during which he should have reigned alone. But if we reckon xlviii years to Sesortasen I. with perhaps a fraction over (and this seems rather than xlv to have been the reading of the papyrus), then perhaps cutting off 8 or 9 years from the beginning, and 7 or 6 from the end of his xxxviii, we may just succeed in reducing the time that Amenemhe II. reigned alone to the xxiii years allowed him by Eratosthenes.

If, as is possible, though the name Concharis cannot be connected with him, Amenemhe II. be the king really alluded to under the names "Timæus" and "Concharis," in whose time according to Manetho (in his 5th year Syncellus has it) "the Shepherds" became the chief power in Egypt, it results that this change took place either immediately on the death of Sesortasen I., or within one year after it.

IV. *Sesortasen II., Ra-sha-cheper.* — The papyrus has clearly xix years, possibly with some fractional months and days after them. On the monuments his 11th year has been found; and, according to Sir G. Wilkinson, his 3rd year is named as coinciding with the 35th of Amenemhe II., in an inscription at Assouan. If so, his first year should be concurrent with the 33rd, or possibly in part with the 32nd, of his father. And the text of Eratosthenes' list giving only xxiii years to Amenemhe II., reckons, as it seems, his full xix to Sesortasen II., whom with Sesortasen III. it consolidates into one generation with lv years. 19. Dec. 14, B.C. 1909, to Dec. 9, B.C. 1890.

V. *Sesortasen III., Ra-sha-karu, or Khakaru* (Concharis?). The papyrus has certainly xxx, and we may suppose that it had v besides in the place for units, since it is clear that the thirty-third generation of Eratosthenes, with lv years, is a consolidation of these two kings; and, even with his full xix to Sesortasen II., xxxvi must be given to Sesortasen III. to make up the number. Manetho, in the lists of Africanus, seems to transpose these two kings, putting down Sesortasen II., under the name of Lachares, with only viii years, to follow after Sesortasen III., to whom, under the name of Sesostris, he gives xlviii (ascribing to him at 36. Dec. 9, B.C. 1890, to Nov. 30, B.C. 1854.

the same time acts belonging to Sesortasen I. and to Rameses II. and III.). However, the joint sum of his two reigns (viii + xlviii =) lvi, scarcely differs from that made by Eratosthenes, and may be reconciled with it, if only we suppose one of the two sums viii and xlviii, of which it is composed, to have been obtained originally by rounding off a fraction. The monuments are said to have supplied as yet no later date of his reign than the 14th year. It is to be observed further that in the series of the Karnak Chamber either one of these two kings consolidated by Eratosthenes (and, if either of them, it should be Sesortasen II. who has the shorter reign) is omitted, or else Amenemhe III. is omitted, which the length of his reign and the greatness of its monuments makes unlikely, unless there was some special ill-will to his memory, like that which has caused the omission of the Memphite pyramid-builders from the monumental lists.

49, from Dec. 2, B.C. 1860, or 43 from Nov. 30, B.C. 1854, to Nov. 20, B.C. 1811. Erat.

VI. *Amenemhe III., Ra-en-ma.*—The papyrus has plainly xl years, and perhaps also viii in the place of units, so as to vary as little as possible from Manetho, whose list gives him, under the name Ammeres, viii years. And this may be correct for the units; but the monuments marking a 44th and even a 45th year of the reign, show clearly that four decades have been omitted. (For the knowledge of the 45th year of this king, marked in an inscription at Sarabeit el Khadeem, the writer is indebted to Mr. Birch of the British Museum.) In the lists of Manetho, as given by Eusebius, though he seems in general to have merely copied, or else to have altered for himself in copying from Africanus, there is a remarkable variant. For, after the two kings answering to Sesortasen II. and III., though in inverted order, he ceases, after his slovenly manner, to transcribe the names, and gives in general terms to "their successors" (*οἱ δὲ τούτων διάδοχοι*), a space of xlii years, made perhaps by doubling each of the two reigns of viii years, and adding the iv of the last reign of the dynasty. And in these earlier dynasties (earlier, that is, than Dyn. XVI of the Chronicle), Eusebius has not the same reason as below (though he still has *some* reason) for making arbitrary alterations.

At any rate, he would have seemed to come very near to Eratosthenes, if only he had given his xlii years to the two Amenemhes III. and IV., instead of including also under them another reign, the last of the dynasty. For, in the list of Eratosthenes Amenemhe III., under the name Mares, with xliii years, makes the last of a series plainly taken from the same kings as belong to Dyn. XII. of Africanus; and as Amenemhe III. and IV. were certainly colleagues for some part at least of the reign of the latter, if not for its whole duration (their names being found conjoined more than once in the same inscriptions), it is not unlikely that the two are consolidated in the list of Eratosthenes into a single generation. And in the series of the Karnak chamber, where Amenemhe IV. is still to be seen, Amenemhe III., as some think, though he had by far the longer reign of the two, is omitted altogether. But if we would reconcile the xliii years given to Amenemhe III. (with or without Amenemhe IV.) by Eratosthenes, with the xlv at least shown to be his by the inscription at Sarabeit el Khadeem, or with the xlviii which we have made for him by uniting the decades of the Turin MS. of Eratosthenes and of the monuments with the units of Manetho, we must suppose that Amenemhe III. was associated by Sesortasen III. some five or six years before his death.

9 from Nov. 20, B.C. 1812, or 8 from Nov. 20, B.C. 1811, to Nov. 18, B.C. 1803. Erat.

VII. *Amenemhe IV.*, *Ra-ma-khru*, ix years + iii months + xxvii days, according to fragment No. 72 of the papyrus, which for the two last reigns of the dynasty, and for its sum, has still all the figures for the years, months, and days perfect. Nevertheless in the lists of Africanus this king has only viii years instead of ix, a difference which is easily accounted for, if we suppose only one year of his reign, or a little more, to have been concurrent with the last part of the reign of Amenemhe III., after whose death he reigned on 8, or something less than 8, years alone. But if this were so, we must no longer suppose Amenemhe IV. to be consolidated into one generation with his predecessor in the list of Eratosthenes. Or, again, it is conceivable that both Amenemhe III. and IV., if they were brothers, were associated or made district kings under Sesortasen III., and that Amenemhe III. reigned on xliii, Amenemhe IV. only viii years after the death of their father.

4. Nov. 18, B.C. 1803, to Nov. 17, B.C. 1799. VIII. *Scemiophris, or Ra-Sebeknefru*, iii years + x months + iv days, according to the papyrus. In the Manetho of Africanus, the reign is filled up to iv years. In the list of Eratosthenes, who had only a limited number of generations into which to compress all the kings of whatever dynasty whom he named or alluded to, the last two reigns of Dyn. XII. of Africanus are unnoticed, and the compilers of his series pass to kings of another lineage.

Thus the sum given by the papyrus at the end of the dynasty in fragment No. 72 (viz. ccxiii years + i month + xvii days) may be exhibited by adding up the eight separate reigns, as still recoverable from fragments 64 and 67, or filled up conjecturally by comparison with other authorities. For in whole years the eight reigns (9 + 48 + 38 + 19 + 36 + 48 + 9 + 3) have 210 years: we know that the fractional months and days of the last two reigns add 1 year 2 months, and 1 day; and we may presume that the fractional months and days of the six earlier reigns, if we had them, would make up the 1 year + 11 months + 16 days that are still wanting.

If Amenemhe I. were separated in the papyrus, as he is in the lists of Manetho, the sum of the papyrus for the remaining VII kings would be 205 years. That of Manetho in the lists of Africanus for these same VII kings is only 160 years. But with the addition of the xvi of Amenemhe I., appended to Dyn. XI, and of the other xliii which we suppose to be only nominally attached to the XVI kings of the same Dyn. XI, but really to represent the reign of Sesortasen I., we have 219 years, reconcilable perhaps with the sum of 213 given by the papyrus for all the reigns of the dynasty. But Eratosthenes, omitting all merely concurrent years, makes from the beginning of the 8th year of the 49 imperfect of Sesortasen I. (which should be 42 full years before the end of Dyn. XVII of the Chronicle), that is, from Thoth 1, or Dec. 30 in B.C. 1974, to the death of Amenemhe III., a sum of 163 years (which would need an addition of three more years to Amenemhe II., if Sesortasen I.

reigned not 48 but only 45 years and some months: and then instead of 163 we should have 166 years). Again, if to 163 or 166 we prefix (9 + 7 =) 16 years, and append for the last two reigns of the dynasty (8 + 4 =) 12 years unnoticed by Eratosthenes, we shall have 191 or 194 chronological years; and the dynasty will begin from Jan. 3, B.C. 1989, and will reach to Nov. 17, B.C. 1799, 133 years after the commencement of the ascendency of the Shepherds by the capture of Memphis, 1 year before the death of the patriarch Joseph, and 51 years before the expulsion of the Shepherds by Amosis, or at least before his coronation at Memphis. But that it really ended, whether then or a little earlier or later, without reaching down to the war with the Shepherds, appears also from the monuments (see the "Tomb of Aahmes," illustrated by M. de Rougé), and from an hieratic papyrus already mentioned more than once, which show that at the beginning of the war of independence only one native prince, named Ra-s-kennen, and he the last of Dyn. XI of Africanus, not of XII, was reigning in Upper Egypt. The 30 remaining years of Amenemhe II. from the end of his 8th (or 33 from the end of his 5th) year would seem to end in B.C. 1902; and the 19 of Sesortasen II. beginning in B.C. 1909, would end in B.C. 1890, 12 years before the exaltation of Joseph. So the thirty-seven Asiatics (Aamou) who are represented in a tomb at Beni-Hassan with their wives and children and asses bowing down and bringing gifts of game taken in hunting, in the 6th year of Sesortasen II., would seem to have submitted themselves to be "bondsmen" in B.C. 1903, 34 years before the family of Jacob came into Egypt. The 36 years of Sesortasen III., if they commenced from after the full 19 of Sesortasen II. in B.C. 1890 would end in B.C, 1854; and the seven years of famine, during which, as we suppose, it was that Upper Egypt also became subject to the Shepherds, would lie between his 19th and his 26th year, B.C. 1871—1864. So his victory over the frontier tribes, read by some Pennou, in Nubia, which is recorded by an inscription at Semneh and connected with the 21st day of Pharmouthi the eighth month, and, *as it is said*, also with the celebration of one of the three season-festivals, and with the 8th year of the king, should be fixed to July 26th of the Julian year B.C. 1882 anticipated, without the Gregorian correction; since this should be the 8th year of the reign; and Thoth 1 was then at Dec. 8. But how Pharmouthi 21 = July 26, being the 10th day before the 1st of the ninth month Pachons, then at August 5th, should have been then the day of a season-festival, or how that season of the year at which it then was should have been suitable for gaining any victory, is not apparent.

If there be here no error, it is the actual observation of Sirius which seems to be indicated as fixing the recurrence of the festival of the summer season, though the date specified, July 26, is five or six days too *late* for it, the first appearance of Sirius being taken for the latitude of Memphis, or a little higher, to be at July 20.

According to M. Biot the heliacal rising of Sirius, which in B.C. 3285, and on Pachons 1 (had the Egyptian months then existed), coincided with the solstice and with the rise of the Nile, might be taken practically to coincide with the same for 500 years on either side of that date, though, as time went on, Sirius rose at an increasing interval after the solstice. In B.C. 2783, he says, that is 315 years after the Flood, the interval between the solstice and the heliacal rising of Sirius (then at Thoth 1) was as yet only 3 days; so that the first settlers of the Delta may well have taken the appearance of Sirius to mark the commencement of the season. Ten centuries later (after 1003 years and 8 months), that is, in B.C. 1780, when the movable Thoth had fallen back two whole seasons *of the zodiac*, and was at Nov. 12, the appearance of Sirius on the 20th July coincided with the 11th of Pachons, 10 or 11 days after the solstice; and Pachons 1 being equivalent to July 10, the *signification* of the Egyptian *tetramenia*, as expressed in hieroglyphics, *then* corresponded to the actual seasons. And in B.C. 1322, when the Sothic Cycle expired and was renewed, the interval, M. Biot says, between the summer solstice and the appearance of Sirius on July 20 amounted to as much as 14 or 15 days.

If, then, the Egyptians had still continued to attach the season-festival to the actual appearance of Sothis in the 19th century before Christ, though it was then 9 or 10 days later than the solstice, it would be easy to find the date of any year in which the festival of the summer season was marked at Pharmouthi 21. One would only have to count back the days from Thoth 1 to Pharmouthi 21, which are 135, and multiply these by 4; and then going back from B.C. 1322, when the appearance of Sirius was at Thoth 1, we should obtain the year B.C. (135 × 4 = 540) 1862, as that in which it was at Pharmouthi 21, which, however, seems to be the 18th, not the 8th year of Sesortasen III. [Any error of a day or two in the actual observation, if it affected the date of the festival in any particular year, would make the date before Christ 4 or 8 years lower than this, not higher. And, in the same way, any difference of a more southern latitude affecting the date would also make it lower, not higher. So M. Biot makes a difference of 6 days between the appearance of Sirius at Memphis and its appearance at Syene: and so the epoch of the renewal of the Cycle, which is B.C. 1322 for Memphis, is put by him at B.C. 1302 for Thebes.]

[On the other hand, if it be supposed that the festival of the summer season was no longer in the 19th century before Christ conjoined with the appearance of Sothis, but rather with the solstice and the rise of the Nile as calculated and perceived by the Egyptians, then, if we take the year B.C. 1780, when Pachons 1 = July 10 nearly coincided, according to M. Biot, with the solstice, and go back 10 days from Pachons 1 to Pharmouthi 21, these 10, multiplied by 4, give us the number of years, viz. 40, which we must go back from B.C. 1780 in order to find the 10th of July and the solstice coinciding in Pharmouthi 21, and this we find in B.C. 1820. But if B.C. 1882 was the 8th year of Sesortasen III., and the season-festival was connected with the solstice, this being 62 years earlier than B.C. 1820, the date on the inscription ought to have been, not the 21st, but rather the 5th of Pharmouthi.

Possibly the addition of the 5 ἐπαγόμεναι, ascribed by one writer to Asseth, by another to Saites, and so probably really made under the Shepherd kings with whom Sesortasen III. was contemporary, may have been made after his 8th year, perhaps about the year B.C. 1780, and may have been joined with some other change in the calendar. And hence there may be a difficulty in accounting for monumental dates of an earlier time. Or perhaps this particular date which has now detained us, if rightly read and rightly represented in all other respects, may have been connected not with a victory of Sesortasen in his 8th but with a victory or dedication in his 18th, or with a dedication by Amenemhe III., who should be on the throne in B.C. 1820. For his accession, after 55 years reckoned to his two predecessors, being according to Eratosthenes in B.C. 1854, his remaining 43 years (supposing him to have been previously associated for 6) will end in 1811. Then, if 8 are to be reckoned separately to Amenemhe IV., after less than 2 of association, those 8 will end in B.C. 1803; and the 4 of the last reign of the dynasty will end in B.C. 1799, 51 years before the commencement of Dyn. XVIII. But if Amenemhe IV. was altogether concurrent with Amenemhe III., the dynasty may have ended 8 years earlier, in B.C. 1809. Or again, on the other hand, it may have ended 4 years later than B.C. 1799 or than B.C. 1809, if there should be an error, and an error uncompensated, in the list of Eratosthenes, in giving only 23 chronological years to Amenemhe II., who may possibly have reigned 4 years only and some months with Sesortasen I., and the remaining months of that year and 27 years alone, and 6 more only with Sesortasen II. associated.]

The great works commenced, according to Manetho, by Sesortasen III. (under the name Lachares, Lamares, or Lampares), and others ascribed elsewhere to Sesostris, with whom also Manetho identifies him, though in the *place* of his predecessor, and those certainly executed or completed by his successor, Amenemhe III., between B.C. 1854 and B.C. 1811, may be accounted for in like manner with those of the contemporary pyramid-builders of Memphis, by that change of relations between the kings and the populations subject to them which was consequent upon the famine.

Dynasties XI XV. XVII. of Manetho concurrent.

The list of Eratosthenes being symmetrically arranged, so as, after the first 190 years of the Chronicle, to exhibit a period of 443 years twice over, once for Lower and once for Upper Egypt, the 443 of Lower Egypt being divisible into 156 + 184 + 103, and the 443 of Upper Egypt into 103 + 184 + 156, the bulk of the 184 years is made on the former side to consist of a representation of the Memphite Dyn. IV of Africanus, on the latter side of Dyn. XII, as shall be explained more at length hereafter. So Dyn. XII and Dyn. IV of Africanus, by this very fact, that they are placed parallel one to another, and over against one another, both of them representing the same 184 chronological years which in the Chronicle belong to the Shepherds, are covertly confessed by Eratosthenes' informants to have been contemporary with the Shepherds and with one another; and also to have been *tributary* to the Shepherds; since the Shepherds, according to the Chronicle, during those 184 years had the chief power in Egypt. Of their chronological displacement in the list of Eratosthenes (for they are thrust down so as even to invade the first 69 years of Dyn. XVIII) this is not the place to speak.

It has been said above that the XVI kings of Dyn. XI of Africanus, with the usual average of 24½ years, ought to have begun before Dyn. XII of Africanus; and this they are known to have done; for one of the kings, named Nantef, is mentioned in an inscription as reigning in Upper Egypt three generations, that is, at least 90 years, before a certain date in the reign of Sesortasen I., viz. his 33rd year. Also it has been said that they ought to have lasted after the end of Dyn. XII even to the commencement of Dyn. XVIII; and this, again, seems to be confirmed by the monuments, as the left side of the Karnak Chamber shows VII kings of Dyn. XII (one king, either Sesortasen II. or Amenemhe III., being omitted) imbedded, as it were, in another Diospolite series of XIII names, the first of which is the Prince Nantef who has no cartouche, while the last is Ra-s-kennen the king who alone was reigning in Egypt at the commencement of resistance to the Shepherds. In the list of Eratosthenes, too, there are three other Theban names following, as well as eight preceding, those of Dyn. XII of Africanus, though it may be doubted whether these three are any continuation of the kings of Dynasty XI of Africanus, since the last of Dyn. XI, Ra-s-kennen, ends the eight preceding. The later three may be suspected to be rather a representation of Dynasty XIV, i. e. of the kings on the right side of the Karnak Chamber, whom the Theban priests would not perhaps be likely to omit altogether, even though they had omitted one or two of the less important dynasties of *Lower* Egypt, viz. Dyn. II and Dyn. V of Africanus. The space to which they were limited by Eratosthenes, even with the admission of the "443 years of the Cycle," precluded, of course, any full exhibition of all the concurrent dynasties.

Dyn. XVI. XXX Nubians in three lines? 216. Dec. 28, B.C. 1966, to Nov. 4, B.C. 1750? or somewhat later?

We come next to the 184 years of Dyn. XVI of Manetho (XIV of Africanus), the kings of which we should have expected to find described as Nubian or Diospolitan, and in number not to exceed VIII or IX. Or, if the knowledge that Manetho was confined by his scheme within certain limits had prepared us to find three or four concurrent lines consolidated into a single dynasty, still, even then, four lines so consolidated would give no more, or certainly not many more than XXXVI kings. But now we find in the text of Africanus a number of no less than LXXVI kings, and the designation Xoites, which sounds as if taken from a city of *Lower* Egypt, though perhaps, like the designations Elephantinite and Thinite, it may admit of being interpreted in a sense different from that which first suggests itself. For *Kes*, *Χοῦς*, or Cush, being the name given by the Egyptians as well as by the Hebrews to the Nubians or Ethiopians, *Κοσῖται*, or by metathesis of the vowel, *Ξοῖται*, might very well be formed from this name by any one who chose to turn it into Greek.

But whatever were the designation (whether Diospolites or Xoites), or the number of the kings (whether XXX, XXVI, or XXXVI), of that dynasty which stood as Dyn. XVI in the series of the original Manetho with the sum of 184 years, it must be supposed to have presented a distinct line, or several lines of one distinct family consolidated; and by the place that it holds in the lists its kings must have belonged to Upper Egypt. For the fact that the Shepherds of Dyn. XVII (XV of Africanus) who lived in the Delta follow in the lists is no objection, seeing that these were strangers, and moreover suzerains of all Egypt, who would naturally be named, if they were named at all, after all the separate lines of native dynasties, and immediately before that sovereign dynasty which expelled them, and united all Egypt under a single sceptre. And since, out of three groups of Diospolite kings exhibited both separately on numerous monuments, and collectively on the left and right sides of the Karnak Chamber, two groups have already been identified with Dynasties XI and XII of Africanus (XIV and XV of Manetho), it follows that the remaining Diospolite or Xoite-Nubian dynasty of Manetho is probably the same as the remaining monumental group of the Sevekhoteps and Neferhoteps found on the right side of the Karnak Chamber. These kings appear to have been connected by blood with the lineage of Amenemhe I., and by locality with Upper Egypt and Nubia. As for their number, the whole series of the right side of the Karnak Chamber being only XXX, of whom half perhaps may have been found also on separate monuments, while LX (omitting one or two *princes*) may be the whole number of kings on *both* sides of the Karnak Chamber, it is probable that this may have been the source of the LX kings of Ptolemy of Mendes and Africanus; and that the original Manetho had not more than the half, i.e. XXX, if Dyn. XIII of Africanus was derived from his Dyn. XVI; or not more than XXXVI or [illegible], if Dyn. XIV, with its designation of Xoites and its doubtful number of LXXVI kings, was derived from his Dyn. XVI. The number LXXVI may probably have been derived from hieratic MSS. similar to that of Turin, in which the names of the Sevekhoteps and Neferhoteps appear with a prodigious multiplication of short reigns of one, two, or three, or at most five years each.

One may conjecture that the original Manetho, ejecting those names of the hieratic papyri which were merely genealogical, and perhaps making of them one division of his Manes, with their short "reigns" expanded into month-years, so reduced the group or groups of these kings to something like the number exhibited on the right side of the Karnak Chamber. Then Ptolemy of Mendes, who even for his interpolations most probably used *some* materials, when he made two dynasties out of one, may have found it convenient to vary the designation, and may have purposely made the number of kings in the first dynasty of the two to correspond with that of the Karnak Chamber, [and their number in the second to correspond with that of the same kings in the hieratic papyri. Or both the numbers LX and LXXVI may have been derived from two consecutive groups of royal names in the papyri, and the coincidence of the first number with that of the Diospolites of the Karnak Chamber *may* have been only accidental. Among the four mythological dynasties of Manes (whom we suppose to be royal names ejected from the hieratic papyri) of the original Manetho, besides two of Thinites and Memphites, there are two with 1817 and 5813 month-years, reducible respectively to 151 and 484 full years, which may have come from the Diospolite and Nubian genealogy of the same papyri. But 151 + 484 years make a sum of 635, from which if we deduct the 184 given by the original Manetho to his Dyn. XVI (the years of the present Dyn. XIV of Africanus), there remain 451, agreeing within 2 with the sum of the interpolated Dyn. XIII of Africanus. And if we suppose the number of kings in those two dynasties of Diospolite and Nubian Manes in which it is not specified to be according to the same average as that which Manetho specifies for the Manes called Memphites, the 151 Diospolite and 484 Nubian years will give in all (XXX + XCVI =) CXXVI kings, short by only ten of CXXXVI, which is the sum of the kings in the two Dynasties XIII and XIV of Africanus thrown together. Nor is even this seeming difference real; for in the remaining dynasty of Manes, where the number of X Thinite kings is specified, the average is lower than for the Memphites, being something under three full years instead of 5 to each king, so that we may well suppose that the number of kings of the Diospolite and Nubian Manes, had they been specified, would have made up together the full sum of CXXXVI, which is made by adding together the kings of Dynasties XIII and XIV of Africanus. Not that we are to suppose that Ptolemy of Mendes followed any such process as we have been now following with the Manes of the original Manetho; but no doubt he took both the number of kings and the years of each king direct from the same hieratic papyri from which Manetho also had extracted and transposed them, when he multiplied their short reigns into month-years.]

Assuming the number of kings in Manetho's Dyn. XVI (represented in its sum of years at least by Dyn. XIV of Africanus) to have been originally only XXXVI or XXXI, or XXXVI at the most, and taking XXX as the mean, thirty reigns, if consecutive, with the ordinary average of the Chronicle and Eratosthenes, viz. 24¾ years, would cover 891 years, whereas there are only 477 years between Menes and the head of Dyn. XVIII; and the Nubian kings cannot have commenced before the conquest of Nubia by Sesortasen I. But the accession of Sesortasen, at least to the sovereignty of all Egypt, being at B.C. 1974, 226 years before that of Amosis the founder of Dyn. XVIII, the interval from his conquest of Nubia was of course less. On the other hand, the 184 years of Manetho's Dyn. XVI would give to XXXVI kings about 5⅑ years each, to XXX scarcely more than 6, and to XXXVI only 5 years, to say nothing of the XX or LXXVI kings of the text of Ptolemy and Africanus, to whom it would give in the one case only three years, in the other less than two years and a half each; averages which suit well enough the numerous and short reigns of parts of the Turin papyrus, but which for actual historical reigns are altogether improbable. But the number of 184 years (like that of 43 given to the XVI kings of Dyn. XI of Africanus) is perhaps inserted merely as an allusion to something else which does not appear on the surface; and it is not to be supposed that the Nubian line or lines of kings so commenced in fact, and so ended, as to coincide exactly with the 184 years of supremacy reckoned by the Chronicle to the Shepherds from their capture of Memphis to the coronation of Amosis in the same city. Perhaps some light may be gained by putting together the following indications:—

First, on the left side of the Karnak Chamber there are, in XXXII cartouches, at least *four* lines of kings who reigned in Middle or Upper Egypt, in the Thebaid or north of the Thebaid; and these lines appear to have been more or less contemporaneous one with another. So by analogy we should expect the XXX names on the right side, especially as they are of less important kings, to be also divisible into three or four lines. Again, Nubia, after its conquest by Sesortasen I., is known to have received (either from him or from Sesortasen III.) an organisation similar to that of Egypt, being divided into an Upper and a Lower Country, each with Nomes of its own (and the division of Egypt itself into Nomes is by some ascribed to Sesortasen or Sesostris). It would be natural then that from some date in the joint reign of Amenemhe I. and Sesortasen I. rather than from the year in which the Shepherds took Memphis, i. e. during 216 or 214 perhaps rather than 184 years before Dyn. XVIII, Nubia should have had at least two lines of concurrent princes, one for the Upper and one for the Lower Country; while a third line of the same stock may have ruled towards the southern frontier of Egypt. And these, being of one lineage, may have been all consolidated by Manetho into one dynasty, to suit his limited number of XXIII dynasties of kings, just as Eratosthenes is obliged to consolidate reigns and kings and allusions to whole dynasties, to suit his limited number of (XV + LXXVI =) XCI generations, and his space of (443 + 1881 =) 2324 years. Again, as regards the Turin papyrus, though we suppose it to be rather a pedigree of regal families than a list of true reigns, and many of its kings to have been even infants who died young, or others who never actually reigned, but only stood for a time in the way of succession, or were the ancestors of such as succeeded afterwards, still, even so, the vast number of names given in the papyrus to this lineage as compared with others, implies not only that it was nearer to the time when the list was made, and important from some connection with the kings of Dyn. XVIII or XIX, then reigning, but also, over and above all this, that it must have been sub-divided into at least two or three concurrent lines. Putting the number of lines at only two, and the kings of Manetho who actually reigned at XXXVI, so as to agree with the number on the right side of the Karnak Chamber, and their whole continuance at 216 instead of 184 years, 18 joint reigns would have an average of only 12 years each; whereas if we allow three lines, they would have the much more probable average of about 18 years, which is also more agreeable to the indications of the Karnak Chamber, and of other separate monuments, connecting several of these kings not only with Nubia, or with places of common interest, such as Abydos or Thebes, but with other localities between the Thebaid and the southernmost frontier of Nubia.

Dyn. XVII. vi Shepherds. 260, from Jan. 8, B.C. 2007, or 184 from Dec. 20, B.C. 1932, to Nov. 4, B.C. 1748.

In Dyn. XVII of Manetho (XV of Africanus) if the VI Shepherd kings had 259 years and 10 months, as he gave them, and as it has been proposed above to allow, they will have commenced under the Memphite Dyn. XVII of the Chronicle (under that part of it which belongs to Dyn. III of Africanus), in B.C. 2007, 76 years before their capture of Memphis in B.C. 1932, the date from which they are reckoned by the Chronicle to have become paramount, or at least superior in some sense to any other dynasty still co-existing with them in Upper Egypt. This is certainly more probable than that they came into Egypt as hostile invaders, took Memphis at once, and contenting themselves with that conquest carried the war no further. We may even conjecture that their mode of living and acting together, and the ease with which they were used to move about, may have made them serviceable to the native kings under whom they first came in; that Sesortasen I. may have used them in gaining or asserting his supremacy, or in conquering Nubia; and that after his death they felt their power; the native Egyptians down to that time having had no considerable wars or armies; nor having their population so concentrated in cities as afterwards. In the Turin papyrus (fragment No. 30) there is a series of *figures* ("73, 72, 63, 95, 0, 95, 70, and [2]4 years") looking like the *lives* of 7 or 8 kings of a long-lived family, agreeing with such a series of long *reigns* as is ascribed to the Shepherds by Manetho; and the one or two short lives intermixed by no means lessen the probability that they really belong to this dynasty; while vestiges of four or five *names* on another fragment, No. 112, look like those of strangers, and have the spaces between the lines agreeing well in width with those between the lines of the figures.

This perhaps is the place to consider an objection which may be brought from the monuments. They may be thought to prove not only that Sesortasen I. and his co-regent Amenemhe I. (who together make the first generation of Dyn. XII for Eratosthenes) were sovereigns of all Egypt, and no vassals of the Shepherds; but also that Sesortasen III. was equally so; for he also is declared by inscriptions in Nubia to have won victories there in the 6th and 8th years of his reign; and centuries later he was worshipped there as a local god by his successors of Dyn. XVIII. Further, his names are said to have been found not merely on any statue which may have been appropriated and transported by a later king, like the granite lions of Amenoph III. found at Gebel Barkal (Napata), or the statue of a Sevekhotep, now in the Louvre, said to have been found at Bubastis, but on granite fragments of plinths belonging to the great temple at *Tanis*. And this fact (the sculptures being assumed to be contemporary with the names on them) would seem to indicate that he also, no less than Sesortasen I., had ruled from Nubia to the Delta. But if this be admitted, it follows that the intermediate kings Amenemhe II. and Sesortasen II. were also independent sovereigns of all Egypt; and so we have four or five kings equalling in number of generations but exceeding in years Dyn. XVII of the Chronicle; while yet all these are preceded on the monuments by at least one other king, Papa Maire, who distinctly wears both crowns of Upper and Lower Egypt, and yet cannot be referred to the Tanite Dyn. XVI of the Chronicle. Some similar presumption, but of less weight, might be drawn from inscriptions made late in the reign of Amenemhe III. at Toura, (where his 43rd year is marked,) or in the Sinaitic peninsula, where his 45th has been found, and also from the magnitude of his works, if he was the author of the Nilometer at Semneh, and the builder or finisher of the Labyrinth in the Fayoum. On these last signs we need not dwell, as quarries and mines would be accessible to friends and tributaries; and in other respects the same that has been said of the vast works of the Memphite pyramid-builders (who also brought granite from Syene and copper from the Sinaitic peninsula) applies here. But conquests in Nubia, and still more the erection or decoration of a temple in Tanis, seem certainly at first sight to imply a sovereignty over all Egypt; and in that case the authority of the Chronicle and its historical series must be given up.

But the Chronicle, as has been remarked before, was obliged in all cases alike to make out a single consecutive series of generations and dynasties, though it may well have happened, and seems to have happened in fact, that at some time or other the two kingdoms of Upper and Lower Egypt were nearly evenly balanced, and neither of them, strictly speaking, exercised sovereignty over the other. Let it be supposed that upon the death of Sesortasen I. the Shepherds reduced Memphis, and that from this same point the Memphite Dyn. XVII of the Chronicle ends, and the 184 years of its anonymous Dyn. XXVII of the Shepherds begin; then, since it is said that the Shepherds "violently took Memphis," while for all the rest of Egypt this is *not* said, but the contrary, that they reduced it, whenever they did reduce it, "in a marvellous manner, easily, and without a blow," we must suppose that in the first instance the remaining kingdom of the Amenemhes and Sesortasens in Upper Egypt continued unattacked, independent, and flourishing, though the Shepherds of the Delta, and the city and dependencies of Memphis, were no longer under them. As for Manetho's assertion that the Shepherds burned the cities and massacred or enslaved all the inhabitants, these embellishments need not here be sifted, as they are put by Manetho himself *after* the subjugation of all Egypt, *Upper* as well as Lower; while really they are borrowed from another subjugation made above 300 years later by the Asiatic sun-worshippers. But we might admit without difficulty, if it seemed more in accordance with the monuments, not only that down to the eighth year of Sesortasen III. the kingdom of Upper Egypt continued to be independent, but that it continued independent *throughout*, were it not for the express testimony of Manetho, who certainly would not exaggerate the depression of the native dynasties, that the Shepherds subjugated not only Lower but also Upper Egypt, making the native rulers their vassals and both countries tributary. The same too is implied by a hieratic MS. already alluded to, certain particulars in which may be brought to bear upon another part of the objection from the monuments still remaining. "At that time," it is said, "there was no king [i. e. no native king] in Egypt, except that Ra-s-kennen ruled in Upper Egypt; and the Shepherd king Apophis [seemingly the second of that name], who held Heliopolis and reigned in Avaris, sent to Ra-s-kennen requiring him to co-operate in building a temple for the god Sutech [a name of Typhon occurring also in composition in earlier Tanite-Memphite names in the list of Eratosthenes, and there rendered in Greek Ἄρης] *at Avaris.* And Ra-s-kennen held a council with his chiefs on this demand;" and their refusal to obey this requisition of the Shepherds seems to have been the commencement of that revolt which put an end to their dominion. Now at Tanis and Avaris the Shepherds had for building temples no stone at all; but for limestone they would need the services of their vassals the kings of Memphis and their viceroys in Heliopolis to send them blocks from the quarries of Toura; and for granite, or alabaster if they wanted it, they would need the services of the kings of Upper Egypt, whether these were only friends or vassals. The requisition addressed to Ra-s-kennen by the last Shepherd is not likely to have been the first of its kind, but implies others to which his predecessors both of Dyn. XI and of Dyn. XII of Africanus, and their Nubian contemporaries of Dyn. XIV of Africanus equally, had submitted from the time that they became subjects. And before that time, since the change was without violence, earlier kings of the Thebaid, such as Sesortasen II. and III., though independent, may well have assisted the Shepherd suzerains of Lower Egypt, no less than the Memphite tributaries of the same Shepherds, in quarrying and transporting granite from the Nubian frontier. Nor is there any thing to show that Sutech, the local God of the Sethroitic Nome, and of the country on the "Saitic," i. e. Sethroitic arm of the Nile, was of foreign introduction; or that he had already become odious at the commencement of the Shepherd rule over Lower Egypt, or during the reign of the three next successors of Sesortasen I. in Upper Egypt. It is quite possible then that Sesortasen III. may have assisted as a friend and ally the contemporary Shepherds of the Delta, in adding to a temple at Tanis, especially to one founded previously by his own ancestor Sesortasen I.; and that in consequence his name, or the names of other contemporary Nubian kings, should be found on its sculptures. It is to be remembered at the same time that the name of Sesortasen III. *might* occur on sculptures not contemporary, added afterwards by kings of Dyn. XVIII, who would be sure to do all they could to efface the memory of the Shepherds even in the Delta, and would commemorate rather even there such kings of Upper Egypt (of Dyn. XII of Africanus) as had been their contemporaries, whether independent or tributary. Lepsius indeed remarks that he "could not find on the site of Tanis those traces of Dyn. XII which seem from the indications attached to his published engravings to have been copied there by Major Burton;" but on the other hand names of the Sevekhotep family are said to have been found more recently at Tanis, besides the Colossus in the Louvre thought to have come from Bubastis. This latter, like the Lions of Amenoph III., may have been moved; and M. Brugsch even thinks that he has discovered upon it the name of a place in *Upper* Egypt, whence, in that case, no doubt it was brought.

Admitting one or other, or both, of these explanations, the question still remains, at what time, and in what way which was at once "marvellous, easy, and without violence," did the Shepherds become suzerains over the powerful and flourishing kingdom of Upper Egypt, for such the monuments declare it to have been? Exactly the explanation needed is to be found in the occurrence of the seven years' famine, and its prediction, through Joseph, to the Shepherd-king Apophis: for then all the rest of the Egyptians, after exhausting their own resources and their money, were forced to sell first their cattle, then their lands, and lastly their own liberties to *that* king whom alone Joseph had instructed, and for whom alone all his provisions had been made. (Gen. xii. 34, 35.) And if so, when "all the neighbouring *countries* had recourse to Joseph," it would by no means follow that any other native dynasty, in any other part of Egypt, was then changed (though all such would necessarily become subject, *ἀπ' ἄκρων ὁρίων Αἰγύπτου ἕως τῶν ἄκρων*), or that it was reduced to any galling servitude, any more than the immediate population of Lower Egypt, who confessed to their preserver that he deserved his name of Zaphnath Pa-anch, for that he "had saved their lives." On the contrary, as after two years of the famine the whole population had sold not only their lands but themselves as serfs, and the king from that time had to choose between feeding them in idleness or employing them on public works for their bread, it is probable that the tributary kings also, through whom any part of Egypt was governed, would obtain a vast increase of personal power, and a superabundance of disposable labour. And even if the Nubian victory of Sesortasen III., which has been placed above in B.C. 1882, or 1879, eleven years, or eight years before the famine, had been attached to a later date, as it would be, if all Manetho's years were successive, this need not have caused any great difficulty. We might even have imagined that the famine itself, with the knowledge that there had been throughout corn in Egypt, produced a pressure of the tribes from the interior towards the Nubian frontier, which it was an important success to repel. It is true that in the list of Africanus (and no doubt also of the original Manetho), Sesortasen III. is identified with the Sesostris of Herodotus, and has the acts of Rameses II. and III. ascribed to him; whereas in Herodotus it is clearly the immediate successor of Mœris, "before whom none had done anything very great," that is, Sesortasen I. the successor of Papa Maire, who was the great conqueror. And if this seems to any one to forbid the idea that Sesortasen III. became a tributary, it may be replied, that this manifest falsehood is rather a sign that there was in the reign of Sesortasen III. something to be dissembled and written backwards, so as to read in a sense precisely contrary to the truth, according to the received Egyptian method in such cases. So Sesortasen III. (in spite of a throne-name very like "Concharis") is purged of all suspicion of ignominy; and, on the other hand, public works are distinctly ascribed to this "Sesostris" which the Hebrew or Greek Scriptures ascribe to Joseph. Such are the measuring and dividing of the lands, the introduction of surveys, the making of canals, the mounding-up of cities, and the removal of the people into them, which same thing (together with the enslavement of the people) Manetho ascribes to the tyranny of the Shepherds, and Herodotus to that of the Memphite pyramid-builders, contemporaries of the Shepherds, and ruled by a Typhonian influence. Lastly, the importance attached to the earliest ascertainment of the probable rise of the Nile, and the institution of a regular gauge or Nilometer at Semneh in Nubia, seems to hint at something which already, not very long before the reign of Amenemhe III., had drawn great attention to this subject.

It does not appear, then, that there was any real difficulty in placing those dynasties which were known to have existed, and which were named by Manetho, a number of them being distinctly named from separate localities, while the designations of others from the capitals of the two countries as Memphite and Diospolite admit of two senses, one narrower, for strictly local lines, and another wider, for lines connected with Memphis or Thebes only by origin, by occasional not permanent residence, and by general sovereignty. Eratosthenes must have been overpersuaded not because the Theban priests proved to him that the dynasties enumerated *could* not have co-existed within the limits marked by the Chronicle, but because they asseverated, on their own knowledge of their national history and monuments, that they *had not* so co-existed, in fact. The result was a compromise, and the composition of a scheme neither that of the Chronicle nor that of Manetho, yet going far enough towards that of the Chronicle to show what would have been the outline, if Eratosthenes had insisted on a perfect agreement with it; and adding collateral indications besides; whereas, had he insisted on the priests confining themselves for the first ten dynasties of kings to the 477 years of the Chronicle, and exhibiting only one continuous series, we might have had no indications whatever except of those Dynasties I, III, VI, and XII of Africanus, out of which the series would have been collected. And this reveals precisely what was that difficulty which made the priests declare such a scheme to be impossible. For omitting (which was a thing of course) the Shepherds, they would have had to omit also *either* the pyramid-builders of Memphis, which was impossible as regarded the Greeks, *or* their own later Sesortasens and Amenemhes of Dynasty XII of Africanus, Sesortasen III. the deified organiser of Nubia, and the builders of the Labyrinth and the pyramids of the Fayoum; but this again was quite impossible for their own Theban patriotism, and scarcely more admissible than the omission of the Memphite pyramid-builders, even as regarded the Greeks.

Before leaving this subject of the earlier contemporary dynasties, there are still two points connected with Manetho's exhibition of them which require attention. It has been seen that he has swelled the average length of the reigns in his six dynasties of Lower Egypt from 24½ to 31½, or over 30 years. This, if the rest were equally expanded, or even had the full ordinary average, would hint that his historical materials were insufficient for the space which he had, for cyclical or other reasons, predetermined to fill. But when three dynasties of Upper Egypt follow, all curtailed in their average, and two of them much more curtailed than the six dynasties of Lower Egypt had been lengthened (two or three distinct lines being in one of them blended together, and a whole line found on one of the monuments of Upper Egypt—the Abydos tablet—being perhaps unnoticed), it is clear that it was not from want of materials that he amplified the dynasties of Lower Egypt, but merely from partiality to his own country; while the excessive compression of the kings of Upper Egypt (expanded again, in spite of limited space, in the Theban lists of Eratosthenes), shows not only a partiality contrary to that which sculptured the Karnak Chamber, or wrote the Turin

MS., but also an absolute superabundance of historical materials to be compressed within some predetermined limits. But hence two questions arise: first, if Manetho thus showed a wanton partiality to Lower Egypt, how can he have removed Menes himself, the founder of the monarchy, with two whole dynasties of his descendants, from Tanis, where they are placed by the Chronicle, to connect them with the unimportant city of This, "Teni," in Upper Egypt? And, secondly, if it has been rightly said above that Manetho had no cyclical scheme, what was there to prevent his exhibiting all those lines of Upper and Lower Egypt which had ever existed with at least its full sum of historical years to each, even though he might patriotically honour the kings of Lower Egypt by exaggerating a little the average length of their reigns?

In answer to the first question, it may be said that probably the original Manetho did *not* name Menes *Thinite* at all, but named his first two dynasties of kings simply *Tanite*, "Τανιτῶν," like the Chronicle; ~~or perhaps with some slight difference, of which traces may remain in the Θενίτης, Θηνίτης, Θεεινίτης, of the MSS.~~; while the present reading of the Manetho of Africanus is probably derived from the list of Eratosthenes. This list, being made out by the priests of Upper Egypt, is called "a Theban list," and a list of "Theban kings" distinguished by Syncellus from "Egyptian." By a corruption analogous to that which changed Τανίτης into Θενίτης, but going a step further, Θινίτης itself in the list of Eratosthenes becomes Θηβινίτης, and approaches to "Theban." But the first step was probably this:—Menes, the founder of the whole monarchy, appeared and still appears (as at the Ramesseum at Thebes) at the head of the monumental and hieratic lists of *Upper* as well as Lower Egypt. Thus he was both a Theban and the head of all later Theban kings; and since one of the fullest and most remarkable of these monumental lists (for the series of the Thothmes Chamber of Karnak began only from the first *Memphite* dynasty) was that of the Temple of Osiris in the sacred city of Abydos, and the priests who worked for Eratosthenes would have this no less than the Karnak Chamber in their minds, and This, "Teni," though a place of no importance in itself, was the civil capital of the Nome containing Abydos, Menes, through the temple and tomb of Osiris, belonged in some sense also to This, "Teni;" and the similarity of the two words in Greek suggested the idea of transferring him with two whole dynasties, also found with him at Abydos, to Upper Egypt, and naming them all not Tanites, but Thinites. Ptolemy of Mendes, being as much Greek as Egyptian, and living under the Romans when Alexandria had an undisputed pre-eminence, may, even as a Mendesian, have been as ready for the sake of Osiris to honour Abydos as Tanis; and so he may have followed Eratosthenes, whose Egyptian Chronicle he doubtless had before him when he undertook to compile his own re-edition of Manetho on a broader basis.

As regards the second question, though Manetho had no *cyclical* scheme, and even purposely avoided falling into one (perhaps because there were then Greeks at court who understood what the cycle was, or for some other reason), he by no means went to work without any scheme at all; but having gone down parallel with the Chronicle to the end of 2922 + 217 real years from the Creation, and having given the last 239 of these (22 + 217) to kings, and wishing still to place more kings before coming to the 1881 real years still to be numbered from the true date of Menes to the death or flight of Nectanebo II., he found in the 40 and in the 443 years "of the Cycle," that is, of the real current Cycle, thrown back by the Chronicle, a precedent for throwing back or reduplicating as many years ("of the Cycle," past or future, as he pleased. That he stopped exactly where he did, when he was short by 26 of having either reduplicated or anticipated and thrown back *all* the 1461 years of the current Cycle, has been explained already by the supposition that he purposely avoided everything of a cyclical form, and that he desired to mark his date for Alexander at B.C. 331, in the same way in which the Chronicle had marked its own epoch of B.C. 305; while if he had gone beyond "the Cycle," that is, the true current Cycle, the only one he alluded to, in throwing back and anticipating years, he would have gone beyond the utmost expansion of that earlier scheme which he was following, even while varying from it in details, and would have been introducing fictitious years of arbitrary fabrication unconnected even by analogy with former precedents, and borrowed from future cycles, which had not as yet, like the Cycle current, even an inchoate existence, or a name by which they could be designated.

From the head of Dyn. XVIII downwards, we have at length only one consecutive series in the lists of Manetho, to compare with that of the Chronicle. On coming to this point Manetho has already paralleled three years more of the 1881 of the kings of the Chronicle than the 477 composing its Dynasties XVI, XVII, and XXVII. Consequently the head of Dyn. XVIII does not seem to coincide exactly in the two schemes, but according to the *apparent* chronology of Manetho it is depressed to B.C. 1745, instead of standing at B.C. 1748. But this difference need not occupy us, for we shall soon see that Manetho in the details of his lists (no less than in his narrative) is regardless of true chronology, though he compensates omissions purposely made at certain points of history by corresponding insertions of unchronological years in other places; so that the true chronology is represented in its general outline, and hinted even as regards details, at least to the initiated. So then, neglecting Manetho's depression of the head of Dyn. XVIII to B.C. 1745 as only apparent, we understand from it only that we have already 3 years in hand to go towards filling up the first void which may occur below; or rather, to speak more exactly, we have 2 years and 10 months, since Dyn. XVII (XV of Africanus), as restored from Josephus, was 2 months short of 260 full years. But in point of true chronology Manetho's two Diospolite Dynasties XVIII and XIX of 333 + 209 = 542 years, are identical and ought to be coincident with Dynasties XVIII and XIX of the Chronicle, (though XVIII is by it called Memphite,) with 348 + 194 = 542 years; these 542 years beginning from B.C. 1748, and ending in B.C. 1206. The Diospolite Dyn. XX of the Chronicle, again, is for 135 years of its 228 chronologically identical with Dyn. XX of Manetho, from B.C. 1206 to B.C. 1071. Its remaining 93 years

Union of all Egypt, from B.C. 1748 downwards.

(reaching chronologically to B.C. 978) are transferred by Manetho to Tanites of Lower Egypt, for whom he creates a new dynasty of his own, his Dyn. XXI, raising the sum of its years from 93 to 130 by the help of 37 unchronological years brought up from times far below. Irrespectively of its apparent undue depression by (2.10m. + 37 =) 39 years and 10 months (as if to B.C. 938), his Bubastite Dyn. XXII is commensurate within one year and identical with the Tanite Dyn. XXI of the Chronicle, a dynasty which has 121 years, from B.C. 978 to B.C. 857. Dyn. XXIII of Manetho, also Tanite, supplies in its 89 years both 1 year lacking to his preceding Dynasty XXII, and 48 (reaching chronologically to B.C. 809) to match the 48 of the Tanite Dyn. XXII of the Chronicle, and 19 (reaching to B.C. 790) to match the 19 of its Dynasty XXIII (which though called Diospolite is identifiable with the two reigns and 18 years of Osorchon and Psammis in Dyn. XXIII of Manetho); and lastly, it contains 21 years besides, reaching on to B.C. 769, and telling towards the 44 of the Saite Dyn. XXIV of the Chronicle. This is identical with Manetho's own Dyn. XXIV, to which however, as being ignominious, he allows only one king, Bocchoris, and instead of 44 only 6 years. So at their end (in B.C. 763) he would be still short of the end of the same dynasty in the Chronicle by 17 years, had he not created above an undue depression to the amount of 40 years, or, as we must reckon, of 39 years and 10 months. But the deficit now found at the end of his Dyn. XXIV absorbing only 17 of these surplus years, his Ethiopian Dyn. XXV, which is identical with Dyn. XXV of the Chronicle, and nearly commensurate, having 40 only instead of 44 years, begins, according to the *apparent* chronology of Manetho, nearly 23 years lower than according to the chronology of the Chronicle (in B.C. 723 instead of 746), and ends nearly 19 years later than according to the chronology of the Chronicle, viz. in B.C. 683 instead of 702. So that under the dislocated chronology of Manetho it may perhaps be implied that the whole period of Ethiopian rule lasted as long as (44 + 19 =) 63 years from the first conquest of Egypt by Sabaco to the death of Tirhakah. So then beginning his

Saite Dyn. XXVI, identical with the Memphitico-Saite XXVI of the Chronicle, at B.C. 683, he needs for it only 158 years, instead of 177, to make it end in B.C. 525, coincidently with the end of the 177 years which the same Dyn. XXVI has in the Chronicle. But in point of fact he gives it only 150 years and 6 months according to the lists of Africanus, the remaining 7 years and 6 months, being represented by 4 months added to the 124 years of the Persian Dyn. XXVII, with 6 years (really only concurrent) of Amyrtæus constituting Dyn. XXVIII (unknown to the Chronicle), and 1 year and 4 months added by the lists of Africanus in Dyn. XXIX to those 57 years which Dyn. XXIX and XXX together should contain according to the Chronicle. Of these additions, making in all 7 years and 8 months, 2 months may be regarded as the complement due to that fraction of 10 months in Dyn. XVII of Manetho (XV of Africanus) which has been noticed above, but which has since, for convenience, been neglected in our reckonings. The remaining 7 years and 6 months fill up what is lacking on Dyn. XXVI; but they do so only by thrusting up, according to the *apparent* chronology of Manetho, the beginning of his Dyn. XXVII of Persians from Jan. B.C. 525, where it is put by the Chronicle, to May of B.C. 533, nearly 4 years before the death of Cyrus. But it is said expressly in the heading of Dyn. XXIII of Ptolemy of Mendes and Africanus (and the specification was no doubt copied from the original Manetho), that Cambyses "reduced Egypt in his *fifth* Persian year," which certainly began in Jan. B.C. 525. We see then in what light years interpolated by Manetho (whether above or below his chief suppressions on Dynasties XXIV, XXV, and XXVI) are to be regarded. They are to be regarded in the places where they occur as mere compensations, notes of restorations to be made elsewhere by such as understand the true succession and course of the history. And thus much having been said of the general chronology, we may now consider each one of Manetho's later dynasties by itself.

Dyn. XVIII. xvi Diospolites. Nov. 4, B.C. 1748, to Aug. 9, B.C. 1400.

It is certain that Dyn. XVIII of Manetho, which expelled the Shepherds, is one with Dyn. XVIII of the Chronicle: yet there is a remarkable difference in its designation,

Manetho naming it "Diospolite," but the Chronicle a little earlier "Memphite;" whence in the scheme of Eratosthenes it is feigned *not* to be coincident with Dyn. XVIII of Manetho, but to contain other earlier kings half Memphite by origin, just as the kings of Dyn. XVIII of Manetho were by connection half Nubian. But earlier still, when Herodotus first visited Egypt, the Memphite priests, far from claiming those kings as Memphites, ignored their whole dynasty as Ethiopian. For they told him that in the whole course of their history there had been XVIII Ethiopian kings, and one queen: — Herodotus says, "one queen, a native Egyptian woman," and identifies her with Nitocris: but this was perhaps only his own addition; as there were certainly more queens than one, and his informants probably meant the queen Hatasu (included under the name Amensis or Amesses in Manetho), sister of Thothmes III. Subtracting from the XVIII the III Ethiopian kings of Dyn. XXV. who were too well known to be omitted, there remain XV kings and one queen suiting well the lists of Manetho and the monuments for Dyn. XVIII, and for no other. And no doubt the kings of that dynasty all reigned over Nubia as well as Egypt, and its founder was connected by origin and intermarriage with Nubian and even with *black* Nubian blood. This Nubian connection of the dynasty explains in some degree, as has been said above, the great development given on the right side of the Karnak Chamber, and still more in the Turin papyrus, and in Dynasties XIII and XIV of Africanus, to the genealogy of the Nubian kings derived from Amenemhe I. It explains also the widespread notion of later times that the monarchy, civilisation, and religion of Egypt had descended the valley of the Nile from Ethiopia, that is from Nubia, to Thebes. The same idea, in a form near to the truth, is expressed by Manetho when he represents the native kings (whether the chronology be exact or mythical matters little) flying from Asiatic strangers into Ethiopia, abiding there for a time, and thence redescending to expel the Shepherds, as by an avenging whirlwind, in the compound persons of the Sethoses and Rameseses. That Dyn. XVIII was most properly called Diospolite the ruins of Thebes, which it first raised to greatness, sufficiently attest:

and they prove further the connection of its kings not only with the Nubians of Dyn. XVI of Manetho (XIV of Africanus), but also with the older local Diospolite line of Dyn. XI, and the Memphite-Diospolite line of XII of Africanus. But to explain fully the designation "Memphite" given it in the Chronicle, we must remember that Memphis had long been the chief capital of the district, "country," and older kingdom or empire of Lower Egypt; and that this kingdom, *never destroyed by the Shepherds*, was obtained a little before their expulsion, and before the capture of Avaris, by Amosis the founder of Dyn. XVIII, not by conquest, like the eastern Delta, but probably by marriage with an heiress; so that Memphis under the kings of Dyn. XVIII preserved its honour as the elder of two co-ordinate capitals. The two crowns, the white and the red, were worn separate or united at will; and there was a close union of the Upper and Lower kingdoms, without either one being incorporated into the other. The ruins too of Memphis, where the Colossus of Rameses II., the Sesostris of Herodotus, is still seen, the relation of Herodotus concerning the propylæa about the temple of Phtha erected by his successors, and a number of recent discoveries and inscriptions, show that great works were executed there too by the kings of Dyn. XVIII, the eldest son of the king, the heir-apparent to both crowns, being sometimes the local viceroy. So Artapanus, a writer of no great weight, certainly, but one whose stories must have had some source, and who was quoted in the time of Augustus by Chæremon in a passage already alluded to, only reverses perhaps the truth when he makes the king who expelled the Shepherds, "Ph-Almanoth" (a name more like Amenoph than Amoses), to have been properly "king of Memphis, and to have given his daughter Μέῤῥις (for he had no son) in marriage to Chenephres, the Χέβρων seemingly of Manetho, who reigned in the parts *above* Memphis, (βασιλεύοντι τῶν ὑπὲρ Μέμφιν τόπων), there being then a number of kings at once in Egypt." But in truth it was the king of Upper Egypt, Amosis, who expelled the Shepherds, and he perhaps married a surviving daughter and heiress of Ph-Almnphthis, or Thamphthis, the last king of Memphis of Dyn. IV, or gave his own daughter to a son-in-law named Χέβρων, or Χενεφρῆς, a collateral of Upper Egypt. For the name "*Merit*," in composition, is borne on the monuments by a sister of Amenoph, daughter of Amosis. So it was possible for a native of Lower Egypt, if only a little partial to his own region, to view the kings of Dyn. XVIII as Memphites, they being the legitimate heirs of the elder kingdom, though no doubt more immediately connected by blood, in the male line at least, with Upper Egypt and Nubia; and though they made their general residence (eventually at least) in the upper capital. In the time of Manetho, Alexandria having long eclipsed all the older capitals, Lower Egypt could better afford to give Thebes its due, and to name from it this line of great kings who plainly made it their chief city, and whose tombs were known to be there. But in the time of Herodotus, just after the re-establishment of the Persian dominion, the two rival countries and capitals had nothing left but to make the most of past glories. And Thebes having had a long succession of great dynasties, against which Memphis had little to set except Mœris, and a share in the compound personage of Sesostris, and the pyramids, a keen jealousy emboldened the Memphite priests, in conversing through interpreters with a Greek who might never visit Thebes (and in fact did not visit it until long after, too late to add more than a note or two to his earlier work), to be silent about the wonders of Thebes, and even indirectly to ignore and stigmatise its chief dynasty, Dyn. XVIII, as Ethiopian.

With regard to the true chronological place and construction of Dynasties XVIII and XIX, it has been seen above, in a passage extracted by Josephus from Manetho's Third Book, that Manetho acknowledged 13 years of servitude to Asiatic strangers, while a king named Amenoph, whose reign in Egypt was followed by their invasion, was surviving as an exile in Ethiopia, till his son Sethos "also called Rameses" was old enough to return with him and expel them. Josephus could not see distinctly where this king Amenoph, or the 13 years of his exile, were placed, but supposed them to be intended to follow *after* Sethos son of Amenoph and head of Dyn. XIX in the lists, and his two successors Rapsakes and

Amenephthes; "for Rameses-Sethos" himself being identified elsewhere with Ægyptus, in whose eighth year Danaus fled to Greece, this seemed to put *him* out of the question. But at any rate the story was clearly connected by Manetho with Dyn. XIX. But the lists, as ascertained through the help of Josephus, reveal the fact that not 13 exactly, but 15 years, have been suppressed by Manetho out of the 348 belonging to Dyn. XVIII, and have been transferred to Dyn. XIX. And assuming that his Egyptian names and reigns are trustworthy and historical, the question is, to what part of Dyn. XVIII do the 15 years so suppressed and transposed chronologically belong? Where are we to detect the intervention of a time of disgrace and servitude under impious Asiatics, whose memory was odious, like that of the Shepherds and the Hebrews, and whose names have been suppressed? The monuments enable us to answer this question with something like certainty; for they prove that between the reigns of Amenoph III. (the Memnon of the Greeks), the eighth king of the dynasty (the same name too as in Manetho), and of Horus, seemingly his son, there really intervened a king who worshipped not the gods of Egypt, but mutilated their effigies, and worshipped only the solar disk. Women and others come out to implore his clemency as to a conqueror: the native Egyptians crouch before him as in fear: Asiatics, with beards and hooked noses, are in his suite: and lastly, this king and the other members of his family are distinguished by a peculiar malformation, a thickness about the loins and hips, precisely similar to that of certain figurines in earthenware found in Mesopotamia. Several of these, which are in the British Museum, will enable any one who pleases to make the comparison for himself. This sun-worshipping king, with one or two others, one of them a local "king of Thebes," named Ai, who appears in his suite, and who reigned with him or after him, certainly intervened between Amenoph III. and Horus; for they have defaced the monuments and the tomb, and have appropriated the cartouches of Amenoph III., while Horus has in like manner defaced their monuments, and cut in his names over theirs. Their dominion certainly lasted for some years, one would think at least fifteen, to judge from the number of their monuments still remaining, and the size and magnificence of some tombs (at Tel-el-Amarna),—which however, being incomplete, hint its sudden termination. And though they thus certainly existed, their names are uniformly omitted from all the later monumental lists, as those of the Rameseeum and Medinet Habou, and of the Abydos tablet, and probably also from the written list of Manetho in Josephus; though it is true that some make them to be the source of the name Achencheres in the last-named list. The reader therefore will judge (apart from all minor questions of detail) how far it is probable or certain that we have found both the true place of the 15 years suppressed or transposed by Manetho, and also the cause of their transposition. The next step is to read his myth afresh, and to distinguish in it those historical elements which either clearly suit the monumental indications for the interval between Amenoph III. and Horus, or are not inconsistent with them. Now according to Manetho there was an invasion: the invaders were Asiatics, Shasou, akin to the earlier Shepherds. Like them they were impious towards the gods of Egypt, doing violences from which the earlier Shepherds had abstained. The time of their invasion was not only after the expulsion of the earlier Shepherd kings, but after the Hebrew shepherds had settled in Palestine: and when they entered Egypt they came themselves from or through Palestine, of which therefore it seems, of the coast at any rate, they were already masters. As for the advance of Amenoph to meet them, and his religious scruple, which made him to return to Memphis without fighting, and retire thence to Ethiopia, this probably is an allusion to the march of another Amenoph (Amenoph II.) after the Hebrews, whom he overtook at the Red Sea, and returned "without a battle." But Amenoph III., to judge from the indications of the monuments, was already dead, and buried in the tomb which he had prepared for himself (the tomb was afterwards defaced and his palace destroyed), when the sun-worshippers became dominant in Egypt; and we may conjecture that they came in at first "without a battle," having some claim to the succession, for Taia, queen of Amenoph III., seems to have been of their lineage; and there is in the Vatican a scarabæus of his 11th year, on which she is represented together with her husband as worshipping the sun's disk. Or else, if some son of Amenoph III. disputed their entrance, he was defeated; and he may have fled to Ethiopia. The atrocities of setting fire to cities, and roasting and eating Apis, if not pure fables borrowed from the Persian Ochus, (which there is no sufficient reason to assert,) agree with the express assertion of a conquest, and not with any mere internal change or succession. Lastly, the survival of Amenoph III. to return with his son merely to see poetical justice satisfied, and then die, and the identification of the son with Sethos I. and II. and with Rameses II. and III., all blended into one person, is of course mythical. Yet even this is to a certain extent illustrated by the monuments, which show that the first military exploits of Seti I. and his son Rameses II. were in fact performed in warring against the Shasou, i. e. the Arabian or other Shepherds, who, though no longer lords of Egypt, were still formidable beyond the frontier; and it was after these had been overcome that their wars extended to the Khita and the Rotennou, apparently the Hittites and the Chaldæans. It was probably the fact that the word *Shasou* designated at once the elder Shepherd kings, the Hebrew shepherds, and all Arabs and other Asiatic nomads, that suggested to Manetho the idea of blending four distinct histories into one myth, which for its complete inversion of the truth and the proportions and complexity of its falsehoods is certainly remarkable.

That account of the 15 years suppressed by Manetho in the middle of Dyn. XVIII, which has been obtained by the comparison of his lists and narrative with the Chronicle and with the monuments, may be further illustrated from sacred history. For according to the joint scale of the Scriptures and Josephus and of the Chronicle the reign of Amenoph III. seems to end at June 22 B.C. 1588, in the year after that in which Joshua died; and nine years later, in B.C. 1579, the Hebrews were subjugated by a king named in the Hebrew text Chushan Rishathaim, in the LXX. *Χουσαρ-σ-αθαὶμ*, in Josephus *Χουσάρθης*, variations which show the proper name to be Chousan, Chousar, Choushan, or Choushar, the syllable Ri or Ri-*s* to be omissible, and Sathaim or *s*-Athaim to be an adjunct. And this king is called "king of the Arabs," those of Irak perhaps, towards the mouth of the Euphrates, (who would be named Shasou by the old Egyptians, and would be likely enough to be sun-worshippers,) "and of the Mesopotamians," the malformation of whose figurines has been noticed above. (Sennacherib, it may be remarked in passing, is in like manner called king of the Arabians in the second book of Herodotus.) But in all ages a conqueror taking possession of Judæa from the north would be on his way to Egypt; or if he had swept down the coast and conquered Egypt first, he would not think his possession of it secure till he had also reduced the hill country of Palestine. On the other hand, if he suffered reverses in Palestine, he would have to evacuate Egypt; or, if he first lost Egypt, Syria also would be emboldened to rebel. But according to our scale, Chushan being defeated by Othniel, the Hebrews, after a servitude of 8 years, regained their independence in B.C. 1571, two years after Egypt, according to Manetho harmonised with the Chronicle, had thrown off the yoke of the sun-worshippers. For so the accession of Horus is put at June 18, B.C. 1573. But according to Manetho's own lists, as they stand, with the head of Dyn. XVIII apparently depressed by 3 years, the independence of Egypt would be recovered only in 1570, in the next year after the victories of Othniel. And apart from this, as Manetho has been detected already in his narrative cutting off two years from the sun-worshippers, writing 13 instead of 15, though his own lists when examined reveal the error, it is likely enough that these two years are not all that he has suppressed; and that for their recovery of independence the Egyptians were in fact indebted to the victories of Othniel. Even the monumental name of the sun-worshipping king in Egypt and that of the Arabian or Mesopotamian in the Bible seem to be only variations, analogous to those of other names admitted to be the same. And the Egyptians in writing hieroglyphically foreign names were used to naturalise them in a manner, so that the sounds expressed and the emblems employed to express them should bear an Egyptian sense. The position of the name proper and the adjunct in the hieroglyphical name Athin-Ra-Quashan is like that of other names with their adjuncts, as "Amon-meri [or Mi] Rameses," "Amon-mi-Shishonk," which in Greek become Rameses-Miammous and Shishonk-Miammous. So too we should read Athin-Ra or Ra-Athin-Quashan. The fact that the syllable Ra in the hieroglyphical name is only a determinative accounts for the variations of the Greek and the Hebrew, as if it were all one to write Choushan *Ri-s*-hathaim or Choushan-Sathaim. The final syllable *in* looking like the Chaldee plural, it is natural to find it in the Hebrew *aim*. The *s* or *sh* in the middle of the name, as written in Hebrew, may be merely euphonic, to divide the two open vowels. As regards the *s* or *sh* (permutable in Egyptian with *kh*) in the proper name itself, it certainly seems to be wanting when the name is read "Khouen"; but if the name Sa-*hou*-ra is found written in Greek Asaou*ch*is, it is not impossible that Kh*ou*'-en also might become Chou*ch*an or Chou*sh*an. Bunsen and Lepsius themselves tell us that the hieroglyphic group, which in this name they agree to read "Khou," is proved by a Greek rendering, "*ὐεστε*," to have had sometimes the sound of "*Ouash*" or "Quash," which will justify us perhaps in writing the name Quashan. And if in the Hebrew the determinative Ra or Re precedes instead of following the word Athin which it determines, this impropriety is more than balanced by our finding the same syllable 'Ρη treated in the Greek as a superfluity, and omitted altogether, Χουσαρ-σ-αθαὶμ being the LXX. rendering of the Chushan-ri-sh-athaim of the Hebrew text. At any rate, having an Arabian and Mesopotamian conqueror, with a name so nearly alike, in Palestine *at the very time*, we can scarcely avoid identifying him with the sun-worshipper of the Egyptian monuments; especially as these Shasou are made by Manetho to come *from Judæa*, and at the invitation of those other Shepherds (not really identical with the Hebrews), who according to him "are sometimes called Arabs," and who had long before been expelled from Egypt. If this identification be ultimately established, it will be the oldest of all known synchronisms of sacred and profane records. And hence light may be thrown on several expressions of Manetho; as, for instance, when Amenoph the son of Pepi predicts that there should come σύμμαχοι, allies, to take the part of the lepers, i. e. of the Hebrews oppressed by the kings of Dyn. XVIII. For though the Hebrews were no longer in Egypt to be assisted, and the Arabs of Chushan were not exactly their allies, yet they being themselves subjects and *so* allies of the Arabians, the invasion which came through and from their country came in a manner from them; and individuals of them may even have attended Chushan into Egypt. And when Manetho says that the whole time of the Shepherds in Egypt from first to last was 511 years, if we remember how Avaris (Heberland), the residence probably of Abram himself, had been "Typhonian from the beginning," the Egyptians having already in Abram's time been plagued there for his sake, it may be that the 511 years are reckoned from those first plagues of the time of Abram to the expulsion of the Arabian "Hierosolymites," the sun-worshippers, whose irruption from the side of Palestine was the fourth and last inroad of Shasou. For the call of Abram being in B.C. 2084, and Abram going down into Egypt shortly after, the 511 years if reckoned from that descent would end within a year or two after B.C. 1573. The only other point from which one might expect the 511 years to be reckoned is from the commencement of the Shepherd Dyn. XVII of Manetho (XV of Africanus). But so they would end not with any Amenoph, or Sethos, or Rameses, but in the 7th year of Achencheres, the 13th king of Dyn. XVIII, supposing the 15 years of the sun-worshippers to have been inserted between the reigns of Amenoph III. and Horus.

Not having before us the actual reigns of the kings of Dynasties XVI, XVII, XXVII, and XVIII of the Chronicle, with their years, months, and days, we cannot tell what fractions at the end of Dyn. XXVII and again of Dyn. XVIII may have been cut off by it, and reckoned to the following dynasties XVIII and XIX, when it made Dyn. XVIII, after 477 full years from Menes, begin from November 4 (then Thoth 1, of the movable year) in B.C.

1748, and end with the last day of the movable year in B.C. 1400; nor, consequently, from what day the *actual* reign of Amosis began, it being perhaps antedated somewhat when put technically at Nov. 4, B.C. 1748. For though the years and fractions given by Josephus from Manetho for the reigns of Dyn. XVIII happen to join together into exactly 333 years, needing 15 full years more to equal the 348 of Dyn. XVIII in the Chronicle, it is not to be thought that the actual accession of Amosis was on the Egyptian new year, Nov. 4; that the sun-worshippers again held Egypt for exactly 15 years from June 22 (not then near to the new year), B.C. 1588 to June 18, B.C. 1573; and again that the last king of the dynasty, Amenoph, ended his reign of 19 years and six months exactly on the eve of the new year, or within a fortnight of it (since Manetho did not exhibit fractional *days*, but rounded them off to months), in B.C. 1400. The Egyptians, as a general rule, did not fill up fractions remaining over, but cut them off, and antedated the following reign or dynasty so as to include them. Consequently, if Manetho and the author of the Chronicle both reckoned the actual reign of Amosis to begin from the same point, and gave it from that point Manetho's length of 25 years and about 4 months, it would have probably *in addition* in the Chronicle when antedated technically from Nov. 4, B.C. 1748, some fraction remaining over from the sum of the *actual* reigns of the three earlier dynasties. Whether the Chronicle and Manetho did in fact both alike reckon the actual reign of Amosis with 25 years and 4 months from one and the same point, is another question. The Chronicle probably made his actual reign, as head of a sovereign dynasty, begin not from his first Theban accession but from his coronation at Memphis, which according to the monuments (see the "Tomb of Aahmes," illustrated by De Rougé) was a year later, and which in that case (the season for war for that year being over) must have been either on or after Nov. 4 of B.C. 1748, and if after, not long after, since the inundation was then over, and the season for opening the next campaign was already approaching. And Manetho is understood by Josephus to reckon the 25 years and 4 months of the actual reign of Amosis not only like the Chronicle from an accession in Lower rather than Upper Egypt, but from the "expulsion of the Shepherds;" that is, from the capture of Avaris, which according to the monuments was several years later, seemingly in his *fifth* year: for Josephus writes thus:—"*Μετὰ τὸ ἐξελθεῖν ἐξ Αἰγύπτου τὸν λαὸν τῶν ποιμένων εἰς Ἱεροσόλυμα, ὁ ἐκβαλὼν αὐτοὺς ἐξ Αἰγύπτου βασιλεὺς Τέθμωσις ἐβασίλευσε μετὰ ταῦτα ἔτη εἴκοσι πέντε καὶ μῆνας τέσσαρας, καὶ ἐτελεύτησε.*" But Manetho, if the words *μετὰ ταῦτα* are from him, is not here writing history properly so called, but fable in all but the list of reigns itself; and even that he introduces with a mythical name for its first king. And in a precisely parallel case, where he introduces the first king of Dyn. XIX, Sethos II., mythically blended with others, and named Rameses, he says that "*after* expelling his brother Danaus he reigned 59 years," whereas his own lists, containing at that place no separate reign of 8 years, nor any brother Danaus at all, show plainly that the 8 years in question, if any one is so scrupulous as to inquire after them, are identical with the first 8 years of Sethos II. himself, while, as Rameses, he is pursuing his foreign and mythical conquests. And so Josephus too reckons, when, casting up the whole 59 years of this Sethos-Rameses, he says that "from the Exodus *of the Shepherds* to the flight of Danaus were 393 years." So no weight is to be attached to the words "*μετὰ ταῦτα*," and the like, in the case of Amosis, whose reign of 25 years and 4 months was most likely taken by Manetho from some hieratic MS. giving it from his original Theban accession, and not, like the Chronicle, from his coronation at Memphis, still less from the "expulsion of the Shepherds." In that case the date for the death of Amosis, and all the dates following down to the death or the fabulous expulsion of Amenoph III. inclusively, when reduced to the scale of the Chronicle, will be earlier by one full antedated year *at least* than they would seem to be if Manetho's actual reign of 25 years and 4 months were to be reckoned from the coronation at Memphis, or from the first of Thoth a little preceding.

But as the precise date of the coronation at Memphis, and

the length of the actual reign of Amosis reckoned from that date by the Chronicle and increased somewhat (unless it were celebrated purposely on the new year) by antedating from Thoth 1, and the date of the actual Theban accession preceding, from which alone, as we suppose, Amosis reigned 25 years and 4 months, are unknown,—we shall draw out first, but only provisionally, the chronology of the dynasty as it would seem to follow from the written lists if its *actual* commencement in Manetho's lists and its technical commencement in the Chronicle were both alike from Thoth 1, = Nov. 4 in B.C. 1748. Then,

1. *Tethmosis*, "after expelling the Shepherds," would reign from Thoth 1 = Nov. 4, B.C. 1748, 25 years and 4 months to Feb. 26, B.C. 1722.

2. *Chebron*, would reign 13 years, from Feb. 26, B.C. 1722, to Feb. 22, B.C. 1709.

3. *Amenoph I.*, 20 years, 7 months, from Feb. 22, B.C. 1709, to Sept. 15, B.C. 1689. And his death seems to be 5 years after the flight of Moses from Egypt, Moses having been born in the 13th of Amosis.

4. *Amessis*, his sister, 21 years, 9 months, from Sept. 15, B.C. 1689, to June 12, B.C. 1667 (or, according to a various reading given by Theophilus of Antioch, as if from Josephus, 21 years, 1 month, from Sept. 15, B.C. 1689, to Oct. 15, B.C. 1668).

5. *Mephres*, 12 years, 9 months, from June 12, B.C. 1667, to March 11, 1654, his death seeming to approach within a month of the Exodus; March 11 of anticipated Julian reckoning, but without the Gregorian correction, being in B.C. 1654 equal, or nearly, to March 29 of true reckoning, 18 days later. (But with the reading of Theophilus mentioned above Mephres would reign from Oct. 15, B.C. 1668, to July 8, 1655, and die in the year before the Exodus; and then all the following dates would be 8 months earlier.)

6. *Mephramouthosis*, 25 years, 10 months, from March 11, B.C. 1654, to Jan. 3, B.C. 1628. (Theophilus gives a variant of only 20 years and 10 months.)

7. *Thmosis* is said to have reigned 9 years and 8 months, from Dec. 25, B.C. 1629, to Aug. 29, B.C. 1619.

8. *Amenoph*, 30 years, 10 months, from Aug. 29, B.C. 1619, to June 22, 1588. (In his 5th, B.C. 1614, on the death of Moses, the Hebrews under Joshua would enter Canaan, and in the spring of 1589 Joshua died.) Here would follow

[A void of exactly 15 years, thrown down to Dyn. XIX, but really needed between Amenoph III. and Horus; that is, seemingly, between June 22, B.C. 1588 and June 18 B.C. 1573. In the 9th of these, on the death of all the Elders who outlived Joshua, the Hebrews would be subjugated by Chushan-Rish-Athaim (*Χουσαρ-σ-αθαὶμ*, *Χουσάρθης*, *Χουσαχὰρ*), and remain in servitude to him 8 years, from B.C. 1579 to 1571.]

9. *Horus*, 36 years, 5 months, from June 18, B.C. 1573 to Nov. 11, B.C. 1537.

10. *Achencheres*, his daughter, 12 years, 1 month, from Nov. 11, B.C. 1537 to Dec. 8, B.C. 1525.

11. *Rathotis*, her brother, 9 years, from Dec. 8, B.C. 1525, to Dec. 6, B.C. 1516.

12. *Achencheres*, 12 years, 5 months, from Dec. 6, B.C. 1516, to May 2, B.C. 1503.

13. Another *Achencheres*, 12 years, 3 months, from May 2, B.C. 1503, to July 27, B.C. 1491.

14. *Armais*, 4 years, 1 month, from July 27, B.C. 1491, to Aug. 31, B.C. 1487.

15. *Ramesses*, 1 year, 4 months, from Aug. 30, B.C. 1487, to Dec. 28, B.C. 1486.

16. *Armesses Miammou*, 66 years, 2 months, from Dec. 28, B.C. 1486, to Feb. 10, B.C. 1419. In his 53rd, B.C. 1433, the Hebrews would be subjugated by Jabin, king of Canaan, a connection probably of Ramesses Miammou, who, after warring with them, married a princess of the Khita.

17. *Amenoph*, 19 years, 6 months, from Feb. 10, B.C. 1419, to the eve of Thoth 1 = August 9, B.C. 1400. In his 6th the Hebrews would regain their independence through the victories of Deborah and Barak. Sisera sounds like an Egyptian name; and this triumph of the Hebrew shepherds just 13 years before the death of Amenoph may possibly have suggested the number 13 instead of 15 for the duration of an earlier disgrace put under another Amenoph, and to be followed by the glorious reign of a Sethos-Rameses.

With this general outline of the chronology, bearing in mind the uncertainties noticed above, and the variant of Theophilus for the reign of Amesses, and having already disentangled and placed what relates to the sun-worshipping Shepherds, we may approach the remainder of Manetho's fable, which is still complex, and separate in it what relates only to the Hebrews from what relates to the Shepherds properly so called.

The king who really expelled the Shepherds and founded Dyn. XVIII is nowhere named by Manetho by his true name Amosis. For in Theophilus, though he is quoting from Josephus, and in Syncellus, who writes "Ἄμωσις ὁ καὶ Τέθμωσις," this is only a gloss, a fair one indeed in this sense that the Tethmosis of Manetho, as expelling the Shepherds and founding a dynasty, *must* so far be one with Amosis; but quite groundless, if the meaning be that Manetho is writing historically, and that Amosis really bore both names. But so far as the Shepherds are made to blend with the Hebrews, and their expulsion is put down mythically (as a first step) by 93 or 94 years, Alisphragmuthosis or Misphramuthosis (i. e. Thothmes III.) is rightly named as the king who waged the great war with them; that is, *mutatis mutandis*, whose tyranny in the land of Avaris immediately preceded and led to the Exodus. In a tomb of his time at Thebes, in which the making of bricks for the temple of Ammon is represented, the labourers (mixed with native Egyptians of the conventional red colour) are light-coloured bearded Asiatics, having officers of their own, who are seen measuring the daily task, while taskmasters much darker than the red Egyptians, of a purplish or chocolate colour, showing a Nubian connection, stand over them in the attitude of command, or sit by with rods in their hands. And though the scene is at Thebes, that is no reason for doubting of its representing the Hebrews, who being in such numbers in the Delta, and all reduced to this slavery, some of them might well be found also at Thebes; and they are certainly to be first thought of even there, and rather than any other more distant Asiatics. So we see Thothmes even to this day waging his war against the Hebrew shepherds, who later, no doubt, were all without exception concentrated near Avaris "by condescension of the king Amenoph," as Manetho says, when he was vacillating whether to let them go or not. It was *not* however, according to Manetho, under Misphramuthosis that the [Hebrew] shepherds were actually expelled, but under his son Thouthmosis or Tethmosis; that is, to speak historically, under Amenoph II. the son of Miphra-Thothmosis or Thothmes III. And Manetho himself elsewhere (when the Hebrews already settled in Palestine are to be confused with other Shepherds, Arabs, really their oppressors, and to be made to come down again *in* them to be finally ejected as lepers), having no longer anything to fear from a name now removed to a distant time and belonging to another king, admits that it was the name Amenoph, not Thothmes, to which some humiliation had attached through the lepers and the shepherds of Jerusalem. But in his earlier myth, in which the Hebrews, as such, are not named, the earlier Shepherds being brought down, so as to cover them, to the true time of the Exodus, he shrinks from naming Amenoph II., and makes Misphragmuthosis supply half of his own compound name as a name for his son: and even this he varies again in the lists, putting in them "Mephres" first as the father, and "Miphrathmuthosis" second as the son, that the two may not be too clearly recognised. The son then of these two it is who besieged the [Hebrew] shepherds within that strong wall with which they had surrounded the whole region of Avaris, the wall being the Divine Power which protected them, and exempted them when it plagued the Egyptians. And despairing at length of reducing them to submission, he consented to their departure; and they went out towards the desert, towards Syria. [From this point the continuation is given by the other myth of the lepers and the Hierosolymites.] And the king Amenoph, whom some even of his own priests had warned that he was fighting against a Typhonian power, marched [after them] and came up with them; but he returned without having joined battle; and [not caring perhaps to be too near to "the field of Zoan"] he went up from Memphis to Thebes, and there abode; while the lepers and Hierosolymites, under Osarsiph-Moses, i. e. under Joseph and Moses, for the bones of Joseph went up with them, [after an interval of 40 years,] settled in that country of which [600 years later] they made Jerusalem the capital. And thence, under another Amenoph, these Hierosolymite Shepherds, blended with the sun-worshipping Arabs, are called down as his brethren by Joseph-Moses and the lepers (i. e. by themselves, as if they were still in Egypt), to avenge their own wrongs, and to be once more and finally expelled. Some of the expressions put by Manetho into the mouth of Joseph-Moses, the priest of Heliopolis and leprous lawgiver, remind one of the invitation sent by the true Joseph to his father and brethren, when he "informed them of all his state, and promised to supply them with all things necessary in abundance, to give them the good of the land of Egypt, to make them eat the fat of the land, bidding them make haste and come down without thinking of their property; for the good of all the land of Egypt should be theirs; so they accepted the invitation with great joy, and came immediately." One expression in Manetho's fable is even more appropriate in the mouth of the true Joseph who ruled Egypt than in that of the representative of the lepers. For among other promises to the Hierosolymites there is one to "take their part and stand by them," whenever there should be need: "ὑπερμαχήσεσθαι δὲ ὅτε δέοι." For though Manetho meant this of armed co-operation, the offer of *occasional* assistance only, and the preposition ὑπὲρ, imply something of security and superiority in him who offers it. Even the numbers in the two fables are remarkable; the 511 years going back to the first Shepherd Abram; the number 80,000 for the lepers derived from him, when first reduced to bondage 94 years before the Exodus, a number perhaps not very different from the true: the force of the Shepherds set at 240,000 fighting men, that is, the full number at which the Egyptian army on the Syrian frontier *was usually stated;* their apprehensions from the quarter of Assyria, covering perhaps allusions to the exploits of Abraham, as well as to much later apprehensions of the Egyptians and actual invasion. But had the true force of the Hebrews at the time of the Exodus been named, viz. 600,000 men, they would have seemed too strong for their oppressors; and if they were confessed to be unarmed, then an unarmed multitude [with the rod of Moses] had put to shame all the armies of the Egyptians with their gods. So they are numbered at only 240,000, but these fighting men; and the king Amenoph has 480,000, exactly double the number, all mighty men of valour, with which to overpower them; so that there is no room even to suspect that his return "without a battle" could be owing either to weakness or overthrow.

From the fables of Manetho there originated the definite historical error of confounding the Hebrews with the earlier Shepherds and Shepherd-kings (Hykshôs), under whom they had entered Egypt (the later sun-worshippers not being known or thought of), and their Exodus with the expulsion of the latter. Ptolemy of Mendes having given the synchronism of Amosis and Moses, with whom he joined Inachus, and Josephus having accepted the same as clearly asserted by Manetho, and as honourable to his own nation, they were followed by nearly all later writers, both Gentile and Christian. Only in some rare instances do we find traces either of some older and truer Egyptian tradition, or of some juster apprehension of the mixed nature of Manetho's fables. So in one passage, already noticed above, Syncellus writes that there was a sort of consensus that Joseph came into Egypt and rose to power under the Shepherds, and more particularly "in the 17th year of Apophis," an assertion which we have seen to be justified by the mixed scale of the Scriptures and the Chronicle, taking the names of the last four Shepherds with the last 184 of their years as they are given by Josephus, but which makes the Exodus to be, as it ought to be by the same scale, not under Amosis in B.C. 1748, but 94 years later. So again in a passage of Clement of Alexandria, who follows miscellaneous sources not always reconcileable with one another, it is said that the Exodus was "345 years before the epoch of the Sothic Cycle;" the only inaccuracy in which statement is this, that its author supposed Moses to have been born in the very first year of the dynasty, and counted from the accession of Amosis to the Exodus only 81 years. For B.C. 1322 + 345 gives B.C. 1667: and if we deduct 81 from B.C. 1748, we obtain the same year, 1667. But really the particulars related in the first chapter of the Book of Exodus require some years to have elapsed between the first accession of the "king who knew not Joseph," and the order for exposing all the male children of the Hebrews. Not that one need think every thing that is mentioned to be included in the interval, or that the cities of Pithom, Rameses, and On (which last is added in the Greek) were built or walled by the Hebrews before the birth of Moses. This and other particulars may be mentioned by anticipation in a condensed narrative. On the other hand there is nothing in the name Ramesses in the Hebrew, or in the designation of the land of Goshen as γῆ Ῥαμεσσῆ in the LXX., to justify the inference that the Exodus was after the time of Rameses the Great, who seems to have rebuilt Avaris and to have renamed it from himself. Else by the same rule it might be shown that some of the prophets wrote after the foundation of Alexandria, since Alexandria is named in the LXX. version of their books. This proves only that Ezra, or some other reviser still older, may have introduced into the text that name by which the place was known when the older name Avaris (Hawar) was entirely disused; though it is not impossible that the name Rameses may be as old as Moses himself, if Amosis, having a son named Rames, or Rameses, as the monuments show him to have had, named one of the cities which he fortified in the Delta after his son. But the other explanation is sufficient.

The indications derived from Manetho's fable that the Exodus took place not under Thothmes III. (Mephres), but under his son Amenoph II., would not of themselves be difficult to explain and set aside, if there were any sufficient reason to believe that the king of Egypt himself was drowned in the Red Sea: but the fact is, that they agree much better with the sacred narrative than does the commonly received opinion. The Scriptures introduce the account of the Exodus by marking the death of a king. "And it came to pass, in process of time, that the king of Egypt died, and the children of Israel sighed by reason of the bondage . . . and God heard their groaning . . . and had respect unto them." (Exod. ii. 23, 24, 25.) Hereupon Moses is sent from the Burning Bush on Mount Sinai to deliver them. This was, according to St. Stephen (Acts vii. 30), when 40 years were expired, " πληρωθέντων," were *complete*, from the time of his flight, his flight itself having been *in* his *fortieth* year, but before its completion: " ὡς δὲ ἐπληροῦτο αὐτῷ τεσσαρακονταετὴς χρόνος," κ. τ. λ. (Ib. v. 23.) But at the end of the 40th year from the Exodus, when Moses died, he was 120 years old. (Deut. i. 3, and xxxiv. 7.) So that the Exodus was just about the time when his 80th year was complete; and the death of the king of Egypt, the mission from the Burning Bush, and the Exodus, were all within one year, the first when Moses had not completed, the last when he had just completed, his 80th year. " Moses was fourscore years old, and Aaron fourscore and three years old, when they spake unto Pharaoh." (Exod. vii. 7.) But on looking at the Egyptian list of Dyn. XVIII, as given by Manetho, we find Amenoph I., the king under whom Moses should fly from Egypt, dying only five years afterwards: therefore *he* cannot be the king from whose death the history of the Exodus commences. But after him there follows a queen called Amesses for 21 years and 9 months; and after her there is only Thothmes III , called in the lists Mephres (the Misphragmuthosis of Manetho's narrative); so that this last is necessarily the king whose death is specified, though some predecessor seems also to be alluded to when it is said to Moses that "*all* the *men* are dead that sought thy life." Thothmes, therefore, whom the Scripture joins, as if already on the throne 40 years before, with the actual persecutor of Moses, died some time in the summer or autumn of B. C. 1655; and the Exodus, being in the spring following, should be in the first *actual* year of his son Amenoph II., called Mephrathmuthosis in Manetho's lists, but Thuthmosis or Tethmosis in his narrative; an inference from the Scriptures as compared with the lists which agrees with the indications elicited above from Manetho's own fabulous narrative. Not only does the Scripture say nothing of the king being drowned, but Miriam in her song, dwelling with emphasis and repetition on "all Pharaoh's cavalry, his chariots and horsemen," "Pharaoh's chariots, his chosen captains," hints that neither the king himself nor the infantry of his army had entered the sea. "For the cavalry of Pharaoh went in, with his chariots and horsemen, into the sea; and the Lord brought again the waters of the sea upon them." "And the waters returned, and covered the chariots and the horsemen, and *all* the host of Pharaoh *that came into the sea after them*; there remained not so much as one of them." "And all the women went out after Miriam with timbrels and dances, and Miriam answered them [with this burden], Sing ye to the Lord, for he hath triumphed gloriously; the horse and his rider hath he thrown into the sea." (Exod. xv.) It is true that verse 15 of Psalm cxxxv. has been made to say in English, that "as for Pharaoh and his host he *overwhelmed* them in the Red Sea:" but this is an inaccurate paraphrase, owing to a peculiarity of expression in the Latin which was not understood. In the Psalms, as translated from the original Hebrew in the Anglican Bible, it is said more guardedly that he "*overthrew* Pharoah and his host in the Red Sea," with a marginal variation, "or *shaked off*," which last is the correct translation. For in the original Hebrew the word is נִעֵר, in the Greek *ἐκτινάξαντι*, in the Latin *excussit*: "*τῷ ἐκτινάξαντι Φαραὼ καὶ τὴν δύναμιν αὐτοῦ εἰς θάλασσαν ἐρυθρὰν*," *κ. τ. λ.* "Et excussit Pharaonem et virtutem ejus *in* mari rubro;" i. e. "who flung off or dashed back Pharaoh and his pursuing force *into* or *in* or *at* (the Hebrew preposition covers equally the three senses) the Red Sea;" "into," if one thinks of them as a cloud of hornets, all of them dashed back, many of them falling into the sea, and some, it may be, falling on the bank; "in," because the act of discomfiture itself was done in the midst of the sea, not because Pharaoh personally, or all his force to a man, were overthrown or overwhelmed by bodily drowning; "at" needs no explanation. As for ecclesiastical writers, they, no doubt, have mostly held the commoner opinion, which seems recommended by a sort of poetical propriety, till we notice that in other instances also the type is in some marked feature left imperfect, to show that the full reality is still to come. Thus Joseph dreamed that the sun and the moon, and the eleven stars, meaning his father *and mother*, and his eleven brethren were to bow down to him. And when his eleven brethren and his father came into Egypt, he being then the lord of the land, the whole might have seemed to be accomplished and terminated, but that the *mother* was dead long before. Leah also had died, and had been buried at Hebron by her husband. So it was clear that Joseph was only a figure, and that the true and perfect Joseph was yet to come, who should be adored by his *mother*, as well as by his father and his brethren. So also there is another and more complete Exodus, in which all the hosts of evil, *with their king*, are to be overwhelmed for ever.

Some perhaps are not yet satisfied, but insist on having a Pharaoh to be drowned; and if they can find traces of a king who reigned less than a year between Thothmes III. and his son Amenoph II., or like to imagine such a king without traces, this idea in itself is certainly admissible. The Egyptians would be sure to suppress the memory of a reign so disastrous, which might leave no monuments; and its imperfect year, if all subsequent to Oct. 12, B.C. 1655, might be covered by the ante-dated accession of his successor. But the monuments seem to forbid this supposition. And Thothmes III. cannot be surrendered to them without causing much greater difficulties. It is true that as we have drawn out the chronology, making the 25 years and 4 months of Amosis to begin from Nov. 4, B.C. 1748, and giving Amesses 21.9$^{m}$., according to our present text of Josephus, Thothmes III. seems to die suspiciously near the time of the Exodus, in the spring of B.C. 1654. And the monuments supply another indication, approaching still nearer to a *proof*, that he and no other is the king under whom the Exodus took place. For in the mounds of Heliopolis, one of the cities according to the LXX. which were fortified by the labour of the Hebrews, many sun-baked bricks bearing the stamp of Thothmes III. have been used, which, on being broken, show that they were made *without straw*; whereas ordinarily the earth of which these bricks are made is held together by a mixture of chopped straw. It is impossible not to see how this singularity is accounted for by the Scriptures. The demands made by Moses and Aaron in favour of the Hebrews had led only to an aggravation of their servitude. Straw was no longer supplied to them. They were required to get it for themselves as they could, and yet to deliver the same tale of bricks. So when in spite of all the threats of the taskmasters the bricks fell short, and their native officers were beaten, and they complained to Pharaoh, instead of obtaining any redress they are again told by the tyrant that they are only idle, and are absolutely required to make the full tale of bricks as before. The consequence, though it be not written, is easily seen. They would make with straw as many bricks as they could, and fill up the tale required, when straw fell short, by making bricks without it. So there is a strong probability that the bricks found bearing the name of Thothmes III., and made without straw, were made at that particular time. Yet after all, this amounts to no positive proof that Thothmes III. was still on the throne. If indeed it had been several years after his death that the tyranny was so aggravated, it would have been next to impossible that bricks made for his successor should be found still bearing his name; but within a few months only after his death, if a multitude of 600,000 men were forced to work against time in making bricks, it is next to certain that they would still continue, in some cases, to use the old moulds for a reason similar to that which obliged them to make some of the bricks without straw.

But for the appearance exhibited by the lists, as if Thothmes III. died within a month of the Passover in B.C. 1654, this is only on the double assumption, shown above to be altogether improbable, that the actual reign of Amosis, the head of the dynasty, according to Manetho, as well as his reign technically antedated according to the Chronicle, began from Thoth 1, that is, from Nov. 4 in B.C. 1748, and that its length was reckoned both by the author of the Chronicle and by Manetho alike to have been 25 years and 4 months from this date. According to Manetho's own *apparent* chronology Thothmes III., even with the two assumptions above mentioned, would live on till the spring of B.C. 1653, three years after the Exodus, Manetho having thrown up from the time of anarchy preceding Dyn. XXVI to the head of his whole series of kings three years, which depress all dates below them, so that the head of Dyn. XVIII would be thereby depressed from Nov. 4, B.C. 1748, to B.C. 1745. And besides this, the preceding Dynasty XVII (XV of Africanus) ending according to the mixed lists of Josephus and Africanus, as pieced together by us, with a fraction of 10 months, and the actual reign of Amosis following with its 25 years and 4 months, this latter reign in technical reckoning, such as that of the Chronicle, would be antedated so as to include the last ten months of the Shepherds; and all the dates of Dyn. XVIII would be one year higher than if the actual accession of Amosis had been at the new year, and the Shepherds instead of 259.10$^{m}$. had ruled 260 full years and had left no fraction. So Thothmes III. would die not at the end of March B.C. 1654, but at the end of March B.C. 1653. Or if Dyn. XVIII were made to begin without antedating from the actual end of Dyn. XVII, two months before the new year, then Thothmes III. would die not at the end of March, but at the end of January, in B.C. 1654, *two* months too early for the Exodus.

Thus far we have been dealing only with the lists of Manetho for Dyn. XVIII; for though it is idle to dwell on figures or even names in lists purposely adulterated like those of Eusebius and Syncellus, original lists, or what come to us as if copied from such, are to be taken as either simply true, or at least as reconcileable with truth. They must not be altered to suit indications of other writers, or even of monuments; still less to introduce new arrangements and theories of our own: for they are the only possible framework which all investigators can agree to follow, at least provisionally and conventionally, and to which all fresh accessions of knowledge can be attached. And in a work like the present, aiming only at a general and conjectural reconstruction of the written schemes of the Chronicle, Manetho, Eratosthenes, and Ptolemy of Mendes, it is not absolutely necessary to discuss questions of detail raised from the monuments by students who, however acute and laborious, are far from having obtained as yet any complete outline of history to substitute for that of the lists. Still, as the monumental notices of Dyn. XVIII are very numerous, and its monumental names and succession may be paralleled to a great extent with those of the lists, and as some facts attested by the monuments seem to set aside our foregoing reasonings based on the lists alone, some notice of the monuments, both for this and for the following dynasties, may be expected by the reader, and shall be given.

As regards the reign of Amosis, the founder of Dyn. XVIII, his 22nd year is found marked in the quarries of Masarah, nearly opposite to Memphis; and in an inscription in the tomb of an officer of the same name, Aahmes Pensuben, at El Kab, which has been illustrated by Mr. Birch and M. De Rougé, a number of battles or campaigns are mentioned as having occurred during the war with the Shepherds between the accession of Amosis and his *sixth* year, when Avaris had already been taken. The owner of the tomb alluded to was born according to his own account of himself under the king Raskennen; on the accession of Amosis he "was still a child," that is, under age; nevertheless he went with him to the war against Avaris (Hawar), seemingly in his first year. The place was not taken, and the campaign having necessarily ended at least four months before the end of the Egyptian year, which about B.C. 1748 was at November 4, the king went to Memphis, and was there *crowned*. So that, although Avaris was still unreduced, the kingdom of Memphis, which had existed throughout under native princes vassals to the Shepherds, was now already united to the kingdom of Upper Egypt. And from this coronation it was, no doubt, that the author of the Chronicle would make his Dyn. XVIII, expressly named by him *Memphite*, commence, just as he had made the preceding Dyn. XXVII of the Shepherds and their 184 years of sovereignty commence not from their first settlement in the Delta, but from their reduction of Memphis, irrespectively of the kingdom of Upper Egypt, which continued independent until long afterwards. Considering the season at which the new year then was, it is not impossible that it was selected for the day of the coronation in preference to the anniversary of the king's actual and first accession in Upper Egypt. After this a second, a third, and a fourth battle or campaign before Avaris are mentioned, the last ending in a repulse; but the *fifth* mention of hostilities ends with the capture of Avaris; and the sixth is connected with the siege of another place, Scharhana, supposed to be beyond the Syrian frontier, and it is expressly fixed to the *sixth* year of the king. After having conquered the Shepherds, the inscription continues, the king made a campaign in Chentnefer, (that is, in the more distant parts of Nubia, near the gold region,) and there also he was victorious. "So he was master both in the south and in the north." After all this there are still mentioned two later expeditions into Nubia under the same king Amosis, the latter of them occasioned by a revolt, and another under his successor Amenoph I., when Aahmes, who relates his own exploits, was now a general. His life of service is said to have continued even to the [beginning of the] reign of Thothmes III., which by the lists would imply a space of ($25.4^m. + 13 + 20.7^m. + 21.9^m. + 1 =$) 82 years, so that if he were only 16 years old when he first accompanied Amosis to war, he would seem by the lists to have been at least 98 at his death. But to return to Amosis: His queen (or one at least, and the principal of his queens, if there were two) named Aahmes Nofriari was honoured and worshipped even to the end of the dynasty in an extraordinary way, and above her husband. She appears on many monuments both with him, and after his death with his successor, with the titles "Royal Daughter, Royal Wife, and Royal Mother," wearing sometimes the double crown or *pshent*, and painted not yellow (the conventional colour for Egyptian women), nor red or chocolate-coloured like Egyptian and Nubian men, but coal-black, which is a clear sign of the Ethiopian connection of this dynasty. For one or two of the Sevekhoteps and Neferhoteps, kings whom we have placed chiefly in Nubia and have referred to Dyn. XIV of Africanus (XVI of the original Manetho), have been found painted black in the same manner. One of these may be seen on a granite altar in the museum at Leyden.

It may be remarked in passing that the Ethiopian connection, and in part origin, of Dyn. XVIII throws light on a passage in the book of Numbers (xii. 1), where it is mentioned that Moses had once "married an Ethiopian woman;" for such a circumstance becomes very intelligible if he were bred up as the adopted son of "Pharaoh's daughter," when the queen-mother was herself an Ethiopian, and naturally had other ladies from Ethiopia about her. A Jewish fable in Josephus makes Moses go himself into Ethiopia with the command of an army; and thus far there is nothing to dispute against, since we know that in his earlier life also he "was mighty both in words and in deeds;" and the *southernmost* parts of Ethiopia were still unconquered, or they might rebel. But when it is added that as he was in the enemy's country the king's daughter fell in love with him, and purchased his hand by betraying her father's capital to the Egyptians, such an account of his Ethiopian marriage falls to the ground before the much more probable and natural explanation which is hinted by contemporary Egyptian monuments.

Amosis and the black queen Aahmes Nofriari are uniformly followed not only on particular contemporary monuments, but in the monumental lists of Thebes and Abydos, by Amenoph I., who was certainly the son of Amosis, but cannot be shown to have been succeeded by any son of his own. Between Amosis and Amenoph on the monuments there is no trace of the name "Chebron," nor of any other intervening king. But *after* Amenoph there is a king, Thothmes I., the chief element of whose throne-name "*Chepr*" may possibly be the source of the name "*Chebron*," and who *must* be identified with the Chebron of Manetho, unless Manetho be supposed first to have interpolated before Amenoph I. a king purely fictitious, and then to have suppressed after him a real king by way of compensation, which is not probable. Of Thothmes I. the monuments record a campaign *in Mesopotamia* in his second year, and they give the name of his queen "*Aahmes*," who seems to be the same with a sister of Amenoph I. named Amon-merit and Aahmes. Amon-merit may perhaps be the source of the Μέῤῥις, daughter of Παλμανώθης, head of the dynasty, and wife of Χενεφρῆς (Che*m*-br-*es* for Chebr-*os* or Chebr-*ou*), in the passage cited above from Artapanus. And in the Alexandrian Chronicle Χενεβρὼν (Che*m*bron for Chebron) is named as the king under whom Moses was brought up. We may conjecture then that Thothmes I., or, as he is called by Manetho, Chebron, married the daughter of Amosis, the sister consequently of Amenoph I., named after her mother Aahmes, and that he reigned after Amenoph I. by her right, not by his own; yet that he was a collateral of the family of Amosis, and so her cousin, the name "Thoth" in composition appearing first with him, while the termination "*mes*," equivalent to the Greek γενής, and the Latin *genitus*, is characteristic of the whole lineage of Amosis, properly written Aahmes (Luni-genitus). And if so, and if either he himself or his chief wife and queen, the daughter of Amosis, were older than her brother Amenoph I., this might perhaps account for his name having got before that of Amenoph I. in some genealogical list which Manetho followed. Leaving then the *reigns*, apart from the names, to stand *for the present* in the order of Manetho's list, but transposing the two names of Chebron or Thothmes I. and Amenoph I., as the monuments require, so that Amenoph succeeds Amosis and reigns 13 years, and Thothmes I., succeeding Amenoph, reigns 20 years and 7 months, we shall have seemingly in all ($25.4^{m}. + 13 + 20.7^{m}. =$) 58 years and 11 months from the actual Theban accession of Amosis to the end of the reign of Thothmes I.

After Thothmes I. and his queen Aahmes, who is styled "Royal Wife, Divine Spouse, Lady of Both Countries, and Great Royal Sister," and who appears also as regent, and seems to have survived her husband, we find on contemporary monuments a *queen*, whose original name was *Hatasu*, but who reigned by the names *Chnum-t-amen* and *Ra-ma-ka*. At the beginning of her reign she is represented as being yet quite a young woman, and has a consort, Thothmes II., *Ra-aa-en-cheperu*, whom some call her brother, and who may really have been a cousin. He is inserted in the later monumental lists of Abydos, the Ramesseum, and Medinet Habou, Hatasu being omitted; while in Manetho's lists on the other hand Thothmes II. is omitted, and a queen, not identifiable however in name with Hatasu, but named "Amesses," appears in the place where either Hatasu or her consort might be expected. Associated with Hatasu, besides Thothmes II., there appears also later on contemporary monuments (from which he has afterwards effaced her name to reduplicate his own) her younger brother, or half-brother, Thothmes III., who is found both on separate monuments of his own, and in the later monumental lists, and in Manetho's written lists. The 16th year of Hatasu or Ramaka, having her brother Thothmes III. then associated with her, but *taking precedence of him*, is marked on a stele at Wadi-Magara; and the Karnak inscription illustrated by Mr. Birch, connecting the 5th campaign of Thothmes III. with his 29th year, and his 10th campaign with his 35th, shows that his first campaign was not later than his 25th year, nor, probably, earlier than his 23rd, and so justifies the inference that the 21 years and 9 months which precede his place in Manetho's lists really represent that portion of his monumental reign which preceded his first campaign. For Manetho in Josephus gives to his queen "Amesses" described as "sister" to the king preceding her, that is to Amenoph I., a reign of 21 years and 9 months [or 21 and 1$^{m}$. according to the reading of Theophilus], and to Thothmes III., who follows her under the name of Miphres, a reign of 12 years and 9 months. If these two reigns were thrown together on the supposition that Thothmes III., when he came to reign alone, antedated his accession, and reckoned his years from the death of his father Thothmes I., they would give us for the whole monumental reign of Thothmes III. a space of 34 years and 6 months [or 33 and 10$^{m}$]. But the Karnak inscription marks a sixteenth campaign of this king, which cannot have been earlier than his 41st year, and probably was not so early: and in another inscription, as it is said, even his 47th has been found; so as to justify the inference that, besides the 21 years and 9 months preceding his first campaign, 13 other years, *following* the 12 years and 9 months allowed him by Manetho, have been cut off from the end of his reign, which really from first to last covered a space of 47 years and 6 months [or 46 and 10 months]. This being so, the next question is where to find in the lists the 13 years wanted? Have they been simply reckoned by Manetho to the next reign, so as still to stand in their true chronological places? or have they been transposed to some other place not their own? For the first supposition the monuments, as will appear below, leave no room. But if we cast our eyes upwards above the reign of Thothmes III., we see just that number of 13 years which we want joined with a name which the monuments have forced us to eject or transpose from the place where it stands, so as by this very fact to suggest a suspicion that the years are to be transposed too, and perhaps separately. This suspicion becomes certainty when we consider the details already referred to of the life of Aahmes Pensuben, who having entered upon service while yet only a lad in the first year of Amosis, is recorded to have been still living, and seemingly still serving, under Thothmes III., that is at least during the year of his first campaign dated by himself, we suppose, as his 23rd. But 82 years of service, which would thus be given to Aahmes if all the reigns named by him are to be computed according to the lists, are so improbable, as of themselves to make one doubt whether the lists are really to be so applied. And when we have proof from other sources that 13 years have been *suppressed* in the lists a little lower down, and transferred to some other place than their own, it is clear that the unchronological addition, the place of which it would have been our business to detect, has shown itself here of its own accord, and needs not to be searched for elsewhere. Even when the 13 years given in the lists to Chebron have been transposed, so as to make the requisite addition to the reign of Thothmes III., bringing it up from the 12 years and 9 months of the lists to 25 years and 9 months, Aahmes Pensuben will still be scarcely less than 85 years old, and will have seen at least 69 years of service, if he served both in the first campaign of Amosis and in the first campaign of Thothmes III. his fourth successor. It is remarkable that Aahmes Pensuben, though he mentions serving the queen Ra-ma-ka (i. e. Hatasu), and nursing her daughter (who seems to have died young), adds this separately, while the series named before in connection with his military service is the same as that of the monumental lists: "I served," he says, "the king *Ra-neb-peh* (Amosis); I served the king *Ra-ser-ka* (Amenoph I.); I served the king *Ra-aa-cheper-ka* (Thothmes I.); I served also the king *Ra-aa-en-cheper* (Thothmes II.)," with other matter between each name; and then in the next column, "I served also the queen *Ra-ma-ka* (Hatasu); I nursed her daughter the princess *Ra-nofreon* deceased;" . . . and lastly is mentioned his still living and serving "the king *Ra-men-cheper*" (Thothmes III.).

We infer then that the 20 years and 7 months given in the lists of Manetho to Amenoph I. really cover the two reigns of that king and his brother-in-law Thothmes I.; and that of the joint sum of the two reigns Amenoph probably had 13 years (since Manetho must have had *some* reason for cutting off 13 years, rather than 12 or 14, from the reign of Thothmes III.), and Thothmes I. or Chebron may have reigned the remaining 7 years and 7 months.

Lastly, we may suppose that the "Amesses" of Manetho, being the daughter of Amosis, sister of Amenoph I., wife of Thothmes I. and mother of Hatasu, having been left a widow, with her children all as yet quite young, continued to govern for them as regent, either till her death, or till the marriage of her daughter with Thothmes II. So the 21 years and 9 months in Manetho's lists may be a consolidation of the two female regencies of Aahmes and Hatasu, mother and daughter, into one, the name of Aahmes prevailing because she was originally the heiress, and the title of her daughter (to say nothing of her daughter's consort) was derived from her.

After the death of Thothmes III. the monuments require us to allow with Manetho *at least* 25 years and 10 months and 9 years and 8 months (making in all 35 years and 6 months) to the two reigns of Amenoph II. (called in the lists of Manetho Misphra-muthosis) and Thothmes IV. respectively. But the following reign, that of Amenoph III., the monuments *force* us to extend beyond the length of 30 years and 10 months given for it by 5 full years, as its 36th current year has been found marked. What may have been the purpose of Manetho in suppressing and transferring elsewhere the last years of a legitimate reign either in this case, or in the similar case of Thothmes III., is hard to determine. One may *suspect* that it was done in order to obscure the true sequence of history at two points of time connected with great national calamity and reproach.

After Amenoph III. two successors at least, Amon-anchut, with his 4th year marked, and the sun-worshipping king Khouen or Quashan (with a local "king of Thebes" named Ai in his suite) are interposed by the monuments before they give us Horus, the next name to Amenoph III. in Manetho's lists. The time of the sun-worshippers, reckoned seemingly as 15 full years from Thoth 1 to Thoth 1, exclusively of such odd months as no doubt also belonged to them, having been suppressed by Manetho and prefixed to Dyn. XIX, must be restored so as to come in after the death of Amenoph III., if, as is said to be the case, the reign of the sun-worshipper preceded that of Amon-anchut. The reign of this latter, omitted in all the lists, is no doubt reckoned by them to Horus, from whose 36 years and 5 months the 5 years added by the monuments to his father Amenoph III. will have to be subtracted.

After Horus, except one name, and that illegible, thought by M. Mariette to be the Rathotis of the lists, the monuments give us nothing till the time of the king commonly known as Rameses I., grandfather of Rameses the Great. His monumental name "Rames*sou*, or Arme*ssou*," is probably the source of the "Armesses" or "Armais" of the lists. His successor Seti I. *must* be the Rameses of the lists on the same principle by which Thothmes I. has been identified above with Chebron. For it cannot be supposed that Manetho omitted entirely such a king as Seti I., one of the most illustrious for his victories and for his monumental records, to substitute, in the very place belonging to him, a merely fictitious and supernumerary Rameses unknown to the monuments. But as Manetho in a fable which blends Seti II. and Rameses III. together with Seti I. and Rameses the Great all into one person says of Seti II. that "he was also named Rameses" (Σέθως ὁ καὶ Ῥαμεσσῆς), so here in his lists he goes further, and names Seti I. simply "Ramesses," omitting his more proper name Sethos. It is indeed possible that the name Rameses was applicable to all the kings descendants of Ramessou-Armesses or Rameses I., whether they took it in their cartouches or not. The title Mi-amon also, afterwards a distinctive surname of Rameses II., was taken occasionally by the father; and many circumstances combined to blend the reigns, the names, and even the persons of the two kings, father and son, into one. Still it is certainly strange that Manetho should here omit the name Sethos altogether and name only Rameses, while Diodorus and other later writers, on the other hand, omit the name Rameses, and merge Rameses the Great himself in his father under the name "Sesoosis," which is only a variation of Sethos or Sethosis, meant by them to represent "Sesostris."

Rameses II. (the Great) who should have been Rameses III. if his father were truly named Rameses, follows next, with the innumerable and magnificent monuments of his long reign. What is strange—stranger even than Manetho's omission of the name of his father — is that this great king, with his reign of over 66 years, has dropped out from one of the lists, the list of Africanus; or at least from that copy of the list of Africanus which Syncellus transcribed; for in the list of Eusebius, also copied, though unfaithfully, from Africanus, he is found. The name of his son and successor on the monuments, Merienphtha, being identified with the Amenophis of the lists, concludes the dynasty.

On a general review we shall now be able perhaps to distinguish on what grounds the Chronicle reckoned to this Dyn. XVIII *fourteen generations,* while the monumental lists of Thebes and Abydos give a series of *thirteen* legitimate *kings;* and the written lists of Manetho and his epitomists count *sixteen* or *seventeen* names, while the actual reigns of all kinds, if thrown together, seem to have been not fewer than twenty-two.

(Generation I., reign i.) *Aahmes, Ra-neb-peh,* and his black queen, *Aahmes Nofriari.* In his 1st Theban year he warred against Avaris, but did not take it. In the same year, when the season for war was over (in the summer of

24. Nov. 4, B.C. 1748, to Oct. 29, B.C. 1724.

B.C. 1747), he was *crowned* at Memphis. In his 5th, seemingly, he took Avaris and expelled the Shepherds. In his 6th, he seems to have been still occupied with the remains of the war with the Shepherds, but no longer within the frontiers of Egypt. After his 6th year, he was free to turn his arms southwards, and was victorious in further Ethiopia, as he had been in the Delta and on the Syrian frontier. In his 22nd year he quarried stone at Toura for the temples of Phtha at Memphis and of Ammon at Thebes. This is his latest date as yet found.

As his Memphite accession, and with it the commencement of Dyn. XVIII is put by the Chronicle at Thoth 1, = Nov. 4th of the anticipated and uncorrected Julian year B.C. 1748, and as so put is no doubt antedated (unless, indeed, the coronation was deferred for five months or more after the campaign, and then celebrated on the very day of the new year), it follows that the actual coronation and accession of Amosis at Memphis must have been in B.C. 1747, some short time after the season for war was over, and when the water season was approaching or had commenced. So if we calculate that it was probably not much more than five months, nor much less than three, before the end of the Egyptian year, and take four months as a mean, we may assume that the coronation was on or about July 2, B.C. 1747, and that the actual Theban accession of Amosis had been one year, more or less, but necessarily, and at the least, eight months earlier. As for the 25 years and 4 months given him by Manetho, Manetho's own method requires that they should date from some *actual* accession, whether Theban or Memphite; and there can be little doubt that they date, in fact, historically and chronologically from his first actual accession at Thebes, while the later Memphite accession (technically antedated from Thoth 1 preceding) is certainly the epoch of the Chronicle. Manetho, no doubt, presents the 542 years of his Dynasties XVIII and XIX as parallel to the same 542 years of the same dynasties in the Chronicle, and as consequently coinciding for their commencement in Thoth 1 = Nov. 4, B.C. 1748. But he himself is at no pains to make this parallelism more than apparent, having in his series above the head of Dyn. XVIII three years (in our patched reconstruction two years and ten months) thrown up from times far below, so that the first year of Dyn. XVIII and all the rest are really depressed by three places below the points of coincidence required for them as they are paralleled with the years of Dynasties XVIII and XIX of the Chronicle. Nor is this enough, but Manetho adds to these two inconsistent reckonings a third equally inconsistent with them both, when he says expressly that the 25 years and 4 months of Amosis are all to be reckoned to him from "after the expulsion" of the Shepherds, i.e. from after the capture of Avaris, which we now know from the monuments to have been in his *fifth* year, and certainly not on Thoth 1, in B.C. 1748, nor on Thoth 1 at all. But without considering that apparent chronology of Manetho which is freely disregarded by himself, having put the Memphite accession of Amosis at July 8, B.C. 1748, and the Theban a year earlier, we have only 24 years and 4 months to reckon to his actual reign, as included within the limits of Dyn. XVIII of the Chronicle, or 25 full years to his technical reign as antedated from Thoth 1 = Nov. 4 in the autumn preceding. Thus the Memphite reign, as antedated by the Chronicle, differs from the actual Theban reign of Manetho by 4 months, which having been depressed by Manetho so as to begin within Dyn. XVIII of the Chronicle, and having been by us ejected, will leave a void below at some point or other, where Manetho must have suppressed four months really belonging to the dynasty. We reckon, then, 4 months of the reign of Amosis as already past at the commencement of Dynasty XVIII; and then the remaining 24 full years common to Manetho and the Chronicle will begin, according to the chronology of the Chronicle, from Thoth 1 = Nov. 4, B.C. 1748, and will end Oct. 29, B.C. 1723.

(Generation II. reign ii.) *Amenhotep I., Ra-sor-ka.* His queen is named Aah-hotep, though some think Aah-hotep was a wife of Amosis. The 1st year only of Amenoph I. has been found. If he reigned 13 years, his actual reign would be coincident, or very nearly, with his reign as 13. Oct. 29, B.C. 1723, to Oct. 25, B.C. 1710.

technically reckoned from Thoth 1 = Oct. 29, B. C. 1723, to Thoth 1 = Oct. 25, B.C. 1710, when Moses would be in his 25th year.

7. Oct. 25, B. C. 1710, to Oct. 24, B. C. 1703. (Generation II. reign iii.) *Thothmes I., Ra-aa-cheper-ka*, consort and probably cousin of *Aahmes Merit-amon*, sister of Amenoph I. and daughter of Amosis, the Amesses of Manetho, who seems to have reigned on after the death of her husband till her daughter *Hatasu* was of age and married. She, if any one, of the princesses known to us from the monuments, should be that "daughter of Pharaoh" who took up Moses from the water, and educated him as her own son. Probably what is asserted of her is true, that she had no other son really her own. If her consort Thothmes I. (whose 2nd year only has been found on the monuments) reigned in all 7 years and 7 months, his 7 years, as technically reckoned, would lie between Oct. 26, B.C. 1710, and Oct. 24, B.C. 1703, his death being 7 months later, May 22, B.C. 1702. At this time Moses was 32 years of age; and since he declined to become the son of Pharaoh's daughter, and "preferred the reproach of Christ to the riches and pleasures of Egypt," we may infer that they were once within his reach, and that it would have suited the policy as well as inclination of his adoptive mother to marry her daughter Hatasu, as soon as she was of age, to him rather than to some collateral, who might use the rank of king-consort only for the aggrandisement of his own branch. After the death of Thothmes I. one may suppose it was, and during the regency of Amesses, included probably under the next reign of Manetho, that Moses had the fullest opportunity of showing himself "mighty both in words and in deeds," and worthy of that rank to which the queen-mother would have raised him. And after he had declined to become, in the strictest sense, "the *son* of Pharaoh's daughter, he was married so as to be free to acknowledge his true kindred, and yet to such a wife as showed a connection with the court. And his position, even after the marriage of the princess Hatasu, under her consort Thothmes II. was still such, that he thought the Hebrews, his brethren, "would understand how that by his arm God would deliver them,"

so soon as he stood up in their behalf and showed himself ready to represent them. "But they understood not."

(Generation III, reign of Manetho IV, not in the monu- 22. From Oct. 24, B.C. 1703, to Oct. 18, B.C. 1681.
mental lists.) Under the name Amesses (*Aahmes* of the monuments) Manetho seems to have included both the regency of Aahmes, and the longer reign of her daughter *Hatasu*, named as queen *Chnum-t-amen*, *Ra-ma-ka*, which again includes that of her consort *Thothmes II.*, *Ra-aa-en-cheper* (reign IV of the monumental lists, omitted by Manetho). Hatasu seems to have reigned not only as regent and guardian of Thothmes III. (probably only her half-brother), but also by her mother's right and her own. How long precisely her mother Amesses was regent, and whether Hatasu with Thothmes II. reigned from her mother's death, or rather from the time of her own marriage, while Amesses was still living, is uncertain. Only it would seem that the regency of Amesses can scarcely have lasted more than six years, whether it be covered by the 7 years and 7 months of Thothmes I., or by the 21 years and 9 months of the Amesses of the lists. For the 2nd year of Thothmes I. and the 16th year of Hatasu have been found. And so, even if Hatasu reigned only 16 years current in all, which is the minimum possible, there would be but 6 years current preceding them at the head of Manetho's 21 years and 9 months for the regency of her mother. The whole joint reign as reckoned technically would have 22 years, from Oct. 24 B.C. 1703 to Oct. 18 B.C. 1681, and would leave a fraction of 4 months over ending Feb. 15 B.C. 1680. Within this space the marriage and the joint accession of Hatasu and her consort Thothmes II. cannot well be placed later than Thoth 1 = Oct. 22, B.C. 1697. In the 3rd year after this it was, in B.C. 1694, that the king, who should be Thothmes II. the consort of Hatasu, "sought to slay Moses," and Moses fled from Egypt. It seems to be hinted by what was said to Moses nearly 40 years later, upon the death of Thothmes III., viz. that "*all* the *men*" in the plural, who had sought his life, were then dead, that Thothmes III., though no doubt only a boy, was already on the throne in B.C. 1694, that is, in the 9th year after the death of his

father, when there were only 13 years more and some months of the actual reign of his sister Hatasu still to come. So this date would be in her 3rd year, if she reigned *only* the 16 years current which are required by the inscription of her 16th, and which in that case may have begun from Oct. 20, B.C. 1697, after her mother's actual regency had lasted 5 years and 5 months, reckoned technically as 6 years, from the death of Thothmes I. But the reign of Hatasu may very possibly have had more than this length of 15 years and 4 months; and she may have associated her half-brother Thothmes III. with herself from the first; or even it may be that the regency during her own minority was administered by the queen-mother Amesses in their joint names. But these points are at present only matters of conjecture. Thus much however appears, that the consort of Hatasu, Thothmes II., was still living in B.C. 1694 when Moses fled from Egypt (since there was then a Pharaoh who sought to slay him); and consequently it is not open to suppose that it was only upon his death that she strengthened herself by associating in the throne her half-brother Thothmes III., not yet old enough to be any cause of jealousy.

48. From Oct. 24, B.C. 1703, or 26 from Oct. 18, B.C. 1681, to Oct. 12, B.C. 1655.

(Generation III, reign of Manetho V, of the monumental lists V.) *Thothmes III., Ra-men-cheper* (who in some of the numerous variants of his name has the title *Mi*[*-ph*]*-ra*). He appears with his sister the queen Hatasu or Ra-ma-ka, but as subordinate to her, at Wadi Magara in an inscription of her 16th year. His own second year *as reigning alone* is marked at Assouan; but generally his years are antedated from the death of his father; and so his 5th campaign is connected in the great inscription from Karnak with his 29th year, his 6th with his 30th, and his 10th with his 35th year. His 16th campaign is named, though its date is wanting. In his 42nd year he erected a sitting statue still preserved to "his brother" (that is, the consort of his sister, and probably his cousin), Thothmes II.; and elsewhere even his 47th year is said to be found. His conquests extended as far as "Nineveh" and the banks of the Tigris; and the list of the tributes paid to him from conquered countries has been in part preserved by sculptures on his additions to the great temple of

Karnak. Under him the oppression of the Hebrews reached its highest point; and from his death it is that the narrative of the Exodus begins. But if the death of his father Thothmes I. be conjecturally fixed to May 22, B.C. 1702, when he was a boy perhaps 5 years old, his own death, if placed 47 years and 6 months later, will be at Nov. 11, B.C. 1655, 5 months or thereabouts before the Exodus. But if in point of fact the Theban accession of Amosis should have been somewhat earlier than we have estimated, or if the variant given by Theophilus of Antioch of 21 years and 1 month instead of 9 months for the reign of Amesses should be more than a mere error, the death of Thothmes would be proportionably earlier, though by another and separate line of reasoning it may be concluded that it did not precede the Exodus by so much as a full year. The reign would be reckoned technically by the Chronicle at 48 years from Oct. 24, B.C. 1703, to Oct. 12, B.C. 1655.

25. Oct. 24, B.C. 1655 to Oct. 5, B.C. 1630.

(Generation IV, reign of Manetho vi, of the monumental lists vi.) *Amenhotep II., Ra-aa-cheperu*, son of Thothmes III. If his actual accession be rightly put at Nov. 11, B.C. 1655, then as technically antedated his reign would be reckoned from Oct. 12 preceding in the same year, and the Exodus would seem to be later in his first year by one month than it was in truth. His 3rd year only is marked, in a temple founded by him at Amada in Nubia.

10. Oct. 5, B.C. 1630, to Oct. 3, B.C. 1620.

(Generation V, reign of Manetho vii, and of the monumental lists vii.) *Thothmes IV., Ra-men-cheperu*, son of Amenoph II. His 4th year is marked at Sarabeit el Khadeem, and his 7th on the great obelisk of Thothmes III. now standing at St. John Lateran's at Rome; it is mentioned also that this same obelisk remained in the hands of the workmen 35 years, from the death of Thothmes III. to some date not given in the reign of Thothmes IV. But according to the reckoning of the lists (which this inscription justifies) Amenoph II. should reign 25 years and 10 months from Nov. 11, B. C. 1655, to Aug. 31, B. C. 1629; and Thothmes IV. 9 years and 8 months from Aug. 31, B. C. 1629, to May 1, B. C. 1619. The two reigns make together only 35 years and 6 months. So the inscription on the obelisk would seem to have been dated within 6 months before the death of Thothmes IV. But in technical reckoning Amenoph II. will have 25 years from Oct. 12, B.C. 1655, to Oct. 5, B.C. 1630; and Thothmes IV. will have 10 years from Oct. 5, B.C. 1630, to Oct. 3, B.C. 1620; leaving 7 months to be reckoned to his successor.

36. Oct. 3, B.C. 1620, to Sept. 24, B.C. 1584. (Generation VI, reign of Manetho viii, of the monumental lists viii.) *Amen-hotep III., Ra-neb-ma*, son of Thothmes IV. by a queen, *Maut em shoi*, whom some suppose to have been of Asiatic origin; and they would account from hence for a certain peculiarity of features which appears in Amenoph III. and his successors down to Horus inclusively. That *Taia*, the queen of Amenoph himself, was of Asiatic origin is less doubtful, as she appears with him on a scarabæus of his 11th year worshipping the sun's disk, a devotion not indigenous in Egypt; and she is specially honoured on the monuments of the sun-worshippers who after the death of Amenoph ruled Egypt; so that one may collect that they were Egyptians only by half-blood, if at all, and that it was through Taia that they claimed the crown. That some unpopularity attached to his memory afterwards (unless indeed Egypt was violently over-run, as Manetho says it was, by foreign enemies), is rendered probable by the fact, that his tomb has been most carefully defaced; and that his temple-palace, to the approaches of which the colossus called Memnon and its fellow belonged, has been completely destroyed. His 36th year being marked on the monuments, we must suppose him to have reigned 35 years and 10 months at least, instead of the 30 and 10 months of the lists; and his reign may be placed conjecturally between May 1, B.C. 1619, and Feb. 20, B.C. 1583, 6 years after the death of Joshua. But in technical reckoning he will have 36 years, reaching from Oct. 3, B.C. 1620, to Sept. 24, B.C. 1584, and he will leave 5 months *to be reckoned* to his successor.

5. Sept. 20, B.C. 1588, to Sept. 19, B.C. 1583? (Generation VII, not in Manetho, nor in the monumental lists.) *Amon-anchut, Ra-neb-cheperu*, said to have been a son of Amenoph III. who certainly reigned before Horus; and as he is omitted by Manetho, while Horus another son of Amenoph III., with a long reign, is made to follow imme-

diately after his father, we may infer that the years of Amon-anchut (whose 4th current year is found) are included within the reign of Horus in the lists. The fact, however, that the foreign dependencies of Egypt and their tributes continued unchanged during his reign looks rather as if he came *before* the sun-worshippers.

16. Sept. 21, B.C. 1584, to Sept. 20, B.C. 1568.

(Generation VII, not in Manetho, nor in the monumental lists.) The sun-worshipping king *Quash-an* [*Ra*]-*athin*, whether he followed, or as is more commonly thought preceded Amon-anchut, certainly had a reign of some length, as the sculptured tombs at Tel-el-Amarna attest; and not only his 6th and 8th year but his 12th is said to have been found. Lepsius asserts that he also was a son of Amenoph III.; and, if so, no doubt his mother was *Taia*, whose peculiar worship of the sun's disk he undertook to establish in Egypt, while he defaced the effigies of the god Ammon and the names in which Ammon entered into composition. It is said that he had himself taken at first the names "*Amenhotep IV.*, *Ra-nefer-cheperu*," and that afterwards he defaced his own scutcheons, and cut in over *one* of them a new name, viz., *Chouen-Atin* or *Chouen-Atin-ra*. But if we take the narrative of Manetho only for our guide (and there is little doubt that under his impious Hierosolymite Shepherds the sun-worshippers who ruled Egypt after Amenoph III. are meant), we shall rather conjecture that Quashan was an Asiatic of the same country and religion and kindred with Taia, than that he was her son by Amenoph III. (though it is true that he honours Amenoph III., and even Thothmes IV., on his monuments as well as Taia). And if he were also the son of an Egyptian princess, or had married a daughter of Amenoph III. and Taia, he may have set up a claim to the throne of Egypt on the death of his father-in-law, and may have enforced it by a successful invasion. Manetho himself suggests the idea that the invaders had a party in Egypt with which they were not unconnected by blood. Other indications, besides those that have been already mentioned, look the same way. A local king of Thebes named *Ai*, with the throne name *Ra-cheper-cheperu-iri-ma*, whose tomb has been most completely defaced at some time after his death, appears in the suite of Quashan as his subordinate; and while the other foreign dependencies of Egypt and their tributes remain in his time unaltered, *Mesopotamia*, as it is said, is *not* named in the list as a tributary country, but Egypt itself *is*. If we take instead of 13 years given in Manetho's narrative to the impious Asiatics the 15 full years reckoned from Thoth 1 to Thoth 1, prefixed by him to the head of his Dyn. XIX, and reinsert them in their proper place, so as to follow after the death of Amenoph III. (unless Amon-anchut can be shown to come first), it will be *necessary* either to destroy of ourselves that character of full years which Manetho has given them, or to add to them such odd months as are wanting to fill the interval between the death of Amenoph III., Feb. 20, B.C. 1583, and Thoth 1, that is, Sept. 24, next following. Thus we shall have to add 7 months, 3 months more than the compensation we wanted to find room for; this excess showing perhaps that the Theban reign of Amosis began really not 4 but 7 months earlier than Nov. 4, B. C. 1748, or else giving us a fraction of 3 months overrunning (as was to be expected) the end of the dynasty, and covered in the Chronicle by the first year of Dyn. XIX as technically antedated. For convenience sake we shall proceed as if the latter were the case. Thus the actual reign of the sun-worshippers, having 15 full years and 7 months, will begin from Feb. 20, B. C. 1583 (nearly 6 years after the death of Joshua), and will end nearly with the Egyptian year at Sept. 20, B.C. 1568 (in the 4th year after the commencement of Othniel's judgeship). But in technical reckoning they will have 16 years, from Sept. 24, B. C. 1584, to Sept. 20, B. C. 1568. It is plainly unlikely that the actual reign of the sun-worshipping king, suppressed by Manetho, should have lasted just 15 years to a day, and doubly so that it should have begun and ended with the Egyptian year; just as it was unlikely that the apparent parallelism of the sum of Manetho's actual reigns for his Dynasties XVIII and XIX with that of XVIII and XIX of the Chronicle should be true and chronological. But there is no great improbability in supposing an actual reign, like that of Horus, following after times of servitude or usurpation, to have been dated originally from the new year.

[This is the place for noticing another method which might have been pursued. If, for instance, after showing that Manetho's two Dynasties XVIII and XIX of actual reigns could not well lie concurrently with Dynasties XVIII and XIX of the Chronicle between Thoth 1, B.C. 1748, and Thoth 1, B.C. 1206,—and further that the actual reign of Amosis was probably reckoned by Manetho from an earlier and the technical reign of the same king by the Chronicle from a later accession, we had abstained from attempting to estimate the precise number of months by which his coronation at Memphis was later than Thoth 1 in B.C. 1748, and had drawn out the chronology of the dynasty at first tentatively upon Manetho's own suggestion, *as if* its years were coincident with those of the Chronicle, though that might in fact be untrue, reckoning upon this principle we should have made the reign of Amenoph III. end not at Feb. 20, B.C. 1583, but 4 months later, that is at June 20 in the same year. We should then have had to place the 15 years prefixed by Manetho to his Dyn. XIX; and as these in his series are full years coincident with as many of the Chronicle, running from Thoth 1 to Thoth 1, they could not have joined on to the preceding reigns at June 20 in B.C. 1583, but would have required 3 months to be prefixed to them; and this done, they would be technically antedated from Thoth 1 preceding the death of Amenoph, and would count for the Chronicle as 16 full years. Again, after the end of the 15 full years, i. e. after Thoth 1 = Sept. 23, B.C. 1568, instead of reaching only to the accession of Horus, calculated upwards from the end of the dynasty, viz., from Thoth 1 = Aug. 9, B.C. 1400 (for from Aug. 9, B.C. 1400, 168 years and 3 months take us up to June 20, B.C. 1568), we should have overrun his accession by 3 months. To avoid this we must either have displaced and thrust down everything below to the extent of 3 months, while we kept all above unchanged, or we must have made a second addition to the 15 full years of the sun-worshippers by suffixing to them 9 more odd months. Thus only could they both retain their original character of *full years lying between Thoth 1 and Thoth 1*, and also coalesce with the 179 years and 9 months of the dynasty above, and the 168 years and 3 months below, without unequally disturbing the relative position of any years or months on either side. But the result of the whole process (besides that the sun-worshippers instead of 15 years would have 16, which is not improbable) would be this, that we should have for the whole dynasty not 348 but 349 years, lying still with the same improbability as before between Thoth 1 and Thoth 1, but also (which is an impossibility) lying chronologically within Thoth 1 = Nov. 4, B.C. 1748, and Thoth 1 = Aug. 9, B.C. 1400. Those two fractions then which we have supposed to be inserted in the middle at Manetho's own suggestion, would force out each of them a fraction equal to itself one at either end; and we should have 3 months forced up and projecting above the chronological head of the dynasty, and 9 months forced down and overrunning below its chronological end. The consequence would be that all the dates above Thoth 1 = Sept. 24 in B.C. 1583 would be one Egyptian month later than we have now fixed them; the death of Thothmes III., for instance, would be at Dec. 11, instead of Nov. 11 in B.C. 1565, only 4 months perhaps instead of 5 before the Exodus (though an interval of 5 months was not at all too much), but all dates below the accession of Horus (which would be at March 19, B.C. 1567) would be 9 months lower than we shall have to place them according to our own calculation of the probable date of the coronation of Amosis at Memphis. But it is time to return from this digression.]

31. Sept. 20, B.C. 1568, to Sept. 12, B.C. 1537. (Generation VII, reign of Manetho IX, and of the monumental lists IX.) *Hor-em-hebi, Meri-amon, Ra-tseser-cheperu, Sotep-en-ra*, son of Amenoph III. The remains of his pylon at Karnak described by M. Prisse are important as proving that his actual reign was later both than that of the sun-worshipping king Quashan, and than that of Amon-anchut, blocks from buildings erected by them with their sculptures and cartouches turned inwards having been used as materials in its walls. In like manner the fact that the sun-worshipper Quashan has appropriated in some cases the cartouches of

Amenoph III. demonstrates him to have been later than that king. Amon-anchut being omitted by Manetho and also by the monumental lists, and Horus being made to follow immediately after his father Amenoph III., there is no reason to doubt that the 36 years and 5 months given to Horus in the lists are antedated so as to cover the whole reign of Amon-anchut, if Amon-anchut was his immediate predecessor, whether it had only the 4 years current required by the date found or any longer continuance. That his nominal reign in the lists includes also the 15 years and 7 months of the sun-worshippers and the last 5 years cut off from the life of Amenoph III., is an idea in itself by no means inadmissible. It is certainly presented by Manetho as doing so, and the monuments oppose no difficulty, as no date beyond his 9th year has been found; and even after deducting (5 + 16 + 4 =) 25 years, there would still remain 10 years and 5 months for his actual reign. But whatever may be the truth historically, since Manetho's lists give no more years than the precise number required for the chronology of the dynasty, we cannot afford to suppress any years of the lists, but must reckon them all as chronological until they are actually displaced by others recorded on the monuments but omitted by Manetho, and requiring to be reinserted. So the 5 years cut off from Amenoph III., having been discovered by help of the monuments, necessarily displace 5 years from some place or other in the lists; and at no place can the compensating suppression be made with more probability than at the end of the nominal reign of Horus. But this reign cannot be supposed to be antedated so as to include at its head the last 5 years of the life of Amenoph III. (together with the 16 following years reckoned technically to the sun-worshippers) until we have at first ascertained the existence of a suppression of 15 years and 7 months elsewhere. Meantime the idea that the nominal reign of Horus may really include in part at least the time of the sun-worshippers (whom Amon-anchut may possibly have preceded) is favoured by a recent discovery in the Serapeum at Memphis; an Apis-tomb, connected by an inscription with the name of Horus, having been found, in which, instead of the usual mummy in a sarcophagus, only some burnt bones of a bull had been deposited, wrapped up together in muslin. The chamber besides showed signs of haste, secresy, and poverty accompanying the burial. And the adjoining tomb of the preceding Apis seemed to have been purposely destroyed; so that there may possibly be here some confirmation of Manetho's story that the impious "Hierosolymites" not only forced the priests of Apis themselves to slay or sacrifice him, but afterwards roasted and ate him. But to leave these questions:— If we cut off from the reign of Horus the 5 years which have been restored to his father above, it will then have 31 years and 5 months, including at their head probably 5 years actually belonging either to Amon-anchut or to the sun-worshippers; and these 31 years and 5 months, beginning at Sept. 23, B.C. 1568, will end Feb. 9, B.C. 1536. But in technical reckoning the reign will have 31 years from Sept. 23, B.C. 1568, to Sept. 12, B.C. 1537.

For the interval between Horus and Ramessou, or Rameses I., the Armesses or Armais, probably, of the lists, an interval, according to the same lists, of 49 years and 9 months, the monuments have hitherto afforded nothing but a single name of one king, and that illegible, found by M. Mariette in the Serapeum at Memphis. But according to Manetho's lists there should be four reigns, as follows:—

12. Sept. 12, B.C. 1537, to Sept. 9, B.C. 1525.

(Generation VIII, reign of Manetho x, not in the monumental lists.) *Achenchres*, daughter (i.e. of Horus), 12 years 1 month, as if from Feb. 9, B.C. 1536, to March 8, B.C. 1524. In technical reckoning 12 years, from Sept. 12, B.C. 1537, to Sept. 9, B.C. 1525.

9. Sept. 9, B.C. 1525, to Sept. 7, B.C. 1516.

(Generation VIII, reign of Manetho xi, not in the monumental lists.) *Rathotis*, her brother, 9 years; as if from March 8, B.C. 1524, to March 6, B.C. 1516; or in technical reckoning 9 years, from Sept. 9, B.C. 1525, to Sept. 7, B.C. 1516. (Perhaps the king whose name has been found in the Serapeum.)

12. Sept. 7, B.C. 1516, to Sept. 4, B.C. 1504.

(Generation IX, reign of Manetho xii, not in the monumental lists.) *Achencheres I.*, 12 years 5 months, as if from March 5, B.C. 1515, to Aug. 1, B.C. 1503; or technically, 12 years from Sept. 7, B.C. 1516, to Sept. 4, B.C. 1504.

13. Sept. 4, B.C. 1504, to Sept. 1, B.C. 1491.

(Generation IX, reign of Manetho xiii, not in the monumental lists.) *Achencheres II.*, 12 years 3 months, as if from Aug. 1, B.C. 1503, to Oct. 31, B.C. 1491; or technically 13 years, from Sept. 4, B.C. 1504, to Sept. 1, B.C. 1491.

4. Sept. 1, B.C. 1491, to Aug. 31, B.C. 1487.

(Generation X, reign of Manetho xiv, of the monumental lists x.) *Ramessou, Ra-men-peh*, commonly called Rameses I. His mother's name is said to be Tii, which some have read Titi, and sought to identify with Rathotis of the lists. Again, she is identified with the wife of *Ai*, the local king of Thebes, and vassal of Quashan. She is also said by some to have been the daughter, and it is considerately added "the youngest daughter," of Amenoph III. Thus Rameses I. is made to be grandson of Amenoph III., the grandfather having had a reign of at least 35 years and 10 months, and the grandson succeeding to the throne ($16 + 31.5^{m} + 12.1^{m} + 9 + 12.5^{m} + 12.3^{m} =$) 93 years and 2 months after his death. The lists and notices of Manetho, on the contrary, interpose at least three generations, of Horus, Rathotis, and Achencheres (for the two kings named Achencheres, even if two persons, are not likely to be *two* distinct generations) between Amenoph III. and Rameses I. His name we have identified in the lists of Manetho with Armesses or Armais, which, like Ramessou itself, Rampses, and Rapsakes, is only a Greek variant for Rameses. His 2nd year has been found; and if he reigned the 4 years and 1 month given him in the lists, they will reach from Oct. 31, B.C. 1491, to Nov. 29, B.C. 1487. In technical reckoning he will have 4 years, beginning from Sept. 1, B.C. 1491, and reaching to Aug. 31, B.C. 1487.

1. Aug. 31, B.C. 1487, to Aug. 30, B.C. 1486.

(Generation XI, reign of Manetho xv, of the monumental lists xi.) *Seti I., Mi-amon*, or *Merien-amon, Merienphtha; Ra-en-ma.* He "defeated the Shasou (i.e. Shepherds) even to the wretched land of Kanāna;" and, accompanied by his son, he extended his conquests to Mesopotamia. He founded the palace-temple of Gourneh, and the great hall at Karnak, which were both finished by his son. His 1st year only is found marked, at Speos Artemidos in the Heptanomis. He seems to be often confounded with his son, the glory of conquest and the name Mi-amon being common to them both. And perhaps his son was associated with him almost from the beginning. The single year and four months given him in the lists under the name of Ramesses, as if *he* were the Σέθως ὁ καὶ Ῥαμεσσῆς of Manetho's fabling narrative, will reach from Nov. 29, B.C. 1487, to March 28, B.C. 1485 (or technically from Aug. 31, B.C. 1487, to Aug. 30, B.C. 1486), and this one year may be the time that he reigned alone; for it is difficult to think that his whole reign was really so short. His tomb alone, which is most gorgeous, and worthy of a long reign like that of his son, is a strong sign to the contrary.

66. Aug. 30, B.C. 1486, to Aug. 14, B.C. 1420. (Generations XII and XIII, reign of Manetho xvi, of the monumental lists xii.) *Rameses II. Mi-amon, Ra-tseser-ma,* with *and* without the adjunct *So-tep-en-ra,* which gave occasion to Rosellini to divide him into two kings, whom he calls Rameses II. and Rameses III. The 62nd of Rameses II. has been found on his monuments, which are extremely numerous, and of great magnificence. On them his conquests both in inner Africa and in Asia are represented with much detail. The colossus of "Sesostris" seen by Herodotus at Memphis, and the stelæ at the river Lycus (El Kab), in Phœnicia, both still visible, bear his names. (The colossus has both the ordinary throne-name and the variant.) It is Rameses II. who is often called the Great.

A date on some fragments of a calendar from Elephantine, now in the Louvre, found mixed with other fragments bearing the name of Thothmes III., but by the style of sculpture belonging rather to the age of Rameses II., at least in the opinion of M. Brugsch, gives the heliacal rising of Sirius so as to indicate according to M. Biot for the latitude of Elephantine the year B.C. 1444. Now this year cannot possibly belong to the reign of Thothmes III.; but it ought to be the 43rd year of Rameses II., whose 66 years and 2 months seem to lie between March 28, B.C. 1485, and May 11, B.C. 1419. In technical reckoning he would have 66 years, from Aug. 30, B.C. 1486, to Aug. 14, B.C. 1420. His oldest son *Scha-em Djam,* who was viceroy of Memphis, being known to have died before his father, who was succeeded by the thirteenth of his numerous sons, Merienphtha, the only one of them all who reigned after him, and the reign itself amounting in length to two full life-generations, one may suppose that the author of the Chronicle would reckon this as a double generation, the sons who died before their father being in strictness his Generation XIII; though it would come to the same thing if Thothmes II. and Hatasu above were reckoned as Generation III, Thothmes III., though brother to Hatasu, being counted separately for Generation IV. So the *fourteen* generations of the Chronicle would be identical with the *thirteen* names of kings which appear in the monumental lists.

20. Aug. 14, B.C. 1420, to Aug. 9, B.C. 1400.

(Generation XIV, reign of Manetho xvi, of the monumental lists xiii.) *Meri-en-phtha, Bai-en-ra,* thirteenth of the sons of Rameses II. His 4th year has been found. His 19 years and 6 months should lie between May 11, B.C. 1419, and Nov. 7, B.C. 1400, so ending 3 months after Aug. 9, then the end of the Egyptian year. But as technically reckoned by the author of the Chronicle Meri-en-phtha would have 20 years from Aug. 14, B.C. 1420, to Aug. 9, B.C. 1400, and the overrunning fraction of 3 months would be included within the first year (technically antedated) of the following dynasty.

But the XVI reigns of Manetho, at the ordinary average of 24¾ years, should give 396 years for the dynasty; and even consolidated as the Chronicle consolidates them into XIV of its *generations,* they should give 343 years. So then the 348 years of the Chronicle are justified rather than 333, which is the *apparent* sum of Manetho.

Dyn. XIX. VIII Diospolites. 194 yrs. from Aug. 9, B.C. 1400, to June 21, B.C. 1206.

The Diospolite Dynasties XIX and XX of Manetho's lists, with VII kings in 194 years, (15 of his *apparent* sum of 209 having been restored to Dyn. XVIII,) and XII kings in 135 years respectively, if thrown together make a sum of XIX kings in 329 years; while the same dynasties in the Chronicle, with V generations in 194, and VIII in 228 years, make a total of XIII generations in 422 years.

But XIX Diospolite kings admitted by Manetho himself to have existed, (and not fewer than XXIII actual kings appear at Thebes on the monuments, before we come to the Tanite-Bubastite name Shishonk,) have an average in 329 years of only 17 years and about 4 months each, while with the 422 years of the Chronicle they have 22 years each, which is still 2¼ years under the ordinary average. So the chronology of the Chronicle is implied to be the true rather than his own by Manetho's own lists. And much more does this appear, if we take the two dynasties separately. For the Chronicle having for Dyn. XIX only V *generations* in 194 years, with an average of 39 years nearly to each generation, Manetho, making only one or at most two more actual *reigns* than the Chronicle makes *generations*, has still an average of 27$\frac{5}{7}$ years to each; while in his Dyn. XX, twelve reigns in 135 years have an average of only 11 years and 3 months each, which is clearly inadmissible. For Dyn. XIX the names of the monuments may be compared with the V generations of the Chronicle and the VII reigns of Manetho thus:—

First, after Meri-en-phthah II., the last king of Dyn. XVIII, there appears (on particular monuments only, but not in the monumental lists),

(Actual reign i.) *Ra-men-ka Sotepenra ; Amonmeses Hak-Djam.*—In an inscription at Gourneh he is said to have been "bred by Isis, *in the city of Khev* (Aphroditopolis), to reign over all beneath the sun." Lepsius thinks his name has been supplanted at Gourneh by that of Siphthah (though *he* also is from the same city of Khev). His name, and the fact that he is suppressed as illegitimate, favours the idea that he is the source of the Armais or Danaus of Manetho, whose 8 years seem in the lists of Africanus to be deducted from the 59 given to Sethos by Manetho according to Josephus, as if they were covered by the last reign of Dyn. XVIII.

(Actual reign ii.) *Khou-Ra-Sotepenra* : *Siphthah-Meri-en-phthah II.* His queen Ta-tecser takes precedence of him in their joint tomb; so perhaps she was a daughter of Meri-en-phthah I. On his standard he has the title "Risen *in Khev;*" and a dignitary named Bai boasts of having "established him on the throne *of his father.*" These two kings being suppressed, we come to the king who stands seventh in the series of nine at Medinet Habou, viz.:

(Generation I of the Chronicle; reigns or *names* of Manetho i and ii, and of the monumental lists i; actual reign iii.) *Seti Meri-en-phtha, Ra-tseser-cheperu, Meri-amon,* son of Meri-en-phtha I., and grandson of Rameses the Great. He seems to have thought of appropriating the tomb of Merienphthah II. Siphthah; but afterwards he made a tomb for himself. He should be the original of that "Sethos son of Amenophis" who took refuge as a child when only five years old in Ethiopia. Afterwards perhaps, under Siphthah, he obtained the title of Prince of Kush; for a prince Seti appears under Siphthah with this title, and with that of "Fan-bearer." The romance of the "Two Brothers," translated by M. De Rougé, was written for the same Prince Seti.

59. Aug. 9, B.C. 1400, to July 25, B.C. 1341.

(Generation II of the Chronicle, *name* of Manetho iv, of Medinet Habou viii., i. e. 2d of the dynasty; actual reign iv.) *Set-necht* or *Nechtset,* and *Amon-necht*; *Ra-tseser Schau-Meri-amon;* probably son of Seti II., and so the second generation of the Chronicle; but apparently consolidated by Manetho with his father and his son into one reign under the double name of "Σέθως, ὁ καὶ Ῥαμεσσῆς." This king has appropriated the tomb of Siphthah-Merienphthah II. and Ta-tseser; but he appears together with Rameses III. (his son) receiving homage from an umbrella-bearer named Hora; and the title taken by Rameses III. in the same sculpture, "Hak On," may have been given him in his father's lifetime.

66 yrs. begin from accession of Set-necht, July 25, B.C. 1341,

(Generation III of the Chronicle, name of Manetho i and ii; of series at Medinet Habou ninth and last, i. e. 3d of this dynasty; actual reign v.) *Rameses III., Hak-On; Ra-tseser-ma, Meri-amon.* He was probably son of the preceding, and certainly son of a king; for he says to Ammon, "I am established on the throne of my father, as thou didst establish Horus on the throne of his father Osiris. . . . . I have not usurped the place of another." (*MS. of Mr. Harris,* quoted by M. De Rougé.) Though he clearly is the king spoken of in Manetho's myth as "having *fleets* as well as armies and cavalry," and extending his conquests towards the East, he has no such name as "Sethos," to say nothing of Ægyptus, nor any brother "Armais." Still less is he the head of Dyn. XIX. So we must look for the source of "Armaus" either in the Armesses of the list of Africanus

and end at the death of Rameses III. July 9, B.C. 1275. (His accession, after 20 of Setnecht, at July 20, B.C. 1321 ?)

preceding the place in Dyn. XVIII where Seti I. Meriamon, or Mi-amon, and his son Rameses II. Minmon, are misnamed or dropped out (and this is the view which best suited Eusebius; and it may be true notwithstanding that it suited him); or we must resolve the myth into its separate elements, and suppose the story of the two brothers or cousins to belong partly to Amon-meses and Seti II. at the head of Dyn. XIX (though Seti II. was no great conqueror), and partly to the conqueror Rameses II., blended with Seti I. and II., and with Rameses III. From the paintings in the palace-temple of the last of these kings at Medinet Habou, executed after, but probably not long after, his 12th year, it seems that the epoch of the Sothic Cycle, when the heliacal rising of Sirius, July 20, coincided with the first day of the moveable Thoth, was connected with his reign. This, if calculated for the latitude of Memphis, or thereabouts, would indicate July 20 in the year B. C. 1322; and when the Sothic Cycle is mentioned by later writers this is the year always understood: but by actual observation *at Thebes* the year, according to M. Biot, would be B.C. 1300 [or 1302]. And Herodotus speaking in part of that Rameses-Sesostris who was nearest to his own time, and who had the *fleet*, and so was said to have crossed into Thrace, puts his accession "less than 900 years before his own time;" that is, some time later than B. C. 1350. So it seems that Manetho has done with Sethos II. the head of his Dyn. XIX much as he has done with Amosis, the head of his Dyn. XVIII, making of him a fabulous personage, with names and acts which do not all belong to any one king in that place, but partly to Sethos I. and Rameses II. many years above, and partly to Rameses III. many years below. The 26th year of Rameses III. has been found on the monuments, the Apis-bull numbered 15 by M. Mariette having died in that year, while his Apis No. 9 died in the 55th year of Rameses II. Minmon. And supposing him to be intended by "Rapsakes" the second king of Manetho's list, the (59 + 66 =) 125 years given to the first two reigns of the dynasty would take us from B. C. 1400, the head of Dyn. XIX, to B.C. 1275; or, if 8 were deducted as belonging to the usurpation of "Armaus or Danaus," to

B. C. 1283, so as to cover the actual Theban as well as the Memphite coincidence of the movable new year with the heliacal rising of Sirius. At Medinet Habou one sees on the wall a series of ten sons of Rameses III. sculptured with their names; and the names of the *eldest four* have been inclosed afterwards in royal rings, showing that they reigned after their father. This makes one suspect that the words following the *first* name "Sethos" in Manetho, "after whom the eldest of his sons, Rapsakes, reigned 66 years," originated in the fact that after the *third* legitimate king and generation, Rameses III., the *four* "eldest of his ten sons" (with even a fifth perhaps, not one of the eldest, included) reigned successively, who all having the same family name, and all being of one and the same generation, might be consolidated into one reign. But the 66 years given to Rapsakes (according to Josephus) with the 59 of Sethos, ὁ καὶ Ῥαμεσσῆς, preceding may be supposed to cover the *actual* reigns over against which they stand.

Five sons of Rameses III., 52 years, beginning from July 9, B.C. 1175.

(Generation IV of the Chronicle, reign or *name* of Manetho iii, actual reign vi.) *Rameses IV., Hik-ma-Miamon: Ra-tseser-ma, Sotep-en-Amon*; the first of the ten sons of Rameses III. at Medinet Habou. In his 2nd year "the Rotennu prostrating themselves bring their tributes, and all the Aamu tremble before him." He founded a fortress at Hammamat to secure the commerce of the Red Sea. A variant of the name of this king, according to Lepsius, with his third year marked, appears also at Hammamat (whom we shall call Rameses IV. *bis*); and connected with the same Rameses IV. *bis* is a high-priest of Ammon named Rameses Nechtu, son of Meri-*Bast*, Prefect of the Palace and Director of Public Works, whose son Amenhotep appears as high-priest under Rameses IX. of Lepsius, the last king, if Rameses IV. *bis* is only a variant, of this dynasty. But M. de Rougé thinks that he is a separate king; and if so, he must have reigned next after the sons of Rameses III., making the fifth generation of the Chronicle, and leaving no room in the dynasty for any other later reign, unless it were of such a kind as not to make a separate generation. But, until further discoveries decide the question, we may treat Rameses IX. of M. de

Rougé, i. e. *Rameses Mati* or *Mama Meriamon, Ra-hik-ma Sotepenamon*, as being only a variant of Rameses IV. And unless this is so indeed, the tomb of the eldest son of Rameses III. is hitherto unknown.

(Generation IV of the Chronicle, name V of Manetho? actual reign vii.) *Rameses V., Amen-ha-chopeschf Meriamon; Ra-tseser-ma Se-cheper-en-ra.* His cartouches having been supplanted by those of Rameses VI. (second of the four *elder* sons of Rameses III.) at Biban Moluk, he must be inserted here; and his name being the same with that of the *eighth* son of Rameses III., he may perhaps have taken advantage of the minority of a nephew or niece, who never reigned, to occupy the throne. *If so,* the rings about the names of the eldest four sons of Rameses III. at Medinet Habou were not added there one by one, as each brother succeeded to the throne, but at some time *after this reign of Rameses V.*, which was disregarded as illegitimate. It is celebrated, however, in an inscription at Silsilis for abundance and good order.

(Generation IV of the Chronicle, name iii of Manetho, actual reign viii.) *Rameses VI. Amon-ha-chopeschf Neter-hak-On; Ra-neb-ma Miamon;* second of the ten sons of Rameses III. at Medinet Habou. He has left a fine tomb, perhaps the most complete of all, with astronomical paintings. These exhibit the heliacal rising of Sirius at the end of the night of Thoth 15, i. e. 15 days later than in the palace of Rameses III. at Medinet Habou. And this indicates that 60 years had already passed from B.C. 1322, if it had been at Memphis; but from B.C. 1300 or 1302, more probably, in fact, as these paintings were executed at Thebes. So towards the end of the reign of the second son of Rameses III. we should be already at the year 1240 B.C. Apis No. 16 of M. Mariette died under Rameses VI., his preceding Apis, No. 15, having died under Rameses III.

(Generation IV of the Chronicle, name of Manetho iii, actual reign ix.) *Rameses VII. At-amen(?) Neter-hak-On; Ra-tseser-ma Miamon Sotepenra;* third of the ten sons of Rameses III. who appear together at Medinet Habou.

The 5[illegible] years (Generation IV of the Chronicle, name of Manetho iii, actual reign x.) *Rameses VIII. Seti-chopeschf Miamon; Ra-tseser-ma Khou-en-Amen;* fourth of the ten sons of Rameses III. This and the four preceding reigns make up together the *fourth* of the five *generations* of the Chronicle; and this king should be at least the *fifth* of Manetho's seven, if he made two out of the five sons of Rameses III., or only the fourth perhaps, if he gave only six distinct reigns.

end at his death, June 26, B.C. 1223.

(Generation v of the Chronicle, name of Manetho vii, actual reign xi or xii.) *Rameses IX.* [XI. of Lepsius, X. of De Rougé] *Siphthah Se-scha-en-ra Miamon;* discovered by M. Mariette in the tomb of his Apis No. 17, on an open vase found in that tomb inclosing a second similar but smaller vase, also open, with the name of *Rameses Scha-em Djam* (Rameses IX. of Lepsius). Hence, if the vases had only been found closed and covered, it might perhaps have been collected that this Siphthah II. was the immediate *successor* of Scha-em Djam, who might have died during the 72 days of the Apis obsequies; the preceding Apis, No. 16 of M. Mariette, having died under Rameses VI. But after the Apis No. 17, whose tomb unites the two kings Siphthah and Scha-em Djam, the next following Apis, No. 18, is buried by Scha-em Djam alone, so that he and not Siphthah must have been the successor, *or at least the survivor;* and the two, who may have been co-regnants, may be presumed in any case to have constituted together only one generation, the fifth and last of the Chronicle. The high-priest Amenhotep, who appears as contemporary of Scha-em Djam, being son of another high-priest Rameses Nechtu occurring under Rameses IV., the reign of Scha-em Djam is already at as wide an interval after Rameses IV. as is convenient. And lastly, while Manetho's number of six kings, not to say seven, seems to need two to follow after the sons of Rameses III., and he has actually two short reigns at the end of his dynasty, Siphthah to all appearance reigned only a short time, and might readily coalesce with his successor so as to make only one generation for the Chronicle, while his reign of 5 or 7 years is scarcely enough alone to bring us on to B.C. 1206 from the death of the last survivor of the sons of Rameses III., even though it be true that when the tomb of

7. June 26, B.C. 1223, to June 24, B.C. 1216.

Rameses VI. was painting, 60 years had already elapsed from B.C. 1302. On putting these considerations together, it may seem probable that after the sons of Rameses III. had reigned, from B.C. 1275, 52 years at the most, to B.C. 1223 (this number results after the suppression of the 28 years which we had to suppress), Siphthah and Scha-em Djam followed,—Siphthah, who should be the younger of the two, being co-regnant with Scha-em-Djam for 5 or 7 years, and Scha-em-Djam surviving for 12 years instead of the 7 given by Manetho. The five years which have certainly dropped out from some one reign or other in the list of Africanus, are thus conjecturally restored by us to this last reign of the dynasty. This may well seem more probable that that Siphthah alone had a reign of much more than 5 or 7 or 12 years, and concluded the dynasty. But it is to future discoveries alone that we must look for a solution of the question. [Since the above was written, the author has been informed by Mr. Birch that a date late in the 16th year of Scha-em-Djam has been found mentioned in a hieratic papyrus belonging to Mde. D'Orbiney.]

17. June 26, B.C. 1223, to June 1, B.C. 1206. (Generation v of the Chronicle, name of Manetho vi, actual reign xi or xii.) *Rameses X., Scha-em-Djam Merer-Amon; Neferkaura Sotepenra* (XI. of De Rougé, IX. of Lepsius). "Lepsius," says M. de Rougé, "improperly puts under him *both* the high-priest Amenhotep, and his father the high-priest Rameses Nechtu, son of Meri-*Bast*, who was really contemporary with Rameses Mati, or Mama, Mia-mon (the Rameses IV. *bis* of Lepsius, but Rameses IX. of M. de Rougé).

Whatever becomes of Rameses IX. of M. de Rougé, the *fifth* and last generation of the Chronicle, which follows next after that of the sons of Rameses III., must include the last two reigns and *names* of Manetho. And having for these two reigns two monumental names inseparably connected together, and connected also through the high-priest Amenhotep and his father with the reign of Rameses IV., the only question is, which of the two, Siphthah or Scha-em-Djam, is to be put first? and how are the 17 years of Manetho's last two kings (5 + 5 dropped out + 7, making 17) to be apportioned between them? On the one hand, the synchronism of Thouoris or Polybus, Manetho's last name, and Troy, plainly indicates that neither the place of that king as the last of the dynasty, nor probably the length of his reign, differ from those really given him by Manetho: on the other, the monuments prove that, of the two kings, one, whose reign certainly exceeded the 7 years of Thouoris, no less certainly survived the other. For it appears from the discoveries of M. Mariette in 1853 not only that Scha-em-Djam, who was found conjoined with Siphthah in one Apis-tomb, buried another later Apis, No. 18, alone, but also that he erected at Memphis monolith columns 40 feet high, with immense architraves bearing his names, works which seem to imply a reign of some length. In his own tomb he boasts of his victories, and a scribe attests that "all the peoples of the North are his subjects." But what is most important is this, that in the same tomb there is an astronomical painting resembling that of the tomb of Rameses VI.; and the indications of the rising of Sothis and other stars being the same in both, this proves that the interval of time between the two was less than 60 years. For in those paintings, the risings of the stars being noted only for the beginning of the morning of the first, and the end of the night of the fifteenth day of each month, no change would be made (according to M. Biot's explanation) till the difference in the risings of the stars amounted to 15 days, which would be only after an interval of 60 years.

So then we are precluded on several grounds from widening the interval between Rameses VI. and Scha-em-Djam, or supposing the latter to have belonged to the following Dynasty XX; and yet, of the two kings found conjoined, Siphthah, who *cannot* stand *last*, rather than Scha-em-Djam, must be Thouoris who *does* stand last in Manetho's dynasty. Manetho then, it would seem, in this instance as in others was regardless of true chronology, and the synchronism connected with the reign of Thouoris, and probably even the name itself, belongs only to the *apparent* chronology of his lists. And, this being understood, there is no difficulty in explaining how Thouoris or Siphthah, with his short reign of seven years, may have come to be placed after another king seemingly his successor but of the same generation, perhaps a brother, who survived him, and had much the longer reign of the two. It is only necessary to suppose that the two were colleagues in the throne during the whole reign of the elder, or during some part of it, and that the elder, whose name would naturally be put first, outlived the younger. But the last two reigns of Manetho, having together (5 + 7 = ) 12, or rather 17 years, (if we are right in restoring to *them* those other 5 which have dropped out, and which are required by the sum of his dynasty,) take us from B.C. 1223 to B.C. 1206; and so the kings placed between Rameses VI. and Scha-em-Djam inclusively would not seem to require an interval between the paintings in the two tombs of more than 60 years. Lastly, the date in the D'Orbiney papyrus enable s us to confirm the conjecture that Scha-em-Djam reigned the whole of those 17 years which in Manetho's lists belonged seemingly to the last two names; and, consequently, that the 7 years placed last do not belong chronologically to the king meant by Thouoris at all, but to the name Ammenemes preceding, from which they are detached only to indicate the length of the shorter and concurrent reign. But as regards the apparent chronology and the synchronism of Thouoris (whose reign seems to begin in B.C. 1213) with Troy, this synchronism, as asserted, must be understood to attach to the 7th or 6th year preceding the death of Scha-em-Djam and the end of Dyn. XIX. It is remarkable that Dicæarchus also, who wrote perhaps about B.C. 322, puts Phrouron, or Nilus, 436 years above the first Olympiad, that is, at B.C. (776 + 436 = ) 1212, while his Sesonchosis = Sesostris, is put 2500 years higher than Nilus as the *first king and conqueror* after Horus. Sesostris so would be put, according to Manetho's scheme of 3555 years of kings, at the 178th year *after* Menes; but according to the scheme of Ptolemy of Mendes and Africanus, if we go up 2500 years from Thouoris and Troy, we shall find the place of this Sesostris 1318 years below Menes at the 25th year of Papa-Maire, the predecessor of Sesortasen I., which last was really the earliest Egyptian conqueror. But for Thouoris and Troy the date of Dicæarchus appears from what has been said above to agree exactly with that of the original Manetho.

The small number of *five* generations given by the Chronicle to Dynasty XIX seems to be justified and explained, Rameses V. being inclosed between four brothers who all together make but one generation; Amon-meses and Siphthah, in like manner, being inclosed between the last king of Dyn. XVIII Menephthah I. and his son Seti II. of Dyn. XIX, whose cousins they probably were; and the later Siphthah of M. Mariette seeming fit enough to coalesce with his co-regent and successor, with whom he was found conjoined, into a single generation. The actual kings of the dynasty, meantime, being no fewer than twelve, will give in 194 chronological years a seeming average of only 16 years and 2 months. But if the three illegitimate kings are omitted, and their years reckoned to the legitimate reigns, and if the later Siphthah is consolidated with his co-regent and successor, the remaining *eight* kings will have an average of 24 years and 3 months each.

To account for the number of "VII kings" (though perhaps Manetho never enumerated more than VI reigns), given in the heading of the list of Africanus, is not so easy, nor perhaps of any importance. Counting the two names Sethos and Rameses united mythically in the first reign, but really belonging to distinct kings, there are no doubt seven *names*; but to these there are only six *reigns*. And besides one king, there are also five years wanting in the list of Africanus to complete the sum 209 given for the dynasty, the VI reigns (51 + 61 + 20 + 60 + 5 + 7) making only 204 instead of 209 years. It is not safe to restore the 5 years wanting to the *second* reign (though we know from Josephus that the original Manetho gave it 66, and not 61 years), because Ptolemy of Mendes seems purposely to have cut off 13 years in all from the first two reigns; viz., 8 from the first, to suit the story of Danaus and Egyptus, and 13 from the first and second together, to suit, however inconsistently, the story of Sethos having been 13 years an exile in Ethiopia *after* the reign of his father (though *he*, too, was fabled to live on) while the Hierosolymites held Egypt. The 5 years which have dropped out must be added somewhere below the first two reigns; and this being done, either with or without the insertion of a name (as if another Rameses or Amenemes had dropped out) to make up the *seven* kings, we must next restore from Josephus the figures of the original Manetho for the first two reigns. We then have 59 + 66 + 20 + 60 + 5 + 5 + 7, amounting in all to 222, more by 13 than the sum given both by Manetho and by Ptolemy to the dynasty. For Ptolemy, cutting off 13 years from Manetho's first two reigns, but keeping his sum, necessarily added an equal compensation below. We have therefore now the 13 years thus added by Ptolemy to cut out from any of the later reigns which most invite such reduction; and, besides these, there are in Manetho's own sum of 209 *fifteen* unchronological years already restored to their true place in Dyn. XVIII, and now to be cut out from whatever part of this Dyn. XIX. it suits best; so in all 28 years are to be deducted.

As regards his VII kings, five of them at least may be pointed out with certainty in those actual and legitimate reigns which are the sources of the V Generations of the Chronicle. The three illegitimate kings, and any other who was only a co-regent, he might possibly omit. But such reigns as those of Seti II., Setnecht, Rameses III., the "eldest son" of the same Rameses III., and Seha-em-Djam, he could not fail either to name or to indicate. This being so, he must be supposed to have consolidated the sons of Rameses III. into two reigns, one of the eldest, and the other of the rest, or perhaps all of them into only one reign. For had he named them all four separately, he would, after naming the last of them, have already had seven actual legitimate kings, without any room for others to succeed them. The fifth generation of the Chronicle containing, as has been concluded above, two actual kings, these, if named separately, would bring up Manetho's number of reigns to six, so as to agree with our present lists. And perhaps it is more probable that no seventh was ever distinctly named by Manetho, than that he named separately one only out of the four (or five) sons of Rameses III., consolidating the rest, or that he named separately one or two of the illegitimate kings, while he consolidated four legitimate kings into one. Neither chronological reasons, nor perhaps the five generations of the Chronicle, allow of the supposition that the dynasty ended with the last survivor of the sons of Rameses III.

After finding in the first reign Sethos II. and Rameses III. blended together into one mythical personage, we need not wonder if the following names and sums given for the reigns are difficult to identify. As for the names, "Rapsakes" is no doubt only a variation of Rameses, which is the family name common to nearly all these kings. ("Amenephthes," too, or Amenophis may be derived from an element almost equally common in the names of this dynasty.) And the designation "the eldest of his sons" coming after the *name* of Rameses III., however misplaced and blended with that of Sethos II., looks so far like a consolidation of the eldest four of the ten sons of Rameses III. The name "Rameses," as it occurs again in the fourth place, holds the place really belonging to the sons of Rameses III.: and if "Rapsakes," already in some sense identified with them, were put down from his connection with the mixed and mythical Sethos, ὁ καὶ Ῥαμεσσῆς, to stand after the distinct Rameses who is fourth in the lists, this latter would rise up into the third place, the true place of Rameses III.; and the Amenephthes who stands before him might then represent his father, whose name will form Ἀμενέχθης or Ἀμενέφθης, *Amen-necht*, as well as Setnecht; and so the first four kings would be restored to their true positions. The fifth name in the list of Africanus, "Amenemes," might also be connected with any one of three names which may seem to lay claim to this place; Amenmeri or Meri-amen being an element almost as common in the names of this dynasty as Rameses itself, and entering into the cartouches both of Rameses IX. of De Rougé, of the later Siphthah of M. Mariette, and of Scha-em-Djam his successor, whom Lepsius makes not to follow but to precede Siphthah. As for the name "Thouoris" or Phouoris, with the rendering Nilus, there is no trace of anything like it on the monuments. It seems rather to be an Egyptian accommodation of the Homeric name Polybus, which would write or pronounce equally Phriouv or Phiouro; and no more may be meant by it than this, that the last king of Dyn. XIX is *chronologically* one with the Πόλυβος of Homer, the contemporary of the war of Troy, 436 years according to Dicæarchus before the first Olympiad, i. e. (776 + 436 =) 1212 B.C.

As regards the *reigns*, considered apart from the names, the first two reigns of 59 and 66 years (if we let these sums stand, as we may, especially if Sethos was only five years old when he fled to Ethiopia) will take us at once from Thoth 1 in B.C. 1400, where Dyn. XVIII of the Chronicle ends, to B.C. 1275, 25 years below the epoch of the Sothic Cycle as observed at Thebes, and 47 below the same epoch for the latitude of Memphis; so that the reign of Rameses III., containing the Sothic epoch, and the *four* actual reigns preceding it, are fully covered. "Amenephthes," whom we have identified with the father of Rameses III., being thus already taken in, his separate 20 years may be omitted as part of those 28 years which we have to suppress; and in no case would it have been possible to think of *adding* them to the next following reign, whether covering only one king or four kings consolidated, for it has already 60 years of its own. Even after deducting from this sum the 8 years which we still have to suppress (the last reign or reigns of the dynasty claiming rather the addition of those five other years which we have to *restore*), the 52 years which remain are certainly quite enough for the elder four of ten sons to survive after a long reign of their father. And these 52 years bring us to B.C. 1223. Then, if we suppose Siphthah to be "Thouoris," and leave him his short reign of only seven years, only chronologically transposed, these go on to B.C. 1216; while, lastly, with the addition of those five that have fallen out from the list of Africanus, Amenemes or Scha-em-Djam will have to himself *as surviving alone* 10 instead of 7 years, and will close the dynasty coincidently with the close of Dyn. XIX of the Chronicle at B.C. 1206. According to the *apparent* chronology of Manetho however the 194 chronological years of this dynasty would begin 3 years, or rather 2 years and 10 months, later than Thoth 1, B.C. 1400, and would end 2 years and 10 months later than Thoth 1 in B.C. 1206.

Dyn. XX. x. i Diospolites. 228 yrs. from June 21, B.C. 1206, to April 25, B.C. 978.

135 years of vii Ramessids. June 21, B.C. 1206, to May 19, B.C. 1071.

Besides the monumental names hitherto enumerated, there still remain to be paralleled with Dyn. XX the following monumental kings:—

1. (Generation I of the Chronicle?) *Rameses XI.* (?) [X. of Lepsius, XIV. (?) of De Rougé]; *Meri* or *Mi-Amon, Amonha-chopesch: Ra-cheper-ma-Sotepenra.* His place is disputed. M. Mariette is quoted as saying that he reigned at least 17 years.

2. *Ra*[*meses XII.* (?)] [unplaced by Lepsius, but given as No. 523 in his Pl. xli.] *Ra-neter-cheper, Sotep-en-Amon.* De Rougé observes that at two places the order of succession is uncertain, and that there are in all three or four names of Ramessids which can be placed only conjecturally. The two places, he says, are, first, after the sons of Rameses III., and, secondly, before his Rameses XII. (?) under whom Her-Hor appears first as a subject, but with such titles as prepare one to find him afterwards on the throne.

3. (Generation II of the Chronicle?) *Rameses XIII.*? [unplaced by Lepsius, but given as No. 524 in his Pl. xli.]; *Ra-hik-ma Djam-tseser: Rameses Merer-amon.*

And allowing for the three monumental names thus conjecturally placed in Dyn. XX, or for others which ought to be placed here instead of these, two full average generations, i.e. 49 years, they will reach from B.C. 1206 to B.C. 1157.

4. (Generation III of the Chronicle?) *Rameses XIV.*? *Miamon II.* [XII. of Lepsius and of De Rougé, XIV. of Rosellini]; *Ra tseser-ma Sotepenra.* Five Apis-bulls, No. 19 to No. 23 were buried in his reign, and their tomb in the gallery of Rameses II. seemed to M. Mariette to come next after that of his Apis No. 18, which died under Rameses X. [VIII. of Bunsen]. A priest named Bekenphthah appears in command at Memphis under both reigns. Lepsius, however, has placed two kings between them; and the priest Bekenphthah was not necessarily the same person.

From a stele in the Louvre, explained by Mr. Birch and M. de Rougé, it appears that this king being in Mesopotamia to receive his tributes (among which precious wood from "*Ta-neteru*" is mentioned), he accepted the daughter of the Prince of Bachtan, and on his return made her queen with the name *Neferou-ra.* In his 15th year, Epiphi 22, there arrived at Thebes an embassy with presents from the father of the queen Neferou-ra, asking the king of Egypt to send him a physician to prescribe for a younger sister of Neferou-ra, named *Bent-reschit,* who was suffering from some strange malady. The physician, being sent, declared that she was possessed by a spirit, which he had no power to expel. In the 26th year of the king, the 1st of Pachons, there came a second embassy, asking him to send one of the gods of Egypt to contend with the spirit. The king thereupon, taking one image of the god Chons before another of the same god but by a different and superior title, prayed the latter to send the former to Bachtan, giving him his own divine virtue to heal the prince's daughter. So the image was sent in its naos, mounted on a bark, with a cortège of boats to convey it down the Nile, and one chariot and an escort of cavalry for its land journey. After a voyage and journey of one year and five months from Thebes it arrived at Bachtan. The prince with his chiefs and his soldiers met the god, and prostrated themselves before him: when he was brought into the presence of Bent-reschit, she was instantly relieved, and the spirit within her welcomed his fellow demon thus: "Welcome, great God, Expeller of Rebels [a title of Chons]! the city of Bachtan is thine: its people are all thy subjects: I myself also am thy slave. I will return whence I came, that thou mayest be satisfied as to the object of thy journey: only, may it please thy Majesty to order that a festival be celebrated in my name by the Prince of Bachtan." Hereupon the god was pleased to say to his prophet, "The Prince of Bachtan must make a handsome offering to this spirit." The Prince, who meanwhile had been standing apart with his guards in profound awe, gave magnificent gifts both to the god Chons himself and to the spirit, and celebrated a festival in their honour: after which the spirit departed in peace whither he would. The Prince in ecstacy said within himself, This god must remain in Bachtan: I will not have him return to Egypt. So he abode there three years and nine months; after which, one night the Prince in a dream saw the god come out of his naos in the shape of a golden hawk, and fly away in the direction of Egypt; and awaking he found himself [unwell]. So he sent back the god with great honour and pomp; and he returned safely to the temple of Chons at Thebes, which he re-entered on the 19th day of Mechir, in the 33rd year of the king, and gave all the rich presents he had received to the superior Chons, without reserving anything for his own special sanctuary. [From De Rougé's "*Etudes sur une Stele Egyptienne*," &c., Paris, 1858.]

Having reckoned above two average reigns of this dynasty to B.C. 1157, a third average reign would go on to B.C. 1132. Or, if the actual reign of Rameses XI. be supposed to begin in B.C. 1157, his 15th may be put at B.C. 1142, his 26th at 1131, and his 33rd in 1124. At any rate one may guess with some probability that the true date of the journey of the ark of Chons was later than the year B.C. 1149; and that between the first and second embassies of the Prince of Bachtan something had been heard of another Ark, which was carried about in Palestine.

5. (Generation IV of the Chronicle?) *Rameses XV.?* [XIII.? of De Rougé, and XIII. of Lepsius.] *Scha-em-Djam Neter-hak-On, Merer-Amen: Ra-men-ma Sotep-en-Phtha.* Under him first *Her-Hor* appears as high-priest of Ammon, and as yet only a subject, with the titles of "Head of Public Works," and "Fan-bearer on the left of the King;" but he is also "Chief of the Army," and "Chief of the Two Countries;" and he wears the uræus in the king's presence. His 18th year, according to M. de Rougé, is found on the monuments.

6. (Generation V of the Chronicle.) *Her-Hor-Si-amon;* the same as was mentioned above, but now with all the royal titles, his title of "High-priest of Ammon," being made into a throne-name. He is represented with Set and Horus; Set crowning him with the red crown of Lower Egypt, Horus with the white crown or *pshent* of Upper. His wife is named *Netem-Nit*, i. e. "Delight of Neith," according to M. de Rougé, who thinks this name indicates a connection with the Delta. This is the last king who thanks Ammon that "the chiefs of all the lands of the Rotennou fall down daily with their tributes at his feet." After his death De Rougé thinks

that Smendis, or whoever is alluded to by that name, founded an independent and contemporary dynasty in the Delta, the Tanite Dyn. XXI of Manetho. To this he supposes the kings bearing the names read by Lepsius "*Petuchanu,*" but by himself "*Hor-Psev-en-schan,*" to belong; and he identifies with this name the "Psusenes" and "Psinaches" of Manetho, observing that Shishonk I., the founder of the Bubastite Dyn. XXII of Manetho (the *Tanite* XXI of the Chronicle), is connected by the priesthood of Ammon with the priestly Diospolites descended from Her-Hor; and that he takes in his standard the title of "Uniter of the Upper and Lower Countries," which *therefore* had before been divided. Lepsius thinks Her-Hor himself the head of Manetho's Tanite Dyn. XXI. But it is plain that the XII Diospolite reigns of Manetho's Dyn. XX must include a line contemporary with the Tanites of his Dyn. XXI for 93 years at least; since the 135 years given by Manetho to the XII Diospolites of his Dyn. XX are plainly insufficient; and even with the full number of 228 years, which they have in the Chronicle, the average length of their reigns will not exceed 19 years. It has been observed that of the numerous sons of Her-Hor several seem to have borne Asiatic names.

The Rameseid kings end at his death, May 19, B.C. 1071.

7. Perhaps an unplaced Rameses. De Rougé places here Rameses X. of Lepsius, whom we have made to be IX., giving as a reason that the son of Her-Hor named *Pianch,* otherwise capable of being regarded as his successor, abstains from taking the royal titles, and is only "High-priest of Ammon," holding certain other high offices besides. Lepsius thinks this is best explained by supposing that Pianch died before his father. But, if so, De Rougé asks, how should he have the title of High-priest, which his father and his father's descendants *retained to themselves* when they took the royal standard and titles?

Five descendants of Her-Hor, 93 yrs. from May 19, B.C. 1071, to April 26, B.C. 978?

8. (Generation VI of the Chronicle, or VII?) *Pinetem I.* (not *Pisem*) son of Pianch, and grandson of Her-Hor. He has titles of two classes, and keeps those which suit a subject after he has taken the royal titles and standard. Also he does not inclose his name in a cartouche, but leaves this distinction to the two princesses *Hent-ta* and *Rakamat*

(names recurring in the Tanite-Bubastite Dyn. XXI of the Chronicle, Dyn. XXII of Manetho), who were probably the heiresses of the Ramessids and his wives. His legends are found chiefly on the temple of Chons, where are also two cartouches ascribed by Lepsius to Pinetem II., and perhaps rightly, though they *may* have been taken later in life by Pinetem I., as his name has been found inclosed in a ring on a piece of leather: and these two cartouches are accompanied by the princess Hent-ta offering to Maut.

9. (Generation VII or VIII of the Chronicle ?). *Ra-men-cheper*, son of Pinetem I., and high-priest, takes a double cartouche. The princess seen with him is named *Tsi-en-Chev*, which shows some connection with the first kings of Dyn. XIX. The same name reappears in Dyn. XXII.

[10. (?) *Psev-en-schan I.*, or *Petuchanu I.*, is here inserted by Lepsius (who found the name on bricks at *Tanis*) as father of Pinetem II. But on the pylon of Horus at Karnak a high-priest Pinetem is distinctly described as "son of Ra-men-cheper." De Rougé therefore argues that Psev-en-schan is probably one of the contemporary Tanites, whose independence commenced from after the death of Her-Hor.]

11. (?) (Generation VIII or IX of the Chronicle ?) *Pinetem II.*, son of Petuchanu according to Lepsius, but of Ra-men-cheper according to De Rougé.

12. (?) *Petuchanu II.*, according to Lepsius (or *Psev-en-schan II.*) whose daughter Rakamat was married to Osorkon the second king of Dyn. XXII of Manetho, or XXI of the Chronicle. De Rougé doubts of the genealogy of the ancestors of Shishonk I. given by Lepsius, and thinks the Tanites had regained Thebes, and married the Theban heiresses, arguing from the fact that the priestly names at Thebes have been defaced, and that the names Rakamat and Hent-ta appear in connection with Dyn. XXII of Manetho (XXI of the Chronicle), Hent-ta being the name of the mother of the Queen Keromama in that dynasty. Shishonk I., as has already been said, takes on his banner the title of "Uniter of the Two Countries."

The number of XII kings given by Manetho is thus made

out, or nearly made out; but it is not probable that this series of names is either quite accurate or quite complete.

Again, the VIII generations of the Chronicle are pretty clearly identifiable; Her-Hor, with his son, grandson, and great-grandson making four in the lower part of the dynasty, Rameses XV.(?) and XIV.(?) (XIII.(?) and XII. of De Rougé and Lepsius) being clearly two more, while the three unplaced Ramessids may sufficiently represent the first two generations of the dynasty.

All the names given above (except those of *Psev-en-schan I.* and *II.*, which M. de Rougé does not admit) are found at Thebes, joined with indications of the decay of the older Ramessid family, and of a transition of power, through the assumption of the royal prerogatives and titles, to the high-priests of Ammon. The last seven names show of themselves that even though connected in some way, as they no doubt were, with the preceding Ramessids, they were on the whole of another lineage. But there is no sufficient evidence to show that these last seven kings were connected principally, either by origin or residence, with Tanis or its neighbourhood in Lower Egypt; still less to identify their names with the names given by Manetho for his Tanite Dyn. XXI. Taking all the thirteen names as they are found on the monuments at Thebes, or elsewhere, their number justifies that given by Manetho for the kings of his Diospolite Dyn. XX; but it requires, as has been remarked already above, the 228 years of the Chronicle for the true duration of the dynasty; seeing that XII kings in 135 years would reign on an average only 11 years and 3 months apiece; and the average of 19 years, which would be given by the sum 228, is quite as short as there are any indications in the way of decay or disorder to account for. The repetition of one and the same name Rameses for fourteen or fifteen kings, made known by the monuments, affords an opportune explanation both of the growing negligence of Manetho in Dyn. XIX, where he consolidates names, and of his total omission of names in his Dyn. XX, the number of kings only being there stated. And though it is true that the last six or seven names are no longer Ramessids, still, as these were Thebans, and even at Thebes perhaps of doubtful legitimacy, most of whose years he cuts off from Dyn. XX of the Chronicle and transfers to a new interpolated dynasty of "Tanites," it is not wonderful that his disposition to treat the Ramessids only in the aggregate extended to these also. With the knowledge that we have of the style of his narrative, so entirely unhistorical, in which his extracts from the hieratic lists were incidentally inserted, we can understand a treatment of this Dyn. XX which in any true historian or antiquary, even though a native of Lower Egypt, would have been inexplicable.

Dyn. XXI. iv or v Tanites. 93, from May 10, B.C. 1071, to April 25, B.C. 978.

As regards his Tanite Dyn. XXI, if we had not the older Chronicle as a guide, and if Manetho's own number of Theban kings in his Dyn. XX, and the number of Theban names on the monuments, had not already required the restoration of the 93 years cut off by him from the Diospolites of the Chronicle, we should have had no little difficulty. For we should have found the accession of Shishonk I. (identified by the Theban monuments with the conqueror of Judæa, and the first monumental Tanite or Bubastite king) depressed in the lists by an older Tanite dynasty to Feb. 10, B.C. 938, 39 years and 10 months below Thoth 1, in B.C. 978, i. e. nearly 39 below the death of Solomon. And lower down the accession of the last Ethiopian king Tirhakah would have seemed to stand by the lists at Dec. 12, B.C. 702, nearly 10 years too low for the synchronism of the 14th year of Hezekiah. But the monuments afford no traces of Manetho's Tanite Dyn. XXI, regarded as a sovereign dynasty of all Egypt. The Theban monuments take us directly from the XII Theban kings of Manetho's anonymous Dyn. XX to Shishonk I. the head of his Bubastite Dyn. XXII. This Dyn. XXII of Manetho agrees in its sum within one year with the Tanite Dyn. XXI of the Chronicle; nor is there any real difference in its designation. And its commencement according to the Chronicle, at April 25, B.C. 978, just exhibits Shishonk I. as contemporary with Solomon as well as with Rehoboam. Manetho, by leaving six of its kings anonymous, seems to hint that as many names of his Dyn. XXI are their representatives above. And lastly, having already seen 93 years to be reclaimed not only by Dyn. XX of the Chronicle, but even by Manetho's number of XII Diospolites of his own Dyn. XX, we shall find the remaining 37 years of his Dyn. XXI to be no less certainly due to other places far below. On putting these indications together, the result is that this first Tanite Dyn. XXI of Manetho vanishes, chronologically at least, leaving his Diospolite Dyn. XX in possession of 93 of its years, so as to coincide *really* in its ending with Dyn. XX of the Chronicle, at B.C. 978. The remaining 37 years, or 36 of them (since one year is wanted to make Manetho's Bubastite Dyn. XXII equal the Tanite-Bubastite Dyn. XXI of the Chronicle) with 3 more (or 2 and 10 months) by which Manetho has been in advance of the Chronicle from the beginning, making 40 in all, or 40 short by 2 months, remain in hand, as a surplus, to insert below whenever we find ourselves falling short of the Chronicle.

At the same time, as has been said above, it does not follow either that the names of Manetho's Tanite Dyn. XXI are fictitious, or, even if they are, that there was not some connection between the later kings of Dyn. XX and Lower Egypt to which Manetho might allude through his interpolated Tanite Dynasty XXI. Shishonk I., the true founder of the first Tanite-Bubastite dynasty which appears on the monuments, might have been already independent in Lower Egypt before he became master of Thebes, or could quarry stone at Silsilis. Even his father and grandfather, or those of his wife, and others before them (since every house must have had a beginning), might have been growing in power in the Delta as the Theban families were declining and divided. And the precise degree of their power, the titles taken by them, and the spot of their residence and their origin, are points on which we must look to the monuments and to fresh discoveries for information.

Now the names of the following Dyn. XXII of Manetho, as Mr. Birch has pointed out, are very peculiar, quite unlike those of the Thebans of XVIII, XIX, and XX, whether Ramessids or others, and showing traces rather of some Assyrian or Babylonian connection, being such as Shishonk,

Osorkon, Nimrot, Keromama. And Lepsius has published in his Königsbuch the pedigree of Shishonk I. from his sixth ancestor. These six names, which are *Bouecouãa, Maõsen, Nebneza, Petut, Shishonk*, and *Nimrot*, have no accompanying emblems of royalty. The grandmother however of Shishonk I., *Mehtenhont*, wife of his grandfather Shishonk, after whom he seems to have been named, was a king's daughter; and his son and successor Osorkon I. married *Rakamat*, daughter of *Psev-en-schan* or Petuchanu II., the last king according to Lepsius of the Diospolites, whom he, to accommodate them to Manetho's lists, calls Tanites. And the name Psev-en-schan, or as he writes it Petuchanu, having been found by him on bricks in the mounds of Tanis, may seem to indicate, for the two kings of this name at least, a real Tanite connection; for which reason M. De Rougé is for separating them from those other names, found at Thebes, which belong certainly to the descendants of Her-Hor. Signs however of some connection between the highpriests of Ammon at Thebes and the Eastern part of the Delta have been noticed as existing at a much earlier date under Dyn. XIX, when a highpriest of Ammon, Rameses-Nechtu, was named under Rameses IV. as son of Pet-*Bast*, *Bast* being the great goddess of Bubastis. But whatever becomes of Manetho's Dyn. XXI, those alliances which are indicated by the monuments, especially by the pedigree alluded to, sufficiently account for the rise of the family of Shishonk I.; and they make it probable that he had already begun to reign in Lower Egypt some time before he became master of Thebes. So the last name, "Susenes" (which is probably only a varied form of Shishonk), in Manetho's Dyn. XXI may be admitted perhaps as designating one and the same king with the first name "Sesonchis" of his Dyn. XXII, but representing an earlier reign or co-regnancy before he became sovereign of all Egypt. Of the remaining six names of Manetho's Dyn. XXI two, the second and the fifth, another Psousenes and an Osorkon, look like anticipations of names of his Dyn. XXII; two more, the first of the dynasty and the fourth, Ismendes and Amenophthis, remind one of the Diospolitan dynasties at the expense of which this has been fabricated; another, Nephercheres, the third, takes us back to far earlier times; while the sixth, Psinaches, which alone remains, even if identified with Petuchanu, would scarcely suffice to make all the 6 or 7 later Diospolites into a real Tanite dynasty of which Manetho should have only corrupted the names. But none of these six as they stand, as kings, receive any countenance either from the Tanite-Bubastite pedigree of Shishonk I. published by Lepsius, or from those Diospolite names of the monuments which he would identify with the Tanite Dyn. XXI of Manetho. Still they probably indicate the growing importance in Lower Egypt of some Tanite family.

Dyn. XXII. ix Bubastites, 169. April 25, B.C. 978, to March 14, B.C. 809.

But as regards Dyn. XXII of Manetho, which we have now made to coincide with XXI of the Chronicle, recent discoveries have enabled us to fill up the six names left blank by Manetho; and the list of the IX actual kings is given by Lepsius as follows:

1. *Shishonk I.*, Σέσωγχις (his 21st year occurs on the monuments): Manetho gives him . . 21
2. *Osorkon I.*, Ὀσόρθων: Manetho gives him . 15
3. *Takelot I.* (his 12th is marked at Karnak)
4. *Osorkon II.* (his 23rd is on an Apis-stele)
5. *Shishonk II.* The three are anonymous in the lists, and have together 25 [29?] years. } 29?
6. *Takelot II.* Τακέλωθις (his 14th is on an Apis-stele): Manetho gives him . . . . . 13
7. *Shishonk III.* (In his 28th an Apis was born which died in the 2nd of Pichai, aged 26 years. So Shishonk III. reigned *over* 51 full years, and the Apis-bull was allowed to live over 25 years)
8. *Pichai* (grandson of Shishonk III?—his 2nd occurs).
9. *Shishonk IV.* (An Apis died in his 37th.) Manetho again throwing together these last three reigns without names gives them all a sum of only . . . . . . . 42

Sum given 120

On a stele found in the tomb of that Apis which died in the 37th of Shishonk IV., Horpeson, the dedicator, priest of Neith, names fifteen generations of his own family, so going back six generations above the head of Dyn. XXII of Africanus. And to the eleventh degree backwards he names both father and mother. He was in the sixth degree from a king of the reigning family; and from this ancestor upwards the kings of the dynasty are named as his ancestors, while the highest six (above Shishonk I.) are probably the citizen ancestors of the Bubastite family, reaching seemingly to the times of Her-Hor (whom Lepsius supposes to have been himself by origin from Tanis, and so the founder of Manetho's Dyn. XXI).

After adding, as above, 4 years to one of the reigns or sums of reigns in the present text of Manetho's lists, to produce the sum of 120 given for the dynasty, and after further adding one year more from the 37 unchronological years of his Dyn. XXI to raise the sum of this dynasty to 121 years to coincide with the 121 which it has as Dyn. XXI of the Chronicle,—if we divide 121 by 9, we obtain an average length of reign for the IX kings of only 13 years and 3 months; whereas the Chronicle gives to the 121 years of its Dyn. XXI only VI generations with an average even so of only 20 years and 2 months, representing perhaps the actual reigns. Again, therefore, the number of kings given by Manetho forces us to the conclusion that he has improperly compressed into 120 years those IX kings which in the Chronicle are divided between its two Tanite Dynasties XXI and XXII, the former with six generations and reigns in 121 years, the latter with three generations or reigns in 48 years. And the indications of the monuments justify this inference, showing that the years assigned by Manetho are far from representing the true length of the reigns. The genealogy too has been made out with sufficient fulness to show that, apart from any care for the average length of reigns, the author of the Chronicle had no such reason to make six of the nine actual reigns into only two generations as the consolidations exhibited by Manetho would suggest, or as the monuments in other cases, as in that of the four sons of Rameses III., have been seen to afford.

So, then, the first six generations, or perhaps the first *seven* actual reigns, of these nine Tanite or Bubastite kings (and their special residence seems to have been at Bubastis, though the Chronicle names only Tanis, the original capital of the Delta), take us, according to the Chronicle, from B.C. 978 to B.C. 857; and the remaining three generations, or perhaps only *two* actual reigns, take us on to B.C. 809, when we have already exhibited the Tanite Dyn. XXII of the Chronicle, and are advanced 48 years into the 89 of Manetho's Dyn. XXIII, which he also calls Tanite. The first name in this dynasty, Petubast, is displaced, unless he were concurrent, by the continuance of the preceding kings, and must be put down over the heads of his two successors, Osorchon and Psammis, whose 18 full years in the list of Africanus identify them pretty clearly with the two generations in 19 years, making Dyn. XXIII of the Chronicle. The names certainly indicate the same lineage with the Tanites and Bubastites preceding; but the Chronicle may have had some ground, notwithstanding, for calling them, as it does, Diospolites, just as, in Dyn. XXIV, both the Chronicle and Manetho designate as Saites kings whose names (Petu*bast*, and perhaps Takelut) still show traces of the Tanite-Bubastite lineage. So with

Dyn. XXIII. ii Tanites. 19, from March 14, B.C. 809, to March 9, B.C. 790.

1. { *Osorkon IV.*, 'Οσόρχων of the monuments, and
2. { *Psimut*, Ψάμμους, whose name occurs at *Thebes*,

we have advanced to B.C. 790, and have completed Dynasty XXIII of the Chronicle, and (48 + 19 =) 67 years of the 89 of Dyn. XXIII of Manetho, having 22 still remaining to go, with the names of Petubast and Zet put down, and with the single name of Bocchoris with only 6 years, which constitutes his Saite Dynasty XXIV, towards the three generations and 44 years of the Saite Dynasty XXIV of the Chronicle. This dynasty also is represented on the monuments by two out of its three names, viz.—

Dyn. XXIV. iii Saites. 44. March 9, B.C. 790, to Feb. 26, B.C. 746.

1. *Pet-si-bast*, Πετουβάστης, and

[2. Ζήτ, or whatever is the true name, has not yet been discovered on the monuments]

3. *Bek-en-ranf*, Βόκχορις. An Apis-bull, No. 34 of M. Mariette, died in the 6th year of Bocchoris; and this Apis

being buried in the same chamber with Apis No. 33, which died in the 37th year of Shishonk IV., with signs of his being the immediate successor, M. Mariette concludes "that during the 89 years of Manetho's Dynasty XXIII no Apis appeared." But we have seen that the first 48 years of the 89 of Manetho's Dynasty XXIII are really covered by the IX kings of his Dyn. XXII, of whom Shishonk IV. is the last. Supposing, therefore, the Apis No. 34 to have been born in the 37th year of Shishonk IV., and Shishonk to have reigned no more than 37 years, the true interval *cannot* comprise *less* than the 19 years of Dyn. XXIII of the Chronicle + two years for two out of the three reigns of Dyn. XXIV + 5 years of Bocchoris, in all 26 years; nor, on the other hand, *can* it contain *more* than 19 + 38 + 5, that is, in all 62 years. Between these extreme limits it must be determined, in default of fresh discoveries, approximatively, by considering how far we may venture to go on the one hand in extending the life of the bull beyond the *minimum* of 26 years, and on the other in shortening the reigns of the first two kings of Dynasty XXIV, Bocchoris being certainly the third and last. If Petubast reigned only 12 years, and Zet, or whoever was the second king, only one, the bull's life, if he were born in the year of his supposed predecessor's death, would still be extended to the length of 39 years.

According to one writer, Τεχνᾶτις, which is only another form of writing Τακέλωθις, according to another *Tnephactos*, which may be a corruption of the same, was the father of Bocchoris. But leaving this question, which further discoveries alone can solve, we observe that Manetho, at the end of this ignominious Saite Dyn. XXIV, is short of the end of the same in the Chronicle by 16 years, which we must supply from the 36 unchronological years of his Dyn. XXI still available. With 16 of these allowed to reckon as depressing the years below them, his Dyn. XXIV may be made to end coincidently with the same Dyn. XXIV in the Chronicle at B.C. 746.

The Ethiopian Dyn. XXV of III Generations in the Dyn. XXV. III Ethiopians.
Chronicle, and of III actual reigns according to Manetho, is 63. Feb. 26,

B.C. 746, to Feb. 11, B.C. 683.

fully illustrated by the monuments, which exhibit its three kings, Sabaco, Sevechus, and Taracus of the lists, thus:—

1. *Shabak*, Σαβάκων. (An Apis-bull, No. 35, died in his 2nd year; and in the same chamber were found traces of the cartouches of his successor Shabatok, connected perhaps with the burial of another bull.)

2. *Shabatok*, Σεβίχως.

3. *Tahark*, Ταράκης. Mechir 13 of his 24th is marked on a stele as the date of the death of the Apis No. 36.

But the monuments seem to indicate that the reigns of these three kings lasted longer than the 40 years of Manetho, or even than the 44 of the Chronicle (for Manetho again falls short by 4 years), so as to justify the assertion of Herodotus that the Ethiopian Sabaco (for he blends the three kings into one) ruled Egypt "above 50 years." But in this, as in other cases, the Chronicle might have some fair ground for assigning them only 44 years (and of course it would give them as few as possible). If, for example, as has been said above, it were after 44 years that Tirhakah "voluntarily retired from Egypt," making Napata his capital (of which the monuments afford proof), while Egypt from that time began again to be governed by native rulers, though divided, and still for a time indirectly and partially under Ethiopian supremacy: so when the 40 years of Manetho have been filled up to 44, and his Dynasty XXV made to end in B.C. 702, where it ends according to the Chronicle, his 40 surplus years unchronologically inserted above (37 of them in his Dyn. XXI and the other 3 long before) are reduced to 19, still uncompensated, which depress the end of the Ethiopian dynasty from B.C. 702, where it is put by the Chronicle, to 683, as if that dynasty really lasted not only 44 years to the time when Tirhakah ceased to reign personally in Egypt, but in all to his death 63 years; and it is highly probable that this was really the case.

Anarchy, 8. Feb. 10, B.C. 683, to Feb. 9, B.C. 675, or dodecarchy, 20, to Feb. 6, B.C. 463.

Manetho, then, having already covered by years unchronologically placed above in his Dyn. XXI, or earlier, 19 of those years which the Chronicle reckons to its Dyn. XXVI, or, to speak more exactly, 19 all but two months (Dynasty XVII of Manetho as restored from Josephus having had a sum of 259 years and 10 months which we have been reckoning as 260 current years), it is plain that he still wants 158 years, or 158 years and 2 months, to make his Dyn. XXVI of IX Saites end coincidently with the Memphitico-Saite Dynasty XXVI of the Chronicle, which has VII generations in 177 years. But, in fact, Manetho gives to his IX Saites only 150 years and 6 months, seemingly less by 7 years and 8 months, but really by 8 years and 2 months, than what are wanted. Respecting the true chronological place of this deficit there can be no doubt, as the conquest of Egypt by Cambyses is the point from which both Manetho and the Chronicle in common make the next dynasty, that of the Persians, to commence; and there is no room for the insertion of any years into the lists of Manetho between the accession of Psammitichus I. and the conquest of Cambyses. It follows, therefore, that the 8 years and 2 months wanting have been omitted by Manetho from the same place with the 19 years last considered, of which they were chronologically the continuation. And we shall see that Manetho compensates for his omission of these 8 years and 2 months, by an unchronological insertion of them below, where they can have no place, just as he compensated above, by an unchronological anticipation in his Dynasty XXI or earlier, for those (16 + 4 + 19 =) 39 years of the Saites and Ethiopians of Dynasties XXIV and XXV which he determined to omit at their true places. So we need not make any difficulty at finding that, according to his *apparent* chronology, his Saite Dynasty XXVI would end, and Cambyses ("in his 5th Persian year") would conquer Egypt as early as May in B.C. 533, that is, in the 4th year before the death of Cyrus. But understanding what he himself understands and hints (though on the surface he seems quite regardless of chronology), we may use by anticipation and place next after the Ethiopians, from Dec. 8, B.C. 684, to Feb. 9, B.C. 675, all those 8 years and 2 months which we shall find inserted where they can have no true chronological place below. These 8 years and 2 months will consist, first, of the 6 months of Psammicherites, the ninth and last king of Manetho's Dyn. XXVII, these being really included in the 3 years of

Cambyses, whose conquest is antedated by some 6 months, so as to be set at the *beginning* of his 5th Persian year. Next there are 4 months added to the 124 years of the Persian dynasty. Then the whole 6 years of Dyn. XXVIII of Manetho are unchronological; and lastly, 1 year and 4 months added by him to his Dyn. XXIX. These additions, making in all 8 years, besides 2 odd months (the old debt due as complement to the fraction of 10 months of Manetho's Dyn. XVII of the Shepherds), take us from Feb. 11, B.C. 583 (strictly Dec. 8, B.C. 584), to Feb. 9, B.C. 575, whence there are 150 true years to the end of the 44th of Amasis and the beginning of the 5th Persian and 1st Egyptian year of Cambyses, Jan. 2, B.C. 525, where the Chronicle also ends its Memphitico-Saite and commences its Persian dynasty.]

Dyn. XXVI. v Kings. 138. Feb. 6, B.C. 663, to Jan. 2, B.C. 525.

It is plain, both from the monuments and from Herodotus, that Psammitichus I. was really the founder of this Saite dynasty; and the monuments prove that the whole space covered by the five kings from Psammitichus to Amasis inclusive (Psammicherites being included as aforesaid in the 5th year of Cambyses), amounted to 138 years lying between Feb. 6, B.C. 663, and Jan. 2, B.C. 525. Manetho, therefore, in giving to the five kings only (54 + 6 + 6 + 19 + 44 =) 129 years, falls short of the true sum of their reigns by 9 years, which must be taken from the three nominal reigns of (7 + 6 + 8 =) 21 years which in his lists precede the accession of Psammitichus I. After this deduction, 12 years still remain attached to three names preceding that of Psammitichus I., and covering the interval from B.C. 675, to B.C. 663. Thus the whole interval from the retirement of Tirhakah from Egypt to Napata to the accession of Psammitichus I. is collected from Manetho and the Chronicle to have been (19 + 8 + 12 =) 39 years, and the whole interval from the death of Tirhakah and the end of Ethiopian supremacy to the accession of Psammitichus is 20 years, which last 20 years must be supposed to contain the dodecarchy of Herodotus and the "anarchy" of Diodorus. But the first three names of the dynasty in Manetho's lists are probably meant to cover indirectly—and the first two generations of the VII of the

Chronicle certainly cover—the whole 39 years which intervened between the retirement of Tirhakah and the accession of Psammitichus I. So VIII nominal kings of Manetho would have an average of 22 years, while the VII generations of the Chronicle have an average of 25 years and something over 2 months each. But if Manetho's lists were taken simply as they stand, IX actual kings, in only 150 years and 6 months, would seem to have average reigns of only 16 years and between 8 and 9 months each; and if even the last king were omitted, the remaining VIII in 150 years would have only 18 years and between 8 and 9 months each.

Necho I., the father of Psammitichus I., is named by Herodotus, not indeed as having actually reigned, but as having had some apparent title for reigning, on account of which he was slain by the Ethiopian Sabaco, a name which with Herodotus covers equally Sevechus and Tirhakah, while Psammitichus I., then very young, was saved by being carried into Syria. Of the two preceding names, Stephinates and Nechepsos, intended perhaps to connect Psammitichus I. with the native Saites who had reigned before the Ethiopian invasion, neither Herodotus nor the monuments afford any trace. But the monuments, especially at Thebes, do exhibit other names belonging to the interval between Tirhakah's withdrawal to Napata and the accession or undisputed sovereignty of Psammitichus I. A king named *Kasto* or *Kasen* is found, and his daughter *Amuniritis*, whose cartouches, according to Lepsius, are respected, while those of her consort, a king named *Pianchi*, are defaced. She and her husband may be the source of the "'Αμμερὶς, Αἰθίοψ," who heads Dyn. XXVI with 12 years in the list of Eusebius, though whence precisely Eusebius obtained so important a variant is not easy to conjecture. The name Pianchi belongs also to two other kings, successors of Tirhakah at Napata, and no doubt of the same family. A daughter of Pianchi and Amuniritis again, named *Sepunteput*, being married to Psammitichus I., brought to aid him in establishing his new dynasty both a title to Theban legitimacy and an Ethiopian connection; though as a separate line of kings reigned after Tirhakah at Napata, Psammitichus, in spite of this connection, had still need to keep an army on his southern frontier. Kasto or Kasen, then, with his queen, and their daughter the queen Amuniritis with her husband Pianchi, may represent the first two of the VII generations given by the Chronicle to its Dyn. XXVI; and the whole series of the Chronicle may be exhibited from the monuments as follows:—

(Generation I.) *Kasto* or *Kasen*. He began to reign under Tirhakah, on his withdrawal to Napata in Ethiopia, Feb. 15, in the year B.C. 702?

(Generation II.) *Ammuniritis* (Ἀμμερίς?) and *Pianchi* (Αἰθίοψ?), who reigned at least 12 years according to an inscription on the bandages of a mummy in the British Museum, mentioned by M. Mariette. The time given to these two generations, answering to the first three names of Manetho's IX kings, ends Feb. 6, B.C. 663.

(Generation III.) *Psamtik I.* 54, from Feb. 6, B.C. 663, to Jan. 23, B.C. 609. From his accession to the end of the 44th of Amasis, viz. Jan. 2, B.C. 525, the whole interval is shown by the monuments to be 138 years; consequently his accession is to be put at Thoth 1, B.C. 663. An important inscription, connecting the reign of Psamtik I. with that of Tirhakah is thus given by M. Mariette from a stele of his Apis, No. 37:—"In the year 20, Mesori 20 [Jan. 15, B.C. 643?] under the king [Psamtik I.] was manifested this Apis, living towards heaven [i. e. he died]. This God was conducted to join the good Amenti [i. e. was buried] in the year 21, Paophi 25. He was *born* in the 26th of the king [Tirhakah] and conducted into Ptah-hat-ka [i. e. was installed at Memphis] Pharmouthi 9. [This stele was] made in the year 21 [of Psamtik I.]." M. Mariette observes, that he would have been glad to translate the last words "[Il] fit [sa vie] en 21 ans," "He lived in all 21 years," but the form for duration of life is too uniform and too well-known to admit of any doubt. To which we may add, that the whole inscription is beautifully cut, and the figures and names as clear as could be wished. Unless therefore any one should imagine that the date for the birth of this Apis was really unknown, and was put conjecturally in the 26th of Tirhakah, as being the year of the death of his predecessor, it is necessary either to bring down arbitrarily the 26th of Tirhakah below B.C. 683, which we have found to be indicated by Manetho as the year of his death, or else to admit that this Apis-bull lived at least 40 years. If the 26th of Tirhakah is put down below B.C. 683, it follows that his first had not yet begun in the 14th year of Hezekiah, B.C. 709; and the difficulty hence arising is only awkwardly palliated by supposing, without other grounds, that Tirhakah was already, in B.C. 709, associated with his father, though his years were reckoned afterwards from his later accession after his father's death. But it seems that this Apis, No. 37, attracted far more veneration than any of his predecessors, no less than 168 votive stelæ, 53 of them dated, having been found, as M. Mariette relates, in his tomb. This extraordinary veneration must certainly have had *some* cause; and extraordinary longevity is the most natural cause, in such a case, that the imagination could suggest. It is just the explanation which would have commended itself even without proof; but being forced upon us, as it is, by separate chronological indications, it is certainly not to be rejected. The day of the bull's death, according to the stele above mentioned, was 20 Mechir, i.e. Jan. 15, and so seemingly at the end of the 20th year of Psammitichus I.; and M. Mariette observes that all the dates of the dated stelæ found in the tomb fall within the 70 days of the funeral, during which alone on such occasions the tomb remained open. He adds that this was the last Apis buried in the older Apis-cemetery of Rameses II., and before the inauguration of the magnificent new galleries of Psammitichus I., in which the next Apis, No. 38, was buried by that king, in his 52nd year. So here again there was an interval between these two Apises of 32 years. Only in this case it is open to suppose that there may have been another bull between, whose tomb has not been found; or else that there was an interval of some years between the death of No. 37 and the birth of his successor, though in general "the search of the Egyptians for their Apis did not last long." After these two Apises, the next, No. 39, was born in the 53rd year of Psammitichus I., Mechir 19, and he died in the

16th year of Necho, on the 6th day of the second month, Paophi, aged 16 years, 7 months, and 7 days.

(Generation IV.) *Necho.* 15, and part of a 16th, Jan. 23, B.C. 609, to Jan. 19, B.C. 594. The Apis No. 40 of M. Mariette, was born in his 16th year, Paophi 7; was installed in the 1st of Psamtik II., Epiphi 9; and died in the 12th of Ouaphre, Pharmouthi 12, aged 17 years, 6 months, and 5 days. Hence it seems that the 16th of Necho's actual reign is imperfect, and that part of the first year of the actual reign of Psamtik II. enters into the same civil year. Consequently the whole of that civil year will technically be reckoned as the first of Psamtik II., though Necho may still have technically as well as actually a sixteenth year, when his accession is antedated so as to cover the fractional months of his predecessor.

(Generation V.) *Psamtik II.* 6, from Jan. 19, B.C. 594 to Jan. 18, B.C. 588. The Apis No. 40, above mentioned, shows him to have reigned 5 years complete, and a sixth, identical in part with the 16th of his predecessor.

(Generation VI.) *Ouaphre-het.* 19, from Jan. 18, B.C. 588 to Jan. 13, B.C. 569. The Apis No. 40 died in his 12th; but the next Apis, No. 41, was not born till the 5th of Amasis. Two stelæ at Leyden and Florence, giving the births of two men in regnal years of Necho, and their deaths in regnal years of Amasis, both fix the interval between the year named of Necho and the year of the same number of Amasis, to be 40 years. Wherefore, as the 16 of Necho and the 6 of Psamtik II. have been found to make together only 21, Ouaphre-het must have had 19 years complete.

(Generation VII.) *Aahmes.* 44, from Jan. 13, B.C. 569, to Jan. 2, B.C. 525. The Apis No. 41 was born in his 5th year, Thoth 7, and died in his 23rd, Phamenoth 6, having lived 18 years and 6 months. The 44th of Amasis is found on the monuments; consequently his accession, reckoned up from Jan. 2 in B.C. 525, should be at Jan. 13, in B.C. 569, and that of Necho at Jan. 23, in 609; and that of Psamtik I. at Feb. 6, in B.C. 663. Lastly,

*Psamtik III.*, the Psammenitus of Herodotus and Psammicherites of the lists of Manetho and his ninth king, appears on the monuments; but he has no place chronologically, as his 6 months are included in the 5th Persian year of Cambyses, in the course of which he conquered Egypt, and from the beginning of which commences his technical or antedated Egyptian reign.

According to our scale of sacred Chronology, combined with that of the old Chronicle, the Egyptian accession of Sabaco being fixed to Feb. 26, B.C. 746, the dealings of Hoshea, king of Israel, with So, Sua, or Segor (probably Sevechus of the lists), should be about B.C. 724, 3 years before the capture of Samaria, in B.C. 721, or perhaps a little earlier; the coming forth of Tirhakah from Ethiopia to meet Sennacherib, in the 14th of Hezekiah, should be in B.C. 713.

Dyn. XXVII. v Persians. 124. Jan. 2, B.C. 525, to Dec. 2, B.C. 402.

The Persian Dyn. XXVII of Manetho, with VIII actual kings in 124 years and 4 months, is of course *really* identical and coincident (the 4 months being unchronological, and having been already anticipated at their true place) with Dyn. XXVIII of the Chronicle, which has V generations in 124 years. It takes us from Jan. 2, in B.C. 525, to Dec. 2, in B.C. 402, i. e. to the end of the second antedated or technical year of Artaxerxes Mnemon, the five *generations* of the Chronicle being plainly derived from the five principal *reigns* of Cambyses, Darius Hystaspes, Xerxes, Artaxerxes Longimanus, and Darius Nothus, yet not to be confounded with them as if their end was necessarily coincident with that of the last reign of the five alluded to. Manetho, naming the three short actual reigns of Artabanus after Xerxes, and of Xerxes II. and Sogdianus after Artaxerxes Longimanus, omits, which is remarkable, the Magian Bardas after Cambyses, though he reigned seven months and the second Xerxes only two. And in order to avoid naming a ninth king, Artaxerxes Mnemon, or rather to gain in appearance two years above, six years instead of four are given by him (in the list of Africanus) to Cambyses, although it is distinctly said, in the heading of the dynasty, that he reduced Egypt "in his fifth," not his third, "Persian year." And his three years, increased to four by including the seven months of the Magian usurper, reach from B.C.

525 to B.C. 521. On the monuments are found for this dynasty—

(Generation I., reign i.) *Kambatet.* 4, from Jan. 2. B.C. 525, to Jan. 1, B.C. 521. He also appears by the name of *Ramesout*; for on his first conquering Egypt, he was enthroned as a legitimate Egyptian king, and took this Egyptian name, and was instructed in all the mysteries of Neith at Sais, and confirmed the priesthood in their privileges: he appears besides in the Serapeum as a devout worshipper of Apis; all which explains the assertion of Herodotus, *ὅτι οἱ Αἰγύπτιοι οἰκηϊεῦνται τὸν Καμβύσεα.* So his violence or madness was only after his return from Ethiopia. An Apis born in his 5th (whence it appears that *he* reckoned his own years in Egypt from his Persian accession) on the 28th day of the 5th month, and which died in the 4th year of Darius on the 3rd day of the 9th month, is said to have lived 7 years, 3 months, and 4 days. Assuming the actual accession of Cambyses to have been soon after the new year, this Apis would be born early in June B.C. 525, and may have been stabbed by Cambyses on his return from Ethiopia. And it seems that he did not die so very soon after his wound. The stele on which the death of this Apis is recorded was misread at first, so as to make him live eight years instead of seven, and it is not the only instance where such mistakes, having had attention drawn to them, have been subsequently corrected. So in another stele, IIIIIii∩ is the year of Amasis in which another Apis was either born or installed; and Lepsius reads this 17, De Rougé more correctly 25. For this same Apis is recorded to have been buried by Cambyses in his 6th year, in the 11th month; that is, if his actual accession had coincided with his technical or antedated accession, in November, B.C. 524, when he may have been on the point of commencing his Ethiopian expedition. Now, if II, as read by Lepsius, was originally written on the stele, this Apis at his death would be 29 years old; but if ∩, as read by De Rougé, he would be only 17, which is certainly more probable.

(Generation II., reign of Manetho ii, actual reign iii.) *Ntarioush*, Darius. 36, from Jan. 1, B.C. 521, to Dec. 23, B.C. 486. He built most of the great temple in the larger

Oasis, and takes there titles identical with those of the old Egyptian kings.

(Generation III., reign of Manetho iii, actual reign vi.) *Kheshirsh*, Xerxes. 21, from Dec. 23, B. C. 486, to Dec. 18, B. C. 465 (under whom Achæmenes was Satrap of Egypt 24 years, from B. C. 484 to B. C. 460).

(Generation IV., reign of Manetho v, actual reign vi.) *Artachsheshes*, Artaxerxes. 41, from Dec. 18, B. C. 465, to Dec. 8, B. C. 460. In his 5th year Inaros revolted, B. C. 460. He was crucified probably in B.C. 455. Herodotus visited Egypt soon after the Persian dominion had been re-established, in B. C. 450? In the 15th of Artaxerxes the Athenians sent a fleet to restore Amyrtæus, whose name has been found on the monuments; but the project came to nothing.

(Generation V., reign of Manetho viii, actual reign ix; and a 10th actual reign, of Artaxerxes Mnemon, follows.) *Darius Nothus*. 19, from Dec. 8, B.C. 424, to Dec. 3, B.C. 405; but he has not hitherto been met with on the monuments. In his 10th year Amyrtæus succeeded in establishing himself, and reigned in the Delta 6 years, when his son Pausiris was allowed to succeed him as viceroy. Or this may have been earlier, in B. C. 484.

Dyn. XXVIII of Manetho, with its one Saite king, Amyrtæus, and his six years, really contemporary and included within the 124 years of the Persians, is no doubt intended as a substitute for the anonymous Dyn. XXVII of the Chronicle with its 184 years, which have been accounted for by Manetho pretty nearly at their true chronological place, above Dyn. XVIII. The six unchronological years of his Dyn. XXVIII have been anticipated by us and inserted in their true place, in the early part of Dyn. XXVI, to which they belong by allusion. On the monuments *Amunrut*, i. e. Amyrtæus, occurs in conjunction with his throne-name; and the first part of the name of his son Pausiris, *Pef* . . . . . and a throne-name read *Chebash*, which however Lepsius has not connected with Pausiris.

Dyn. XXIX of Manetho, like XXVII, has an unchronological addition of one year and 4 months, which any one who saw merely that Dyn. XXVIII is not to be allowed to thrust up that of the Persians, might think intended to serve with the 4 odd months of XXVII as a patch to fill the void produced by drawing up the head of Dyn. XXVII to the 3rd instead of the 5th year of Cambyses, and so leaving the first two years of Artaxerxes Mnemon uncovered by it below. But the unchronological nature of all these dislocations of Manetho has been sufficiently explained already; and both this and other similar additions have been anticipated at the head of Dyn. XXVI. So, without further noticing the odd year and 4 months, Dyn. XXIX with 19 and Dyn. XXX with 38 years have together 57 years, the same number as Dynasties XXIX and XXX of the Chronicle, though their division in it is different, being into 39 and 18 years; and the 57 years will begin *really*, though not apparently, for both Manetho and the Chronicle alike, from Dec. 2, B.C. 402, and will also end for both alike simultaneously at Nov. 18, B.C. 345.

As regards the actual reigns of Manetho and the monuments, and the generations of the Chronicle, the monuments exhibit the names of

(Dyn. XXIX, Generation I, of the Chronicle, reign i.) *Naifaurut*, Nepherites, with a throne-name like what is mentioned above as *Chebash*. If he had 6 years, they would be from Dec. 2, B.C. 402, to Dec. 1, B.C. 396.

(Generation II of the Chronicle, reign ii.) *Hakor*, Achoris. His 13 years would lie between Dec. 1, B.C. 396, and Nov. 28, B.C. 383, and would include the single year of Psammuthis consolidated by the Chronicle.

(Reign iii.) Some traces seemingly are given by Lepsius of *Psamtik IV.*, who is written in the list of Dyn. XXIX "Psammuthis," in like manner as Psamtik III. is written above in the lists of Dyn. XXVI. From Nov. 28, B.C. 384, to Nov. 28, B.C. 383?

(Reign iv.) Of *Nepherites II.* no trace has been found. His 4 months would no doubt be covered by the next reign as technically antedated. And it is to be remembered, that though we can only guess *where* the addition has been made, we *know* that one year and four months out of the twenty years and four months given to this dynasty by Manetho are unchronological and fictitious.

(Generation III of Dyn. XXIX of the Chronicle, reign i. of Dyn. XXX of Manetho.) *Nect-hor-heb*, by some erroneously supposed to be the name of Amyrtæus; but really it is Nectanebo I., whose 18 years begin from Nov. 28, B. C. 383, and end Nov. 23, B. C. 365.

(Reign ii of Manetho's Dyn. XXX.) *Teos*, or *Tachos*, has not been found. His 2 years seem to reach from Nov. 23, B. C. 365, to Nov. 23, B. C. 363, and to belong to the 39 years of Dyn. XXIX in the Chronicle, though the reign would not be noticed as a separate generation.

(The single generation of Dyn. XXX of the Chronicle, reign iii of Manetho.) *Necht-nebef*, Nectanebo II., whose 18 years, antedated technically from Nov. 23, B. C. 363, and including the odd months of the reign of Tachos, end Nov. 18, B. C. 345, 15 years before the *cosmocracy* of Alexander.

Of the above seven kings of Manetho's lists, Nectanebo II., there can be no doubt, represents the single generation of Dyn. XXX of the Chronicle, and Nepherites II., with his 4 months, as certainly would be covered by the antedated accession of Nectanebo I., while the collective sum of the other reigns, as they now stand in the list of Africanus, needs a further reduction of one entire year to make it true and historical. On the other hand, the reigns of Nepherites I. with 6 years, of Achoris with 13, and of Nectanebo II. with 18, were probably both in the Chronicle and in reality distinct generations; and as the Chronicle cannot have made more than III generations in its Dyn. XXIX, the Shepherds of its Dyn. XXVII requiring IV, it seems to be *certain* that Psammuthis with 1 year, and Teos or Tachos with 2, were not alluded to as distinct generations by the Chronicle, and most probable, without being absolutely certain, that the 184 years of its anonymous Dynasty XXVII were really covered, as Manetho's lists indicate, by only *four* Shepherd kings.

After Dyn. XXX, the only point still remaining to be noticed is this, that Manetho, in the structure of his scheme above, has indicated the year B. C. 331 as the epoch to which he meant by allusion to bring down his history, and from which he made the empire of Alexander and the Macedonians over Egypt to commence. For having found in the Chronicle the "443 years of the Cycle" lying between B.C. 305 and A.D. 139 thrown up, he threw up in like manner, and reduplicated, 978 more of the years of the Cycle, viz. all those which had passed from its commencement in B.C. 1322 to the end of the monarchy in B.C. 345. And of the 40 (now alone remaining) between Nectanebo and the Lagidæ, which had all been thrown up in effect, though unnamed, by the Chronicle, Manetho threw up only 14, so marking the interval between Nectanebo and Alexander. Thus he threw up the whole 1461 years of the current Cycle, all but 26, marking at once by this very fact, that 26 alone were not thrown up, the 26 years' interval between Alexander and the Lagidæ, and avoiding the incidental and partial admission of a cyclical element which was foreign to his scheme. At a later period, when the Macedonians were no longer in power to be complimented, and the memory of the last Persian government had become less odious by lapse of time, Ptolemy of Mendes made of the interval between Nectanebo II. and Alexander the last of a scheme of XXXI Dynasties, all of kings successors of Menes.

In conclusion, if we neglect the first 21 cycles or 30,681 nominal years of the Chronicle, as resolvable into the 2922 properly belonging to its XIII Gods, and if we further neglect the 341 fictitious years added to make all time seem to have run in cycles, the remainder of its years, being all full and real, amounting in number to (2922 + 14 + 26 + 217 + 443 + 1881 =) 5503 civil years, and lying ostensibly between Aug. 25, B.C. 5844, and Nov. 18, B.C. 345, but really and *chronologically* between April 26th, B.C. 5361, and July 20, A.D. 139, may be paralleled with the years of Manetho as follows, unchronological years and positions being printed in red:—

| | |
|---|---|
| *Chronicle.* | 30,000 years of the Sun (Dyn. I) + 681 + 900 + |
| *Manetho.* | . . . . . . . . . . . . . . : 900 + |
| *Chron.* | 2000 . . . . . . . . . of XIII Gods (Dyn. |
| *Man.* | 2000 [presented as 24,000] of . . Gods, Demi- |

*Chron.* { II to XIV incl.) from April 26, B.C. 5361, to
*Man.* { gods and Manes from April 26, B.C. 5361, to

*Chron.* { May 2, B.C. 2463 + 22 of the same XIII Gods,
*Man.* { May 2, B.C. 2463 + 22 transferred from the Gods

*Chron.* { completing the first 2,922 years of human time in
*Man.* { of the Chronicle to Menes (Dyn. VIII of Manetho,

*Chron.* { two pseudo-cycles, commencing from May 2, B.C.
*Man.* { of viii Thinites, I of Africanus), from May 2, B.C.

*Chron.* { 2463, and terminating at April 26, B.C. 2441.
*Man.* { 2463, and terminating at April 26, B.C. 2441.

[Here the Chronicle inserts and adds to the XIII Gods 341 fictitious years, foreign to Manetho's scheme, in order to make time seem to have begun from a Sothic epoch, viz., from July 20, B.C. 5702, 341 years earlier than April 26, B.C. 5361.]

*Chron.* { + 14 past years "of the Cycle," really lying
*Man.* { + 14 past years "of the Cycle," really lying

*Chron.* { between Nov. 18, B.C. 345, and Nov. 15, B.C.
*Man.* { between Nov. 18, B.C. 345, and Nov. 15, B.C.

*Chron.* { 331, thrown up and added to the XIII Gods.
*Man.* { 331, thrown up and transferred to Menes, ending with the 36th year of the 253 of Dynasty VIII (I of Africanus). Thus, after seven mythological Dynasties, the *first* XXII and XIV, or in one sum the FIRST XXXVI YEARS of the First Dynasty of the kings in Manetho's Book I., indicate by their origin those two points in the true Egyptian chronology at which his historical narrative is made to begin and end, if one only sets aside all those years, (14 + 443 + 978 =) 1435 in number, which are originally "years of the Cycle current in Manetho's time," thrown up, or even thrown up *and* reduplicated, and which therefore, as interposed among other true years anterior to B.C. 1322, are plainly unchronological. So, *in terms of the true reckoning*, the reign of Menes is feigned to have begun from after the 2900th year of the Gods: that is, from

May 1, B.C. 2461, 236 years higher than in the Chronicle, and these 236 true and chronological years, falsely added to the monarchy, together with the 14 thrown up and marking the interval between the end of Manetho's last dynasty of kings and Alexander, and also the last historical date to which Manetho brings down his work, constitute together the 253 years of the first Dynasty of viii Thinite kings headed by Menes. It was no doubt in order to make the three sums 22, 14, and 217, go exactly into the dynasty, that Manetho not only increased by 6 decades the 190 years which the same dynasty has in the Chronicle, but also made the further remarkable addition of *three units*, really taken from the head of Dyn. XXVI, far below, and depressing everything below them, through nearly all the dynasties, till at length the void left by them is reached and filled.

*Chron.* { + 26 more *past* years of the Cycle, really lying
*Man.* { : — These 26 years are *not* thrown up by Ma-

*Chron.* { between Nov. 15, B.C. 331, and Nov. 8, B.C.
*Man.* { netho. If they had been, he would have re-

*Chron.* { 305, thrown up and added to the XIII Gods,
*Man.* { duplicated and thrown up the whole 1461 years

*Chron.* { together with the preceding 14, (the whole of the
*Man.* { of the Cycle current in his own time, which began

*Chron.* { forty years being purposely undescribed,) +217
*Man.* { in B.C. 1322, and was to run out in A.D. 139. +217

*Chron.* { of the VIII Demigods, making Dynasty XV (after
*Man.* { transferred to kings, *ending with the* 253*rd and last*

*Chron.* { which follow XV dynasties of the kings) from
*Man.* { *year of Dynasty VIII (I of Africanus,)* from

*Chron.* { April 26, B.C. 2441, to Feb. 3, B.C. 2224+443
*Man.* { April 26, B.C. 2441, to Feb. 3, B.C. 2224+443

*Chron.* { of the Cycle . . still future, . . . really
*Man.* { of the Cycle *partly* still future, partly past, really

*Chron.* { lying between Nov. 8, B.C. 305, and July 20,
*Man.* { lying between Nov. 8, B.C. 305, and July 20,

*Chron.* A.D. 139, cast up in fifteen blank generations, not
*Man.* A.D. 139, cast up and transferred to kings, mak-

*Chron.* constituting any one of the thirty dynasties, nor
*Man.* ing the 302 years of Dyn. IX (II of Africanus),

*Chron.* given either to the Gods, or to the Demigods, or to
*Man.* of ix Thinites, and the first 141 of X (III of Afri-

*Chron.* mortal kings after Menes: —These years thrown
*Man.* canus) of ix Memphites +978 *past* years of the

*Chron.* up by Manetho are absent from the Chronicle for
*Man.* Cycle, from July 20, B.C. 1322, to Nov. 18, B.C.

*Chron.* the same reason that the 341 inserted by the
*Man.* 345, reduplicated and thrown up, as the Chronicle

*Chron.* Chronicle for a cyclical purpose are absent from
*Man.* had thrown up the other (40 +443 =) 483 years

*Chron.* Manetho, the author of the Chronicle having no
*Man.* of the Cycle lying between Nov. 18, B.C. 345, and

*Chron.* need of room in which to place concurrent lines of
*Man.* July 20, A.D. 139. These 978 years make the

*Chron.* kings, any more than Manetho had need of that
*Man.* remaining 73 of Dyn. X (III of Africanus), the

*Chron.* precise number of 341 years which would make
*Man.* 277 of Dyn. XI (IV of Africanus), the 248 of Dyn.

*Chron.* time to have run in cycles from the beginning.
*Man.* XII (V of Africanus), the 197 of Dyn. XIII (VI of Africanus), the 59 of Dyn. XIV (XI of Africanus), concluding Book I. of Manetho, and lastly the first 124 years of Dyn. XV (XII of Africanus) in Book II.

*Chron.* +the first 22 +14 or together the first
*Man.* +the FIRST XXII + XIV or together the FIRST

*Chron.* 36 years of the monarchy, viz., of the viii Ta-
*Man.* XXXVI YEARS of the monarchy, according to true

*Chron.* nite generations, headed by Menes, with 190 years.
*Man.* consecutive chronology, indicated by the remainder of *thirty-six* years included in and ending the 160 of Dyn. XV (XII of Africanus.) The same number

XXXVI, composed of 22 of the Gods and 14 of the Cycle, marking the beginning and the end of Manetho's historical narrative, having been already noticed at the head of Manetho's whole series, chronological or unchronological, of kings in connection with the name and epoch of Menes, its repetition here, at the true epoch of Menes according to the Chronicle, is no doubt a covert indication that here, at this point, Manetho makes as it were a new beginning; and they who would distinguish the true chronological series of years (however it may be in places dislocated by suppressions and compensations), must reckon from hence, as if Menes had been set at the 36th year before the end of Dyn. XV (XII of Africanus). And accordingly, taking this hint, and reckoning from hence, we find that there follow in all *fifteen dynasties*, and 1881 years to the end of the fifteenth and last of them, which, it is needless to say, is precisely the number of dynasties and precisely the number of years given by the Chronicle to the Egyptian monarchy from Menes to Nectanebo II.

And we can see a certain parallelism between the commencement of Manetho's Book I. or of that portion of it which contained dynasties of kings and years chiefly unchronological, and this covert *recommencement* in Book II. indicating the true chronological series of the history. As the first regal dynasty of Book I., with the number *thirty-six* at its head, was made to contain the remainder of the true years of the Gods and Demigods transferred to kings, while (443 + 978 =) 1421 fictitious years "of the Cycle" thrown up, or 1297 of them, were to follow in six more dynasties to the end of Book I., – so in commencing Book II., its first dynasty (Manetho's eighth of kings, fifteenth of the XXX) is made to unite the remainder, viz. 124, of the fictitious years of the Cycle thrown up with a commencement of *thirty-six* of those true and historical years of the monarchy which were to follow after it in all the rest of Book II. and in Book III., and which were to be identical in their number, 1881, and parallel in their number of *fifteen* dynasties, with the 1881 years and *fifteen* dynasties given by the Chronicle to the kings from Menes to Nectanebo II. So the (36 + 217 =) 253 of Dyn. VIII (I of Africanus), and the (124 + 36 =) 160 of Dyn.

XV (XII of Africanus) are analogous to one another and symmetrical, in Books I. and II.

*Chron.* The *first* 36 years of Menes and the Monarchy
*Man.* The *last* 36 years of Dyn. XV (XII of Afric.),

*Chron.* reaching from Feb. 3, B.C. 2224, to Feb. 22, B.C.
*Man.* reaching from Feb. 3, B.C. 2224, to Feb. 22, B.C.

*Chron.* 2188, + the remaining 154 of the 190 of Dyn.
*Man.* 2188, + the first . . 154 of the 184 of Dyn.

*Chron.* XVI of the viii earliest Tanite kings, from Feb. 22,
*Man.* XVI (XIV of Africanus) of Xoites, from Feb. 22,

*Chron.* B.C. 2188, to Jan. 14, B.C. 2034, + 103 viz. the
*Man.* B.C. 2188, to Jan. 14, B.C. 2034, + 103 viz. the

*Chron.* whole continuance of the second sovereign dynasty
*Man.* last 30 of Dyn. XVI (XIV of Africanus), and

*Chron.* of kings, being Dyn. XVII . . . . . . of
*Man.* the first 73 of Dyn. XVII (XV Africanus) of

*Chron.* iv Memphites, from Jan. 14, B.C. 1034, to Dec.
*Man.* vi Shepherds, from Jan. 14, B.C. 1034, to Dec.

*Chron.* 20, B.C. 1932. + [184 of iv Shepherd kings
*Man.* 20, B.C. 1932. + 184 of vi Shepherds, from

*Chron.* transposed, so as to stand unchronologically as
*Man.* the 73rd to the 257th of the 259 years $10^{m}$. of

*Chron.* Dyn. XXVII in the Chronicle, from Dec. 20,
*Man.* Dyn. XVII (XV of Africanus), from Dec. 20,

*Chron.* B.C. 1932, to Nov. 4, B.C. 1748] : ——The 2
*Man.* B.C. 1932, to Nov. 4, B.C. 1748. + $2.10^{m}$. *un-*

*Chron.* years and 10 months of Manetho, if reckoned here
*Man.* *chronologically occurring here* at the end of Dyn.

*Chron.* as chronological, would depress the head of Dyn.
*Man.* XVII (XV of Africanus,) but needed as compen-

*Chron.* XVIII and all the dates below, until their effect
*Man.* sation for years and months suppressed before

*Chron.* were compensated by some unchronological sup-
*Man.* Dyn. XXVI. These 2 years and 10 months have

*Chron.* pression. But it is best not to let them count
*Man.* originated in an addition of three units to Dyn.

*Chron.* here, so as to destroy the manifest identity and
*Man.* VIII (I of Africanus), made to obtain for *it* that

*Chron.* parallelism of the 348 + 194 = 542 and 333 + 209
*Man.* *commencement, and for Dyn. XV* (XII of Afric.),

*Chron.* = 542 years of the two following Dynasties XVIII
*Man.* *that remainder of* (XXII + XIV =) XXXVI *years which*

*Chron.* and XIX of the Chronicle and Manetho. In this
*Man.* *has been noticed above.* That there is now a frac-

*Chron.* and other similar cases the unchronological surplus
*Man.* tion of 10$^{m}$. and another of 2$^{m}$. corresponding to

*Chron.* years or months must be only carried to account as
*Man.* it below in the sum of Dynasties XXVI, XXVII,

*Chron.* compensation available for filling voids below.
*Man.* and XXIX, may perhaps be owing to the way in which our reconstruction has been obtained, namely, by patches, partly from the lists of Africanus, and partly from the original Manetho of Josephus. . . . . .

*Chron.* + the first 165 years of the 348 of the xiv "Mem-
*Man.* + the first 165 years of the 333 of the xvi "Dios-

*Chron.* phites" of Dynasty XVIII, from November 4,
*Man.* polites" of Dynasty XVIII, from November 4,

*Chron.* B.C. 1748, to Sept. 24, B.C. 1583. + 15 years of the
*Man.* B.C. 1748, to Sept. 24, B.C. 1583. — suppressed

*Chron.* Sun-worshippers, from September 24, B.C. 1583,
*Man.* by Manetho, but compensated by an addition

*Chron.* to September 23, B.C. 1568. + the remaining 165
*Man.* of 15 prefixed to Dyn. XIX. + the remaining 165

*Chron.* years of the 348 of Dyn. XVIII, from Sept. 23.
*Man.* years of the 333 of Dyn. XVIII, from Sept. 23.

*Chron.* B.C. 1568, to Aug. 9, B.C. 1400. : — not histo-
*Man.* B.C. 1568, to Aug. 9, B.C. 1400. . 15 *prefixed to*

*Chron.* rical, nor to be found in this place in the Chronicle,
*Man.* *Dynasty XIX.* in lieu of 15 suppressed above,

*Chron.* { + the 194, i.e. the whole continuance of the v Dios-
*Man.* { + the 194 remaining of the 209 of the vii Dios-

*Chron.* { polites of Dyn. XIX, from Aug. 9, B.C. 1400, to
*Man.* { polites of Dyn. XIX, from Aug. 9, B.C. 1400, to

*Chron.* { June 23, B.C. 1206. + 135 of the 228 of viii
*Man.* { June 23, B.C. 1206. + 135 [of vii?] of the xii

*Chron.* { Diospolites of Dyn. XX, from June 23, B.C. 1206,
*Man.* { Diospolites of Dyn. XX, from June 23, B.C. 1206,

*Chron.* { to May 19, B.C. 1071. + the last 93 of the 228
*Man.* { to May 19, B.C. 1071. + the first 93 of the 130

*Chron.* { years of the viii Diospolites of Dyn. XX, (with
*Man.* { of [iv of?] the vii Tanites . . of Dyn. XXI, (with,

*Chron.* { a separate and contemporaneous line of Tanite
*Man.* { the last iv or v of the xii Diospolites of Dyn.

*Chron.* { kings, perhaps reigning in the Delta,) . from
*Man.* { XX reigning contemporaneously at Thebes), from

*Chron.* { May 19, B.C. 1071, to April 25, B.C. 978. : —
*Man.* { May 19, B.C. 1071, to April 25, B.C. 978. + 37.

*Chron.* { absent here from the Chronicle, but found in 37
*Man.* { viz. the last 37 of the 130 *years* (*also* three of the

*Chron.* { years suppressed by Manetho below + 1, viz. the
*Man.* { vii Tanite *kings*) of Dyn. XXI. . : absent

*Chron.* { first year of the 121 of the vi Tanite genera-
*Man.* { from Manetho, but covered by 1 of the 37 unchro-

*Chron.* { tions of Dynasty XXI, extending from April 25,
*Man.* { nological years of his Dyn. XXI, from April 25,

*Chron.* { B.C. 978, to April 25, B.C. 977 + the remaining
*Man.* { B.C. 978, to April 25, B.C. 977 + the whole. .

*Chron.* { 120 of the vi Tanites of Dyn. XXI, from April
*Man.* { 120 of the ix Bubastites of Dyn. XXII, from April

*Chron.* { 25, B.C. 977, to March 26, B.C. 857. + the whole
*Man.* { 25, B.C. 977, to March 26, B.C. 857. + the first

*Chron.* { 48 years belonging to the iii Tanites of Dynasty
*Man.* { 48 years of the 89 of the iv Tanites of Dynasty

*Chron.* XXII, identical with the last three of the ix
*Man.* XXIII. (Really these 48 belong to the last three

*Chron.* Bubastites of Manetho's Dynasty XXII, not to
*Man.* of the ix Bubastites of his Dyn. XXII, and are

*Chron.* Petubast, who is either a contemporary or else put
*Man.* to be transferred to them from the names

*Chron.* up out of his true place, from March 26, B.C.
*Man.* Petubast and Osorchon), from March 26, B.C.

*Chron.* 875, to March 14, B.C. 809, + 19 years, (being the
*Man.* 875, to March 14, B.C. 809, + 19 more of the 89

*Chron.* whole sum) of the ii Diospolites of Dyn. XXIII,
*Man.* of the iv Tanites of Dyn. XXIII, viz. 9 to be

*Chron.* who are identifiable with Osorchon and Psammous
*Man.* brought up and given to Osorchon from the 31 of

*Chron.* in Dynasty XXIII of Manetho, Petubast being
*Man.* Zet, and 10 of Psammous, (22 years being left

*Chron.* put up to carry years not belonging to him,
*Man.* to Zet to divide with Petubast, as put down,)

*Chron.* from March 14, B.C. 809, to March 9, B.C. 790, + 28,
*Man.* from March 14, B.C. 809, to March 9, B.C. 790, + 28,

*Chron.* viz. the . . . first 28 of the 44 of Dyn. XXIV
*Man.* viz. the remaining 22 of the 89 of Dyn. XXIII

*Chron.* of the *three* Saites identified with Petubast and
*Man.* belonging to the kings Petubast and Zet together,

*Chron.* Zet of Manetho's Dyn. XXIII, and Bocchoris
*Man.* and the 6 of a third, *the single* Saite Bocchoris,

*Chron.* of his XXIV, from March 9, B.C. 790, to
*Man.* of Dyn. XXIV, from March 9, B.C. 790, to

*Chron.* March 2, B.C. 762, + 16, viz. the remainder of the
*Man.* March 2, B.C. 762. — These 16 are suppressed by

*Chron.* 44 of Dyn. XXIV, from March 2, B.C. 762, to
*Man.* Manetho, but compensated by 16 of his unchrono-

*Chron.* Feb. 26, B.C. 746. + 40 of the 44 of the iii
*Man.* logical years above. + 40 of . . . . . . the iii

*Chron.* Ethiopians of Dynasty XXV, from February
*Man.* Ethiopians of Dynasty XXV, from February

*Chron.* 26, B.C. 746, to February 16, B.C. 706, + 4
*Man.* 26, B.C. 746, to February 16, B.C. 706, : –

*Chron.* remaining of the 44 of Dynasty XXV, from
*Man.* These 4 are suppressed by Manetho, but

*Chron.* February 16, B.C. 706, to February 15, B.C.
*Man.* compensated by 4 of his unchronological years

*Chron.* 702, + 19, being the first 19 of the 177 of the
*Man.* above : – These 19 are suppressed by Manetho,

*Chron.* vii "Memphite" generations of Dyn. XXVI,
*Man.* but compensated by 19 of his unchronological

*Chron.* probably to the death of Tirhakah, from Feb. 15,
*Man.* years inserted *above*, in the latter part of his

*Chron.* B.C. 702, to Feb. 11, B.C. 683; + 8 more of the
*Man.* interpolated Dynasty XXI . These 8 are

*Chron.* 177 of Dyn. XXVI, commencing from Feb. 11,
*Man.* suppressed by Manetho, but compensated by 8

*Chron.* B.C. 683, and extending to Jan. 15, B.C. 675.
*Man.* of his unchronological years inserted *below*.

*Chron.* + 12 more of the 177 of Dyn. XXVI (making
*Man.* + 12, being the first 12 of the 150, 6^m^. of the ix

*Chron.* 49 in all, to the end of its 2nd generation), to the
*Man.* Saites of Dyn. XXVI, reaching, in truth, to the

*Chron.* accession of Psammitichus I., Jan. 12, B.C. 663:
*Man.* end of the 3rd name or generation of the ix, the
three first of whom really *could* only have 12, not
21, of the 150 years, there being certainly as many as 138 after the accession of Psammitichus I. But the first three names really cover also the preceding 27 years suppressed:

*Chron.* from Jan. 15, B.C. 675, to Jan. 12, B.C. 663 +
*Man.* from Jan. 15, B.C. 675, to Jan. 12, B.C. 663 +

*Chron.* 138 remaining of the 177 years . . . . of Dyn.
*Man.* 138 of the remaining 150 years and 6^m^. of Dyn.

*Chron.* { XXVI, from the accession of Psammitichus I.,
*Man.* { XXVI, from the accession of Psammitichus I.,

*Chron.* { Jan. 12, B.C. 663, to a little before the death of
*Man.* { Jan. 12, B.C. 663, to a little before the death of

*Chron.* { Amasis, and the commencement of the 5th Persian
*Man.* { Amasis, and the commencement of the 5th Persian

*Chron.* { year of Cambyses, Jan. 2, B.C. 525, + 184 of the
*Man.* { year of Cambyses, Jan. 2, B.C. 528 : — These

*Chron.* { iv(?) generations of the anonymous Dyn. XXVII,
*Man.* { 184 years, with the names of the Shepherds, are

*Chron.* { which have been restored above to their true
*Man.* { given by Manetho exactly in their true chrono-

*Chron.* { place, so as to precede the kings of Dynasty
*Man.* { logical place, in his Dyn. XVII (Dyn. XV of

*Chron.* { XVIII : — Absent from the Chronicle, really
*Man.* { Africanus + 6 months, the last of Dyn. XXVII,

*Chron.* { covered by the first year of its Dyn. XXVIII of
*Man.* { really contained in the Egyptian reign of Cam-

*Chron.* { the Persians, antedated from Thoth 1 of the 5th
*Man.* { byses, as antedated from the beginning of his 5th

*Chron.* { of Cambyses, + 124 of the v Persians of Dyn.
*Man.* { Persian year, + 124 of the viii Persians of Dyn.

*Chron.* { XXVIII, from the beginning of the 5th of Cam-
*Man.* { XXVII, from the beginning of the 5th of Cam-

*Chron.* { byses to the end of the 2nd of Artaxerxes
*Man.* { byses to the end of the 2nd of Artaxerxes

*Chron.* { Mnemon, these last two years being consolidated
*Man.* { Mnemon, the last 2 years being unchronologi-

*Chron.* { in the v generations of the Chronicle, from
*Man.* { cally forced up, and given to Cambyses, from

*Chron.* { Jan. 2, B.C. 528, to Dec. 2, B.C. 402. : — Absent
*Man.* { Jan. 2, B.C. 528, to Dec. 2, B.C. 402. + 4 months

*Chron.* { from the Chronicle], as being really covered
*Man.* { unchronologically added to Dyn. XXVII, telling

*Chron.* { by the first year of the next dynasty : — Absent<br>
*Man.* { in compensation of suppressions above + 6 years

*Chron.* { from the Chronicle ; being a substitute for its<br>
*Man.* { also unchronological, constituting with one name,

*Chron.* { anonymous Dyn. XXVII + 19 of the 39 years<br>
*Man.* { Amyrtæus, Dyn. XXVIII + 19 of the 21. 1m.

*Chron.* { of the iii Tanites of Dyn. XXIX, from<br>
*Man.* { of the iv Mendesians of Dyn. XXIX, from

*Chron.* { Dec. 2, B.C. 402, to Nov. 28, B.C. 383 : — Ab-<br>
*Man.* { Dec. 2, B.C. 402, to Nov. 28, B.C. 383 + 1. 4m.

*Chron.* { sent from the Chronicle, the whole year and the<br>
*Man.* { unchronologically added to Dyn. XXIX, telling

*Chron.* { 4m. being all equally unchronological. + 38, being<br>
*Man.* { towards compensations needed above, + 38, being

*Chron.* { the last 20 of the iii Tanites of Dyn. XXIX,<br>
*Man.* { the . . 38 of the iii . . . . . . . . .

*Chron.* { and the 18 of the single Tanite of Dyn. XXX,<br>
*Man.* { . . . . . . . . Sebennytes of Dyn. XXX,

*Chron.* { from Nov. 28, B.C. 383, to Nov. 23, B.C. 363, and<br>
*Man.* { from Nov. 28, B.C. 383, to Nov. 23, B.C. 363, and

*Chron.* { Nov. 18, B.C. 345. + 14 [+ 1 = 15] years on to the<br>
*Man.* { Nov. 18, B.C. 345. + 14 years to Alexander, (Nov.

*Chron.* { *Cosmocracy* of Alexander, viz. Nov. 15, B.C. 330,<br>
*Man.* { 15, B.C. 331,) these 14 being alluded to, but not

*Chron.* { these 15 years being alluded to perhaps by the<br>
*Man.* { contained, in the 3555 years of Manetho's kings.

*Chron.* { text of the Chronicle, but not distinguished in the structure of the scheme itself, nor contained in its 1881 years of kings, nor in its whole period of 35,525 years.

The scheme of 48,863 years, preserved by Diogenes Laertius, having no intermixture of fictitious or unchronological years, but only its round month of cycles, viz. (30 × 1461 =) 43,830 cosmical rather than nominal years, prefixed, all its remaining years, being 5033 in number, and divisible into 2922 + 217 + 1881 + 13, or into 900 + 2000 + 22 + 217 + 22 +

14 + 1845 + 13, to Alexander, are strictly chronological, and need no separate comparison to parallel them with the true and chronological years either of the Chronicle or of Manetho, to the foregoing exhibition of which they afford the strongest and the most satisfactory confirmation.

# CHAP. III.

## ERATOSTHENES.

We come next to Eratosthenes, the father of technical Greek chronology, who was born at Cyrene in Olymp. 126, α′, B.C. 276, early in the reign of Ptolemy Philadelphus. Invited from Athens by Ptolemy Euergetes in his 8th year (B.C. 239?), he became about B.C. 226, chief librarian at Alexandria, where he wrote many learned works, and died at the age of 80 or 82 in Olymp. 146, α′ or γ′, B.C. 196 or 194. A list of Egyptian kings, called "Theban," was made out with the assistance of the priests at Thebes from names and notices which they supplied, and rendered from their vernacular Egyptian into Greek, by Eratosthenes at the special desire of his sovereign. And a portion of this list, consisting of XXXVIII out of the XCI names (XV + LXXVI) of the whole series, has been preserved to us by Syncellus, from the disciple and successor of Eratosthenes, Apollodorus of Athens, who ended his own chronography about 145 years before Christ.

From internal evidence supplied by this list we see that Eratosthenes had before him both the Old Chronicle and the work of Manetho, and that what he sought from the priests of Thebes was not help to make out directly from the monuments or from their hieratic papyri an independent series of his own, but help to select from Manetho's lists, or from whatever sources they preferred, names of kings with which to fill up the *blank generations* of the Chronicle, a document which, as he perceived, contained already a continuous chronological series scientifically adjusted. In order to make such a selection he naturally needed native help; and as Manetho, who presented all the early dynasties as successive, and the author of the Chronicle, who in his Dynasties

XVI and XVII (especially so long as the true place of Dyn. XXVII was unperceived) seemed to have scarcely room for all the known lines of early kings, were both natives of Lower Egypt, it was reasonable to hope that at Thebes, if anywhere, there might be found an independent local tradition, and the historical knowledge necessary to throw light on the subject.

It is to be regretted, for some reasons, that Eratosthenes did not succeed in making the priests his assistants simply execute his own idea. Had he done so, we should have seen distinctly from what dynasty or dynasties of Manetho they selected names to fill up or parallel the IV generations and the 103 years of the "Memphite" Dyn. XVII, and the unspecified number of generations and 184 years of the anonymous Dyn. XXVII of the Chronicle. But he ventured — or rather he allowed the priests for him — to improve upon the Chronicle by adding to its 1881 years of the monarchy those XV abstract and undynastic generations, which were placed by it between the Demigods and Menes, and described merely as "443 years of the Cycle." It was admitted then, the priests might suggest, even on the face of the Chronicle itself, that there had been after the Gods and Demigods fifteen generations at least of men, during which Egypt had been inhabited; and if so, there must have been rulers; and the names of these rulers, they might add, were legible on the monuments, in their hieratic papyri, and in the dynasties of Manetho. The point being once yielded to add these XV generations and 443 years, it followed that either some new founder of the monarchy must be pretended, anterior to Menes, or that Menes and his VII Tanite successors with their 190 years must be put up by 443 years, the XV generations and 443 years preceding this dynasty in the Chronicle being transposed so as to intervene between it and that Memphite dynasty of IV generations and 103 years by which in the Chronicle it is immediately followed. The device by which the Theban priests palliated this difficulty recalls to mind a criticism said to have been passed upon Eratosthenes himself, namely, that he treated history *geometrically*. They put Menes and his Tanites or

Thinites (whose names appeared in the temple at Abydos in the Thinite nome, and were so naturalised in Upper Egypt) at the head of all; (they could not do otherwise;) but as these 8 kings in 190 years had an average of something *under* 24 years, while the XV generations of the Cycle, to be taken in at once and prefixed, had in their 443 years an average of 29½ years each, they reduced the eight Tanite generations of Dyn. VIII of Manetho (I of Africanus) to *five*, continuing to the five the full sum of 190 years: and after these they inserted a selection of *ten* names or generations with 253 years; and again they added *five* more with 190 years; so that, taking the whole *twenty* generations together, one might at will either regard the 190 years of Dyn. XVI of the Chronicle, with Menes at their head, as standing first, and the XV generations and 443 years of the Cycle as following and interposed between them and the IV Memphite generations and 103 years of Dyn. XVII of the Chronicle, *or* reckon the XV generations with 443 years of the Cycle first, as they actually stand in the Chronicle, and then the 190 years of Dyn. XVI of the Chronicle *after* the 443, in their proper place, so as to be followed immediately by 103 years, as Dyn. XVI is followed by Dyn. XVII in the Chronicle. Understood in this latter way the 190 years of the Chronicle would be, it is true, disjoined from Menes; but Menes was not *named* by the Chronicle; and its designation "*Tanites*" might be supposed to be still applicable in some sense to the earliest of those kings who followed next after Menes and the XV generations of the Cycle. The compression of VIII generations or reigns with a lower average than 24¾ years into V with the extraordinary average of 38 years each, was a change requisite for the exhibition of the XX generations with the symmetry above described. For if they had allowed eight generations twice over to the 190 years, once at either end of the 443, the seven generations or names of kings intervening could not have had a lower average than one of 36 years; whereas, with the contrivance actually adopted, the high average of the first V generations, or rather the exceptional length of the first two of them on which all the excess is thrown, might be excused by their antiquity; and after these the ordinary average of 24¾ was preservable throughout, one actual historical reign of enormous length, that of Phiops, enabling the priests to exhibit the 190 years the *second* time in only five generations without any great difficulty.

Still, when they had at starting suppressed three of the generations of the Chronicle, and so increased the average length of the reigns in one of its dynasties, this involved the necessity of making a compensatory addition of three generations, and a consequent reduction of the (particular) average length of the reigns in some one at least of the dynasties of the Chronicle still remaining after the 190 years of its Dyn. XVI had been amalgamated with the 443 of the Cycle. So, then, if there occurred below other additional reasons for varying, they would no longer be likely to make a point of preserving the *particular* averages of the Chronicle in filling up *any* of its dynasties. Only, the particular average length, viz. 29½ years, of the XV generations of the Cycle being exhibited for their 443 years, whether reckoned from the accession of Menes or from after the conclusion of his dynasty, the *general* average of 24½ years, given by the Chronicle in its 1881 years of kings to its LXXVI royal generations, would be necessarily exhibited also, so long as the same 1881 years were reckoned separately, apart from the 443 years of those XV generations in which the average is much higher, or at least apart from some one or more of them on which the whole excess of (5 × 15 =) 75 years producing their higher average may be concentrated. In fact it is so contrived that the kings named even for the XV generations and 443 years of the Cycle, whether reckoned before or after those of the 190 years of Dyn. XVI of the Chronicle, seem to have generally the average of 24¾ years or thereabouts, the whole *excess* of 75 years, which really raises their average to 29½, being divided between only *three* generations of 62, 79, and 100 years.

Again, it is to be regretted, on some accounts, that Eratosthenes could not make a point of adhering to the *particular* average lengths of the generations in spaces corresponding to each *particular dynasty* of the Chronicle. For the particular averages of its dynasties vary much; and the variations are closely connected with the real history and actual lives, and reigns of kings, underlying their artificially adjusted generations. Thus a very long average in any dynasty of the Chronicle, as in XXVII and XIX, hints either remarkable longevity in the reigning family, joined with peace, security, and prosperity, or else the inclusive reckoning of intervals of anarchy, doubtful succession, or national disgrace, which the native priests were unable or unwilling to cover with a true series of actual reigns. Averages on the other hand shorter than 24½ years in any dynasties of the Chronicle, as in Dyn. XXII and others, show that the actual kings alluded to had short reigns, though not so short nor otherwise such as to cause them to be omitted and consolidated with the longer reigns to which they were adjacent.

A third point in which Eratosthenes, if he had tasked his informants to the utmost, and had made the most of the royal command, might perhaps have extracted from them some closer approaches to the truth of history, is in the method adopted for reducing the length of Manetho's dynasties within the bounds, not indeed of truth, but of that limited addition of 443 years which he allowed them to make to the 1881 years of the monarchy. With the exception of some single reign in some one of the dynasties, Manetho, we may presume, would not needlessly falsify the *units* which he found in the hieratic lists either in the sums of particular reigns or in those of dynasties; but he would make such additions or subtractions as he needed in whole *decads;* and the Theban priests, only one generation later, must have been perfectly able to detect his additions of fictitious or concurrent or suppressions of historical and successive years. But the reductions in the list of Eratosthenes have been made by suppressing whole reigns, years and names together; or sometimes, as it seems, in consolidating two reigns the name only was taken from one of the two and the figures only from the other, so as to afford an obscure hint of the historical existence of both. Thus, when dealing with Dyn. VIII of Manetho (I of Africanus) which they rightly reduced by 63 years from 253 to 190, the sum of the Chronicle, having a reason for also consolidating the eight generations into five, the priests made this double reduction of the years and the generations by one process, whereas one might have hoped that they would first cut off the six decads and the three units from those particular reigns to which they had been unchronologically added by Manetho, and then add the true years of the three names to be suppressed to the other adjacent reigns. But to have done this would have interfered with their purpose of concentrating upon the first two reigns the whole of that excess of 67½ years by which the five generations, if taken together, must exceed the ordinary average.

The Chronicle, in its first two consecutive dynastics, XVI and XVII, *taken together*, has XII generations, with an average in (190 + 103 =) 293 years of 24 years and 5 months to each. But Manetho, in his six dynasties of Lower Egypt, numbered VIII to XIII (I to VI incl. of Afric.) naming (viii + ix + ix + viii + ix + vi =) xlix kings, and making the sum of their years to amount to (253 + 302 + 214 + 277 + 248 + 197 =) 1491, has an average length of $30\frac{21}{49}$ years and between 4 and 5 months for each actual reign, showing a systematic addition of nearly one fourth part to the ordinary average (viz. $24\frac{5}{12}$) of the Chronicle. Thus his average is higher even than that of 29½ years given by the Chronicle to its XV generations of the Cycle, though *they* are mere abstract lives, and not reigns; whereas the average ought certainly to be less to any considerable number of actual reigns than in an artificial chronological series in which very short reigns are consolidated with longer, as we see done in the astronomical canon of Ptolemy. We should therefore be justified in assuming that Eratosthenes of himself would probably have estimated the sums allowable as historical for Manetho's first six dynastics of viii, ix, ix, viii, ix, and vi kings, conjecturally and approximatively at 198, 222¼, 220½, 198, 222¼, and 148¼ years, and would then have shortened the sums actually given by Manetho, so as on the whole to suit this estimate, yet perhaps so as not to let the changes made on its account affect the units. For Dyn. VIII of Manetho (I of Afric.) we know from other sources that the true chronological sum was 190 years, being 8 *less* than were allowed by our estimate. Of the following dynasties, Dyn. IX (II of Afric.) would have 222 years allowed instead of 302 or 222½; Dyn. X. (III of Afric.) would have 214, Manetho's own sum, since it is 8½ *under* the estimate; Dyn. XI (IV of Afric.) would have 177 perhaps, instead of 277 (the sum given) or 198; Dyn. XII (V of Africa.) would have 228 instead of 248 or 222½; and lastly, Dyn. XIII (VI of Afric.) would have, besides its own 147 due to it by the average, compensatory additions of (6 + ½ + 8½ + 21 =) 36 — 6½ = 30½ years due to Dynasties VIII, X, XI, and XII (I, III, IV, and V of Afric.) by the average, but excluded by us above in fixing their sums, and as yet uncompensated. So Dynasty XIII (VI of Afric.) will have its sum brought up to 150½, or rather to 177, as we must fix it if the units of the sum given are to be preserved, instead of having either the 197 years of Manetho's lists, or the 147 of our estimate based upon the average of the Chronicle. At first sight it would seem that the sum for Dynasty XI (IV of Afric.) should have been made higher by two decads, and that for Dynasty XIII (VI of Afric.) lower by two decads; but it is certain from other sources that Dyn. XI (IV of Afric.) had a somewhat *shorter* continuance not only than 198, but even than 184 years, and the units of the sum given being 7, 177 is the highest sum admissible. And in Dyn. XIII (VI of Afric.) the exceptional reign of Phiops of 94 years, exhibited by the lists, quite justifies our addition made on other grounds of mere calculation to the sum of the dynasty, which, with such a giant inclosed in it, could scarcely fail to exhibit some disturbance of the ordinary average. Thus, with 190, 222, 214, 177, 228, and 177 years, making a sum in all of 1208 years, we should have for Manetho's xlix reigns very nearly the ordinary average of 24¼ years, an addition of 4¼ years only to the whole sum being needed to give it exactly. And with this average so obtained, the sums of each of the dynasties would still continue to exhibit the same units as in the unreduced lists of Manetho, excepting only in his Dyn. VIII (I of Afric.), to which we know him to have attached a very peculiar addition of *three* units (just those needed by the calculation above), really belonging to Dyn. XXVI far below, and so not rightly separable on any reduction, unless special compensation were provided for them elsewhere. Eratosthenes, however, and his assistants, who used the lists of Manetho only in subordination to the chronology of the Chronicle, certainly reduced the first dynasty of kings, from 253 years, not to 193 as Manetho's scheme would have required, but to the 190 of the Chronicle. It is true that the units of Manetho's sums, whether in this or in the other following dynasties (in which latter there is no reason to suspect him of having varied from the hieratic lists), are of less importance than they would have been, if all Manetho's additions had consisted simply of fictitious decads of years. As it is, his additions were no doubt made in great part, if not entirely, by adding up unchronologically all the years of certain reigns which were in part only associate and concurrent; and so the units in the sum total of the years both concurrent *and* chronological of any reign or dynasty *cannot* be taken to represent those which would have appeared if only the chronological years had been added up together. Still, as Manetho's are the only sums we have to begin with, it is best in reducing them to the average of the Chronicle and Eratosthenes to alter them no more than the process really requires.

On coming to the dynasties of *Upper* Egypt, for which he had no undue partiality, the conduct of Manetho is reversed. From the end of his last Memphite dynasty, Dyn. XIII. (VI of Afric.), to the end of his Dyn. XVI (XIV of Afric.) inclusively, he gives us no more occasion to suspect him of lengthening unduly the reigns of the kings. On the contrary, in two out of these three dynasties of Upper Egypt, he even suppresses their names, and manifestly curtails their years; so that Eratosthenes, instead of *reducing* their sums to the average length of the Chronicle, would have rather to *add*, or to estimate how many years ought to be understood to have belonged historically to each of those dynasties.

It is true that lower down, in the last-placed of all the early dynasties, viz., in that of the Shepherds, immediately preceding Dyn. XVIII, the sum of 259 years and 10 months, given to only six kings, seems again to call for reduction; since, at an average of 24½, they could claim only 147 years.

But there are signs that the Shepherd kings were really long-lived; and the Chronicle also seems to have reckoned only *four* of them to the 184 years of its Dyn. XXVII, being the time of their ascendency or supremacy. It is more probable, too, that they had been already for some time settled in the Delta before they "took Memphis," than that they became dominant on first coming in, all at once; especially as Manetho himself has given his readers to understand that there was *no fighting*, as with invaders, on their first coming in, but that they *presumed* afterwards, with a *strange audacity*, to make themselves masters. And lastly, it is most unlikely that Manetho, after having discontinued during three whole dynasties his former excessive average, should suddenly break out again into exaggeration merely to do honour to the Shepherds, even though they *did* belong locally to the Delta. It is safest, therefore, to suppose that, since the average of 43 years and 8 months has been allowed by him to kings whose memory was odious, and of whom scarcely any monumental traces have escaped, this average, however wonderful, did not exceed the truth.

But leaving this discussion about a dynasty which the Theban priests, as limited by Eratosthenes, would be sure to omit, let us return to those *three* of the "Upper Country" which in Manetho's lists follow next after the *six* of the Lower, that is, of Tanis, Memphis, and Central Egypt. Whether there were really only three in all for Upper Egypt, or whether Manetho did full justice only to those of the "Lower Country," while he compressed the dynasties of the Upper into half their number, we need not as yet decide; but we already begin to suspect that the latter was the case, when we notice how he has dealt with the *names* and *years* of those three dynasties of Upper Egypt which he has admitted.

To the first of them, Dyn. XIV (XI of Africanus), connected locally with Thebes (or with Hermonthis on the west bank, which seems to have been the original city), Manetho gives XVI kings, a number parallel to the XVII of the two consecutive Dynasties X and XI (III and IV of Africanus), connected locally with Memphis. But of the names of these kings he mentions *not one;* and while he has given to the XVII Memphites no less than (214 + 277 =) 491 years, reducible for Eratosthenes to (220½ + 177 =) 397½, he gives to the XVI Diospolites only 43, that is, less than 3 years apiece. The truth is, that he suppresses altogether both their names and their years, attaching only in appearance to their dynasty a number of 43 years, which he had a reason for wishing to distinguish, and again appending the name of Amenemhe I., with 16 years, so as to isolate it at the end of his Book I. for a similar reason. Eratosthenes, therefore, would have to seek from the priests the names of the XVI kings of Dyn. XIV (XI of Afric.), to whom he would be prepared to allow about 392 years.

In Dyn. XV (XII of Africanus), also called Diospolite, though not specially connected with the locality of Thebes, Eratosthenes would find VII, or, taking in Amenemhe I., VIII kings, *all named*, with 160 or 176 years; so that only an addition of 11½ or of 20 years would be needed to bring them up to his average. The priests might tell him, from their hieratic papyri, that the 43 years nominally attached to Manetho's Dyn. XIV (XI of Afric.) belonged really to the following Dynasty XV (XII of Afric.); and that if they, and the 16 of Amenemhe I., were added to the 160, the sum obtained, viz. 219, would *exceed* the true sum of the dynasty by 6 years.

But in the third and last of Manetho's early dynasties of Upper Egypt, whether called Diospolite or Xoite (that is, Nubian), Eratosthenes had before him as many perhaps as XXXVI or XXX kings, about whose names and historical continuance he would need information, the sum of 184 years given to them being scarcely more admissible for XXXVI or XXX, or even for XXVI, than that of 43 was for XVI kings. This sum, which affords to the kings only 5 years and 4 months, or at most 6 years each, would suggest of itself the suspicion that either Manetho had some reason for wishing to distinguish the number 184, and therefore only attached it to a line of XXXVI kings whose true historical duration he suppressed; or else, if the 184 years truly and alone belong to this dynasty, that he had some reason for *compressing several distinct lines of kings into one;* or, lastly, that the text of his lists is corrupt, and that it originally had some smaller number of kings. Thirty-six kings (to say nothing of LXXVI which appear in the text of Ptolemy of Mendes and Africanus), if consecutive in one local line, would cover, according to the ordinary average, 882 years, being nearly double the whole space of 477 years allowed by the Chronicle between Menes and Dyn. XVIII, and more than double the time which any other local line, or consecutive lines, preceding have appeared to fill; the two Dynasties, VIII and IX (I and II of Africanus), *even if* both locally connected with the *city* itself of Tanis, having claimed only (190 + 222 =) 412, the two consecutive Dynasties X and XI (III and IV of Africanus) at Memphis having claimed only (214 + 177 =) 391, and the single continuous line of the local Thebans, viz. Dyn. XIV (XI of Africanus), claiming only 392 years. But to suppose a line of Upper Egypt, and one, too, comparatively unimportant, to run back 400 years above Menes, or to have commenced even contemporaneously with the earliest Memphites or Diospolites, to say nothing of the still earlier Tanites, would be either plainly absurd, or in the highest degree improbable. Eratosthenes, therefore, would of himself, no doubt, see that the XXXVI Xoite kings of Dyn. XVI (XIV of Afric.) (supposing that number, or XXX, or even XXVI to have been in his text), must be a consolidation of several contemporaneous lines, all perhaps of the same blood, which, if exhibited in generations, so as to suit the space of 184 years, would not exceed the number of VIII. And the Theban priests would tell him, that there had really been in the southern parts of Upper Egypt, and in the "Lower and Upper Countries" of Nubia, a numerous family of kings, making a great show in the hieratic papyri, whose Egyptian blood was derived in part from a daughter of Amenemhe I., or Sesortasen I., and whose commencement dated from some point of time later than the conquest of Nubia; so that their continuance, if reckoned from the death of Sesortasen I. (or the capture of Memphis by the Shepherds), in B.C. 1932, to the accession of Amosis, the head of Dyn. XVIII, in B.C. 1748, would be just 184 years. But no doubt they had really commenced from 20 to 30 years earlier than the death of Sesortasen I., so as to cover in all perhaps, in nine or ten generations, a space of about 216 years.

Taking all the regal dynasties of Manetho's Book I. as seemingly consecutive, and *unreduced*, Eratosthenes had before him in the collective sum of the *years*, viz. 1491, of the first six dynasties, those, that is, of *Lower* Egypt, exactly *three times* the true chronological number of (190+103+184=) 477 years intervening according to the Chronicle between Menes and Dyn. XVIII (as if it had been meant to allude under this triple repetition to each of the three chief divisions of the Delta, Memphis, and Central Egypt); and besides this sum of thrice 477 years, viz. 1431, there was yet further contained in the 1491 a fractional remainder of 60 years, capable of coalescing either with the 43 years of the first dynasty of Upper Egypt, Dyn. XIV (XI of Africanus) into the sum of 103, or with the first 124, the only unchronological, years of the second dynasty of Upper Egypt, Dyn. XV (XII of Africanus), into the sum of 184 years; while, after the first 124 of Dyn. XV, its remaining 36 years (124+36=160), and the 184 given to the third and last of the early dynasties of Upper Egypt, and all the years of the remaining dynasties, are *upon the whole* consecutive and chronological, forming a sum of 1881 years in *fifteen* more complete dynasties, parallel to the 1881 years given by the Chronicle in its last *fifteen* dynasties and LXXVI generations for the duration of the monarchy.

So, in fact, Manetho having, besides the 1881 years of the Chronicle, 1674 additional years of kings, of which (22+217 =) 239 only are in themselves, though not in their attribution, chronological, and having given of these 1491 (which are thrice 477, and 60 over) to his six early dynasties of *Lower* Egypt (and 16 inconvenient years he isolated between his Dynasties XIV and XV, so as to include them in his Book I), he gave to the three early dynasties of *Upper* Egypt *no other unchronological years* than two complementary sums, the one of 43 years which he attached to the first, and the other of 124 which he attached to the second of the three dynasties in question, that these same sums might both coalesce with the remainder of 60 years belonging to the sum of the six dynasties of Lower Egypt, so as to make with it, or rather to indicate, the one of them the sum of 103, the other the sum of 184 years. This will be made clearer by the following table, in which all Manetho's unchronological years, and years of Gods and Demigods unchronologically transferred to kings, are printed in red.

### Table A, of 1674 Years

either essentially unchronological, or transferred from Gods and Demigods to Kings, in Books I. and II. of Manetho.

In Dyn. VIII, IX, 253 = (22 + 14 + 217) or (190 + 63) + 302 = 555
In Dyn. X, XI, 214 + 277 = 491
In Dyn. XII, XIII, 248 + 197 = 445

Sum of the years of the Six Dynasties of Lower Egypt . . 1491

But this sum of 1491 is equivalent to

190 + 103 + 184 = 477
190 + 103 + 184 = 477 But 60
190 + 103 + 184 = 477 43

(1431 + 60) + 43 of Dyn. XIV of Upper Egypt = 103
124 of Dyn. XV of Upper Egypt in Book II.

184

Sum total of years of kings unchronological or transferred in Books I. and II. of Manetho 1674, originating in 22 of the XIII Gods + 14 of the Cycle thrown up + 217 of the VIII Demigods + (978 + 443 =) 1421 of the Cycle thrown up.

### Table B, of 1881 Years

which are chronological and parallel *on the whole* with the 1881 years of the Kings in the Chronicle, the places of particular suppressions (in red) and of compensations made by Manetho being distinguished by brackets, and by the marks for minus – after the sums of years suppressed, and for plus + before the sums of years or months interpolated.

36 (being the last 36 of Dyn. XV, XII of Afric.) of Upper Egypt .
184 of Dyn. XVI, of Upper Egypt .
257 of Dyn. XVII, of the Shepherds } = 477 = { 190 / 103 / 184
{ [+2.10m] of the same Dyn. XVII : 165 of Dyn. XVIII

: [15 – of the same] : 168 years to the end of the same Dynasty XVIII : [+15 prefixed to Dyn. XIX] : 194 really belonging to the same Dynasty XIX.

Sum of the chronological years of Book II., 1020 years and 10 months, which with 124 unchronological at the commencement of the same Book make a sum total of 1144 years and 10 months.

Book III. has 135 of Dyn. XX : 93 of Dyn. XXI : [+37 of the same] : [1 – on Dyn. XXII] : 120 of the same : 89 of Dyn. XXIII : 6 of Dyn. XXIV : [16 – on the same] : 40 of Dyn. XXV : [21 – on the same] : [27 – on Dyn. XXVI] : 150 of the same : [+6 months of the same] : 124 of Dyn. XXVII : [+ 4 months of the same] : [+6 years of Dyn. XXVII] : 19 of Dyn. XXIX : [+1 year and 4 months of the same] : 38 of Dyn. XXX.—Sum of Book III, 860 years and 2 months; which with the 1020 years and 10 months of Book II. make the sum total of chronological years in the last fifteen dynasties (with the 36 ending Dynasty XV) to amount to 1881.

But as regards the *reigns* or *generations* of the first ten dynasties of kings, six of Lower and three of Upper Egypt, and one of the Shepherds, being the materials which Eratosthenes or his assistants would have in the first instance to review and prepare, and then to use in covering with names $(190 + 443 + 443)$ or $\left(\begin{array}{c} +156+103+184 \\ 34+156+103+184+156= \end{array}\right)$ 1076 years of the Chronicle, these ten dynasties, the six with their reigns reduced, and the three with their reigns expanded, to the average length of 24½ years which Eratosthenes, following the Chronicle, would allow for kings, (the Shepherd dynasty alone being unaltered,) are exhibited below in the table C. In this the kings of each dynasty are represented by the numbers 1, 2, 3, &c. in the upper one of two lines, and the reign of each king as reduced or expanded (the units of Manetho being preserved), is set in the lower line immediately below that number in the upper line by which he is represented, the whole being arranged within the chronological spaces (viz. 190 + 103 + 184, in all 477 years) of the

Chronicle. For the sake of clearness, that the whole may be seen and referred to together, the generations finally selected or compounded by Eratosthenes or his assistants, with the years given to each, are also subjoined in two other similar lines parallel to the kings and the reigns of Manetho. In both of the two parallel schemes, of Manetho and Eratosthenes, those kings or generations which belong also to the Chronicle are printed in small capitals; and in the series of Manetho the figures indicating kings or reigns which (whether as reduced or unreduced) are found also in the scheme of Eratosthenes, are all printed in red. Where kings or reigns of Manetho are omitted by Eratosthenes for want of room, but are still alluded to, or in some way implied to have existed, this is signified by a plus sign + placed where the name or reign so alluded to should have stood, if it had been expressly reckoned. And where any king or reign is entirely omitted and unnoticed by Eratosthenes, this is indicated in like manner by a minus sign—in the place which should have belonged to it. Manetho's second dynasty of Tanites (all but its last two reigns, put up into a place not their own) ,his dynasty of Elephantinites, and the dynasty of the Shepherds, being all entirely omitted (though the existence of the second dynasty of Tanites is perhaps alluded to) by Eratosthenes, these three dynasties have each of them in the table only the two lines of figures properly belonging to it, without any parallel lines for the scheme of Eratosthenes. This omission of three lines of kings with 302, 248, and 260 years respectively, brings down the sum of Manetho's unchronological years by 810, from 1674 to 864; and the 864 when the average is reduced become 674; so that if Eratosthenes had had no *additions* to make on Dynasties XIV and XVI of Manetho, (XI and XIV of Afric.) there would have been only (674—443=) 231 years too many for him to place; indeed only (231—156=) 75 years too many; since, as we shall presently find, he makes room for five more early generations of Upper Egypt than he could otherwise have placed by depressing the head of Dyn. XVIII to the extent of 156 years. But before entering into the details of his scheme we must complete our review of his materials.

## TABLE C.

| YEARS OF THE CHRONICLE. | DYN. XVI. 190 YRS. | XVII. 103 YRS. | XXVII. 164 YRS. |
|---|---|---|---|
| Dyn. VIII. IX. Man. | I II III IV V VI VII VIII | 1. 2. 3. 4. | 5. 6. 7. 8. 9. |
| Yrs. reduced. - - | 32. 27. 21. 23. 20. 26. 18. 26. | 28. 19. 27. 17. | 41. 17. 25. 48. 30. |
| Gen. of Erat. - - | I II III + + IV V + | — — — — | — Dyn. X. 6. |
| Yrs. of Erat. - - | 62. 59. 32. + 19. + 18. + | — — — — | — — — 79. |
| Dyn. X. XI. Man. | 1. 2. 3. 4. 5. | VI VII 8. 9. | 1. 2. 3. 4. 5. 6. 7 8. |
| Yrs. reduced. - - | 26. 29 7. 17. 16. | 19. 42. 30. 26. | 29. 43. 26. 38. 15. 12. 10? 9. |
| Gen. of Erat. - - | + 7. 8. 9. 10. | XI XII [+ +] | [13. 14.] 15. 16. 17. 18. + 19. |
| Yrs. of Erat. - - | + 6. 30. 26. 20. | 16. 22. [+ +] | 13. 10. 29. 37. 31. 33. + 35. |
| Dyn. XII. Man. - | 1. 2. 3. | 4. 5. 6. 7. | 8. 9. |
| Yrs. reduced. - - | 28. 13. 20. | 17. 20. 44. 9. | 44. 33. |
| Dyn. XIII. Man. - | 1. 2. 3. | - - - IV 5. | 6. |
| Yrs. reduced. - - | 20. 33. 7. | - - 24. 1. | 12. |
| Gen. of Erat. - - | + + + | - - XX 21. | 22. |
| Yrs. of Erat. - - | + + + | - - 100. 1. | 6. |
| Dyn. XIV. Man. | 1. 2. 3. 4. | 5. 6. 7. 8. | 9. 10. 11. 12. 13. 14. 15. 16. |
| Yrs. *augmented* - - | 25. 24. 25. 24. | 25. 24. 25. 24. | 25. 24. 25. 24. 25. 24. 25. 24. |
| Gen. of Erat. - - | 23. 24. 25. 26. | + + + + | + + + + 27. 28. 29. 30, |
| Yrs. of Erat. - - | 22. 12. 8. 18. | + + + + | + + + + 7. 12. 11. 60. |
| Dyn. XV. Man. - | | 1. II | 3. 4. 5. 6. 7. 8. |
| Yrs. of Man. - - | | 16. 46. | 38. 48. 8. 8. 8. 4. |
| Gen. of Erat. - - | | 31. XXXII | 33. + 34. 35. — — |
| Yrs. of Erat. - | | + 42 | 23. + 58. 43. — — |
| Dyn. XVI. of Man. | | 1. | 2. 3. 4. 5. 6. 7. 8. 9. |
| XIV. of Afric. - | | 1. | 2. 3. 4. 5. 6. 7. 8. 9. |
| four concurrent | | 1. | 2. 3. 4. 5. 6. 7. 8. 9. |
| lines of Nubians - | | 1. | 2. 3. 4. 5. 6. 7. 8. 9. |
| Yrs. *augmented* - | | 25. | 24. 25. 24. 25. 24. 25. 24. 25. |
| Gen. of Erat. - - | | — | + + + + 36. 37. 38. + |
| Yrs. of Erat. - - | | — | + + + + 5. 19. 63. + |
| Dyn. XVII. Man. | | 1. 2. | III IV V VI |
| Yrs. *unreduced.* - | | 19. 44. | 35.7m. 61. 50.1m. 49.2m. |

*Sums of the kings and years of the above dynasties of Manetho as reduced, and of Eratosthenes as actually specified,*

| | | | | |
|---|---|---|---|---|
| *Man.* | VIII, IX | ( I, II, Afric. | ) VIII + VII | Tanites? 193 + 222 yrs. |
| *Erat.* | VIII, IX | ( I, II, Afric. | ) V — | Thinites 190 — yrs. |
| *Man.* | X, XI | ( III, IV, Afric. | ) IX + VIII | Memphites 214 + 177 yrs. |
| *Erat.* | X, XI | ( III, IV, Afric. | ) VII + VII | Memphites 201 + 178 yrs. |
| *Man.* | XII, XIII | ( V, VI, Afric. | ) IX + VI | Memphites 228 + 167 yrs. |
| *Erat.* | XII, XIII | ( V, VI, Afric. | ) — III | Memphites — 107 yrs. |
| *Man.* | XIV, XV, XVI | (XI, XII, XIV, Afric.) | XVI + VIII + XXXVI | Thebans 392 + 176 + 184 yrs. |
| *Erat.* | XIV, XV, XVI | (XI, XII, XIV, Afric.) | VIII + V + III | Thebans 150 + 163 + 87 yrs. |

The parallel lines in the Scheme D, and the figures in Table C, are the same thing, except that the parallel lines in D exhibit to the eye the chronological spaces in their true relative positions and proportions, while the reigns or generations subdividing them are to be found in the Table C.

## Scheme D.

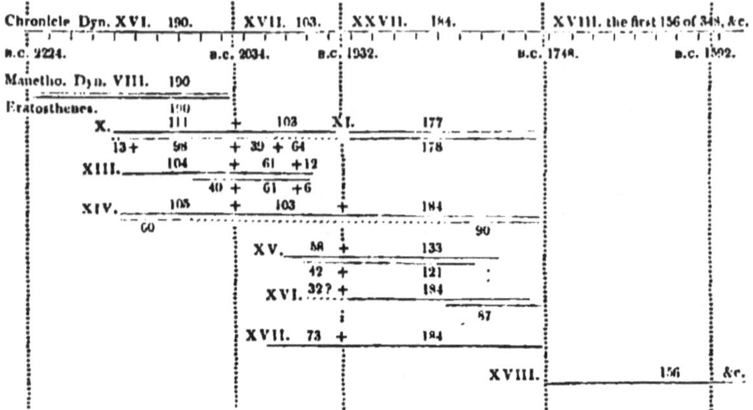


That reduction which we have seen to be called for by the average length of the reigns in the first six royal dynasties of Manetho, Eratosthenes and his assistants unfortunately could not make uniformly and naturally, because those XV new generations in 443 years which were to be inserted among the kings of the Chronicle had an average length not of 24½ years each, but of 29½, not so much as 1 year less than the average length of reign of Manetho's XLIX kings. On the other hand they could not give to the generations of the first dynasty of kings those 63 years by which Manetho had increased their average without departing from the framework of the Chronicle. So they retained and marked its sum of 190 years, suppressing or consolidating three of the VIII generations of the Chronicle, and three of the VIII corresponding names of Manetho, whereby the remaining five obtained an average length of 38 years each, the excess however being all concentrated upon the first two reigns. And the like they did again, after interposing ten generations, as has been said above, marking the 190 years a second time in five generations as before, by the help of a transposition of two of the shorter reigns in Dyn. XI (IV of Afric.) from the bottom to the top of their dynasty, and by the help of 64 years of a whole century given in a single generation to Phiops of Dyn. XIII (VI of Afric.). Having thus made a space answering to Dyn. XVI of the Chronicle at both ends, and in each case with only five generations, they were able to give to the intermediate ten generations (which have 253 years, and are capable of coalescing on either side with the five adjacent into fifteen generations with 443 years) an average of something over 25 years, being little more than the average of the Chronicle, instead of the $30\frac{1}{3}$ of Manetho, or the $29\frac{1}{2}$ of the generations of the Cycle. Thus, when it might have seemed natural rather to follow uniformly the average of Manetho, or something very near it, as agreeing with that properly belonging to the XV generations of the Cycle now inserted among the kings, they showed their sense of its inaccuracy; and at the same time they cleverly disposed of that excess which they were obliged to introduce somewhere, by lumping it all together in two or three places where it could cause no historical error. For in Dyn. VIII (XVI of the Chronicle, I of Afric.) it is easy to restore the three names suppressed; and for Dyn. XI (IV of Afric.), though they omitted one name and transposed two others, the sum of years, viz. 178, approaches within 6 to the 184 of the parallel Dyn. XXVII of the Chronicle, and so probably represents the true duration of the tributary Memphites. The intervening generations *represent* really 201, but as placed only 195, years of Dyn. X (III of Afric.), 156 of them seeming to be anterior to Dyn. XVII of the Chronicle, 39 seeming coincident with its first 39 years, and 6 seeming to run on unchronologically, merely to depress the 178 following years of Dyn. XI (IV of Afric.), so as to end together with the 184 of Dyn. XXVII of the Chronicle. But when Dyn. XI (IV of Afric.) is put down to its true chronological place, and when the whole of the 103 years of Dyn. XVII of the Chronicle, instead of only 39, are interposed between it and the end of the VIII Tanites, coincident seemingly with the end of the 156th but really of the 162nd year of the earliest Memphites, it is by no means to be thought that these latter continued only for 39 years into the space of Dyn. XVII of the Chronicle; on the contrary, it is certain that they continued during the whole 103 years, to the time of the Shepherd domination. So either 64 years and two or three kings are to be added to those of Eratosthenes, making XI or XII kings in all, and 265 years, if the Memphites began only 28 years after Menes the founder of Memphis; or else, if the number of 201 or rather 214 years is their whole duration, their line, ending when the Shepherds took Memphis in B.C. 1932, cannot have begun earlier than in B.C. 2145, 79 years after Menes; and the first reign of 79 years really covers two kings and 51 out of 64 years omitted below. And this no doubt is the more probable supposition.

Independently of any general principle as to the average length to be admitted for the reigns of the kings, the admission of the consecutive series of the Chronicle, making only 477 years from Menes to Dyn. XVIII, and the substitution of its sum of 190 years for the first Tanite dynasty, instead of the 253 of Manetho, would of itself render a proportionate reduction of the years of Manetho's five following dynasties inevitable. Otherwise it would be impossible to make the sums of Manetho's dynasties lie within the limits of the Chronicle. For if we give with the Chronicle 190 years only to the first Tanite dynasty, and suppose, as seems at first natural, Manetho's second dynasty of Tanites (not Thinites) to follow it, as kings of the same lineage and locality, only subordinate, or perhaps of a younger branch, after the supremacy had passed to Memphis, the sum of Manetho, viz. 302 years, unreduced, and beginning from the end of the 190 of the earlier Tanites, would not only extend through the 103 years of Dyn. XVII of the Chronicle, which should be its natural limit, but also through all the 184 of the Shepherds of Dyn. XXVII of the Chronicle, which is highly improbable, and, more than this, through 15 years of Dyn. XVIII, which is plainly absurd. So again as regards the two Memphite dynasties X and XI (III and IV of Afric.), which are certainly consecutive, with (214 + 277 =) 491 years, even if they were supposed to begin with Menes himself, still the first of them would run 24 years into Dyn. XVII of the Chronicle, and the second, after covering its 79 remaining years and all the 184 years of the Shepherds (who yet set up a *new family* at Memphis), would run on 14 years into Dyn. XVIII, which again is plainly absurd.

But if it be supposed that the second Tanite dynasty was contemporary with the first, as if two divisions of the city of Tanis separated by the water, or two cities both in the same region of Tanis, had each its own line of kings,—and if in like manner it be supposed that Dyn. XII (V of Afric.) of Elephantinite-Memphites (that is Memphites perhaps of the East Bank) were contemporary with those of Dyn. X or XI (III or IV of Afric.), and those of Dyn. XIII again (VI of Afric.) with those of Dyn. X (III of Afric.),—then, and in every case the reductions made in the principal dynasties will require a similar reduction to be made of all other dynasties grouped together with them and originally similar to them in the average lengths of their reigns.

But besides the books of Manetho, and the Chronicle, and those hieratic sources used by Manetho which would be equally known to the priests at Thebes, a word must be said of other materials. For though, when it is said that Manetho wrote "from the sacred records of the temples," or that Eratosthenes made out his Theban list of kings "from the monuments," the records and monuments intended are no doubt only the hieratic papyri, and there is no probability that either Manetho, or Eratosthenes, or the priests his assistants, had ***studied*** the ***monuments*** properly so-called with a view to history; still there were at Thebes itself, and at Abydos in the Thebaid, some monumental lists of kings, especially that of Rameses II. at Abydos, and that of Thothmes III. at Karnak, so remarkable, that the Theban priests having them before their eyes could not fail to think and speak of them when consulted by Eratosthenes.

Of the Abydos tablet, which seems to have exhibited in its uppermost and second lines (26 + 25 =) 51 cartouches of kings, much need not be said. Its series may probably have commenced with Menes and his seven Tanite successors, who would so be naturalised as "Tenites," This or *Teni* being the civil capital of the nome in which Abydos and its temple were situated. For in other monumental lists of Dynasties XVIII and XIX, Menes, though singly, or with only one other intermediate link, viz. either Mentuhotep Ra-neb-kher, or Sesortasen I., stands at the head. But the first 14 names in the upper line and the first 8 at least in the second are broken away; and the 12 names remaining entire in the upper line are scarcely to be identified with *any one series* in Manetho's lists. In the second line the XII legitimate kings of Dyn. XVIII ending with Rameses II., are immediately preceded by the kings of Dyn. XV (XII of Africanus.)

The Thothmes Chamber of Karnak demands a more particular attention; and as there will be occasion to refer to it in detail, the relative position of its kings shall be here exhibited in a tabular form:

| | *g* | *c* | *a* | *e* *h* | |
|---|---|---|---|---|---|
| Thothmes III. offering. | 1] [7 6, 5, 4. | 8, 2, 1.] | [1, 2, 3, | 4, 5, 6, 7, 8, | Thothmes III. offering. |
| | 5, 4, 3, 2, 1,] | [1, 2, 3. | 9, 10.] [10. | 9, 8, 7, 6, 5, | |
| Thothmes III. offering. | 2, 3. 4. 5, | 6, 7.] 6, | 3, 2, 1,] | [1, 2, 3, 4, | Thothmes III. offering. |
| | 1] [13.+12, 11. 10. | 9, 8, 7, | 4, 5, 6, | 7, 8, 9, 10.] | |
| | | *d* | *b* | *f* | |

*a b* is a line dividing the wall of the chamber immediately opposite to the entrance from top to bottom: *c d* and *e f* are the two corners; the spaces to the right of *e f* and to the left of *c d*, are the side walls to the right and left of the spectator as he enters. The figures on the four lines represent LXI kings, all seated, with his name (generally, but not always, the throne-name) added to each. They all face towards Thothmes III., who is represented four times over, standing before a table of offerings, and "offering to his ancestors the kings of Upper and the kings of Lower Egypt." So the four lines of kings to the right of the spectator are all *dos-à-dos* to the four lines to his left, the whole being divided by the line *a b* into two distinct groups.

It seems, however, that in this Theban monument of the fourth king of Dyn. XVIII, the distinction of the "Upper and Lower Countries" divides not so much the Delta and the region of Memphis from the Thebaid, as the district of Thebes itself and Central Egypt, including Memphis, from the more southern regions and the Lower and Upper Nubias. For of the four parallel lines of seated kings to the left of the spectator, who must be meant for the kings of the Lower Country, *none* are from the Delta, but the first seven may perhaps be identified with Manetho's earliest Memphite

Dynasty X (III of Africanus). At any rate Eratosthenes was made so to identify them. After these seven names (*some* names of kings belonging to this and other dynasties being as it seems omitted), there follow next, sitting and facing the same way, but to be read as if turned into the faces of the preceding, four kings certainly identifiable with Dyn. XIII of Manetho (VI of Afric.), which is called Memphite by him, but which no doubt reigned in Central Egypt, in the parts south of Memphis. After them there is a series of XIII names, the first of them styled only Prince, which are identifiable with Dyn. XIV of Manetho (XI of Afric.), both by their antiquity, by their number, approaching to XVI, and by their known connection with the locality of Thebes or Hermonthis. In the midst of these, sitting and facing apparently the same way, but really in inverse order, as if sitting into their faces, is a shorter line of VII kings, identical with those of Manetho's Dyn. XV (XII of Afric.), called by Manetho Diospolites like the former, but not like them locally residing at Thebes. So the group of the kings of the *Lower* Country, on the left hand side of the chamber, consists in all of four lines or dynasties of kings, connected with that part of Egypt of which Memphis was the northernmost and Thebes the most southern capital. But among these kings of the Lower Region we find no trace of either of Manetho's two Dynasties VIII and IX (I and II of Afric.) of Tanites, nor of his Dyn. XI (IV of Afric.) of those Memphites who built the Great Pyramids and were contemporaries of the Shepherds, nor of the kings of his Dyn. XII (V of Afric.), called Elephantinite. The names, so far as they remain and are legible, of the other four dynasties which *are* represented, though not without omissions, are as follows:—

Dyn. X (III of Afric.), IX Memphites.
1. *Ra-smen-teti*...? Gen. VI ? of Erat.
2. lost .......... Gen. VII ? of Erat.
3. lost ............ Gen. VIII ? of Erat.
4. *Assa* ......... Gen. IX ? of Erat.
5. *Aan* ......... Gen. X ? of Erat.
6. *Sahouru* ...... Gen. XI ? of Erat.
7. *Snefrou* ...... Gen. XII ? of Erat.

Dyn. XIII (VI Afric.), VI Memphites.
1. *Teti*............ — — —
2. *Papa* ......... Gen. XX of Erat.
3. *Meranre*...... Gen. XXI of Erat.
4. *Nepherchere* Gen. XXII of Erat.

Dyn. XIV (XI Afric.), XVI Diospolites.
1. *Nantef I., Prince* — —
2. *Mentuhotep I.* Gen. XXIII ? of Erat.
3. *Nantef II.* ... — — —
4. *Nantef III.* ... — — —
5. [*Nantef-aa* ?] Gen. XXIV ? of Erat.
6. *Nantef V.* ... Gen. XXV ? of Erat.
7. [*Ra-neb-toti*?] — — —
8. *Ra-sneferkar.* Gen XXVI ? of Erat.

9. *Ra-neb-kher* ...Gen. xxvii? of Erat.
10. *Ra-nub-cheper* Gen. xxviii of Erat.
11. *Tsescrenra* ... Gen. xxix? of Erat.
12. *Necht-en-ra* } Gen. xxx of Erat.
13. *Ra-sekenn* }
Dyn. XV (XII of Afric.) viii Diospolites.
1. *Ra-cheper-kar* Gen. xxxi. of Erat.
2. *Ra-s-hotep-het* Gen. xxxii of Erat.
3. *Ra-nub-karu* Gen. xxxiii of Erat.
4. [*Ra-khakaru?*] Gen. xxxiv of Erat.
5. [*Ra-en-ma?*] ...Gen. xxxv of Erat.
6. *Ra-ma-khrou* — — —
7. *Ra-sebek-nefrou* — — —

Thus on the left side of the chamber there were (7 + 4 + 13 + 7 =) xxxi names. On the other, to our right, for the kings of the Upper Country, there were xxx names; of which latter perhaps about half have been found also on other separate monuments. And as these both by their number, by their ascertained connection of lineage with Amenemhe I. and Sesortasen I., and also with the kings of Dyn. XVIII, and by their local connection with the southernmost part of Egypt and with Nubia, are clearly identified with Dyn. XVI of Manetho (XIV of Africanus), and their continuance must have been chiefly during those 184 years which are indicated by their sum in Manetho's lists, we may collect both that Manetho's genuine sum of the kings of this dynasty was either xxx or xxxvi rather than lxxvi, and also that several lines of kings, of the same lineage and general locality, are here consolidated into one. The symmetry of the two groups for the Upper and Lower Countries of itself suggests that as there are certainly four distinct lines in the one case, so there are probably three or four in the other; and the number of kings, if there are xxxvi, makes it plainly impossible to suppose that they were all consecutive. The names preserved on the right hand side of the Karnak Chamber are not here given, as Eratosthenes takes from them only three or four, and those are not identifiable. Their division in the scheme above into three dynasties or lines is merely conjectural, to show the sort of order in which the cartouches on the right side must be supposed to read, analogous to the order of those on the left.

With these materials for selection and compression before them, the Theban priests were called upon by Eratosthenes to draw out a list of generations of kings, either answering exactly to the lxxvi of the Chronicle in 1881 years, or at most only adding xv more generations with 443 years.

It is plain, therefore, that of the 1674 years of Manetho which are either unchronological altogether or unchronologically transferred to kings after Menes, they would have had to omit 1231, even if they had wished to adhere to Manetho's scheme as closely as possible. But this they were not likely so to adhere to as to favour unduly the early dynasties of Lower Egypt at the expense of those of Upper.

The first and simplest idea, seeing that Manetho had given nearly all his unchronological years to the six dynasties of Lower Egypt, would have been to retain for the dynasties of Upper Egypt the whole sum of 477 chronological years from Menes to Dyn. XVIII, which they already possessed in the scheme of Manetho, (only substituting some of those Diospolites of his Dynasties XIV, XV, and XVI, whose names and years he in great part suppresses, for the Shepherds, to whom he gives 260 years,) and then simply to prefix 443 unchronological years with names selected from the dynasties of Lower Egypt, instead of the much greater number given them by Manetho. But this would have required the distinct introduction of a line of kings with 443 years anterior to Menes and his seven successors, which could not be thought of. And as these eight Tanite kings, wherever they might seem to be placed, necessarily held the first 190 true and chronological years of the monarchy, their distinct enumeration as Thinites at the head of all left to the Thebans after the insertion of 443 unchronological years, only 103 + 184 = 287 of those 477 chronological years which by the scheme of Manetho, if *they* had been given in full, and the Shepherds neglected as only contemporaries, they would seem to occupy. The first operation then was not merely to *prefix* 443 unchronological years in XV generations, but to amalgamate these, as has been said above, with the first 190 chronological years, so that they might be reckoned with Menes, at the head of all, or after the 443 years apart from Menes at pleasure; and its result was the following scheme, the first 443 years of which may be regarded as corresponding to the thrice 477 and the remainder of 60 of the first six dynasties of kings of Manetho; while the rest begin and proceed concurrently with his 1881 chronological years; i. e. from after the 124th year of his Dyn. XV.

## SCHEME E.

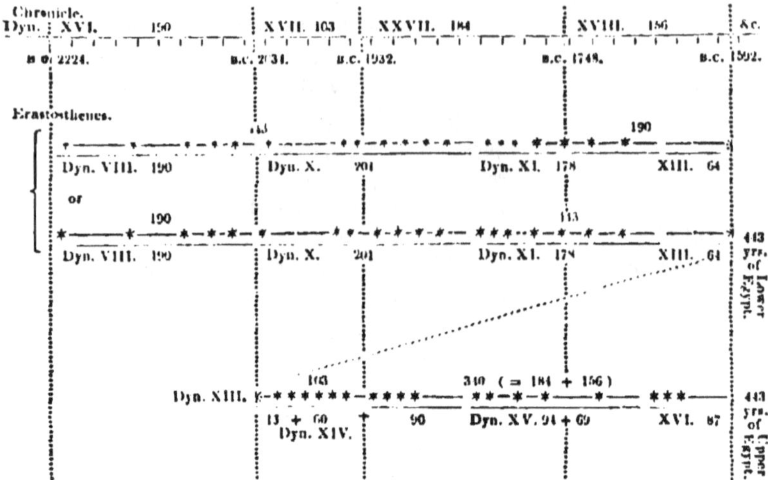


For the composition of these XX generations with (190 + 443 =) 633 years, Menes and his VII successors were put first, only compressed into five, with their full sum according to the Chronicle of 190 years. After them VII Memphite generations with 201 years, made out of the last two kings of Manetho's Dyn. IX and seven of the IX of his Dyn. X (II and III of Afric.), though with a covert allusion under the 13 years of the next generation belonging to Dyn. XI (IV of Afric.) to the 13 years still wanting to complete the 214 of Dyn. X (III of Afric.). And these seven Memphite generations of Eratosthenes seem to be meant to correspond to the first VII cartouches of the Thothmes Chamber of Karnak, though it is not easy to identify the names preserved there with those of Manetho's lists. Then follow beyond a doubt the kings of Manetho's Dyn. XI (his second of Memphites), only with VII names instead of VIII, and those not all of them identifiable, nor in the same order as with Manetho. And these, who as tributaries of the Shepherds and as being of evil memory are omitted in the Thothmes Chamber, but who as the builders of the pyramids would be required by Eratosthenes, have 178 years, short by six only of 184, the full period of the Shepherd domination.

Lastly, the 443 years to be inserted, if the 190 are reckoned first, or the 190, if the 443 are understood to be prefixed, are completed by the first 64 years of the full century given to the single generation of Phiops, the fourth king of the Memphite Dyn. XIII of Manetho, but the second of the same family of kings as he appears in the Thothmes Chamber. So his *generation* is ambiguous, and capable of being reckoned with either the one or the other of the two series into which it is divided. But it belongs rather to the first, being wanted to complete the five generations of the second exhibition of the 190 years, answering to the five generations of their first exhibition.

Supposing now for the moment those 443 years which we have been considering to be consecutive, and identical or concurrent with 443 of the chronological years really following, according to the scale of the Chronicle, after the 190 of the first Tanites, it follows, since (190 + 443 =) 633 exceed 477 by 156, that they overrun by 156 years the head of Dyn. XVIII, to which, however, the name of Phiops is certainly unknown, and under which there is no room for any concurrent lines. Consequently, for such as knew the true Chronology, it would be clear that, however presented, the 443 years, *if all consecutive*, must have begun 156 years *before the end of the first dynasty of Tanites*. And if, as was actually the case, it were desired after the first 190 years of Tanites to exhibit the sum of 443 twice over, once for Lower Egypt and once for Upper, the second series of 443 being made to commence after the second exhibition of 190, as the first series began after the first exhibition of the same number, then it follows in like manner that the second series of 443 also will run 156 years into the chronological space of Dyn. XVIII; and this time (since we may not add any more unchronological or concurrent years than the first 443 already placed above), there will be a real chronological depression of the head of Dyn. XVIII to the extent of 156 years, unless some of its kings are named in the series, which is not the case. The fact is, that besides those 184 years of the anonymous Dyn. XXVII of the Chronicle which Manetho restored to their true place and to the Shepherds, and which the Theban priests, suppressing the Shepherds, gave to kings of Upper Egypt, there were in the Chronicle years of anarchy and foreign rule not really belonging to those adjacent generations to which they were added, and in one or two long dynasties generations of a length altogether exceptional. So that 156 years might easily be spared and thrown up from below to make room for some of the kings of Upper Egypt anterior to Dyn. XVIII, and to produce a symmetrical equality and parallelism between the early unchronological or contemporaneous dynasties of Lower and the early chronological dynasties of Upper Egypt, after the first Tanites, who were the common source and trunk to the kings of both the Lower and the Upper Countries.

The two series then of 443 years are exhibited apparently only as consecutive, but really in the following form: —

### SCHEME F.

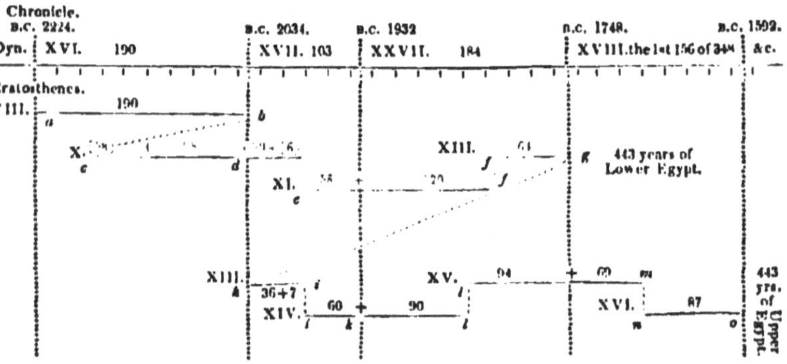

Since the 443 years of the cycle transferred to kings answer in the scheme of Eratosthenes to the whole 1674 unchronological years of Manetho, and besides them there are no other years by origin unchronological, but only a series of 1881 years of kings all historical, though the kings occupying them may be sometimes placed unchronologically, —and since, by marking the sum of 190 years belonging to

Dyn. XVI of the Chronicle not only as if at B.C. 2667 *before* but *also* at B.C. 2224 *after* an exhibition of the 443 added years, the scheme of Eratosthenes hints that this latter is the true chronological epoch of Menes, we may accept this hint, and act upon it. Then Menes and his Tanite successors being moved down will of themselves tend to depress the whole series of the 443 added years as reckoned after them, so as to make it become concurrent and parallel with 443 of the chronological series, answering to the 103 and 184 years of Dyn. XVII, and to 156 years more of Dyn. XVIII of the Chronicle. But as no concurrent dynasties can be continued below the head of Dyn. XVIII (B.C. 1748), which united all Egypt under one sceptre, it follows, that as soon as 287 of the 443 unchronological years have been depressed so as to occupy concurrently the interval between Dyn. XVI and Dyn. XVIII of the Chronicle, the remaining 156, at top, will simply stand aside when displaced by the bringing down of Menes and his Tanites, and will become parallel and concurrent with the last 156 years of their dynasty.

Thus we obtain, for a first step, those relative positions within the spaces of the Chronicle which are exhibited in the scheme F, and which in figures stand as subjoined:—

$$190\,(=34 + \begin{cases} 156 + 287\,(=103 + 184) \\ 156) + 287\,(= 103 + 184) + 156. \end{cases}$$

If the two spaces of 287 years were each filled in the scheme of Eratosthenes by generations dividing naturally into two pairs of dynasties commensurate, or nearly so, with the two Dynasties XVII and XXVII of the Chronicle, and with one another, while the names given for the last 156 years (those of the first 156 years could cause no difficulty) were identifiable with names of Dyn. XVIII of Manetho, nothing would remain for us to do. But this is by no means the case; and though the scheme, as stated generally, is now intelligible, the particular generations and dynasties entering into its spaces do not at once resolve themselves into two parallel successions, but need to be examined in detail before we can tell either which years and names will give way when the extremities inclosing them are compressed, or what relative places, under the influence of such compression, they will assume, or lastly, which years and generations will remain to constitute the true and principal dynastic succession of the Chronicle.

If we look first to that one of the two series which comes first in the lists both of Manetho and of Eratosthenes, we recognise at once in it a representation of Dyn. XI of Manetho (IV of Africanus), lying in scheme F between the points *e*, *f*, B.C. 1990 and B.C. 1812, i. e. between the 45th year of Dyn. XVII and the 120th of Dyn. XXVII of the Chronicle. But we know from the lists of Manetho that no one native dynasty ruled Memphis both before and under the Shepherds. It is expressly said of the Shepherds, that they took Memphis by force, and that the kings of Dyn. XI (IV of Africanus) who were their contemporaries and tributaries were *not* of the same lineage with the kings of Dyn. X (III of Africanus) preceding. And in the scheme of Eratosthenes we have VII earlier Memphites immediately preceding the names taken from Dyn. XI (IV of Africanus). So then we may confidently identify these two lines in the lists of Eratosthenes with Manetho's first two dynasties of Memphites, and may with no less certainty assert that they only partially cover their true chronological places, the point at which the one line ended and the other began being not really at B.C. 1990, but at B.C. 1932, 58 years lower down. The same is plain even from the sight of the lines themselves in the scheme E, where the 178 years lying between *e*, *f*, are all of one dynasty, and equal within 6 to the 184 of the Shepherds of the Chronicle, and there is nothing else with which to parallel those 184 years but portions of Dyn. X and XIII (III and VI of Africanus), amounting in all to only 109 years, that is, to the 103 of Dyn. XVII of the Chronicle, with the addition of those 6 years by which 178 fall short of the 184 of the Shepherds. So then these 178 years must be moved down so as to lie between B.C. 1932 and B.C. 1754, displacing all but 6 of the 64 years of Dyn. VI that follow. And since the 58 years so displaced cannot be thrust down below B.C. 1748, into the space of Dyn. XVIII, nor can 6 of the 64 be really separated from the

58, it follows that the whole 64 must be anterior to the whole 178 of Dyn. XI (IV of Africanus,) and they will rise up over their heads when they are thrust down, leaving the last 6 years of the 184 of the Chronicle vacant. And either they will thrust up the whole of Dyn. X (III of Africanus) so as to make it begin in B.C. 2206 instead of B.C. 2200, only 28 instead of 34 years after Menes, while the last 39 years of Dyn. X, together with the 64 of Phiops, make up the 103 years of Dyn. XVII of the Chronicle; or else, since the end of Dyn. X ought not to be parted from the commencement of XI, one must suppose the 201, (or with an addition of 13, indicated below by Eratosthenes, the 214) years of Dyn. X (III of Afr.) to have begun historically in B.C. 1932 + 201 or 214 = 2132 or 2145, and the last 64 of their years to have been parallel with the 64 of Dyn. XIII forced up by putting down Dyn. XI (VI and IV of Afr.). In either case, the 103 years of the Chronicle would be paralleled by 39 years of Dyn. X, with the first 64 of Phiops of Dyn. XIII (III and VI of Afr.); on which composition of it two remarks are obvious, *first*, that it exhibits *less* than *three* generations instead of the *four* of the Chronicle; and *secondly*, that though a very long-lived king may have been sovereign of all Egypt only for part of his whole reign, that part should not be the *first*, nor the middle, but rather the *last*.

Passing now to the second series of (287 + 156 =) 443 years, which are all upon the whole chronological, we find the space of 103 years, answering to Dyn. XVII of the Chronicle, marked at its outset clearly enough, and dovetailed into the second exhibition of the 190 of its Dynasty XVI preceding. For while the last five generations of the unchronological 443 years admit also of being reckoned as if following the same 443 years, and representing Dyn. XVI of the Chronicle, (27 + 31 + 33 + 35 of Dyn. XI of Manetho with the first 64 of Phiops of Dyn. XIII making 190 years), the remaining 36 of Phiops with 1 + 6 of his two successors of the same dynasty, and 22 + 12 + 8 + 18 = 60 of the first four Diospolites of Dyn. XIV (XI of Africanus) of Upper Egypt, make the sum 103, which in the Chronicle follows upon the 190 years, ending in B.C. 1932; and thence again to the true commencement of Dyn. XVIII, in B.C. 1748, are 184 years. And it is remarkable how here a compensation is inserted or hinted for the three generations suppressed in both the first and the last of the two exhibitions of the 190 years of the Tanites. For Phiops, both by the number of his years, and by the relation in which he stands to both the series, contributing to both the sums 190 and 103, may well be regarded as a *double* generation; and if he be viewed in that light, we have instead of Dynasties XVI and XVII of the Chronicle with 190 and 103 years in VIII + IV = XII generations, two spaces of 190 and 103 years in V + III + IV = XII generations, the designation of the Chronicle "*Memphite*" entering into the composition of the whole sum of 103, while the IV Diospolites grouped by themselves after three compensatory generations correspond to the IV generations connected with the same 103 years by the Chronicle. So from this point, however he may vary in detail, Eratosthenes has on the whole no element of disturbance remaining, either as to the number of generations, or as to their average duration. He has already prefixed and inserted the XV new generations "of the Cycle," with their peculiar average of $29\frac{1}{3}$ years, and he has paralleled V + III + IV = XII of the LXXVI generations of kings (all at least but one *name;* for Phiops is a double generation only in effect, but a single one in name, and this *name* he will insert later). And from this point he has still remaining LXXVI − XII = LXIV of the generations of the Chronicle to be paralleled or made out according to its general average of $24\frac{1}{2}$, in 1588 years.

But though the *years* of the second series of 443 years in the scheme of Eratosthenes are in themselves chronological, and identical with as many of the Chronicle, the names and generations filling them are by no means in their true chronological places, any more than those of the former series were found to be, when it was brought within the historical spaces of the Chronicle. It was hinted however already, in the older scheme of Manetho, as we have seen, that his Memphite Dyn. XIII (VI of Africanus), which contains Phiops, was really connected with the 103 years of the Chronicle, since the remainder of 60 at its end (and at the end of all the six dynasties of Lower Egypt) coalesces with the 43 attached to Dyn. XIV (XI of Africanus) into 103. It was also hinted that the first part of Dyn. XV (XII of Africanus) is connected with the same period, since the 43 years nominally attached to Dyn. XIV really belong to Dyn. XV. Again, it was hinted that the next following space of the Chronicle, that of its 184 years, is connected with the remaining years of Dyn. XV, (XII of Africanus,) since the sum of the unchronological years given to it, viz. 124, coalesces with the remainder of 60 years of the Memphites of Lower Egypt into 184. These hints in the scheme of Manetho would prepare us to anticipate that connection of his Dyn. XIII (VI of Africanus), with the 103 years which we find in fact to be distinctly exhibited by the scheme of Eratosthenes, in which Phiops twice over, once alone and once with his two successors, contributes towards the exhibition of that sum. It is true that these two presentations of him are plainly inconsistent with one another. His 64th year cannot be at once the *last* of the 103, as it appears to be in the first series of 443 years when the names of Dyn. XI (IV of Africanus) are transposed to their true places, and his 65th *at the same time* be the *first* of the same 103, (the 64th having been concurrent with the last year of the 190 of Dyn. XVI of the Chronicle,) as appears to be the case by the second series of 443 years in the scheme of Eratosthenes. But whatever may be the solution, it seems pretty clear that in *some way or other* he must be connected with the 103 years. And if so, and if he enters into these not only as contemporary, but as being himself one of the IV generations covering them in the Chronicle, and his reign in this relation must be looked for at the end, not at the beginning or the middle, of his 100 years; — and if further it is really hinted by Manetho that the 43 years detached from his Dyn. XV (XII of Africanus) belong to the same 103 years, then we must look in the generations of Eratosthenes for names answering to Dyn. XV (XII of Africanus), and see if they afford us at their head anything like the 43 years we want.

In point of fact, on looking downwards, we do find a

group of four, or *nominally* five generations (XXXI and XXXII, XXXIII, XXXIV, XXXV), plainly identical with Dyn. XV of Manetho (XII of Africanus), though they commence seemingly no less than 157 years after the 100th and last of Phiops, and no less than 90 after the distinct exhibition of the 103 years in the scheme of Eratosthenes has been completed. At the same time they also overrun the head of Dyn. XVIII by 69 years; so that their position, no less than that of the names from Dyn. XI (IV of Africanus) in the former series of 443 years, is plainly unhistorical; and we may confidently thrust them up not only so as to stand clear of Dyn. XVIII, but so as to come into contact with the last year of Phiops, or rather with the single year of his successor, since the first generation from Dyn. XV (XII of Africanus) in Eratosthenes has not 43, but only 42 years. So, by the help of Manetho's hints, we may obtain from below (42 + 1 =) 43 years for the last chronological part of Dyn. XVII of the Chronicle; and then we have only to inquire how many years of the latter part of the life of Phiops are to be added to them to make the third of its four generations: and this inquiry is readily answered, on considering that in the former series of 443 years we found the Memphite Dyn. X of Manetho (III of Africanus) beginning apparently 156 or 162 years before the end of the Tanites, and projecting 39 into the 103 years of the Memphite Dyn. XVII of the Chronicle. We may fairly infer, then, that these 39 years really constitute the first two generations of the 103, though 64, or 51 *at least*, of those 162 which have been thrust up, as if concurrent with the Tanites, may belong historically to the interval between the 39th year of Dyn. XVII of the Chronicle and the 1st of its Dyn. XXVII. There will be room, therefore, in Dyn. XVII of the Chronicle for 21 of the last years of Phiops; and the whole series of its IV generations (five actual reigns being reckoned as four) will consist of 17 + 22 + 21 + 1 + 42 = 103 years, belonging to Dynasties XI, XIII, and XV of Manetho (III, VI, and XII of Africanus).

Independently of any hints given by Manetho's scheme, if we look only to the names with which the (287 + 156 =) 443 chronological years of Eratosthenes from B.C. 2034, to B.C.

1992, are covered, we see first a remainder of (36 + 1 + 6 = ) 43 years of Dyn. XIII of Manetho (VI of Africanus); then IV generations in 60 years seemingly representing the first four kings of Dyn. XIV of Manetho (XI of Africanus), and completing the exhibition of the 103 years of the Chronicle (when yet the historical commencement of the first Diospolites should be a good deal earlier than even the *commencement* of Dyn. XVII of the Chronicle); then again IV more generations, or five reigns compressed into four, seemingly of the same dynasty as the preceding, but taken from its end instead of its beginning, for the last name is that of the king *Ra-sekenn* (Σοικύνιος) who immediately preceded Dyn. XVIII. And these four or five kings are put up over the names taken from Dynasty XV of Manetho (Dynasty XII of Africanus) which next follow, just as in the former series of 443 years the Memphite contemporaries of the Shepherds were put up unchronologically (yet in agreement with Manetho's order), and after the completion of their 178 years Phiops of Dyn. XIII of Manetho (VI of Africanus) was made to end the 103, and even the 190, years of the Chronicle. So now also the enumeration of Eratosthenes keeps to the order of Manetho. He completes his selection of VIII names from the XVI of Manetho's Dyn. XIV (XI of Africanus) before he approaches those of Dyn. XV (XII of Africanus); and by taking 4 kings from the top, and 4 (or by implication 5) from the bottom of Dyn. XV, and putting up the latter so as to seem to be consecutive with the former, while Dyn. XV (XII of Africanus) is put down below them, he hints both at the existence of those intermediate 6 kings whom he omits for want of room, and also at the true points to which the commencement of Dyn. XIV (XI of Afric.) is to be put up, and its termination is to be put down.

For since those five generations (XXXIV to XXXVIII) concluding the second series of 443 years, which Eratosthenes has placed in 156 chronological years belonging to Dyn. XVIII of the Chronicle and of Manetho, cannot possibly stand where they are, but must be put up above the head of Dyn. XVIII in B.C. 1748,—if, on their moving up, we were to suppose *all* the generations preceding, of *both* series, as lying previously within the first 477 years of the monarchy, to give way and rise up *equably*, the consequence would be that the head of the earlier concurrent or unchronological series of 443 years would be thrust up from B.C. 2190 to B.C. (2190 + 156 =)2246, 122 years above Menes. Or, if we were only to suppose the preceding generations of the *second* or chronological series of 443 years all to give way *equably*, when pressed upwards from below, still, even so, the 65th year of Phiops would be thrust up from the head of the 103 years of the Chronicle where it seems to stand in B.C. 2034 to B.C. (2034 + 156 =) 2190, that is, it would become concurrent with the 35th year of Menes. But both these results being inadmissible, and Phiops being doubly connected, once on either side, in both the two series, with some part or other of the 103 years, and so less capable of giving way than any name or group of names below him, we must suppose that when the later generations of the second or chronological series of 443 years are thrust up from below, while Phiops its highest generation remains fixed above, the series will part asunder at one or other of the points of junction of the dynasties or parts of dynasties composing it, so that 156 of its years may be free to move up and to stand as merely concurrent and parallel to as many chronological years which refuse to be displaced. But the whole series consisting of 43 years of Dyn. XIII (VI of Africanus), 60 + 90 of Dyn. XIV (XI of Africanus), 163 of Dyn. XV (XII of Africanus), and 87 of Dyn. XVI (XIV of Africanus), the points of junction between distinct dynasties are only three; and of the three, that between Dynasties XV and XVI (XII and XIV of Afric.) is out of the question, as the last two generations of Dyn XV have themselves to move up out of the chronological years of Dyn. XVIII. Nor is it suitable to select the juncture between Dynasties XIV and XV (XI and XII of Afric.), since Dyn. XIV, the first of Upper Egypt, is known to have both preceded and accompanied and outlasted the second dynasty of Upper Egypt, viz. Dyn. XV (XII of Afric.), which follows it in the lists, and has only half its number of kings. There remains then only the juncture between the Memphite Dyn. XIII and Dyn. XIV of the earliest Diospolites (VI and XI of Africanus); and against supposing the series to part asunder at *this* point there is no shadow of an objection.

Let this latter supposition then be admitted; and the head of the earliest Diospolite dynasty, Dyn. XIV (XI of Africanus) thereupon rises 156 years above the apparent end of Dyn. XIII (VI of Africanus) of the Memphites of Central Egypt; that is, it rises 156 years above B.C. (2034 – 43 =) 1991 to B.C. (1991 + 156 =) 2147, the 78th year after Menes, a date which is not inadmissible for the commencement of a line of XVI kings known to have ended at or a little before B.C. 1748; for so they would have in all a continuance of about 400 civil years. Further, since the eight names inserted from this dynasty in the series of Eratosthenes have only 150 years, their last year named will stand as seemingly parallel and concurrent with the single year of the successor of Phiops, the last *king* of Dyn. XIII (VI of Africanus); and the years which will stand as parallel and concurrent with the six of the *queen* Nitocris, the last six, that is, of the same Dyn. XIII, will be the first six of the Diospolite Dyn. XV (XII of Africanus). So by this method also, without having recourse to any covert hints given by Manetho, the first generation, or the first two generations (for there are two *names*, and nominally two generations, XXXI and XXXII, with only a single sum of 42 years) of Dyn. XV (XII of Africanus), are brought into contact with the end of the reign of Phiops. For the single year of his successor would not count as one of the IV generations of the Chronicle, but would be consolidated with one or other of the adjacent reigns, probably with the reign following, so as to make for that reign not the sum of 42 given it by Eratosthenes, but 43 years, which it seems to have in the reckoning of Manetho as attached to his Dynasty XIV (XI of Africanus). It will be remembered that after the second exhibition of the 190 years of the Chronicle, when certain generations were inserted from Dyn. XIII (VI of Africanus) into the following space of the 103 years of the Chronicle as compensation for the three suppressed in the exhibition of the 190 years, it was noticed that the compensation was *imperfect*, the century of Phiops, which in point of length is fully adequate to representing two or even three generations, had three been needed, being yet but a single generation the *name* of which belongs strictly to the second exhibition of the 190 years, though 36 years of his *life* without any name make the first part of the 103 following. So *one* name, a *name* only without years, was still wanted to complete the compensation, in order that V + III + IV = XII generations of Eratosthenes might answer to the VIII + IV = XII of the Chronicle. This deficiency then is now supplied by that double generation (XXXI, XXXII), with two *names* of two kings who were coregnant but a single sum of 42 years, which stands at the head of Dyn. XV (XII of Africanus) in the list of Eratosthenes, and which, when moved up into its true place, so as to stand in contact with Phiops and his successor, is found to complete the exhibition of the three compensatory names in such a way that, while all standing together, they have little or no bulk of years between them. For the successor of Phiops has but one year; and Nitocris, 6 of whose 12 years have been transferred to Phiops and so cut off from the end of the dynasty, being only a queen, might be understood to be concurrent with the main line of the Chronicle, even if we had not the first 6 years of Dyn. XV (XII of Africanus) standing parallel to her reign and in contact with Phiops or his successor. And, lastly, the mere *name* of Amenemhe I. (however it was written for Eratosthenes), though conjoined with that of Sesortasen I. at the head of Dyn. XV (XII of Africanus), leaves the chronological sum of 42 years single and entire to the reign of the latter king.

But the collocation of the eight names taken from Dyn. XIV (XI of Africanus) is not yet final or exact. Though all from one and the same dynasty, and intended no doubt to be regarded in the first instance as either all actually themselves consecutive, or as representing as many years of the same line which were so, they are nevertheless divided into two distinct groups of *four* names each; and of these the first group, as it stands originally, is made to cover part, viz. the last 60 years, of the 103 years of the Chronicle: but the later group is made to cover part, viz. the first 90 years, of the

184 years of the Chronicle. Hence, when the names and years belonging to Dyn. XV (XII of Africanus), are moved up, so as to seem to take possession of the last 66 years of the 103, and the first 97 of the 184 of the Chronicle, between B. C. 1997 and B. C. 1842, the eight names taken from Dyn. XIV (XI of Africanus) with their (60+90=) 150 years seem at first to be thrust up, as if all consecutive, so as to begin in B. C. (1997+150=) 2147. But so soon as we notice that the last name of the later one of their two groups of four names each is that of *Ra-Sekenn*, the last king of the dynasty, known as such from the Thothmes Chamber and from other monuments, we perceive that the two groups are really taken the one with 60 years from the top and the other with 90 from the bottom of the whole series of the XVI kings, and that the seven or eight names omitted are those of the intermediate space. So when at length the earlier four have been put up so as to begin from B.C. 2147, and the later four have been put down again so as to end at or before B.C. 1748, the two groups between them, though in themselves making out only half the number of kings belonging to their dynasty, and less than half its years, either actually cover, or at least have covered by passing over it, the whole historical space of the dynasty. The idea of so representing Dyn. XIV (XI of Africanus), by taking its first kings who preceded, and its last who outlasted Dyn. XV (XII of Africanus), might naturally enough be suggested by the order of their cartouches in the Thothmes Chamber of Karnak, where the shorter though more important line of Dyn. XV (XII of Africanus), is interposed, and as it were imbedded in the midst of them.

As regards the three generations (the last with 63 years representing seemingly two reigns) which both originally and after having been moved up seem to follow after the names of Dyn. XV (XII of Africanus), and which as finally placed fill the space of the last 87 of the 184 years of the Chronicle, and so perhaps hint the existence of 97 more years preceding, it appears both from Manetho's lists and from the Thothmes Chamber that if they belong, as they must be presumed to belong, to Dyn. XVI (XIV of Africanus), they are only a representation of it, having less than half that number of *generations* which by the ordinary average should go to a sum of 184 years, and less than half that sum itself of 184 years which is given by Manetho to their dynasty. Still, since, as finally placed, after having been moved up out of the space of Dyn. XVIII, the three generations of this Dynasty XVI (XIV of Africanus) are exhibited as both connected with and completing the 184 years of the Chronicle, while the same sum of 184 is also their own in Manetho's lists, we may perhaps see in this their position a hint that, though unnamed for want of room, four or five more generations, with 97 years at least, of kings of the same lineage were understood by Eratosthenes also, or his assistants, to have preceded the three or four generations named. And though the last 87 years of this Dynasty XVI (XIV of Africanus) seem to follow the names taken from Dyn. XV (XII of Africanus), still, as they have no real continuity with them, but are the continuation of a distinct line which had begun long before, the place of these 87 years is no hindrance to the admission that Dyn. XV (XIV of Africanus) may have had a continuance of 12 years or more, as it appears from the lists of Manetho and from the Turin papyrus to have had, after those 163 years which alone are noticed by Eratosthenes. In like manner it may have had some 16 years of Amenemhe I. and Sesortasen I., unnoticed by Eratosthenes, previously to the commencement of the same 163 years.

Lastly, to come to the main point of the whole: When we considered first and separately the first series of 443 years, the result obtained, as regards Dyn. XVII of the Chronicle, was this, — that it seemed to be composed of two reigns or generations of Dyn. X (III of Africanus) with 39, and a third, or part of a third, of Dyn. XIII (VI of Africanus) with 64 years; and we remarked that there ought to be in it not three generations only, but *four*, including the *last* part perhaps, but not the beginning nor the middle, of the century of Phiops. Now, from the examination of the *second* series of 443, we have obtained this fresh result, that the head of Dyn. XV (XII of Africanus) is placed in contact with the end of the reign of Phiops or the single year of his successor, which is the same thing, as a reign of one year would certainly be consolidated, and unnoticed in the generations of the Chronicle. So the first double generation of Dyn. XV (XII of Africanus) in the list of Eratosthenes, which is no doubt the conjoint reign of Amenemhe I. and Sesortasen I., being fixed to 42 years, we may place these 42 at the end of the 103 years of the Chronicle between B.C. 1932 and B.C. 1974. The single year of the successor of Phiops takes us back to B.C. 1975. And as we had a beginning made above for Dyn. XVII of the Chronicle in two reigns or generations and 39 years of Dyn. X (III of Africanus), reaching from B.C. 2034 to B.C. 1995, it is easy to see how many years, viz. 21, of the latter part of the long reign of Phiops intervene for the time of his sovereignty. So we have for the four generations of Dyn. XVII of the Chronicle in the list of Eratosthenes the following generations and names: —

Dyn. XVII of the Chronicle, 103 yrs. Jan. 15, B.C. 2034, to Dec. 20, B.C. 1932.

| | | |
|---|---|---|
| Gen. XI. | *Sirius*, or *Gneurus* (*Tseserirenra*, or *Sahoura*) reigned 18 years, but as suzerain . . . . . . . . . . . | 17 |
| Gen. XII. | *Chnoubus Gneurus* (*Snefrou*) . . . . | 22 |
| Gen. XX. | *Apappous* (*Papa Maire*) . . . . . . . | 21 |
| Gen. XXI. | *Echescosokaras* (*Meranre*) . . . . . | 1 |
| Gen. XXXI. | *Peteathyres* (*Amenemhe I.*) } | 42 |
| Gen. XXXII. | [*Sesortasen I.*] . . . . } . . . . | |
| | Sum of the years of Dynasty XVII . . | 103 |

This will be the series, if we suppose the two names belonging to Dyn. X (III of Africanus), viz. Sirius and Chnoubus Gneurus, who cannot be *at once* the occupants of the *first* 39 years of the 103 of the Chronicle and the *last* kings of their own dynasty, to belong really to the 39 years, and that the remaining 64 years of Dyn. X (III of Africanus) with the kings belonging to them and unnamed are, 51 of them, thrown back and covered by the 79 years of the first reign, while the rest are indicated by the 13 years of the first name taken from Dyn. XI (IV of Africanus). Else, if the two kings named last by Eratosthenes in his representation of Dyn. X (III of Africanus) were supposed to occupy only unchronologically the first 39 years of Dyn. XVII of the Chronicle, but to have reached chronologically to the end, or to within 13 years of the end, of their own dynasty, and so also of the end of the 103 of Dyn. XVII of the Chronicle, one would have to seek the names belonging to the first 39 years of the 103 higher up in the list of Eratosthenes.

But the last 21 years only of Papa Maire (who is the Apappous of Eratosthenes and the Phiops of Manetho) having been included in the series between B.C. 1995 and B.C. 1975, his first accession or birth will rise to B.C. 2074; so that he will be really contemporary with the latter part of the first Tanite dynasty; and his three predecessors of Manetho's lists, though unnamed by Eratosthenes, may be understood to take us up some 70 years higher to about B.C. 2144, viz. to the 81st year after Menes. Nor are these years perhaps left entirely without indication in the scheme of Eratosthenes; seeing that, if we had allowed it, the five generations unchronologically placed in 156 years of Dyn. XVIII, when thrust up, would have raised the accession of Pape Maire 156 years above the point at which it seemed to stand, i.e. (156+64=) 220 above B.C. 2034 or 30 above Menes. And though this was inadmissible, yet if the operation had been deferred till we had first found the true accession of Phiops *as suzerain* to be as low as B.C. 1995, and we had then raised up the 156 years and names unduly depressing Dyn. XVIII, the effect upon the same accession of Phiops (if it could have given way) would be to carry it back 156 years from B.C. 1995, to B.C. 2151, a date which, if taken to *indicate* the commencement of his dynasty, differs by only 7 years from that commencement which we have calculated for it on other grounds.

The result arrived at in respect of the composition of Dyn. XVII of the Chronicle is strongly confirmed by the monuments; nay it is even required by them: for they prove beyond a doubt that Papa Maire and Sesortasen I. were sovereigns of all Egypt; and they connect Sesortasen I. with some earlier Memphite kings, especially *Aan* and *Tseserirenra*, of Dyn. X of Manetho (III of Africanus). Herodotus too, though without himself understanding what he was told, has transmitted to us native Egyptian testimony to the same effect. For he was informed that Mœris and his successor Sesostris (the king who first conquered Nubia), in comparison of whom none of their predecessors had done anything remarkable, reigned shortly before the pyramid-builders of Memphis, and their contemporary the Shepherd.

In the Chronicle the Shepherd kings, though unnamed, misplaced, and put out of sight for the Greeks, were still placed as one of the sovereign dynasties, with the number of their generations, probably IV, and the sum of the years of their supremacy, viz. 184, indicated for Egyptian readers. And Manetho gave them their whole duration, with VI names, and in their true chronological place, as if he had no thought of keeping up the former sensitiveness and dissimulation respecting them. He *indicated*, besides, the chronological period of their dominion, viz. the 184 years of the Chronicle, no less than the 103 years after which they followed. He even made 184 the formal sum of one of his dynasties, viz. Dyn. XVI (XIV of Africanus), to which it can scarcely be believed historically to belong. But in the scheme of Eratosthenes the Shepherds are totally suppressed, no less than in the monumental lists of Dyn. XVIII, without any hint whatever either of their existence, or of the 184 years of their domination. And that, although the chronological framework of the Chronicle was taken for a basis, and though its other sums of 443, 190, and 103 years, were all marked twice over, (the 443 being even repeated a third time), its sum of 184 alone being omitted. And not only so, but the dynasties, or parts of dynasties exhibited, were so arranged, in accordance with the order of Manetho, as by no means to exhibit those kings of Lower or Upper Egypt who were really contemporaries of the Shepherds, like the Memphites of Dyn. XI (IV of Africanus), as filling those 184 years, or the greater part of them, which were necessarily marked off for such as knew the scale of the Chronicle between the end of the 103 years and the head of Dyn. XVIII.

The relation of the first XXXVIII generations and 1076 years of Eratosthenes to as many years and generations of the Chronicle, to the first ten dynasties of Manetho's kings, and to the double series of the Chamber of Thothmes III. in the temple of Karnak, with the true positions of the dynasties of Manetho and of the generations of Eratosthenes within the chronological spaces of the Chronicle, have been drawn out and exhibited above in the tables and schemes C, D, E, F, to which the reader will find it useful to refer as he follows the subjoined enumeration:—

The XV generations and 443 years "of the Cycle" are exhibited by Generations I to XV inclusively:

Also, by Generations VI to XX, exclusively of the last 36 years of Generation XX.

The VIII Tanite kings and 190 years of Dyn. XVI of the Chronicle, and the VIII Tanites and 253 years of Dyn. VIII of Manetho (I of Africanus), are represented by Generations I to V inclusively, with the 190 years of the Chronicle:

Also, by Generations XVI to XX, with 190 years, exclusively of the last 36 years of Generation XX.

The ten generations, VI to XV inclusively, having 253 years (which coalesce on either side with the 190 of Generations I to V, *or* XVI to XX inclusively, into 443 years), they are equal, but only by chance, to the *unreduced* sum of Manetho's first dynasty of kings, Dyn. VIII (I of Africanus).

The IX generations, VI to XIV inclusively, seem to indicate by their number and the sum of their years, viz. 224, the IX kings and the 224 years of Manetho's second dynasty of Tanites, Dyn. IX (II of Africanus), 224 being the remainder after the last two reigns with 79 years have been cut off from its original and unreduced sum of 303.

The VIII generations, VI to XIII inclusively, with the sum of 214 years, the 79 years of the first of them being compounded out of two distinct reigns, viz. the last two of Manetho's Dyn. IX (II of Africanus), *indicate* the IX Memphite kings and the 214 years of Manetho's Dyn. X (III of Afric.).

The VII generations, VI to XII inclusively, the first of them covering three names and the sums of *two* reigns, represent with their 201 years (all but 13 years indicated below under a *name* not wanted, and belonging to the next dynasty), the IX Memphites and 214 years of Manetho's Dyn. X (III of Afric.).

The VII generations, XIII to XIX inclusively, with 178

years, represent the VIII Memphite kings and the whole historical duration of Manetho's Dyn. XI (IV of Africanus).

Dyn. XII of Manetho (V of Afric.), with its IX Elephantinite (or Heliopolite?) kings in 218 years, is not alluded to.

The III generations XX to XXII inclusively, with 107 years, represent the last three of the VI Memphite kings of Manetho's Dyn. XIII (VI of Africanus), and the last 107 of their 177 years, 6 years being transferred from the last reign, that of Nitocris, to the *generation* or life of Phiops, so that the two, instead of having 94 and 12, have 100 and 6 years respectively.

The last 36 years of Generation XX, and the two following Memphite generations, XXI and XXII, being compensatory of three names out of the VIII of Dyn. XVI of the Chronicle suppressed above, these, with IV more Diospolite generations, XXIII to XXVI inclusively, making VI or VII generations with 103 years, represent the IV Memphite generations and 103 years of Dyn. XVII of the Chronicle, and are joined on, through Phiops, to the second exhibition of the 190 years of Dyn. XVI of the Chronicle.

The 39 years of Generations XI and XII, from the 2nd of Sirius, with the last 21 of Gen. XX, the 1 of Gen. XXI, and the 42 of Generations XXXI and XXXII, make up the 103 years of Dyn. XVII of the Chronicle.

The 184 years of Dyn. XXVII of the Chronicle, lying between its Dynasties XVII and XVIII, are unnoticed.

The last 36 years of Generation XX, with the eighteen generations following, make a sum of 443 years, parallel to those 443 years "of the Cycle," covered with kings from Manetho's six early dynasties of Lower Egypt, which may be reckoned either from Generation I to XV inclusively, or from Generation VI to the 64th year of XX inclusively. The present sum of 443 years is occupied by kings of Upper Egypt, and seems to cover a chronological space beginning with the 1st year of the 103 of Dyn. XVII of the Chronicle, and ending with the 156th of its Dyn. XVIII.

The VIII generations, the last of them covering two reigns, from XXIII to XXX inclusively, with 150 years, may be regarded as equivalent to the 1st, 2nd, 3rd, and 4th, and to the 13th, 14th, 15th and 16th of the XVI Diospolites of Dyn.

XIV of Manetho (XI of Africanus), with less probably than the half of the true historical sum of their years.

The v generations, xxxi to xxxv inclusively, xxxi and xxxii being two names but with a single reign, and xxxiv being a consolidation of two kings, represent six out of the viii reigns of Manetho's Dyn. XV (XII of Africanus), which *seems* to have in all 43 + 16 + 160 = 219 years, though of these 59 are detached, and mentioned under the preceding dynasty. The 163 years of Eratosthenes are the 163 lying chronologically between the commencement of the 42nd year preceding the death of Sesortasen I. and the end of the last year of Amenemhe III. If 16 years at the top, and 12 at the bottom, unnoticed by Eratosthenes, were added, the whole chronological sum would be brought up to 191 years.

The iii generations xxxvi to xxxviii inclusively (the last of them representing at least two reigns), with 87 years, are a representation of the latter part of the Diospolite Nubian or Xoite Dyn. XVI of Manetho (XIV of Africanus); and when put up, so as to stand clear of Dyn. XVIII, they fill the last 87 of that sum of 184 years which is given to them by Manetho, but which belongs to Dyn. XXVII of the Chronicle.

The xvi generations from xxiii to xxxviii inclusively, or rather the xv (since one is merely a *name*, without years, completing the compensation of the three names suppressed in Dyn. XVI of the Chronicle), having a sum of 340 years, are intended, with the first reign of the following series not copied by Syncellus, or rather with 8 of its years, to parallel the xiv generations and 348 years of the "Memphite" Dyn. XVIII of the Chronicle, as if that were *not* identical with the Diospolite Dynasty XVIII of Manetho, with xvi reigns and 333 years.

Before proceeding to exhibit the list of Eratosthenes in the actual text of Syncellus, and to comment on it in detail, it will be proper to notice and account for a mistake made by Syncellus respecting the space of time covered by that portion of the list which he transcribes. We have been assuming, as a matter of course, that Eratosthenes' entire series of xci generations, being the lxxvi generations and 1881 years of the kings of the Chronicle, with its xv preceding generations "of the Cycle" added, ended at the same point of time with the last or fifteenth dynasty of the kings of the Chronicle, that is, with its Dyn. XXX, and with Dyn. XXX of Manetho, viz. at the last Persian conquest of Egypt by Darius Ochus, in B.C. 345; and that it began, in appearance at least, 443 years earlier than the series of the kings of the Chronicle, viz., in B.C. 2667, instead of B.C. 2224. But Syncellus, going seemingly upon some words of Apollodorus, which he does not quote, supposes the first XXXVIII generations of Eratosthenes in (443 + 190 + 103 + 184 + 156 =) 1076 years, which he transcribes, and which really run five generations and 156 years into Dyn. XVIII of the Chronicle, ending in B.C. (2667—1076 =) 1592, to begin from his own "year of the world 2900, 124 years after his era of the Dispersion and of the accession of Menes, A.M. 2776;" and to end with his "A.M. 3975," (it should have been A.M. 3976,) 1165 years before the close of his A.M. 5141 where he puts the end of Dyn. XXX of Anianus. That is, he makes the series of Eratosthenes (really one with that of the Chronicle) to end 68 years too low. For from B.C. 1592, where the 1076 years according to the scale of the Chronicle really end, to B.C. 345, where Dyn. XXX and the native Egyptian monarchy really ends, there are (1592 − 345 =) 1248 Egyptian years; while Syncellus between his A.M. 3975 (3976), where he makes the series of 1076 years which he transcribes to end, and his A.M. 5141, where he makes Anianus' Dyn. XXX to end, (15 years before the Chronicle) has only 1165 years; so that the remaining LIII generations and 1248 years of the Chronicle and of Eratosthenes (which cannot be curtailed) would end (83 − 15 =) 68 years later than B.C. 345, supposing Syncellus' A.M. (5141 + 15 =) 5156 and his last year of Dyn. XXX to end together (which they ought to do, but do not) in B.C. 345. It is clear that in putting the head of the whole series 124 years *after* his own epoch of Menes, Syncellus must be going upon some inference from words of the author whom he followed, and must have obtained the date for the commencement of the 1st, and we may add that for the end of the 38th, generation of Eratosthenes from some notice, in the chronography of Apollodorus relating, or seeming to himself to relate, to the end of the whole series. But that Eratosthenes shifted the end of a series of XCI generations taken from the Chronicle, and with it the end of Dyn. XXX both of the Chronicle and of Manetho and the epoch of the conquest of Ochus, by 68 years, from B.C. 345 to B.C. 277, is manifestly impossible. And the date itself which comes out seems to explain the origin of the mistake made by Syncellus, who took some words really relating to the date of *Manetho's writing*, which might well be in terms of Anianus' or Syncellus' reckoning about (A.M. 3976 + 1248 =) A.M. 5224, or B.C. 277 (= B.C. 277 also according to the vulgar era), when *Eratosthenes* was only just born, as if they related to the date to which Eratosthenes, following the Chronicle and Manetho, brought down his series of (XXXVIII + LIII =) XCI generations of Theban kings.

The words with which Syncellus prefaces that portion of the list of Eratosthenes which he has transcribed into his own chronography, and so preserved to us, are as follows:—

"Apollodorus, the chronographer, has inserted another list of XXXVIII kings of the Egyptians who are called Thebans, covering 1076 years, which commenced in (after) the year of the world 2900, and ended with the year of the world 3975 (3976). The knowledge of these, he says, Eratosthenes obtained in the form of a series of names with short notices in the Egyptian language, by command of the king, and rendered them into Greek as follows:—"'Ἀπολλόδωρος χρονικὸς ἄλλην Αἰγυπτίαν τῶν Θηβαίων λεγομένων βασιλείαν ἀνεγράψατο βασιλέων λη', ἐτῶν ͵αος'· ἥτις ἤρξατο μὲν τῷ ͵βϡ ἔτει τοῦ κόσμου, ἔληξε δὲ εἰς τὸ ͵γϡοε' ἔτος τοῦ κόσμου· ὧν τὴν γνῶσιν, φησὶν, ὁ Ἐρατοσθένης λαβὼν Αἰγυπτιακοῖς ὑπομνήμασι καὶ ὀνόμασι κατὰ πρόσταξιν βασιλικὴν τῇ Ἑλλάδι φωνῇ παρέφρασεν οὕτως."

*Dynasty XVI of the Chronicle, VIII of Manetho, I of Africanus, of VIII Theinite or Thinite kings, with 190 years.*

From March 3, B.C. 2224, to Jan. 14, B.C. 2034.

"α'. Πρῶτος ἐβασίλευσε Μήνης Θηνίτης, Θηβαῖος· ὃ ἑρμηνεύεται Αἰώνιος· ἐβασίλευσεν ἔτη ξβ'." "*Menes* was the first king who reigned in Egypt. He was of *Teni*, a Theban (i. e. of the Thebaid). The name is equivalent to *Æternus;* he reigned 62 years." He no doubt stood at the head of the series of kings recognised as their ancestors by the Thebans of Dynasties XVIII, XIX, and XX, both on other monu-

*Menai*, 30. March 3, B.C. 2224, to Feb. 23, B.C. 2194.

ments, on some of which he is still visible, and especially in the temple of Osiris built or rebuilt by Rameses II. at Abydos in the Thinite nome; and hence perhaps we may derive a sufficient explanation of the designations "Thenite" and "Theban." The syllable *men* in Egyptian had the same sense as the root of *μένω*, *μονὴ*, *maneo*, in Greek and Latin.

Athothis I. 27. Feb. 23, B.C. 2194, to Feb. 17, B.C. 2167.

"β΄. Θηβαίων β΄ ἐβασίλευσεν Ἀθώθης υἱὸς Μηνέως ἔτη νθ΄· οὗτος ἑρμηνεύεται Ἑρμογένης." "*Athothis*, son of Menes, reigned 59 years. His name means *Hermogenes*." Thus far the names of Eratosthenes are identical with those of Manetho and of the Turin papyrus; and the years of these first two kings are taken, with an addition of three units only to the second, from the *unreduced* figures of Manetho, who gives Menes 62, and Athothis 57 years, which last we suppose to have been 56 and some odd months. It is to be noticed how the expression "Θηβαίων ἐβασίλευσε," "reigned over the Thebans," goes with the designations "Thinite" and "Theban," and explains the sense in which these kings are appropriated by the Theban priests in making out *their* list for Eratosthenes.

Athothis II. 21. Feb. 17, B.C. 2167, to Feb. 11, B.C. 2146.

"γ΄. Θηβαίων Αἰγυπτίων γ΄ ἐβασίλευσεν Ἀθώθης ὁμώνυμος ἔτη λβ΄". "*Athothis II.* reigned 32 years." Here the name is entirely different from the third name in Manetho's list, which is Κενκένης; but the years of his reign are the same within one; for Kenkenes of Manetho reigned 31, and Manetho's text may have had 31 and some months, which in the list of Eratosthenes (which had no fractions) were rounded off to a full year. And on other grounds it is certain that the five kings of Eratosthenes are identical with five out of the eight of Manetho, though only the first two names are clearly the same in both lists. Whatever may be the cause, the names of Eratosthenes from this point to the end of his whole series are far from being generally or certainly identifiable; but happily so many are identifiable, and at such intervals, as to enable us to distinguish clearly the general order of the whole, and the dynasty to which each name separately belongs.

The name Athothis in this list of Eratosthenes pervades in a manner the whole of the first dynasty of kings, being repeated no less than four times, and in connection with every one of the five kings named except Menes. And Menes himself is elsewhere said to have been instructed by Thoth. And as the 4th and 5th names of Eratosthenes are the 6th and 7th of Manetho, and each king is said to have been the son of his predecessor, the name Athothis is by implication connected also with the 5th and the 8th kings of Manetho, though they are omitted in order to reduce the eight to five generations. This prominence given to the name Athothis may remind one of a passage in one of Eusebius's extracts from Sanchoniathon, in which it is said that "Cronus (i. e. Ham) going southwards, gave all Egypt to *Thoth*, to be his kingdom," that is, to some patriarch so named, as if Thoth or Athothis, rather than Menes, were the founder of the Egyptian monarchy. And again, in another passage, it is said that the names of their gods were taken by the Egyptians and others partly from ancestors and other great men, and especially "from some of their own kings." If this were so indeed, then, since they are the oldest Egyptian kings, and Manetho himself records the deification of Apis and Mnevis and of the Goat of Mendes as introduced later, one might suspect that it was Menes or Mnevis who gave his name to the Bull of Heliopolis, the names being really identical (*Menai*), and that, instead of Athothis, his successor, being named from the god Thoth, or Hermes, it was in reality the god Thoth who was named from the king; especially as Manetho describes this same king as doing things suitable to the god his namesake, being a builder and physician, writing books, and prescribing the method of embalming, and, as we may understand, the whole ceremonial of the dead. But the name was certainly given in later times to at least one ancestor much older that the time of Menes. In the pseudo-Manetho quoted by Syncellus the records of the first times, in allusion to the antediluvian world, are fabled in a story borrowed from Berosus to have been inscribed on certain stelæ by the *first Thoth*, and after the Flood to have been written thence in Egyptian hieroglyphics and in hieratic books by Agathodæmon *son* of the *second Thoth* and *father* of *Tat*, that is, of a *third Thoth*. And these last-named three should be kings, for they deposited what they wrote "in the sanctuaries of the temples of Egypt."

[Ouenephes, 23 yrs. Feb. 11, B.C. 2146, to Feb. 6, B.C. 2123. Athothis III] 19 yrs. Feb. 6, B.C. 2123, to Feb. 1, B.C. 2104. Miebaes [26 yrs. Feb. 1, B.C. 2104, to Jan. 25, B.C. 2078.]

"δ'. Θηβαίων ἐβασίλευσε δ' Διαβιῆς υἱὸς Ἀθώθεως, ἔτη ιθ'· οὗτος ἑρμηνεύεται Φιλέτερος." "*Diabies*, son of Athothis, 19 years." The name is that of Μιεβαῆς or Μιεβιδὸς, Manetho's 6th king. The gloss Φιλέτερος too is probably a corruption of Φιλόταυρος, that is, Lover of the Divine Bull, or Beloved by the Divine Bull, as has been well remarked by Bunsen. The 4th king of Manetho, *Ouenephes*, is suppressed by Eratosthenes, all but the three units of his 23 years, the addition of which to the 2nd and 3rd generations has been noticed above. The 5th king, *Ousaphaidos*, is also omitted, but he contributes his *reign* of 19 years and some months, the latter omitted by Eratosthenes, to the fourth generation, the *name* for which, *Miabies*, is taken from Manetho's 6th king. From the sense of the name Miebaes it appears that when it was given the Bull was *already* a recognised divinity; yet Manetho, who would not be likely to make that worship *less* ancient than it really was, says expressly that it was introduced in the time of Kaiechos, the 2nd king of his second dynasty of Tanites, that is of his Dyn. IX (II of Africanus). So then it would seem to follow that Kaiechos, the 2nd king of the Tanites of Dyn. IX (II of Africanus), was more ancient than Miebaes, the 6th king of the Tanites of Dyn. VIII; and the two Tanite dynasties, instead of being successive in one and the same city, would seem to have been contemporaneous in two distinct cities of the same Tanite district, though Dyn. IX commenced in any case at some time later than the accession, and probably later than the death of Menes. A similar inference might be made from the name Κωχώμη, mentioned by Manetho in connection with the 4th king of his Dyn. VIII, Ouenephes, who he says first began to build the pyramids at Κωχώμη; for this name is thought by some to mean "*The place of the Black Bull.*" But the inference in this case is of little weight, since a *place*, as "Ramesses," or "Alexandria," may be designated by that name by which it was familiar to the writer, even though he chance to be speaking of it at a time when the name was not yet given.

Smenpses, 18 yrs. Jan. 25, B.C. 2078, to Jan. 21, B.C. 2060.

"ε'. Θηβαίων ἐβασίλευσε ε' Πεμφῶς υἱὸς Ἀθώθεως, ὅ ἐστιν Ἡρακλείδης, ἔτη η'." "*Semphos*, son of Athothis, 8 years." The gloss shows that Σεμφῶς is the true reading, *Sem* or *Smen* being elsewhere also rendered Ἡρακλῆς. The name is then fairly identifiable with *Semen-pses,* the 7th king of Manetho, and the reign of 8 years is also from the 18 of the same king, the units only being retained, and the decad suppressed. The 8th king of Manetho, *Bieneches,* and the 4th, *Ouenephes,* are indicated in the list of Eratosthenes no otherwise than by the fact that the first two reigns of Menes and Athothis, with 62 and 59 years, look as if they were both double generations.

[Bienneches, 26 yrs. Jan. 21, B.C. 2060, to Jan. 14, B.C. 2034.]

So Menes with 30 + 32, Athothis with 27 + 32, Athothis II. with 21 + 11, Miebaes with 19, and Semphos with 8 years, hint under only five names the eight actual reigns which are consolidated, and exhibit, in such a way as suits the purpose in view, their true sum of 190 years.

*Dynasty X of Manetho, III of Africanus, of* IX *Memphite kings, with* 214 *years.*

Eratosthenes for these has only VII names, ending with the seventh king, as it seems, of the IX, but giving to his VII names 201 years, and *indicating* the full sum of 214 years, and the full number of IX kings.

Dyn. X. of Manetho. IX Memphites, 214 yrs. B.C. 2145 to 1932.

"ϛ'. Θηβαίων Αἰγυπτίων ἐβασίλευσεν ϛ' Τοἴγαρ, ἄμαχος, [Σούτεχ-Ῥα, or Στοῖχος, Σούτεχος, Ἄρης, ἄμαχος?] Μομχεῖρι Μεμφίτης, ἔτη οθ'. Οὗτος ἑρμηνεύεται Τίσανδρος [so read for Τήσανδρος], περισσομελής." The adjunct Μεμφίτης, "of Memphis," marks the transition from the Tanites or Theinites to the Memphites. This king however is identified beyond all doubt —not with any one of Manetho's *first* IX Memphites, but with the *last but one,* the *eighth,* of his *second* dynasty of Tanites, viz. of Dyn. IX (II of Africanus). For both Manetho and Eratosthenes mention that he was a giant, περισσομελής; and the reign of 79 years (made out of 78 and some months) given him by Eratosthenes, is plainly compounded of the two sums 48 and 30 of *Sesochris* or *Set-ochris* the giant and *Cheneres,* the last two kings of Manetho's Dyn. IX (II of Africanus). After thus beginning his " Memphites " with a single name seemingly of a stranger, but covering or indicating probably two reigns besides the first of the IX Memphites of Manetho's Dyn. XI (III of Africanus), Eratosthenes continues with *six* more names, which are clearly a representation of Manetho's

[*Akoun?* 34 yrs. Jan. 5, B.C. 1996, to Dec. 27, B.C. 1962; and 13 of the 26 yrs. of *Asesherph?* to Dec. 23, B.C. 1916. *Nechcroph?*] 28 yrs. Feb. 11, B.C. 2145, to Feb. 4, B.C. 2117.

Dyn. X (III of Africanus), since they are "Memphites," preceded by a consolidation of the last two reigns of Manetho's Tanites, and followed by VII names taken from the later Memphites of Manetho's Dyn. XI (IV of Africanus). There is no doubt then as to their character, though their names as they stand in the list of Eratosthenes are disappointing; and in spite of plausible conjectures, for which the corrupt state of the text gives abundant room, no single name of all the seven has as yet been identified in a manner completely satisfactory. Nor is there much, if any help, to be obtained from the sums or order of the particular reigns.

The two kings *Sesochris* and *Cheneres*, if *rightly* placed, as they are placed by Manetho, at the end of the *second* dynasty of Tanites, should be at the earliest contemporaries of the *last* two or more kings, not the *first*, of that earliest Memphite dynasty which began in B.C. 2145, 79 years after Menes, and ended, after continuing for 214 years, in B.C. 1932, when the Shepherds took Memphis. But if they were *wrongly* placed by Manetho, and the Theban priests for Eratosthenes were in fact correcting Manetho when they placed Sesochris (or *Ra-Soutech?*) at the head of the Memphites, the only way of accounting for Manetho's error will be by supposing that in some hieratic papyrus which he followed the *rubric* marking the commencement of a new line of kings was put two names too low; or else that he himself put it too low in his own list through copying inattentively from a papyrus in which it had stood right. In either case the blunder imputed to him is too gross to be probable. But *if it were so indeed*, its correction would involve this consequence, that while the kings of the second Tanite line were *reduced* to VII from IX, those of the earliest Memphite line would be *increased* from IX to XI, and would claim by the ordinary average of the Chronicle and Eratosthenes a duration of 269½, instead of 220½ or 214 years; so that, as they certainly ended when the Shepherds took Memphis, in B.C. 1932, they should have begun as early as B.C. 2201, only 23 years later than the accession of Menes. But Eratosthenes gives no hint either of more kings than IX, or of more years than 214 for the dynasty; and these two numbers he *does* indicate in that indirect way which alone was possible within his limits. And though he makes VII kings from Dyn. XI of Manetho (IV of Africanus) to follow next after these first VII of his own Memphites whom we are now considering, still, as he makes his first Memphites with 201 years seem to end, and his later to commence, not at B.C. 1932, but 58, or rather 64, years earlier, so that the last two of the seven names of his first Memphites cover the first 39 years of the 103 of the Memphite Dynasty XVII of the Chronicle, we may infer that the two names, and 51 of the 64 years omitted but needed to the historical completion of the dynasty, are covered by the two consolidated Tanite reigns and the 79 years of the giant Sesochris or Stoigar Momcheiri; and that this consolidation was put up at the head of the early Memphites because it was desired, while naming VII only out of their IX kings, to make the last year of the seventh name mark the point at which the sovereignty kept in view by the Chronicle passed out of this line to a king of Dyn. XIII of Manetho (VI of Africanus). If any one reject this view, he must suppose that the last king of the VII named by Eratosthenes as if from the IX early Memphites of Manetho (only with 13 years more than are expressly given him), was historically the ninth and last of the dynasty, ending his reign in B.C. 1932, and that the first 79 historical years of the dynasty, and its first three historical kings, whoever they were, are covered by the single name of Mom-cheiri, with the sums of two reigns taken by some strange blunder or caprice of the Theban priests from the latest Tanites of Manetho. There remains, it is true, a third hypothesis, viz. that *both* the 79 years, covering two kings *added* to the IX of Manetho's Dyn. XI (III of Africanus), are historical above, and at the same time that Manetho's last two kings and 64 years are omitted by Eratosthenes, and need to be added to complete the historical continuance of the dynasty below. But thus it would have XI kings and (64 + 201 =) 265 years to say nothing of 13 more, which are indicated only, and not actually reckoned to its names, in the list of Eratosthenes; and the 265 years, if they ended in B.C. 1932, must have begun in B.C. 2196, only 28 years after Menes, a date seemingly inadmissible, and nearly identical with that which has been already noticed above as consequent upon the admission of XI instead of IX kings, if their duration were according to the ordinary average of 24½ years to a reign.

It will be best then perhaps to suppose that the first (64 − 13 =) 51 years of the first Memphite generation of Eratosthenes really and chronologically form part of the last 64 of the dynasty lying between B.C. 1995 and B.C. 1932; and further to notice that the remaining (201 − 51 =) 150 years are unchronologically depressed as regards their relative position; for the last-named king of the dynasty (not really the last, but the 7th) seems to overrun by 6 years the commencement of the 184 years of Dyn. XXVII of the Chronicle; whereas the later Memphites of Dyn. XI of Manetho (IV of Africanus) certainly commenced at the *beginning* of the 184 years in question, and the 6 years by which their 178 fall short of 184, are really the *last* six, not the first six years of that period. After the deduction of 51 years the first Memphite generation of Eratosthenes will still have (79 − 51 =) 28 years left, answering exactly to the reign of Manetho's first Memphite king, *Necherophes* or *Necherochis*, who has twenty-*eight* years. A monumental name with which the first historical Memphite of Eratosthenes may with much probability be connected, is the first of the VII earliest names in the uppermost line of the Karnak Chamber on the left hand side (of the spectator). This name is read *Ra-s-men-teti*, with an additional character, the sense and pronunciation of which are still disputed. Mr. Birch would read it *kherp*, which with *Ra* prefixed might be the source of the *Ne-cheroph-is* of Manetho. For the rest, the syllable *smen*, and in the same characters, occurs also in other private names in composition with *pet*, as "*Pet-Smen*," like *Pet-Amon* or *Petu-Bast*; so that *Smen* should be a name of some deity, rendered Ἄρης by Eratosthenes, perhaps of Σούτεχος or Στοῖχος, who was the local god of that district in which Tanis was situated: or it may be one with *Sem* or *Smem*, as in the name *Smen-pses*, which is rendered Ἡρακλείδης. Whatever be the true account of the first name, the agreement from this point between the series of Eratosthenes and that exhibited on the left hand side of the Karnak Chamber is so close, that there can be little doubt that it was designed.

Stoichus, 6 yrs. Feb. 4, B.C. 2117, to Feb. 3, B.C. 2111.

"ζ. Θηβαίων Αἰγυπτιων ἐβασίλευσεν ζ Στοῖχος υἱὸς αὐτοῦ· ὅ ἐστιν Ἄρης, ἀναίσθητος, ἔτη ϛ'." "*Stoichus* son of the preceding, 6 years." The name is probably that of the deity Soutech, who is the same as Set, with a Greek termination; and there are many instances where Set, under the eighteenth and nineteenth dynasties, appears or is named in such a manner as to explain and justify the rendering Ἄρης. It seems probable, when one notices both the form of the preceding name *Stoigar* and the double gloss ἄμαχος and τίσανδρος, that it is really the same, only with "*Ra*," perhaps, in composition, Στοῖχρος or Στουγαρῆς for *Soutech-Ra*, and a gloss from the sound resembling *okr*, which means "*victorious*." Further, the notice added, that he was *son* of the preceding, suffices of itself to prove that the preceding name, *Stoigar Mom-Cheiri*, ("*Set-okr, Ker-en-ra of Memphis?*") represents not only the last two *Tanites* of Manetho's Dyn. IX (II of Africanus), or whatever they stand for, but also one other really Memphite king, the first as we have presumed of Manetho's Dyn. X (III of Africanus), that is, Necherophes or Necherochis. And the name "*Stoichos*, son of *Setochris*," *may* be identifiable with Manetho's *fourth* name *Mesochris*, if this latter be a contraction of *Mes-Setochris*, the syllable *mes* being in sense equivalent to "*son*." Or the *M* beginning the name may be a corruption for Σ. The epithet ἀναίσθητος, "senseless," is no part of the gloss on the name, but, like περισσομελὴς attached to the name preceding, it is a notice descriptive of the person. Lastly, the source of the reign of 6 years may be found in the 7 years (6 and some months) of Manetho's 3rd name, 6 suiting better than the 29 or 30 of Manetho's 2nd name to follow after a reign of 79 years. The second cartouche in the Karnak Chamber, which should answer to *Stoichus*, is wanting.

*Ra-Tsesor-mi?* 30 yrs. Feb. 3, B.C. 2111, to Jan. 26, B.C. 2081.

"η'. Θηβαίων Αἰγυπτίων ἐβασίλευσεν η' Γοσορμίης, ὅ ἐστιν Αἴτησις παντὸς [so correct for Αἰτησιπαντὸς], ἔτη λ'." "*Tsesor-mi*, 30 years." The suffixed syllable "*mi*," meaning "*beloved*," may be the source of the gloss Αἴτησις παντὸς, "*Desire of All*;" and the essential element of the name, "*tsesor,*" is the same which alone constitutes the second name of Manetho's nine, viz. *Tosor-thrus*, or *Sesor-thus*, which are identical, except that in the former of the two readings from the text of Africanus the syllable *Ra* entering into the composition of the name is expressed, while in the variant of Eusebius it is omitted. The reign too agrees; for the *Tsesor-phra* of Manetho has 29 years, and, we may suppose, some months, and the *Tsesor-mi* of Eratosthenes has 30 years. The notice in Manetho, that he was reckoned and named by the Egyptians as another Esculapius for his skill in medicine, agrees well with the epithet in Eratosthenes "*Mai*" or "*Mi,*" "*Desire of All.*" The corresponding cartouche in the Karnak Chamber is again wanting.

Mares, 26 yrs. Jan. 26, B.C. 2081, to Jan. 20, B.C. 2055.

"θ'. Θηβαίων Αἰγυπτίων ἐβασίλευσεν θ' Μάρης, υἱὸς αὐτοῦ· ὅ ἐστιν Ἡλιόδωρος, ἔτη κϛ'." "*Mares,* that is Heliodorus, the Gift of Ra the Sun-god, 26 years." Both *Ma-res* and *Tureis,* the third name of Manetho's nine, will bear the rendering *Heliodorus* or *Gift of Ra;* and the units of the two lists, being 6 in Eratosthenes, and 7 as rounded off in the edition of Ptolemy of Mendes and Africanus, agree together. The whole sum however, 26, seems to consist of the 17 years of Manetho's fourth reign, with an *addition* of nine more years given by Manetho to the *seventh* reign but not allowed by the Theban priests to stand in that connection. The corresponding cartouche in the Karnak Chamber reads *Assa;* and Bunsen supposes this Assa to be the same with *Assa Tet-cheres* of the Memphite tombs, who however is probably a later king, viz. the last but one of Dyn. XII of Manetho (V of Africanus).

An-Houphou, 20 yrs. Jan. 20, B.C. 2055, to Jan. 15, B.C. 2035.

"ι'. Θηβαίων Αἰγυπτίων ι' ἐβασίλευσεν Ἀνώυφις, ὅ ἐστιν Ἐπίκομος, ἔτη κ'." "*Anoyphis,* which means the *Longhaired,* 20 years." This name is compound, and as it might equally be written Ἀὰν Ὦυφις, or Ἀὰν Σώυφις or Σάοφις, it agrees at once and perfectly both with the fifth name, *Soyphis,* of Manetho's nine, and with the corresponding cartouche in the Karnak Chamber, which reads *Aan.* That the name in the list of Eratosthenes is really thus compounded is proved by the gloss Ἐπίκομος, "*Longhaired,*" the same interpretation being given to the name *Souphis* or *Saophis,* the monumental *Khoufou* or *Shouphou,* in the following dynasty. The 20 years of the reign in the list of Eratosthenes are the 16 of Manetho's fifth reign, with an *addition* of 4 more, transferred from his *seventh.* So the 4th and 5th reigns of Eratosthenes, with (26 + 20 =) 46 years, equal together the 4th and 5th of Manetho, with (17 + 16 =) 33, and contain besides 13 years transferred from Manetho's 7th reign.

"*ια'. Θηβαίων Αἰγυπτίων ια' ἐβασίλευσε Σίριος, ὅ ἐστιν Υἱὸς Κόρης, ὡς δὲ ἕτεροι, Ἀβάσκαντος, ἔτη ιη'.*" "*Sirius* (as if *Si-iri-us*), which means *Son of the Pupil of the Eye,* or according to others *Not to be Fascinated by the Power of any Eye,* 18 years." Here also perhaps a harmony may exist between the three lists. For the word *tseser,* which Eratosthenes elsewhere renders *κράτος,* power, and which is the main component element of Manetho's sixth name, *Toser-tasis,* is found in composition on the monuments with the character for the pupil of the eye, pronounced "*iri*" in the name *Tseser-iri-en-ra,* from which *Sisires* or *Sirius* might readily be formed; and the monuments exhibit this king in conjunction with *Aan* (who should be his predecessor) as honoured by Tsesortasen or Tosor-tasis I. their descendant. But "*power or lordship of the pupil of the eye*" would admit the gloss *ἀβάσκαντος,* i.e. "*not to be mastered by the eye of another;*" while, if considered in connection with the syllable *Ra,* the sense "*power of the eye of Ra*" might perhaps be rendered "*son of the eye of Ra,*" as "*Athothis*" was rendered above "*Hermogenes,* i.e. *son* of Thoth." But it is probable that some of these glosses were merely from the *sound,* and not from any true etymology; and so *Sirius* might be interpreted as if it were *Si-iri-en-ra,* "son of the eye of Ra," or *Si-en-iri,* Ra being dropped. The corresponding cartouche in the Karnak Chamber reads *Sahou-ra;* and as both the word *Sahou* and the character with which the word is written represent the dogstar, it might naturally be *translated* by the name of the same star, *Sirius,* in Greek. But whether *Sahoura* and *Seserirenra* of the monuments and *Tosertasis* and *Sirius* of Manetho and Eratosthenes are all one and the same king under two names, like *Aan* and *Haophou,* or rather the list of Eratosthenes under the name and the gloss of its eleventh

*Sahou-ra,* 18 yrs. Jan. 15, B.C. 2035, to Jan. 10, B.C. 2017.

generation blends together two monumental kings, one of whom is omitted by the Karnak Chamber and the other by Manetho, is a different question. That there may be great variations sometimes in writing the names of the same king is sufficiently proved by the fact that in a papyrus of late date the Egyptian name *Sahou-ra* has been found rendered in Greek as *Asychis*, the syllable *ra* being neglected, and the aspirate being transposed so as to make "Sa-ou*h*" or "Sa-ouc*h*," instead of "Sa-*h*ou," and so Ἀσαῦχις or Ἀσῦχις. The 18 years of the reign of *Sirius* in the list of Eratosthenes are short by only 1 of the 19 of Tosertasis in that of Africanus. It must be admitted, however, that *if Tseser-ir-en-ra* is the monumental name alluded to under the "Toser-*tas*-is" of Manetho, Manetho is guilty of an inaccuracy like that which appears lower down in his lists when the true Tosertasis, *Sesortasen I.* of Dyn. XV (XII of Africanus) is given as "*Gesongoses*," a corruption coming very near to the name of *Sesonchis* or *Shishonk*, the head of a much later dynasty.

*Snefrou, 22 yrs. Jan. 10, B.C. 2017, to Jan. 5, B.C. 1995.*

"ιβ'. Θηβαίων Αἰγυπτίων ιβ' ἐβασίλευσε Χνοῦβος Γνευρὸς, ὅ ἐστι Χρύσης Χρύσου υἱὸς, ἔτη κβ'." "*Chnoubus Gneurus*, which means *Chryses* the son of *Chryses* (in English, *Gold* the son of *Gold*), 22 years." The 22 years are one of them from the sixth and 21 from the *seventh* reign of Manetho, which, with the name Aches, has 42 years. Of these 42, 13 have already been added to the 4th and 5th reigns; 21, with 1 other detached from Manetho's 6th reign, are now allowed to the 7th; and the remaining 8 must be understood to be put down to the 8th king. It being required that the 6th and 7th of these earliest Memphites should mark both the number of generations and the number of years contributed by their dynasty towards the IV generations and the 103 years of Dyn. XVII of the Chronicle, the 42 years of Manetho's 7th reign opposed a difficulty. But when 13 of these were transferred to the 4th and 5th reigns above, and 8 more cut off and given to the 8th reign below, the 6th and 7th reigns, standing with (19 + 21 or 18 + 22 = ) 40 years, approached so nearly to the sum desired, viz. 39, as to need no further alteration: for it would be understood that the 6th king might have been already on the throne of Memphis for one year before the death of the 8th and last Tanite king of Dyn. XVI of the Chronicle. But as regards the names, there is no correspondence beween that of *Aches* in Manetho (who is probably the *Aa-karou*, or *Aakou* of the monuments), and the *Chnoubus Gneurus* of Eratosthenes; and it appears that though the reign of 22 years, to judge by its units, is taken from Manetho's seventh, the king to whom it is given is rather Manetho's eighth, the name *Σίφουρις* of his lists being easily reconcilable with the monumental form *Snefrou*, designating the seventh and last of those Memphite kings who make the earliest and uppermost series on the left hand side of the Karnak Chamber. So *Aches* and *Kerpheres*, the 7th and 9th kings of Manetho, instead of *Siphouris* and *Kerpheres*, his 8th and 9th, will be the two kings reckoned as 8th and 9th for Eratosthenes by the Theban priests, and omitted both by them and, as it seems, also by Thothmes III. in arranging the series of the Karnak Chamber, probably for this reason, that they were of less importance when the sovereignty or precedence for all Egypt had passed to another line, viz. to a king of Dyn. XIII (VI of Africanus) not locally resident at Memphis. As for the years of these two kings omitted, they have already, all of them at least but 13, been thrown up and added to Manetho's first reign of 28 years at the head of the dynasty; and a length of 79 years given to one reign alone and of itself (even without any knowledge of the *sources* of its figures) hints plainly enough that two actual reigns are suppressed somewhere.

The Theban priests wishing their own 6th and 7th Memphites to mark the first 39 years of Dyn. XVII of the Chronicle, and having for this end cut off the historical continuance of Dyn. X from B.C. 1995 to B.C. 1932, being 64 years, adding to the 28 years of the 1st Memphite 51 of these, and to the 4th and 5th adding 13 other years (which look like but *are not* the complement of the 64), they gave, irrespectively of these 64 years, in agreement with Manetho, a sum of 97 years to the first five Memphites. But then giving to their 6th and 7th names only (18 + 22 =) 40 more years, making with the 64 thrown back 104, they had in

Manetho's last 4 reigns a sum of 117, being 13 years more; as if *either* 13 years of the first 64 still remained to be thrown back, *or else* Manetho's 9th king had lived on after being displaced by the Shepherds, and the dynasty, ending in B.C. 1932, had really lasted only 201 years from B.C. 2132. These last 13 years they indicated ambiguously by the help of their next following generation, which belongs in itself to another dynasty. For if we regard *only* the *sources* of the 79 years of Eratosthenes's first "Memphite" king, his reign is clearly double, and only double. So when we have ended the 7th generation, we have as yet only 8 actual reigns *indicated*, and still want one of the IX of Manetho, the full number of the dynasty. We have also at this point made out only 201 years, wanting still 13 of the full sum of 214. But when we go on to the next name of Eratosthenes, so as to have counted IX kings with Manetho, we find that this name has 13 years, just the number wanted to complete our reckoning of the years as well as of the kings of Dynasty X of Manetho (III of Africanus).

Lastly, as regards the name of Eratosthenes' seventh and last king of the early Memphites taken from the IX of Manetho's Dyn. X, and from the IV of Dyn. XVII of the Chronicle:—Granting that the seventh name of the Karnak Chamber, *Snefrou*, may probably be identical with the *Σίφουρις* of Manetho, and that the full titles taken by Snefrou at Wady Magara agree well with the opinion that he was *one*, whether the first or the second, of the four sovereign "Memphites" of Dyn. XVII of the Chronicle, still, it may be asked, what resemblance is there between the names Siphouris or Snefrou, and Chnoubus Gneurus? Certainly there is none whatever. And yet this name in the list of Eratosthenes is by no means one of those which cause most difficulty; and its examination gives some insight into the sources of such wide apparent discrepancies in writing, and still more in translating and explaining, the names of kings. For even in very early times, before the custom of taking two cartouches (one of which may be called the personal or *family-name*, the other the *throne-name*) had become fixed and uniform, there were in use three other names, which have been called the *Standard*, the *Vulture and Uræus*, and the

*Gold Horus names.* Sometimes all five names, the three just mentioned being even included in one long cartouche, are exhibited on the monuments in order. Now *nub* or *chnoub* is the Egyptian word for *gold,* and the hieroglyphical emblem, both for this word and for gold itself, is the basis of one of those three forms of regal names and titles which have just been mentioned. . So if the king whose ordinary cartouche reads Snefrou or Snefouris were specially connected with the Gold or Gold Hawk title, and if he were the second king who used it, his father having introduced it, this would satisfactorily account for the name *Gnoubus Gneuv-r-us,* Χρύσης Χρύσου υἱὸς, given him in the list of Eratosthenes. The circumstance too of such an assumption and introduction of a new royal title and emblem by the father and his son, would agree well with those other signs which indicate these same kings to have been the first two of the sovereign Dynasty XVII of the Chronicle. In point of fact, Snefrou does appear on the monuments with the *Gold Hawk* title; and either his name, or a variant of *Tseser-ir-en-ra* (which belongs more probably to a later king), is the earliest as yet known to be joined with it. Bunsen even mentions, as a variant of the name Snefrou, a *cartouche* found in the neighbourhood of Memphis reading *Chnoub-ra,* which would be identical with the Greek name Χρύσης. And as another indication that the Gold title was the special distinction of Snefrou and his father, and that they first introduced it, it may be noticed that while it is not found connected with any earlier name, as *Assa* or *Aan,* the names following that of Snefrou in the Karnak Chamber, both those of Dyn. XIII (VI of Africanus), *Papa, Meran-re,* and *Nepherchere,* and those of the later Memphites of Dyn. XI (IV of Africanus), seem all to take it on the monuments.

So for the 214 years of Dynasty X of Manetho (III of Africanus), Eratosthenes has *first* 51 out of its *last* 64 years. These lie really between B.C. 1995 and 1945 (the remaining 13 to the end of the dynasty in B.C. 1932 being *indicated* only at the last, after 201 have been actually *reckoned* to it). The 51 years just mentioned, together with the 28 of Manetho's first Memphite reign, making together the sum of

Manetho's last two Tanite reigns (which we suppose to have had 78 years and some months), this sum of 79 years with one name, is followed in the list of Eratosthenes by two reigns with 6 years and 30 years, parallel to Manetho's 2nd and 3rd reigns with 29 and 7 years, only in inverse order, and with the odd months rounded off differently. Then there commences a difference, the two following reigns of Manetho, the 4th and 5th, having only 17 and 16 years, (together 33) and the 6th 19, while the 4th and 5th names of Eratosthenes have 20 and 26 (together 46), and the 6th 18, which last generation of Eratosthenes, like his 2nd and 3rd, differs from the corresponding reign of Manetho only in the manner of rounding off the odd months. But in the 4th and 5th names of Eratosthenes there is an excess of 13 years added to them at the expense of the 7th reign of Manetho, the purpose of the transposition being this, to exhibit in the 6th and 7th places two reigns answering to the first two of the four sovereign generations of Dyn. XVII of the Chronicle, which had, as it seems, together 39 years, and which left after them 64 years of the same Dyn. XVII of the Chronicle, and also 64 parallel years of Dyn. X of Manetho (III of Africanus) still to run. Now in the lists of Manetho the sum given to the 6th reign, viz. 19 or 18, according as its odd months were cut off or filled up, suited well enough; and the units of the next, the 7th reign, opposed no difficulty; but its four decads, if added, would have made for the two reigns 60 years, instead of the 40 or 39 which were wanted. And if 21 years had been simply detached, and added to the last two reigns of the dynasty, still these having already (30 + 26 =) 56 years of their own, and there being a previous excess of 1 year on the 6th reign, there would have been a continuance after the end of the 7th reign of 77 years instead of 64: that is, there would have been in all 13 years too many. These then are the 13 years added above, 9 of them to Manetho's 4th, and 4 to his 5th reign, which seemed to interrupt the historical parallelism discoverable between the first three reigns of both lists. But the difference being now accounted for, the 18 and 22 years of Eratosthenes's 6th and 7th names are identifiable with the 19 and (42—21 =) 21 of Manetho's 6th and 7th reigns; and we can see that the 8 years wanting to Manetho's last two reigns, to complete the sum of 64, would be transferred to them in the reckoning of Eratosthenes from the preceding reign, so that the 8th reign would have 38 instead of 30 years. Then, of the 64 years so obtained for the last two reigns, which are not expressly named as generations by Eratosthenes, nor in the Karnak Chamber, 51 having been prefixed unchronologically at top, as part of the 79 years of Momcheiri or Sesochris (and 13 other unchronological years of Manetho having been restored to the 4th and 5th reigns), the final 13 years of the dynasty are also indicated by a double use of the sum of Generation XIII of Eratosthenes, which in itself is really the first of seven taken from a different Memphite dynasty, viz. Dyn. XI of Manetho (IV of Africanus). In figures alone the parallelism between the list of Eratosthenes and Manetho stands thus:—

[*Aucheru*, 38 yrs. Jan. 5, B.C. 1995, to Dec. 26, B.C. 1958. *Kerph-re*, 13 yrs. to Dec. 23, B.C. 1945, and 13 more to Dec. 20, B.C. 1932.]

*Man.* . . . . 28) : 29+7 : 17—— : ——16 : 19 . (21+9+4+8) : 30 : (13+13.)
*Erat.* ([38+13]+28) : 6+30 : (17+9) : (4+16) : 18 : .23 *tr* : *tr.* : [13]

What historical justification there may have been for the reduction of Manetho's 6th and 7th reigns from 19 and 42 to 18 and 22, and for the distribution of the 21 years cut off among several other reigns, above and below, we have not the means of determining. It is enough that we can see the nature of the changes made, and the motives prompting them.

*Dynasty XI of Manetho (IV of Africanus)* VIII *Memphites of another family with* 177 *years; for whom Eratosthenes has* VII *generations with* 178 *years.*

The beginning of this dynasty being fixed to the date of the capture of Memphis by the Shepherds and the commencement Dyn. XXVII of the Chronicle in B.C. 1932, its 178 years must lie chronologically between B.C. 1932 and B.C. 1754, and must leave unparalleled a space of 6 years at the *end* (not the *beginning*) of the 184 years of Dyn. XXVII of the Chronicle. In the list of Eratosthenes, however, as exhibited in Scheme F, at p. 299, VII names taken from the Memphite contemporaries of the Shepherds follow, according to the order of Manetho's dynasties, immediately after the VII names taken from Dyn. X (III of Africanus), and seem to lie between B.C. 1989 and B.C. 1812, *e* and *f*, being themselves

Dyn. XI of Manetho. VIII Memphites, 178 yrs. B.C. 1932 to 1754.

followed by 64 years, *f*, *g*, taken from Dyn. XIII (VI of Africanus), which 64 years seem to end at B.C. 1748, the head of Dyn. XVIII. But the last 64 years of Dyn. X (III of Africanus) and its last two names being *omitted* by Eratosthenes, if these 64 years, which *must intervene* before Dyn. XI (IV of Africanus) can commence, are inserted, or (which comes to the same thing), if the 64 of Dyn. XIII (VI of Africanus) lying between the points *f*, *g*, and the 178 years of Dyn. X (III of Africanus) lying between *e*, *f*, be transposed, the consequence is that the 178 years of Dyn. XI (IV of Africanus) will appear to end at B.C. 1748, where the 64 seemed to end before, and the last 64 of Dyn. X (III of Africanus), concurrent seemingly though not really with the first 64 taken from Dyn. XIII (VI of Africanus), will appear to project 6 years into the space of Dyn. XXVII of the Chronicle. But this exhibition of the 6 years lacking to Dyn. XI (IV of Africanus) of the full space of 184 years, as if they were at the beginning instead of at the end of the Shepherd dominion, and were covered by a continuance of the earlier Memphites, being certainly unchronological, the 150 (or 137) chronological years given by Eratosthenes to the first VII Memphites of Dyn. X (III of Africanus) must be put back in scheme F by 6 places, so as to begin in B.C. 2145 (or 2132) and to parallel the first 39 years only of Dyn. XVII of the Chronicle from B.C. 2034 to B.C. 1995 (instead of paralleling, as they now seem to do, 45 of its years), and so as to leave a void space of 64 years instead of only 58 to the head of Dyn. XXVII of the Chronicle at B.C. 1932; so that the 178 years of the Memphites of Dyn. XI (IV of Africanus) may begin from B.C. 1932, and end in B.C. 1754, leaving a void of 6 years to the head of Dyn. XVIII in B.C. 1748. Their chronological position being thus fixed, we may proceed to consider the generations themselves.

Out of the VIII names of Manetho no less than six, viz. the two Suphises, Mencheres, Ratoises, Bicheres and Thamphthis, being the 2nd, 3rd, 4th, 5th, 6th and 8th, are certainly or probably identifiable in the lists of Eratosthenes, whose 7th and only remaining name is a reduplication of Mencheres. Three of Manetho's names, viz. the first king, Soris, and the seventh, Sebercheres, do not appear. But to identify the sums of the reigns, or to trace in those of Manetho the sources of those of Eratosthenes, is a more difficult matter. Still, in a general way, one can see what was the main cause of the variations in the two lists. For the priests who arranged the list of Eratosthenes had already at the end of their representation of Dyn. X (III of Africanus) made out (v + vii =) xii generations and (190 + 201 =) 391 years; and it was necessary for them now to make their next three generations exhibit exactly the sum of 52 years, so completing the 443 years "of the Cycle" with the fifteenth generation. And when this was done, they had again to find four generations which one with another should have 31½ years each, or together 126 years, so as with the first 64 years of Apappus of Dyn. XIII (VI of Africanus) to exhibit for a second time the 190 years of the Chronicle in *five* generations, after the 443 years "of the Cycle," in like manner as the same 190 years had once already been exhibited in five generations at the beginning. But the viii reigns of Manetho having originally the sums

29 + 53 ? + 66 + 63 + 25 + 22 + 10 ? + 9,

or, as reduced to the average length of 24½ years, perhaps

29 + 43 + 36 + 23 + 15 + 12 + 10 + 9,

were far from offering any facility for exhibiting either of the two sums required, whether at the top or the bottom of the dynasty. For supposing that the 8th reign were consolidated, so as to leave to the dynasty the same sum of 177, or as Eratosthenes made it of 178 years, as before, the first three reigns would make unreduced 148, and after reduction perhaps 108, instead of only 52 years; and the remaining four reigns would make as reduced only 69 instead of 126 years. It is true that, if taken as they stood originally and unreduced, they would make 129 years, which would have needed but a slight alteration to suit the purpose desired; but thus the first three kings (two of them being the two Souphises, whose long reigns were famous among the Greeks through the association of their names with the two greatest pyramids, and through the writings of Herodotus) would have had to be compressed within the space of 52 years, affording for the first three kings only 17 years apiece, which was clearly out of the question.

To attain the end desired they devised, as it seems, the following process: First, to get rid at the end of those four reigns which were too short, and to obtain three as short as they wanted at the beginning, they transposed the fifth and sixth kings *Ratœses* and *Bicheres*, written *Rauosis* and *Biyres* in the list of Eratosthenes, so as to make them the first and the second; and instead of the reigns of 25 and 22 years which they have in Manetho's lists, the second only of the two reigns, viz. the 22 years of Bicheres, with its odd months filled up so as to become 23, was divided between the two kings. So the dynasty commenced with the name of *Rauosis* with 13 years, constituting Generation XIII; and *Biyres* followed with 10 years, constituting Generation XIV; after which Manetho's *first* reign of 29 years, now become the *third* of the dynasty, was given to *Saophis I.* the builder of the great pyramid, the *name* of *Soris*, from which the 29 years were taken, and the *reign*, viz. 63 years, of Souphis I., to whom the 29 years of Soris were now given, being both suppressed. Thus the first three reigns having 13 + 10 + 29 years, made up the requisite sum of 52, and the 443 years "of the Cycle" were completed, with the average of 29½ years, by the fifteenth generation. The king suppressed, Soris, was still indicated in a covert way for the Egyptians themselves by the *reign* originally belonging to him. Then, towards the exhibition of the (190 − 64 =) 126 years needed in the four next following generations, the 66 years of *Saophis II.*, having their odd months filled up and four of their six decads suppressed, furnished one reign of 27 years, and to its true possessor; and the two reigns of Soaphis I. and Saophis II., viz. 29 and 27 years, if put together, made up a reign of 56 years, explanatory of the sums of years connected by Herodotus with the names of these kings. The 63 years of Manetho's fourth reign, increased like the preceding reign by a unit by filling up the odd months, was preserved and divided between two kings of the same name, Mencheres I. and Mencheres II., corrupted into *Moscheres* and *Mosthes*, the latter serving as a substitute at any rate for Manetho's seventh king, *Sebercheres*, who was suppressed. Having thus three generations of the requisite length, it remained only to add to Manetho's last name, *Thamphthis*, the 25 years abstracted from Ratoises and since left unappropriated (they being shortened first by one decad), and also the 11 (made out of 10 years and some odd months) of Manetho's seventh king, Sebercheres, similarly vacated by the suppression of his name. But (15 + 11 =) 26 being added to the 9 years belonging to the eighth and last king *Thamphthis* in Manetho's lists, give him a reign of 35 years; and with this he appears as *Pammes*, making Generation XIX in the list of Eratosthenes. And so Generations XVI, XVII, XVIII, and XIX have together 126 years; and with 64 more of the following generation XX of Phiops of Dyn. XIII (VI of Africanus), they complete the second exhibition of the 190 years in five generations. We now continue with the names.

"ιγ΄. Θηβαίων Αἰγυπτίων ιγ΄ ἐβασίλευσε Ῥαύωσις, ὅ ἐστιν Ἀρχικράτωρ, ἔτη ιγ΄." "*Rauosis*, which means Chief Ruler, 13 years." The gloss Ἀρχικράτωρ of itself justifies Bunsen's conjecture that this name was written *Rasosis*, and that it is the *Ra-tseser* of the monuments, the word *tseser* and its sign being repeatedly rendered into Greek by the word *κράτος*. The same conjecture is also confirmed by the form in which the name appears in Manetho's lists with *t* instead of *u* as *Ra-tæs-es*. That he was really the fifth not the first king, but has been transposed so as to stand first, and why this was done, and whence his 13 years are derived, has all been explained already; so that the pyramid built by him must not be taken to be older than the three great pyramids of the Suphises and Mencheres, as if its founder had reigned from B.C. 1932 to B.C. 1919; but rather we must suppose that Ra-tseser was buried in his pyramid about the year B.C. (1748 + 31 =) 1779. The 22 years and some months filled up to 23 years and given by Eratosthenes to this king and his successor Biyres, (to whom the whole 22 originally belonged when he stood as sixth in the lists of Manetho,) besides answering their special purpose in the adjustment

[Sor, 29 yrs. Dec. 20, B.C. 1932, to Dec. 13, B.C. 1903. Or] 23, to Dec. 14, B.C. 1909.

of the scheme of the first fifteen generations of Eratosthenes, are made also in a secondary way to ind'cate 13 years, otherwise omitted from the preceding dynasty.

"ιδ'. Θηβαίων Αἰγυπτίων ιδ' ἐβασίλευσε Βιΰρις ἔτη ι'." "*Biyris*, or *Biyres*, 10 years." This name varies from Bicheris, the sixth name in Manetho's list, much as the preceding name, Rauosis, varied from Ratœses, viz. by the substitution in the middle of it of an open vowel or diphthong for a consonant. His reign, originally the sixth, and consisting in Manetho's lists as unreduced of 22 years and some months, is the source, as has been explained above, both of the single decad given to him as the second generation of the dynasty by Eratosthenes, and also of the 13 years given to his predecessor Rauosis, as the first.

Besides completing the XV generations and 443 years "of the Cycle" with an average of 29½ years to each generation, this fifteenth generation of Eratosthenes completes an indication of Manetho's Dyn. IX (II of Africanus) of IX Tanite kings, with an allowance of 224 instead of 302 years. For the last king but one, the 8th, of that dynasty, viz. Sesochris the giant, having been substituted for or blended with the first king of the earliest Memphites, with both the 8th and 9th reigns of Dyn. IX unreduced attached to him, the remainder of the sum of the Tanite dynasty (302 − 78) is a sum of 224 years. But if we suppose it so to be hinted, that after cutting off in a manner 78 years, the remainder of 224 was to be allowed, not for the preceding VII, but for all the IX kings together, and count nine names, as if of Tanites, blended with and hinted under as many Memphites, from the compound reign and name of the giant to his eighth successor inclusively, that is, to this fifteenth generation of Eratosthenes, at which we now are, we find that the nine generations (79 + 6 + 30 + 26 + 20 + 18 + 22 + 13 + 10) make together exactly that sum of 224 years which would remain to Manetho's dynasty of the later Tanites, after reducing it by 78 years, that being also almost exactly the reduction required by the ordinary average for a line of IX kings. As for the historical chronology, since the last two Tanite reigns have been employed to *indicate* 51 years of the last 64 of the earliest Memphites, and of Dyn. XVII of the Chronicle, leaving 13 years still to run, while a continuance of 10 years more seems to be indicated afterwards for the Tanites themselves, we may guess (though with little certainty, having only such imperfect and indirect hints to go upon), that the 224 years of the IX later Tanites ended either in B.C. 1935, three years before, or else in B.C. 1919, twenty-three years after the capture of Memphis by the Shepherds, and the commencement of Dyn. XXVII of the Chronicle. And if so, the 224 years must have begun either in B.C. (1935 + 224 =) 2158, or in B.C. (1919 + 224 =) 2142, only 66 or 83 years after Menes. In either case it seems clear that the designation "*Tanite*," as given by Manetho to these kings (for we assume throughout that the designation *Thinite* is no earlier than the time of Eratosthenes), is to be understood not in the strictest sense, as if they lived and reigned in the city itself of Tanis. But they must have been by origin from Tanis, and of the same lineage with Menes and his seven successors, i.e. with the Tanites of Dyn. XVII of the Chronicle; and they must have reigned in some city of the Tanite region of the Delta, perhaps separated only by the water. For the city and nome of Tanis seems to have been double; and two cities and districts, divided only by the water, had from early times the white and the red crowns as their separate emblems. But it is time to return to the later Memphites, who are not like these Tanites merely alluded to, but are expressly named by Eratosthenes.

"*ιϛʹ. Θηβαίων Αἰγυπτίων ιεʹ ἐβασίλευσε Σαῶφις, Κομάστης, κατὰ δὲ ἐνίους Χρηματιστὴς, ἔτη κθʹ.*" "*Saophis*, that is, the *Long-haired*, or, according to some, the *Extortioner*, 29 years." He is plainly Saophis I., the builder of the great pyramid, and the second king of the dynasty, though the reign of 29 years here given to him belongs properly to Soris the first king, who is supplanted by the two names brought up from below. But after reckoning the 23 years which the two have brought with them, and understanding them to cover the name of Soris omitted, the only chronological disturbance as yet occasioned is this, that the accession of Saophis I. is put up 6 years higher than it ought to stand, so as to be at B.C.

Khouphou, 50. Dec. 14, B.C. 1909, to Dec. 2, B.C. 1860. Or 43, from Dec. 13, B.C. 1903.

(1932 − 23 =) 1909, instead of B.C. (1932 − 29 =) 1903. As regards the true length of his reign, we have not the means of determining it; yet the exaggeration in Manetho's list even of the long reigns of 50 and 53 years named by Herodotus, and the magnitude of the works executed by these kings, joined with the knowledge that the symmetry of their scheme for the exhibition of the first XX generations would force the Theban priests to take liberties both with the names and with the reigns of this dynasty, incline one to suppose that the reigns of the two Suphises, at least, were longer than they seem to be by the list of Eratosthenes. At the same time it is to be borne in mind, that if there was in this Memphite family the same frequency of associations in the throne and joint reigns as we know there was about the same time in Upper Egypt, in the family of the kings of Manetho's Dyn. XV (XII of Africanus), many reigns might with equal truth be said to have had two or more very different sums of years.

As regards the double gloss on the monumental name Shouphoo, or Khoufou (identifiable with Χέοψ of Herodotus, and Chemmis, or Chembis, of Diodorus), Κομάστης, i.e. "*Comatus*," is intelligible, and has occurred above in connection with 'Αν-ωυφὴς, or Σαῶφις (*Aan-Khoufou*), of Dyn. X (III of Africanus). How the other gloss, Χρηματιστὴς, may also be connected with the sound or sense of the Egyptian name is not so clear; but one can see in it an allusion to that same unpopularity which is mentioned by Herodotus as attaching to the names and works of these kings.

Khaf-ra, 57. Dec. 7, B.C. 1880, to Nov. 23, B.C. 1823. Or 27, from Dec. 2, B.C. 1850.

"*ις′. Θηβαίων ις′ ἐβασίλευσε Σαῶφις β′, ἔτη κζ′.*" "*Saophis II.* reigned 27 years." The 27 years are made out of the 66 years, with some odd months, which the same king had, we may suppose, in Manetho's lists. So the four generations of Eratosthenes, down to this point, are in fact equivalent to the three first reigns of Manetho for the same dynasty, with four decads cut off from both the second and the third reigns, besides that the first and the second reigns are transposed. Instead of the 29 + 63 (= 40 + 23) + 66 (= 40 + 26 and some months), or 67 of Manetho, Eratosthenes has 23 (subdivided unchronologically into two reigns, and equal to 63 − 40) + 29 + 27 ( = 67 − 40). And the reigns of the two Souphises, according to the list of Eratosthenes, viz. 29 and 27 years, if put together, make 56, the sum given by Herodotus to the second; for he writes that the one of the two reigned 50 and the other 56 years, and that the two, being *brothers*, reigned in all 106 years. So the units of the joint sum of Herodotus are exhibited by Eratosthenes, and only so many decads as are historically improbable for two *brothers*, or cousins, are cut off and disallowed. Manetho, it is to be remarked, makes the joint sum of the two reigns (63 + 66) to be 129 years, which is higher by 23 even than the joint sum of Herodotus. Herodotus was told that the construction of the causeway and other preparations for building the great pyramid of Cheops, or Khouphou, occupied that king for 10 years, and the building itself for 20 more, so that his "extortion and tyranny" would seem to have distinguished the last 30 years of his reign, or perhaps somewhat less, since we have learned from the pyramid itself that Souphis I. did not live to see it quite completed. Pliny has preserved a statement that "*the three* pyramids," those, that is, of *Shoophou*, or Souphis I., *Khaphra*, (the Souphis II. of Manetho and Eratosthenes, the Κέφρην of Herodotus, and the Chabryes of Diodorus,) and Mycerinus, *Mencheres*, "were built in a space of 78 years and 4 months," a time which agrees well enough with the relation of Herodotus, if only we suppose it to be exclusive of the 10 years of preparation named as preceding. Let us suppose, then, that Souphis I. really reigned in all the 50 years given to him by Herodotus, and that these commencing in B.C. (1932 − 29 = ) 1903, after the 29 of Soris (whose name has been found on the monuments, and is legible on a fragment of the Turin papyrus, but is connected with no great or known pyramid), ended in B.C. (1903 − 50 = ) 1853. Then, though he really died *before* his pyramid was completed, we may perhaps assume that the 20 years of its construction were meant by the informants of Herodotus to be reckoned to his death. If so, it should have been commenced in the year B.C. (1853 + 20 = ) 1873, that is, after the end of the fifth year of the seven years of plenty; and its unusual proportions may have been suggested afterwards by the superabundance of labour which first came to be at the disposal of the kings in Egypt, whether suzerains or tributaries, four years later, after the second year of the famine. Let us suppose, again, the successor of Shoufou, Shafra, or Khaphra, the Κέφρην of Herodotus, to have really reigned in all 56 years, as Herodotus says he did, but that for 20 of these he was merely associated with Shouphou, we shall then have at his death in B.C. (1853 − 36 =) 1817, fifty six years (20 + 36 = 56), during which the construction of the two great pyramids had been going on; and we shall have to fix the following reign of Mencheres at 22 years and 4 months, if the 78 years and 4 months of Pliny were meant to end at his death, though it is true that the third pyramid was left by Mencheres unfinished. Hence it would seem that, besides reducing Manetho's sums of 63 and 66 years for the two Souphises, by 13 and 10, to the 50 and 56 of Herodotus, we must cut off, as years merely concurrent, from Souphis II. 20 more of the 56 years left to him, and no less than 40 from the 63 years of Mencheres, so that instead of 29 + 63 + 66 + 63, or 29 + 50 + 56 + 63, the first four reigns will have 29 + 50 + 36 + 23 = 138 years; and the last of the four, that of Mencheres, will end in B.C. (1817 − 23 =) 1794, leaving (1794 − 1748 =) 46 years only to be divided among the last four kings of the dynasty, of whom one only, and he too as the builder of another pyramid, Ratœses, or Rauosis (*Ra-tseser*), is known to us from the monuments. And there will be no doubt as to the manner of apportioning the reigns of these four kings, since the units of Manetho for the four last reigns suit exactly, while their whole sum shows an excess of two decads, and there are only two out of the four reigns from which a decad can be retrenched. Instead, therefore, of 25 + 22 + 10 + 9 years (the 10 for the seventh reign, the last but one, being recovered from Syncellus's sum of the dynasty), we must reckon 15 + 12 + 10 + 9, which make together 46 years, and carry us down from B.C. 1794, to B.C. 1779, B.C. 1767, B.C. 1757, and finally to B.C. 1748. But with this last date for the end of the dynasty it will have in all the full space of 184 years, which are 6 too many to suit the sum of Eratosthenes, who gives it 178, and

7 too many to suit the sum of Manetho, who, as reduced but without change of his units, gives it only 177 years. We must suppose, then, to suit the sum of 178 years, that Soris, the first king, reigned alone only those 23 years which are virtually given to him by Eratosthenes, and some months over technically reckoned to his successor; and that Souphis I. followed with 50 or with 44 current years, according as 23 or 29 are reckoned to Soris. But to suit the sum of Manetho we must suppose that the *actual* reign of Soris, which he reigned alone, had not commenced from Thoth 1, in B.C. 1932, but was antedated when reckoned by Eratosthenes at 23 years, whereas, for Manetho, who gave the actual reigns only with their odd months, the time that Soris reigned alone was only 22 years, and his successor Suphis I. would have either 50 or only 43 years according as 29 or only 22 were reckoned to Soris. So we recover and complete that exhibition of Manetho's units which we had sacrificed for a moment as to one point by admitting the 50 years of Herodotus for the second reign.

"ιζ'. Θηβαίων ιζ' ἐβασίλευσε Μοσχέρης, 'Ηλιόδοτος, ἔτη λα'." "*Moscheres*, which means *Given by Ra* the Sun-god, reigned 31 years." Mencheres or Moncheres (for the σ is only a corruption), the Mycerinus of Herodotus, is certainly the king who built the third pyramid, which though smaller surpassed the pyramids of Shouphou and Shafra in its workmanship, and was partly faced with Ethiopian granite, as is still to be seen. This granite would be of itself an indication (if any such additional indications were needed) that the Memphite kings who built the great pyramids lived *after* the conquest of Nubia by Sesortasen I., rather than *before* it: and certainly, *if* they *had* been earlier, it would have been unaccountable that the Memphite priests should have told Herodotus that, down to the time of Sesostris *the first conqueror of Nubia* and his immediate predecessor *Maire*, none of their kings had waged any great war, or left any monuments that were remarkable. The force of this latter confession is unfelt because the name "Sesostris" was made to cover at once and confound together Sesortasen I. and Rameses II. and III.: and Herodotus being told, and truly, that the

*Menkaura.* 23. Nov. 23. B.C. 1823, to Nov. 17, B.C. 1800.

pyramid-builders followed at no long interval after Sesostris the first conqueror of Nubia, he put them down after Rameses II. and III., in doing which he was of course deceived. But the general error of ascribing to the builders of the pyramids too high an antiquity rests only on their apparent place in Manetho's lists, and on the presumption, groundless in itself though purposely suggested to Greek readers, that all Manetho's dynasties were consecutive. The pyramid of Mencheres is said to be double in its construction, as if begun and ended by two different founders. It contains two distinct sepulchral chambers, in the chief of which was found the sarcophagus of Mencheres himself. This was lost at sea; but the wooden case or outer coffin of the same king, with his name on its surface, is to be seen in the British Museum, and has been illustrated by Mr. Birch. The reputation for piety ascribed to him by Herodotus is illustrated by the manner in which his name is honoured in the "Ritual of the Dead," for it is there mentioned that he reopened the temples. The gloss on his name, Ἡλιόδοτος, "Gift of the Sun," is probably derived only from the last two syllables, *kar* and *Re*.

*Ra-tseser?* 15, Nov. 17, B.C. 1800, to Nov. 13, B.C. 1785. Blyris, 12, to Nov. 10, B.C. 1773. *Sevaouch-re?* 10, to Nov. 8, B.C. 1763.

"ιη'. Θηβαίων ιη' ἐβασίλευσε Μοσθὴς, ἔτη λγ'." "*Mosthes* reigned 33 years." This name is no doubt a reduplication of Mencheres, only more than ordinarily corrupted; the whole reign of 63 years and some months given by Manetho to Mencheres being split into two of 31 and 33 years respectively. It is curious that on a monument from a tomb of Memphis, now at Berlin, another Mencheres, the seventh king of Manetho's Dyn. XII (V of Africanus), is similarly reduplicated, there being two kings, one named *Men-ker-Hor* and the other *Men-ker-Re*, instead of only one, followed as in Manetho's list by *Tat-chere*, and seemingly also by *Ounos*. It is *possible* therefore that in this case also in Dyn. XI (IV of Africanus) the name and reign of Mencheres may cover two actual kings. Certainly the story about the religious king Mencheres repeated by Herodotus would indicate rather a short than a long or average reign. But whether there were two Mencheres or only one, if the death of the pious king was late in B.C. 1794, or in 1793, that of the patriarch Joseph having occurred early in B.C. 1798, one may divine the meaning of those few years of piety and happiness which just then as a gleam of sunshine gladdened Egypt in the midst of her mysterious oppression by a Typhonian power. The six years of festival which the malice of those who knew not Joseph imagined afterwards to mark and celebrate the epoch of his death (though his influence was destined still to oppress Egypt for 50 more years), are a sort of set-off and compensation for those seven harvests (including six full years of plenty) on which his influence and the influence surviving him was based.

"ιθ'. Θηβαίων ιθ' ἐβασίλευσε Πάμμης, Ἄρχων Γῆς [so we may correct for Ἀρχόνδης], ἔτη λϛ'." "*Pammes*, that is *Ruler of the Land*, reigned 35 years." The name is no doubt a corruption of *Thamphthis*, the ninth and last of the dynasty in Manetho's lists; and the reign is made up, as has been explained above, by adding to the 9 years properly belonging to the last king of the dynasty the 25 years of Manetho's fifth reign. The gloss Ἄρχων Γῆς, suggests the idea that the name may possibly be compounded of the two words "*Djamto*," that is, *Sceptrum mundi*.

Pammes, 9. Nov. 8, B.C. 1763, to Nov. 5, B.C. 1734.

Dynasty XII of Manetho (V of Africanus), of IX kings certainly of Memphite connection, but called Elephantinites, whom we suppose to have been Heliopolitans or Memphites of the East Bank, is neither expressly noticed, nor, so far as the writer can see, even covertly alluded to by the list of Eratosthenes. So it justifies the opinion formed on other grounds, that these kings, wheresoever they reigned, were contemporaries of those of Dyn. X or XI (III or IV of Africanus), perhaps partly of both, and of secondary importance. One might conjecture that Manetho's *second* line of Tanites or Thinites really reigned at Heliopolis; and that there also, as at Memphis, a new line, namely that called by Manetho Elephantinite, was substituted by the Shepherds, and continued during the 184 years of their supremacy over Lower Egypt. But these are questions upon which, at present, nothing can be safely concluded; and it is to the study of the monuments alone that we must look for information.

Two observations, however, respecting Dyn. XII of Manetho (V of Africanus), may be made in passing. The first is this, that the names of most of its kings are identifiable in the tombs near Memphis, and are associated there with those of the pyramid-builders, *Outseserkerf, Nepherchere, Tseserirenra, Karenra, Menkerhor* and *Menkere, Tutchere,* and *Ounos,* being probably or certainly the 1st, 3rd, 4th, 5th, 7th, 8th and 9th kings of Dyn. XII of Manetho. The second observation is connected with the elements "*kar*" and "*re*" entering the former into five out of the nine names of this dynasty in the lists, the latter into all of them except one. These two syllables, *kar* and *re,* appear first in composition in the sixth name of the later Tanites of Dynasty IX of Manetho, viz. *Chaires,* or *Cher-res,* and are both repeated in the three remaining names of that dynasty. In Dyn. X (III of Afric.) of the earliest Memphites, *Re* seems to enter into composition, and to be noticed as entering into composition, in Manetho's 2nd, 3rd, 4th, 8th, and 9th names, though perhaps it is not really an element in them all; and *kar* seems to enter into four of them, the 1st, the 4th, the 7th, and the 9th. In Dyn. XI (IV of Africanus), the same two elements occur together in three out of the VIII names, viz. the 4th, the 6th, and the 7th: but in Dyn. XII (V of Afric.) they occur together in five out of the IX names, and *Re* alone in three of the remaining four. Another element, "*nepher,*" which appears first in the 7th name of Dyn. IX (II of Afric.) in union with the other two, and makes the name *Nephercheres,* reappears in the same conjunction in a later Nephercheres (the 3rd name) of Dyn. XII (V of Africanus). But in the upper line of the tablet of Abydos two out of these three elements in conjunction, viz. *nepher* and *kar,* making the name *Nepherchar,* with or without the addition of *Re,* are reproduced in no less than eight cartouches out of a series of thirteen which occur together; and the element *kar,* with or without the *Re,* but without the *nepher,* occurs in three more; so that from one name only of the thirteen, *Mer-en-Hor,* both the *kar* and the *nepher* are absent. This comparison might perhaps justify the inference that the kings of Dyn. XII of Manetho (V of Africanus), and also those of the series of the Abydos tablet, whether that series be simple or complex, are continuations rather of the last Tanites, and more closely connected with them by blood, than with the Memphites of either Dyn. X or XI, with whom, however, they were not unconnected. The names *Sesochris*, *Mesochris*, and *Ouserchere*s in Dynasties IX, X, and XII, *Chaires* and *Cheneres* of IX and *Cheres* of XII, *Nephercheres* of IX and XII, *Sesorthos* and *Tosertasis* of X, *Ratoises* of XI, and *Rathouris* and *Sisires* of XII, *Saophis* of X and XI, and Mencheres of XI and XII, are names respectively identical or similar; while in the series of the upper line of the Abydos tablet, besides the family names *Nepherchere* and *Cher-re* running through it all, we find a *Menchere* connecting it with Dyn. XI and XII, a [*Neb-*]*bi* [*nefer*]*-chere*, reminding us of *Bicheres* of Dyn. X, a [*Ma-*]*tatchere*, like *Tatchere* of Dyn. XII., a *Nepherchere Khantou*, somewhat resembling *Thamphthis* of Dyn. XI, a *Meren-Hor*, which takes us to Dyn. XIII, besides a *Papa* and an *Ounos* in composition in two names not regal, looking like names of governors under the Shepherds Apophis and Janias.

*Dynasty XIII of Manetho* (*VI of Africanus*) *VI Memphites of Central Egypt, with* 177 *years, partially exhibited in the list of Eratosthenes by III generations with* 107 *years.*

Dyn. XIII. 107 of its 177 years from Jan. 24, B.C. 2074, to Dec. 29, B.C. 1968.

If, in passing to this dynasty, the list of Eratosthenes begins not with the first king of Manetho's list, *Othoes*, *Ati*, or perhaps *Teta*, who is also its first king in the Karnak Chamber, but with *Apappus*, that is *Phiops*, or *Papa*, the last king of Manetho's six, and the second of the four of the Karnak Chamber, the reason for this is not merely want of room to place all the kings even of those dynasties which are distinctly exhibited; but rather because it was desired, while following the order of Manetho, to follow also and mark, though in a general way, the composition of Dynasty XVII of the Chronicle. For this reason it was that, after enumerating the first seven kings of the early Memphites, (the sixth and seventh making the first two generations of Dyn. XVII of the Chronicle,) the last two, who did not enter into the composition of Dyn. XVII of the Chronicle, were omitted. And now, for the same reason, after the unchronological interposition of the later Memphites of Dyn. XI (IV of Africanus), justified by their historical continuity, and by the order of Manetho, the first king or kings of Dyn.

XIII (VI of Africanus), who do not enter into the composition of Dyn. XVII of the Chronicle, are omitted, and that king, *Apappus*, is named in whom the sovereign line of the Chronicle, broken off with the seventh king of Dyn. X (III of Africanus), is to be resumed and continued.

Besides this, the long reign of Phiops of 94 years, if placed next after Generation XIX in the series of Eratosthenes, was very capable of being turned to account; whereas if any other king or kings of the same dynasty had been named first, it would have caused no slight difficulty. As it is, Phiops being placed as Generation XX, the 64 years still wanted towards the second exhibition of the 190 of the Chronicle in five generations are readily supplied. It is true that these 64 years fall far short of his whole sum, so that as a generation he becomes ambiguous, contributing part of his years to one sum of the Chronicle and the rest to another. But this, far from being a blemish, is actually an improvement to the symmetry of the scheme. For thus, in the first place, it is *indicated* that the 103 years of the Chronicle, which the last part of the years of Phiops are made to begin, are not *really* separable from the 190 which his first 64 years complete; though the contrary seemed to be asserted when Menes and his Tanites or Thinites were named, and their 190 years exhibited for the first time, as preceding the 443 years "of the Cycle," and as separated by them from the 103 years of Dyn. XVII of the Chronicle. Again, the two short reigns following Phiops in Manetho's list were very fit to be inserted as part of the compensation due for the suppression of three out of the VIII generations belonging to Dyn. XVI of the Chronicle. For thus two out of three compensating generations, necessarily to be inserted somewhere, were inserted so as to be in actual contact with the five of which they were the complement; and though the name and generation of Phiops was, strictly speaking, the last of the five generations of the 190 years, still the remainder of his years, being extraneous to that sum, and no fewer than 36, were an abundant *indication* of one additional generation; so that it might stand at once for a promise of one of the compensating generations due, and also as a link uniting all the three compensating generations with the preceding sum of 190 years, and with the five generations to the last name of which it belonged.

It is to be noticed that in the list of Eratosthenes advantage is taken of the distinction between *generations* and *reigns*, to reckon to the generation of Phiops the whole century of his *life*, though its first six years are expressly excluded by Manetho from his *reign*. This change is virtually a transfer of half the last reign of the dynasty to Phiops, since the same number, viz. six years, which are added to him, are suppressed out of the twelve of Nitocris. And the motive is plain, namely, to make the two reigns, which were to stand as compensatory of *names* suppressed above, to have as few *years* attached to them as possible, and to obtain as many years as possible to give to those four generations which were meant to be paralleled with the four of Dyn. XVII of the Chronicle, and which properly should have had to themselves the whole space of 103 years, instead of sharing it with two or three names displaced, or compensatory of others displaced, from the preceding 190 years of its Dyn. XVI.

A point of interest in connection with this peculiarity of reckoning the whole century of his *life* to Phiops is the indirect confirmation which it affords to the suspicion that the designation *Thinite*, given by the "Manetho" of Africanus to his Dynasties I and II, is not really from the true and original Manetho, but from his re-editor Ptolemy of Mendes, and originally from Eratosthenes, with whose Greek as well as Egyptian chronology Ptolemy of Mendes was well acquainted. For in the case of Phiops we have a clear proof that the compiler of the Manetho of Africanus had before him, and followed in some things, the list of Eratosthenes. For though a notice of the original Manetho is repeated, that Phiops "succeeded to the throne at the age of six years, and reigned to the age of a hundred," that is, certainly only ninety-four years, the author, while preserving this notice, has himself reckoned the whole 100 years to the sum of his Dyn. XI (XIII of the original Manetho); and this by no mere error, as the sums of that and of the other dynasties (noted by Africanus), and the larger sums entering into the scheme of the author, sufficiently prove. Those expressions, then, in the same lists of Africanus which represent Menes and his successors as "Theinites" or "Thebans," and as "reigning over the Thebans," may well be from the same source.

*Papa-Maire, 94 years, Jan. 24, B.C. 2068, to Dec. 31, B.C. 1975. Or 21, from Jan. 5, B.C. 1995, to Dec. 31, B.C. 1975.*

"κ'. Θηβαίων κ' ἐβασίλευσεν 'Απάππους, Μέγιστος· οὗτος, ὥς φασι, παρὰ ὥραν μίαν ἐβασίλευσεν ἔτη ρ'." "*Apappus*, which means *Very-Great*, reigned, as is said, 100 years, all but one hour." He is the *Phiops* of Manetho, who reigned 94 years, and lived to 100; and the *Papa Maire* of the monuments, who is called by Herodotus Mœris, and who is said to have been the first king who did anything very remarkable. He appears on the monuments with the double cartouche, of *family* or *personal*, and *throne-name*, the use of which in later times became universal, though for some time after his reign, as also before it, an intermediate fashion of inclosing both names, or even all the royal names and titles, in one compound or elongated cartouche, was occasionally used. The vast number of royal names mentioned by Herodotus and Hecatæus, and still exhibited or indicated by the Turin papyrus, does not seem to have been swelled, as one might have suspected, by feigning double cartouches to represent twice the true number of kings; for in the fragments of the Turin papyrus two cartouches are not given to any one king; but many of the names, especially those of the Nubian connection, are long and compound, exhibiting in one the two cartouches belonging to the king named, which in some cases are found separately on the monuments. The names in the uppermost line of the Abydos tablet have also many of them a like compound character. Papa Maire is represented in the Karnak Chamber not by his throne-name *Mai-re*, but by his personal name *Papa*. He occurs elsewhere double, on one and the same monument, as if he were two kings, being seated *dos à dos* to himself, with the name Papa on one side and Maire on the other, and on one side wearing the white crown of the Upper and on the other the red crown of the Lower Country, to which latter he may have succeeded perhaps in right of his queen *Anch-set-mire*, mother of his son Nepherchere, if she were a daughter of

Snefrou. His *Gold Hawk title* has *three* hawks, over the emblem for *cnoub*, gold, as if he might be styled " *Chryses III.*" His *sixteenth* year of sovereignty, and seemingly also his *eighteenth* is marked; and he appears in several places in connection both with *Teti* or *Teta* who preceded him, and with *Meranre* and *Nepherchere*, who were perhaps his sons, or his son and son-in-law or grandson. The same two kings appear also in the Karnak Chamber as his successors, and represent probably the last two reigns of the dynasty, though the one of them died in the second year after his father, and the other, having died before his father, was represented, as we may collect, by his widow Nitocris, who " reigned by right of her deceased husband." Pliny mentions " two plain obelisks without hieroglyphics," which may be a sign of these being also the most ancient, as erected one of them by the king *Marres* and the other by *Phios*, that is really both by this king Papa Maire, one of his names being on one of the two and the other on the other. And an altar of dark granite with the names of places and deities around it, now preserved at Turin, shows that already, before the conquest of Nubia, the power of this king was exerted on the Nubian frontier, and that blocks of granite were quarried there and brought down the Nile, though not in such quantities nor in such vast masses as afterwards, when Sesortasen I. set up his obelisks, and when the Third Pyramid was faced in part with Ethiopic stone. The gloss *μέγιστος* is derived naturally from the name *Apopi*, which signifies a giant, and also " the great dragon," or serpent, the oldest representative of evil and darkness in the Egyptian mythology, as appears from many places in the " Ritual of the Dead."

In B.C. 2007, the 67th year of the life of Papa Maire, if the figures of Manetho's Dyn. XVII are to be trusted, those Shepherds who 86 years later became suzerains of Lower Egypt first settled in the Delta. Whether Philistines or Arabs by origin, their names seem to be Egyptian, that of their first king *Saites* connecting him with the *Saitic* or *Seth-ro-itic* nome and its local deity, that of *Apachnas* having a purely Egyptian sound, *Janias* and *Asseth* being the names of native kings of Manetho's Dynasties X and XII, *Aan* and *Assa*, while *Apophis*, a name taken by more than one Shepherd king, was perhaps borrowed from *Papa Maire*, whose long life and reign may have attracted admiration.

With the 64th year of Apappus we have the completion of the 443 years "of the Cycle" in fifteen generations, as made out after first exhibiting, in five generations reduced from eight, the 190 years of the Tanites of Dyn. XVI of the Chronicle, with Menes at their head. For 79 + 6 + 30 + 26 + 20 + 18 + 22 + 13 + 10 + 29 + 27 + 31 + 33 + 35 + 64 make together 443 years.

Also we have at this point the completion of the first exhibition of the 103 years of Dyn. XVII of the Chronicle, as entering into the composition of the 443 years of the Cycle unchronologically taken in, the same 103 years being to be exhibited again in the second series of 443 years, which from its apparent coincidence with as many years of the Chronicle, from the 190th to the (190 + 443 =) 633rd year of the kings after Menes, we call chronological. For if we begin with those 39 years of Sirius and Chnoubus Gneurus which, when their merely apparent depression of 6 years has been rectified, coincide with the first 39 of Dyn. XVII of the Chronicle, and eject the seven names taken from Dyn. XI of Manetho (IV of Africanus), as inserted only in appearance between the 39th and the 40th years of Dynasty XVII of the Chronicle, then 17 years of Sirius + 22 of Chnoubus Gneurus + 64 of Apappus make together 103 years.

Lastly, we have also at this same point the completion of the second, and of what we may call the *chronological*, exhibition of the 190 years of Dyn. XVI of the Chronicle in five instead of eight generations, so as to suit the supposition that the 443 years "of the Cycle," with their fifteen generations (62 + 59 + 32 + 19 + 18 + 79 + 6 + 30 + 26 + 20 + 18 + 22 + 13 + 10 + 29, making together 443), have been reckoned first in their original order as they stood in the Chronicle, instead of being transposed and inserted unchronologically between the 190 years of Dyn. XVI and the 103 of Dyn. XVII of the kings of the Chronicle.

"κα'. Θηβαίων κα' ἐβασίλευσεν Ἐχεσκοσοκάρας ἔτος α'."

The reign of only one year identifies this corrupt name with the *Menthe-suphis* of Manetho. In the Turin papyrus also (Fragments 42, 43), though the names of Apappus and his successor are lost, their *reigns* are clearly identifiable, the one having 90 years and some units, probably 4, and the next following it having only 1 year and 1 month; after which we see the name *Nitocris*, but its figures again are lost. In the Karnak Chamber, and in the tombs of Chenoboschion, the name of *Papa* is followed by two other names of the same line, which may safely be presumed to represent the last two reigns of Manetho and the Turin papyrus, though instead of the female name *Nitocris* these monumental lists have that of *Nepherchere*, whom we suppose to have been her husband. The intermediate king, then, with whom we are now occupied as constituting Generation XXI of Eratosthenes, is the *Meranre* of the Karnak Chamber, and of other monuments.

"κβ′. Θηβαίων κβ′ ἐβασίλευσε Νίτωκρις, γυνὴ ἀντὶ τοῦ ἀνδρὸς, ὅ ἐστιν 'Αθηνᾶ Νικηφόρος, ἔτη ϛ′." "*Nitocris*, a woman, reigned *in place of her husband* 6 years. The name means '*Athene* (*Neith*) *the Victorious*.'" The gloss is clear, and in this instance, at least, not taken from the mere sound, as the name is written in the Turin papyrus *Nit-okr*, and it recurs similarly compounded in later times. Whether she really reigned only 6 years, or the 12 which Manetho gives her, cannot be determined from the Turin papyrus, as the figures belonging in it to her name are broken away; but since we can discern a motive for shortening her reign, we may suppose that the six years added in the list of Eratosthenes to Apappus are six which have been cut off from Nitocris. Of Manetho's notice that she "built the third pyramid," that of Mycerinus, something has been said elsewhere. That her beauty and ruddy complexion also are borrowed by Manetho from the Greek Rhodopis may be suspected. Her courage covers perhaps an allusion to the story in Herodotus of her avenging (and at Memphis, as it would seem) the death of her brother. If there were any truth under these stories, we should have to suppose that the king assassinated was Meranre, brother of her deceased husband

Nepherchere. But the long life of Apappus, and the facts that the elder of his two associated sons, Meranre, survived him by only one year, while the younger had already died before him, lead one to suspect that Meranre also died a natural death, and that, when her brother-in-law died, the widow of Nepherchere was no longer distinguished either by youth or beauty, but reigned securely as a local queen, under Sesortasen I. It may be remarked that the female name *Nitocris*, ending Dynasty XIII (VI of Africanus), and the notice that she had reigned not as regent for a son, but "instead of a deceased husband," shows of itself what it was that caused this second transition of the sovereign power to a new line, Sesortasen I. becoming suzerain by the failure of the male line of Dyn. XIII (VI of Africanus) on the death of Meranre, just as Papa seems to have become suzerain on the death of Snefrou. For there is, or was, at Gizeh, the tomb (not a pyramid) of a prince, named *Nepher-iri-karu*, who has the titles of the *King's High Justiciary, King's Guardian of the Divine Apis*, and *Director of the Royal Household*; and this prince, who was no doubt heir to the throne, died before his father *Snefrou*. On the other hand, the queen of Papa Maire, named *Anch-set-Mi-re*, who was the mother of the king *Nepherchere*, husband of Nitocris, was herself the daughter of a king, we may suppose of Snefrou.

Both the two kings of Manetho's Dyn. X (III of Africanus) who make Generations I and II of Dyn. XVII of the Chronicle, viz. *Sahou-ra* and his son *Snefrou*, appear on contemporary stelæ at Wady Magara in the Sinaitic peninsula as conquerors, though the hostilities undertaken by them and their victories had probably no further object or result than the undisputed possession of the copper-works on the spot where they are recorded. These copper-works are constantly designated afterwards as the "mines of Snefrou." Both these two kings, in the stelæ alluded to, are represented like Sesortasen I. in Nubia, and like other later Pharaohs, clutching a fallen enemy by the hair of the head, and holding in the other hand a mace uplifted, ready to strike. The tablet of Sahoura is divided into two compartments, in one of which, to the left of the spectator, he is represented twice over, as if he were double, once wearing the white and once wearing the red crown. In the other compartment, in which he is striking his prostrate enemy, he wears the white crown. These two crowns one may suspect to have been first used to distinguish the Upper and Lower cities and districts of the Tanite kingdom; then, later, to distinguish the Upper or Memphite kingdom (with the symbol of the White Crown and the White Fortress), from the Lower capital and kingdom of Tanis; and lastly, to distinguish the whole Lower region of Memphis and the Delta from the Thebaid and Upper Egypt, to which the white crown was then finally attached. But the history of the two crowns, and of the other customary emblems and titles referring to lordship over two regions, an Upper and a Lower, is a subject only for conjecture. At present no more can be affirmed with certainty than this, that the use of the two crowns, and that of the other double emblems and titles, in later times by no means always imports sovereignty over the whole extent of Egypt. Still it is important to notice that *Sahoura* and *Snefrou*, and after them *Papa Maire*, are the earliest kings at present known to be represented on any monument as if they were double, wearing separately or uniting in one two distinct crowns. The same two kings, Sahoura and Snefrou, are also the earliest who are known to have taken as their special device the gold hawk, or Horus, which appears in the titles of later kings, both preceding the standard-title when uninclosed, or surmounting it when it is inclosed in the standard itself, and which also, in connection with the collar, the sign for gold, and for the word *nub*, forms what is afterwards known as the *Gold Horus title*. In the stele of Sahoura the father at Wady Magara the order in which his titles appear is this: First, there is the gold hawk, or Horus, not surmounting, as it does later in the Gold Horus title, the sign for *nub*, but alone: next follow the signs for the words *Neb Schaou* ("Lord of the Diadems"), that is, we may presume, "Lord of the two Crowns," since with later kings these words are placed under or after the Vulture and Uræus, which are symbolical of the Upper and Lower regions; and even without the addition of the words *Neb Schaou*, the Vulture and Uræus over the sign for the word *Neb* are translated "Lord of the Diadems." In the stele of Sahoura neither the Standard nor the Gold Horus title, nor the Vulture and Uræus title, appears as yet in its complete form. The gold Horus has not the collar under it, nor are the Vulture and Uræus seen before the words *Neb Schaou.* Hence it may seem that the gold Horus here preceding the title "Lord of the Diadems," is simply equivalent to the standard title of later kings, as that always goes first, and is sometimes written uninclosed; for in ancient times the same title or device as was written under or after the Vulture and Uræus, was also associated with the standard. In this case of Sahoura, after the gold Horus, and the title *Neb Schaou* (Lord of the Diadems), there follow the sprig and the bee, which, in later times always precede the throne-name of the king, as the goose and the disk of the sun, *Si Ra* ("Son of the Sun"), precede his family name. The sprig and the bee too, pronounced *Souten Kheb,* are interpreted in later times to mean King of the Upper and King of the Lower Countries. After these, inclosed in the usual ring, there is the name *Ra-Sahou,* or *Sahou-ra;* and subjoined, a little below the cartouche, are the signs for the words *Neter-Aa* (the "Great God"). In the stele of his son Snefrou the titles are fuller: there is the oblong standard ending with a long fringe, surmounted by the gold Horus wearing the double composite crown afterwards known as the *pshent,* and containing the device *Neb-Mat,* "Lord of Justice," instead of the title "Lord of the Diadems" which would have been in the standard of his father. The standard is to the right hand side in the stele, a little below. Above there is an elongated cartouche containing first the sprig and the bee, then the vulture and uræus, each of them surmounting the sign for *Neb* (Lord), so as to be equivalent to "Lord [of the diadem] of the Upper," and "Lord [of the diadem] of the Lower Region," though the word *schaou* (diadems) is not expressed. After the vulture and uræus there follows the title *Neb-Mat* (Lord of Justice), the same that is also contained in the standard. Then follows the gold hawk, perched on the collar, the sign for *nub* (gold), exhibiting for the first time, so far as is known, the Gold Horus title in its full form. Lastly, the name itself, *Snefrou*, closes and completes the cartouche, under which is subjoined uninclosed the title "*Neter-Aa.*" Below this there is another small cartouche containing simply the name *Snefrou*, without any repetition of titles before it, but with some of those signs which usually follow royal cartouches subjoined.

It may naturally be inferred from these titles that it was *Sahoura* who first took the title *Lord of the Diadems*, as with him these words appear *alone*, and his son Snefrou, though he retains and perpetuates their sense, can no longer take them alone as a distinctive device: secondly, that it was *Snefrou* who first took the *full* Gold Horus title, which is repeated by other kings after him, but always with some distinctive addition. Also, in reference to the opinion that the gold hawk of Sahoura preceding his title "*Neb Schaou*" is simply his standard title written at full, but uninclosed in the standard itself, it is to be noticed that in the elongated cartouche of the son, Snefrou, where the title *Neb Mat* corresponding to the *Neb Schaou* of Sahoura and belonging also to the standard occurs, it is not preceded by the pshented or double-crowned hawk which surmounts the standard, but is preceded by the vulture and uræus, and followed by a gold hawk like that which came first in the titles of his father, only now in a different order, and placed over the sign for *nub*. But even if the gold hawk and the "*Neb Schaou*" of Sahoura at Wady Magara be merely his standard title, still, he may have also taken the gold hawk for his special device, and may on that account be the Χρύσης of Eratosthenes. And whether Snefrou merely completed the Gold Horus title by placing the collar, the sign for gold, under the gold hawk of Sahoura, or originated it altogether by taking the gold hawk which had only surmounted the standard or preceded the standard title of Sahoura and making of it with the collar a separate and additional title, in either case, there may be enough to account for his being designated Χρύσης Χρύσου υἱὸς, the Gold Horus King, son of the first Gold Horus King.

After all, the gloss may be erroneous, and the double "gold" of Snefrou may refer not to a father and a son, but to the "*gold* hawk," and the collar, the sign for the word *nub*, meaning "gold," over which it was placed.

After Sahoura and Snefrou, their successor in Dyn. XVII of the Chronicle, Papa Maire, who appears to have associated with himself his two sons Meranre and Nepherchere, takes for his Gold Horus title *three* gold hawks perched on the collar, the sign for gold, the eldest son, *Meraure*, taking *two*, and the younger, *Nepherchere*, only *one*, but with an additional sign to distinguish it from the earlier single hawk of Snefrou.

The name *Sahoura* having been found marked on blocks of stone belonging to the northern or lesser pyramid of Abouseer (which seems to have been once 257 feet square at its base and 162 high), and the name *Ra-tseser* having been found in the middle pyramid of Abouseer (which was 274 feet square at the base and 171 high), it has been concluded that these are the tombs of two of the Memphite kings of Dyn. X of Manetho (III of Africanus). But this conclusion has been too hastily drawn. The name *Ra-tseser* (either with or without the addition of *en*) certainly belonged to more than one king; and though it suits perfectly one name, viz. the second, *Tosorthrus* or *Sesorthrus*, of Manetho's Dyn. X (III of Africanus), who first, according to Manetho, introduced in building the use of squared stones,—and that may *possibly* be the name found by Perring on a block taken as he says from some earlier building and built into the pyramid of Reegah,—the same monumental name suits equally well *Ratœses* the immediate successor of the Suphises and Mencheres in Manetho's Dyn. XI (IV of Africanus). And, as found in the middle pyramid of Abouseer, it is accompanied by the Gold Horus title, with the collar, the sign for *nub*, not found with the Gold Horus of Sahoura; and at Wady Magara also, where a stele of this same king *Ra-tseser* is to be seen, the gold Horus title is perfect and distinct, and shows the sign for the word *Neter* (God or Divine) added, so as to distinguish it from the Gold Horus title of Snefrou. The name *Sahoura* too may just as well be identified with *Seberchercs* of Dyn. XI of Manetho, or with *Sephres* or *Sisires* of XII (IV and V of Afr.), as with the *Sirius* of Eratosthenes; especially as a monumental king named *Sahoura* appears in tombs near the pyramids associated with the kings of Dyn. XI and XII (IV and V of Afr.), all of them together being preceded by Shouphou. So in the tomb No. 16 of Lepsius, now set up in the museum of Berlin, two out of three brothers are styled priests of the three deified kings *Shouphou*, *Sahoura*, and *Nepher-iri-kar-re* or *Nepher-en-kar-re;* while the eldest of the three, who outlived the two younger, is priest also of a fourth deified king, *Ra-tseser* or *Ra-en-tseser*, who therefore *seems* to have died after the other three. A fifth king, *Aseskerf*, probably *Kerpheres*, is named in the same tomb, but seemingly as if living. Again, in tomb 89 of Lepsius, *Khaphra*, *Menkaura*, *Aseskerf*, *Outses-erkerf*, and *Sahoura* are named. In two tombs (south of the 7th, 8th, and 9th pyramids of Gizeh as marked by Perring) in which he recognised a representation of the end of the sarcophagus of Mencheres, the cartouche of *Ra-tseser* also was found; and in No. 5 of Pl. xxvii. of Burton's "Excerpta Hieroglyphica," in a tablet from a tomb near Gizeh, Anubis is besought to "give to the loyal bard N. a good embalmment and other blessings in the abode of the god Ra, of the goddess Athor, and of the pure gods *Nepher*[*kar*]*re*, *Sahoura*, and *Tseserenre*." Of the king named in a double cartouche *Assa* and *Tetkare*, and occurring in tombs of the same locality and connection as the above, it has already been observed elsewhere that he is certainly not the *Assa* of the Karnak Chamber, but the last king but one of Manetho's Dyn. XII (V of Africanus).

Lastly, as regards the name *Sahoura*, since it has been found rendered into Greek Ἄσυχις, we may presume that the Sahoura whom recent discoveries have connected with the north pyramid of Abouseer is the Asychis to whom a pyramid is ascribed, with whatever inaccuracy as to details, by Herodotus. And if so, certainly he was represented to Herodotus as having lived not before but after Mencheres.

• But as regards the pyramids, since we have been led to mention them in connection with the kings of Dyn. X (III of Africanus), this perhaps is the place for adding a few more words, not to describe or identify them in detail, but to mark out in a general way their number and probable connection as monuments with Manetho's first six dynasties of the kings of Lower Egypt, and with his Dynasty XV.

It seems to be asserted by Manetho that Ouenephes, the third king after Menes, was the first who built a pyramid for his tomb, viz. the earliest of those built at a place called *Ko-chome.* Reckoning from this beginning, and presuming that all the remaining kings of Manetho's first six regal dynasties of Lower and Central Egypt would build pyramids in like manner, we are prepared to find traces of any number of pyramid-tombs of kings not exceeding 5 + 8 + 9 + 8 + 9 + 6 = 45, besides lesser pyramids of queens or princesses, since Herodotus tells us of the existence of some such; and recent discoveries have confirmed the accuracy of his information. But in guessing at the historical antiquity or connection of particular pyramids we have two landmarks to keep in view: First, there is the admission of the Memphite priests that, previously to the time of Papa Maire and his successor Sesortasen I., the first conqueror of Nubia, no one of their numerous kings had waged any great war, or left any monument which was very remarkable. The pyramid-tombs then of the kings preceding Papa Maire should not be of any very admirable workmanship, nor of stupendous dimensions. But we may presume that the earlier of them all would be also the smaller, and that, as time went on, they would be likely to increase somewhat in size, and to improve in execution, each king emulating his predecessor: also, that their relative sizes would be some indication of the length or shortness of the reigns during which they were constructed: further, that they would probably be found in groups representing more or less the dynasties with which each group was connected; and that if circumstances made one part or another of the Libyan hill a common locality for all, the group of pyramids nearest to Memphis would probably contain the tombs of many of the local Memphite kings. It may be presumed too that the pyramids of those kings who were at any time suzerains, or who were nearer to the quarries, and built in the vicinity of their own city, would on the whole be rather larger and better built than those of others who were only contemporaries and subordinate, or who resided at a distance and built their tombs in the necropolis of their neighbours. Secondly, as we know that the pyramids of the largest size, or otherwise most remarkable, were built at Gizeh by the Suphises and Mencheres during about 78 years beginning from B.C. (1932 – 29 = 1903 – 23 =) 1880; and as the same social changes which then placed a superabundance of labour at the disposal of the Memphite kings operated over all Egypt, we may presume that the next largest and most remarkable pyramids, after those of the Souphises and Mencheres, would be those of the contemporary kings of Dyn. XII (V of Africanus). The Shepherds themselves probably did not build pyramids; else they as suzerains ought, no doubt, to have built the largest of all; and it seems sometimes even to have been said that they did. And besides some kings of Dynasties XI and XII (IV and V of Africanus) some two or three kings of Dyn. XV (XII of Africanus), viz. Sesortasen III. and Amenemhe III. and IV. who governed in the Fayoum, while the greatest pyramids of the Memphites and Elephantinites were building, would be likely to leave great pyramids also. And, to speak generally, after the fashion of building vast pyramids had once come in, though later kings could not but fall short somewhat of their predecessors when the first sudden and temporary change caused by the famine had passed away and had left only its modified and permanent results, still it may well be conceived that the pyramids even of the shortest and least important reigns, even to the end of Dynasties XI, XII, and XV (IV, V, and XII of Africanus), would continue to exceed in size those even of the longest and most important reigns of any earlier dynasties.

Upon these principles, if we take those XXXIX pyramids which were all that Col. Howard Vyse and Mr. Perring in 1837 could discover, and of which they have given the measurements, and if of these we set aside only the six which are as satellites to the pyramids of Cheops and Mycerinus as being probably the tombs of their queens and daughters, and allow all the rest, viz. XXXIII, to be the tombs of as many kings, —then, as we know the two great pyramids of Gizeh to belong to kings ii and iii of the local Memphites of Dyn. XI (IV of Africanus), we may make a probable guess that the two next greatest will be the works of their contemporaries and neighbours, the Elephantinite Memphites or Heliopolites of the East Bank, who will be kings iii and iv of Dyn. XII (V of Africanus). And, again, we may guess the two next greatest (which are at some distance southward, at Illahoon and Meydoom) to belong to two other kings also parallel and contemporary (who will be v and vi) of Dyn. XV (XII of Africanus), the kings of which are known to have left such monuments in the Fayoum. Having thus begun three parallel series, we have 5 later reigns of Dyn. XI, 5 of Dyn. XII, and 1 at least of Dyn. XV, without counting its last two short reigns. In all then we have of the same three dynasties eleven more kings, to whom we may apportion those eleven pyramids which come next in point of size. And after thus placing conjecturally the (7+7+3=)17 largest pyramids, and reserving the two ruins at Biahmou, in the Fayoum, as given both by Herodotus and by local tradition to the earlier times of Papa Maire, we may revert to that point of time at which the building of the largest pyramids in all the three dynasties commenced, and go backwards from it step by step from the greater of the pyramids still remaining to the lesser, and from the later to the earlier kings. So we may make out, as a rough approximation, the following table, apportioning xx of the most considerable pyramids to as many kings of Dynasties XI, XII, and XV (IV, V, and XII of Africanus); the first column indicating the dynasty of Manetho and the reign of the same dynasty, the second the years of the reign, and the third the modern site from which the pyramid paralleled with the reign is named. Of the four columns of figures which follow, the first two give in English feet the present length of the base, or the greatest length, if the sides are unequal, and the present perpendicular height, and the remaining two give the original length of the base, and the original height, as calculated by Mr. Perring, or, from his data, by M. Bunsen. The decimals of the exact measurements, as being irrelevant to our purpose, are omitted:—

| Dyn. of Man. | Reign. | Years. | Site of Pyramid. | Base. | Height. | Origl. do. | do. |
|---|---|---|---|---|---|---|---|
| Dyn. XI. | i. | 29. | Abou-roash? - - | 320. | — | 342. | — |
| | | | Abouseer, small Δ? - | 54. | 20. | 75. | — |
| " | ii. | 43. | Gizeh, Great Δ. - - | 746. | 450. | 767. | 479. |
| " | iii. | 36. | Gizeh, 2nd Δ. - - - - | 690. | 447. | 705. | 457. |
| " | iv. | 23. | Gizeh, 3rd Δ. - - - - | 352. | 203. | 352. | 219. |
| " | v. | 15. | Sakkara, No. 3, Gt. Δ - | 350. | 190. | 399. | 200. |
| " | vi. | 12. | Abouseer, Gt. Δ. - - | 325. | 164. | 359. | 227. |
| " | vii. | 10. | Abouseer, Mid. Δ. - - | 213. | 107. | 274. | 171. |
| " | viii. | 9. | Abouseer. N. Δ. - - | 216. | 118. | 256. | 162. |
| Dyn. XII. | i. | 28. | Zawiet-el-Arrian? - - | 300. | 61. | — | — |
| " | ii. | 13. | Reegah? - - - - - - | 123. | 49. | — | — |
| " | iii. | 20. | Dashour, N. stone Δ. - | 700. | 326. | 719. | 342. |
| " | iv. | 27. | Dashour, S. stone Δ. - | 615. | 319. | 616. | 335. |
| " | v. | 20. | Lisht, S. Δ. - - - - - | 450. | 68. | — | — |
| " | vi. | 34. | Lisht, N. Δ. - - - - - | 360. | 89. | — | — |
| " | vii. | 19. | Dashour, unfinished Δ | — | — | — | — |
| " | | | Dashour, small stone Δ | — | — | — | — |
| " | viii. | 34. | Dashour, S. brick Δ. - | 300. | 90. | 342. | 125. |
| " | ix. | 23. | Dashour, N. brick Δ. - | 300. | 156. | 342. | 267. |
| Dyn. XV. | v. | 36. | Illahoon - - - - - - | 560. | 130. | — | — |
| " | vi. | 43. | Illahoon - - - - - - | 530. | 224. | — | — |
| " | vii. | 8. | Howara - - - - - - | 300. | 106. | 383. | — |

Of the remaining pyramids, no less than 10 are at Sakkara, the proper cemetery of Memphis, and they suggest by their very site, and by the scale of their relative proportions, that they belong to the IX earlier kings of Memphis, of Manetho's Dyn. X (III of Africanus). Beginning then from the smallest, this group will stand as follows:—

| | | | | | | | |
|---|---|---|---|---|---|---|---|
| Dyn. VIII? | vii. | 18. | Sakkara - - - - - | 120. | 28. | — | — |
| or X? | viii. | 26. | Sakkara - - - - - | 120. | 28. | — | — |
| Dyn. X. | i. | 28. | Sakkara, No. 7. - - | 140. | 27. | — | — |
| " | ii. | 29. | Sakkara, No. 1. - - | 210. | 59. | — | — |
| " | iii. | 7. | Sakkara, No. 4. - - | — | — | 220. | 62. |
| " | iv. | 26. | Sakkara, No. 2 - - | 210. | 108. | — | — |
| " | v. | 20. | Sakkara, No. 8. - - | 240. | 87. | — | — |
| " | vi. | 18. | Sakkara, (see below) - | — | — | 309. | 60. |
| " | vii. | 22. | Sakkara, No. 9. - - | 250. | 40. | — | — |
| " | viii. | 38. | Sakkara, No. 5. - - | 245. | 75. | — | — |
| " | ix. | 26. | Sakkara, No. 6. - - - | 270. | 80. | — | — |

Of these the one between No. 8 and No. 9 is a building of pyramidal but irregular form, the original dimensions of which seem to have been at the base 309 feet N. and S., by 217 E. and W., and at top 263 by 181, while the original height was in the centre 56, and at the ends 60 feet. This mass is called

*Mustabat el Pharaoon*, i.e. the "Throne of Pharaoh:" and supposing it to be the tomb of a king, we shall have in all at Sakkara eleven royal tombs (besides one which we have given on account of its size to Dyn. XI), being two more than are required to parallel the IX reigns of Dyn. X (III of Africanus). But for the remaining tombs of all those early kings of Lower Egypt, (viz. 3 of Dyn. VIII and 9 of Dyn. IX, making 12 in all,) besides those of any kings of Dynasties XIII and XV anterior to B.C. 1932, who may have built pyramids, we must have recourse to the traces of additional pyramids discovered by Lepsius and the Prussian expedition: for Lepsius considered himself to have found traces more or less distinct of above fifty pyramids in all in Lower or Central Egypt, though some of those added by him to the list are confessed to have been *very* small, and therefore not likely to have been tombs of kings.

So then there is no superabundance of pyramids now extant in point of number, nor any pyramids of incalculable antiquity, nor much difficulty in classifying those which are known, and assigning them, in a rough and general way, to the kings of Dynasties X, XI, XII, and XV, (III, IV, V, and XII of Africanus). But if one wishes to go further, and to assign each pyramid to its proper founder, and especially if one wishes to distinguish the tombs of the first two Memphite suzerains, Sahoura and Snefrou (the pyramids of Papa Maire and his queen Anch-set-mire we may find at Biahmou), or if it be said that Sesortasen I. and his colleagues, Amenemhe I. and II., may probably have left a pyramid, or pyramids, no less than Papa Maire, and if so, their pyramids must be among those still known, and greater doubtless than any of earlier kings, it must be confessed that these are questions which at present admit of no satisfactory answer.

But before we pass with Eratosthenes to the dynasties of Upper Egypt, there is still something to be noticed in conclusion respecting his representation of Dyn. XIII of Manetho (VI of Africanus). Why it was introduced only from the birth of Apappous or Phiops, its fourth king, his three predecessors in Manetho's lists being unnoticed, and why, on the other hand, its last two short reigns (which one might have expected the Theban priests to omit) are *not* omitted, and why the 12 years of Nitocris are reduced to 6, has been explained above. But one purpose which the priests had in view, and which has not yet been noticed, was this,—to exhibit and mark, as if at the *commencement* of the 103 years of the Chronicle, the same sum of 43 years which Manetho had marked as belonging to the *end* of the same 103 years, by attaching it to his Dyn. XIV (Dyn. XI of Africanus), his first dynasty of Upper Egypt. The circumstance that the double generation of Apappous exceeded by many years the number of 64 needed to complete the 190 years of the Chronicle, joined with the necessity of inserting somewhere three supernumerary generations to compensate for the three suppressed on the 190 years of the Chronicle, suggested the idea of imitating, only in inverse order, that device of Manetho by which he first exhibited, as attached to his sixth and last dynasty of Lower Egypt, a remainder of 60 years, and then exhibited another sum of 43 years as its complement in connection with his earliest dynasty of Upper Egypt, the two together making up the 103 years of Dyn. XVII of the Chronicle. So Eratosthenes, in like manner, was made by the Theban priests to exhibit first a remainder or surplus, not of 60 but of 43 years, attached to the sixth dynasty of Lower Egypt, and running over from the 190 years of the Chronicle, and then another sum, not of 43 but of 60 years, as its complement, in connection with the earliest dynasty of Upper Egypt, the two together making up the 103 years of Dyn. XVII of the Chronicle.

The true date of the end of Dyn. XIII is ascertainable from the scheme of Eratosthenes by the help of that composition of Dyn. XVII of the Chronicle which it indicates. For when the double generation (XXXI and XXXII), representing the joint reign of Sesortasen I. and his colleague, is put up by 156 years (which it is, so soon as the head of Dyn. XVIII is allowed to rise up to its true historical place in B.C. 1748), its first year stands immediately below the single year of the successor of Apappous, and commences apparently in B.C. 1997, 66 years instead of 42 before the true end of Dyn. XVII of the Chronicle. We have then, on recognising it as the 4th generation of that dynasty of the Chronicle, to move it down again so that the end of its 42nd and last year may coincide with the known date for the end of the same dynasty in B.C. 1932, Phiops, who has already before been recognised as the third generation of the same dynasty, being drawn down also. Thus at length the end of the single year of the successor of Apappous will be in B.C. (1932 + 42 =) 1974; and the 6 years of Nitocris, or rather the 12 (the 6 cut off from her by Eratosthenes being restored), will be reckoned from thence, and will give B.C. (1974 − 12 =) 1962 for the end of Dyn. XIII of Manetho (VI of Africanus). And reckoning upwards we shall have B.C. (1974 + 1 + 100 =) 2074, for the birth of Apappous and the commencement of those 107 years of his dynasty, which find a place in the scheme of Eratosthenes.

Towards determining the total duration of this dynasty, and the exact date of its commencement, Eratosthenes affords no help, but only a general hint through a date preceding by 6 years the commencement of its fourth reign. As regards the monuments, it is remarkable that both in the Karnak Chamber and in the tombs of Chenoboschion, *Teti*, who may be "*Tithoes Pete-Such-os*," the founder of Crocodilopolis, is the only predecessor (unless a name read *Ati* be *Othoes*, the head of the dynasty and a distinct king) whose name has as yet been found associated with that of *Papa Maire*, the Phiops and Apappous of Manetho and Eratosthenes. And it is to be remembered that, if the latter was only a child of 6 years old at his first accession, he must necessarily have had guardians reigning for him and with him for some considerable time; and these, if relatives, having been once associated in the throne, might probably figure in the lists as reigning on to their deaths; so that both the absence of their names from the monuments (*if* they are really altogether absent) may be in part accounted for; and the true historical duration of the dynasty may be suspected to have been something less than we have collected from the lists.

It may also perhaps be questioned whether 42 years only are to be reckoned to Sesortasen I. as suzerain with Eratosthenes, or 43, as seems to be hinted by Manetho; and whether the single year of the successor of Phiops (whom we identify with *Meran-re* of the Karnak Chamber and of other monuments) really belongs or not to the sovereign Dynasty XVII of the Chronicle. That it does belong to it seems to be the safest conclusion; both because this is indicated by the scheme of Eratosthenes, and because the mere shortness of this king's reign by no means justifies any suspicion that he did not succeed to the whole authority and pre-eminence of his father, with whom he had probably been for many years previously associated. On the other hand the female name Nitocris of itself suggests that the sovereignty or pre-eminence over all Egypt would be likely enough at her accession to pass into another line. So, when 43 years are hinted at by Manetho in connection with his Dyn. XIV (XI of Africanus) as if representing the time during which the sovereignty over all Egypt was with the first king or kings of his next following Dynasty XV (XII of Africanus), this may be explained and reconciled either by supposing that the single year of his predecessor Meranre is consolidated, and covered by the 43 years of Sesortasen I., his accession as suzerain being antedated by one year, or by supposing (though this is contrary to the usual practice) that the 43 years of Manetho are the last 43 years *current* of the reign and life of Sesortasen I. And it is certain that when these 43 and the 16 of Amenemhe I. are added to the 160 years expressly given by Manetho to his Dyn. XV (XII of Africanus), Manetho's gross sum of 219 years exceeds that of the Turin papyrus for the same dynasty by nearly 6 years. But if Meranre is *not* reckoned to Dyn. XVII of the Chronicle, Papa Maire will have in it 22 instead of 21 years, and Dyn. XIII of Manetho will begin and end later by one year than we have calculated.

*Dynasty XIV of Manetho, of* XVI *Diospolites in about* 392? *years, partially exhibited by Eratosthenes in two groups of* IV *Generations each, with* 60 *and* 90 *years respectively.*

That the eight generations to which we now come are really a representation of Dynasty XIV of Manetho (XI of Africanus) cannot be proved by any identification of names, since Manetho gives none; but it is placed beyond a doubt by other considerations: First, there is the fact that Eratosthenes has hitherto been following the order of Manetho's dynasties, and that after Dyn. XIII (containing Phiops and his two successors) Dyn. XIV is the next in order, with only two more native dynasties following it (both of them represented in the series of Eratosthenes) before one comes to Dyn. XVIII. Again, there is the parallelism already noticed between the remainder of 60 years on the six early dynasties of Lower Egypt and its complement of 43, connected by Manetho with his Dynasties XIII and XIV, and the similar remainder or overplus of 60 and its complement of 43, exhibited in connection with Dyn. XIII of Manetho and some other line of kings following it by Eratosthenes. These kings, therefore, may be presumed to belong to Dyn. XIV of Manetho, unless there be any proof to the contrary. Also, we have seen how closely the series of Eratosthenes has followed hitherto the order of the cartouches which are to the left hand side (of the spectator) in the Karnak Chamber; at least from the first Memphite name (for the Tanites are not there given); since in both alike there is a series of VII Memphites, representing Dynasty X of Manetho; and in both alike one sees the last three names of Dyn. XIII of Manetho; though it is true that VII generations from Dyn. XI of Manetho (IV of Africanus), absent from the Karnak Chamber, are enumerated by Eratosthenes, and Teti, the predecessor of Phiops, is absent from the series of Eratosthenes, though he appears in the Karnak Chamber. The female name, too, of Nitocris may probably have been represented in the Karnak Chamber by her husband Nephercheres. But these discrepancies are perfectly intelligible. And the next series in the Karnak Chamber, which is made to inclose within itself seven cartouches from the distinct line of Dyn. XV of Manetho (XII of Africanus), is fixed beyond a doubt by the tombs of its kings found near Thebes, and by other monuments, to be a representation of a line of above XIII Diospolites, one of whom (and he not the first nor the second) was born more than 90 years before the first accession of Sesortasen I. in B.C.

1980, while the last of them was the immediate predecessor of Amosis the head of Dyn. XVIII of Manetho (and also of the Chronicle). There is no doubt, then, that this monumental line is identifiable also with Manetho's first and earliest Diospolite dynasty, which, to judge by analogy only, should have rather more than the XIII names or generations representing it in the Karnak Chamber. For instead of the IX names of Dyn. X, the Karnak Chamber has only VII; and instead of the VI of Dyn. XIII, it has only IV; and lower down, instead of the VIII of Dyn. XV, it has only VII. And Manetho gives expressly to his Dyn. XIV *sixteen* kings, while to judge from the monuments, and from the analogy of Manetho's lists compared with the monuments in other cases, its actual kings may probably have even exceeded this number. And after once finding proof of its strictly local connection with Thebes, or Hermonthis, and of its having commenced long before Dynasty XV (XII of Africanus), and continued after it, down to the time of Dyn. XVIII, one must view it as parallel in Upper Egypt and contemporary with the local Memphite succession of Manetho's two consecutive Dynasties X and XI in Lower Egypt. But these two last-named dynasties having (IX + VIII =) XVII kings in a space of 214 + 178 = 392 years, we might expect the Diospolites of Upper Egypt, beginning either at the same time with the Memphites, or a few years later (for they would not be likely to begin *earlier*), to last nearly the same time. It so happens that 396 years is exactly the duration which an estimate based upon the average of 24¾ years would assign to XVI reigns, so that if the sixteenth and last king of these Diospolites ended at the commencement of Dynasty XVIII, in B.C. 1748, while the Memphites of Dyn. XI of Manetho (IV of Africanus) ended 6 years earlier, the accession of the first king of the Diospolites should be estimated to have been in B.C. (1748 + 396 =) 2143, 26 years later than that of the first Memphites, and 105 years after Menes.

Assuming, then, as admitted by the reader, that those eight generations of Eratosthenes to which we are now come are a representation of some part of the XVI reigns of Dyn. XIV of Manetho (XI of Africanus), and of some part of the cartouches numbered 1 to 13, at p. 293, in the 2nd, 3rd, and 4th lines to our left in the Karnak Chamber, we have next to observe that the VIII generations (XXIII to XXX inclusively), are divided into two groups of four each, which must be considered separately.

The first group, consisting of Generations XXIII, XXIV, XXV, and XXVI, with 22+12+8+18, amounting in all to a sum of only 60 years, represents in the whole scheme of the (XV + LXXVI =) XCI generations the IV generations of Dyn. XVII of the Chronicle, a dynasty which in it is called Memphite. Nor is this designation unintelligible; seeing that, of the four kings chiefly alluded to under the IV generations, the first two have been found to be from Manetho's Dyn. X (III of Africanus), and so strictly and locally Memphites; and the third, Phiops, has been found to be from a dynasty (Dyn. XIII), which is called by Manetho Memphite though in a wider sense, and further, to have inherited in right of his wife the sovereignty of the two local Memphites preceding; while the fourth and last king, Sesortasen I., appears on contemporary monuments to name the earlier Memphite kings as his personal ancestors. And Eratosthenes, having now paralleled both the XV generations "of the Cycle," and V out of the VIII of Dynasty XVI of the Chronicle, in two sums of 443 and 190 years, and having also appended two more generations, and 36 *years* of a third, in compensation for the III suppressed, it is plain that the IV generations of Dyn. XVII of the Chronicle stand next in order, and that they are now represented by his next four generations; though four Diospolites of Upper Egypt are substituted for those four Memphite sovereigns of the Chronicle with whom either they, or some other kings of their much longer line, were really contemporary.

These IV generations, being meant to correspond to the IV of Dyn. XVII of the Chronicle, ought naturally also to have had to themselves the full space of 103 years, instead of only completing it by a complementary sum of 60 years, after its first 43 years have been already exhibited. Thus they seem to have to themselves only 15 years each. But this is owing partly to the reign of Phiops having more years than could well be included in the 190 preceding, and partly to the necessity of inserting three compensatory generations somewhere (and wherever they were inserted, their years would reduce the length of some adjacent generations of the Chronicle). Lastly, it is owing also to a desire of exhibiting a surplus of just 43 years running over from the preceding Memphites, and answering to that surplus or remainder of 60 years which Manetho exhibits at the end of the same Memphites, in order that it may be followed by a compensatory sum of 60 years from the Diospolites of Dyn. XIV (XI of Africanus), just as Manetho's remainder of 60 years is followed by a complementary sum of 43 years attached by him to the same Diospolites of his Dynasty XIV (XI of Africanus).

This parallelism of the 60+43=103 years of Manetho and 43+60=103 years of Eratosthenes, being understood, it will be understood also that though 60 years only are given in the series of Eratosthenes to his Generations XXIII, XXIV, XXV, and XXVI, this number is by no means to be taken for historical; but rather the whole sum of 103 years belonging to those four generations of the Chronicle for which they stand is indicated as really belonging to these four also. And as, in dealing with Menes and his four successors, who seemed to occupy the whole sum of 190 years belonging to the VIII Tanites of the Chronicle, no one would think that three of Manetho's VIII names were really to be suppressed as unhistorical merely because omitted by Eratosthenes, so here in like manner, in dealing with the IV generations which are curtailed of their proper average by the addition of three supernumerary and merely compensatory generations within the space of the 103 years of the Chronicle, one must not hesitate to restore to them their full historical sum of 103 years, their right to which, far from being rendered questionable, is rather indicated and held in trust for them, by those compensatory generations.

Allowing them, then, instead of 60, the full 103 years of the Chronicle, or, if any one prefer it, at the least that sum of 98 years which they would claim according to the usual average, it follows next to inquire to what part of the whole dynasty, and of its 392 years, are these IV generations and their 103 or 98 years to be referred? No one of the IV names being identifiable with any certainty, we can only conjecture that they represent the earlier part of the dynasty, both because we have found that they are liable to be moved up by 156 years from the chronological point at which they first seem to stand in the scheme of Eratosthenes; that is, so as to end in B.C. 2047 instead of B.C. 1932; and also because the last name of the *later* group of IV names seems to be identifiable with that of the last monumental king who immediately preceded Amosis, which shows that those four names, with their years, are taken from the last part of the dynasty. And if so, it is most symmetrical and most agreeable to analogy to suppose that the earlier and separate group is taken from the earlier part of the dynasty, the middle part, for which there was no room, being perhaps represented indirectly by that contemporary Dyn. XV (XII of Africanus) which was really both preceded, and accompanied, and outlasted, by the Diospolite of Dyn. XIV (XI of Africanus). And with this supposition the order of the cartouches in the Karnak Chamber agrees so well (as may be seen by referring to p. 293), that it may be even thought to have itself suggested the idea of taking from the top and bottom of Dyn. XIV its first and last years, so that, when these were referred to their true historical and chronological places, the generations representing the next dynasty (Dyn. XV of Manetho, XII of Africanus) should be inclosed within them, and they, being partly prefixed to its head above, and partly appended to it below, should supply what was wanting to it, whether in point of antiquity or continuance, towards the exhibition of a full Diospolite series.

"κγ'. Θηβαίων κγ' ἐβασίλευσε Μυρταῖος Ἀμμωνόδοτος, ἔτη κβ'." "*Nantef Mentuhotep?* reigned 22 years." Possibly Μυρταῦος may be a corruption of Ναvταῦος, and Ἀμμωνόδοτος a free translation of *Mentuhotep*, Mentu, the god of the earlier city Hermonthis, on the west bank of the Nile, being rendered by Ammon, because he in later times was the chief deity of Thebes, which was named from him No-Amon, or Diospolis. In the same way these kings themselves are called Thebans and "Diospolites;" though Thebes as distinct from Hermonthis is unnamed on the altar of Papa-Maire; and notwithstanding that Sesortasen I. founded the sanctuary of Karnak, it was not till the time of Dyn. XVIII that the city on the right bank of the Nile rose to importance. Whatever becomes of our guess as to the two names, the sense of "Ammonodotus" can scarcely be extracted as a gloss out of "Myrtæus;" and, if Eratosthenes was to place a selection from the first names of this line as it appears at Karnak (not having room for all), the name with which he would most naturally begin would be that of Mentuhotep, which stands as No. 2 of the line at p. 293, since this Mentuhotep appears as the first king. But though his is the first cartouche, his name is preceded by another not inclosed in a cartouche, nor accompanied by royal titles, but having the title of *Erpa*, or *Prince*. It may be conceived then that the two names were joined together so as to hint at once at two distinct generations, *Nantef*, as the family name and the name of the prince who was the founder of the house, being put first, and *Mentuhotep*, the proper name of the second ruler of the Nantef line, who was however the first king, being conjoined. Further, the name *Ammonodotus* serves to mark the transition from the Memphites of Manetho to the Diospolites, just as the gloss or epithet Μεμφίτης, attached to Στοῖχαρ Μομχεῖρι, marked the transition from the still earlier Tanites or Thinites to the Memphites. Making then of this a double generation, and paralleling the two names with the first two names of the dynasty in the Karnak Chamber, we must make an addition to our former estimate, and allow to the four Generations XXIII, XXIV, XXV, and XXVI of Eratosthenes, 103 or 98 years as directly, and 24½ more as indirectly, connected with them: and as we have set aside the sums of years nominally attached to the four generations, we must be content to give to all the reigns alike one uniform and average length, only noticing such chronological indications as may be anywhere applicable. It is to be remembered, also, that our date for the commencement of the Diospolite line, besides being in itself conjectural, depends in some degree upon the date which may be assigned not only to the

*Nantef*, prince, 25 years. From Thoth 1, B.C. 2139 to B.C. 2114 ?

*Mentuhotep I.* 24 years. B.C. 2114 to B.C. 2090 ?

commencement of the earliest Memphites, but also to the commencement of the second or secondary line of Tanites, especially if these latter are supposed to have reigned at Heliopolis; for the foundation of Hermonthis was certainly later than that of Heliopolis or On, seeing that one of its early names is *On-Res*, "On of the South," and its local god Mentu or Mentu-Ra is twin-brother to the god Atum of Heliopolis. In later times the form *Amon-Munt* also occurs. Assuming, therefore, that the earliest Memphite dynasty commenced as early as B.C. 2145, and that the second dynasty of the Tanites commenced at Heliopolis in B.C. (1932 + 225 =(2154) there is no difficulty in allowing that the Prince Nantef, the founder of his house, may have begun to rule at Hermonthis, or "On of the South," as early as B.C. (1748 + 39: =) 2148; and from this point we shall reckon downwards.

"*κδ'. Θηβαίων κδ' ἐβασίλευσε Θυοσιμάρης, ὅ ἐστι Κραταιὸς, Ἥλιος* [so perhaps we should transpose and read the gloss *Κραταιὸς, ὅ ἐστιν Ἥλιος*] *ἔτη ιβ'*." "*Thuosimares*, 12 years." The 3rd and 4th representatives of the line in the Karnak Chamber are both named *Nantef*, and probably they had no second cartouche; but if standards and standard titles were already in use, the name of Eratosthenes may possibly have been derived from the standard. To judge from its appearance its Egyptian elements should be *tseser* (*κράτος*) *ma* (the cubit) and *Re*; and we find on monuments two later Nantef kings of the same family name into whose throne and standard names the elements *ma* and *Re* enter. These are *Ra-tap-ma-kherp* and *Ra-her-her-ma-kherp*. If the gloss is only Κραταιὸς Ἥλιος, it cannot be complete nor closely accurate, as the syllable *ma* is left by it unexplained.

"*κε'. Θηβαίων κε' ἐβασίλευσε Θίνιλλος, ὅ ἐστιν Αὐξήσας τὸ πάτριον κράτος, ἔτη η'*." "*Thinillus*, which means *Who increased the power of his father*, 8 years." The king alluded to is no doubt a Nantef, and the gloss might be obtained from the name of one of the kings of this family. For there is one who adds to his personal name *Nantef* the peculiar suffix *Aa*, meaning *great*; and the syllable *tef*, which in names of this family is generally, but not invariably, annexed to the root, *Hann* or *Nan*, is, in sound at least, equivalent to the Greek πατρὸς αὐτοῦ, and may be the source of the word πάτριον in the gloss. The sense of the root is *to bring*, as to *bring tribute.* But the King *Nantef-aa* could not be paralleled with any earlier name of this dynasty in the Karnak Chamber than No. 5, even though we were to allow that the adjunct *Aa* might be omitted, and that a king who is known to have had a double cartouche might be represented in the Karnak Calendar by his personal name, as seems to be the case with Papa Maire. For of the three earlier Nantefs, Nos. 1, 2, and 4, in the Karnak Chamber, the first has no cartouche at all, and only the title of *Erpa*, "Prince;" and all the three, together with No. 2, who is Mentuhotep I., have only the title of *Horus*, not the full royal titles, *Souten Kheb* (the sprig and the bee) or *Neter-Nepher* "the Good Deity," which are added alternately to the later cartouches, probably from No. 5 inclusively. No. 8 is unfortunately wanting, but it may be supposed to have contained the name *Nantef-aa;* indeed either it or No. 7 must have done so, unless this king was omitted altogether, which is not probable.

We are acquainted through the monuments with several names of this line which may be presumed to be among the earliest, inasmuch as they are contained in a single cartouche. The tomb of one of these, *Si-Ra-Hann-aa*, is mentioned as the second of ten regal tombs (all but that of Amenoph I. connected with Dyn. XIV), which were examined under Rameses III. The papyrus Abbott containing the report of this examination, which has been illustrated by Mr. Birch, is now in the British Museum. From the simple form of the name one might be tempted to identify the king *Han-aa* even with the *Prince Nantef*, the founder of the dynasty, who is No. 1 in the Karnak Chamber. His name being found inclosed in a cartouche in the papyrus alluded to is no proof to the contrary. Still, it may be safer to suppose that he is *Nantef II.* The name *Mentuhotep* also occurs with the title *Si-Ra* inclosed in a single cartouche; and if any where this single cartouche is unaccompanied by other titles proper to Mentuhotep II. or III., it may be ascribed, conjecturally at least, to the first of the name, Mentuhotep I.

*Nantef II.* 25 years. B.C. 2090 to B.C. 2065 ?

*Nantef III.* 24 years B.C. 2065 to B.C. 2041 ?

Another *Nantef* taking only a single cartouche with the title of *Horus*, and a standard bearing the device *Uah-anch*, is known from a stele found at Semneh, in Nubia, and now preserved in the Leyden Museum. The stele itself is dated in the 33rd year of Sesortasen I., which if reckoned from his first accession, and so as to allow between 48 and 49 years for his whole reign, may have begun some months after Dec. 24 of B.C. (1932 + 17 =) 1949, that is, in B.C. 1948. The deceased person to whom offerings are made in this stele, and whose name was *Nantef-akr*, tells us himself, in the inscription, that it was in the reign of *Hor Uah-anch Si-Ra Nantef* that the father of the father of his father was made scribe of the canal of the great cemetery of Abydos. But even if we suppose the deceased Nantef-akr who speaks to have been born as late as B.C. (1948 + 32 =) 1980, about the time of the first accession of Sesortasen I., and to have died at the early age of 33, which is improbable, and reckon backwards 30 years from any appointment of his father, about the time of his own birth, to a similar appointment of his grandfather, and again 30 years to that appointment of his great-grandfather which is mentioned, this latter appointment will not be later than B.C. (1980 + 60 =) 2039. But as the life of the deceased Nantef-akr may be estimated with more probability at 50 or 60 than at 33 years, the date alluded to in the reign of the *Horus, Uah-anch Nantef*, may have been as early as B.C. 2065; and his reign should be the *fourth* average reign of Dyn. XIV of Manetho; and since he has only the title of *Horus*, we may identify him, under the name of *Nantef III.*, with the cartouche No. 4 at Karnak.

*Nantef IV.* 25 years, B.C. 2041 to B.C. 2016.

After him we may insert conjecturally, as *Nantef IV.*, a king who has no longer only the title of *Horus*, but the full royal title of *Souten Kheb* (the sprig and the bee), but still with only a single cartouche. Of three Nantefs whose wooden sarcophagi found near Gourneh are now in the Museums of London, Paris, and Berlin, this one seems to be the earliest, as the other two are known to have taken the double cartouche. All the three coffins and their cases are much alike in form and appearance, being covered all over with gilding, but showing their antiquity by their comparative simplicity, and by a certain inferiority of workmanship. That of the king whom we call Nantef IV. was bought from the Anastasi collection for the British Museum, together with a jasper scarabæus said by the Arabs to have been found in it. But this assertion may be disregarded as untrue. For they had destroyed the mummy of the king Nantef, and had substituted for it the mummy of a priest taken from another tomb in the same neighbourhood. Wherever found, the scarabæus bears on it the cartouche of a king named *Sebek-em-saf* belonging to this same Dyn. XIV of Manetho (XI of Africanus); and, besides the cartouche, there is on it an extract from cap. 64 of the Ritual of the Dead, which is said, in a rubric in some copies of the Ritual, to have been found at Hermopolis, and carried away thence by a prince named *Har-tetef*, in the time of the king *Mencheres*. It was found inscribed on burnt bricks painted blue placed under the feet of the god Thoth, and supposed to have been written by the god's own hand. The king *Sebek-em-saf*, therefore, and his scarabæus, must seemingly be later than the time of the Memphite king Mencheres, if he is the Mencheres alluded to; and the prince *Har-tetef*, if of the Nantef family, must have been a remote descendant of the king named by us Nantef IV., whose gold diadem with its uræus is at Leyden, and whose coffin, with its single cartouche, is in the British Museum.

This king cannot be identified with any one of those who were represented in the Karnak Chamber, as its Nos. 1, 2, 3, and 4 have only the title of *Horus*, and No. 5, which is blank, is wanted for the king *Nantef-aa*, who is known to have taken a double cartouche. But as the Karnak Chamber had only XIII names in all from this line, and so certainly omitted three of Manetho's XVI kings, there is nothing strange in our finding a king who appears to have been thus omitted. It may even be that not one only but two of those omitted are among the earlier names of the dynasty. For we have calculated this dynasty to have begun perhaps in B.C. 2139, only 6 years after the earliest Memphite dynasty (X of Manetho, III of Afric.); and if after this we take the first six names of these Thebans, as they stand at Karnak, to represent the first six of their line without any omissions, we shall have the fifth (or for certain the sixth) Theban name in possession of full royal titles, and seemingly also of the double cartouche, two generations before the Memphite suzerain Snefrou, who stands seventh of his line, and three before Papa Maire, whose double cartouche is otherwise the earliest known. And a consideration of the monumental names of Theban kings probably identifiable with Nos. 5, 6, and 7 in the Karnak Chamber, points the same way. For we know of two Nantef kings and one Mentuhotep of the earlier part of Dyn. XIV. who all have the double cartouche; and the last-named of the three has the *Vulture and Uræus*, and the *Gold Horus titles* besides. All these three are less likely to have been omitted in the Karnak Chamber than other earlier kings. But if we give to them the cartouches Nos. 5, 6, and 7, and make them at the same time to have been the 5th, 6th, and 7th kings of the XVI of the whole line, they will be the contemporaries of the three Memphite suzerains Sahoura, Snefrou, and Papa Maire, and will seem to have led the way in introducing, rather than to have followed others in adopting, the double cartouche, which is not seen on the monuments of Sahoura or of Snefrou. This is possible, indeed, seeing that the later Memphites and Elephantinites, or Heliopolites, who were tributaries under the Shepherds seem to have continued (with only occasional exceptions) to use the single cartouche when the double was used not only by the Shepherds, their suzerains, but also by every petty king in Nubia and Upper Egypt. Still, we must not unnecessarily so place any monumental names as to imply that this was so. But it is most likely that those Diospolites of Dyn. XIV who during their lives used the double cartouche were later than Papa Maire, and followed a custom previously introduced by him. And it is most likely that any Theban king, as Mentuhotep II., who takes the *Gold Horus* title, or the titles *Neb-iri-t*, *Neb-teti*, was later than Snefrou, and followed in these points a custom previously introduced by him or by his father.

*Nantef-Aa.F.* 24 years. B.C. 2016 to B.C. 1992.

A papyrus probably found in the same tomb with the sarcophagus and mummy of the king *Nantef-aa* or of his successor (both now in the Louvre at Paris), but purloined and sold separately by the Arabs, seems to require that the king in whose tomb it was found should be placed one generation later than Snefrou. In this most ancient and curious writing which has been illustrated by M. Chabas, and which consisted originally of moral sentences in two parts, the author, a "Royal Relative," whose name was *Ptah-hotep*, and who had reached when he wrote his last words the great age of 110 years, mentions the names of three kings, all seemingly of the Memphite Dynasty X of Manetho (III of Africanus), and identifiable with cartouches which appear in the uppermost line to our left in the Karnak Chamber. These names are *Assa, Ur-Aan* (Sahoura?) and *Snefrou*, whose accession is alluded to as the most recent, and as following upon the decease of *Ur-Aan*. But according to our conjectural estimate, based only on the average length of reigns, the king *Nantef-aa*, in whose tomb this MS. is said to have been found, would reign from B.C. 2016 to B.C. 1992; while the accession of Snefrou, according to the indication of Eratosthenes should be in B.C. (2034 − 18 =) 2016.

The sarcophagus of *Nantef-aa*, whom we call *Nantef V.*, and identify with No. 5 of the Karnak Chamber and with the *sixth* of Manetho's XVI kings, resembles closely that of the earlier Nantef in the British Museum, which possesses a limestone pyramidion of the same king. On the sarcophagus in the Louvre there is only a single cartouche with the family or personal name, and the adjunct *aa;* but on the pyramidion in the British Museum, taken also no doubt from his tomb, he has both the throne-name, *Souten Kheb, Ra-Tap-ma-kherp*, and the personal name, *Si-Ra Nantef-aa.* The standard name is *Hor Tap-ma.* It is mentioned in the inscription on the coffin that this king was buried by "his brother, the king Nantef," whom we shall call *Nantef VI.*, and identify conjecturally with No. 6 of the Karnak Chamber. The outer cover of the sarcophagus of Nantef-aa is in the Museum at Berlin, and exhibits his name like the inner. His tomb is named in the papyrus Abbott as the fourth of the ten examined in the time of Rameses III.

*Nantef VI.* 25 years. B.C. 1992 to B.C. 1968.

Side by side with the sarcophagus of Nantef-aa there stands in the museum of the Louvre another similar sarcophagus, still covered by its outer case, which exhibits the name of a king Nantef, whom we may suppose to be the son of the preceding, or the brother who buried him. We shall identify him as *Nantef VI.* with No. 6 of the Karnak Chamber, the first cartouche of this line which has the title *Neter Nepher Makhrou* (the *Good Deity*, the *Justified*) peculiar to a deceased king; and joined with *Neter Nepher*, the title *Neb Teti*, "*Lord of the Two Regions,*" which afterwards, together with *Neb Schaou*, "*Lord of Diadems,*" is often either added to or substituted for the titles *Souten Kheb* and *Si-Ra* prefixed to the throne-name and to the personal name of kings. The sarcophagus of this king exhibits a double cartouche; but one of the two names (the throne-name, with the sprig and the bee) has been put in on the breast, as if at some later time, to facilitate recognition, in black pigment over the gilding. The names are *Souten Kheb*, *Ra-her-her-ma-kherp*, *Si-Ra-Nantef*. The fact that the throne-name was added afterwards seems to indicate that when Nantef VI. died (which should be, according to our estimate, about B.C. 1968, 6 years after the death of Papa Maire), the official use of the double cartouche was not as yet a settled custom in this Diospolite family, seeing that none of those three sarcophagi of Nantefs which have been found bore it originally. And if so, we must suppose the pyramidion of *Nantef-aa*, with its double cartouche, to have been added in like manner, and placed in his tomb, not only after his own death but also after the death of his brother.

*Mentuhotep II.* 21 years. B.C. 1968 to B.C. 1944.

The king *Mentuhotep II.*, *Ra-neb-teti*, whom we place next, and whom we suppose, with his throne-name, *Ra-neb-teti*, to have once filled the cartouche No. 7 of the Karnak Chamber now destroyed, could not well have been placed *earlier*, whether in the other blank cartouche No. 5, or as a king omitted, because he has all the royal titles; not merely the double cartouche, but also the *Vulture and Uræus* title, and the *Gold* or *Gold Horus* title; and this fact seems to require that he should be placed one or two generations after Snefrou. He takes one and the same title, *Neb-teti*, three times over, in his standard, with the Vulture and Uræus, and in one of his cartouches, where, with the usual prefix, *Ra*, it constitutes his throne-name. In an inscription on the Kosseir road, published by Major Burton, he speaks of himself as having done something with the help of an *officer* named Amenemhe. The title *Neb-teti* or *toti* having appeared already in the Karnak Chamber in connection with kings of Dyn. XIII, and in this Dyn. XIV in connection with the cartouche No. 6, which we call Nantef VI., while Nantef V. and VI., if we have rightly placed them as Nos. 5 and 6 of the Karnak Chamber, have the elements *Ma-re* both in their throne and standard names, it is possible that the Θυοσιμάρης of Eratosthenes may have been made from *Neb-toti Mare*, the *Neb* (which signifies Lord) being dropped. And if, at the same time, the Greek name *Thinillus* is formed from *P-Hannou-aa* or *P-Hannou-ef* (both of which variants for Nantef-aa may be justified from the papyrus Abbott of the time of Rameses III.), while the adjuncts *tef-aa* are the source of the gloss, it will seem that in the list of Eratosthenes the order in which the two brothers are named by the Karnak Chamber is reversed.

The eighth name in the Karnak Chamber is preserved, and reads *Snepherkar;* and we may perhaps venture to identify this name with the Σευφρουκράτης, or Σεμφρουκράτης, who stands as Generation XXVI in the series of Eratosthenes. The Greek gloss is Ἡρακλῆς, Ἁρποκράτης. If there is any truth in this conjecture, it will carry us on to the conclusion that whether Eratosthenes went himself to Thebes in the first instance, or only sent to the priests there a notice of what he wanted, he did not remain till they had completed their task, nor receive from their lips the explanation of the names of the kings in the series which they had made out for him. On the contrary, he probably received at Alexandria in writing the list made out for him, according to his directions, by the priests at Thebes; and he translated the names into Greek, or added glosses upon them, with more or less success, sometimes so as to suit the true etymology, sometimes from the mere sound, and with such native assistance as happened to be at hand, and which happened not to be of any great value. In the particular case which we are now considering the Egyptian name caught at by the ear and written in Greek Σεμφρου-

Snepherkar 24 years. B.C. 1968 to B.C. 1924.

*κράτης*, and mischievously corrected by Bunsen by omitting the *ρ*, justifies the gloss attached to it, *Sem* being commonly rendered in Greek by "Heracles," and *Sem-pa-chrot* (Hercules the Child) being fairly paraphrased by "Heracles, Harpocrates." But the Egyptian name really written in the Egyptian list sent to Eratosthenes was not *Sm* (Heracles), *ph* (the definite article *the*), and *chro-t* (child), but Senphrchra, with the *r*, omitted by Bunsen, but faithfully retained as he heard it by Eratosthenes, and without the final *t* of the word *chrot* (child). After this, or any other similarly suspicious name and gloss, the reader may consider how far the words of Apollodorus, transcribed by Syncellus, justify the explanation that has been suggested: "ὧν (τῶν Θηβαίων λεγομένων βασιλέων) τὴν γνῶσιν (φησὶν) ὁ Ἐρατοσθένης λαβὼν Αἰγυπτιακοῖς ὑπομνήμασι καὶ ὀνόμασι κατὰ πρόσταξιν βασιλικὴν τῇ Ἑλλάδι φωνῇ παρέφρασεν οὕτως." He *received* them written in Egyptian characters and names *from others*, and *himself* translated, paraphrased, or glossed them in Greek.

The fourth Diospolite name in the list of Eratosthenes, whether rightly identified or not with the 8th name, *Snepherkar*, of the Karnak Chamber, is certainly made to close and complete the space of the 103 years of the four generations of Dyn. XVII of the Chronicle; and these 103 years we know end chronologically in B.C. 1932. But the 8th Diospolite reign, whether of Manetho or of the Karnak Chamber, if calculated approximatively according to the average length of 24½ years to each reign, would end as we have seen in B.C. 1924, a date which differs by only 8 years from the historical end of Dyn. XVII of the Chronicle.

The second group then of four more Diospolites, making generations XXVII, XXVIII, XXIX, and XXX of Eratosthenes, so far as their apparent and original position is any indication (since they seem to cover the first 90 years of the 184 of Dyn. XXVII of the Chronicle), ought to be parallel to the 9th, 10th, 11th, and 12th reigns of Manetho, but not to Nos. 9, 10, 11, and 12 of the Karnak Chamber, unless its series were complete and parallel, without omissions, to that of Manetho. But in point of fact, the fourth and last Diospolite of this second group, instead of carrying us from B.C. 1924, or rather from 1932, only 98 or 90 years to B.C. 1834, is fixed by his name to end four generations or 94 years later, concurrently with Dyn. XXVII of the Chronicle; so that these four names, covering originally and apparently the *first* 90 years, and by the identification of the last of them with *Ra-Sekennen* covering the last 90 years, cover in one way or another the whole 184 years of Dyn. XXVII of the Chronicle, and indicate not only all the five remaining names of the Karnak Chamber, but also those other three reigns of Manetho which in the Karnak Chamber are omitted.

*Mentuhotep III. 29 years. B.C. 1924 to B.C. 1895?*

"κζ'. Θηβαίων κζ' ἐβασίλευσε Χουθὴρ Ταῦρος, τύραννος, ἔτη ζ'." "*Chuther Taurus*, a tyrant, 7 years." The gloss, if it be a gloss, must be a distortion rather than a true rendering of the sense, as no king would style himself tyrant, though he might be proud of being styled Most Absolute.

Supposing No. 9 of the Karnak Chamber to be the 10th of Manetho's XVI kings, and Generation XXVII of Eratosthenes to correspond to it, the monumental king is *Mentuhotep III.*, both whose cartouches as well as his standard title and his Vulture and Uræus title are known. The throne-name is *Ra-neb-kher*, the title taken in the standard is *Kher-teti*, and the same is taken with the Vulture and Uræus. In these names one certainly cannot recognise at first sight either the *Chuther* or the *Taurus* of Eratosthenes: but still, going upon more general grounds, we may remark, first, that Mentuhotep III. is a king whom the Theban priests would not be likely to omit, seeing that in monumental lists and in tombs of the time of Dyn. XVIII he is sometimes named, when all other ancestors are omitted, as the sole connecting link between Amosis and Menes. Sometimes, in a similar way, Sesortasen I. is named. It is clear then that from some cause or other considerable importance was attached to him. Again, it is known from a magnificent stele brought from Abydos, and now in the museum of Turin, that he had a very long reign, for the inscription on this stele names his 44th year. And lastly, it is observable that the 8th and last name of this Diospolite line in the list of Eratosthenes, having a sum of 60 years attached to it, plainly indicates at least *two* actual reigns, and without looking away to Manetho, the *fifth* name before the end of this line in the Karnak Chamber is *Ra-neb-kher*, the throne-name of Mentuhotep III. Perhaps then in the list of Eratosthenes two kings, Mentuhotep II. and Mentuhotep III. (the first of whom does not appear in the Karnak Chamber), are consolidated together; and while one of the two names given, viz. Ταῦρος, is from the Neb-*Tot-re* of Mentuhotep II., the other, which is put first, *Χουθὴρ*, is from the Neb-*kher-ph-re* of Mentuhotep III. It is plain that there is a close analogy between the names and titles of Mentuhotep II. (*Hor-neb-toti* and *Ra-neb-toti*) and those of Mentuhotep III (*Hor-kher-toti* and *Ra-neb-kher*); and it is possible that in the list of Eratosthenes the two may have been consolidated together; and that while one of the two names given, viz. *Χουθὴρ*, is from the "*Neb-kher-ph-re*" of Mentuhotep III., the king primarily intended, the adjunct, Ταῦρος, is from the "*Neb-tot-re*" of Mentuhotep II. Or the Ταῦρος also may be from *Toti-hor* in the standard title of Mentuhotep III., or a translation from the sound of the syllable *kher*, since *ka* means a bull. The title *Neb-to*, or *Neb-toti* (lord of the worlds), might give some colour to the gloss *τύραννος*, in the sense of despot, or absolute lord. The tomb of Mentuhotep III. is the tenth and last named in the papyrus Abbott.

*Hannouf*, 25 yrs. B.C. 1895 to B.C. 1870. Reign XI? "*κη'. Θηβαίων κη' ἐβασίλευσε* Μευρὴς, Φιλόσκορος, *ἔτη ιβ'*." "*Meures*, which means the *Lover of the Eye*, 12 years." The sound of this name and the gloss agree well together, and indicate the Egyptian elements *mi* or *mer*, "loving," and *iri*, the pupil of the eye. But No. 10, the cartouche which should correspond in the Karnak Chamber, has nothing resembling these elements, either in sound or sense; nothing at least peculiar to that king. For though the title *Neb-iri*, taken by Snefrou and by other kings after him, might make Νευρὴς or Μευρὴς, and would answer sufficiently to the gloss Φιλόσκορος, this title is given in the Karnak Chamber to at least one king earlier than No. 10, viz. to No. 9, who with the "*Neter Nepher*" has the adjuncts *Neb-toti*, *Neb-iri-t;* and as the similar title *Neb-toti* (with which *Neb-iri* sometimes alternates and sometimes is conjoined, with a certain regard to symmetry, in the Karnak Chamber) is given to No. 5, as we suppose, and certainly to Nos. 6, 7, and 8 of these Diospolites, it is probable that the title *Neb-iri* was applicable to them also. The name No. 10 in the Karnak Chamber reads *Ra-nub-cheper*. The personal name, which occurs conjoined with this in the papyrus Abbott, is *Hannouef* or *Nannouef*. The tomb of this king is the third of the ten named in the papyrus Abbott.

*Tseser-en-ra, 24 years, B.C. 1870 to B.C. 1846.*

Reign XII? "κθ'. Θηβαίων κθ' ἐβασίλευσε Χωμαέφθα, Κόσμος Φιλήφαιστος, ἔτη ια'." "*Chomaephthah*, which means the *World loving Phthah*, reigned 11 years." The gloss seems to justify Bunsen's correction of *To*-mac-phtha; and then the gloss and the name agree together. But there is nothing either in the corresponding cartouche, No. 11 of the Karnak Chamber, or in any other cartouche near it, to throw light on such a name. The cartouche No. 10 reads *Tseser-en-ra*, reminding us of some earlier kings of Lower Egypt who bore the same or a similar name, with the character for *iri* included in it; so that if this variant were familiar and interchangeable, it might be the source of the Μευρὴς of Eratosthenes. The personal name and other titles of Tseser-en-ra are not known.

Twelve average reigns having brought us down only to B.C. 1846, and Eratosthenes having now only one more name from this line, and that the name of a king, *Ra-Sekenn*, who is known with certainty to have died about a century later, it is necessary, after one more name from the Karnak Chamber, to insert two of those names with which the monuments enable us to fill up the number of Manetho's XVI kings. The monuments it is true exhibit more kings than we can place in succession, more at least than we can place consistently with Manetho's number of XVI reigns, and with our own reckoning of full average reigns to each king. But the actual reigns are usually more numerous than the names of any monumental or written succession; and some of the kings whose tombs are known to have existed at Thebes may have been associated with others. Indeed there are signs that before the commencement of Dyn. XVIII the royal title was given to many princes at once in Upper Egypt. One in particular, styled in his cartouche, "*Ahmes, the son of Pear*," is named in the papyrus Abbott as a king, though he was living after the accession of Amenoph I., and has only the title of prince given to him on contemporary monuments. His tomb is named in the papyrus as the ninth of those ten which were examined in the time of Rameses III.

*Necht-en-re*, 25 yrs. B.C. 1846 to B.C. 1821.

*Necht-en-re.* The personal name of this king, who is No. 12 of the line in the Karnak Chamber, has not yet been found. He may perhaps have reigned at a time somewhat later than that to which we are now assigning him.

*Sebek-em-saf*, 24 yrs. B.C. 1821 to B.C. 1797.

Two kings of the same name, *Sebek-em-saf*, one of them with the throne-name *Ra-khet-schaou*, and the other with that of *Ra-Ha-shetito*, seem to have belonged to this dynasty. The names of the latter of the two are known from the papyrus Abbott, his tomb being the *fifth* of the ten examined in the time of Rameses III., and the only one which was found damaged.

One reason for giving to these two kings together, or to one of them (if only one belongs to Manetho's Dyn. XIV), the 14th rather than any earlier reign is this,—that they may be exhibited as reigning either contemporaneously with or after the Memphite king Menchere, the builder of the third pyramid. For since chapter 64 of the "Ritual" is said to have been found at Hermopolis in the time of Menchere, it is obvious that *Sebek-em-saf*, whose scarabæus with an extract from that chapter upon it is in the British Museum, should be later than Menchere, or at least not earlier. But the reign of Menchere, apart from any years during which he may have been associated with his uncle or predecessor, has been estimated above to have commenced in B.C. 1823, and to have ended in B.C. 1800.

*Ra-neb-en-chent*, and *Kames*, 25 yrs. B.C. 1797 to B.C. 1772.

Two other kings who appear, or who did appear, in a tomb at *Der-El-Medineh*, as if intervening between Mentuhotep III. and Ra-skennen the last king of Dyn. XIV (XI of Africanus), are named *Ra-neb-en-chent* (so read by Mr. Birch, instead of *Ra-spen-neb*, as it is given by others) and *Kames*. The tomb of the latter is named eighth of those examined in the time of Rameses III., and the report of that examination in the papyrus Abbott supplies his throne-name *Ra-uat-cheper.* It is clear from a number of indications that these two kings were among the most recent predecessors of Amosis the founder of Dyn. XVIII; while others named on the same monuments, as the king *Aahotep,* seem to represent the Nubian family of his black queen *Aahmes Nofriari.*

*Ra-sekenn, 24 yrs. B.C. 1772 to B.C. 1748.*

"κθ'. Θηβαίων κθ' ἐβασίλευσε Σοικύνιος, 'Ωκὺς, or 'Οξὺς, [so we may correct for 'Οχο], Τύραννος, ἔτη ξ'." "*Sĕkunn,* which means *Sharp, Tyrant,* reigned 60 years." The gloss agrees with the name, which according to Bunsen may mean an *axe* or *scimetar,* from a root, *sken* (σχεν), signifying to *cut.* Here at last we can satisfactorily identify the name given by Eratosthenes with that cartouche, No. 13, in the Karnak Chamber with which it ought to correspond. And the identification, not only from its being almost the only one, but also from the place of this king being known to be at the end of the dynasty, is of the utmost value; as so the series of Manetho, of Eratosthenes, of the Karnak Chamber, and of the actual reigns of this line being ascertained to coincide at their end, one may go backwards from this, as from a known point, in making out conjecturally and approximatively that agreement and parallelism which is implied to have existed from the beginning. The slight difference between the *Ra-sekenn* of the monuments and the *Sekenn* of Eratosthenes disappears entirely when one considers that the ordinary prefix *Ra* in royal names may be either added or omitted at will; a good instance and illustration of which is furnished by the papyrus Abbott already alluded to. For in naming the first of the ten royal tombs examined, viz. that of Amunoph I. of Dyn. XVIII, both whose names are perfectly well known, and do not vary on the monuments, the Report gives his throne-name not in the ordinary form, *Ra-sor-kar,* or *Sor-kar-re,* but simply *Sorkar,* without the *Ra.* So too we have found the older name *Sahou-ra* rendered in Greek by *A-saouch-is.*

In the papyrus Abbott the tombs of two kings of one and the same throne-name, *Ra-Sekenn,* being named together as the sixth and seventh of the ten examined, and the personal names being also *almost* the same, the one already known as belonging to the predecessor of Amosis being *Ta-aa-ken* and the other known only through the papyrus being *Ta-aa-aa*, we shall not be far wrong in inferring that the two were either brothers, or a father and son, who reigned for some short time together. And the *reign* of Eratosthenes, as distinct from the *name*, having no less than 60 years, two full thirds of the whole space of 90 years given to this group of four generations, it seems intended to hint the existence of several actual kings, for whom *as generations* there was no room. At any rate, if we look no further than to the XIII names of the Karnak Chamber, and, having identified its last cartouche, No. 13, with Generation XXX of Eratosthenes, inquire whether then his Gen. XXVII is to be identified with No. 10 of the Karnak Chamber (in which case Mentuhotep III. would be omitted), it may be replied that not only is it probable in itself that this second group of four generations made out from Dyn. XIV would commence with *Mentuhotep III*, but it is also shown so to commence in truth by the circumstance that the last of the four reigns is in its length plainly double, so as to require us to understand and reckon at least *five* actual instead of only four nominal generations.

Space of Dyn. XXVII of the Chronicle, IV kings, 184 yrs. B.C. 1932 to B.C. 1748.

Thus the second group of Diospolites in the scheme of Eratosthenes, with its four names and 90 years, following, as it does ostensibly, after the 103 years of the Chronicle, so as to begin concurrently with the first year of the 184 of Dyn. XXVII of the Chronicle, and yet being fixed by its fourth name *Sekenn* to end together with the last year of the same 184, represents in fact the whole of those 184 years, and all the actual reigns of Manetho's Diospolite Dyn. XIV which properly belong to the same space. And having ostensibly only IV generations for that space, it alludes, though in a very indirect way, to those IV generations of the Shepherds which according to the Chronicle and to Manetho really covered the same 184 years, the four Shepherd kings reigning one with another above 46 years each.

*Dynasty XV of Manetho, ostensibly of* VII *Diospolites, with* 160, *but really of* VIII *with* (43 + 16 + 160 = ) 219 *years, partially represented by Eratosthenes under five generations with* 163 *years.*

That the next five generations are a representation of Dyn. XV admits of no doubt; for though the first name *Peteathyres* can only doubtfully be traced in the throne-name of Amenemhe I. with the article prefixed *P-etep-het-re*, and though Generation XXXII has really fallen out, the name which follows as if it were Generation XXXII, and which is itself followed by XXXIV, being "*Amenemhe II.*," shows that one of the two preceding names, XXXII or XXXI, must be identifiable with Amenemhe I.: and, if so, the other must be identifiable with Sesortasen I. And, after Amenemhe II., the next two names, though corruptly written, are identifiable with Sesortasen II. or III. and Amenemhe *Ma-re*. Besides which the figures of Eratosthenes show that they belong to the reigns of Dyn. XV as exhibited by Manetho and by the much earlier Turin papyrus. Dyn. XV. VIII Diospolites, 191 yrs. B.C. 1989 to B.C. 1799.

The odd months and days of the Turin papyrus, and the odd months of Manetho, being rounded off to whole years, their respective exhibitions of this dynasty and that of Eratosthenes may be paralleled with one another in the manner exhibited below: —

Turin MS. { (9 : – : –) / (3 + 4 + 34 + 8) (8 + 23 + 7) / (7 + 11 + 1) (1 + 31 + 5) / (5 + 42 + 1) (1 + 8) + 4

Man. { [40 + 3] : (9 + 3 + 4) / (1 + 34 + 8) (8 + 23 + 7) / (7 + 41 ——) (2 + 1 + 5) / (5 + 2 + 1) (—— 8) + 4

Erat. (34 + 8) + 23 + (7 + 11 + 1) + (31 + 5) + (42 + 1) ——

Turin MS. . . . 9+49+38+ 19+37 +48+9+4=213
Man. . [43+]16+46+38+ 49+ 8 + 8+8+4=219
Erat. . . . —— 42+23+(19+36)+43 —— =163

Between the three exhibitions there is no real discrepancy. It is necessary only to observe that the Turin papyrus leaves unnoticed the 7 years during which Amenemhe I. reigned on as associated with Sesortasen I.; and that Manetho, in order to exhibit a sum of 43 years in connection with his Dyn. XIV, abstracts 40 years from Amenemhe III. and 3 from Sesortasen I.; or, if any one prefers, he may say that Manetho takes all the 43 from Sesortasen I.; and makes them good, all but 3, by transferring to Sesortasen I. from below 40 of the years of Amenemhe III. Manetho also neglects to reckon one year during which Amenemhe IV. was associated with his predecessor, giving him only 8 years instead of the 9 of the Turin papyrus. In consequence of this omission, instead of exceeding the sum of the Turin papyrus by the whole 7 years of the survival of Amenemhe I. which he reckons, but which the papyrus omits, he exceeds by only 6 years, having a sum total of 219, while the sum total of the papyrus is 213. Eratosthenes omits the 16 years of Amenemhe, and begins the reign of Sesortasen I. from the time when he began to reign alone as sovereign of all Egypt. He omits of course all concurrent years; and he takes leave of the dynasty after the reign of Amenemhe III., without carrying us on to its end. Thus, to complete that chronological exhibition of it which he supplies, we must prefix to his 163 years the 16 years of Amenemhe I. and Sesortasen I. at top, and annex the (8 + 4 =) 12 years of Amenemhe IV. and Sevek-nefrou at the bottom; and these additions will bring up the chronological years of the dynasty to the sum of 191.

The monuments, which for this dynasty are numerous, go far to explain and justify the chronological arrangement of Eratosthenes, showing distinctly that two kings were frequently associated together in the throne; though it is true that we should scarcely have collected from the monuments alone that the separate reign of Amenemhe II. was to be reduced to so few years as 23, though we might perceive that they just admitted the possibility.

The first year of the 163 taken from Dyn. XV (XII of Africanus) being so placed in the scheme of Eratosthenes as to seem to coincide with the 91st of Dyn. XXVII of the Chronicle, beginning in B.C. 1842, the last year of the 163 seems in consequence to coincide with the 69th of Dyn. XVIII ending in B.C. 1679. But when the 69 years of Dyn. XV and the 87 following them which are taken from Dyn. XVI of Manetho are all put up so as to stand clear of the commencement of Dyn. XVIII in B.C. 1748, the first year of the 42 given by Eratosthenes to his double Generation XXXI-XXXII seems to begin in B.C. (1842 + 156 =)

1998; seeming also at the same time to be in contact with the single year of Meranre of Dyn. XIII, and to begin the last of the four generations of Dyn. XVII of the Chronicle. But as this identification of the double Generation XXXI-XXXII of Eratosthenes requires that its 42nd year should end together with Dyn. XVII of the Chronicle in B.C. 1932,—and as besides the reign of Papa Maire as suzerain, and as making the third generation in Dyn. XVII of the Chronicle, cannot be put earlier than in B.C. (2034 − 39 =) 1995, the double Generation XXXI-XXXII of Eratosthenes is thereby put down again by 25 years, so as to begin not in B.C. 1998 but in B.C. 1974. And from hence accordingly we shall begin to reckon:—

"λα'. Θηβαίων λα' ἐβασίλευσε Πετεαθυρῆς, [καὶ

"λβ. Σίστωσις? . .] ἔτη μβ'" "*Peteathyres* [and . .] reigned 42 years." *Peteathyres* may possibly be formed from the throne-name of Amenemhe I., *P-hetep-heth-re*, with the definite article prefixed, instead of the formative *S*. But though Amenemhe I. is the first king of Dyn. XV, if the list were given in full, he should not be named at all in connection with the last 42 years of Sesortasen I. Yet in one way or another he must here be named, or alluded to, as the next following generation is "Amenemhe II.," which requires an Amenemhe I. to have preceded. Again, if the list of Eratosthenes adhered to the order of the Karnak Chamber, even though Amenemhe I. were named, Sesortosis I. should be named first; but now the name Peteathyres, which seems always to have stood first, offers some resemblance to the throne-name of Amenemhe I., but none whatever to any name of Sesortasen I. The fact that the number λβ' is now attached in the MSS. of Syncellus to the name of Amenemhe II., while λδ' follows, is however a sign that the two numbers λβ' and λγ' originally belonged to Ἀμμενεμῆς α' and β' which have become consolidated; so that the only restoration needed is to supply after "λβ' [Ἀμμενεμῆς α', ἔτη μβ'·

*Sesortasen I., 42 yrs. Dec. 30, B.C. 1974, to Dec. 20, B.C. 1932.*

"λγ'.] Ἀμμενεμῆς β', ἔτη κγ'." "*Amenemhe II.*, 23 years."

*Amenemhe II. 23 yrs. Dec. 20, B.C. 1932 to Dec. 14, B.C. 1909.*

But a further question remains as to the years to be given to the two generations λα' and λβ' when restored; for there are no signs in this place of any years being wanting; and Syncellus checks his own figures by telling us after each generation to what year of the world according to his reckoning, it brings him. In Goar's edition of Syncellus the number *μβ'* is only added in the margin as a variant, while the text for Generation XXXI has "*Πετεαθυρὴς ἔτη ιϛ'·*" and Bunsen divides the 42 years into two sums of 16 and 26, giving the 16 to Peteathyres and the 26 to Ammenemes I. But the number of 16 years, if it existed originally, could have no other sense than that of *indicating* the number of years which might have been given to Amenemhe *if* his reign had been inserted; for none of the 42 years divided by Bunsen could historically or chronologically be reckoned to him.

Perhaps in this place *Peteathyres* is really the throne-name of Amenemhe I. which was inserted so as to have no separate years attached, the 42 belonging either to Generation XXXII alone or in seeming conjunction with Generation XXXI. For we may remember with respect to the three generations suppressed out of the eight of Dyn. XVI of the Chronicle that 36 *years* only (without a name) have been hitherto inserted as compensation for one, and two names with as few years as possible for the other two; so that a name—a mere name, if possible, without years — is still wanted. And since by its final and chronological adjustment the head of the 163 years of Dyn. XV has been placed in the scheme of Eratosthenes in actual contact with both the two compensating names taken from Dyn. XIII, while the 36 years have disappeared, it may hence be understood why Amenemhe I., a mere name without any years, is here inserted; and also, why the order of the Karnak Chamber is departed from; for thus the three compensatory names of Meranre with only 1 year, Amenemhe I. with none, and Nitocris with 6, but those only concurrent and not in the main line of the succession, stand all together.

*Sesortasen II. and III. 55 yrs. Dec. 14, B.C. 1909 to Nov. 30, B.C. 1854.*

"λδ'. *Θηβαίων λδ' ἐβασίλευσε Σιστοσιχέρμης* (corrupted perhaps from *Σεσόρτωσις*, *'Ερμῆς*) *'Ηρακλέος κράτος, ἔτη νε'.*" "*Ses[or]tosis*, the *Strength of Hercules*, reigned 55 years." The reign, as appears from a comparison with the figures of Manetho and the Turin papyrus, is the joint sum of the two reigns of *Sesortasen II.* and *III.*, whose names being identical seemed to invite consolidation. Besides this, it seems that in the Karnak Chamber also only one of these two kings was named, unless indeed Amenemhe III. be the king omitted, which is less likely, and would need some special explanation. The gloss Ἡρακλέος κράτος is probably meant to allude to the great deeds ascribed by Manetho to Sesortasen III., whom he identifies with Sesostris, as if it had been said, "This was the Egyptian Hercules." With a like meaning it is said elsewhere that the Egyptians considered this king to have been the "first," that is, the greatest, and the greatest conqueror "after Osiris," that is, after the reigns of the gods. For Osiris-Dionysus first went as a conqueror over the earth, and in union with him the combats and victory of Horus also were celebrated; and on the monuments of the time of Rameses II. and III., and in hieratic papyri celebrating their exploits, we find applied to them the very words "first after Horus," which are put back and transferred by Manetho to Sesortasen III. whom he for reasons of his own magnifies, rather than Sesortasen I. And hence Dicæarchus imagines that Sesonchosis, by whom he means Sesortasen I., was *first*, that is, not only the first and greatest conqueror, but also the first king, after Osiris and Horus, confounding him with Menes. The word κράτος in the gloss has its source in the principal element of the name, viz. *tseser*, which Eratosthenes repeatedly renders by κράτος, while the Ἡρακλέος is from the last part of the name *sen*, as if it had been *Sem*. But this is without any true foundation in the etymology; the final syllable *sen* being really the formative of the plural, so that *Tsesor-t-sen* is equivalent to Οἱ Κρατοῦντες, *Potentes*, *The Powerful*. There may also be some allusion to the gigantic stature ascribed to this king by Manetho, as also to Rameses II. by others. What may be the source of the word or epithet Χερμῆς or Ἑρμῆς does not appear.

"λε'. Θηβαίων λε' ἐβασίλευσε Μάρης ἔτη μγ'." "*Mares* reigned 43 years." *Ma-re* or *Ma-t-en-re* is the throne-name of Amenemhe III., whose name probably stood next in the Karnak Chamber to that of Sesortasen III., though both are now lost. His 45th year being marked at Wady Magara, while the units in Manetho's list indicate that he reigned in all 48, we must suppose that he was associated in the throne with Sesortasen III. five years before the death of that king.

For the two remaining names of the dynasty, though they both appear in the Karnak Chamber, there was no room in the scheme of Eratosthenes, whose 163 chronological years having begun with the 17th year of the dynasty, 42 years before the end of Dyn. XVII of the Chronicle, in B.C. (1932 +42=) 1974, end with the 121st year of the Shepherds of Dyn. XXVII of the Chronicle in B.C. (1932+121=) 1811, and leave still (8+4=) 12 chronological years to the completion of the 191 years belonging to Manetho's Dyn. XV in B.C. 1799.

Dyn. XVI. 216 yrs ? B.C. 1964 to 1748.

*Dyn. XVI of Manetho, of* XXXVI *Nubian kings (equivalent to* VIII *generations) in* 184 *years, for which Eratosthenes gives expressly* III, *or by implication* IV *generations, and its last* 87 *years.*

Though the names given are not identifiable, we may safely presume that the three generations to which we are now come are a representation, however partial, of that dynasty, viz. XVI (XIV of Africanus), which follows next after Dyn. XV in Manetho's lists, and of that group of kings of the Upper Region which occupies the remaining side, that to the right of the spectator, in the Karnak Chamber.

To say nothing of the number of LXXVI kings which is given to this dynasty in the lists of Africanus, and probably in the hieratic papyri (as appears from the fragments of one of them preserved at Turin), the number of XXXVI kings, which may have been that of Manetho, and the number of XXX which is exhibited to our right hand side in the Karnak Chamber, being both utterly incompatible with Eratosthenes' limited number of XCI generations, and with the sum of 184 years given by Manetho to the dynasty, it is no more than was to be expected if Eratosthenes has followed not the number of kings given, but the number of years, and allowed to these latter such a number of generations, viz. about VIII, as suits best his general average, though he may not have room in which to place more than a portion of them even after they have been so reduced.

It is not wholly beyond our power to explain how the kings of the right hand side in the Karnak Chamber, of Manetho's Dyn. XVI, and still more those of the corresponding portion of the hieratic lists, should be so numerous, and should yet be reducible to VIII generations, or X at most, and to 184 or at most to about 216 years. It has been observed elsewhere, that not only is the idea of XXX or more of these kings having been consecutive in a single line in itself inadmissible, but the symmetry of the Karnak Chamber requires us to suppose that as there are four distinct dynasties grouped together in that half of the Chamber which is to our left on entering, so also there are a number of lines, whether fewer or more than four, in the other half to our right. It has been observed too by Mr. Birch, that just at the commencement of Dyn. XVIII a number of names of princes and princesses are found inclosed in cartouches; and to some of these who appear on monuments of the time of Amunoph I. with a cartouche, but with the title only of prince, the title of *king* is given afterwards in the hieratic papyri, as is done in the papyrus Abbott with the name of "*Ahmes, son of Pear.*" Now, of those names which are still legible to our right hand in the Karnak Chamber, about half have been identified on contemporary monuments, found either in Upper Egypt, (at Abydos for instance, at Coptos, and on the road to Kosseir,) or in Lower or Upper Nubia. And, besides these names common to other monuments with the Karnak Chamber, a number of others have been found, plainly of the same lineage and connection, who are not to be seen in the Karnak Chamber, but who *are* some of them identifiable in the much fuller exhibition of the same group preserved in the Turin papyrus. In two instances at least, where a king of this group is named in a contemporary inscription, the king's father and his sons, and other members of his family being named with him, it appears that the *father* was *not a king;* while the names of one or more of the sons appear in the fragments of the Turin papyrus *as kings,* after the name of the king their father, but without any trace of the name of the grandfather.

A king whose cartouche in the Turin papyrus exhibits the family name *Nepherhotep*, conjoined with a throne-name beginning *Ra-scha* . . , the remaining sign *kherp*, or as some read it *sechem*, being lost, was found by M. Brugsch on a rock in the isle of Sehèl, at the first cataract, with a number of other personages of his family, and he has given us the list as follows:—" 1. The Divine Father *Ha-anchef;* 2. the Royal Mother *Kama;* 3. the Royal Wife *Senebsen;* 4. the Royal Son *Hathor-si;* 5. the Royal Son *Sevek-hotep;* 6 the Royal Son *Ha-anchef;* 7. the Royal Daughter *Kama;* 8. the Royal Grandson *Neb-anch;* 9. the [Keeper of the Seals?] *Senebj.*" The same names of some of this family are found also on the rocks at Assouan and in the isle of Konosso. And in the Turin papyrus we find the king *Ra-scha-kherp Nepherhotep* preceded in the list by a king named *Ra-kherp-ka Sevekhotep* (without any mention of his father *Ha-anchef*), and followed by two of the three sons whose names have been copied by M. Brugsch from the rocks of the first cataract, viz. *Ra-Hathorsi* (the rest is broken away), and *Ra-scha-nepher Sevekhotep.* These then had the title of king after their father; but the third son and the grandson, whose names are with theirs on the rocks, do not appear in the papyrus.

Again, M. Brugsch gives from the Königsbuch of Lepsius the names of a number of personages of the family of another king named Sevekhotep, as follows:—" 1. The Divine father [who therefore was not a king] *Mentuhotep;* 2. the Royal Mother [who therefore seemingly was daughter of a king] *Sonhet-hetou;* 3. the King *Sevek-hotep II.*; 4. the Queen *Nena;* 5. the Prince *Seneb;* 6. the Princess *Souhet-hetou-Font;* 7. the Princess *Anch-t-mati;* 8. the Prince *Sevekhotep;* 9. the Princess *Souhet-hetou;* 10. the Princess *Hont;* 11. the Prince *Mentuhotep.*" This king M. Brugsch would identify with a Sevekhotep in the Turin papyrus whose throne-name is broken away; and it may well be the same, as he is followed in the papyrus by a king *Ra-kherp-s . . . teti Sevekhotep,* who may also be the Prince Sevek-hotep who occurs as son of the king Sevek-hotep, commonly called Sevekhotep II. But whether his brother the prince Mentuhotep also reigned after the father does not appear, as the two next following cartouches have their latter halves broken away.

So then in each of these two instances we obtain from the monuments and from the Turin papyrus a little collateral line or dynasty of kings, consisting of two or three names, followed, it may be, by more, which are all omitted as subordinate and unimportant in the Karnak Chamber. And yet there is such an affinity in the whole group, that in the Turin papyrus the two monumental kings whose fathers are now known *not* to have been kings are not distinguished by any rubric. Hence we may understand, that though they might omit *some* of those numerous royalties of the same lineage which are exhibited by the hieratic papyri, a number of the more important of them would naturally be retained and exhibited by those who arranged the Karnak Chamber; and those retained, no less than the more numerous group of the papyri (no less we may add than the four dynasties in the other half of the Chamber to our left), would have to be reduced within very different limits, if it were desired to exhibit only, and in one series, the number of generations and of consecutive years covered by the XXX or XXXVI kings.

When first put up, so as to stand clear of Dyn. XVIII, the 87 years taken by Eratosthenes from Manetho's Dyn. XVI, while they occupy the last part of the 184 years given to them by Manetho, and really belonging to the Shepherds of Dyn. XXVII of the Chronicle, with whom they were for all that time contemporary, seem also to form a continuation to Dyn. XV (XII of Africanus), from after the death of Amenemhe III. But when the position of Dyn. XV has been finally rectified, and Generation XXXIII of Eratosthenes, that is, the separate reign of Amenemhe II., has been made to begin in B.C. 1932, so that the reign of Amenemhe III. ends in B.C. (1932—121=) 1811, and that of Sevek-nefrou 12 years later, in B.C. 1799, then the 87 years taken by Eratosthenes from the Nubian Dynasty XVI, and commencing in B.C. (1748+87=) 1835, appear to be, as they really are, part of a separate dynasty, concurrent only in part with Dyn. XV, but outlasting it, and ending at the same point with Dyn. XIV, with which also it is concurrent. But for its commencement we have no other indication than the sum of 184 years given to it by Manetho. If this sum were historical, we should have to say that the XXXVI kings of Manetho must be reducible to at most VIII generations, and to not fewer than four separate lines. But it is clearly improbable that the precise sum of 184 years should belong at once to the Shepherd supremacy over Lower Egypt, and to three or four lines of kings in Upper Egypt and in the two Nubias, which cannot be supposed to have all risen and fallen together with the Shepherds. Even the tributary kings of Memphis, who did really begin from the same point with the 184 years of the Shepherd supremacy, did not last precisely to their end; while in Upper Egypt there is no trace of the Shepherds having become predominant till much later. And, besides this, as we know that Sesortasen I. conquered Nubia, and as we know that the numerous kings of Dyn. XVI were connected by blood with him or with his partner Amenemhe I., and names of the same formation are found in Nubia in contemporary inscriptions of his reign, we may infer that he not only conquered Nubia, but also organised its government after the manner of Egypt; that so the true historical duration of Dyn. XVI may have been perhaps about 216 rather than 184 years; and that one or more of the successions grouped together in it may have had as many as IX, or even X, actual kings. But the 184 years of Manetho, like some others of his numbers, are merely an indication of the 184 years of the Chronicle. And, if so, then in the scheme of Eratosthenes also the same 184 years, indicated as belonging to Dyn. XVI of Manetho by his Generations XXXVI, XXXVII, and XXXVIII, occupying 87 years before Dyn. XVIII, are really, though in a very indirect way, an indication of Dyn. XXVII of the Chronicle. And viewed thus, the three generations of Eratosthenes, with a fourth indicated (for the last has 60 years), like the last four of his representation of Manetho's Dyn. XIV, afford a parallel to the IV generations of Dyn. XXVII of the Chronicle, as well as a hint of the 184 years chronologically belonging to them.

"λϛ'. Θηβαίων λϛ' ἐβασίλευσε Σιφόας ὁ καὶ Ἑρμῆς, υἱὸς Ἡφαίστου, ἔτη ε'." "*Siphoas*, or *Thoth*, which means *son of Phtha*, reigned 5 years." From the gloss, *υἱὸς Ἡφαίστου*, Bunsen naturally wishes to read Σιφθᾶς; but the other gloss, Ἑρμῆς, requires rather Σι-θὼθ, which with a Greek termination might make Σιφόας. The two glosses then are seemingly mere guesses from the sound.

"λζ'. Θηβαίων λζ' ἐβασίλευσε Φρουρῶν, ἤτοι Νεῖλος, ἔτη ε' [ιθ'.]" "*Phrouro*, or *Nilus*, reigned 19 years." The sum of Syncellus, who passes here from his A.M. 3889, to his A.M. 3894, justifies Bunsen's correction of 19 for "5 years;" and the gloss agrees fairly with the name, as "*iour*," (the river, the Nile,) with the article prefixed, will make *Phiourr*, or *Phrour;* and we find the same name, with the same gloss, at the end of Manetho's Dyn. XIX, in Θούωρις, who is identified with Πόλυβος, or Nilus. But to what king the allusion may be in the list of Eratosthenes we have no means of discovering.

"λη'. Θηβαίων λη' ἐβασίλευσεν Ἀμουθανταῖος, ἔτη ξγ'." "*Amouthantæus* reigned 63 years." As no gloss is added, and there is no list of names to which we can refer, it is hopeless to inquire after the owner of this name, into which either *Amon* or *Mouth*, and the family name *Hantef*, may perhaps enter. All that is clear is that for some reason or other it was desired to indicate under one sum at least two actual generations, so that the three are equivalent to four. But to what end four should be preferred to three, when even with four the representation of the dynasty is so imperfect, is not clear; unless it were for this, that the number of four generations in connection with the 184 years given to this dynasty by Manetho, and shown to end in B.C. 1748 by the scheme of Eratosthenes, might hint that as it stands in Manetho's lists it is really and chronologically concurrent with Dyn. XXVII of the Chronicle, just as the same had been hinted already for the latter portion of Dyn. XIV with its four names.

At this point Syncellus ceases to transcribe from Apollodorus, without having given us as yet any name from Manetho's Dyn. XVIII, but having brought us, according to his own apprehension, in some sense or other to the end of a series: for he says:—

"'Η τῶν λη' βασιλέων τῶν κατ' Αἴγυπτον λεγομένων Θηβαίων, ὧν τὰ ὀνόματα 'Ερατοσθένης λαβὼν ἐκ τῶν ἐν Διοσπόλει ἱερογραμματέων παρέφρασεν ἐξ Αἰγυπτίας εἰς 'Ελλάδα φωνὴν, ἐνταῦθα ἔληξεν ἀρχὴ, ἀρξαμένη μὲν ἀπὸ τοῦ βϡ' κοσμικοῦ ἔτους ἔτεσιν ,ρκδ' μετὰ τὴν σύγχυσιν τῶν γλωσσῶν, λήξασα δὲ εἰς τοῦτο τὸ ,γϡοε' τοῦ κόσμου ἔτος." That is, "The line of the XXXVIII kings, called in Egypt Theban, whose names Eratosthenes had sent to him from the sacred scribes at Diospolis, and rendered them with glosses into Greek, *ended here*, having commenced from the year of the world 2900, and ending at this year of the world 3975, which has been last named." It should have been "commencing from after A.M. 2900, and ending at the end of A.M. 3976." For Syncellus and those whom he follows, make 2776 years *complete* to the Dispersion; and he allows from thence 2365 years of the 3555 of the original Manetho, cutting off as inadmissible 656 before, and 534 after the Flood, and saying that the remaining 2365 end with the year of the world 5141, which means that they so end in the scheme of Anianus. After what has been recited above, he continues thus:—"Τῶν δὲ τούτοις ἐφεξῆς ἄλλων νγ' Θηβαίων βασιλέων ὑπὸ τοῦ αὐτοῦ 'Απολλοδώρου παραδεδομένων τὰς προσηγορίας περιττὸν ἡγούμεθα ἐνταῦθα, ὡς μηδὲν συμβαλλομένας ἡμῖν, παραθέσθαι, ἐπεὶ μηδὲ αἱ πρὸ αὐτῶν." "But the continuation of LIII other names of Theban kings, which is given by the same Apollodorus, I think it superfluous to insert here, as they make nothing to our purpose, though in truth the same may be said equally of the rest which have preceded."

So Syncellus omits the LIII following names, being the remainder wanting after XXXVIII to complete the whole scheme of the LXXVI royal generations and 1881 years of the Chronicle, with the XV generations and 443 years "of the Cycle" prefixed; and he leaves us to make them out for ourselves as we can; only, with the certainty that he has now brought us to the commencement of Dyn. XVIII of Manetho and the Chronicle, that great dynasty, most properly called Diospolite, which, after overthrowing the Shepherds, united both Upper and Lower Egypt (and both the Nubias too during some centuries) under a single sceptre. For having followed hitherto the order of Manetho's dynasties, and having given already twice over to native kings of Lower and Upper Egypt the chronological space of the Shepherds, that is, of Dyn. XXVII of the Chronicle, identical with the larger and more important part of Dyn. XVII of Manetho (XV of Africanus), the Theban priests had nothing now to do but to continue with the single series of the Chronicle and Manetho, from the first name of Dyn. XVIII, the chronological space of which they have already encroached upon to the extent of VII generations and 156 years. And as the actual kings named or counted by Manetho for his XV Dynasties from XVIII to XXX inclusively, are now all to be placed or omitted as if between B.C. (1748 – 156 =) 1592 and B.C. 345, in LIII instead of LX generations, and in B.C. (1592 – 345 =) 1247, instead of B.C. (1748 – 345 =) 1403 years, the first thing needed is to review Manetho's names, comparing them with those of the Chronicle, and to see how far we can go in ascertaining which names would be omitted or consolidated; and, when this is done, we shall have a list not very greatly differing from that omitted by Syncellus; one which will serve at any rate to show *how* the scheme of Eratosthenes must have been completed, though in what form the names appeared, or with what reigns attached to them, we cannot always even attempt to conjecture.

But before attempting thus to recover, at least approximatively, the arrangement of the LIII remaining generations, there are two points which demand notice:

First, the use sought to be made of that difference which exists between the designation and description of Dyn. XVIII by the Chronicle and by Manetho; for the Chronicle makes it a dynasty of "XIV *Memphite* generations in 348 years," while Manetho makes it a dynasty of "XVI *Diospolites*" in 333 years. There can be no doubt that these are really one and the same dynasty, with the same kings and the same years, beginning historically from the same point, and ending at the same point one with the other; though Manetho seems to depress the head of the dynasty by an unchronological insertion made at the very beginning of his kings, and originally consisting of 3 years, but reduced since to 2 years and 10 months; and though he also transposes 15 years from the middle of the dynasty to the end, and prefixes them to Dyn. XIX. This he does for a reason similar to that for which the Chronicle also itself had misplaced and suppressed as far as was possible, consistently with its purpose, one whole dynasty with its 184 years. There can be no doubt either that the Theban priests who filled up for Eratosthenes the framework of the Chronicle, as enlarged by themselves, knew this at least as well as we can know it. So we must not suppose that in their own minds they distinguished betwen Dyn. XVIII of the Chronicle and Dyn. XVIII of Manetho. Still, as we have now had some experience of their methods of *indicating* what they do not distinctly exhibit, and of making the same generations serve the purpose of double or even treble indications, it will be nothing strange to find that in order to conceal more effectually all traces of the Shepherd Dynasty, and that they may not be distinctly understood to have thrown it back to its true place from the place where it was named unchronologically by the Chronicle, they affect to regard Dyn. XVIII of the Chronicle and of Manetho as two distinct dynasties, and indicate both of these, and others after them, in such a way, that at length the two series may blend together, long after the 184 years of Dyn. XXVII of the Chronicle have been anticipated and placed ambiguously so as neither to betray what they really are, nor that they had been purposely transposed by the Chronicle and are now put back to their true places, but not in connection with their true owners. So after paralleling the XV generations "of the Cycle," and the first (V + III + IV =) XII of the royal generations of the Chronicle, those, that is, of its Dynasties XVI and XVII, they insinuate that their next twelve generations (XXVII to XXXVIII inclusively) which may be regarded as indicating fourteen generations, (XXXI and XXXII being reckoned as only one, but three others, viz. XXX, XXXIV, and XXXVIII, being double,) are, in spite of the designation "Memphite," a representation of the XIV generations and 348 years of Dyn. XVIII of the Chronicle, the series named having 340 years, and the remaining 8 being to be added from the next reign. Thus, while in truth they were making the earlier Thebans invade the space of Dyn. XVIII of Manetho, and depress it so as to begin 156 years too low, they made as though they had done the very reverse, putting up Dyn. XVIII of the Chronicle 184 years too high, so as to begin, as it does ostensibly, immediately after Dyn. XVII, and so as to occupy both the 184 years really belonging to Dyn. XXVII, and also the first 156 (and 8 more) of its own years, leaving the rest to be reckoned by a double reckoning as making the commencement both of Dyn. XVIII of Manetho with 333, and of Dyn. XIX of the Chronicle with 194 years.

This point having been noticed, we must consider more particularly both the causes and the consequences of the inroad already made on the space of Dyn. XVIII of the Chronicle.

If we put together the last thirteen dynasties of the Chronicle, as they stand, from the head of Dyn. XVIII, (Dyn. XXVII included, with its IV anonymous kings and 184 years,) they have in all 64 generations in 1588 years, showing an average of nearly 25 years to each generation, that is, something above the ordinary average of the Chronicle, notwithstanding the presence of many short reigns in the later dynasties. But this high average is caused mainly by the fact that the anonymous Dynasty XXVII to its 184 years has only IV generations, and in part also by some other spaces of anarchy or of illegitimate reigns being added on to particular dynasties, so as to swell the average length of their reigns. Thus 15 years at least of kings not recognised are reckoned by the Chronicle to Dyn. XVIII, and 59 perhaps to Dyn. XIX. On the ejection of Dyn. XXVII (supposing it to be restored to its true place above Dyn. XVIII, and with only IV kings), the twelve remaining dynasties, viz. XVIII to XXX inclusively, with LX kings and (1588 —

184 =) 1404 years, being now all consecutive and in their true places, will have an average length of 23 years and 4 months to each reign, being 1 year and 2 months *under* the ordinary average of $24\frac{1}{2}$ years. And this is the series which Eratosthenes would have had to make out, had he not already given VII of these LX generations, and 156 of their years, to names of other "Theban" kings, anterior to Dyn. XVIII. But having done that he has only LIII generations and 1248 years of the Chronicle left to parallel, and all his names, if answering to those of Manetho's lists from the head of Dyn. XVIII downwards, will be of course unchronologically depressed to the extent of 156 years, and will depress all below them till some part of history is reached where Manetho supplies no names, and where the priests choose rather to bridge over a chasm with Theban names unchronologically placed, than to supply new and more accurate information to their Greek questioner. Also, as 156 years are fewer by 18 than what would belong to any VII generations of Dyn. XVIII of the Chronicle, according to its particular average (XIV in 348 giving $24\frac{12}{14}$, or nearly 25 years), the average length of the last LIII generations of Eratosthenes would necessarily be something more than that of the last LIII of the Chronicle (Dyn. XXVII not being included), viz. something over $23\frac{1}{2}$ years, instead of $23\frac{1}{3}$ years. But this is of no moment, as Eratosthenes does not follow closely the particular averages of the Chronicle, and irrespectively of this minute difference his last LIII generations, omitted by Syncellus, commencing from Sept. 26, B.C. 1592, answer exactly to the last LIII of the Chronicle (Dyn. XXVII not being included), commencing from Sept. 21, B.C. 1574. The next question is, how may these generations have been filled up?

We have been following the dynasties of Manetho hitherto conjointly with the divisions or spaces of the Chronicle, so doubtless Eratosthenes would continue to do so still; the more so as now there is in general but one line of sovereigns for all Egypt. And so we might suppose at first that the only thing to be done is to compress Manetho's more numerous actual kings by consolidation to the number of the

Chronicle, as we can do with certainty in most of the dynasties. Thus in Dyn. XVIII, where Manetho has XVI kings (or XVI and one queen), and the monumental lists have XIII kings, it is easy either to reduce these latter to XII, as we shall do below, or make them up to the XIV of the Chronicle by considering Rameses II. as a double generation, and admitting some additional name, such as that of *Amen-Anchut*. The VI names again given by Manetho for Dyn. XIX admit of being reduced to the V of the Chronicle by the consolidation of one short reign of only 5 years. The IX monumental kings who are identical with the IX of Manetho's Dyn. XXII, suit exactly the VI of Dyn. XXI, and the III of Dyn. XXII of the Chronicle. Two kings contained in Manetho's Dyn. XXIII are indentifiable with the two of Dyn. XXIII of the Chronicle; and the two others and the single king of Manetho's Dyn. XXIV with the three of Dyn. XXIV of the Chronicle. The three Ethiopians are the same in Dyn. XXV according to both schemes. Dyn. XXVI presents no difficulty, the last of Manetho's IX kings, with only 6 months, being really contained in the 5th year of Cambyses, and the three predecessors of Psammitichus I. in Manetho's lists being no doubt set aside by the Theban priests for two monumental names connected with Upper Egypt. Instead of the VIII Persians enumerated by Manetho in his Dyn. XXVII, the Chronicle, under the V generations of its Dyn. XXVIII, indicates beyond a doubt the five principal reigns of Cambyses, Darius, Xerxes, Artaxerxes Longimanus, and Darius Nothus, consolidating the months of Artabanus, Xerxes II., and Sogdianus, as well as those of the Magian, and three years of Artaxerxes Mnemon, which Manetho himself also has left unnoticed. If two kings with 1 year and with 4 months respectively, and another with 2 years, in Manetho's Dynasties XXIX and XXX were consolidated, the remaining IV kings would be identifiable with the III kings of Dyn. XXIX and the single king of Dyn. XXX of the Chronicle. And so for Dynasties XVIII, XIX, XXI, XXII, XXIII, XXIV, XXV, XXVI, XXVIII, XXIX, and XXX of the Chronicle, we should have from Manetho and from the monuments a series of (14 + 5 + 6 + 3 + 2 + 3 + 3 + 7 + 5 + 3 + 1 =) 52 names to fill up the LIII anonymous generations of the Chronicle.

But this method alone does not quite carry us through. There still remains one long dynasty, Dyn. XX of the Chronicle, with VIII generations and 228 years, of which we have as yet taken no account. Manetho, with fewer years (a difference which is nothing to our present purpose), gives it XII kings; and these, if the reigns had been given, might have been reducible by consolidation of short reigns, or of reigns not constituting distinct generations, to the VIII of the Chronicle. But in Manetho's lists, as they now stand, *no names are given*, and it seems that this was so from the first, no hieratic list being transcribed by him for this dynasty, though no doubt he added in his narrative some notice by way of explanation, as that all the kings were of the same family, or that they all had one and the same family name, (viz. Rameses,) with the preceding. If the Theban priests named, as they were certainly able to name, these kings, whose tombs and other monuments were before their eyes, the introduction of VIII more names for this dynasty would force us (since we have LII already without them) to suppress either above or below VII of those which we have already enumerated. But it is probable that the Theban priests availed themselves of the fact that Manetho had left this dynasty anonymous in order to gain room for some of those VII generations of Dyn. XVIII which they at the same time displaced and thrust down from above. For the Greeks the names already known through Manetho were as good as any others, or rather preferable; and there was nothing objectionable in covering the space belonging to Dynasties XIX and XX with names thrust down unchronologically from Dynasties XVIII and XIX, seeing that this is only what they had been doing throughout, no names having stood hitherto in their true chronological position. This then was the reason that they suppressed (if they did suppress them, as seems most probable) *five* perhaps out of the eight kings due to Dyn. XX, not that they were unable to name them, but that they wanted their room for names less convenient for omission, which they had depressed from above. Dyn. XXI of Manetho would naturally be unnoticed, for Manetho himself reckons to his Dyn. XX Diospolites enough to cover all those 93 years of Dyn. XXI which are chronological as they stand, and not merely thrown up from other places below; and the Theban priests would not go out of their way to place either his fictitious or his contemporary Tanites of Lower Egypt. So they probably made Manetho's VI names of Dyn. XIX, consolidated into V to suit the Chronicle, and all depressed from above, together with only three others really taken from the monumental kings of Dyn. XX, and from its end rather than its beginning, to exhibit the VIII generations given to that dynasty by the Chronicle.

We may now subjoin a conjectural and approximative reconstruction of the last LIII generations of Eratosthenes and Apollodorus, omitted by Syncellus, but needed to complete those (XV + LXXVI =) XCI generations and (443 + 1881 =) 2324 years of the Chronicle, which the Theban priests made Eratosthenes allow to the kings from Menes to Nectanebo:

*Continuation of Dynasties XVIII and XXVII of the Chronicle, indicated under Dynasty XVIII of Manetho, with XIV generations and 333 or 348 years.*

"λθ'. Θηβαίων λθ' ἐβασίλευσεν Ἄμωσις, ἔτη κε'." "*Amosis* reigned 25 years." With his 8th year the 348 years of Dyn. XVIII of the Chronicle are completed in XI generations, as expressly reckoned, or in XIV as indirectly indicated; and from this point commences a second exhibition of the 184 years of Dyn. XXVII of the Chronicle, so that the XVIII generations from Generation XXVII to XLV inclusively (that is, the XVIII which have years attached to them, Generation XXXI, which is only a name, being not counted), may be divided *either* into VII with 184 years and XIV with 348, *or* into XIV with 348 and VII with 184 years, thus:—

| | | | | | | | | | | | | | | | | | | |
|---|---|---|---|---|---|---|---|---|---|---|---|---|---|---|---|---|---|---|
| Either | Dyn. XXVII, 184. | | | | | | | Dyn. XVIII, 348. | | | | | | | | | | |
| Gens. | κζ. | κη'. | κθ'. | λ'. | λβ'. | λγ. | λδ'. | λε'. | λς'. | λζ'. | λη'. | λθ. | μ'. | μα'. | μβ'. | μγ'. | μδ'. | με' |
| Yrs. | 7. | 12. | 11. | 60. | 42. | 23. | (29+26). | 43. | 5. | 19. | 63. | (9+17). | 20. | 48 | 26. | 10. | 48. | 15. |
| Or | Dyn. XVIII, 348. | | | | | | | | | | | | Dyn. XXVII, 184. | | | | | |

By detaching the last reign and reckoning it to those following, the same scheme may be regarded as exhibiting Manetho's Dynasties XVI and XVIII, with 184 and 333 years, which might equally with those of the Chronicle be reversed and reckoned the 333 first and the 184 last, if there were any reason for such ambiguity, which there is not, it being only Dyn. XXVII of the Chronicle of which it was desired to conceal the exact place and nature.

"μ'. Θηβαίων μ' ἐβασίλευσεν Ἀμενωφθὶς, ἔτη κ'." "*Amenoph I.* reigned 20 years."

"μα'. Θηβαίων μα' ἐβασίλευσε Μιφρὶς ἔτη μη'." "*Thothmes III.* reigned 48 years."

"μβ'. Θηβαίων μβ' ἐβασίλευσεν Ἀμενῶφις, ἔτη κϛ'." "*Amenoph II.* reigned 26 years."

"μγ'. Θηβαίων μγ' ἐβασίλευσε Τούθμωσις, ἔτη ι'." "*Thothmes IV.* reigned 10 years."

"μδ'. Θηβαίων μδ' ἐβασίλευσεν Ἀμμενῶφις, ἔτη μη'." "*Amenoph III.* reigned 48 years."

"με'. Θηβαίων με' ἐβασίλευσεν Ὧρος, ἔτη ιε'." "*Horus* reigned 15 years.

Here the double exhibition of either 184 + 348 or 348 + 184 years, as if belonging to Dynasties XXVII and XVIII or XVIII and XXVII of the Chronicle, is completed. And Eratosthenes might continue with an indication of Dyn. XIX of the Chronicle as follows:—

| Man. | Remainder of Dyn. XVIII, 333. | | | | | | Dyn. XX, 135. | | | Dyn. XXI, 93. | | | |
|---|---|---|---|---|---|---|---|---|---|---|---|---|---|
| Gens. | μϛ'. | μζ'. | μη'. | μθ'. | ν'. | να'. | νβ'. | νγ'. | νδ'. | νε'. | νϛ'. | νζ'. | νη'. |
| Yrs. | 25. | 25 | 4. | 68. | 19. | (15+38.+6). | 20. | 47. | 52. | 21. | 42. | 7. | 23. |
| Chron. | Dyn. XIX, 194. | | | | | | Dyn. XX, 228. | | | | | | |

"μϛ'. Θηβαίων μϛ' ἐβασίλευσεν Ἀχεῤῥῆς, ἔτη κε'." "*Acherres* reigned 25 years."

"μζ'. Θηβαίων μζ' ἐβασίλευσεν Ἀχεῤῥῆς, ἔτη κε'." "*Acherres* reigned 25 years."

"μη'. Θηβαίων μη' ἐβασίλευσε Ἀρμεσσῆς, ἔτη δ'." "*Armesses* reigned 4 years."

"μθ'. Θηβαίων μθ' ἐβασίλευσε Ῥαμεσσῆς, ἔτη ξη'." "*Rameses Miammous* reigned 68 years."

"ν'. Θηβαίων ν' ἐβασίλευσεν Ἀμενῶφ, ἔτη ιθ'." "*Amenoph* reigned 19 years."

Here in truth we end Manetho's Dynasty XVIII of XVI Diospolites in 333 years. But in consequence of the depression of this dynasty by 156 years, we have now come apparently to the end of the 141st year of Dyn. XIX of the Chronicle. It would have been the 156th, but that Manetho, as has been explained elsewhere, has attached 15 years really belonging to Dyn. XVIII to the first reign of his Dynasty XIX.

"να'. Θηβαίων να' ἐβασίλευσε Σέθως, ἔτη νθ'." "*Sethos* reigned 59 years."

The first 15 of these really belong, as has been just said, to Dyn. XVIII of the Chronicle, and make the difference between its sum of 348 and Manetho's sum of 333 years. But in the present unchronological exhibition of both the schemes these 15, with 38 more years of the same reign, complete the exhibition of the 194 *years* of Dyn. XIX of the Chronicle, the five *generations* of which have been reckoned already. But the remaining 6 years, together with the name, represent the first of the VIII generations of Dyn. XX of the Chronicle. Dynasty XIX of Manetho is equally completed and exhibited, and at the same point with Dyn. XIX of the Chronicle, the only difference being, that for the exhibition of the three Dynasties XVI, XVIII, and XIX of Manetho, the 15 years of Generation XLV are reckoned to the head of Dyn. XIX, instead of being reckoned to the end of Dyn. XVIII; while for the exhibition of Dynasties XVIII, XXVII (or XXVII, XVIII), and XIX of the Chronicle, it is *vice versâ.*

*Dynasty XX of the Chronicle, of VIII Diospolites, in* 228 *years, and Dynasty XX of Manetho with* 135 *and part of XXI with* 93 *years.*

The last 6 years of Generation LI, together with the name *Sethos*, make the first generation towards the representation of this dynasty. Then

"νβ'. Θηβαίων νβ' ἐβασίλευσεν Ἀμενεχθῆς, ἔτη κ'." "*Amen-necht* reigned 20 years."

"νγ'. Θηβαίων νγ' ἐβασίλευσε Ῥαμεσσῆς, ἔτη μζ'." "*Rameses III.* reigned 47 years."

"νδ'. Θηβαίων νδ' ἐβασίλευσε Ῥαμεσσῆς, ἔτη νβ'." "*Rameses* reigned 52 years."

Here is completed the exhibition of the 135 *years* of Manetho's Dyn. XX, but not that of the XII Diospolite *kings* whom he gives to the same dynasty, and who cover 93 years more, so as to end together with the VIII generations and 228 years of Dyn. XX of the Chronicle.

"νε'. Θηβαίων νε' ἐβασίλευσε Θούωρις, ὁ παρ' Ὁμήρῳ Πόλυβος, ἔτη κα'." "*Thuoris,* who is the Polybus of Homer, reigned 21 years."

The five generations which have hitherto been named as if representing the first 156 years of Dyn. XX of the Chronicle, being really depressed from above, the names still wanting to complete the VIII generations of the Chronicle will be taken, we may presume, not from the first of the historical kings of Dyn. XX, but from those at its end, so that they may indicate their five predecessors whose places have been usurped by names depressed and belonging historically to Dynasty XIX.

"νϛ'. Θηβαίων νϛ' ἐβασίλευσεν Ὧρος Σιαμμῶν, ὅ ἐστι Διογενὴς, ἔτη μβ'." "*Her-Hor Si-amon* reigned 42 years."

"νζ. Θηβαίων νζ' ἐβασίλευσε Παντευνῆς, ἔτη ζ'." "*Pinetem* reigned 7 years."

"νη'. Θηβαίων νη' ἐβασίλευσε Μενταύρης, ἔτη κγ'." "*Ramen-cheper* reigned 23 years."

Here, in VIII Diospolite generations, we have completed a representation both of the VIII generations and 228 years of Dyn. XX of the Chronicle, and of the XII *reigns* of Dyn. XX of Manetho, these latter being compressed into VIII generations, and covering 93 more years than the 135 which Manetho allows to their dynasty. Consequently these 93 years must be subtracted from the 130 years of his Dyn. XXI, the concurrent Tanites of which would be set aside in favour of the Thebans really belonging to the same space; while the remaining 37 years of Manetho's Dyn. XXI are transposed by him from their true places and connections, to which we may presume the Theban priests would restore them. So taking the head of Dyn. XXI of the Chronicle now to coincide with the head of Dyn. XXII of Manetho, and having from this point downwards no longer any reason for distinguishing the two schemes, we may continue, simply filling up the blank generations of the Chronicle from Manetho's names:—

*Dynasty XXI of the Chronicle and XXII of Manetho, with* VI *Tanite or Bubastite generations and* 121 *years.*

"νθ'. Θηβαίων νθ' ἐβασίλευσε Σέσωγχις, ἔτη κα'." "*Shishonk I.* reigned 21 years."

"ξ'. Θηβαίων ξ ἐβασίλευσεν Ὀσόρχων, ἔτη ιε'." "*Osorchon I.* reigned 15 years."

"ξα'. Θηβαίων ξα' ἐβασίλευσε Τακέλωθις, ἔτη [κε'?]." "*Takelot I.* reigned [25?] years."

"ξβ'. Θηβαίων ξβ' ἐβασίλευσεν Ὀσόρχων, ἔτη [κθ'?]." "*Osorchon II.* reigned [29?] years."

"ξγ'. Θηβαίων ξγ' ἐβασίλευσε Σέσωγχις, ἔτη [ιζ'?]." "*Shishonk II.* reigned [17?] years."

"ξδ'. Θηβαίων ξδ' ἐβασίλευσε Τακέλωθις, ἔτη ιδ'." "*Takelot II.* reigned 14? years."

Manetho gives no names for the 3rd, 4th, and 5th of these kings; and between all the three he gives only 29 years, and he gives to the 6th king only 13 years. But the 12th year of Takelot I., the 23rd of Osorchon II., and the 14th of Takelot II., have been found marked on the monuments. With the sums conjecturally assigned them, the VI kings have 121 years.

*Dynasty XXII of the Chronicle, with* III *Tanite generations and* 41 *years, the names belonging to Dynasty XXII and the years to Dynasty XXIII of Manetho.*

"ξε'. Θηβαίων ξε' ἐβασίλευσε Σέσωγχις, ἔτη ις'." "*Shishonk III.* reigned 16 years." [But by an Apis-stele he reigned 51.]

"ξς'. Θηβαίων ξς' ἐβασίλευσε Πιχαῆς, ἔτη ις'." "*Pichai* reigned 16 years." [But the only known date of this king is that of an Apis-stele where his second year is marked.]

"ξζ' Θηβαίων ξζ' ἐβασίλευσε Σέσωγχις, ἔτη ις'." "*Shishonk IV.* reigned 16 years." [But on an Apis-stele his 37th is named.]

So perhaps the two generations and 48 years of the Chronicle are really covered by Shishonk III. alone, who with a son who died before him may count for two generations. And if so, Pichai and Shishonk IV. may be contemporaries of the two kings of Dyn. XXIII who had possession of Thebes, and of other kings following.

*Dynasty XXIII of the Chronicle, II Diospolites, in* 19 *years, being the second and third names of Dynasty XXIII of Manetho.*

"ξη'. Θηβαίων ξη' ἐβασίλευσεν Ὀσόρχων, ἔτη θ'." "*Osorchon* reigned 9 years."

"ξθ'. Θηβαίων ξθ' ἐβασίλευσε Ψάμμους, ἔτη ι'." "*Psimout* reigned 10 years."

As *Shishonk III.*, *Pichai*, and *ShishonkI V.* seem by the Apis-stelæ to have reigned between them not only 48 years, answering to the 48 of Dyn. XXII of the Chronicle, but 90 or more years (answering rather to the 87 of Dyn. XXIII of Manetho), we must suppose that Egypt was in the time of these kings again divided; and that the two kings of Dyn. XXIV of the Chronicle, who though probably of the same lineage with the preceding, are called by it "Diospolites," because they had possession of Thebes, were really contemporaneous with part of the 90 years of the three above-named kings of Dyn. XXIII.

*Dynasty XXIV of the Chronicle (part of XXIII and XXIV of Manetho), with III Tanite generations and* 44 *years.*

"ο'. Θηβαίων ο' ἐβασίλευσε Πετουβάστης, ἔτη [κα'?]." "*Petsibast* reigned [21?] years."

"οα'. Θηβαίων οα' ἐβασίλευσε Ζὴτ, ἔτη [ια'?]." "*Zet* reigned [11?] years."

"οβ'. Θηβαίων οβ' ἐβασίλευσε Βόκχορις, ἔτη ιβ' ?" "*Bocchoris* reigned [12?] years."

The names of the first two of these kings not having been found on any Apis-stelæ, we may suppose that they also were contemporaries of the last of the three Tanites named above, under Dyn. XXII of the Chronicle. But since the Apis No. 34 of M. Mariette was buried "in the 6th year of *Bocchoris*," while the preceding Apis, No. 33, which died in the 37th year of *Shishonk IV.*, was buried in the same chamber, it would seem that the division had now come to an end, and that Bocchoris succeeded Shishonk IV. as sovereign of all Egypt.

*Dynasty XXV of the Chronicle and of Manetho, with III Ethiopian generations and 44 years.*

"ογ΄. Θηβαίων ογ΄ ἐβασίλευσε Σαβάκων, ἔτη ιη΄." "*Sabaco* reigned 18 years."

"οδ΄. Θηβαίων οδ΄ ἐβασίλευσε Σεύηχος, ἔτη ιδ΄." "*Sevechus* reigned 14 years."

"οε΄. Θηβαίων οε΄ ἐβασίλευσε Τάρκος, ἔτη ιϐ΄." "*Tirhaka* reigned 12 years."

*Dynasty XXVI of the Chronicle (and of Manetho), with VII Generations of Memphites in 177 years.*

"ος΄. Θηβαίων ος΄ ἐβασίλευσε Καστόης, ἔτη ιθ΄." "*Kasto* reigned 19 years."

"οζ΄. Θηβαίων οζ΄ ἐβασίλευσεν Ἄμμερις Αἰθίοψ, ἔτη κ΄." "*Ameniritis* reigned 20 years."

"οη΄. Θηβαίων οη΄ ἐβασίλευσε Ψαμμίτιχος, ἔτη νδ." "*Psammitichus I.* reigned 54 years."

"οθ΄. Θηβαίων οθ΄ ἐβασίλευσε Νεχαὼ, ἔτη ιε΄." "*Necho* reigned 15 years."

"π΄. Θηβαίων π΄ ἐβασίλευσε Ψαμμίτιχος, ἔτη ς΄." "*Psammitichus II.* reigned 6 years."

"πα΄. Θηβαίων πα΄ ἐβασίλευσεν Οὐάφρις, ἔτη ιθ΄." "*Ouaphres* reigned 19 years.

"πβ΄. Θηβαίων πβ΄ ἐβασίλευσεν Ἄμωσις, ἔτη μδ΄." "*Amasis* reigned 44 years."

*Dynasty XXVIII of the Chronicle (XXVII of Manetho), of V generations of Persians in 124 years.*

"πγ΄. Θηβαίων πγ΄ ἐβασίλευσε Καμβύσης, ἔτη δ΄." "*Cambyses*, from the beginning of his 5th Persian year, reigned 4 years."

"πδ'. Θηβαίων πδ' ἐβασίλευσε Δαρεῖος, ἔτη λϛ'." "*Darius* reigned 36 years."

"πε'. Θηβαίων πε' ἐβασίλευσε Ξέρξης, ἔτη κα'." "*Xerxes* reigned 21 years."

"πϛ'. Θηβαίων πϛ' ἐβασίλευσεν Ἀρταξέρξης, μα'." "*Artaxerxes* reigned 41 years."

"πζ'. Θηβαίων πζ' ἐβασίλευσε Δαρεῖος, ἔτη κβ'." "*Darius Nothus* reigned 22 years."

*Dynasty XXIX of the Chronicle (XXIX and part of XXX of Manetho), with III Tanite generations, in 39 years.*"

"πη'. Θηβαίων πη' ἐβασίλευσε Νεφερείτης, ἔτη ϛ'." "*Nepherites* reigned 6 years."

"πθ'. Θηβαίων πθ' ἐβασίλευσεν Ἄχωρις, ἔτη ιγ'." "*Achoris* reigned 13 years."

"ϟ'. Θηβαίων ϟ' ἐβασίλευσε Νεκτανέβης, ἔτη κ'." "*Nectanebes I.* reigned 20 years."

*Dynasty XXX of the Chronicle (the remainder of XXX of Manetho), of one Tanite generation, in 18 years:—*

"ϟα'. Θηβαίων ϟα' ἐβασίλευσε Νεκτανέβης, ἔτη ιη'." "*Nectanebes II.* reigned 18 years."

Such is the simplest way in which a continuation of the list of Eratosthenes may be constructed from the same materials, that is, from the names of Manetho, as were chiefly used in the earlier part of the same list preserved to us by Syncellus. If any one, noticing the high particular average of the Chronicle in its Dynasties XIX and XX (where V generations in 194 years have nearly 39 years, and VIII in 228 have 28½ years apiece), thinks that the Theban priests would be likely for these dynasties to take a hint from Manetho's numbers of VI and XII kings, and so make room for eight names instead of only three of the Diospolites really belonging to Dyn. XX, there is nothing to forbid this supposition. Only in that case more extensive alterations than those made above would be required; since both the five reigns or generations of Dyn. XIX, as depressed into the space belonging to Dyn. XX, would need to have their years much curtailed; and compensation would have to be made for the five generations added to Dyn. XX, by suppressing somewhere or other below five of those (VI + III + II + III + III + VII + V + III + I =) XXXIII generations which follow it in the Chronicle. But the plan of reconstruction adopted above seems more likely to be near to the truth; and in any case it suffices to illustrate the general outline and proportions which the whole Theban list of Eratosthenes must have exhibited (though under names probably not always to be recognised), had it been preserved to us complete.

# NOTES AND CORRECTIONS

TO

# VOLUME I.

---

| Page | Line | |
|---|---|---|
| 4, | 9, | for "3024" read "3012 vague or 3010 Julian." |
| 4, | 15, | for "about 1504" read "1506 vague or 1505 Julian.", |
| 5, | 6, | for "500" read "about 500." |
| 5, | 21, | for "one great season" read "four great months." |
| 9, | 22, | for *αὐτὸν* read *αὑτὸν* |
| 9, | 27, | for "Ηφαίστου and *οὐκ ἐστι* read Ἡφαίστου and *οὐκ ἔστι*. |
| 9, | 29, | for *τρεις* read *τρεῖς*. |
| 8, | 35, | for *ςη'* read *ςγ'*. |
| 10, | 1, | for *ςκα* read *ςκα*. |
| 10, | 6, | for ζ read ζ'. |
| 10, | 11, | for *δυναστειων* read *δυναστειῶν*, and for *ἰτῶν* read *ἐτῶν*. |
| 10, | 19, | for *πιριζόμενα* read *μεριζόμενα*. |
| 10, | 29, | for *ἐτηριδων* read *ἐτηρίδων*. |
| 10, | 35, | for "ἀλληλα" read "ἀλλήλας." |
| 10, | 38, | for "*του*," read "*τοῦ*," and insert a comma after *τρισμύρια*. Also note that Syncellus, by reckoning only "xxix dynasties" after Phthah, shows that Dyn. XXVII was disregarded by him, though the text itself signifies plainly enough that Phthah is not one of the dynasties. The same appears also from the omission of 184 years required by the sum total, and manifestly belonging to Dyn. XXVII. |
| 16, | 14, | for "a sum divisible by" read "just the sum of." |
| 17, | 32, | before "B.C. 345" insert "in." |
| 20, | 6, | for "of the time of Augustus" read "perhaps of the third century after Christ." |
| 22, | 17, | for "elder" read "older." |
| 24, | 36, | for "Hezekiah" read "Rehoboam." |
| 25, | 14 & 24, | for "the end of" read "Nisan 1 in." |
| 25, | 31, | "in all 48.9m." Strictly speaking, instead of reckoning 4 years to Neriglissar, and 9m separately to Laborosoarchod, Josephus should have reckoned 20 as remaining to Nebuchadnezzar (for he reigned 43 from the spring of B.C. 604, but 44 from his first Syrian campaign in B.C. 605) + 2 of Evilmerodach + 4 of Neriglissar (including the 9m of Laborosoarchod) + 17 of Nabonadius, making in all 49 from Jan. 18 in B.C. 587 to Jan. 5 in B.C. 538. |
| 26, | 5, | for "23," read "24," and line 10, for "eleventh" read "tenth." |
| 26, | 10, | after "from" read "Nisan 1 in." |
| 28, | 2, | for "the end of," read "Nisan 1 in." |
| 29, | 19, | omit the words "and Hippolytus." Hippolytus made only 2242 years to the Flood. |
| 30, | 33, | omit "men of learning and sagacity." |
| 31, | 3, | omit "or 14th." |
| 31, | 20, | for "Herodotus and Plato or Eudoxus", read "Plato and Eudoxus, or at any rate Eudoxus." |
| 31, | 27, | at the words "Diodorus Siculus," &c. see below the note to p. 41, l. 17. |
| 33, | 24, | for "35,864" read "35,064." |
| 34, | 34, | for "$\frac{11}{12}$ths" read "$11\frac{1}{2}$" and for "a fraction" read "a divisor." |
| 35, | 22, | for "in truth, all" read "in truth all" &c. |
| 38, | 22, | for "$29\frac{1}{2}$" read "$29\frac{8}{13}$." |
| 39, | 7, | after "23,220" insert "[really 23,218]." |
| 39, | 17, | for "35,054" read "35,064." |
| 39, | 20, | "*might* substitute" &c. But compare p. 514 and other passages in Ch. IV. which show that the Hieratic scheme did *not* in fact do this, but divided its 35,064 month-years into 23,218+3944+7902. This is to be noted and borne in mind whenever the same numbers 23,220 and 7900 recur, as in pp. 40 and 41. |
| 39, | 22, | after "7900" insert "[really 7902]." |
| 40, | 4, | for "6780" (which is 7900−1120) read "6782", and wherever else the same number recurs. See the last note above. |
| 41, | 7, | &c. In the first series of figures "$\frac{21,915+1305}{23,220}$" should have been "$\frac{21,915+1303}{23,218}$"; and "$\frac{936+5844}{6780}$" should have been "$\frac{938+5844}{6782}$"; and in the second series "23,220 + 6780" should have been "23,218+6782." |
| 41, | 17, | "such season-years," but see p. 628. It does not seem that any of the Egyptian |

Page Line

schemes really contained such season-years. The assertion rests only upon a suggestion made in conversation to Diodórus and for his personal benefit.

43, 37, for "the Demigods" read "a third order of Gods derived from them."

49, 30, "Suidas, following Philo and Porphyry" &c. But if Clinton has good grounds for placing Suidas (whose age used to be considered unknown) "before Strabo," the name Suidas in this and many similar references must be understood only of the present text of Suidas as added to by later transcribers and re-editors.

50, 12, before "ancestor" insert "the."

58, 3, for "cycles" read "pseudo-cycles."

63, 20, for "these;" read "these,"

67, 16, 17, "A Horus was named immediately before Menes." This opinion of M. Brugsch, however, is discarded in Ch. IV. (see pp. 505, 506), after a more careful examination of the Papyrus.

71, 4, for "to give this" read "in order to obtain for this."

71, 6, for "at 29½" read "of 29½."

73, 22, for "and Sogdianus" read "Sogdianus and Artaxerxes Mnemon."

73, 36, for "33½ years" read "23½ years."

75, 9, for "XVI" read "XVI of the Chronicle."

76, 17, "Manetho, whose designation of Menes as *Thinites*," &c. But further on reasons are given for concluding that this designation is only from Eratosthenes, and from the compiler of the lists of Africanus; and that Manetho himself agreed with the Chronicle in naming Menes and his successors *Tanites*. The same note will apply also at p. 77, l. 7, and elsewhere.

79, 6, for "at B.C. 1322" read "in B.C. 1322."

79, 28, 29, for "8" read "7."

80, 3, for "nearly 8" read "above 7."

80, 4, for "8" read "7."

85, 3, for "Hystaspes." read "Hystaspes"

85, 5, for "Dec," read "Dec."

86, 7, for "Apollodorus" read "Apollonius Rhodius."

86, 16, for "B.C. 276" read "B.C. 268" which is Clinton's date.

87, 16, for "about" read "before" the time of the Christian era, &c.; since further on, when the statements of Diodorus come to be examined (in Ch. V.), it will appear that it was probably a good deal earlier, and at some time between B.C. 145 or B.C. 138, when Apollodorus flourished (he may have *lived* much longer), and B.C. 58. Perhaps one may put it conjecturally about B.C. 100. The fact too that a "Manetho of Mendes" is mentioned by Suidas points to the same inference, if Suidas has at length been rightly placed before the contemporaries of Augustus. For though Suidas is quoted for many names and references of later centuries after Christ, the name of an Egyptian writer of a date not far from his own is not so likely to have been inserted into his text afterwards as those of others of later celebrity.

87, 25, for "B.C. 141" read "B.C. 145." Apollodorus however *wrote* his Chronography at some later date than B.C. 138.

87, 27, for "B.C. 60" read "B.C. 58."

88, 7, before "Eratosthenes" insert "and" and omit "and Apollodorus."

89, 10, for "in the first century" read "in the second century." Tatian is put by Clinton from S. Jerome at A.D. 173.

92, 8, for "also Heroes? or" read "i.e. Manes, viz."

93, 1, "Dyn. I," &c. For the Greek text see p. 441, &c.

95, Dyn. XIV the number "LXXVI" should be in red. Also for "XXVI, XXX, or XXXVI?" read "XXXVI."

97, 8, for "A.D. 220" read "A.D. 221."

98, last line, for "which" read "the former of which two."

100, 1, for "and other" read "or."

100, 10, for "Manes and" read "Manes or."

100, 24, for "between two and three centuries" read "perhaps two centuries."

100, 5 from bottom, "possibly" &c. But in Ch. IV. and Ch. VIII. this doubt is retracted; as it appears that Ptolemy of Mendes must have written before the time of Diodorus Siculus.

101, 13, for "the compiler to" read "the compiler of."

102, 12, 13, omit the parenthesis "(though it is slightly uncertain, &c.)." The two MSS. of Syncellus having been examined afterwards, it appeared clear that the defect was only in one of them, which omits the sum of years belonging to Dyn. XIII, and all but the sum of years of Dyn. XIV; so between the two by an error in transcribing one dynasty is lost.

104, 30, "of Dyn. II." For M. Mariette's later discovery of names of Dyn. II of Africanus (IX of Manetho) see the note at p. XXXV of the Introduction.

104, 32, for "Sesorcheres of Dyn. II and other" read "seven."

105, 22, for "eight or ten" read "fifteen or sixteen."

105, 25, for "XXVI" read "XXXVI."

105, 26, for "sometimes gives also princes" read "certainly omits some kings."

105, 27, for "the LX" read "the number LX."

105, 28, for "to include" read "to allude to."

106, 8, for "Demigods, as Thoth" read "Thoth,"

106, 13, omit the parenthesis "(the last of whom is a Horus)."

106, 16, after "Aches" insert "and Siphuris," and omit the words "and Mencheres."

106, 20, after "and" insert "that by."

106, 22, after the name "Mentuhotep" insert "(Ra-neb-kher)" and before "XI" insert "Dyn."

107, 3, at the words "and other [mythical] kings" observe that the "Manes," and these "other [mythical] kings" are really identical for the original Manetho; but the source of this inaccurate distinction may be found in the fact, that in the text of Africanus the designation "Manes" is given expressly only to Group VII.

Page Line

See p. 92, where after the "Heroes" or Demigods there follow three groups of "*other* [mythical] kings," and then "Manes."

107, 6, for "indefinite" read "unnamed."

107, 30, "It is open then to imagine," &c. But this conjecture is set aside in Ch. IV. after a closer study of the Papyrus (see Ch. IV.) So the last 10 lines of this page and line 1 on the next may be regarded as cancelled.

108, 4, after "hypothesis" insert "—even if this sum represented the historical years of the kings or Manes here connected with it, which it does not—"; and see pp 530 and 531. All the rest of this paragraph on p. 1'8 will be set aside further on.

121, 7, after "of" insert "31$\frac{32}{113}$ or."

121, 10, instead of "24$\frac{1}{3}$" read "24$\frac{2}{5}$." And note that 24$\frac{1}{3}$ having been written by some inadvertence in the first instance, the same error is repeated afterwards, and needs the same correction in many other places throughout the work, though it involves no consequences worth notice.

121, 15, for "forty-eight" read "forty-nine."

121, 16, for "24$\frac{1}{3}$" read "24$\frac{2}{5}$."

121, 17 and 18, for "something over 31 years, being very nearly" read "30$\frac{21}{40}$, being not very much below."

121, 19, for "31$\frac{1}{4}$" read "31$\frac{32}{113}$."

121, 21, for "31$\frac{1}{4}$" read "31$\frac{5}{8}$."

121, 23, for "16$\frac{1}{3}$" read "16$\frac{32}{127}$."

122, 7, for "24$\frac{1}{3}$" read "24$\frac{2}{5}$."

122, 30, after "1916," insert "or 1919."

122, 39, for ' varieties" read "variants."

123, 17, &c. Respecting the designations and the number of kings really belonging to Dynasties IV and VII of Manes, see Ch. IV. and the Tables at p. 554.

124, 10, Dyn. XVI, for "LXXVI" read "XXXVI."

124, 14, Dyn. XVIII, after "XVI" insert "or XVII."

124, 15, for "(XXIX + LXXVI =) CV," read (XXIX + XXXVI =) LXV."

124, 20, for "with LXXVI" read "with XXXVI."

124, 21, for "something under 9 years" read "14 years and about 8 months."

124, 22, for "XXXI" read "XXIX."

124, 23, for "24 years and a half" read "25$\frac{28}{35}$, or nearly 26 years."

124, 26, Dyn. XIX. after "of VII" insert "[or only VI"].

125, 19, after "LXVII" insert "[or only LXVI"].

125, 23, for "15 years" read "16 years."

125, 25, for "(LXVI + CV + LXVII =) CCXXXVIII correct and" read "(LXVI + LXV or LXVI + LXVII or LXVI =) CXCVIII?"

125, 28, for "CCXXXVIII reigns" read "CXCVIII reigns."

125, 29, for "scarcely 15" read "17$\frac{169}{193}$ or something under 18."

125, 32 and 33, omit "XXX" and "or XXVI."

125, 38, for "CLVIII" read "CXLIX," and for "3171" read "3371."

126, 1, after "of" insert "22$\frac{83}{149}$ or", and for "20" read "22$\frac{2}{3}$."

126, 2, omit "then."

126, 4 and 5, for "three" and "XXVI" read "four" and "XXXVI," omitting "much."

126, 20, for "approximative" read "approximate."

128, 6, for "the foundation" read "Manetho's date for the foundation or dedication."

128, 19, for "the remaining 22" read "the remaining 21."

130, 31, after "foundation" insert "or dedication."

130, 39, for "23,220" read "23,218."

131, 1, for "6780" read "6782."

132, 19, omit "alone."

132, 21 and 24, omit "probably," and after "903" insert "*chronological*." In Ch. IV, it is shown that the Hieratic scheme gave to kings nominally about 3750 years ending in B.C. 1322, which being, all but 903, really concurrent were spread backwards over years of three kinds so as to look as if successive.

133, 22, "*συγχρόνως*." See, too, page 134, line 5, where Manetho uses the modified expression "*Princes*," which should have been in italics, for those early and concurrent kings.

135, 12, for "24$\frac{1}{3}$" read "24$\frac{2}{5}$."

135, 22, after "two kings" insert ", viz. *Sahoura* and *Snefrou*."

136, 29, for "24$\frac{1}{3}$" read "24$\frac{2}{5}$."

137, 2 and 3, for "24$\frac{1}{3}$," "220," and "117," read "24$\frac{2}{5}$," "222$\frac{2}{3}$," and "119$\frac{2}{3}$."

137, 26, for "171$\frac{1}{3}$" read "173$\frac{2}{3}$," and for "68" read "70$\frac{1}{3}$."

138, 4 and 5, for "24$\frac{1}{3}$" and "58" read "24$\frac{2}{5}$" and "60$\frac{2}{3}$."

138, 9, in the marginal note for Dyn. X, for "204" read "214."

138, 13, for "220" read "222$\frac{2}{3}$."

138, 15, in the marginal note for Dyn. XI., for "174" and "1756" read "177" and "1753."

139, 1 and 4, after "Dyn. IV" and after "Dyn. XV" insert "(of Afric.)"

140, 1, for "220" read "222$\frac{2}{3}$."

140, 15, for "they would have begun 36 or 34" read "they may have begun about (228−178=) 50."

140, 17, omit "36 or 34," and observe that if it be an admissible hypothesis that Dynasties II and V of Africanus, though called Tanite and Elephantinite, were both really Heliopolite, and successive, like the Memphite Dynasties III and IV, then if the later Heliopolites ended together with the later Memphites with the 178th year of Dyn. XXVII of the Chronicle and their 228 years began 50 years before Dyn. XXVII of the Chronicle began, it will follow that the 174 years of the earlier Heliopolites, called Tanites, will have begun (103−50=53, and 174 − 53 = 121, and 190−121 =) 69 years below the epoch of Menes, and about 10 years before the earliest settlement of local kings in Memphis.

140, 19, in the marginal note to Dyn. XIII, for "167," &c. substitute "181, from Feb. 8

Page Line

in B.C. 2132, to Dec. 25 in B.C. 1952," and see Ch. IV. p. 309.

140, 37, 38, 39, for "$24\frac{1}{2}$," "$73\frac{1}{2}$," "$180\frac{1}{2}$," "29," and "$110\frac{1}{2}$," read "$24\frac{3}{4}$," "$74\frac{1}{2}$" "$181\frac{1}{4}$," "30," and "$108\frac{1}{2}$."

141, 2, for "$79\frac{1}{2}$ or 77," read "82 or 81," and for "in the very same year" read "only 3 years," and for "with" read "after."

141, 5, "Tanis." But the Turin Papyrus referred to above shows that though the estimate of 181 years for this dynasty is by chance exactly right, it had 22 of these years below the accession of Sesortasen I. as suzerain, i.e. below B.C. (1932 +42=) 1974, and so began later in proportion, not in B.C. 2142, which would be only 82 years after the epoch of Menes, but in B.C. 2132, which is 92 years after that epoch, and 13 instead of 3 after the estimated commencement of the earliest Memphites.

142, 15, omit the words "still perhaps to be seen at Rome."

142, 22, in the marginal note to Dyn. XIV, for "392 Feb. 10, B.C. 2139" read "396, Feb. 11, B.C. 2143 [or 380 from Feb. 8, B.C. 2127 ?]"

142, 34, omit the parenthesis "(perhaps the same whose throne-name is *Ra-neb-teti*.)" This conjecture would assign a throne-name to a petty king long before the accession of Papa Maire as suzerain, whereas his is at present the earliest double cartouche known. For the same reason omit the similar parenthesis after "Enantef III." And, besides, these first three kings have not the full royal title in the Karnak Chamber, though their names are enclosed in rings, which that of the first of the line, the "Prince Enantef," is not.

143, 6, for "*Ra-neb-cheru*" read "*Ra-neb-cher*."

143, 7, for "44th year" read "46th year."

143, 32, 34, 37, for "$24\frac{1}{2}$," "392," and "85th" read "$24\frac{3}{4}$," "396," and "81st. But probably this date is somewhat too early and as the Turin Papyrus has made us put down the commencement of the central Memphites later by 10 years than it had been put conjecturally, we may perhaps put the commencement of the Diospolites also lower by 16 years than it would have been put by our estimate. Then with 380 instead of 396 years, they will still begin 97 years after Menes, that is," &c.

144, 4, in the marginal note to Dyn. XV, for "1999" read "1989."

144, 12, before "himself" insert "Sesortasen I."

144, 13, for "his successors" read "their successors."

145, 8, for "Egypt," read "Egypt.", and omit all that follows down to the full stop after "Africanus)." The inscription alluded to merely names a certain "*Amenemhe*" as a royal *officer*, at the same time that it contains the cartouche of a *king* named "*Mentuhotep*."

145, 25, the admission made here and elsewhere that Amenemhe I. *may have* reigned "19 years or more" is superfluous, as there are really no traces of any *decade* besides the *nine* years given to him in the Turin Papyrus. The "19" is merely from Bunsen.

145, 33, in the marginal note, for "1980" and "1933" read "1979" and "1932."

150, 34, for "8th" read "7th."

150, 38, for "need" read "involve."

155, 17, for "$24\frac{1}{2}$" read "$24\frac{3}{4}$."

156, 14, in the marginal note, for "XXX" read "XXXVI," and for "216" read "perhaps 216 years."

156, 21, 22, omit "or certainly not many more," and for "XXX" read "XXXVI."

156, 33, for "were the designations" read "was the designation."

157, 19, "As for their number," omit what follows to the words "it is probable" in line 24, and, retaining these words, omit again what follows, and go on in line 26 thus, "that the original Manetho had not more than XXXVI kings." Then omit to "XVI" inclusive in line 30; and after "LXXVI" in line 31 insert "of Africanus."

157, 27, for "merely genealogical" read "of least importance."

157, 29, "with their short reigns expanded into month-years." But in Ch. IV. it is shown that the reigns nominally attached to the Manes are *not* derived from the historical years which belonged to them as kings after Menes in the Papyri.

158, 7, before "to correspond" insert "nearly." But the suggestion itself is needless, and the additions and variations of Ptolemy are sufficiently accounted for in Chap. IV. without it.

158, 8, for "Chamber," read "Chamber." and omit all that follows to after "accidental" in line 14, or even to the end of the paragraph in line 8 of p. 159, as these suppositions are set aside by the examination of the Papyrus itself in Ch. IV.

159, 7, for "them," read "them." and omit what follows. (See Chap. IV.)

159, 11, for "only XXVI" read "only XXXVI," and omit all that follows to "thirty" inclusive in line 12, and insert "thirty-six" before "reigns" &c.

159, 14, for "$24\frac{1}{2}$" read "$24\frac{3}{4}$," and for "735" read "891."

159, 19, for "1975" read "1974."

159, 22, 23, 24, for "XXVI" read "XXXVI," omit "about," and for "7" read "$8\frac{4}{36}$," and omit what follows till after "years," inclusive in line 24.

159, 24, 25, 26, omit "LX or," and after "give" read "only $2\frac{23}{76}$ years," going on with "each" in line 26.

160, 28, "though we suppose, &c." But these suppositions are set aside in Ch. IV by the examination of the Papyrus itself.

161, 1, for "XXX" read "XXXVI," and after "as" insert "nearly."

161, 4, for "15" read "18," and for "$14\frac{1}{2}$" read "12."

161, 6, for "$21\frac{1}{2}$" read "18."

161, 33, "Fragment No. 30" seems however, from the width of the lines, to belong to the earlier part of the Papyrus, and so

Page Line

suits better for the pyramid-builders of Dyn. IV of Africanus. The spaces in Fragment 112 are not so wide.

168, 22, for "24⅓" read "24⅔."

174, 16, "Subtracting," &c. But if the sense of Herodotus is that among the 330 or 331 kings before Sesostris or Rameses III. there had been xviii Ethiopians, we can scarcely reckon the three later Ethiopians of Dyn. XXV at all, but must add to the xvi of Dyn. XVIII the first ii of Dyn. XIX (Rameses III. himself being really the third king of the dynasty), and so the xviii will be made out.

175, 38, "the last king of Dyn. IV of Afric." But it is to be remembered that Manetho's lists of the early dynasties are not all full, nor are the reigns attached to the names given historical.

179, 23, for "elder," read "older."

179, 35, "B.C. 1588." But the monuments, as will appear below, require an addition of at least five years to be made to the reign of Amenoph III., so that his death would not be more than 4 years, instead of 9, before the subjugation of the Hebrews by Chushan Rishathaim.

183, 8, after "it is not to be thought," insert ", at least not on that account." But if it be true, as M. Brugsch asserts from an inscription in which the 23rd year of Thothmes III. is mentioned, that Pachons 3 was the anniversary of the accession of the king named, one may perhaps be justified in assuming that the accession meant was at the same point of time at which the reign of his sister Hatasu (Ramakar) and that of Manetho's Amesses ended, and in reckoning backwards and forwards from this accession the actual reigns according to Manetho's lists, only restoring to Thothmes III. the 13 years cut off from him by Manetho and thrown up so as to make a separate reign. When this is done, we shall find the Theban accession of Amosis to have been for Manetho (21.9m + 20.7m + 25.4m =) 67 years and 8 months above that of Thothmes III.; and from June 17, in B.C. 1682, those 67 years 8 months take us up to Nov. 7, in B.C. 1749, a date later by only three days than Thoth 1, which was then at Nov. 4. And the death of Thothmes III., being 93 years 5 months later than the Theban accession of Amosis, appears to have been at March 11 (or in Gregorian reckoning about March 25), B.C. 1655.

183, 33, "was a year later," &c. But if the coronation at Memphis had been before the end of the first Theban year of Amosis, his Memphite accession would be antedated by the Chronicle, according to its general principle, so as to coincide with his Theban, which coincided in a manner (being only three days later) with the Thoth 1 preceding.

195, 2, "this singularity." The case, however, though rare and remarkable, is not absolutely unique; and more is made of it in the text than was necessary.

196, 35, for "conjectural," read "approximate."

203, 9, for "*Ra-nofreos*," read "*Ra-nofreou*."

204, 1, In the absence of any clue to Manetho's motive for thus cutting off five years or more from the reign of Amenoph III., one may hazard the conjecture that during the last five years of his life he had already associated with himself the sun-worshipping prince Chousan, who was nearly related to himself and to his queen Taia. There may have been a double connection by intermarriages, or it may even be true, as some say it is, that the sun-worshipping prince was the *son* of Amenoph III. and Taia; only in that case it must be supposed that through Taia he had inherited and come into possession of other Asiatic dominions before the death of Amenoph. In this case, since he was disallowed afterwards as illegitimate, and since the years of his reign were suppressed or transposed by Manetho, those last years of Amenoph III., during which he was associated, or declared heir to the throne, may have been suppressed on the same principle. The same cause may explain how it came to pass that though Amenoph III. died in peace, and was buried in the tomb which he had prepared for himself, this tomb was defaced, with a most careful hostility, at some later time, and his palace-temple destroyed. The *sun-worshipper* appears in sculptures not only as honouring the queen-mother Taia, but as honouring also the memory of Amenoph III. whom at Soleb he calls "his father." He therefore cannot be suspected of having violated his tomb.

204, 13, "15 full years," but to be reckoned as 16, if Amosis, instead of the 25 years and four months of Manetho reckoned from his Theban accession, reigned only 24 years and the odd four months from his Memphite accession, as antedated by the Chronicle, and his first Theban year (though counted by Manetho) is really anterior to all the 348 years of Dyn. XVIII of the Chronicle.

205, 36. Going upon M. Brugsch's rendering of the inscription rendered above, we may correct the marginal notes for this and the following reigns of the dynasty in the manner indicated below:—"Amosis, 24 years, technically reckoned from Thoth 1 preceding his coronation at Memphis, i.e. from Nov. 4, in B.C. 1748, to Oct. 29, in B.C. 1724. But his actual reign of 25 years 4 months is from his Theban accession Nov. 7, B.C. 1749, to March 1, B.C. 1723."

205, 38, for "In the same year" read "At the commencement of his second Theban year."

207, 23, "differs from the actual Theban reign by 4 months." But according to the inscription cited by M. Brugsch it differs by one whole year all but three days,

Page Line

and the void to be filled up for Manetho below will be one year, besides the 15 transferred by him to Dyn. XIX.

207, 12, for "a year earlier," read "at Nov. 7 in B.C. 1749," for "24yrs and 4m," read "23yrs and 8m."

207, 15, for "25 full," read "24 full."

207, 21, 28, and 29, for "four months" read "one year."

207, 31, for "25 full" read "24 full."

207, 34, for "1723" read "1724."

207, 5 from bottom, in marg. note for Amenoph I., read "13, reckoned technically from Oct. 29, B.C. 1724, to Oct. 26, B.C. 1711, but actually 13 from March 1, B.C. 1723, to Feb. 26, B.C. 1710."

208, 1, 2, for "B.C. 1723, to Oct. 25, B.C. 1710," read "B.C. 1724, to Oct. 26, B.C. 1711;" and for "25th," read "24th."

208, 4, in marginal note for Thothmes I., for "Oct. 25, B.C. 1710," read "technically 7 years, from Oct. 26, B.C. 1711," and for "1703," read "1704."

208, 16, 17, for "1710," read "1711," and for "Oct. 24, 1703," read "Oct. 23, 1702," and after "his death," continue thus, "being (4 + 7 =) 11 months later, Sept. 22, B.C. 1703."

209, 3. For marginal note to Amesses, read "Technically 22 from Oct. 24, B.C. 1704, to Oct. 18, B.C. 1682; but actually perhaps Aahmes (Amesses) 5yrs and 1m from Sept. 22, B.C. 1703, to Oct. 22, B.C. 1698, and then Hatasu (Ra makar Chnum-t-amen), with her consort Thothmes II., and her younger brother Thothmes III., as associated, 16yrs 8m from Oct. 22, B.C. 1698, to June 17, B.C. 1681."

209, 27, for "1703" and "1681" read "1704" and "1682."

209, 28, for "4 months" &c., read "8 months over, ending June 17, B.C. 1681."

209, 30, for "well" read "in any case."

209, 7, for "5 years and 5 months, reckoned technically as 6 years," read "6 years and 1 month, which technically would be antedated by 11 months, and reckoned as 7 years."

210, 22, marginal note to Thothmes III., read "Technically either 48 from Oct. 24, B.C. 1704, or 26 from Oct. 18, B.C. 1682, to Oct. 12, B.C. 1656; but actually either 47 years and 6 months from Sept. 22, B.C. 1703, or (13 + 12.9m =) 25 years and 9 months from June 17 (Pachons 3 of M. Brugsch's inscription) in B.C. 1681 to March 11, B.C. 1655." But note that this date, March 11, is in the Canicular or uncorrected Julian year B.C. And in the anticipated Gregorian year B.C., the equivalent date will be about March 25 or 26.

210, 37, after "the Tigris:" insert "Babylon also is mentioned:"

211, 4, for May 22, B.C. 1702," read "Sept. 22, B.C. 1703."

211, 6, for "Nov. 11, B.C. 1655, 5 months or thereabouts before the Exodus," read "June 13, B.C. 1655, 10 months or thereabouts before the Exodus," and omit the sentence which follows.

211, 18. In marginal note to Amenoph II., read "In technical reckoning 26 years from Oct. 12, B.C. 1656, to Oct. 5, B.C. 1630; but actually 25 years 10 months from March 11, B.C. 1655, to Jan. 3, B.C. 1629."

211, 20, 21, 22, for "Nov. 11," read "March 11," and for "preceding in the same," read "in the preceding."

211, 23, for "would seem to be later in his first year by one month," read "would be just after the commencement of his second year (being about April 5, in the anticipated *Gregorian* year 1654 B.C.), and would seem to be later in his reign by 5 months than," &c.

211, 26. In marginal note to Thothmes IV., read, "Technically 9 from Oct. 5, B.C. 1630, to Oct. 3, B.C. 1621; but actually 9 years 8 months from Jan. 3, B.C. 1629, to Aug. 29, B.C. 1620."

211, 36, for "Nov. 11," read "March 11," and for "Aug. 31," read "Jan. 3."

211, 37, for "Aug. 31," read "Jan. 3," and for "May 1, B.C. 1619," read "Aug. 29, B.C. 1620."

212, 3, for "25," and "1655," read "26," and "1656."

212, 4, 5, for "10," "1620," and "7," read "9," "1621," and "11."

212, 7. In marginal note to Amenoph III., read "Technically 37 from Oct 3, B.C. 1621, to Sept. 24, B.C. 1584; but actually 36 years 10 months (?), from Aug. 29, B.C. 1620, to June 22, B.C. 1583."

212, 28, for "must" read "may," for "35" read "36," and omit "at least."

212, 30, 31, for "May 1, B.C. 1619," read "Aug. 29, B.C. 1620," and for "Feb. 20," read "June 22."

212, 32, 33, 34, for "36" read "37," for "1620" read "1621," and for "5 months" read "9 months."

214, 2, omit from "and" to "*is*," in line 6, inclusive.

214, 14, for "Feb. 20," read "June 22."

214, 16, for "7 months," read "3 months," and omit what follows down to "the case," inclusive, in line 24

214, 25, 26, for "7," read "3," and for "Feb. 20," read "June 22."

215, 3. The whole paragraph beginning "This is the place," &c., and ending with "digression." on page 216, line 29, is now set aside by the help of M. Brugsch's date for the actual accession of Thothmes III., if only this date has been rightly understood and applied above. Only, at line 28 of page 215, we may retain the observation, that "After the end of the 3 months and 15 full years, or 16 years in technical reckoning now assigned to the Sun-worshippers, (i.e. after Thoth 1 = Sept. 20, B.C. 1568,) we have by the lists of Manetho still remaining to Dyn XVIII 173 years and 3 months, from the accession of Horus, while from Thoth 1, in B.C. 1568 to Thoth 1, in B.C. 1400, when the dynasty must end according to the Chronicle, there is room only for 168 years. We must therefore cut off either from the

Page Line

36 years 5 months of Horus, or from the 15 years 3 months assigned to the Sun-worshippers, five of those six years which we have added above from the monuments to the reign of Amenoph III., when we lengthened it from 30 years 10 months to 36 years 10 months. The remaining year of the six added is accounted for by the fact, that Manetho has depressed into his Dyn. XVIII one (the first year) of Amosis, as dated from his Theban accession, which does not belong to the 318 *years* of Dyn. XVIII of the Chronicle. The odd three months of Manetho which will still remain over (after cutting off five years from Horus), are only what we might expect to find in a list of actual reigns, and they will be covered by the first year of Sethos II., and of Dyn. XIX, as technically antedated by the Chronicle.

217, 24, for "5 years," read "5, or rather 6 years."

217, 32, omit "at."

217, 33, for "15 years and 7 months" read "(5+15=) 20 years."

218, 15 "Sept. 23," read "Sept. 20."

218, 17, for "23," read "20."

220, 37, "His eldest," &c. *Seha-em-Djam, second* originally of the two sons by the Queen *Isinofre*, was probably heir-apparent at the time of his death, and during his viceroyalty at Memphis.

221, 24, for "21½," and "392," read "24½," and "396."

222, 3, for "2½," read "2⅔."

228, 21. In marginal note, for "June 1," read "June 21."

235, 28, for "No. 23" read "No. 23,"

237, 11, for "Rameses XI." read "Rameses XIV."

239, 11, for "Pinetem II." read "Pinetem I."

241, 26, for "nearly 8," read "nearly 10."

242, 12, for "equal" read "equal to."

244, 13. In marginal note, before "169," insert "(121+48=)."

244, 22, The Apis of the 23rd of Osorkon II. was buried by Shishonk II., who then had only the title of Prince.

244, 27. We are told from the Inscriptions of the Serapeum that in the 11th year of Shishonk III. "his son *Osorkon*" is mentioned as *dead*, and the father of his wife Keromama, "the high priest *Nimrot*," is also mentioned as *dead*, but her *grandfather*, the king *Osorkon II.*, is mentioned as *still living*; also, that *Shishonk II.* and *Takelut II.* are mentioned *without the title of king being given to either of them.*

244, 31. If Pichai was the grandson of Shishonk III., as is supposed, his father, who died without reigning, will be the first of the iii generations of Dyn. XXII of the Chronicle; and Shishonk III. (whose actual reign was equal to a double generation) will be the last of the vi generations of Dyn. XXI of the Chronicle, the vii actual reigns making together only vi generations. From what is mentioned of Osorkon II., it appears that Shishonk II. and Takelot II. are the two names which together make only one generation, parallel to that of the high-priest Nimrot, father of Keromama.

245, 11, after XXI. add, "But the opinion of De Rougé, that Her-Hor and his descendants, who are certainly the later Diospolites of Dyn. XX. of the Chronicle [and included under the xii of Manetho's own Dyn. XX], are distinct from the Tanites of Manetho's Dyn. XXI, is much the more probable."

247, 25, insert "But it is certainly possible that the two 'Diospolites' of Dyn. XXIII of the Chronicle may have been contemporary with Shishonk IV."

248, 15, for "above" read "for."

249, 9, "Respecting the true chronological place of this deficit," &c. The case may be more simply, and perhaps more accurately stated thus:— Manetho has one year too many (21 instead of 20) placed *as if* between the death of Tirhakah, in B.C. 683, where he begins his Dyn. XXVI, and the actual accession of Psammitichus I., which really was in B.C. 663, not 662, and below the 44th year of Amasis, he has 8 more unchronological years and 2 months. So having in all 9 unchronological years and 2 months *in* or *below* (and all but one year and six months *below*) this dynasty, he compensates and makes room, as it were, for this excess of 9 years by omitting 9 chronological years between the actual accession of Psammitichus I. and the end of the 44th year of Amasis, having for this interval only 129 years instead of the true sum, which was 138. Hence it is that the sum of his Dyn. XXVI is shorter than it ought to have been by 8 years.

250, 10, the numbers "583," "584," and "575," are misprints for "683," "684," and "675;" but the whole paragraph from "Manetho," &c. on p. 248 to "dynasty." on p. 250 may be set aside, as it is quite clear that *six* years at least out of the nine suppressed between Psammitichus I. and Amasis were suppressed in order to make room for the 6 unchronological years of Dyn. XXVIII, and that these latter 6 years were interpolated on grounds of their own, and not in order to compensate for any previously existing deficit above; and this is indication enough as to the mutual relation of the remaining 3 chronological years suppressed, and the remaining 3 unchronological years interpolated, though it may not be easy to account for each separate interpolation.

250, 39, "indirectly," since they are all really unchronological, and *Necho*, the last name of the three, is that of the father of Psammitichus, who, according to Herodotus, was put to death by Sabaco, or at any rate by Tirhakah.

251, 4, "an average," that is, in the full number of 177 years given by the Old Chronicle to the dynasty.

Page, Line

253, 5, for "at least 40" read "42 or 43."

253, 6, after "years," read "Even if the 26th of Tirhakah be put down as low as B.C. 683 (so as to require only 39 or 40 years for the life of the bull), it follows that his accession was in B.C (683+ 26=) 709, 3 years later than the end of the 14th of Hezekiah, which began in B.C. 1713; and the difficulty," &c.

253, 9, for "709" read "713."

253, 11, after "death," insert "It is more probable that the 26th year of Tirhakah really began at least as early as some point in B.C. 688, so that his accession was not later than the spring of B.C. 714, nor his reign shorter than 31 current or 30 complete years at the least, though in that case the Apis bull must have lived about 45 current years or 44 complete at the least. Indeed it appears that this Apis," &c.

255, 9, 10, 14, for "720," "717," and "709," read "724," "721," and "713."

255, 21, for "of the second" read "of the third."

255, 32, omit "in appearance," and for "two" read "three."

257, 6, before "24" insert "in all for."

257, 9, for "B.C. 460" read "B.C. 424."

257, 16, after "reign" insert "that,"

257, 22, for "484" read "448?"

258, 5 and 6, after "Cambyses, and" insert "interpolating another year besides, and"; and for "first two" read "first three."

258, 10, for "without further noticing" read "without further notice of."

259, 9, "Teos .... His 2 years," &c. The Chronicle having to its two Dynasties XXIX and XXX 39 and 18 years respectively, *either* the 21 years given by Manetho to his Dyn. XXIX are all chronological,—and then these 21, with 18 of Nectanebo I., make the 39 of Dyn. XXIX of the Chronicle, and the 2 years of Teos really begin in B.C. (345+18=) 363, and are included by the Chronicle in the 18 years and the single generation of its Dyn. XXX, while Manetho gives to Nectanebo II. separately the 2 years of Teos over again,—*or else* the 21 years of Manetho's Dyn. XXIX, the 18 of Nectanebo I., and the 2 of Teos, all together make not 41 years, or 40 and 4 months, but only 39 chronological years; and then, in this case, the six names of Manetho make only III generations for the Chronicle, and the 2 years of Teos *end*, and the separate 18 of Nectanebo II. commence, as early as Nov. 23 in B.C. (345+18=) 363, which seems too high for the expedition of Agesilaus.

259, 16, for "the odd months" read "probably in one *generation* the 2 years."

260, 24, for "cycles" read pseudo-cycles."

260, 31. It may be remarked here how two accidents concur, one, that all the 138 years of the Cycle which were to run out after our era were thrown up in the Old Chronicle and other schemes, the other, that the 345 years between Nectanebo and the vulgar era are exactly equal in number to the 341 fictitious years added only in such schemes as were cyclical, but otherwise to be ejected, together with the 4 years which are lost in reducing 4 Sothic cycles from terms of the vague year to terms of the Julian; and the effect of this concurrence is, that any one might collect from the Egyptian schemes a sum of about 5500 years ending either at B.C. 345 or about the vulgar era of the Nativity, according as the 341 fictitious years and the 4 vague years lost by reduction were deducted or not.

273, 5, for "became about B.C. 226," read "succeeded Zenodotus as". Eratosthenes is *mentioned*, according to Clinton, in the Paschal Chronicle as flourishing (ἠγνωρίζετο) at a date indicating B.C. 223, Ol. 139 β'; but as Zenodotus was librarian till about B.C. 240, Eratosthenes probably was invited on purpose to succeed him, and succeeded him at once.

273, 7, for "83," read "82;" and for "194 or 192" read "196 or 194."

273, 16, for "about 141 years before Christ" read "in the year B.C. 145, and is known to have made additions to it as late as B.C. 128."

275, 5, after "24" insert "(viz. $23\frac{3}{4}$)."

275, 7, after "of" insert "$29\frac{8}{13}$ or about."

275, 19, for "$24\frac{1}{4}$" read "$24\frac{2}{3}$."

276, 1, 20, 31, for "$24\frac{1}{4}$," read "$24\frac{2}{3}$."

276, 17, for "$29\frac{3}{4}$," read "$29\frac{8}{13}$."

276, 26, for "(5×15=) 75" read "(443–$371\frac{1}{4}$=) $71\frac{3}{4}$."

276, 29, for "75," read "$71\frac{3}{4}$."

276, 30, for "$29\frac{3}{4}$," read $29\frac{8}{13}$."

277, 6, after "prosperity," insert "or reigns of brothers or cousins in succession,"

277, 10, for "$24\frac{1}{4}$," read $24\frac{2}{3}$."

277, 24, the word "*needlessly*" should be in italics.

278, 9, for "$67\frac{1}{4}$." read $66\frac{1}{4}$." But whatever may have been the case with regard to this particular dynasty, it must be borne in mind that the early reigns of Manetho are now proved to be to a great extent unhistorical in their sums of years, so that the priests could not, perhaps, even if they had wished it, deal with them in the way that is here desired, but were obliged either to take them as they stood, *as if* they needed only a certain reduction to be historical, or else to enter more into details with Eratosthenes than they thought necessary.

278, 19, before "30," insert "$30\frac{7}{13}$ or."

278, 20, for "between 4 and" read "a little over."

278, 21, for "nearly" read "rather more than."

278, 22, for "$24\frac{1}{4}$" read $24\frac{2}{3}$."

278, 23, for "$29\frac{3}{4}$" read "$29\frac{8}{13}$."

278, 33, for "196, $220\frac{1}{4}$, $220\frac{1}{4}$, 196, $220\frac{1}{4}$, and 147," read "198, $222\frac{2}{3}$, $222\frac{2}{3}$, 198, $222\frac{2}{3}$, and $148\frac{1}{3}$."

278, 39, for "6 less" read "8 less."

279, 3, for "$220\frac{1}{4}$" read "$222\frac{2}{3}$."

Page Line

279, 4, for "6½." read "6¾."

279, 6, for "196" read "198."

279, 7, for "218" and "220½" read "228" and "222¾."

279, 8, for "147" read "148½."

279, 9, 10, for "(6+6½+19+2½=)34−1½=32½" read "(8+¾+8¾+21=) 38½−6¾=31½"

279, 14, for "179½" read "(148½+31½=) 179¾." and for "167" read "177."

279, 16, for "147" read "148¾."

279, 22, for "196" read "198."

279, 24, after "admissible" insert "we shall find hereafter the true sum to be 181."

279, 30, after "177" insert "[or 178]." For the "218" which follows read "228," and after the second "177" insert "[or 181]." Then for "1198" read "1208 [or 1213]."

279, 32, for "24½" read "24¾" years, and continue thus, "an addition of 4 years only and ¾ths, or in round terms of 5, to the above sum being needed to give the average exactly. And the sum of Eratosthenes for Dyn. XI and that of the Papyrus for Dyn. XIII of Manetho (IV and VI of Africanus) which have been added in brackets, being 178 and 181 respectively, supply this addition of 5 years."

279, 38, omit the parenthesis "(Just those needed, &c.)"

280, 15, after "concurrent;" insert "and whole reigns the names for which he has suppressed;"

280, 30, for "24½" read "24¾" and for "147" read 148½."

281, 29, after "their" insert "true" and omit "as."

282, 2, 3, 4, for "(220½+177=) 397½" read "(222¾+177=) 399¾."

282, 13, for "392" read "396."

282, 18, for "11½" and "20" read "(173½−160=) 13½ or of (198−176=) 22."

282, 29, omit "or XXX."

282, 31, 32, for "or XXX or even for XXVI" read "to say nothing of LXXVI."

282, 30, for "5 years" read "$5\frac{4}{38}$ years," and omit "and 4 months, or at most 6 years."

283, 6, for "882" read "891."

283, 16, for "392" read "396."

283, 24, for ", or XXX or even XXVI" read "rather than LXXVI."

286, 12, 13, for "[+6 years of Dyn. XXVII]" read "[+6 years of Dyn. XXVIII]."

286, 27, for "24½" read "24¾."

288, 7, from the bottom, for "167" read "177."

289, 5, from the bottom, for "392" read "396."

290, 11, for "30½" read "$30\frac{7}{10}$."

295, 29, "are not here given." They are given in Ch. IV. at p. 501.

303, 23, for "29½" read "$29\frac{8}{13}$."

303, 29, for "24½" read "24¾."

306, 15, for "follow," read "follow;"

319, 10, for "only just born" read "scarcely yet born."

319, 33, "*Menai*," &c. in the marginal note. The reader may note that though this and other following reigns are calculated and marked as if their lengths were all ascertained, this is by no means true in fact, since the reigns or generations of Eratosthenes are reduced from those of Manetho, and those of Manetho do not belong historically, at least not in all the years given to them, to the kings named for each, but are compounded by Manetho partly from the true reigns of the kings named, partly from those of many other kings omitted, and partly also from fictitious years interpolated by himself.

324, 34, for "269½" and "220½" read "272½" and "222¾."

324, 36, for "2201" and "23" read "2204 or 2205" and "about 20."

326, 4, for "24½" read "24¾."

330, 20. Here we are forcibly reminded that the reigns of Manetho are fictitious, since the 39 years of the first two Memphite suzerains of Dyn. XVII. of the Chronicle will not come naturally out of those sums of years which Manetho exhibits; and, after they have been taken, Manetho seems to make his Dyn. X overrun by 13 years the commencement of Dyn. XI by which it was succeeded.

338, 24, for "29½" read "$29\frac{8}{13}$."

338, 32, for "Soaphis" read "Saophis."

340, 16, for "29½" read "$29\frac{8}{11}$."

349, 20, after "177" insert "[*really* 181]."

352, 20, omit "The vast number," &c. down to "character" incl.

352, 39, for "*Anch-sel-mire*" read "*Anch-nes-mire*."

353, 33, for "86" read "76."

355, 26. But indirectly the Papyrus shows that she had 12 years, if we compare the sum of the dynasty presented by the Papyrus with the figures for the reigns in detail helped out, where the Papyrus is defective, by the list of Manetho. See p. 509.

356, 2, "Meranre." A sphinx bearing the name of this king is in the collection of Mr. Larkin at Alexandria.

356, 16, "There is, or was, at Gizeh," &c. This assertion may or may not be accurate. Being found in a work of no authority, it should not have been repeated without further verification.

356, 22, for "*Anch-sel-mire*" read "*Anch-nes-mire*."

362, 11, "Not exceeding 45." But the Turin Papyrus shows that instead of only 49 kings there were as many as 89, from whom the 49 of Manetho are selected and consolidated. And though many of these 89 may have had very short reigns, they might all or nearly all have commenced at least the preparation of a tomb. And, in fact, Dr. Lepsius imagines that he found traces of as many as 60 or 70 pyramids, though some of them must have been very small; and some, or many, may have belonged to queens or to others besides kings. It is true, no doubt, that Manetho in all probability has retained the names of the more important kings who had the longest reigns and left the most conspicuous tombs; but still that comparison which is offered of the 37 Pyramids known to Col. Howard Vyse and Mr. Perring with the names of Mane-

Page Line

tho's early dynasties is put forward in no other sense than as a basis for some broad and general inferences.

366, 1, The name of "*Ounos*" is said to have been found on blocks either connected with this building or in its immediate vicinity.

366, 26, for "Anch-set-mire" read "Anch-nes-mire."

368, 11, "of Manetho." But the Papyrus shows that there were 4 more kings after Nitocris with very short reigns, and that Manetho has suppressed these and thrown up their 10 years, adding these, and 16 other fictitious years besides, to the earlier kings of the dynasty.

368, 16, "Towards determining," &c. But the Papyrus determines its duration to 181 years, which ended in B.C. (1974−12=1962−10=)1952, and therefore began in B.C. (1952+181=)2132, that is, 92 years after Menes.

369, 34, for "392?" read "396?"

371, 27, 29, for "392" and "24½" read "396" and "24¾," and omit "exactly."

371, 35, 36, for "392=) 2139, 6" and "86" read "396=)2143, 2." and "81."

373, 32, before "103" insert "something like."

373, 38, for "98" read "99."

374, 1, 2, for "392" and "98" read "396" and "99."

375, 3, after "Papa Maire" insert "at Turin."

375, 4, after "Karnak," insert "and the cartouches of Amenemhe I. as well as those of the Nantefs and Mentuhoteps have recently been found on remains of contemporary buildings on the west bank."

375, 14, in marginal note to the Prince *Nantef*, for "25 years, from B.C. 2139 to 2114" read "29 years, from Thoth 1 B.C. 2143 [or 29−16=13 years, from Thoth 1 B.C. 2127?] to Thoth 1 B.C. 2114."

375, 31, for "98" and "24½" read "99" and "24¾."

376, 15, for "392=) 2139" read "396=) 2143, though the fact that the actual commencements of Dynasties VIII, X, and XIII of Manetho are ascertained to have been later by 8, 8⅔, and 16 years respectively, than those which we should have calculated for them makes it probable that the commencement of Dyn. XIV also was later, let us suppose by 16 years, than the date calculated for it. So it may have begun in B.C. (2143−16=) 2127; and from either B.C. 2143 or B.C. 2127 we may reckon downwards 396 or 380 years to B.C. 1748."

379, 35, for "2139" and "6," read "2143 or B.C. 2127" and "2 or 18."

383, 19, in the marginal note to *Snefcrkar*, for "24 years B.C. 1968 to 1924," read "25 years B.C. 1944 to B.C. 1919."

384, 28, 29, for "24½," "1924," and "8," read "24¾," "1919," and "13."

385, 13, in marginal note, for "29 years. B.C. 1924" read "24 years. B.C. 1919."

385, 31, after "him." "Probably it was through him that the kings of Dyn. XVIII traced themselves up both to Amenembe I, the head of Dyn. XV of Manetho (XII of Africanus), and to the earlier Memphites and Tanites of Lower Egypt."

385, 38, for "44th" read "46th."

391, 2, after "219" insert "(but really 213)."

393, 7, for "reign" read "accession."

396, 27, omit "probably."

396, 29, after "Turin)" insert "there were no fewer than CXLIII, or even CLXII."

405, 32, after "illegitimate reigns," add "or of reigns not in the right line of descent."

405, 35, for "perhaps" read "either of illegitimate reigns, or of brothers or cousins making only one generation with their predecessors, are reckoned."

405, 39, for "kings" read "generations."

406, 2, before "23" insert "23$\frac{31}{60}$ or."

406, 3, 4, for "1 year and 2 months" and "24½" read "1 year and 5 months" and "24¾."

406, 24, before "something" insert "23$\frac{29}{35}$ or", and before "23½" insert "23$\frac{31}{60}$ or something over."

407, 7, after "of" insert "Thothmes II. or that of."

408, 17, after "they all" insert "or most of them."

413, 29, for "41 *years*" read "48 *years*."

413, 33, after "51." insert "And it is probable that Shishonk III. is more properly the last generation of the preceding dynasty, a prince who died before his father being alluded to as the first of the three generations of Dyn. XXII. of the Old Chronicle."

414, 37, after "on any Apis-stelæ" insert "(the 2nd, *Zet*, has not been found at all)."

415, 11, 12, for "μβ'" and "12" read "μη'" and "18."

415, 15, 16, for "μη'" and "18" read "μβ'" and "12."

END OF THE FIRST VOLUME.

LONDON
PRINTED BY SPOTTISWOODE AND CO.
NEW-STREET SQUARE.

www.ingramcontent.com/pod-product-compliance
Lightning Source LLC
Chambersburg PA
CBHW020449270326
41926CB00008B/544

* 9 7 8 3 7 4 2 8 6 4 9 0 1 *